HISTORY of the A.M.E. CHURCH in ZAMBIA

An Astounding Account of a Revival of a Church

A HISTORICAL SYNOPSIS OF THE CHURCH IN SOUTHERN, EAST & CENTRAL AFRICA

CHARLES KAPUNGWE
with
John Lester C. Membe & David K. Simfukwe

© 2020 Charles Kapungwe (U.S.A). All rights reserved. No part of this book may be reproduced in any form, by Photostat, microfilm, xerography or any other means, or incorporated into any information retrieval system, electronic or mechanical, without the written permission of the author.

Unless otherwise stated Scripture taken from the HOLY BIBLE, NEW INTERNATIONAL VERSION®. Copyright © 1973, 1978, 1984 by International Bible Society. Used by permission of Zondervan. All rights reserved.

published by CharlieKaps®
Auburn, ME 04210

Softcover ISBN: 978-0-578-73728-7

Library of Congress Control Number: 2020917871

CK
CharlieKaps®
Auburn, Maine
2020

Acknowledgments

I would like to thank the Lord for his unmerited favor that he has continuously showered on me. In the midst of great adversity and personal tragedies he continued to show his love for me. When close friends turned their backs on me, he still remained my Anchor and strength. Even in a great turmoil the following stood steadfastly by me and I am grateful to the Lord for them. My appreciation goes to Rev. Leroy Cannon and his wife Helen of Columbia, South Carolina. I would also love to recognize Mr. Eddie Woodin and the Victory Power Team of South Portland, Maine for unwavering support rendered to me both financially and spiritually. My special thanks go to Bro. David Simfukwe, Jr., and Mother Rose Simfukwe of Jacksonville, Florida in U.S., Rev. Samson M. Kapufi, P.E. of Mansa, Rev. Emmanuel Ngalala, P.E. of Samfya, Rev. Wilson Mpundu and Rev. Peter M.P. Mwenya, P.E. of Mufulira and Mother Elizabeth N.L. Simyembe of Kitwe in Zambia for their contribution. Finally, my special thanks go to my late father and my late mother Mr. Amos Kapungwe and Nancy Kapungwe, Mr. Davis Musonda and wife Mary Kapungwe Musonda, my sisters, Foster Kapungwe and husband Joseph Mulenga, Mabel Kapungwe and her husband Barry Lupingula, Fridah Kapungwe, Gift Kapungwe and her late husband Moses Nswana and Cecilia Kapungwe and her husband Jonathan Mwale. Also, my special thanks go to Mr. Robert and Joellyn Rabias, and Mr. and Mrs. Steve Marbert of New Covenant Presbyterian Church in Aiken, South Carolina for their missionary work and building of Trinity A.M.E. Church where I was once a pastor from 1996 to 2000 in Zambia. Other thanks go to Jordan Chapel A.M.E. Church (my childhood church in Kitwe), Calvary A.M.E. Church (our first church to plant in Kitwe) and Trinity A.M.E. Church in Kitwe, Zambia where I was pastor.

Zambia's first Republic President who got Zambia her independence from the British in 1964, Dr. Kenneth D. Kaunda with Rev. Charles Kapungwe at Adam's Mark Hotel in Columbia, South Carolina U.S.A. He was president from 1964 to 1991. 18th March, 2003.

Preface by Charles Kapungwe

There are many capable saints who could have been deserving authors of this work. Their labours for the work of the Lord in the A.M.E. Church in Zambia, qualifies them to be the ones who would have taken up this magnanimous task of penning down the history of this denomination; a denomination which was born out of a deep anguish of souls – souls which had no freedom of worship in the land where their forefathers had been taken to America as slaves from Africa. Thankfully, this task was made easier by two of our predecessors who chose to preserve their work. Also, besides the two, many other people contributed to this work for no single person could have managed to accurately compile this enormous task by himself. Although I was the least of all those great saints in Zambia who could have been considered to compile or write this work, I felt compelled by the Spirit of the Lord to pen down the journey of those who had laboured for the Lord in the African Methodist Episcopal Church in Zambia to keep their memory alive.

"Procrastination is the enemy of time," so I learned. Also, "There are thousands of people who go to the grave daily with undone works," I learned. After watching on the sidelines for years, waiting for my co-labourers and those I deemed more qualified persons than I, to take up the mantle of giving a historical account of the A.M.E. Church in Zambia but to no avail, expediency finally demanded that I take up this mammoth task upon myself. Having lost great men and women who had laboured tirelessly for the Lord, some of them who had been walking miles in villages and towns taking the gospel of the Lord to all corners of Zambia in this Southern-central region of Africa, a country the size slightly larger than the state of Texas, the onus, I felt, was left upon me to investigate the history and the role this denomination has played in the revival of Zambia, which the late President Frederick Chiluba declared as a Christian nation in 1991.

It is my prayer that posterity will not judge us harshly when it reads this important history. It is also my prayer that many shall learn from those whom God had raised and had laboured tirelessly for their Master because learning history helps us to understand the present and plan for the future. From the great works of the late Rev. John Lester C. Membe, Rev. David K. Simfukwe, Rev. Henrique Matenda Lukamba, Rev. Warren K. Simyembe, Rev. Samson Mulonga Kapufi, Rev. David Dafite Khomela, Rev. Caleb Ngoma, Rev. Cuthbert Katebe, Rev. Henry Alimasi, Rev. Isaac C. Mumpanshya, Rev. Daniel Mkhwanazi, Rev. Peter M.P. Mwenya, Rev. Wilson Mpundu, Mother Elizabeth Nelinya Simyembe, Mother Daisy Katebe, Mother Rose Simfukwe and many servants who have gone ahead of us, I felt that keeping their memories in this collection of works was going to be worth the trouble and time of investigating what the men and women of the Lord had contributed to what we now are a part of a major revival in Zambia. Join me in keeping their memory alive and that of our Lord Jesus Christ whom they laboured for, for decades. God bless you all!

Charles Kapungwe
Portland, Maine U.S.A., January 1, 2020

Preface by Rev. John Lester C. Membe

To the Bishops, Ministers, Missionaries, and members of the African Methodist Episcopal Church, and many others who might be interested to know and understand about the history of the A.M.E. Church in Central Africa. I beg leave to submit this short history book of the Church at the request of our beloved Bishop, the Rt. Rev. John D. Bright, Sr., the Presiding Bishop of the A.M.E. Church, 17th Episcopal District, Central Africa.

First, I give my sincere grateful thanks and glory to God our Heavenly Father, the Father of our Lord and Saviour Jesus Christ. By his wise Providence, he made it possible to the time when something should be done in putting the foundation history of the African Methodist Episcopal Church in the 17th Episcopal District, Central Africa, for our children and the generation to come. They will build on this foundation a full story of the Church of our fathers under their own "VINE" tree in Central Africa, and continue to keep the "BANNER OF THE AFRICAN METHODISM OUTFLUNG." They will keep going ONWARD, FORWARD AND HEAVENWARD, under the great "MOTTO" invented by that great Father of the African Methodism Richard Allen, "GOD OUR FATHER, CHRIST OUR REDEEMER, MAN OUR BROTHER." They will also keep the FIRE BURNING DAY AND NIGHT ON THE ALTER," for THE RACE IS NOT TO THE SWIFT, NOR THE BATTLE TO THE STRONG, BUT TO HIM WHO HOLDS OUT TO THE END. <u>AMEN</u>.

Many of those who witnessed the beginning of the A.M.E. Church in Central Africa have gone to rest with Him beyond the Universe. However, those who are still alive, when asked, cannot remember how it all started; they say it is too long ago for them to remember. Nevertheless, having in my possession some old documents, minutes of conferences, memories and help from people and contributions, etc., I have managed to outline this short account and brief historical sketch of our Church based only on the early stages of the beginning of the A.M.E. Church in this part of Africa.

My personal thanks and appreciation are extended mainly to the Historical Committee of the Zambezi Annual Conference of the A.M.E. Church in which I acted as Secretary. I have their report in my hands which comprised the following names as members of that Committee in 1936 and completed in 1938: Rev. J.A. Daniels (Chairman), Rev. S. N. Sangweni (Vice Chairman), Rev. J.L.C. Membe (Secretary), Rev. D.D. Khomela, Rev. J. Tshaka, Brother E.M. Makghato (Vice Secretary), Rev. S.M. Kamdgshariwa and Rev. J. Marumo. From this Committee's records and other old records and information, I have been helped to outline briefly about the history of the Church in Southern Rhodesia and Northern Rhodesia. So, readers of this short historical sketch are being reminded that the facts contained in this work have been obtained from reliable and authentic account and records, and also information.

No attempt has been made to record in full the history of our church in Central Africa. This will follow this work in sequel. It is hard for a historian to please everybody. Therefore, my work on this little pamphlet is made subject to criticism, additions, amendments and corrections. I also wish to apologize in advance for any error or omission. I also wish to extend my grateful thanks and appreciations to my co-labourers in the "Vineyard" of the Lord who helped me greatly to collect more information and contributions to this little piece of work on the history and expansion of the Church in this country: Rev. Foodson B.S. Washiama, Rev. Benjamin W. Chalomba, and also the Rev. Mundia K. Wakunguma who helped to collect information and contributions to this history of the A.M.E. Church in Barotse Province. Thanks are also due to Rev. N.J. Sichone, Mrs. late Rev. B.B. Chisela, Mrs. late Pastor Augustus Kawala and any other members of the Church in Northern and Luapula Provinces as well as the Copperbelt and other places in this country. Also, thanks go to Rev. D.D. Zimba who took a great part in organizing the work of the Church in the area of Lake Mweru.

There are some people who claim to be the founders of the A.M.E. Church in this country simply because they want to do so to mislead and mix up things. Yet, they came to do the work of the Church started by others but because they were first official leaders of the Church, they are trying to put themselves into that place without any proper evidence to show they did so. The people who helped in doing this work cannot be wrong and ignorant of facts: So, I would like conclude with these words: Avoid the history written by an individual person behind the closed door for fear of being criticized shamefully.

Respectfully and loyally submitted,

J.L.C. Membe

Kitwe, Northern Rhodesia, 30th March 1962

Editorial Comment by Rev. David K. Simfukwe

For many years, the African Methodist Episcopal Church has never published the history of its existence from 1800 to 1962, in Central Africa. Much has been spoken verbally; as a result, many people have never been acquainted about the beginning of the Great African Methodist Episcopal Church in both South and Central Africa.

In 1963, the A.M.E. Church Press at Luanshya appealed through the Voice of Mission in Zambia to all leaders of the Church to produce written and concrete proofs concerning the Church history. However, the cooperation given to the Publication Office by the "DEAN" of the 17th Episcopal District, Father Rev. J.L.C. Membe is beyond thankful expression. As one of the great pioneers of the A.M.E. Church, and the former Secretary of the Episcopal Committee at the Annual Conference of 1962, with Bishop J.D. Bright as the then Conference Chairman, Father Rev. J.L.C. Membe, tried hard to preserve the A.M.E. Church History and we feel that many of you will be very happy to read this History Book concerning the beginning of the Church.

This office gives many thanks to Rev. C.F. Banda of Luanshya A.M.E. Church Press for working hard until the production of the last copy of this History Book. And now, to all the brethren which are with me, unto all the Churches of Central Africa and abroad, grace be to you and peace from God the Father, and from our Lord Jesus Christ, who gave Himself for our sins, that He might deliver us from this present evil world, according to the will of God and our Father; to whom be glory for ever and ever, Amen.

Rev. D.K. Simfukwe, Conference Secretary
13th December 1968

Foreword by Rev. Peter M.P. Mwenya

I am pleased to write this extended Foreword to the History of the A.M.E. Church in Zambia. It is such a joy to experience what I have always desired to see in my lifetime come to fruition: a history book of this church in Zambia. For years I had been deeply troubled and concerned if I were going to ever see this work written for our future generation. Many coworkers and I, who have laboured in this denomination for decades, greatly despaired with concern if ever we were going to see someone document the works that the Lord has done in this church. Although we were aware of some writings that had been done, we knew that such writings were not documented in a modern book that would reach many readers in Africa, America and the rest of the world. Gladly, the effort demonstrated by the Rev. Charles Kapungwe to compile this work serves as a relief to all of us who have laboured tirelessly in this church and have wanted this work to be written.

I had always thought that the Rev. Dr. Paul Bupe was going to write this work. Sadly, the persecution and great opposition that this church has carried out relentlessly against those who have been preaching the gospel, the liberating power of our Lord Jesus Christ and work of the Holy Spirit to all, finally made him to leave too. This opposition made several ministers and laity to leave the A.M.E. Church. While acknowledging the tireless works of our fathers including the labours of the Rev. John Lester C. Membe, we were aware that the traditions the A.M.E. Church had been steeped in for decades left many worshipers bound by powers of darkness. We give God the glory that his liberating message of the cross compelled us to preach the gospel that sets captives free.

What you are about to read is a true historical work that we have been a part of for years. From the mid-1970s through the late 1990s, the A.M.E. Church in Zambia experienced an expansion and spiritual awakening. This came about through the mighty works of the Holy Spirit and it involved resisting of Satan's works. The enemy's works involved use of his people he had put in the Church's leadership in the same way he used the Pharisees and Sadducees to oppose the message of our Lord Jesus Christ. I am grateful to God for the works of the Rev. J.L.C. Membe, Rev. David K. Simfukwe and the Rev. Dr. Charles Kapungwe for this history which you all will find interesting to read. May the Lord grant you the zeal to catch the passion for the lost souls and speak to as many people as possible about the saving power of our God through his Son Jesus Christ and the Holy Spirit.

Rev. Peter M.P. Mwenya
Presiding Elder, Copperbelt West
Mufullira, Zambia, 5th February 2020

Table of Contents

Acknowledgments iii
Preface by Charles Kapungwe v
Preface by Rev. John Lester C. Membe vi
Editorial Comment by Rev. David K. Simfukwe viii
Foreword by Rev. Peter M.P. Mwenya ix
1. Introduction 1
2. Prehistoric Africa 6
3. The Setting – Prehistoric Zambia 14
4. Formation of the A.M.E. Church in the United States of America in 1787 24
5. The A.M.E. Church Reaches the African Continent in 1821 and 1896 26
6. The A.M.E. Church Takes Root in Southern Africa: Extends to Southern
Rhodesia in 1900 31
7. Formation of the A.M.E. Church in Northern Rhodesia in 1929 35
8. First Appointments to Northern Rhodesia in 1931 42
9. The A.M.E. Church on the Copperbelt Province in 1930 44
10. Creation of First Two Districts and Second Appointments to Northern Rhodesia in 1933   56
11. The Great Expansion of the A.M.E. Church in Northern Rhodesia –
Northern and Luapula Provinces in 1932 59
12. The A.M.E. Church in Eastern and North Western Provinces in 1934 73
13. The A.M.E. Church in Southern, Central and Barotse (now Western) Provinces 76
14. Rev. David Dafite Khomela's Version – The First Presiding Elder of Northern
Rhodesia in 1931 81
15. The A.M.E. Church in Tanganyika Territory in 1933 84
16. The A.M.E. Church in Belgian Congo in the Year 1957 105
17. Bishops and Missionaries Who Served the A.M.E. Church in South Africa,
Southern, East and Central Africa 107
18. Rev. John Lester Coward Membe: Founder of the A.M.E. Church in Zambia 122
19. Rev. David K. Simfukwe – The Educator 134
20. Ministers Who Have Served the A.M.E. Church Both in Northern Rhodesia
and Zambia 143
21. Ministers Who Have Served the A.M.E. Church Both in Northern Rhodesia
and Zambia II 167
22. The A.M.E. Church in Zambia and Congo DR Today 218
23. Obstacles and Challenges to Effective Ministry in the A.M.E. Church in Zambia 232
24. Obstacles and Challenges to Effective Ministry in the A.M.E. Church in Zambia:
Leadership Crisis! 257
25. Regression 304
26. God's Powerful Hand in the Revival of A Traditional Church to His Glory &
The Rev. Peter Mfula Pious Mwenya's Story 313
27. Called, Committed and Compelled to Serve: The Story of Charles Kapungwe 331
28. The Legends 419
Reference 470
Index 472

Caution: This book will transform you!

"The Bible is a History Book, but it doesn't play around. It demands a choice."
– Charles Kapungwe, 18th September, 2018

To my children in faith: "Do not fight the Jezebel spirit with gloves on. Get 'em off."
– Charles Kapungwe, 5th October, 2017

Chapter 1
Introduction

The A.M.E. Church has been in existence in Zambia (Northern Rhodesia) since 1929. However, its history has not been widely told. Although this Church has been known among many denominations in Zambia including other Southern, East and Central African nations, a well-written and circulating documentation of its presence and history in this part of Africa has been lacking. In spite of the efforts made by the Rev. J.L.C. Membe, the undisputed founder of the Church in Zambia, the Rev. David K. Simfukwe and other Historical Committee members who once worked on the compilation of the history of the A.M.E. Church in Zambia, their effort could not reach a wider audience because it was documented in a booklet. The Rev. Charles Kapungwe was, therefore, burdened to put this work together including other works not previously documented to share the history of the Church in Zambia, Southern, East and Central Africa.

To put together such a work required collection of materials from many reliable sources. It also required finances and a lot of investment of time. Rev. Kapungwe, the burden bearer, decided to shoulder all the expenses and sacrifice to help preserve the history of this Church. In our society obsessed with misunderstandings and speculations, he wanted this to be categorically known that no other outside organization or individuals ever funded this work! Thus, the first instinct was to reach out to as many people as possible who we thought would be willing to share their stories. Alas, the response was very poor! Rev. Kapungwe then reached out to surviving ministers, spouses or their families who still had information which could be helpful to write such an extensive and important work. He is very grateful to those who heeded to the request.

God's ordained meetings with the Rev. David K. Simfukwe became pivotal moments for him to reconstruct this work. In 1986, while studying clinical medical sciences at Chainama College of Health Sciences in Lusaka, Zambia, Bro. Kapungwe had paid a courtesy call on the Rev. Simfukwe at Ebenezer A.M.E. Church where the latter was Pastor then. Unknown at the time that this meeting would play an important role in this work in future, the Rev. David Simfukwe had painstakingly shared his work to this young man who had wanted to know more about the Church's history. While at home at Chilenje in the mission house, the Rev. showed Bro. Kapungwe his work and it was at this time that Bro. Kapungwe had learned about how the Church had come to Northern Rhodesia and how it had reached various points in Zambia. He had seen the Rev. Simfukwe in many meetings before but this was the first time they ever talked for a long time and just the two of them. The senior minister always wanted to share his knowledge with the younger generation.

The Rev. David Simfukwe, an ardent educator like his wife Mother Rose Simfukwe, strived to disseminate the history of the A.M.E. Church in Central Africa. Unlike our friends in the West, writing books in our part of the world was not vigorously pursued by the church members or Ministers. When I was growing up, we had many books both in vernacular and English which were under Longmans or Oxford University Press written by different authors of the 1950s and 1960s who had influenced Zambian readers and schools. Writers such as Stephen A. Mpashi, Simon Mwansa Kapwepwe, Kenneth D. Kaunda, Dominic C. Mulaisho and later Vernon Mwaanga and others showed us the potential Zambian writers had. However, the Church hardly had any writers to document history. The Rev. Simfukwe not only republished the A.M.E. Church Bemba Hymnal but also wrote or put together a history book, albeit, in the old-fashioned way, through use of the stencil but his efforts, deserve to be applauded, regardless! Subsequently, I saw it fit to amalgamate his work and that of the Rev. J.L.C. Membe with mine to consolidate our story.

It was 22 years later (in 2008) that Rev. Charles Kapungwe was to meet the Rev. David Simfukwe again! This time, they met in Jacksonville, Florida in the U.S.A. At the time, Rev. Kapungwe and Rev. Paul Bupe were studying in the U.S. Rev. Simfukwe had migrated to the U.S.A. with his family as a Permanent Resident. With another brother from Zambia, Rev. Kapungwe visited the Simfukwe family and found that the Rev. Simfukwe had been unwell for a while. In spite of it, he still would read. They went to the library and Rev. Simfukwe sat on the computer for hours reading. He still was willing to pass over his knowledge. He was a teacher who had invested a lot of time and money in educating people, especially the underprivileged children. He was a man who had worked hard and he knew his work needed to be passed on. The duo (with a brother from Zambia) had also met Mother Rose Simfukwe at home.

In 2016, Rev. Charles Kapungwe increasingly became burdened that this work needed to reach a larger audience. This now was 30 years after having first met Rev. Simfukwe in 1986 in Lusaka, Zambia and 8 years after having been together in Florida. Rev. Kapungwe had looked at the work of the Rev. John Lester C. Membe whom he had passively known when Bro. Charles was a youth. He never at the time thought that he would need the work of this pioneer of the A.M.E. Church in Zambia in future, in order for him to tell a comprehensive history and disseminate it to a wider audience both in Zambia and abroad.

Rev. J.L.C. Membe's work offered a pertinent background that this writing needed! Nevertheless, this story wouldn't be possible too without another man, the Rev. David K. Simfukwe who had been entrusted with the story, by the founder and was an ardent educator himself too. Ultimately, another person in Rev. Kapungwe, came a man from a generation which had been burdened to make a difference. It was a generation spoken about by Joel which had received the Holy Spirit and decided to herald the story you are about read.

As mentioned above, the history told earlier came through a booklet. Written using the old technology which utilized the typewriter and a stencil, it was strongly felt by this brother that the work could be lost completely if it was not upgraded and stored into the current information technology systems. Rev. Kapungwe obtained oral history too from many eye witnesses. Also, there were single pages or stapled papers, typewritten or even handwritten work handed down to this history collector which too, would likely have been lost with time. Therefore, to recognize those who had laboured tireless, some of them who had been walking for miles, or were courageous to face authorities at the time when organising meetings and gatherings could easily have been misconstrued as political activism, the history of this Church needed to be told, to keep their memories alive.

The ultimate goal of the writing will also not be met if this work failed to document the change the Church has experienced over the years. This change, like the labour of the pioneers and their successors, is being credited to God. God, through the Holy Spirit and our Lord Jesus Christ, has been responsible in raising a people of power who have been moving by his Spirit and glorifying his name. Therefore, this history also highlights the work of the Holy Spirit in awakening this Church from lukewarmness, formalism, legalism, traditions, rituals and iniquity-related problems which had for years dogged the Church and made it lag behind many other denominations.

This writer recalls the extraordinary insight and understanding Bishop Larry T. Kirkland used to display during his tenure of office in the 17th Episcopal District. The Bishop who had been assigned to the District from 1996-2000, recognized the spiritual warfare the District had been going through and repeatedly sought the guidance of God and the Holy Spirit in his decision-making process on major issues. He was a man who was greatly used by the Holy Spirit. Whenever he discerned a conflict which he came to learn was as a result of the two factions at play (spiritual and natural), he would inform the Annual Conference that he was going to pray about the matter before making a decision. When the Bishop would come the following day, he would inform you of the decision he had made and believers would immediately confirm that such a decision came from the Lord!

A great spiritual divide in Zambia had dogged the Church for decades. Bishop Kirkland, however, had recognized that Pastors who were born again were likely or had been targets of persecution or being undermined. He himself once stated, "When I was born, my mother told me about it but when I was born again, I told my mother about it!" For instance, many of the issues involving the Rev. Wilson Mpundu in Annual Conferences, he handled them wisely by the Spirit of God in contrast to others.

The history of this Church will be incomplete if it does not state missteps of those who went before us. We learned in school the importance of learning history. Learning history helps us to understand the present so we can plan for tomorrow. Therefore, in order for our current generation to understand the current conditions, it has to learn how we arrived here. After that, it has to apply itself to either conforming to the status quo or to changing what it perceives to be wrong or not in conformity with the will of God. The will of God, in our view, is soul winning (evangelism) and discipleship – calling people to repentance, to be born again and to live for Jesus in holiness and reverence of him – not to a denomination.

This is important since our subject matter involves faith in God. It also involves the need to plan for the future – a better future, which must be the desire of every reader or believer in this Church. We also learn history because we are aware that history often repeats itself. Therefore, when a repetition of history which is not in line with the will of God occurs, the Church will be in an ideal position to respond better and in accordance to the will of God.

Lastly, knowledge of history will help us to measure progress. For example, since 1986 when Rev. Kapungwe learned about the history of the A.M.E. Church in Zambia, vis-à-vis the respective years the Church reached or started in a given town or city, it helped him determine the level of growth of the Church in that particular place. He had used this ever since as a spiritual barometer to gauge both Church growth and impediments or weaknesses. Consequently, each time he travelled to a new place, he was able to recall the year the A.M.E. Church was started or when it arrived in the area. This formed a strong basis for him to evaluate the spiritual stand, numerical growth or quality of building structure he saw in that particular area which generally reflected or told a story. In writing this work, therefore, these have been some of the goals which it is hoped will be met or important to learn from or utilize in our future ministry.

This history will be vital for every believer to study. It will be helpful to learn and evaluate personal ministries. It will be important to see and learn about how other people with inadequate facilities and limited resources sacrificed and laboured for their Master by walking long distances or using a bicycle, sailing in boats, traveling by bus or train to go and do the work of God. When we compare our friends with us who happen to have all the facilities and better methods at our disposal today to help us reach communities and nations, we may be challenged to ask ourselves as to how we have fared. We may also ask another question as to what kind of message are we, or have we been delivering?

This book will be useful to Bible students too. It will also be useful to believers wanting to study missions, be involved in missions or those who want to learn about history of Christianity in Southern, East and Central Africa. Learning about the role the Church (other denominations included) played in equipping people through provision of schools and education or teaching them the word of God, and producing native missionaries among themselves in the process, are lessons too important not to be missed.

Understanding the prevailing environment at any given time is important to fathom how the work at hand was affected or influenced. It is important to learn about the political, economic, cultural and spiritual environment that preceded the arrival of the Church here. These factors at play at the time, were going to impact both the spreading of the Word of God and expansion of the Church. Interaction between the Church and other new denominations or already established denominations, together with the regulatory roles of existing Colonial Governments in respective lands, was going to impact Church-planting too. Therefore, knowledge of the condition of the political environment at the time, will aid in understanding the work that God performed through his early missionaries on the continent of Africa, both native and foreign.

We are aware of the fact that such a work would not satisfy everyone. There will be omissions which were not intentional. Something had to be written despite such fears or else nothing could have been. The cost of such a work would be prohibitive if everyone had to be included! Thus, the ones covered here help to give us just an overview and truthful account of the history of the Church in this part of Africa. Also, to help account or cover for appropriate "dispensations" or timeframes covered by the three authors, we decided to run two concurrent prefaces and an editorial comment. This will help capture the history properly and accurately and address the expectation or need of each period or generations among the trio. May the Lord be glorified for all he has done and we thank all who contributed to this work. God be with you all.

Chapter 2
Prehistoric Africa

To cover the history of the A.M.E. Church in Zambia, understanding the context in which this history takes place is of great importance. The region in which the setting happens including the larger context of the continental history at interplay in the unfolding history helps us to understand issues as they unfold. Therefore, looking at Early Africa, the Middle Ages, Africa between 1500 and 1800 and Modern Africa will aid the reader to grasp the background and current trends to help understand the A.M.E. Church's arrival in Southern, East and Central Africa.

It is generally accepted among the scientific community that Africa is the continent where humans first inhabited the earth. This is the finding of many including a British Broadcasting Corporation (BBC) Science Correspondent, Richard Gray (Gray, 2009). As people of faith, though, we recognize that the continent of Africa was one with the Asia or Middle East before the Suez Canal was made and opened in 1869. By 100,000 BC, hunting and gathering of food using stone tools was the norm by modern humans. Humans then spread to Europe and by 5,000 BC, farming spread to Africa. People raised cattle, grew crops and it was believed that at the time the Sahara had been arable land before it became a desert. Writing was inverted in Egypt around 3,200 BC. The Egyptians crafted weapons and other tools at this time out of bronze but most of Africa at the time was cut off from Egyptian civilization by the Sahara Desert. Sub-Saharan Africa was also hindered from contact due to deficiency in good harbours which made access by sea not possible (Lambert, 2018).

Use of stone tools and weapons by farmers persisted until about 600 BC. At this period, use of iron had spread in North Africa and by 500 AD iron tools and weapons had eventually reached the present-day South Africa. In about 480 BC, the City of Carthage, in Tunisia, was founded by the Phoenicians who came from present day Lebanon. Later, Carthage was involved in wars with Rome and in 203 BC the Romans put to the sword the Carthaginians defeating them at the battle of Zama. Rome destroyed the City of Carthage in 146 BC and made them subject to the Roman Empire.

Egypt, however, flourished and its influence spread via the Nile reaching the kingdoms of Nubia and Kush. The duo emerged in what is the present-day Sudan. Also, the kingdom of Axum, an exceedingly civilized kingdom, arose in Ethiopia. "Though often overshadowed by its Egyptian neighbours to the north, the Kingdom of Kush stood as a regional power in Africa for over a thousand years. This ancient Nubian empire reached its peak in the second millennium B.C. when it ruled over a vast swath of territory along the Nile River in what is now Sudan," (Andrews, 2017). It became a trading partner with Rome, Arabia and India and in 4th Century AD, Axum became Christian. Rome continued to grow and in 30 BC, Egypt became a territory of the Roman Empire. In 42 AD, Morocco too fell to the Romans. "However, the rest of Africa was cut off from Rome by the Sahara Desert," (Lambert, 2018).

The Middle Ages in Africa

The Middle Ages began to reshape and alter Africa, especially North Africa. These years left a religious imprint that has persistently remained so for centuries. The Arabs conquered Egypt in 642 and in 698 to 700 they overran Tunis and Carthage and began to control the all coast of North Africa. Since the Arabs were Muslims, they introduced Islam to the whole region of North Africa. However, Ethiopia remained Christian but it was curtailed off from Europe by Muslims. "The Kingdom of Aksum (parts of Eritrea and Northern Ethiopia today) became one of the first empires in the world to adopt Christianity, which led to a political and military alliance with the Byzantines. [Byzantine Empire (Eastern Roman Empire) was continuation of the Roman Empire in the eastern provinces during Middle Ages whose capital was Constantinople (now Istanbul)]. Aksum empire later went into decline sometime around the 7th or 8th century, but its religious legacy still exists today in the form of the Ethiopian Orthodox Church," (Andrews, 2017). Note: Axum is a variant of Aksum.

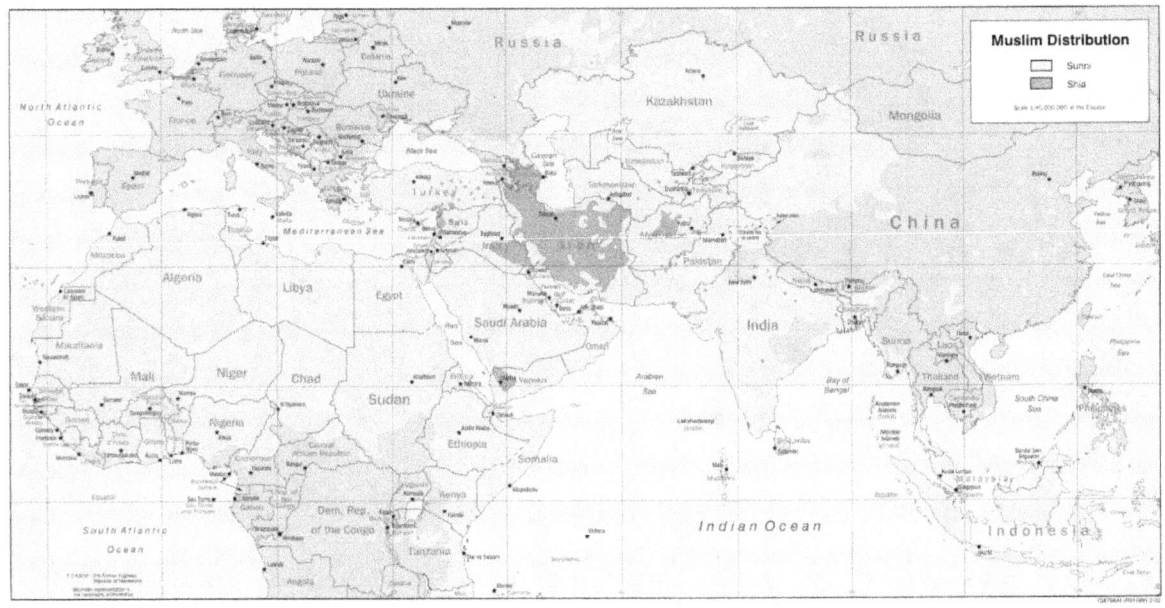

Africa and Asia Muslim Distribution – Open source maps of Africa Yahoo Image Search 9-22-2018

After 800 AD, northern Africa saw the emergent of organized kingdoms. The kingdoms engaged in trade with the Arabs in the north and this contact led to the spread of Islam to northern Africa. Arab traders brought salt and other luxury goods in exchange for gold and slaves from Africans. One such organized kingdom to emerge among early African kingdoms was Ghana. It included regions of Mali, Mauritania and what is the country of Ghana today. Ghana became known as the land of gold by the 9th century and was later to derive its name from this becoming Gold Coast when the British came. Nevertheless, Ghana was destroyed in the 11th century by African raiders from the north.

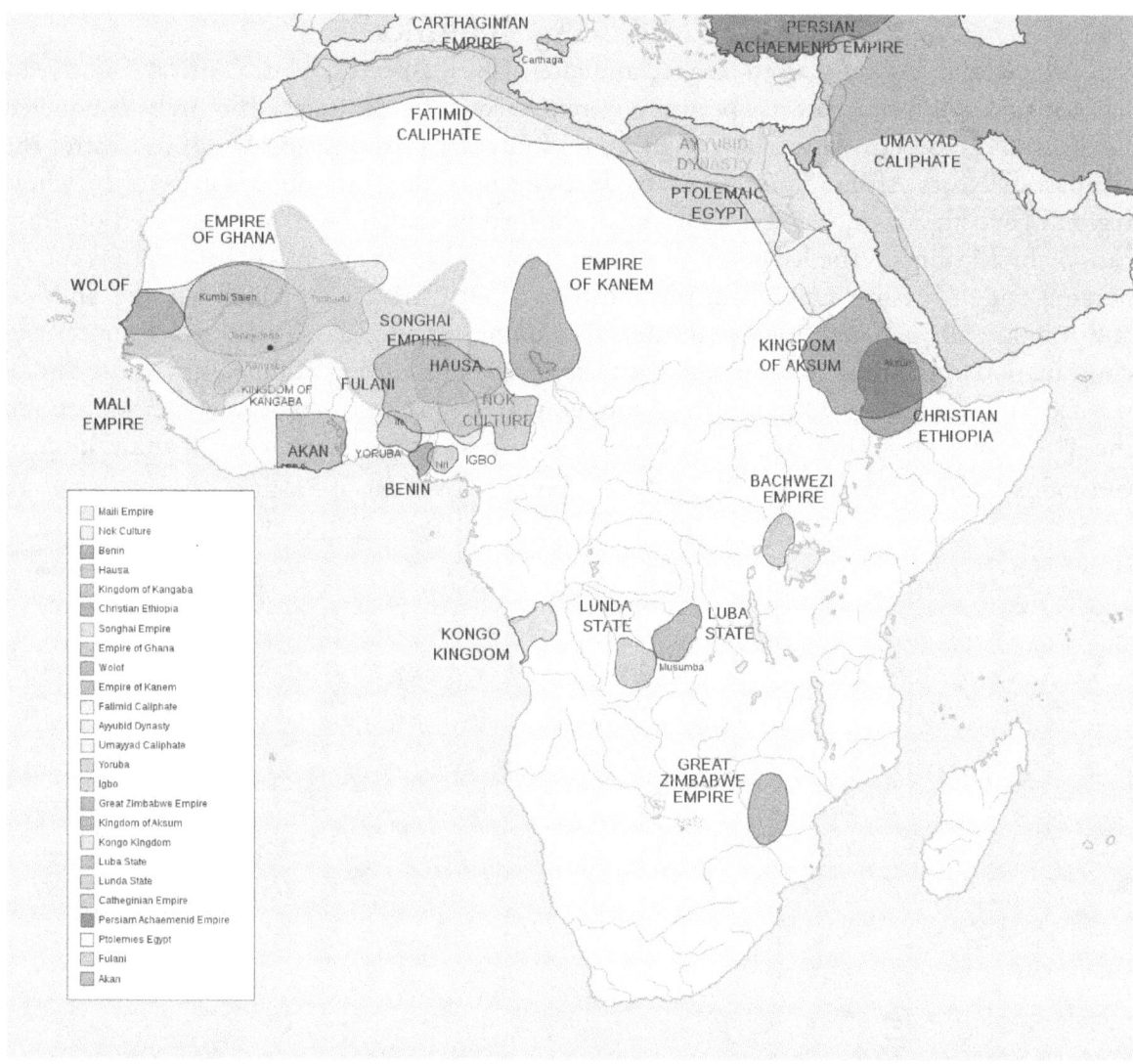

African civilizations map – Precolonial – Open source maps of Africa Yahoo Image Search 9-22-2018

The City of Ife in South-West Nigeria also flourished in the 11th century. It became the center of a great kingdom and from the 12th century Africans who were good at making crafts from Ife, made terracotta sculptures and bronze heads. Nevertheless, Ife began to decline in the 16th century. Benin was another African kingdom which appeared in the 13th century. The old kingdom of Benin was larger than the current country. In the 13th century, the kingdom was prosperous and powerful. The kingdom of Mali began to emerge too in the 13th century. It equally became rich and powerful by the 14th century. The famous city of Timbuktu was in Mali and was a busy market place where salt, horses, gold and slaves were the "merchandise" sold. "Sundiata Keita – sometimes called the 'Lion King' led a revolt against a Sosso king and united his subjects into a new state. At Timbuktu was one institution, Timbuktu Sankore

University, which included a library with an estimated 700,000 manuscripts," (Andrews, 2017). The kingdom of Songhai which arose in the 16th century, however, was destroyed by Mali.

Songhai arose as a kingdom located east of Mali from the 14th to the 16th century. It was on the Niger River. It was strongest around 1500 AD but was obliterated in 1591 by the Moroccans, breaking it up. Near Lake Chad, Kanem-Bornu was another powerful North African kingdom to emerge. It sprung up in the 9th century and remained independent until the 19th century. "For sheer size, few states in African history compare to the Songhai Empire. Formed in the 15th century from some of the former regions of the Mali Empire, this West African kingdom was larger than Western Europe and comprised parts of a dozen modern day nations. The empire enjoyed a period of prosperity thanks to vigorous trade policies and sophisticated bureaucratic system that separated its vast holdings into different provinces, each ruled by its governor," (Andrews, 2017).

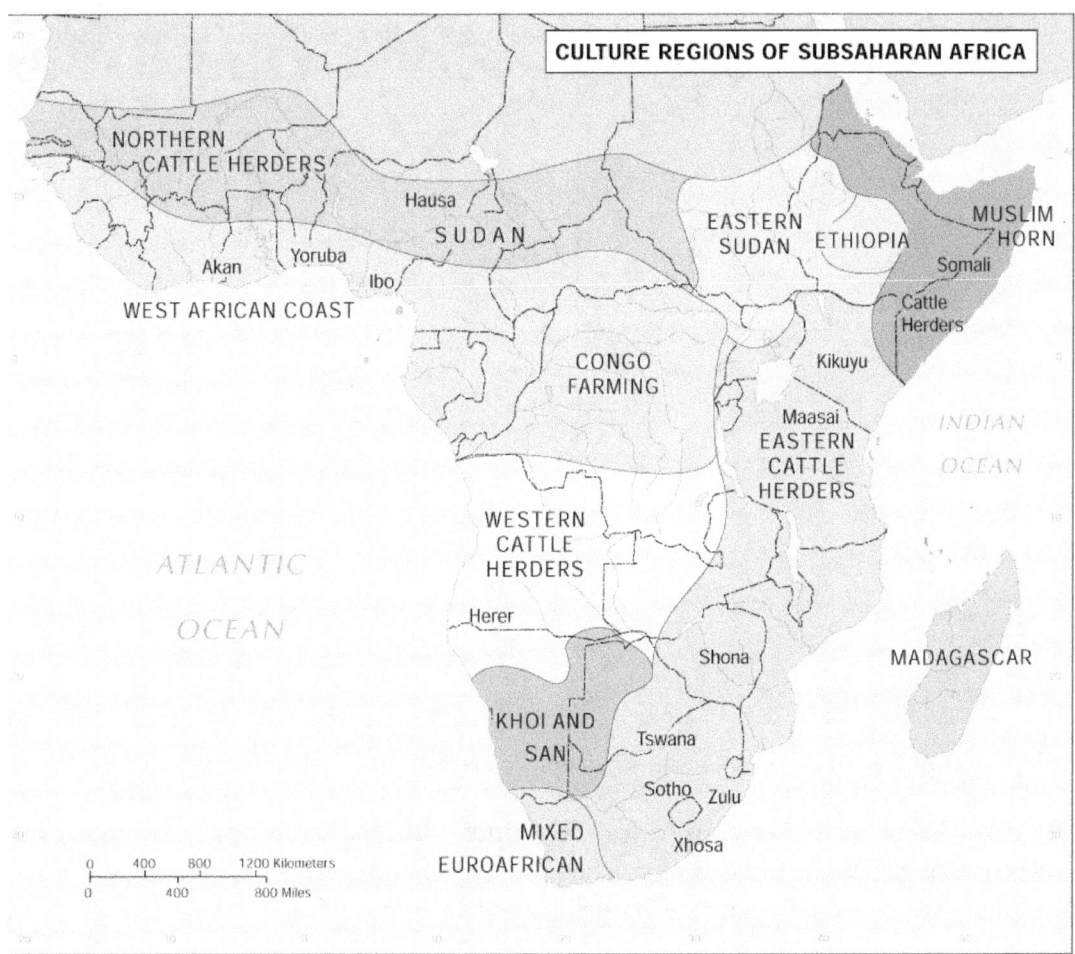

Culture regions of Sub-Saharan Africa – Open source maps of Africa Yahoo Image Search 9-22-2018

Soon, Arabs began to sail down the east coast of Africa. They began to settle in new-found territories such as Mogadishu and the island of Zanzibar. Southern Africa was being organized by ethnic groups too to form organized kingdoms. About 1430, well-built structures from stone known as the Great Zimbabwe were put up. Myths and legends included belief that it was the residence of the Biblical Queen of Sheba but now historians believe it was a capital city of an indigenous empire which thrived between the 13th and 15th centuries. The kingdom ruled over a large portion of modern-day Botswana, Zimbabwe and Mozambique. It was rich in cattle, precious stones and gold and was connected to the Indian Ocean Coast (Andrews, 2017). Ethiopia too was flourishing in the Middle Ages and a well-known church of St. George was built around 1200.

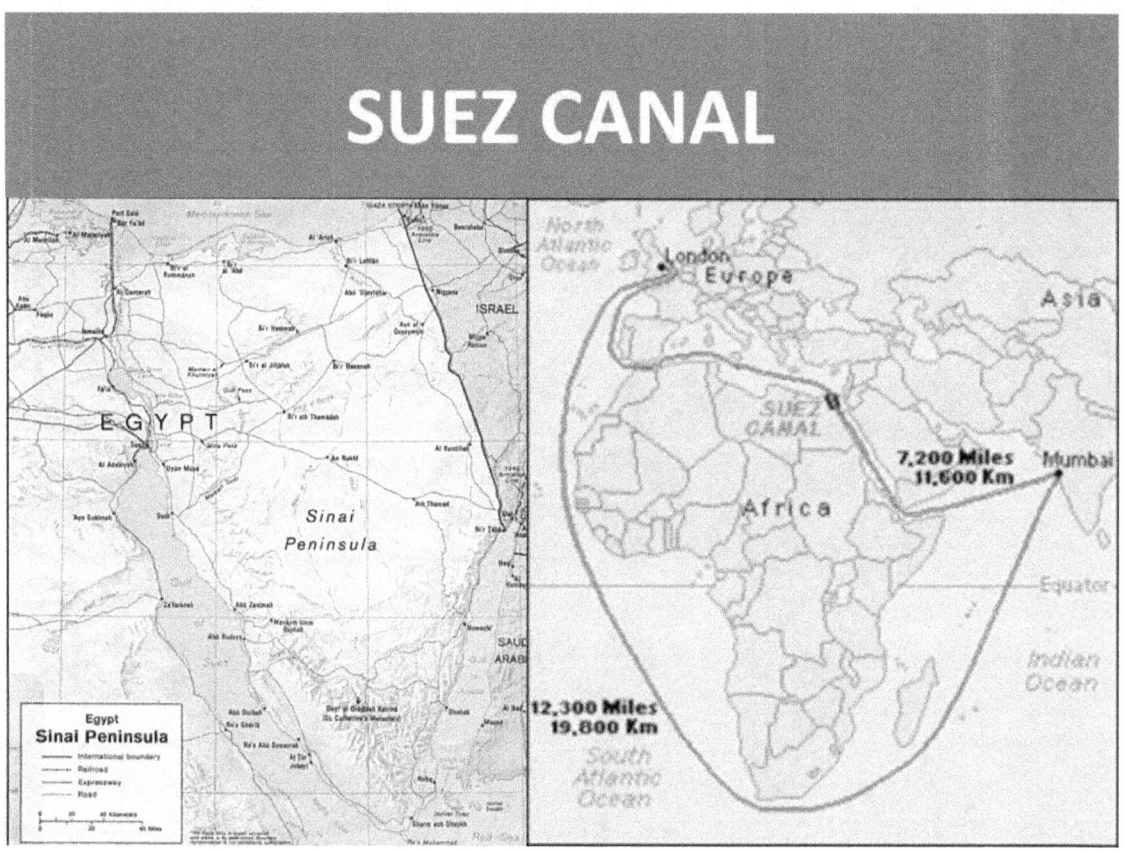

Early Map of Africa and the Suez-Canal – Open source maps of Africa Yahoo Image Search 9-22-2018

Portugal had a keen interest in Africa at the time. Their explorers began to venture out on the west coast of Africa. In 1431, they reached the Azores and in 1445 they reached the mouth of the Congo River. The Portuguese eventually sailed around the Cape of Good Hope in 1488.

Africa's History from 1500-1800

Europeans began the trans-Atlantic transportation of African slaves in the 16th century. Arabs had perpetrated the trade by wooing African kingdoms with gun powder, guns, salt, clothes and other goods in exchange for slaves. The Arabs acted as middlemen for Europeans and slave trade grew becoming a very lucrative business for Arabs, Europeans and Americans. Rev. Charles Kapungwe recalls his grandparents telling them stories of how they used to be warned by their parents or grandparents not to go in certain areas because people were lurking in designated places to catch people whom they sold as slaves. His grandmother on his father's side Mrs. Fanny Mwape Kapungwe was a daughter of an Arab father! *"Kwa Engwe,"* an area where the current Children's Hospital, Arthur Davison's Hospital in Ndola, Zambia is, used to be dreaded for "slave catchers" he recalls. Ndola has a historical tree known as the "Slave Tree" which was one of the spots slave transaction and routes occurred.

Ships from Britain began to bring finished products to Africa. Products included gun powder, alcohol, cloth, metal ware and firearms. They took slaves to America, South America or West Indies. On their way back to Britain they carried sugar from West Indies and cotton, tobacco, rum and lumber from America. The route became known as the "Triangular Slave Trade" and it involved other European nations too besides the British, especially the Portuguese and the Spanish. France had also participated for a while. Raids supported by this lucrative business ensured that slavery was perpetrated and it lasted about 400 years capturing over 12 million Africans. In the 16th and 18th centuries, Barbary pirates from the North African coast robbed Spanish and Portuguese ships and the Turks conquered most of the North African coast in 16th century. Egypt was conquered in 1517 and by 1556 nearly all of North Africa was under the Turks. Interior to the south, Africans continued to build powerful kingdoms. Kanem-Bornu continued to enlarge, thanks to the guns which they bought from the Turks. Ethiopia's power went down in the 16th century; nevertheless, its importance never waned.

Europeans, soon saw potential in the new territories of Africa. The Portuguese settled in Portuguese West Africa (Angola) and Portuguese East Africa (Mozambique) in the 16th century. The Dutch also settled in South Africa establishing a new colony in 1652. They were led by Jan van Riebeeck, an official of the Dutch East India Company.

Africa's Modern History

Europeans took a lot of interest in Africa in the 19th century. They began taking steps to ban slave trade and Britain banned it in 1807. Nevertheless, they took a step to begin colonizing Africa in the 19th century. The British took the Dutch colony in 1814 in South Africa while the French invaded northern Algeria in 1830. It was late in the 19th century that colonization became completed in what had been labeled "The Scramble for Africa" by Europeans from around 1881 to 1914. It was also termed as the "Partition of Africa." However, it was the Berlin Conference of 1884 which formally regulated the partition of Africa. The Germans took South West Africa (Namibia), Togo and Cameroon in 1884 and they got Tanganyika in 1885 while the Belgians took Belgian Congo (now Democratic Republic of Congo). The French grabbed Madagascar in 1896 and extended their influence further in the north by taking Morocco in 1912. The Italians grabbed Libya while the British took Egypt in 1914. When the Italians invaded Ethiopia in 1896, they were defeated by the latter and Ethiopia and Liberia remained the only uncolonised states in Africa (Lambert, 2018).

African Colonies after the Berlin Conference of 1884 – Open source maps of Africa Yahoo Image Search 9-25-2018

In the southern half of Africa, the British further took more countries. They took Southern Rhodesia (Zimbabwe), Northern Rhodesia (Zambia), Nyasaland (Malawi), Bechuanaland (Botswana), Basutoland (Lesotho), Swaziland (Eswatini), Uganda and Kenya. Portuguese West Africa (Angola) and Portuguese East Africa (Mozambique) were already firmly under the control of the Portuguese.

Views concerning imperialism began to change in the 20th century in Europe. European and American churches provided schools and this led to many Africans become educated. This became a catalyst to bringing about change. The wheels of change for independence became inevitable and in the 1950s and 1960s most African countries became independent. In 1960 alone 17 countries gained independence (Lambert, 2018). Angola and Mozambique, however, had to wait till 1975 while Zimbabwe had to wait even longer until 1980. South Africa remained under apartheid until 1994 when Nelson Mandela became president after the law which stopped apartheid was signed by F.W. de Klerk in 1993.

There has been a lot of change in the 21st century with economic growth in many African countries today. However, the threat of a new exogenously introduced disease, HIV from around 1984, has been the trauma against the hope that Africa is now currently rubbing herself with and faith is being put in God for Africa to triumph. Also, currency manipulation, debt impositions, foreign instigated coups, syphoning of wealth, economic destabilization and foreign-induced wars have evolved as new covert slave trade – cancers that Africa has to eradicate to shame her captors.

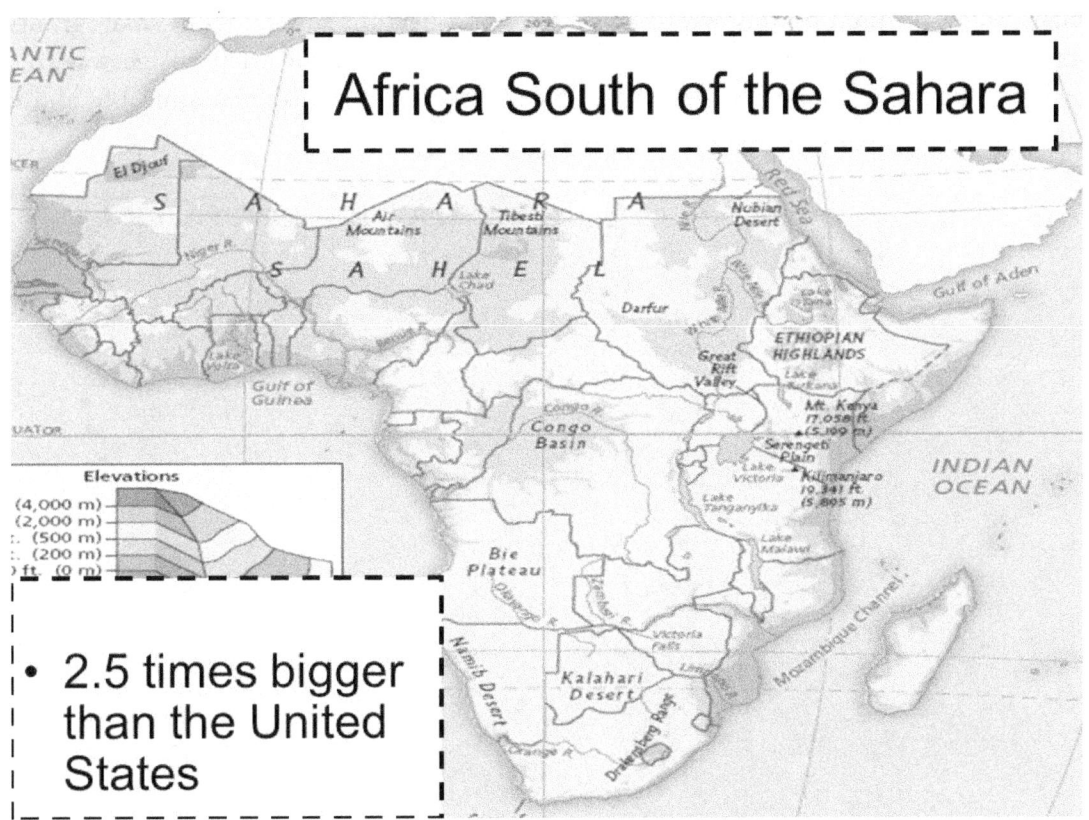

Sub-Saharan Africa: Size – Open source maps of Africa Yahoo Image Search 9-22-2018

Chapter 3
The Setting – Prehistoric Zambia

Northern Rhodesia was inhabited by what were termed as "Bushmen" during the period of Biblical days. The inhabitants gathered food during the stone age and used bows and arrows to hunt and trap animals. They gathered fruits, nuts, caterpillars and locusts. They lived semi-nomadic life and lived in thatched houses. However, in about 4th century groups of Bantu-speaking arrived from the north and settled in different parts of present-day Zambia.

The Bantu were farmers and used iron tools. They planted sorghum, beans, bananas and yams. They raised cattle and goats and used arrows to hunt or tipped arrows to kill trapped animals. They also used pottery which they made and lived in small huts in small groups of about twelve or so. They used slash and burn-type agriculture and each village was by and large self-sufficient in its needs. The Bantu lived alongside the Bushmen amicably and only when the soil appeared to be spent did they relocate.

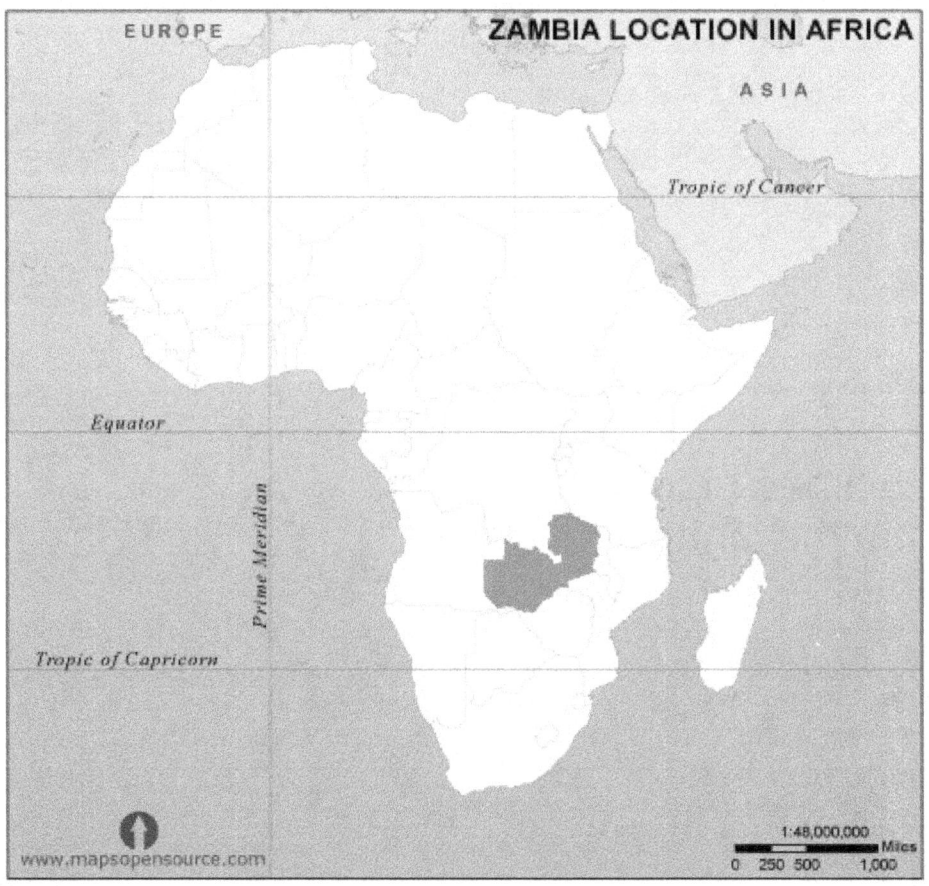

Zambia location in Africa – Open source maps of Africa Yahoo Image Search 9-22-2018

An Advanced Society Emerges in Zambia

A more advanced Iron Age culture, by 11th or 12th century emerged. Long distance trade grew and notable ones are the *"Ing'ombe Ilede"* (A place where the cow lies) near the convergence of the Zambezi and the Kafue Rivers. This area is believed to have had a significant commercial activity and traded in salt among other goods amidst a flourishing culture. Cotton was weaved; copper crafts were made into crosses and were used as currency. They also made copper bracelets and had ivory carving. The area had both a sizable population and some political activity too.

Organised kingdoms grew by 1500. The Chewa in the east, the Lozi in the west and the Bemba and Lunda in the north were the largest. In the 16th century, some men were buried with gold beads and some rulers had glass beads from the Indian Ocean coast. Farmers in the north (the Bemba), practiced slash and burn agriculture known as *"Chitemene."* When the soil was spent, they migrated to new lands. The farmers interacted peacefully with the "Bushmen" for centuries.

Europeans in Zambia

Zambia, being inland, had no direct contact with Europeans. There was interaction with Arab slave traders though. The Portuguese were, however, on both coasts, Portuguese West Africa (Angola) and Portuguese East Africa (Mozambique), sandwiching landlocked Zambia in the middle. The Portuguese, by 1500, brought new foods, maize and cassava from the Americas even though they never went far inland. Raids inland for obtaining slaves by ethnic groups aided or influenced by Arab middlemen were the means by which contacts with Europeans, mostly, the Portuguese in coastal areas occurred.

From the 7th century, the Arabs had been involved in slave trade. The Portuguese were able to sail around the coast of Africa by 1500. Direct contact with the Europeans occurred in the 19th century. Shaka the Zulu, a warrior, arose in the early 19th century in what is South Africa today. He raided other ethnic groups and many fled his dreaded warriors and some groups reached as far north as Zambia. The Makololo fled and crossed the Zambezi in 1830's and went north of the Victoria Falls. They later attacked the Lozi who had a kingdom in the upper Zambezi subduing them. They established the Makololo kingdom but the Lozi took control of their kingdom again in the 1860's.

Other ethnic groups were displaced by the Zulu warriors. The Ngoni migrated away from Shaka in the 1820's and crossed the Zambezi in 1835. They went as far as Lake Tanganyika but later settled in east Zambia. They raided other groups or traders' caravans to obtain their food (Lambert, 2017).

Dr. David Livingstone, the Scottish explorer, physician and missionary was the first European credited to have made contact with inland Zambia. During the trip he reached the Zambezi in 1851. He met the Makololo kingdom and observed the upper class dressed in British cloth which had been sold to Africans by the Portuguese from Portuguese West Africa. He established a mission among the Makololo but it never took off because of deaths of members. He desired to end slave trade by replacing it with normal trade such as supply of cotton (which was grown by Africans and the demand in Europe was high) and ivory in exchange for European goods which were in demand too by Africans. Many Africans who were caught or sold came from small agricultural communities and had the knowhow of how to grow crops. They were now used in the colonies to grow sugar and cotton. Europeans made keyboards and snooker balls out of ivory.

Zambia Under the British

Livingstone was the first European to see the Victoria Falls. He named it after the Queen of England on 16th November, 1855. He also wanted to convert the Africans. He explored inland. Sister Evelyn Chitente, one of our sisters from Central Assembly of God who attended our joint cell group with A.M.E. Church at my home for years in the early 1990's in Kitwe shared an interesting story to me about her father! Her mother was from Thomas' village, Chief Munkanta in Kawambwa District while her father, originally, a Katongo, from Northern Province, after serving a local chief at Mbereshi, had his name changed to Chitente. He had been a sectional leader so people called the place or person *"Kwa Chitente"* (Sectional Leader), hence, the name change. Her dad was Livingstone Mwale Chitente because it was believed that her grandfather, while he was a youth had met Dr. Livingstone!

David Livingstone died in present day Zambia on 1st May, 1873 at Chitambo's Village. The village is located south of the Bangweulu Swamps and north of Serenje. His first trip from the UK was via Cape Town in 1841. He then went north across the Kalahari. He was at Lake Ngami (in Botswana) in 1849 and the Zambezi in 1851. He had taken three expeditions to Africa. There was about 35 years of Europeans' absence after Livingstone. Not much was recorded until 1889 to 1901 when the British came. This followed activities in 1889 where Cecil Rhodes (1853-1902) came into play after setting up British South African Company (BSAC) with the view of carrying out mineral exploration in southern and central Africa. Since Britain did not want to foot the bills over the running of the colonies, the BSAC was seen as the best way to achieve this. Rhodes and his company, therefore, entered into treaties with different African ethnic groups for prospecting and mining rights.

Eventually, after mining activities had begun, the British took claim of the territories. The Lozi, seeking protection from the Ndebele, sought for help from the British in exchange for mining rights even though the area the Lozi lived in was nowhere close to the region where minerals had been discovered – on the Copperbelt. The Lozi also thought this was an opportunity for the British to build schools in the kingdom; therefore, Lewanika signed the document while talking to a representative of BSAC in a mistaken belief that he was a representative of the British (Lambert, 2017).

The king granted permission to the company to mine in "his" territory. This was to be done in exchange for £2,000 a year and protection from the Ndebele. However, the British did not authoritatively deal with the Ndebele until the Ndebele raided the Lozi in 1893 again. Also, it was only until 1897 that money was sent via a representative of the British. Cecil Rhodes entered into other treaties with other ethnic groups, namely, the Tabwa, the Lungu and the Mambwe in 1891 to 1894.

The Bemba and the Ngoni, nonetheless, refused to negotiate. Consequently, they were defeated by force. The Bembas, at first withstood and held on to their position against a small number of British troops sent against them. Through raiding long-distance caravans, the Bembas would obtain arms. However, when the Europeans took more land in Africa, the caravans ceased and the source for power for the Bembas waned. A French Catholic Missionary, Joseph-Marie-Stanislaus Dupont (1850-1930) alias, *"Moto-Moto"* (meaning *"Fire-Fire"*), persuaded and forced himself as Chief of the Bembas amidst succession wrangles among faction groups in 1898. This helped him to invite the BSAC from Fort Jameson and later from Abercorn to the area since the British dreaded the Bemba and it marked the British presence at Kasama.

The Ngoni were defeated by the British using machine guns. The British took their land and cattle and made them wage labourers. When initially Rhodes and his men did not find the minerals (they found copper ore, copper oxide at or near the surface and zinc, they were not hopeful for the mineral wealth), they forced the people to pay a hut tax which led to many able-bodied men find work as wage labourers in South Africa or Southern Rhodesia. Uprising against forced taxes were suppressed through use of force. Imprisonment or burning of huts by the British was usually the punishment! Later in the 1920's below the copper oxide, was found to be huge amounts of copper sulphide and this helped change the economics of the land.

Only about 3,000 Europeans were in the present territory of Zambia by 1914. The majority lived along the line of rail and farms where the Africans provided labour. Indians were traders and worked as middlemen between Africans and Europeans.

Zambia into the 20th Century

With mining projected to becoming a major source of wealth for the British and the BSAC, easy access to the resources became a priority. Also, reliable power supply to giant copper mines was important. Cecil Rhodes dreamed of a road from Cape to Cairo. A railway bridge was constructed from the south in Rhodesia to the north across the Zambezi River. Livingstone was established in 1905 when the railway line was built. The railway line reached Belgian Congo in 1909. Zambia comprised two parts North-Western Rhodesia and North-Eastern Rhodesia. Livingstone, after 1907, was the capital of North-Western Rhodesia while Fort Jameson (Chipata) was the capital of North-Eastern Rhodesia. The two regions were joined in 1911 as Northern Rhodesia with the capital at Livingstone.

Lusaka was established in 1905. Lead mining at Broken Hill (Kabwe) was underway, therefore, Lusaka was to serve the lead mine at Broken Hill. In 1935, Lusaka became the capital of Northern Rhodesia. In 1904, Ndola was founded. At the time, Tanganyika Territory was under the Germans and when World War I broke, about 3,500 Northern Rhodesian troops were used to fight the Germans there. In addition, between 50,000 and 100,000 Northern Rhodesians joined the British Army as porters. The country suffered since a lot of cattle and grain was confiscated for use during war.

By 1923, Britain had begun backpedaling on its earlier positive attitude towards the Africans. This followed its earlier stance of fighting slavery. They also were not in favour of the British South African Company being in control so they made Zambia a British Protectorate in

1923. A legislative council was formed in 1925 and it did not include any black involvement. The colonial secretary made pronouncements in 1929 about future interests of blacks to be important but these words were considered empty by many Africans.

Economic Boom Through Mineral Wealth

Northern Rhodesia quickly evolved strongly financially with the discovery of huge copper and cobalt deposits in 1928. Kitwe, the hub of the Copperbelt, was founded in 1936 and by 1939 Northern Rhodesia was the leading supplier of copper in the world. Northern Rhodesia became a prosperous country. The white population in the mines reached around 4,000 compared to about 30,000 African miners in 1930. Although the price of copper fell in the 1930's the demand for copper grew between 1935 and 1937. More white settlers came from the UK but the majority was from South Africa and the number of whites reached about 13,000 in 1939, threefold the population of 1930 (Lambert, 2017).

Anticipating more whites to come, the British government divided the land into two. There was land exclusively for whites and then another for blacks. They also subdivided shopping centers in the towns or cities into "first class" (mostly for whites) and "second class" for Africans. Nevertheless, most of the lands set aside for the whites remained empty since many whites preferred to have long term settlement in either Southern Rhodesia or South Africa. Africans were, however, left short of land. Compulsory taxation forced Africans to take up jobs as wage labourers for whites. By 1936 about 60% of men who could work in Northern Rhodesia were working away from home. An estimated 60,000 were employed in Northern Rhodesia, mostly as miners. The rest worked on plantations in Southern Rhodesia or Tanganyika Territory.

Huge numbers of men from different corners of Northern Rhodesia and neighbouring states working together in the mines created an important social bond. While absence from their ethnic groups tended to weaken ethnic bonds, they instead created new bonds amongst miners. Instead of seeing themselves as belonging to different ethnic groups, miners tended to see themselves as miners primarily. Africans had no trade union in the 1930's, however, African miners went on strike spontaneously. Work stoppage came with riots but the government used the army to stop them. They recorded loss of life (six miners) and 22 injured.

White miners went on strike in 1940 demanding improved conditions too. The employers conceded and gave them improved conditions. Africans, in spite of still not having a trade union decided to follow suit. Their strike was accompanied by riots and was overpowered by force claiming 17 miners' lives and wounding 64. Subsequently, in 1948, African miners organized themselves and created a trade union. The Railway workers did the same in 1949. African trade unions' presence became a major threat to British rule.

Changes in Northern Rhodesia appeared inevitable in the 1930s. Besides awareness of poor enumerations, inequalities and perceived injustices in political governance by miners, other signs of discontentment elsewhere were appearing on the horizon. Since the late 19th century, missionaries had been establishing schools which gave the local population education. The British government started to provide education to their subjects too in the 1930s. As a result, there was an increase in the number of educated Africans. They took up jobs as clerks, teachers or traders and began to participate in the affairs which concerned them. They started organizing themselves by making welfare associations. By 1933, welfare associations had been established at Abercorn, Kasama and Fort Jameson. Initially, welfare associations fought against local injustices but they evolved to be a voice speaking for the need for independence. Consequently, in 1946, about 14 welfare associations came together and created the Federation of African Societies of Northern Rhodesia.

Positive Outlook in Governance Evolves

The pressure provided from discontentment began to finally yield positive results. The British government in the 1930s and 1940s made concessions to the way governance was going to be carried out. They implemented a new policy of indirect rule. This was to involve African chiefs taking up a role in local administration. Following the Copperbelt unrest in 1935, the government formed urban advisory councils granting urban Africans "advisory" role in the manner towns were to be run. In addition, African provincial councils were formed in 1943. They comprised chiefly traditional chiefs but did have elected members as well.

In the end, an African Representative Council was formed in 1946. It was composed of 25 elected members and 4 appointed members by the Paramount Chief Lewanika of Barotseland in the west of Northern Rhodesia. Later, in 1948 some Africans were appointed to the legislative council and the following year African National Congress (ANC), was formed from the welfare associations which had their beginning in the 1930s. This began the process of challenging the legitimacy of British governance in Northern Rhodesia and a movement towards fighting for independence.

These developments began to unsettle the white settlers in Nyasaland, Northern Rhodesia and Southern Rhodesia. They began to collaborate on how best they could prevent political activism and possible independence by Africans. They chose to form a single territory from the three different colonies. This, it was conceptualized, was going to help them control the Africans easily. In the 1940s, the white settlers vigorously campaigned for amalgamation of the three territories but they were faced with strong opposition from the Africans.

However, a compromise was put into effect by London in 1953. It constituted the formation of a federation. The federation retained autonomy of each of the three governments and was responsible for local administration and its "Native affairs." However, a federal parliament was formed and had responsibility over matters which concerned more than one colony including foreign affairs. Only 6 Members of Parliament (two from each colony) were to be Africans out of the 35 MPs! In addition, only whites were mandated to elect African MPs from Southern Rhodesia to represent Southern Rhodesia in parliament! Also, the African MPs were granted the power to query any legislation they considered racist and to be sent to London to either be approved or vetoed!

The African MPs were going to be tested to this effect by the due process. In 1957 and 1958, the federal parliament passed a legislation that increased the number of African MPs. Nevertheless, it warranted also that the majority of voters were to be white! When the African

MPs sent this legislation to London as provided by the law, London approved it, regardless! Also, during the entire Federation period (1953-1963), the Federal Government weaned off the revenues from Northern Rhodesia copper mines and spent it scantily on Northern Rhodesia! The only big development done in Northern Rhodesia at the time was Kariba Dam which was constructed from 1955-1959 to produce electricity. Interestingly, "Southern Rhodesians made no secret of the fact that they regarded Northern Rhodesia as a resource to be exploited," (Lambert, 2017). A huge lake came into being in 1960-1961 behind the dam leading to resettlement of 50,000 people. Also, many wild animals were rescued in what was known as "Operation Noah."

The Copperbelt Province grew to become one of the richest lands on the continent. Chingola was established in 1943 and Kalulushi was founded as a company town for miners in 1953. It was made a public town in 1958. Despite copper being Zambia's main export by 1950s, Zambia had a huge gemstone industry as well. It included beryl, rubies, sapphires and other precious and semi-precious stones. Consequentially, the white population grew rapidly reaching 50,000 by 1955. This represented a white population of 3% and majority of these new immigrants hailed from Britain. They enjoyed a relatively high standard of living in comparison to the one they had in post-war Britain which was characterized by shortages and rationing. By the late 1950s the average salary for a white worker was £2,071 a year while for a black worker it was £203 a year (Lambert, 2017).

A new bill was announced by the governor introducing a new constitution for the colony. The leader of ANC, Harry Mwaanga Nkumbula welcomed it leading to a split in the party. The more radical members of the party founded the United National Independence Party (UNIP). It was led by Kenneth Kaunda after 1961 and white settlers were destined to lose the grip on the nation. Educated Africans were increasing and after 1953 they were allowed to take up jobs in management in the two major mining conglomerates. Later, in 1955, African miners went on strike. The strike lasted 58 days and ended up in victory. Their grievances were addressed proving that they were getting better organized. Moreover, world opinion was turning against imperialism and in 1960 British Prime Minister Harold Macmillan acknowledged the inevitability of the coming change which was sweeping through Africa demanding for independence.

Zambia Gains Her Independence

The white settlers, however, did not let go of their wishes easily. The British Secretary of State of Colonies proposed a constitution for Zambia which promised to give Africans control. The white settlers pressured the secretary of state to amend the proposal and grant them control instead. Kenneth Kaunda threatened to "Paralyse" the government if the constitution was not reversed. He called for peaceful protests but the protests deteriorated into violence and destructions. The disorder was called "Cha Cha Cha."

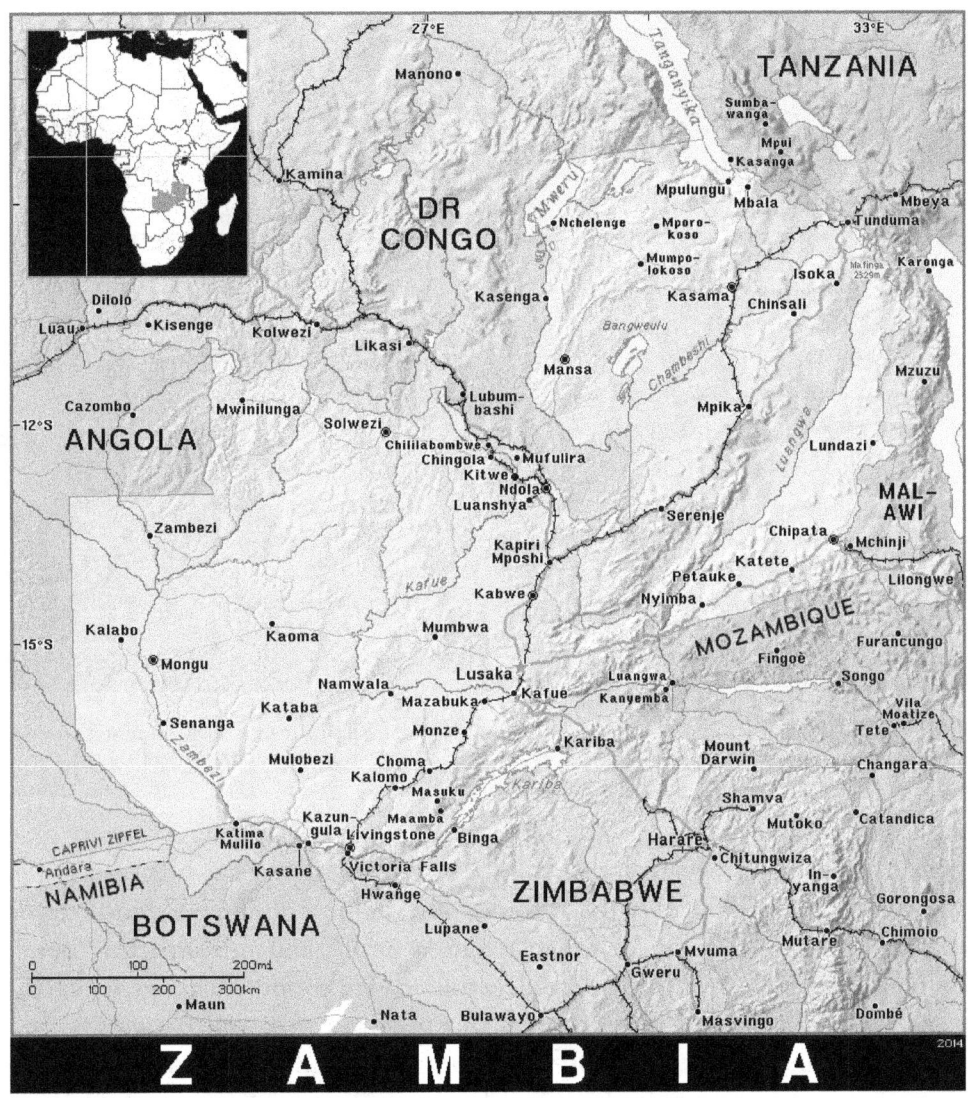

Zambia – Open source maps of Africa Yahoo Image Search 9-22-2018

The British government curved in to the demands by Africans. The constitution was amended giving the Africans a small majority in the parliament. Elections were held in 1962. ANC and UNIP formed a coalition as an incoming government while the British colony readied itself for independence. In 1963, after 10 years of its existence, the Federation of Northern Rhodesia, Southern Rhodesia and Nyasaland was dissolved. Kenneth Kaunda became Prime Minister in January, 1964 following a UNIP victory. In the same year, Zambia was beleaguered by a rebellion which was led by Alice Lenshina of Lumpa Church and the government used force to quell it. Over 700 members were killed at Sione Church at Chinsali, Northern Province on July 24, 1964. Zambia became independent on 24th October, 1964 and Kenneth Kaunda became the first president.

Rev. Paul Bupe and Rev. Charles Kapungwe with Zambia's first Republic leader, President Kenneth David Kaunda at Clarion Town House Hotel in Columbia, South Carolina, U.S.A. 18th March, 2003.

Zambia faced many challenges as a new nation. With hardly 100 university graduates at independence, poor infrastructure and few schools, a plan called First National Development Plan to run from 1965-1969 was hatched to develop the new country. Kaunda devoted most of the resources to the public sector which required health and infrastructure development. He also put finances on education. Large dependence on copper earnings which accounted about 90% was a challenge which the government began to work on to diversify its earnings.

Southern African countries continued to struggle to gain independence. Belgian Congo (Democratic Republic of Congo) which had been acquired by King Leopold II of Belgian as a personal property in 1885, got its independence in 1960. It had been run as an official colony in 1908 after nearly 10 million people had died. Tanzania had gained her self-rule in 1961 from Britain and merged with Zanzibar in 1964 to form one nation. Germany had ruled the territory but lost it to the British after World War I. Botswana gained her independence in 1966 after being a British protectorate since 1885. Swaziland (Eswatini) which had been ruled by Britain from 1903 gained her independence in 1968. Lesotho, first under the British in 1868, was annexed to the Boers of Cape Colony in 1871 and later returned to the British in 1884, got her independence in 1970.

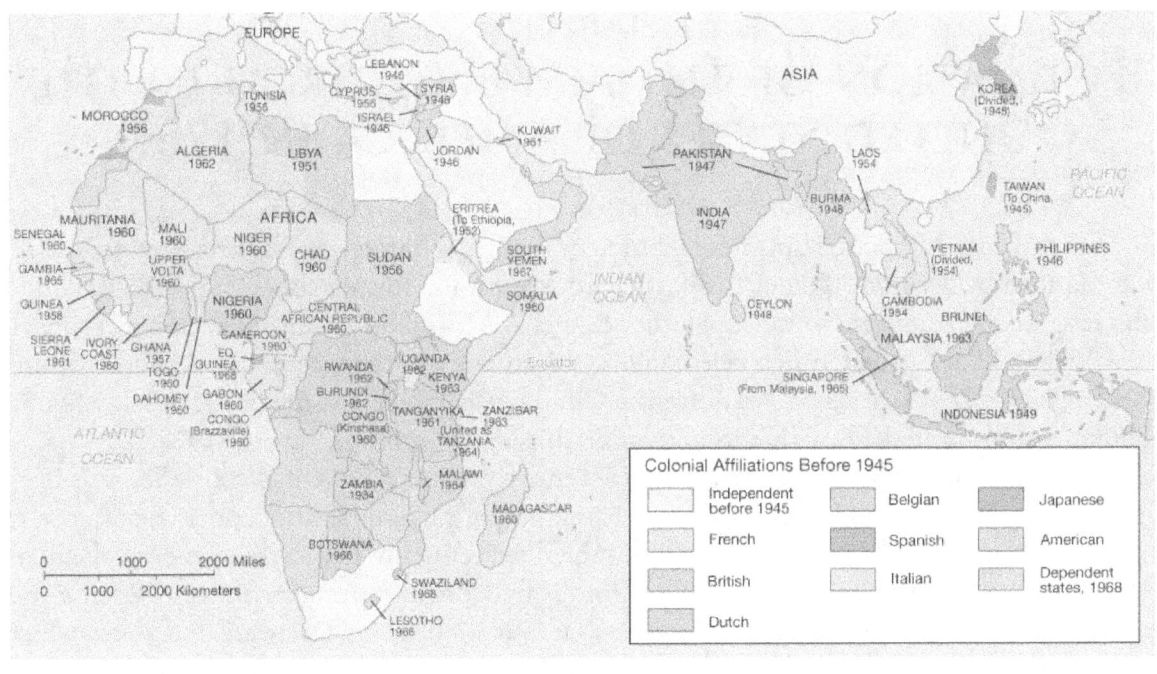

Decolonization

Africa and Asia – Decolonisation – Open source maps of Africa Yahoo Image Search 9-25-2018

However, other Southern African countries were not as fortunate or blessed as the countries mentioned above. Angola's independence came in 1975 after nearly 500 years of Portuguese' rule and it came by the barrel of the gun. Mozambique too, after being under the Portuguese since 1530 obtained their independence in 1975 after a bloody armed struggle. South West Africa (Namibia), first ruled by Germany, then handed over to South Africa after World War I, obtained her independence in 1978 after an armed struggle as well. Southern Rhodesia's (Zimbabwe) liberation came late in 1980 following a bloody war too. Ian Smith had declared a Unilateral Declaration of Independence (UDI) in 1965 which made white settlers form an independent government from Britain. South Africa was the last nation to be liberated. A prolonged apartheid policy induced an African National Congress' armed struggle which resulted in a democracy in 1994 since the coming of the British in 1652. This gives us the setting in which our history is going to be told to help us understand how the A.M.E. Church evolved in Southern, East and Central Africa.

Chapter 4
Formation of the A.M.E. Church in the United States of America in 1787

The African Methodist Episcopal Church or A.M.E. Church, often abbreviated as A.M.E. was founded by Richard Allen in 1787. Richard Allen was a former slave who worked hard to purchase his freedom. He founded Mother Bethel A.M.E. Church in Philadelphia, Pennsylvania in the U.S.A. The Church celebrated its bicentennial existence in 1987 and according to Douglas C. Lyons, at its celebrations; the Church was marked as the oldest Black religious denomination in the U.S. with a total membership of 1.8 million, (Lyons, 1987).

Richard Allen was born in Philadelphia, Pennsylvania as a slave in 1760. Allen was born again at the age of 17. He began to preach the gospel of Jesus Christ and is reportedly to have led his master to the Lord which undoubtedly, eventually led to the owner to facilitate Allen's buying his freedom. He had worked for his freedom and purchased it in 1783 at a cost of $2,000. He began preaching in Methodist circuits in 1781 in Delaware and states which were closer by. Well-known Methodist leaders such as Francis Asbury ensured that doors were open for Allen to preach in many areas. Allen came back to Philadelphia in 1786 and joined the St. George's Methodist Church followed by scores of blacks who were drawn to his prayer services and leadership, precipitating grounds for racial tensions.

St. George had no history of segregated seating prior to 1780. In later years, however, whites demanded that blacks take the chairs around the walls and not the pews. Blacks had an area reserved for them called the "Negro Pew" or "Black Corner," (Christianity Today, 2018). In 1787, a group of blacks sat on new pews which they were not aware had been reserved for whites. When the blacks had knelt down to pray, a white trustee pulled Absalom Jones, a colleague to Allen informing him that he was not to kneel there. When Absalom politely asked to be left until he had finished, the trustee refused and continued to pull him. The blacks, however, continued to pray and after they were done, they walked out.

Racism prompted Allen and his friends to start a new Church. In spite of this push against them, he still wanted to remain in Methodist hoping for the best to come out of it for the Church. Allen and Jones were threatened with expulsion from the Methodist Conference. In spite of this mistreatment they helped to bury many whites who had died in the 1793 yellow fever epidemic after a request was made to him and his followers. Out of love and service, Richard Allen consented in spite of risks of exposure to sickness. Dr. Benjamin Rush, a well-known physician and a signer of the Declaration of Independence, was reportedly quoted to have erroneously infer that "Blacks had immunity to the cursed fever," after observing the unexpected response from blacks and their sacrifice to bury the dead estimated to be over 5,000.

Allen bought an old frame building in 1793 which had been used as a blacksmith's shop. The shop was then relocated to Sixth and Lombard Streets in Philadelphia. It cost $35 and was pulled by a team of horses which the Allens owned, to a new place. It was then turned into a church named Bethel meaning "House of God" (Notable Biographies, 2018). This became Bethel African Methodist Episcopal Church, also known as "Mother Bethel." Bishop Francis Asbury dedicated the building in 1799 and proceeded to ordain Richard Allen as a Deacon.

For a decade and half, Methodist leaders tried to have Bethel A.M.E. Church to be under its jurisdiction as well as their property. However, on January 1, 1816, the Pennsylvania Supreme Court ruled that the church belonged to Allen and his friends. In April of 1816, the church was consolidated and several black Methodist Churches met in Philadelphia and made an agreement that united them as independent African Methodist Episcopal Church (A.M.E.). Richard Allen was ordained as an Elder and then consecrated as Bishop – the first black to hold such an office in America.

Blacks in many parts of the U.S. took leaf at Allen's example and established independent African Methodist Churches. Mother Bethel, the A.M.E. Church in Philadelphia grew to an astounding 7,500-member church in the 1820s. The denomination became by all means the most prominent black institution in the nineteenth century and today has over 6,000 churches and over 2 million members, (Christianity Today, 2018). The Church today (2020) has more than 3 million members worldwide.

Like many ministers, Richard Allen's ministry was supported by his hardworking wife, Sarah Allen. Missionary Sarah Allen (1764-1849) was a famous and well-respected female among worshipers of God of her time. She was recognized as a first female missionary in the A.M.E. Church, a woman who established a first charity organization for women. She was also a leading member who provided aid to runaway slaves in the renowned Underground Railroad.

Not much is known about Sarah Allen before she met Richard in 1802. However, historians think she was born a slave in 1764 but when she met Allen, she was free. Richard Allen's first wife Flora had passed away on March 11, 1801 due to a chronic illness and afterwards Allen had met Sarah on his preaching circuits. They got married in 1802. They had four sons Richard, James, John and Peter and two daughters Sara and Ann. Initially, the women's ministry which involved clothing the clergy whose clothes were worn-out later began helping the needy, not just the clergy. At first, they were called Dorcas Society because the women group was involved in clothing and feeding the poor (Notable Biographies, 2018). The group was also known for evangelization by word of mouth, church organizations founded and attended by women, and accumulation of resources. Richard Allen named the group, Women's Missionary Society or W.M.S.

Richard and Sarah Allen's home became a transit home for runaway slaves. They provided and hid the runaway slaves seeking freedom. They used the celler of the church building and their own home to hide those who were running away from the South and South East to the Northern States and to Canada via the Underground Railroad. They raised funds and helped those who were to resettle. Richard Allen died in 1831 and his wife continued the good works until her death on July 16, 1849 at the age of 85. She died at the home of her youngest daughter Ann Adams in Philadelphia. Sarah Allen and Richard Allen were buried side by side in a tomb under Mother Bethel Church. The site has now been converted into the Richard Allen Museum. Rev. Charles Kapungwe and Rev. Paul Bupe visited the site and sang at the Mother Bethel in 2001 while on tour of the North East with Allen University Concert Choir.

Chapter 5
The A.M.E. Church Reaches the African Continent in 1821 and 1896

The African Methodist Episcopal Church reached the African continent possibly on two fronts. These are Liberia in West Africa and Union of South Africa in Southern Africa. For the former, it must be understood that Liberia and Ethiopia were two countries in Africa which had not been colonised. Also, Liberia was established after the land was acquired by American Colonization Society which resettled the freed slaves from America in 1821 creating a colony at Cape Mesurado. In 1824, the colony became Liberia and the main settlement took the name of Monrovia, which is the capital today. Independence was declared in 1847 (Holsoe, 2018). We therefore, would conceptualize that freed slaves who resettled in Liberia brought the A.M.E. Church to this West African country while a different scenario orchestrated by God's providence and interaction with South Africans brought the Church to the Union of South Africa.

The resettlement of the freed slaves offered the opportunity for the Church to take root in West Africa. It expanded to Sierra Leone, Nigeria and Gold Coast (Ghana), what is collectively known as the 14th Episcopal District today. For Southern Africa, the interaction between the visiting South Africans on tour with a British sponsor to the U.S. offered an opportunity for the Church to take root in South Africa. We will explore the latter in detail since it is the history we are concerned about in this writing. Suffice at this point to state that the A.M.E. Church now is a global denomination. Today, the A.M.E. Church is nearly on all the continents of the world. It is divided into 20 Episcopal Districts. There are 13 Districts in the U.S.A. (including an extension to India – of the 4th Episcopal District), 1 District in Europe, Caribbean and South America and 6 in Africa. There are discussions of creation of more Districts with possibility of dividing the 17th District.

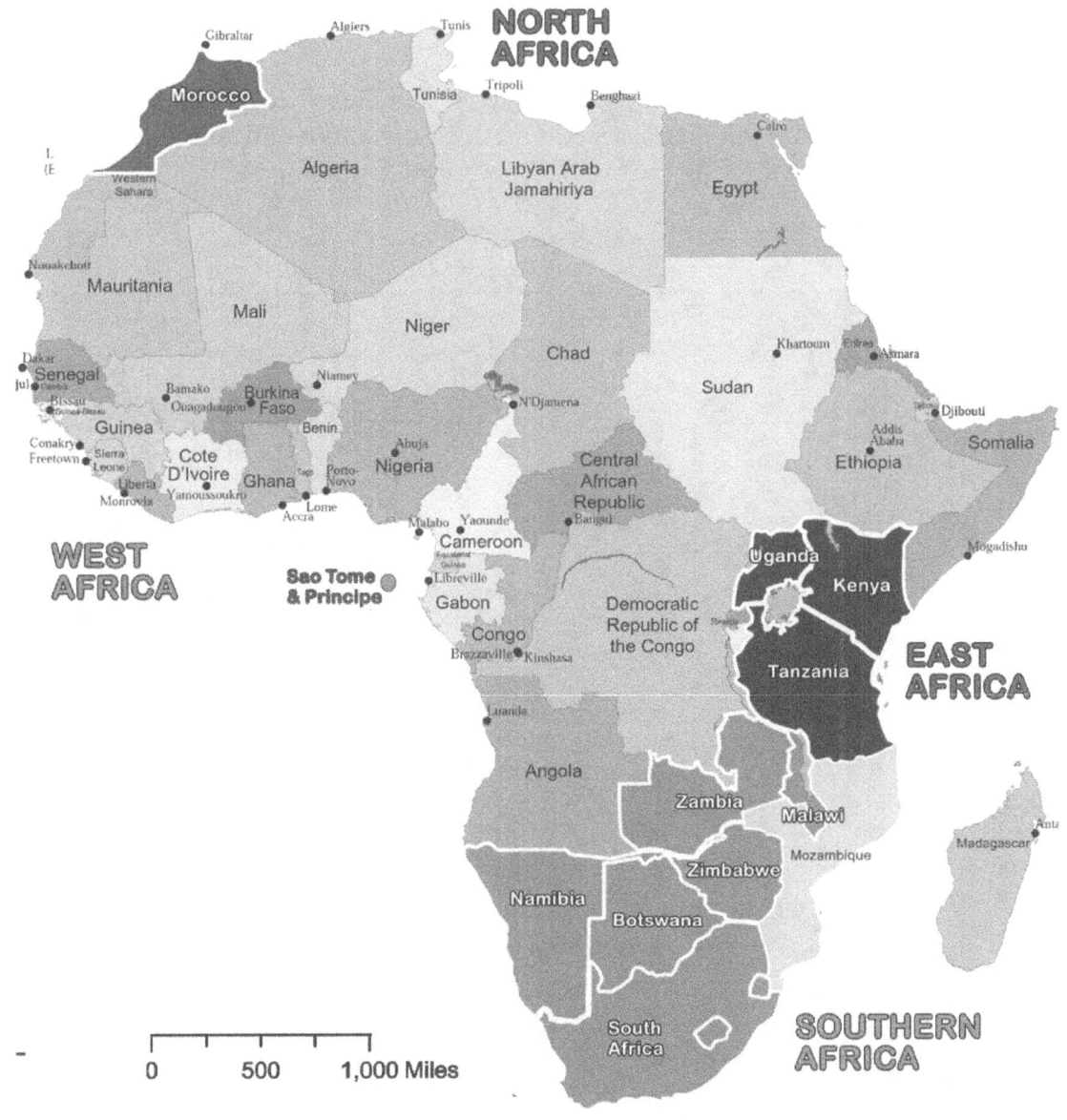

Africa and regional blocks – Open source maps of Africa Yahoo Image Search 9-22-2018

However, according to Annetta Louise Gomez-Jefferson, the A.M.E. Church had been established in 1821 in Sierra Leone. It was established by Rev. Daniel Coker who set up a church there, (Gomez-Jefferson, 1978 p 351). Annetta, quoting Bishop Joseph Gomez, her father, who had been sent to the 17th Episcopal District in 1968-1972, stated that Joseph had wanted to find out about the 17th District following his appointment there. It is this time that he found out about the Church having been established in Sierra Leone in 1821. At the time of Bishop Gomez's appointment, the 17th District comprised Zambia, Rhodesia (now

Zimbabwe), Malawi, Zaire (now Congo DR) and Tanzania. Regardless, the freed slaves settling in Liberia, it must be noted, got there in the same year, 1821. Bishop Cornelius Thaddeus Shaffer visited West Africa in 1902 and established a high school there.

Bishop Henry M. Turner arranged for the Liberia and Sierra Leone Annual Conferences in 1891. Later, the A.M.E. Church reached Ghana in the 1930s and Europa Randal from Sierra Leone is credited with this expansion. This paved a way for the Church to get into Nigeria as well.

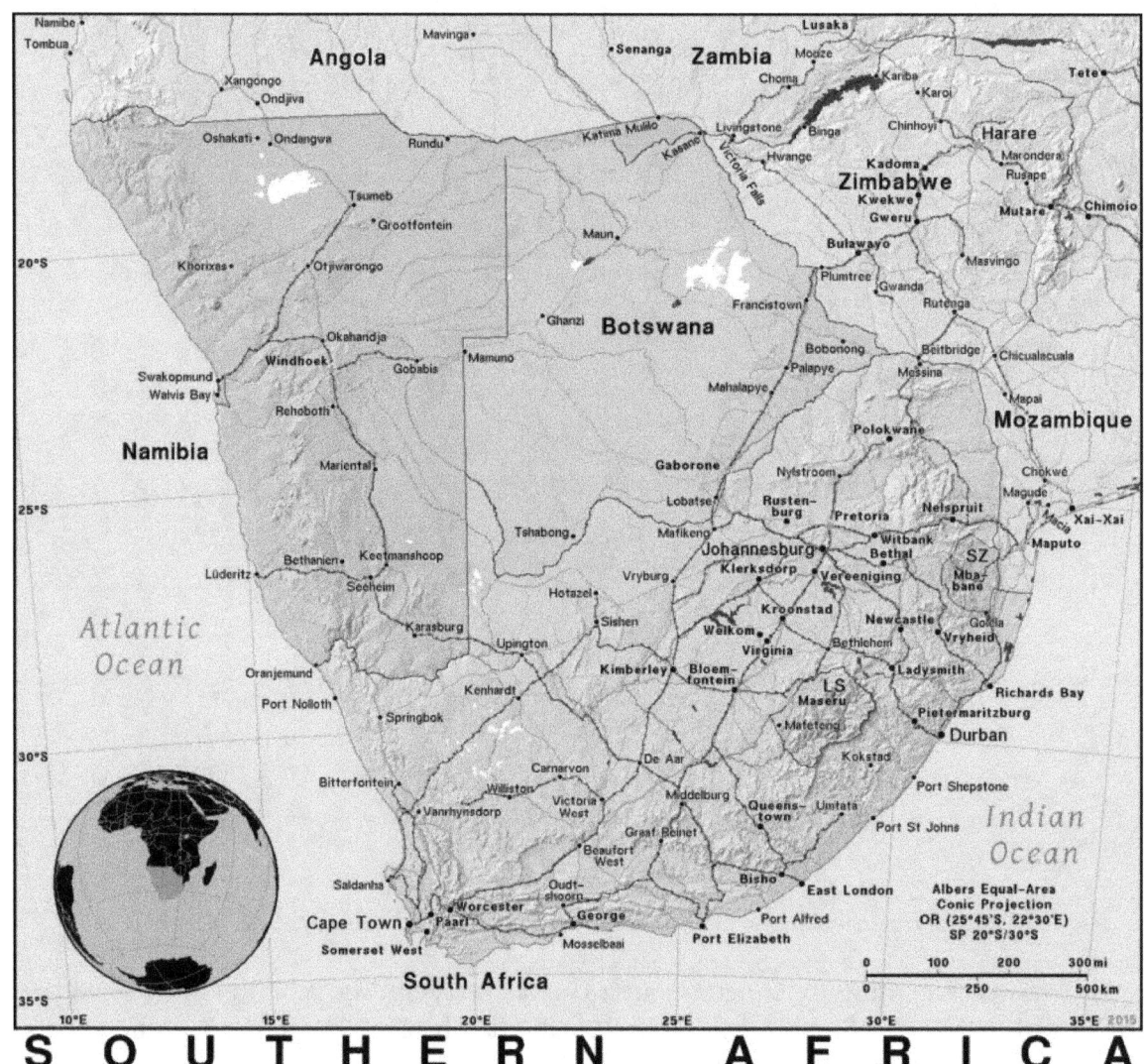

Southern Africa showing South Africa – Open source maps of Africa Yahoo Image Search 9-25-2018

It was 75 years later, however, in 1896 that the A.M.E. Church reached Southern Africa via South Africa. At the time, the country was known as the Union of South Africa. According to Rev. Warren W. Kalo Simyembe, (a Zambian Minister who had studied at Wilberforce Theological College in South Africa in the early 1950s), Rev. Mangena M. Mokone of the Ethiopian Church in Pretoria was the person the Lord used to have the Church find its root in Southern Africa. Prior to 1896, Rev. Mokone's daughter had gone to a concert party where her husband, a gifted singer was performing in Cape Town. While at the concert, an Englishman in the audience had been awestruck by the performance of Rev. Mokone's son-in-law and the choir. He, consequently, offered them a concert tour to England and the United States which they accepted.

After the concert in England, the family proceeded to America. When in the United States, the African Americans were amazed to learn of the presence of blacks in the United States from Africa! They also were surprised that the Africans were Christians. Equally surprised were the South African visitors because they met fellow Africans in America. They were invited to the Negro Church, the African Methodist Episcopal Church and they felt welcome there. Some of the boys and girls who had accompanied the choir were awarded scholarships so they remained behind to study in American high schools, chiefly at Wilberforce College. When Rev. Charles Kapungwe attended Allen University which was established in 1870, from 2000 to 2004 in Columbia, South Carolina, U.S.A. where he graduated with a Bachelor of Science Degree in Biology, he learned that in the early years of the school, at this Historically Black College and University (HBCU), students would start from the first grade and go to high school and university at the same institution.

The students were very excited to study in the U.S. They wrote Rev. Mangena Mokone about the Negro Church in America. The A.M.E. Church, in the end, invited Rev. Mokone and a delegation from his Church to visit the United States to attend the General Conference. When the team was in America, more students were offered scholarships again to study in the U.S. high schools. Eventually, Bishop Henry M. Turner, an A.M.E. Bishop, visited Cape Town in 1896 with the view of establishing the A.M.E. Church in South Africa. Following negotiations with the Union of South Africa Government, a branch was founded in the Union; however, Bishop Turner could not be allowed to stay.

When the students graduated from their different programmes, they headed home. They were the first group of South Africans with University Degrees. They included the first woman graduate. When an opportunity arose to build a school for Africans in 1908, courtesy of the City of Johannesburg, land was set aside for the project. The graduates from America began the school which was named Wilberforce Institute. The Church, later, spread throughout the Union of South Africa. The work of the A.M.E. Church then, continued to grow. In 1900, the Church reached Southern Rhodesia and in 1924, it reached Nyasaland through Rev. Hanock Msokera Chingo Phiri who founded it there. Before this year, the A.M.E. Church had already been established in Basutoland (Lesotho).

The work of the A.M.E. Church continued to grow in Southern Africa. It reached Northern Rhodesia and Bechuanaland in 1929, continued to expand reaching Tanganyika Territory in 1933 and Belgian Congo in 1957. In the recent past, after 2004, the work has expanded to reach Burundi, Rwanda, Kenya and Uganda. Rev. Charles Kapungwe picked up

Rev. Moses Achola, a Pastor of Bethel A.M.E. Church from Nakuru, Kenya at a bus station who had come to attend Bishop Paul Kawimbe's inauguration as President of the Bishops' Council in Charleston, South Carolina in 2008.

This expansion has allowed for creation of additional Episcopal Districts. A redrawn district, for example, of the Twentieth Episcopal District today consists of Malawi, Zimbabwe, Tanzania and Uganda. Also, this expansion was important to the Christian faith on a continent that had had an onslaught of Islam from the north. It marked a buffer to Islam's southward expansion. The A.M.E. Church, however, was not the only Church in Southern, East and Central Africa to provide that barrier. Several denominations mostly by missionaries from Europe, America and within Africa had helped in this great feat. However, today's Christians must not be contented with this. They must take the gospel further north and heed our Master's call to do so and claim North Africa for Jesus.

Chapter 6
The A.M.E. Church Takes Root in Southern Africa: Extends to Southern Rhodesia in 1900

The A.M.E. Church took its beginning in Southern Rhodesia in 1900 from the Union of South Africa. The Church had come to Southern Rhodesia, (now Zimbabwe) from the Union of South Africa (now the present-day country of South Africa) at the time when Bishop L.J. Coppin was the presiding prelate in the Union of South Africa. (In 2002, Rev. Charles Kapungwe, had the privilege of living in Coppin Hall at Allen University in Columbia, South Carolina, named after Bishop Coppin). Therefore, the Rt. Rev. Bishop Coppin played a role in the extension of the Church from the Union of South Africa into Southern Rhodesia.

To help administer the Church in Southern Rhodesia, a number of ministers were appointed. Rev. S.J. Mabote from Krugersdorp, Transvaal in South Africa was appointed as first Presiding Elder. He was tasked with running the entire Rhodesia District helped by three ministers, Rev. Daniel K. Gabashane, Rev. Mikia C. Ncube and Rev. J. Daniel Molebatsi. The Presiding Elder made his base in Salisbury but he experienced difficulties to obtain authorization from the government to run the Church in Southern Rhodesia. Failure to register the Church meant that running the Church was problematic and membership drive was hampered. This led to the team vacating Southern Rhodesia and returning to the Union of South Africa but left behind Rev. Mikia C. Ncube in Bulawayo.

Rev. Ncube succeeded in planting the Church in Bulawayo in 1902. A few members were mobilized. However, persistent difficulties in church administration made the pastor to ask Rev. D.K. Gabashane from the Union of South Africa to come and help him iron out the challenges that the Bulawayo Church was experiencing. Since registering of the Church had proved to be a problem, the Church continued meeting as an "underground" Church. Meetings were done in private homes and in places owned by individuals who some of them, were not even members of the Church. Meetings were also conducted in outskirts of town in the farms.

The Rev. M.C. Ncube invited Bishop L.J. Coppin towards the end of 1902. The Bishop visited Bulawayo in the company of Rev. Abel S. Gabashane. This visit was to be used as an opportunity to discuss with the Southern Rhodesia Government and facilitate for registration of the Church. Bishop L.J. Coppin, therefore, became the first Bishop to reach Southern Rhodesia from the Union of South Africa. He was interviewed by Government Authorities and returned to the Union of South Africa to preside over the Cape Annual Conference at Kimberly, Cape Province in January 1903. Rev. Daniel K. Gabashane was reappointed by the same Conference as Presiding Elder of the Southern Rhodesia District. He was given two pastors, Rev. M.D. Makgatho and Rev. J.D. Molebatsi.

Progress was made this time. Nevertheless, both ministers returned to the Union of

South Africa in 1903 leaving Rev. Makgatho working alone but receiving help only from his first Local Preacher of the A.M.E. Church in Southern Rhodesia, Brother John C. Tshaka. Afterwards, Brother John C. Tshaka was ordained a minister in Southern Rhodesia. Rev. Makgatho continued to minister with his Local Preacher for many years until 1925. He struggled with ministry since he had no place of worship in the town of Bulawayo and his work was unrecognized by the Local Authorities who had not given them a permit. However, through endurance, a few members held up his appointment and he was sustained up to the year 1925.

In 1925, a Joint Session of Transvaal, Natal, Cape Orange Free State and Basutoland Annual Conference of the A.M.E. Church was held at Bloemfontein, Orange Free State in the Union of South Africa. The Conference, presided by Bishop J.A. Gregg, was hosted by Zion A.M.E. Church and it ran from 14th to 18th January, 1925. At this Conference, new changes were made. The Conference appointed the following brethren to the Rhodesia District under the auspices of the Rev. Joseph J. Khaile as Presiding Elder: Rev. J.J. Khaile, P.E., Rhodesia District, Salisbury; Rev. Moses D. Makgatho, Bulawayo S.R.; Bubi circuit: To be supplied, and Rev. Hanock M. Phiri, Pastor of Nyasaland circuit. The Presiding Elder, Rev. Joseph J. Khaile returned to South Africa after a few months, leaving behind Rev. Makgatho alone in Southern Rhodesia while Rev. Phiri was sent to Nyasaland as Pastor of the entire Nyasaland Protectorate from 1925 to 1926 with no Presiding Elder. Both pastors were ordained ministers.

Rev. M.D. Makgatho was ordained as Deacon in 1903 while Rev. H.M. Phiri was ordained as Deacon on 18th January, 1925 at Bloemfontein, Orange Free State. With no money in his pocket, the Rev. Hanock M. Phiri trekked from Nyasaland (now Malawi) to Bulawayo, Southern Rhodesia (Zimbabwe) over 500 miles on foot! Rev. Makgatho, then paid train fare for him from Bulawayo to Bloemfontein, Union of South Africa so he could attend this Conference! Rev. Phiri was ordained as Deacon at this Conference and he received a train fare from the Conference to travel back to Nyasaland where he continued his ministry as a preacher there.

The Conference reappointed Rev. M.D. Makgatho as pastor back to Southern Rhodesia. This was to have him continue the work there as pastor all alone up to the end of 1925. Bishop J.A. Gregg came to Southern Rhodesia in 1926 to negotiate with the government and during this time he reappointed Rev. J.J. Khaile as Presiding Elder of the Rhodesia District and pastor of Salisbury. However, he only served for a year and returned to South Africa. There were only three circuits at the time and were under the Rhodesia District. The circuits were Salisbury, Bulawayo and Nyasaland. Bubi circuit remained on supply for many years and activity there had stopped temporarily.

Bishop J.A. Gregg appointed Rev. Z.C. Mtshwello as Presiding Elder of the Rhodesia District in 1927. The headquarters were at Bulawayo. He was also concurrently appointed as Superintendent of the work of the Church in Southern Rhodesia and Nyasaland Protectorate. However, when Rev. Mtshwello, arrived at the Railway Station in Bulawayo, he was met by government officials who ordered him back to South Africa and was not allowed to preach in Southern Rhodesia.

Bishop Gregg made an impromptu journey to Southern Rhodesia to try and meet the government officials. He had received the news of Rev. Mtshwello's deportation while in Cape

Town and traveled by road by car to Bulawayo where he also met members of the Church in Bulawayo who were not expecting him. He returned to South Africa after talking to the government officials. He reappointed Rev. Mtshwello back to Rhodesia the same year in 1927. The Church grew that year and spread to many places in Southern Rhodesia. Rev. Mtshwello also saw the licensing of local preachers in 1927 under his work. Among the licensed were Brothers Solomon Ngala Sangweni, D.D. Khomela, S.M. Kamdgshariwa, William Nomazele, J.H. Penxa, Johannes Marumo and many others including Brother John Tshaka who had been already a Local Preacher for a number of years.

Creation of the Zambezi Annual Conference in Southern Rhodesia and Three Presiding Elders' Districts in 1929

In 1929, Rev. Mtshwello was appointed as Superintendent of the Church in Rhodesia. This was at the Joint Annual Conference held in Bloemfontein, Orange Free State in the Union of South Africa. The appointing officer was Bishop George B. Young who had just been assigned to the Union of South Africa by the General Conference in the U.S.A. The Conference was held from 16th to 20th January, 1929 which saw the birth of Zambezi Annual Conference and three Presiding Elders' Districts were created namely, Matabeleland, Mashonaland and Bechuanaland Districts. The two Districts of Matabeleland and Bechuanaland were headed by Presiding Elder Rev. Mtshwello with his headquarters at Bulawayo, Southern Rhodesia while Mashonaland District was being headed by Presiding Elder Rev. John Oliver Maya with his headquarters in Salisbury.

The appointments are tabulated below:

Matabeleland and Bechuanaland Districts – Rev. Z.C. Mtshwello, P.E.
1. Bulawayo: Rev. Z.C. Mtshwello, P.E. P.O. Box 36, Bulawayo, Southern Rhodesia.
2. Bembesi: Br. S.N. Sangweni and D. Monyiswa.
3. Gwelo: Bro. Moses Mazingi.
4. Selukwe: Br. N.P. Kameel.
5. Fort Victoria: Br. S.J. Nteeo.
6. Belingwe: Rev. L.R. Legalamitloa.
7. Umzingwani: Br. W. Nomazele.
8. Filabusi: Rev. A.I. Nojekwa.
9. West Nicholson: Br. J. Maqungo.
10. Gwanda & Matobe: Bro J.H. Penxa.
11. Gwai Reserve: Br. J. Marumo.
12. Nyamandlovu: Br. Calvert H. Monne.
13. Gwaai River: Br. Ntulusi.
14. Bubi: Br. J.R. Molefe.
15. Francis Town: Br. David Dafite Khomela.
16. Lobatsi: Br. Stephen S. Mabe.
17. Pitsani: Rev. N.E. Aringonda.

Mashonaland District
    1. Salisbury: Rev. J.O. Maya, P.E.
    2. Mazoe: Supply
    3. Marandellas: Supply
    4. Umtali: Supply
    5. Mondoro: Supply
    6. Hartley: Supply
    7. Gatooma: Supply
    8. Que: Supply
    9. Lower Gwelo: Supply
    10. Kasungu, Nyasaland: Rev. H.M. Phiri, Pastor.

Bishop G.B. Young attempted to buy a farm at Gumtree in the same year 1929. This was for the purpose of empowering the Church but this did not materialize and instead a church was built in Bulawayo. This is the present Young's Chapel A.M.E. Church and is the first building in Southern Rhodesia which was a proud and great monument of the A.M.E. Church in Southern Rhodesia at the time. This made a milestone in the expansion of the A.M.E. Church in Southern Rhodesia. The Church spread to new areas within Southern Rhodesia and then to Northern Rhodesia in 1929.

Chapter 7
Formation of the A.M.E. Church in Northern Rhodesia in 1929

Rev. J.L.C. Membe, founder of the A.M.E. Church in Northern Rhodesia (Zambia).

The A.M.E. Church in Northern Rhodesia began in 1929. Brother John Lester C. Membe, later known as Rev. J.L.C. Membe, founded the A.M.E. Church in Northern Rhodesia. He joined the A.M.E. Church at Victoria Falls Town in Southern Rhodesia in June, under the Rev. J.R. Molefe from South Africa. He used to ride a bicycle from Livingstone, a southern border town in Northern Rhodesia across the Zambezi to Victoria Falls Town, a northern border town in Southern Rhodesia. He would then return home every Sunday after the service. Rev. J.L.C. Membe wrote about his early involvement with the A.M.E. Church and how he eventually started the work in 1929.

Livingstone, Zambia named after Dr. David Livingstone the Scottish missionary, explorer and physician. Mosi-oa-Tunya building. 16th April, 2020. Photo by Sis. Linda Libingi.

Victoria Falls, Livingstone, Zambia named after Queen Victoria by Dr. David Livingstone. The Falls was known as Mosi-oa-Tunya in a local language meaning "The Smoke that Thunders." 16th April, 2020. Photo by Sis. Linda Libingi. (Rainy Season).

While still at Livingstone, he wrote about his ability and desire to reach out to people to share to them about the Church. It is this ability that enabled him to be a man God had raised him to be – a missionary. "I converted one man, a friend of mine called Pengemani (Benjamin) Chanda of Chinsali, a Northern Rhodesia policeman. We went together to Victoria Falls town but after two months he got tired and joined the Watchtower movement. I kept on going all alone. I tried to persuade Rev. Molefe to come to Livingstone to open a branch for one church there, but he told me he had no permit to do so in Northern Rhodesia. He advised me to write to the Superintendent Rev. Z.C. Mtshwello of Bulawayo which I did in November 1928, nevertheless, before I received his reply, I was transferred to Broken Hill as Clerk and Typist in the District Commissioner's Office," writes the Rev. J.L.C. Membe.

"That time the BOMA (British Overseas Management Administration) headquarters were still at Mutwewansofu before the BOMA was moved to Broken Hill. Since there was no A.M.E. Church anywhere in Northern Rhodesia, I decided to go to Wesleyan Methodist Church on Sundays. All this time I had been thinking seriously of the reason why should the A.M.E. Church be in Southern Rhodesia alone and not in Northern Rhodesia.

I began to talk to so many friends about the A.M.E. Church. The first people I converted to the A.M.E. Church were Mr. and Mrs. Aaron Mwenya and his wife Elizabeth from Kawambwa, Mr. and Mrs. John Mwila both from Serenje, Mr. Lazarus Besa and wife from Luapula. All of them were in the Mine Compound. Prayer meetings were being held in Mrs. Aaron Mwenya's house for the time being and on Sundays. These people also influenced their families and brought them to the prayer meetings until they were also joined to the first group as follows:

A Mine Policeman Mr. Meleka Kasongo, Thomas Sonta and wife, Thomas Ngwisha and wife all of them from Mkushi. They were Mine employees except Bro. Meleki Kasongo who came from Solwezi. From Government 5-acre plots who joined us were Mr. Aaron Mpande, Jackson Siyame and wife, Sister Maliya Kayasu and one girl Agness Mvula, and Brother Lester Somanje of the Railways.

When I saw that we were meeting in fear of the Authorities as we had no permit, I approached the District Commissioner Mr. Ebemfield. I asked for the permit to preach in the name of the A.M.E. Church. After having asked me so many questions and about how I could manage to do two things at the same time, as a Government employee and work of the church, I told him I was going to do the Church work at my own spare time. He told me to wait until he found out from the Provincial Commissioner about this.

I wrote to Rev. Z.C. Mtshwello in Bulawayo, to ask him to come and talk with the Government Authorities personally concerning the establishment of the Church in this country. This was important so we could obtain the permit to allow us to start the Church officially. After some weeks, Rev. Mtshwello replied me and said that my letter was receiving attention. I showed this letter to the District Commissioner. He asked me the number of members we have. I told him the number which I told the Rev. Mtshwello 400 although the number was not so. On 18th March, 1930, the following permit was given to me:

NORTHERN RHODESIA GOVERNMENT
PROVINCIAL ADMINISTRATION
<u>LUANGWA PROVINCE</u>

Broken Hill, N.R.
18th March, 1930.

<u>AFRICAN METHODIST EPISCOPAL CHURCH
PERMIT ISSUED UNDER SECTION 9 ORDINANCE 29/1927</u>

Permission is hereby granted Lester Mweni-Membe Siwale to preach in the Broken Hill District for the African Methodist Episcopal Church. This permit is subjected to weekly renewal until the leaders of this church applied for recognition of this Church by the Northern Rhodesia Government.

(SGD) L.A. RUSSEL
PROVINCIAL COMMISSIONER
<u>M A G I S T R A T E.</u>

The very same day I mailed this permit to the Rev. Mtshwello in Bulawayo, Southern Rhodesia. I sent it with a covering letter under registered envelope and asked him to send it back as soon as he could which he did. I repeated to call him to Broken Hill. Rev. Mtshwello told me that he had already sent application to the Government, and that in September last year he sent Rev. Sangweni to interview the Paramount Chief Imwiko of Barotseland about the A.M.E. Church. He also said the Chief told Rev. Sangweni that there was no objection to have the Church established in his country or area.

We worked for the Church the whole year without being visited by the leaders of the Church. By this year, 1930, the membership at Broken Hill was now over 400 which was reported to Rev. Z.C. Mtshwello.

The Application Of Recognition
Sent To The Northern Rhodesia Government

On 25th October, 1930, an application was written to the Northern Rhodesia Government by Rev. Z.C. Mtshwello, the Superintendent of the Church in Southern Rhodesia through the Chief Secretary to the Government, Livingstone. The following is a copy of application: -

African Methodist Episcopal Church
P.O. Box 56,
Bulawayo, S. Rhodesia.
25th October, 1930.

The Secretary of Native Affairs,
Livingstone,
NORTHERN RHODESIA,

APPLICATION FOR GOVERNMENT RECOGNITION OF THE EVANGELICAL WORK OF THE AFRICAN METHODIST EPISCOPAL CHURCH IN NORTHERN RHODESIA.

Sir,

I, the undersigned, I am Superintendent or head of the Church in Bulawayo and for the Colony of Southern Rhodesia. Our Church was established in the United States of America in 1787 and in South Africa in 1893. It is an organization purely for, and under the supervision of, the black people.

I have the honour to and respectfully submit my application as above on behalf of our Church. The following governments have given their official recognition to our Church: - The Union of South Africa, Bechuanaland Protectorate, Southern Rhodesia and Nyasaland.

There are over four hundred Natives who are members of our church and they have asked that the Church be extended to their homes, so we selected Rev. Solomon N. Sangweni to go and interview the Chief Imwiko M. Lewanika of Mwandi, Sesheke concerning these peoples' request. This has been done and Chief Imwiko passed the message on to the Paramount Chief of Barotse tribe.

We want to thank you for the kindness you rendered to us by allowing Rev. Sangweni to visit the Chief in your territory in September last year. In connection with our work, I would mention that we do not participate in the politics of the land and our work is to spread the Master's Kingdom amongst our Native people and to encourage the educational facilities and industry.

We possess two Training Institutions in the Union of South Africa, and over a hundred of day schools in different districts in colonies. We are loyal British subjects under the Throne and Government; in testifying the behaviour of our Church I would refer your Government to the various Governments which have recognized our Church. Our Headquarters in South Africa are in Cape Town, the address being Bishop G.B. Young, M.A., D.D. 28 Walmer Road Woodstock, Cape Town.

Thanking you in anticipation.
I have the honour to be,
Your obedient servant,

(SGD). Z.C. MTSHWELLO.

No reply was made to the above application of October 25th, 1930. The number of membership mentioned in the above application by Rev. Mtshwello was not for Barotse people.

This question was raised at the Conference of 1931, and it was found out that this was made by error for they thought that all Africans in Northern Rhodesia were all Barotse and under the Chief of the Barotse tribe, but that this was the number of membership reported from Broken Hill where, at the time, not even one of the Barotse people were a member of the A.M.E. Church there.

On 6th January, 1931, another application was sent by Rev. Z.C. Mtshwello to the Government of Northern Rhodesia, this one was answered, and the following was the reply: -

---

Ref. No. 85 -1/1.
Office of the Secretary of Native Affairs,
LIVINGSTONE, NORTHERN RHODESIA

APPLICATION FOR GOVERNMENT RECOGNITION OF THE AFRICAN METHODIST EPISCOPAL CHURCH IN NORTHERN RHODESIA

I have the honour to acknowledge receipt of your letter of the 6th inst., forwarding copy of the report of Native Churches Commission 1925 which I return herewith.

With reference to your letter of 25th October, 1930, I am directed to inform you that His Excellency the Governor is prepared to approve the African Methodist Episcopal Church as a society to carry on evangelistic work in Northern Rhodesia within the Barotse Province.

Ministers or Elders of this Church who desire to work in the Territory will be required to produce satisfactory evidence of good character and to obtain, from Magistrate of the District wherein they propose to operate, a license in terms of the Native School Ordinance 1927.

It is also understood that work of the African Methodist Episcopal Church will be open to inspection and supervision by the Native Education Department.

I have the honour to be,
Sir,
Your Obedient Servant.
(SGD). J. MOFFAT THOMSON
SECRETARY FOR NATIVE AFFAIRS.

The Rev. Zephaniah C. Mtshwello,
African Methodist Episcopal Church,
P.O. Box 36, Bulawayo.

The Rev. Z. C. Mtshwello's Visit To Northern Rhodesia

After having received the reply from the Northern Rhodesia Government accepting the A.M.E. Church in Northern Rhodesia, in January 1931, the Rev. Z.C. Mtshwello came to Livingstone in Northern Rhodesia. He came toward the end of January, accompanied by Revs. S.N. Sangweni, D.D. Khomela, C.H. Monne, J.R.M. Molafe and Brother Justin Chingo.

While at Livingstone, the Rev. Mtshwello instructed Rev. S.N. Sangweni to go to Ndola with Brother Peter Phiri. Bro. Phiri was sent by a little group of new members to meet these ministers in Livingstone. Rev. D.D. Khomela was also ordered to visit those other members at Broken Hill to see how they were doing there, and both Reverends Sangweni and Khomela were asked to report back to the Rev. Mtshwello in Bulawayo. The telegram that was sent to me from Rev. Mtshwello asking me to meet him at Livingstone found me gone on tour with the District Commissioner touring the Lenje Reserve. When I came back, the telegram was time overdue already and could not go to Livingstone.

In two days' time, Rev. Khomela came from Bulawayo and found me in my office at Mutwewansofu BOMA. This was before the BOMA Headquarters were moved to Broken Hill Town. As it was a working day, many workers did not meet him, only a few men and women did. He stayed with us the whole day. A small number of people gathered and he preached a short sermon after explaining to the people gathered about the Church. 12 women and 10 men joined the Church. In the evening Rev. Khomela went back to Southern Rhodesia by train. This was the first work in February 1931.

In September 1931, the Rev. Mtshwello sent me a circular inviting those who would be able to get to the Union of South Africa to attend the Joint Session of Annual Conference. The Conference was to be held in Bloemfontein, Orange Free State and was to be hosted by Mount Zion A.M.E. Church from 30th September to 4th October, 1931. Bishop G.B. Young presided over that Joint Session of the Annual Conference. At this Conference, I joined the candidates on Admission Class and was admitted and asked to report to the Zambezi Annual Conference in Bulawayo for record."

Chapter 8
First Appointments to Northern Rhodesia in 1931

At the Third Session of the Zambezi Annual Conference held in the Young's Chapel A.M.E. Church at Bulawayo, Southern Rhodesia in October 1931, first appointments to Northern Rhodesia were made. The appointments included the first Presiding Elder and four recognized circuits with their respective leaders. The appointments also marked the official recognition of the A.M.E. Church's Northern Rhodesia ministry by the Annual Conference.

Rev. David Dafite Khomela was appointed as the first Presiding Elder of Northern Rhodesia District. His headquarters were at Livingstone. At this time the whole Northern Rhodesia was one Presiding Elder's District. The following were the appointments which were made: -

1. Livingstone: Rev. D.D. Khomela, P.E. from S.R.
2. Broken Hill: Bro. J.L.C. Membe, Pastor
3. Ndola: Rev. R.J. Mkwayi, Pastor from S.R.
4. Bro. Benjamin Chisela who was the leader at Ndola, was appointed to Matetsi in S.R.

I have already explained about the beginning of the A.M.E. Church at Broken Hill where the A.M.E. Church started before the Church spread elsewhere in Northern Rhodesia. In the same year 1931, Rev. Khomela the Presiding Elder, asked the Bishop to make another appointment on supply for Broken Hill. His request was based on what he reasoned as "Bro. Membe was a Government employee," but the Bishop replied to him that, "If Bro. Membe had time to organize a church there how could he not be able to do the work of the Church there? He could work as a part time Pastor, except if the work he does as a Government civil servant gives him no time to do so."

However, in February 1932, Rev. D.D. Khomela, the Presiding Elder, brought with him Rev. Jonas Lesapi Honoko from Transvaal, South Africa as full time Pastor of Broken Hill. Consequently, Brother Membe became an assistant Pastor under Rev. J.L. Honoko. A public meeting was called and met near the beer hall at Pullon's Compound, the only Municipal African Location at Broken Hill at the time. At this meeting, over 500 people attended. Rev. D.D. Khomela preached the sermon on the "The Lepers." After his sermon 210 persons were added to the church. Among them who joined the church that day were brothers Abner Bright Kazungu, Ben Thumba, Anderson Sakala, Jackson Chipandwe, Ng'wani Matula, and many others.

The first Church Conference was held a day after the public meeting. It was held under the chairmanship of Rev. D.D. Khomela, Presiding Elder during that visit. At this Conference, the following were elected Local Officers under one Official Board: -

J.L.C. Membe, Secretary and Assistant Pastor, Broken Hill West.
C.A. Mvula, Chief Steward, both sections, also Class Leader Eastern Section.

Anderson Sakala, Treasurer, Eastern Section.
A.B. Kazunga, Local Preacher and Chief Trustee.
Ben Thumba, Assistant Secretary both sections.
Meleki Kasongo, Steward, Western Section.
Thomas Ngwisha, Treasurer, Western Section.
Thomas Sonta, Assistant Treasurer Western Section.
Amon Mpande, Local Preacher, 5 Acre Plots.
C. Guguma, Class Leader.
Naliya, Mulonda, Kanyasu, President Women Missionary Society, Western Section.
Lazarus Besa, Exhorter, Western Section.
Jackson Siyame, Exhorter, Mine Compound.
Maggie Siyame, Vice President, W.M.S.

From this time, the Church spread to the Lenje Reserve in Chief Chipepo's area. Another section was created at Broken Hill Railway Compound. After some time, Bro. Lester Somanje was elected a Class Leader there and at Nine Native Farms. A house which had been built as a communal bathroom was spared us for our Church services by the Location Superintendent at Broken Hill until a Church building of our own was built. The Nine Compound Manager allowed us to hold our Church services in the verandah of a food store but there was always a lot of noise. We therefore, moved ourselves and began to meet at an open place where we built a grass shelter in which to meet.

In June 1932, Presiding Elder Rev. D.D. Khomela came to hold his first Quarterly Conference at Broken Hill from his headquarters at Livingstone. The Quarterly Conference was held on 11th June, 1932. On Sunday June 12, 1932, there was a very big gathering for Church services. 218 persons were baptized and about 116 were received into Full Membership and many joined the Church. This service began at 9:00 a.m. and continued until 10:40 p.m. The money collected at this service including Annual Conference report, certificates, and offerings amounted to £114.31p.

First Main Places of the A.M.E. Church in Northern Rhodesia

Broken Hill, 1929.
Ndola, 1930.
Livingstone, 1931.

Therefore, the beginning of the A.M.E. Church in Northern Rhodesia can be traced to Broken Hill. Broken Hill was the foundation place where the A.M.E. Church started. The second was Ndola. We will give an account of the development of the A.M.E. Church in Ndola in the next chapter which will also highlight the spread of the Church on the Copperbelt Province.

Chapter 9
The A.M.E. Church on the Copperbelt Province in 1930

Beginning of the Church at Ndola – 1930

Many people say that the A.M.E. Church at Ndola started in 1931. However, the beginning of the A.M.E. Church at Ndola dates back to 1930. Its beginning was linked to a group of believers who had returned to Northern Rhodesia from Belgian Congo where they had lived for years and had been employed there. While in Congo, they had been members of the American Methodist Episcopal Church. When they came back to Northern Rhodesia, they had joined a Church called Native Christian Church, the only native Christian Church on the Copperbelt at the time. Consequently, the Native Christian Church became a precursor to the A.M.E. Church as was the American Methodist Church, a derivative of the former at Ndola.

Early in November 1930, the return to Ndola from Congo of a group of Northern Rhodesians helped in the establishment of the A.M.E. Church at Ndola. Brothers Benjamin Ben Chisela, Augustus Kawala, Robert Chibwe, Misheck Zimba, Rain Kalyongo, and Sisters Susie Kawala, Meleki Kapondo, Sarah Chisela, Jessie Zimba and Brother Maxwell Chibiliti, all of them Northern Rhodesians from Luapula Province, returned to Northern Rhodesia and settled at Ndola. In Congo, they were members of the American Methodist Episcopal Church in Elizabethville (now Lubumbashi). Since there was no American Methodist Episcopal Church in Northern Rhodesia, they decided to join a small church called Native Christian Church, the only native church on the Copperbelt at that time.

The Native Christian Church was formed or established by Christian Africans who came from many different countries to search for work on the Copperbelt. There were no other Churches where these people could attend Sunday Services. Therefore, these Africans from many different Protestant denominations, mainly from Free Church of Scotland, Presbyterian Church of Scotland, London Missionary Society, Baptists and many other Churches including the Christian Missions in Many Lands, joined together and formed the Church called "NATIVE CHRISTIAN CHURCH OF THE COPPERBELT" from which the United Church of the Copperbelt took its beginning.

All those men and their wives who came from Congo joined them. Nevertheless, before long, they were not interested in the way services and conditions of worship were carried on as Methodists. This little group decided to resign from the Native Christian Church and be led by themselves. They started to meet by themselves on Sundays and they elected Brother Benjamin Ben Chisela to be their leader. They wrote a letter to Bishop John Springer of Congo asking him to send them a Preacher or a minister to help them at Ndola. Bishop Springer answered them that he had no permit to do so from the Northern Rhodesia Government. However, if they knew where the A.M.E. Church is, they can join it for it is the same if at all there was one in Northern Rhodesia or write to one of the Bishops of the A.M.E. Church there.

Furthermore, Bishop Springer asked these men to meet him at the Ndola Railway Station on Saturday a week before Christmas 1930. He was on his way to Umtali in Southern Rhodesia. These men did so and met Bishop Springer at Ndola Railway Station in the afternoon and he explained to them all about the A.M.E. Church. He also informed them that he knows that the A.M.E. Church is being mentioned somewhere in Southern Rhodesia, it should be in Northern Rhodesia too perhaps. The Bishop left.

When they came back to their place, they continued meeting in the name of the American Methodist Church. The meetings were being held in Bro. B.B. Chisela's house built of grass and mudded inside. At that time, there was no Municipal Location at Ndola; many people had to build their own shelters.

I had a friend of mine Mr. Samson Chisela who worked for a Mr. Owen. We made arrangement of spending our Christmas holiday at Ndola. We left on a motor cycle. When we reached Ndola, we went to his younger brother Benjamin Ben Chisela. We found them holding a meeting discussing the letter from Bishop Springer and the interview they made to him at the Railway Station but could not find the Church which he mentioned to them. Mr. Samson Chisela introduced me to his brother after which I asked them if they could allow me to say something and they agreed. Then I introduced myself as a preacher from the A.M.E. Church at Broken Hill, but that I was a civil servant not a minister. I told them that I have started the Church there myself while the leaders are in Southern Rhodesia but that I do write them and they too do write me.

After some considerable time of explanation about the Church they asked me to organize them too. They asked me to preach to them at the evening service which I did, and they were very pleased. I wrote the address for the Rev. Z.C. Mtshwello on a piece of paper and asked them to write him as I did too so as to make him come quickly to make us put right with the Church. In the next morning, we left for our place. Before we left, they asked me to visit them and help them to organize. After a week I came back, and this time they were now many as they went about to bring all they knew to the new Church. At this time, I helped them to elect officers and went back to Broken Hill.

Early in January 1931, Rev. Hanock Msokera Phiri came from Nyasaland to visit his nephew in Luanshya. He was also going to visit other relatives in the Mines. When he arrived at Ndola, he was accommodated by Mr. Alexander Mwamba. Mr. Ernest Alexander Mwamba was a Senior Clerk in the Government at Ndola in the Provincial Administration who was also a leader of the Native Christian Church at Ndola. At that time the leaders of the Native Christian Church at Ndola were: Mr. Ernest Alexander Mwamba, Aliton Sitambuli, Robert Mbakaya, and some others. Many used to say that Mr. Mwamba and Rev. Phiri were the people who organized the Church at Ndola and were founders of the A.M.E. Church in Northern Rhodesia. I do not know how one can dare say so when he did not do so. When Rev. Phiri came to Ndola, Mwamba was still a Church leader in the Native Christian Church and the persons mentioned above had already started meeting in the name of the A.M.E. Church, can they claim to be founders when they found other people had started something already?

When Rev. Phiri came to Ndola that was the time Mr. Mwamba heard much about the A.M.E. Church from Rev. Phiri. Mr. Mwamba told him that there were some people from Congo and are members of the Church to which you belong. He led them to the men and Rev. Phiri was very pleased to see them and encouraged them greatly. He, being a Minister in the Church for many years, worked hard to encourage them in many ways before he left for Luanshya two days later. He also gave them Bishop's address in Cape Town. Bro. Mwamba was very much interested in the Church in the way Rev. Phiri explained to him, but his difficulty was how to get away from the Church he leads to come to the A.M.E. Church.

Finally, Mr. Mwamba joined the A.M.E. Church before the end of 1931. Mr. Mwamba was a very highly educated man of his time. He became a Church Secretary and took a very active part organizing the Church at Ndola and through his effort many people followed him from the Native Christian Church. He was a very strong and influential man. He brought many other educated men also, Mr. Elijah Chunga and his wife, Mr. Aswell Nkhoma, Rev. A.F. Chambwe, Peter Phiri and wife, Duncan Stewart Banda and wife and many others. Some of the leaders of the Native Christian Church also came to join the A.M.E. Church and their names are Aliton Sitambuli, and Elijah Mpofu.

Many other people who were members of other denominations and those who belonged to no Church came to join the A.M.E. Church in great number. In the same month of January 1931, a letter was sent from Ndola to Rev. Z.C. Mtshwello, Bulawayo, Southern Rhodesia asking them to send a minister to help them organize the Church and to baptize their people. The letter was signed by Brother B.B. Chisela as Chairman and Brother E.A. Mwamba as Secretary. Rev. Z.C. Mtshwello, the Superintendent of the Church in Southern Rhodesia, wrote them back and asked them to send some people to meet him in Livingstone. Accompanying Rev. Mtshwello to Livingstone were Rev. S.N. Sangweni, D.D. Khomela, C.H. Monne, J.R. Molefe, and Brother Justin Chingo. That was in January 1931.

After some talks and some arrangements between them, Rev. S.N. Sangweni was asked to go to Ndola with Brother Phiri. By the beginning of February, Rev. Sangweni and Brother Peter Phiri went to Ndola. In two days' time, the word spread all over the Copperbelt about the new Church from their brothers in America, the A.M.E. Church.

Many people came to see Rev. Sangweni and to make some enquiries concerning the new Church of the black people. Rev. Sangweni stayed at Ndola up to 15th February. He then left Ndola and went back to Southern Rhodesia. Rev. Sangweni came back from Southern Rhodesia with Rev. Z.C. Mtshwello on 7th March, 1931. On this visit, according to the Church Register Book, 300 persons were baptised and 266 were received into full membership of the A.M.E. Church. At the same time, Brother Benjamin Ben Chisela was appointed first Pastor of Ndola circuit by Rev. Z.C. Mtshwello, Superintendent of the Church in Rhodesia.

City of Ndola, Zambia's third largest city and Provincial Headquarters of the Copperbelt Province today showing National Building Society and Bank of Zambia buildings on Buteko Avenue. Photo by Rev. Boyd Mazimba, son of Rev. Joel Mazimba. 10th July, 2020.

On 14th August 1931, Rev. Mtshwello visited Ndola for the second time. Rev. Benjamin Ben Chisela was Pastor of Ndola. On 16th August many more people joined the Church, and also many were baptized and received into full membership in the A.M.E. Church. During the year 1931, the Church spread to Luanshya. In 1932, the Church spread to Mufulira, Kitwe, Chingola and in the Lamba Rural Areas such as Nkana's area, and so forth. From here, the Church began to expand and reached many other provinces in Northern Rhodesia and Tanganyika.

Rev. Charles Kapungwe had reached out to Presiding Elder Samson M. Kapufi in Mansa in 2017. Rev. Kapungwe had phone conversations again in 2018 with the P.E. The Elder was advanced in age and some of the work was being delegated to Rev. Emmanuel Ngalala, the younger minister, to execute. However, Rev. Kapufi had documented some history as well and informed him, "I had been the Secretary of our Father, the Rev. J.L.C. Membe. The younger ministers cannot know nor do they have the information."

Rev. Charles had already received important documentation in English from the Presiding Elder Samson Kapufi. There was also a single undated page, typewritten copy in Bemba which Rev. Kapungwe had to translate into English. It gave a similar account of the history of the beginning of the Church at Ndola. As pointed out above by Rev. J.L.C. Membe, "Many people," he had stated, "Thought that the Church at Ndola began in 1931 when, in fact, it began in 1930." The paper in Rev. Kapungwe's possession indicated (just as Rev. Membe's concerns had been) that the Church at Ndola began in 1931 too. Rev. Membe's version, however, indicated that the Church at Ndola began in 1930 and not in 1931. Rev. Kapufi's history, thus read:

The People Who Began the Church at Ndola

It was in the year 1931, in April, when Ms. Nelia Miyanda and Mr. Gideon Miyanda came to Ndola. They started to worship outside under a Mutobo Tree at Chibolya, the present-day Masala. Those who were meeting with them are:

Br. Benjamin Chisela, Br. Peter Phiri, Bro. Gideon Miyanda, Br. Alexander Mubamba, Bro. Eliya Chunga, Br. Teddy Tongwe, Br. Lazarus Mbiko, Bro. John Mumba, Bro. Abram Nsofu, Bro. Levi Kaluba, Br. Levi Mukumbi, Bro. Matafwali Kindala and Bro. Misheck Zimba, who was the Choir Master.

Women: -

Sis. Janet Jeya, Sis. Megi Mayuru, Sis. Nelia Miyanda, Sis. Nyawandama (Mrs. Mubamba), Sis. Evelyn Chunga, Sis. Jessie Chilongoshi, Sis. Elina Phiri (Mrs. Phiri), Sis. Agness Nsofu, Sis. Nelia Nyanzima, and others.

Mother Janet Jeya was the person who was visiting Circuits. Sis. Nelia Miyanda was the Secretary at the Circuit. In the same month, April, they went to ask Rev. Mtshwello to come and strengthen the church. Bro. Peter Phiri is the one who went to get him. The woman who was presiding over the Women's Annual Conference was Mother Lisabe. The Conference was one from Mansa (Luapula or from the North) all the way to Harare (Salisbury). Mother Miyanda, was the one who often attended the meetings in Zimbabwe (Southern Rhodesia). She also was the one they would send to all other meetings.

Mother Hughes was the first person who came to Ndola. The first bishops were 1. Bishop Bonner. 2. Bishop Jordan. 3. Bishop Ball. Mother Beatrice Lukamba, Mother Fanny Membe, Elina Nekhairo are the ones who could tell what followed afterwards. Women had no Bank Book. They used to give money to men after every gathering and the men are the ones who would take the money to the bank. Author's Note: Mother Beatrice Lukamba passed away in Kitwe on 8th April, 2007 while Mother Fanny Membe passed away in 2015 in Lusaka. She was a member of Bright Chapel in Kitwe for many years until she fell sick and moved to Lusaka to be with her daughter. This document must, therefore, have been written years before these years. Mother Rose Simfukwe indicated that the church in Ndola used to meet at Main Masala before they were allocated a place at Kabushi where Mother Hughes is today.

So, in the year 1931, the Church spread to Luanshya. In 1932, it reached Mufulira, Kitwe, Chingola and in the Lamba rural areas such as Nkana's area, and so forth. From here, the Church began to expand and reached many other provinces in Northern Rhodesia and Tanganyika.

An unidentified girl gives Bishop Robert Pruitt flowers to welcome him at Quinns A.M.E. Church in Chingola for the Annual Conference in 1984. To the Bishop's right is Br. Katoposha greeting a man behind the Bishop. From left to right is Rev. Siusiku (Pastor), Br. Ndelemani alias "Chimozimozi" (Lay Organisation President), Rev. Wilson Mpundu in dark suit and two unidentified brethren.

Beginning of the Church at Luanshya – 1931

The A.M.E. Church on the Copperbelt Province of Northern Rhodesia (now Zambia) branched from Ndola. Brother Ernest Alexander Mwamba of Ndola organized the church at Luanshya from Ndola voluntarily. He was a Government Senior Clerk at Ndola. His first converts at Luanshya were: -

1. Chimpeni Banda
2. Simeon Phiri
3. John Maluti
4. Lamech Chapusa Rowane
5. Nathan Joel Sichone
6. Errit Phiri
7. G. Aliton Muhanga
8. Thomas M. Mukamba
9. Madlopa
10. Chindalo
11. Lazarus S. Saka
12. Janara Soko Chilimina.

Rev. David K. Simfukwe, Sr., who had once been a Pastor at Luanshya wrote about the beginning of the Church there. The following history is attributed to him. The Church in Luanshya started in 1932. (Author's Note: Rev. J.L.C. Membe dates the beginning of the Church at Luanshya to 1931, not 1932). The building was first at Section 3 but when the Mines started their expansions, they demolished the old church building and asked them to be worshiping in the Welfare. The membership and leaders, apparently, were unaware of the plans of demolition.

To the delight of the members the mining company made amends by promising compensation. The company, headed by what was known as the Rhodesian Selection Trust, was tasked with spearheading this compensation. The Trust met the members and took them with their pastor, Rev. Saka L., to a new meeting place. They were given keys and they were amazed! It was a new building with a mission house, had running water and a toilet. The church became what is known as Roan A.M.E. Church and the new facility was comparably better.

From 1932 to 1962, which is 30 years, the church still had less than 20 Full members. Different approaches made by different pastors within these thirty years might have contributed to this low membership. My appointment to Luanshya was in 1961 after my ordination at Bright Temple at Matero by Bishop J.D. Bright. Immediately after my appointment in November, I took position. My main programme was to struggle for membership. I knew that no programme can be implemented effectively without the membership. At that time, I was young and more revolutionary as a student of the Bible College of Ndola. My main task within the year was to print a hymn book which had run out completely. The Church had had no hymn books for the past ten years from the last ones which were done in 1952 when the Church Hymn Book had been printed by our veteran Father J.L.C. Membe.

The publication of this Hymn book raised a big controversy. It went to an extent that in the Annual Conference of 1963 at Kazembe, the Rt. Rev. M.K. Wakunguma offered to resign if Bishop J.D. Bright did not suspend me. I requested the Bishop to appoint someone to pastor Luanshya in order to give chance to Rev. M.K. Wakunguma not to resign. Despite all these sacrifices I made, the Reverend resigned from being a Presiding Elder of the Copperbelt District. Rev. Isaac C. Mumpanshya was nominated Presiding Elder of the Copperbelt instead. Bishop J.D. Bright still confirmed with the church that I should be ordained as an Elder in 1964 in Lusaka Annual Conference. Rev. Kawanda from Solwezi was going to Luanshya.

Year 1964 in the Annual Conference held at Ebenezer A.M.E. Church in Lusaka brought a lot of changes. I was ordained an Elder minister and straight away posted to Luanshya again. This time I consolidated more to such that by 1974, there was no other circuit that could compete with Luanshya. The membership had been very much grown to such an extent that Luanshya had been raised from one single congregation to eight congregations. Thus, I had – Roan, Mpatamato, Kawama, Town, Mikomfwa, Mushili West, Minsenda and Ibenga. With God's help we managed to construct churches at Mpatamato, Kawama, Mushili West and Ibenga. This gave us membership of over 2,000 in all.

I liked ministry and was quite happy to do the work as I did. There was a lot of cooperation with no problem within and around Luanshya. Some of my people who assisted me and my wife, Mother Rose Simfukwe in the development, have now become Pastors in various churches in the country. Some of these members are Brother and Sister Jonas Kachusha, Brother and Sister Ngosa, Brother and Sister Langster Zulu, Brother and Sister Chiluba, Rev. and Sister Chakowela Kaswa, Brother and Sister Mwampanshi, Brother and Sister Chiwelani. Others were Sister Kapende and her children, especially Annie Kapende who was an outstanding young lady in music to such an extent that the A.M.E. Church participated regularly on Radio and Television Broadcasting. My wife and the family enjoyed the good services of two outstanding ministers namely Rev. Ephraim Membe, Rev. and Mother Samuel Yanduli and my first four years of stay was mostly promoted by the beloved Rev. and Mother Baldwin L. Zulu.

Leaving Luanshya at the end of 1974 was like a bomb! I was just taken by surprise when Bishop H.H. Brookins transferred me to Bright Chapel in Kitwe. Although the circuit had just reported K16 to the Conference, I worked hard with my wife. It did not appear as if I had left the place for some time in 1975 when I went to the International Training Institute in Nairobi. The same church by the end of 1975 had paid out K600 arrears and reinstalled electricity in the church and still the church managed to report an amount of K519 to the Annual Conference.

Being glad with the development of the circuit, Bishop H.H. Brookins assigned me to two positions. I was both Pastor of Bright Chapel and Presiding Elder of the Copperbelt. The Bishop decided that Mother Rose Simfukwe and I should go to the United States to study in Chicago at the Institute. Beginning of March 1976, we left for U.S.A. Bright Chapel A.M.E. Church and the Copperbelt were still administered by me through the most dedicated leadership I had left in key positions. This made us enjoy the trip very well.

By the end of October 1976 we came back to Zambia from the United States of America. We found the work quite in super situation. Three weeks later, there was the Annual Conference and my circuit Bright Chapel reported K632. There was no other District that could match the Copperbelt District in reports. Everything was done well as planned.

In 1976, the following were Copperbelt District ministers:

Rev. D.K. Simfukwe, Pastor of Bright Chapel and Presiding Elder of the Great Copperbelt District.
Rev. G.W. Kanyembo – Luanshya
Rev. R.K. Mwenyo – Allen Temple, Mufulira
Rev. M.C.C. Phiri – Chambeshi
Rev. Chiko Banda – Jordan Chapel, Wusakile Kitwe
Rev. Dhlakama – Quinns Chapel, Chingola
Rev. Sichilongo – Brookins Chapel, Chingola
Rev. Elsie Musonda, Mindolo Kitwe (Now Judah A.M.E. Church).
Rev. S. Saka – Twatasha Kitwe, Now (Membe A.M.E. Church)
Rev. Baldwin Zulu – Ndola
Rev. Henry C. Alimasi – Chibuluma
Rev. Kacencete – Nkana

Rev. Foodson B.S. Washiama – Chililabombwe
Rev. Stephen Victor Chambata – Chapula
Rev. Numa D. – Mukutuma; Shimukunami.

The Church had just sent Rev. M.P.P. Mwenya who was previously in Chingola to Ndola Bible College of Central Africa. The year 1977 saw us take full responsibility to develop the church at Bright Chapel and the Copperbelt District. Mrs. Rose Simfukwe concentrated on the Women Missionary Society while I concentrated more on the use of intellectual methods.

A one-week seminar of all the Pastors of the Copperbelt was well-planned for in which we covered:

1. Church Administration
2. Pastoral care and
3. Marriage and ordinance

To this seminar, I give thanks to Rev. Baldwin Zulu who taught on Pastoral Care. I am also grateful to Father Mumba of the Anglican Church who taught on Marriage and Family Care. The seminar had very good results. The entire church on the Copperbelt was happy and made tremendous achievement.

Copperbelt continued to flourish and we made tremendous achievements. The Annual Conference of 1977 recorded an increase in membership and finances throughout all the Copperbelt. Bright Chapel under my charge reported K770 and Mufulira under the Rev. R.K. Mwenyo reported K742, Ndola under Rev. Baldwin Zulu reported K700 while Quinns Chapel and Brookins Chapel in Chingola each reported K500.

The work on the Copperbelt was seen as good and encouraging. I attributed this progress to teamwork. Cooperation was the main reason we saw improvement. Soon, Bright Chapel embarked on mission house building project. In 1977 Annual Conference, I found myself transferred to Lusaka as Presiding Elder. My territory was vast and reached up to Serenje in Central Province and Namwala in Southern Province. This was very interesting and challenging too.

Resolutions in Brief from the Committees – 1968

Committee on Admission recommended the following brothers to go to the 1st Year Studies:
1. Jim Sinyangwe 2. Simon Kabemba 3. Morgan Mtwazi 4. Paska Sikazwe 5. Davies Lusha Hadebe 6. Moses.

The Following People to Repeat Until 1969
1. Benson Mulenga 2. Davison Sikazwe 3. Jackson Kapombe 4. Yona Sichinsambwe 5. David Numa 6. B.J. Kapepe 7. E.L. Munyanta 8. J. Musukuma 9. Laban Mulenga

The Committee on the First Year Study Recommended the Following Brothers to go to the 2nd Year Study:
1. Nekodemu Abakunda 2. Jones Musonda 3. Loti M'kandawire 4. Simon L. Membe 5. Dustone Kanyembo 6. Mateyo Chibanga 7. Anthony M. Muzimba 8. Willy Nkonde 9.

Wilson Dube 10. William Kalyati 11. Bellington Simanwe 12. Alfred Chipesha 13. Ismael Ng'onga 14. Jacob Kapembwa 15. Thomas Chilufya 16. Paska Sikazwe

The Committee on the Second Year Study Recommended the Following Brother to go to the 3rd Year Study:

1. Ephraim Simunyola

The Committee on the Third Year Study Recommended the Following Brothers to go to the 4th Year Study:

1. A.M. Chelemu 2. James S. Sinkala 3. Zebron Chifunda 4. G.F. Masongo 5. J.K. Samukonga 6. Samson Mulambwa 7. Lameck Ng'onga 8. F.T. Sikazwe 9. H. Alimasi 10. P. Musonda 11. G.D. Limani

The Committee on the Fourth Year Study Recommended the Following Brothers to go to Ordination as Elders:

1. Ephraim Mapesa 2. Dauson K. Kawaya 3. Alfred Mulenga 4. Stephen Mulenga 5. Godfrey Chifunda 6. John E. Mwenya 7. Henry Kalaba Waluzimba

Recommendation from the Church Extension – 1968

1. Ndola to be helped with K600 for their church building
2. Chiyanga Church to be helped with K200 to meet their demand for church building
3. Church in Katanga to use the funds in the bank within Katanga Bank and the Secretary of the Conference to send a letter to the Congo Government about some of the requests.
4. Demands from other Circuits could not be met because of short of funds.

Committee on Pensions

The pension should be paid to the people concerned as usual

Other Recommendations:

1. The Presiding Elders should check the number of members, including children in every circuit.
2. The Church should recommend one church building per year in order to build good and permanent buildings.
3. "Picnic Marriages" among our Ministers should not be tolerated, under any circumstances.
4. The Conference to elect a Committee to write the History of the A.M.E. Church in Zambia.
5. A Standing Financial Committee to receive funds both locally and from the Foreign Aid should be formed. Christian friends in the United States think perhaps the Church in Zambia was not thankful on whatever help they had rendered. This was due to the fact that the church hasn't got that Committee. Nobody knows what happens.
6. Discipline must be closely followed.

Beginning of the Church at Mufulira – 1932

1. Thomas Mabula Mukamba, Organiser
2. Benjamin West Chalomba
3. Kayuni
4. Sally Chalomba
5. Nelly Kayuni
6. Dorca Mambwe
7. Dauti Mambwe and
8. Bombechi Mwansa.

Beginning of the Church at Kitwe – 1932

1. Alexander Matako Mwamba, Organiser
2. D.D. Zimba
3. Makisashi
4. Anna Chifuntwe Makisashi
5. Ludia Besa
6. Paul M. Gwamba
7. Mary Gwamba
8. Lilly Golden Mulundu
9. Monika Antonio
10. Wilson Matanda
11. Lista Chipili
12. Libi Kasonge
13. Chiwasha Antonio
14. Nalukonde Elijah
15. Emele Chitundu
16. Ishmaele Tembo.

Center: Rev. Charles Kapungwe (Trinity), Rev. Richard Kasanda (Judah), Br. Gideon Y. Phiri (Calvary) and daughter lower right corner Sis. Musonda Phiri leading in praise at a Joint Kitwe District A.M.E. Churches' donation of clothes and other items to Children in Distress (CINDI) spearheaded by Mrs. Minerva Phiri and the W.M.S., Buchi – Kitwe, 1998.

City of Kitwe (Edinburgh Hotel). Photo: 8th May, 2020 by Robert Moyo.

Beginning of the Church at Chingola – 1932

No information from Chingola was available. However, available information seems to suggest that the Church was first organized in Nchanga Mine Townships. Although the Church was distinctly African, it incorporated Western influence which was noted in its songs. Other denominations observed this during their interaction with the new Church in town.

Beginning of the Church in Lamba Rural Areas, Nkana – 1932

Br. Paul and Sis. Mary Gwamba helped Rev. Henrique Matenda Lukamba and Mother Beatrice Lusati Lukamba organize the Church in Lamba areas of Nkana. In 1945, Mother Elizabeth N.L. Simyembe's father, Rev. Lukamba was appointed Pastor of Nkana Circuit.

Chapter 10
Creation of First Two Districts and Second Appointments to Northern Rhodesia in 1933

Second Appointments

At the 1933 Annual Conference presided by Bishop David Henry Sims, held in the Young's Chapel A.M.E. Church, Bulawayo from 27th February to 3rd March, 1933, two Presiding Elders' Districts were created in Northern Rhodesia. The Districts were known as Livingstone and Ndola Districts. The Presiding Elders' headquarters were at Wankie (now Hwange), in Southern Rhodesia for Livingstone District and in Ndola, Northern Rhodesia for Ndola District. Creation of the first two Districts and second appointments to Northern Rhodesia proved to be a great milestone in the establishment of the A.M.E. Church in Northern Rhodesia.

The following were the appointments for both Districts: -
Livingstone District – Rev. Alfred Innes Nojekwa, P.E.
Wankie: Rev. A.I. Nojekwa, (S.R).
Matetsi: Bro. Sampson Ngulube, (S.R).
Victoria Falls: Bro. Benjamin Ben Chisela (S.R).
Gwaai Reserve: Rev. Solomon Ngala Sangweni, (S.R).
Htlangano: Rev. Calvert H. Monne, (S.R).
Kennedy: Bro. Nathan S. Mhango, (S.R).
Masunkumala: William Z. Masukuma, (S.R).
Dett: Bro. Daniel Kekana, (S.R).
Livingstone: Rev. Phineas Nthoba, (N.R).
Mazabuka: Bro. David Njukwa, (N.R).
Choma: Rev. Johannes Marumo, (N.R).
Feira: Bro. A. Simwanza, (N.R).
Siyacitema: Bro. Isaac Simbeye, (N.R).
Mapansa: Bro. Benjamin West Chalomba, (N.R).
Mumbwa: Bro. Abel Motale, (N.R).
Hvamba: Bro. Halifeyo Mukalane, (Bech. Protectorate).
Lusaka: Rev. David Dafite Khomela, (N.R).
Ayrser Mataka: Bro. Michael Kalizembe, (Bech. Protectorate).
Ngamiland: To be supplied, (Bech. Protectorate).
Ndola District – Rev. H.M. Phiri, P.E., P.O. Box 210 Ndola, N.R.
Ndola: Rev. Hanock Msokera Phiri, P.E.
Fort Roseberry: Br. David Bangwe.

Abercorn: Rev. J.L.C. Membe.
Serenje: Bro. Elijah H. Chunga.
Chisamba: Bro. Peter Phiri.
Broken Hill: Rev. Jonas Lesapi Honoko.
Solwezi: Bro. Nathan Soko.
Namwala: Bro. Isaac Banda.
Petauke: Bro. Aswell A. Nkhoma.
Kawambwa: Bro. James Kakonko Lendeng'oma.
Nuwamba: To be supplied.

Some people would wonder of when the Church reached to all those places in just a short period like that. The Annual Conference had passed a resolution to give an appointment to anybody provided he was prepared to go where there was no A.M.E. Church to start one there and make members for himself. If the person had failed to convert members to the Church, he was not to come back to the Annual Conference for he was regarded as having failed. So, each Presiding Elder had to sit down and just write down names of the people he remembered provided they were members of the Church.

However, when those appointments were brought to them, many refused. Only a few managed to go to their appointed charges to open new fields of labour for the Church. Pastors who were sent to places where the Church had been established already, like Broken Hill, Ndola, and Livingstone in Northern Rhodesia, accepted the appointments.

Those who offered themselves to go to open new fields were as follows: -

1. Rev. Johannes Marumo, Choma, from Southern Rhodesia.
2. Rev. David Dafite Khomela, to Lusaka, from Southern Rhodesia.
3. Rev. J.L.C. Membe, to Abercorn from Broken Hill.

So, in this year, 1933, we had only two Presiding Elders and four Pastors. They were: Rev. A.I. Nojekwa, P.E., Wankie with Rev. J. Marumo as Pastor of Choma and Rev. D.D. Khomela as Pastor of Lusaka. Ndola District: The whole Copperbelt was at that time Ndola Circuit. Rev. H.M. Phiri, P.E., had two Pastors, Rev. Jonas Lesapi Honoko, Pastor of Broken Hill and Rev. Lester C. Membe, Pastor of Abercorn. So, there were only six ministers in both Districts. The Wankie District extended from Wankie to Lusaka, and Ndola District extended from Broken Hill to Abercorn.

Sis. Charity Nakazwe (2nd from left, standing) with fellow YPDers in 1978 at Bright Temple, Matero in Lusaka. She was the daughter of the Pastor in charge Rev. Field T. Sikazwe. Rev. Sikazwe later became P.E. Elder of Copperbelt East District in 1990. Sis. Charity was helpful in bringing about revival in Lusaka during her days as an older youth and we (Charles Kapungwe and Team on the Copperbelt) coordinated well with her in the Midlands. Rev. Sikazwe was Pastor of Bright from 1975 to 1990.

Chapter 11
The Great Expansion of the A.M.E. Church in Northern Rhodesia – Northern and Luapula Provinces in 1932

During the year 1932, a great expansion of the A.M.E. Church took place and reached many parts of Northern Rhodesia. This was done by members and many of them had no official appointments from the Annual Conference. It must be kept in mind that the present Northern and Luapula Provinces were one at the time under the name, Northern Province. The following are some of the main places and the names of persons who first organized the A.M.E. Church voluntarily there:

LWAMFWE: Bro. Office Kabunda, Organiser, 1932.
Bro. Amon Chanda
Bro. Moses Kaitenge
Bro. Barnabas Kubi
Bro. Stephen Chomba
Bro. Daster Shitumba, and many followed them.
Today, (2020), Lwamfwe is in North Mwense District and Rev. Emmanuel Ngalala is the Presiding Elder.

MUSANGU: Bro. Samuel Mambwe, Organiser, 1932.
Bro. Moses Kaunda
Bro. Samuel Katebe
Bro. Jack Kabongo
Bro. Daniel Chishimba
Bro. Koweni Mabu,
Bro. Rain Kalyongo.
Sisters Lelly Koweni and Anna Bwalya.
Today, Musangu is in Mwense North District.

KALENDA: Bro. Matthew Mwelwa, Organiser, 1932.
Bro. Robert Chibwe.
Bro. Foodson Burton Shadreck Washiama
Bro. Kantambo Chilufya, Mankanka
Bro. Richard Chishala, Mankanka
Bro. Luswili Chama, Kashiba
Bro. Daniel Musonda, Kashiba, and Ngwelele Katuna.

Today, Kalenda is in Mwense North District.

MULUNDU: Bro. Semusi Lukokola Kaunda, Organiser, late in 1932.
Bro. Stephen Chomba, and many others whose names are not available. Mulundu is Mwense South District today. The Presiding Elder is Rev. Goodson Mwenya.

KAZEMBE: Bro. James Kakonko Lendeng'oma, Organiser, late 1932.
Bro. Lifai Chibwe.
Bro. Petro Mumba.
Bro. Nicodemus Mpundu
Bro. Maxwell Chibiliti, Mukamba
Goshen Mwemena, Mukamba
Shimose, Mukamba
Robert Chiwaya, Mukamba
Jackson Chama, Mukamba
Sister Silika Katebe, Mukamba
Kazembe is in Mwansabombwe District today. Presiding Elder is Rev. Jonas Chiwele.

LUKANGA: Bro. Peter Mengo, Organiser, late in 1932.
Bro. Reuben Sumba, and many others. Today, Lukanga is in Nchelenge South District with Rev. Philemon Mwaba as Presiding Elder.

ITABWA-KALUNGWISHI: Bro. David Dickson Zimba came to Kalungwishi from Ndola fully licensed Local Preacher. When he came home at Chanda in Chief Mununga's area, Mporokoso in the Mweru Valley, he started to organize the Church there. Itabwa-Kalungwishi is in Chienge District today, and Rev. Richard Kalwa is the Presiding Elder.

CHANDA: Bro. David Dickson Zimba, Organiser, late 1932.
Bro. Mose Mwaba
Bro. Lwangwa
Bro. Ason Chiyambi
Bro. Kapufi Maingwe
Bro. Nsendela
Bro. Chimbabulele
Bro. Chileya Mwansa.
Chanda is in Chienge District today and the Presiding Elder is Rev. Richard Kalwa.

All men mentioned from the beginning included their wives although their wives' names are not mentioned.

In 1934, Brother Ernest Aaron Mvula was appointed Pastor of the Chanda circuit in Kalungwishi area. He made his headquarters at Chanda's village near Nyamfwa where Bro.

D.D. Zimba started. Pastor Mvula extended the Church to the following places in 1934: - Kashiba, Chief Mukupa Katandula.

Bro. David Dixon Zimba, Organiser, and the first members were: - Abel Nsama, Thomas Kapepa, Datson Kaselekela and wives.

CHIBUTA-MPOROKOSO

Bro. James Musalakata Mwape
Bro. Daniel Mwango
Bro. Levi Kabwe and then many others. Chibuta-Mporokoso is in Luapula and today (2020) is in Mporokoso District and Rev. Chansa Mulenga is the Presiding Elder.

Before Rev. Mvula went to his headquarters at Chanda, he appointed Brother James Mwape and Brother Daniel Mwango as Local Preachers. They were to preach at Chibuta, Songa and Lupele but some members of the London Missionary Society and Roman Catholic Church leaders went to Chief Mporokoso and reported to him that there are some men who are preaching in your area in the name of a Church they have never heard of. Chief Mporokoso was worried and went to report to the District Commissioner of Mporokoso. These two young men were summoned to go and appear before the District Commissioner to go and answer charges. The young men Mwape and Mwango were imprisoned for one month for preaching in that area without permission from the Chief and Government.

A letter was sent to the Presiding Elder at Ndola about this case. He was called to come to Mporokoso but Rev. Hanock Msokera Phiri wrote to the Provincial Commissioner at Kasama and told him that he had one minister at Abercorn, Rev. J.L.C. Membe who acts as Presiding Elder's representative; he should be called to deal with the matter in my place. The Provincial Commissioner sent the letter to me at Chiyanga, Abercorn through the District Commissioner of Abercorn and ordered me to go to Mporokoso "about the men of your church who are imprisoned for preaching without a permit."

Really, this puzzled me greatly! I did not know what Rev. Phiri did to put me in that trouble that should have been dealt by him as Presiding Elder. Regardless, I went to Mporokoso on a bicycle (a distance of 225 km or 139.8 miles) and reached there on 16th December, 1934. On 17th December, I went to the BOMA and discussed with the D.C. and the chief, and after some agreed points those two brothers were released from prison after having served the sentence for two weeks. They were ordered not to preach any more until they had been given preaching permits from the Provincial Commissioner at Kasama.

On 18th December, I cycled to Kasama (a distance of 177.2 km or 110.1 miles) for two days. I made an interview with the Provincial Commissioner, who, after some general talks about the Church and its Constitution; I gave him a copy of the Discipline Book of the A.M.E. Church to read. He asked me to see him the next morning. In the next morning, I met the P.C. who told me he was satisfied with our Constitutional Book and the Discipline Book and he issued me with Permits to preach for the two brothers James Mwape and Daniel Mwango.

After two days, I reached Mporokoso and showed the permits to the District Commissioner who also advised me to show these papers to Chief Mporokoso too. In the afternoon I went to Chibuta's village where I found these two men waiting for me. When I gave them the permits from Kasama, they were very pleased and the work of the Church continued safely.

After the trouble ceased in Mporokoso District, the Presiding Elder Rev. H.M. Phiri visited the Province in July, 1934. This was the first and last time that the Presiding Elder visited the Province. He came and found all troubles were no more. This time Rev. Phiri was the Presiding Elder of the whole Northern Rhodesia and Nyasaland.

In 1934, the Church spread very rapidly reaching many areas. It reached as far as Mweru Valley in Chiyenge, Ufipa Province in Tanganyika and many areas. During the year 1935, there was another trouble again in the Mporokoso District arising from some influences by the missionaries of other denominations to the chiefs against the A.M.E. Church. This was done in a pressing manner; therefore, it made the Government and some chiefs ban the Church in their areas. The chief reason was that the A.M.E. Church has turned all their members to the A.M.E. Church and to try to have their members back to their Churches they had to say a lot of false accusations against the A.M.E. Church just to have it banned.

However, Rev. Mvula disregarded the ban. He continued to go there to do his work because in those areas there were hundreds and hundreds of A.M.E. Church members. Nonetheless, he was arrested and was brought to Court before the Magistrate at Mporokoso in November 1935. Rev. Mvula was suspended from preaching in the Mporokoso District. Before Rev. Mvula was sent away, Rev. Phiri, the Presiding Elder, was called from Ndola to come to Mporokoso about Rev. Mvula's case which would be dealt with at Kasama, but the Presiding Elder could not come. He instead referred the Magistrate to me at Abercorn.

I went to Kasama in place of the Presiding Elder. After having pleaded earnestly with the Government Official to just let him be sent away from the Province, Rev. Mvula was ordered to leave the Province and go back to his Presiding Elder at Ndola. However, when I went back to Abercorn, Rev. Mvula went to Tokatoka and Mofwe in Kawambwa District and stayed there. At that time Luapula and Northern Provinces were together as Northern Province. Rev. Mvula started again to preach at Tokatoka in Kawambwa District. When this came to the knowledge of the Provincial Commissioner of Kasama in Northern Rhodesia that Rev. Mvula was still preaching in the Province in which he has been banned the following letter was sent to the Presiding Elder. Rev. Hanock Msokera Phiri of Ndola: -

HAG/FT. M28/90/33 – (1427)

<u>NORTHERN RHODESIA</u>
OFFICE OF THE PROVINCIAL COMMISSIONER,
NORTHERN PROVINCE,
KASAMA,
13th December, 1935.
Hanock Phiri
Presiding Elder,
African Methodist Episcopal Church,
P.O. Box 210,
<u>NDOLA.</u>

Sir,

I have the honour to forward you a copy of the proceedings of the enquiry, held by me at Mporokoso, into the allegation of misconduct against your Pastor Aaron Mvula together with my findings of the case.

2. I regret that you were unable to be present at the enquiry.

3. I sent you these proceedings in order that you may intimate any action you wish to take, before the matter is referred to His Excellency for final decision, and also allow you to communicate with your Bishop.

4. It is clear from the evidence that there is no prejudice against your Church, and that the complaints are against Aaron Mvula personally, and you will be pleased to know that your other ministers have been well received and are popular alike with both officials and natives.

5. With his previous long experience in the Mission field I feel that Aaron Mvula did not act with ignorance of a new-comer overzealous for his Church but was willfully overbearing in his conduct.

6. I must draw your attention to your Pastor Augustus Kawala who, unless he was quite unaware of Aaron Mvula's suspension, took Aaron to the District Commissioner, Kawambwa, to get another Preaching license in a very unworthy manner.

7. Aaron Mvula informs me that he is staying at Tokatoka's village under Chief Chiwoshi in Kawambwa District.

I have the honour to be,
Sir,
Your obedient servant.

(SGD) H.A. GREEN
<u>ACTING PROVINCIAL COMMISSIONER.</u>
Copy to Provincial Commissioner, Ndola.

I have failed to trace the copy of the proceedings of the Commissioner's enquiry concerning Rev. E.A. Mvula's case. I had a copy given me by the Provincial Commissioner on my request. I wrote a letter to the Presiding Elder at Ndola to transfer Rev. Mvula from the Northern Province and he did.

North West Zambia Conference (Luapula Province) and North East Zambia Conference (Northern Province and Muchinga Province) – Past and Present.

North West Zambia Conference (Luapula Province)

Luapula Province (North West Zambia Conference) played a major role in the expansion of the A.M.E. Church in Zambia. The A.M.E. Churches in Luapula began to be established in 1932. Since there were very few Pastors, the expansion was done chiefly by members. Second appointments to Northern Rhodesia were done in 1933. However, Luapula got their first officially appointed Pastor in 1934 to Chanda. After months of consultations and collaboration with retired Presiding Elder Samson Kapufi and Presiding Elder Emmanuel Ngalala from 2017 to 2020, the hardworking ministers were able to provide us with detailed information on the appointments done over the years in Luapula.

Minor differences with Rev. Membe's history were observed on the year of the Church's beginning here. However, it was discovered that many churches began without official Pastors in charge and on many instances were under another charge. Rev. Kapufi, in some instances therefore, indicated that some churches began in 1934 while Rev. J.L.C. Membe dates their beginning to 1932. Such dates were consequently synchronized with the Founder's dates.

The list below shows the respective churches' years of establishment: Lwamfwe 1932, Musangu 1932, Mulundu 1932, Kazembe 1932, Lukanga 1932, Itabwa-Kalungwishi (Chanda) 1932, Chipifya 1934, Puta (Dr. Kawimbe) 1934, Munkombwe 1968, Mukwakwa 1971, Lupiya 1971 and Chienge 1981. Others are Mukunta 1983, Swali 1985, Kalembwe 1985, Chifumbe 1986, James 1988, Mpapwa (Mununga 1999) and Allen 2002. The list also covers some of the Presiding Elders who have served in Luapula.

From left to right: Rev. Emmanuel Ngalala, P.E., Rev. Richard Kalwa, P.E., Rev. Ackim Mpundu and Rev. Philemon Mwaba, North West Zambia Conference (Luapula Province) at the Annual Conference with Lake Bangweulu in the background in Samfya. 2nd August, 2014.

CHURCH HISTORY LUAPULA PROVINCE CHIENGE DISTRICT	PRESIDING ELDER DISTRICTS AND NAMES – Luapula Province 1933-2020
CHURCHES **FIRST PASTOR** <u>CHANDA A.M.E. CHURCH 1932</u> Rev. Ernest Aaron Mvula 1934 Rev. Amose Kaunda 1934 Rev. Robert 1937 Rev. Maingwe Kapufi 1938 Rev. Benson Mulenga 1942 Rev. Peter Mumba 1947 Rev. Maiko Chilambwe 1938/1939 Rev. Ismail Ng'onga 1981 Rev. James Musalakata 1988 Rev. John Mwila 1988/89 Rev. Kabungu Chilupula 1990 Rev. Lameck Chansa 1991 Rev. Manda Mutakwa 1995 Rev. J.K. Chanda 1997 Rev. Bedford Katebe 2001 Rev. Richard Kalwa 2003 Rev. Emmanuel C. Ngalala 2013 Rev. Jonas Musonda 2014	Rev. Hanock Msokera Chingo Phiri – 1934 Rev. J.L.C. Membe 1935 (& Northern P.) Rev. Moses Kaunda – 1939 Rev. A.F. Chambwe – 1939 Rev. Chalomba – 1948 Rev. Maingwe Kapufi – 1959 Rev. Robert Kabala – 1959 Rev. Jonas Musonda – 1978 Rev. Paswell Mpele – 1990 Rev. Chansa Mulenga 2002 (Mporokoso D.) Rev. Goodson Mwenya 2002 (Mwense South D.) Rev. Jonas Musonda 2003 (Mwansabombwe D.) Rev. Muma Musangu 2005 (Nchelenge South D.) Rev. Phillimon Mwaba – 2005 (Chienge District) Rev. Agness Makwaza – 2012 (Kawimbe District) Rev. James Chiwele – 2013 (Mwansabombwe D.) Rev. Richard Kalwa – 2014 (Chienge D.) Rev. Daniel Choma – 2015 (Kawambwa D.) Rev. Paxion Kasanda – 2016 (Nchelenge North D.) Rev. Emmanuel Ngalala – 2018 (Mwense North D.)

CHIPIFYA A.M.E. CHURCH 1934 (Chienge District) – Under Chanda Rev. Ernest Aaron Mvula Rev. Moses Kaunda 1935 Rev. I.P. Kayumba 1937 Rev. Maingwe Kapufi 1960 Rev. Lameck Chansa 1983 Rev. J.K. Chanda 1995 Rev. Ackim Mpundu 1998 Munkombwe A.M.E. Church 1968 Lay Pastor Kamfwa Richard 1977 Lay Pastor Lazarus Mwaba 1982 Lay pastor Darlington Mpundu 1989 Lay Pastor Black Mwila 1993 Lay Pastor Welly Katebe 1998 Rev. Emmanuel C. Ngalala 2002 Rev. J.K. Chanda 2007 Lay Pastor Black Mwila 2010	PUTA (DR. KAWIMBE) A.M.E. CHURCH 1934 Rev. Ernest Aaron Mvula (founder) 1934 Rev. Amos Mpundu 1935 Rev. I.P. Kayumba 1937 Rev. Poleni Kafitisha 1952 Rev. Amon Chanda 1954 Rev. Chakowela Kaswa 1956 (Deacon, late) Rev. Samson Chungu 1958 Rev. Benson Mulenga 1963 Rev. Paswell Mpele 1975 Rev. Kafwanka 1979 Rev. Kubi Lumbwe 1981 Rev. Rev. Mwendapole 1985 Rev. K.P.C. Mwila 1992 Rev. Emmanuel C. Ngalala 2001-2011 Rev. Kelvin Mwitwa 2013 Rev. Ackim Mpundu 2017 Rev. Richard Kalwa 2018
Mukwakwa A.M.E. Church 1971 Rev. Omedu Chikumbi 1983 Rev. Manda Mutakwa 1988 Rev. Emmanuel C. Ngalala 2000 Rev. Ackim Mpundu 2007 Rev. Okey Mwila 2010 Rev. Manda Mutakwa 2011	Lupiya Border A.M.E. Church 1971 Lay Pastor Munkuku Samson 1975 Rev. Benson Mulenga 1977 Rev. Marko Mulenga 1980 Rev. Eunice Kabeka 1987 Rev. Ackim Mpundu 1993 Rev. Mwendapole 1994 Rev. Paswell Mpele 1997 Rev. Richard Kalwa 2007
Chienge A.M.E. Church 1981 (Under Puta) Lay Pastor Charles Manda 1987 Rev. Ackim Mpundu 2002 Rev. Kelvin Mwitwa 2008 Lay Pastor Lumbwe 2011	Mukunta A.M.E. Church 1983 Rev. Lameck Chansa 1989 Rev. Emmanuel C. Ngalala 2001 Rev. J.K. Chanda 2006 Lay Pastor Black Mwila 2009 Lay Pastor Friday Lwamfwe 2011
Swali A.M.E. Church 1985 Rev. Eunice Kabeka (Founder) Rev. Alex Chishimba 2002 Rev. Alfred Lubango 2000 Rev. Ackim Mpundu 2010	Kalembwe A.M.E. Church 1985 Rev. Eunice Kabeka (Founder) Rev. Wales Seya 1997 Rev. Alfred Lubango 2000 Rev. Paul Changala 2000

<u>Chifumbe A.M.E. Church 1986</u> Rev. Eunice Kabeka (Founder) Rev. T.K. Silanda 2001 Rev. Sondashi Mwape 2007 Rev. Emmanuel C. Ngalala 2009	<u>James A.M.E. Church 1988</u> Lay Pastor Black Mwila 1999 Lay Pastor Welly Katebe 2001 Rev. Emmanuel C. Ngalala 2005 Rev. J.K. Chanda 2008
<u>Allen A.M.E. Church 2002</u> Lay Pastor Wellem Kabwe 2002 Lay Pastor Jackson Makwala 2005 Rev. Emmanuel C. Ngalala 2006	<u>Mpapwa A.M.E. Church (Mununga 1999)</u> (Under Chanda) Rev. J.K. Chanda 2002 Rev. Richard Kalwa 2008 Lay Pastor Wellem Kabwe 2009 Lay Pastor Makwala 2010 Rev. Emmanuel C. Ngalala 2011
KAWIMBE DISTRICT	
<u>Thomas A.M.E. Church 1967 (Mansa)</u> Rev. Mary Chalomba Founder Rev. Simuyemba 1972 Rev. Rev. Samson Kapufi 1975 Rev. Jonas Musonda 1981 Rev. Betele Chonde 1988 Rev. Jonas Chiwele 1991 Rev. Daniel Chomba 1999 Rev. Kelvin Mwitwa 2006 Rev. Taylor Siulapwa 2013 Rev. A.K. Chishala 2019	<u>Samson Kapufi Temple 2008 (Mansa)</u> Rev. Samson Kapufi 2008-2010 (Founder) Rev. Jonas Chiwele 2012 Rev. Emmanuel Ngalala 2013 Rev. Makwaza 2018 <u>Allen Temple A.M.E. Church, 1982 (Samfya)</u> Rev. Muvunga (Founder) Rev. William Kabwe 1984 Rev. Mukange 1986 Rev. Laston Mwape 1990 Rev. Chella 1991 Rev. Makwaza 1995 Rev. Chibanga 2004 Rev. Sikazwe 2006 Rev. Bobley Chipawa 2010 Rev. Emmanuel Ngalala 2015/P.E.
MWANSABOMBWE DISTRICT	
<u>Kazembe A.M.E. Church 1932</u> Rev. Benjamin Ben Chisela.	

North East Zambia Conference (Northern Province and Muchinga Province)

Mbala North District Conference at Jordan Chapel (formerly known as Mayanga Mission also known as Chiyanga Mission, started by Rev. J.L.C. Membe). From left Presiding Elder Kennedy Mazimba (with mic), Rev. Licks Simutowe with hands holding glasses, Pastor at Kings Chapel; Kalambo District Presiding Elder Joel Sichilima, reading the Bible, Rev. Weston Silupya behind him with Rev. Kalifwa Sikatunga on his right (blurred face). July 2018, Mbala.

OLD YPDers' Day at Solomon's Temple, Kasama held on 19th August, 2018.

OLD YPDers' Day at Solomon's Temple, Kasama held on 19th August, 2018. Sam Chupah (left, interpreter) and Presiding Elder Rev. Kennedy Mazimba guest speaker, North East Zambia Conference.

Mbala North District Conference at Jordan Chapel (Chiyanga Mission), July 2018, Mbala.

Pastor Mutale teaching the youth. Mbala North District Conference at Jordan Chapel, Mbala. July 2018.

Elijah Simuyemba North East Zambia Annual Conference Sons of Allen President at Jordan Chapel, Mbala, July 2018.

North East Zambia Annual Conference held at Bonner Chapel, Mbala (Host Pastor, Rev. Kennedy Mazimba, P.E., 2019).

****

On 24th November, 1935, I was appointed Presiding Elder of Northern Province, Luapula Province and Tanganyika District with headquarters at Chiyanga Mission, Abercorn. From 1936 there had never been any more troubles in the Church. The A.M.E. Church was now accepted in many provinces and districts where the Church was first refused.

Rev. John Lester C. Membe was appointed to Northern Province in 1932 and the following places are the first main circuits: -

CHIYANGA MISSION (Headquarters). Rev. J.L.C. Membe, the first members were listed as follows:

Simeon Kennedy Simpanya,	Chiyanga	Bro. Chimbini Sampala	"
Numberfour Siwale	"	Bro. Norris Lyonga	"
Ben Chipungu	"	Bro. Mwapeya Chizule	"
Abraham Juma	"	Bro. James Fundi	"
Ferman James Sikazwe	"	Bro. Simon Zombe	Chilwa (Simon Zombe's village)
Sisters: Nelly Peter Namabao	"		
Alice Mwambazi	"	Bro. James Kaziwe	"
Mandalena Chilombo	"	Bro. Simon Fwambo	"
Martha Nakazwe	"	Bro. Island Mapesa	Mapesa's village
Ellen Chewe	"	Bro. Moses Nondo	Kapata
Mulenga Chanda	"	Bro. Dillian Mwananzila	Chisanza
Nansawa Namutowe	"	Bro. Amon Chinkula	"
Elsie Chelemu	"	Bro. Enock Mwananzila	"
Gladys Chelemu	"	Sister Mwaya Kombe	"
Elina Chakupewa	"	Bro. Pintu Changala	Chipwa
Bro. Milton Chitimbwa	Mutono's Village	Bro. Silas Chikapa	"
Bro. Jacob Chisumbe	"	KASAMA:	Bro. Stephen Butanda
Bro. Holland Nonde	"		Bro. Bafula Lesa
Bro. Moses Chinama	Chipulila's Village		Bro. David Munuumo.

SUMMONS: -

During the years 1934 – 1935, many enemies rose against the A.M.E. Church in many places and districts. Missionaries of many districts tried hard to persuade the Government to ban the A.M.E. Church in their areas because many of their Christians were joining the A.M.E. Church in great numbers. Every time we were summoned, the case ended in our favour. The Government assured all the missionaries that people were free to change their faith without being forced to do so. From that time there was peace in the Church and many people had to come from far to join the Church and went to start it in their areas. The way the A.M.E. Church expanded in a few years' time was wonderful.

Chapter 12
The A.M.E. Church in Eastern and North Western Provinces in 1934

Beginning of the Church at Fort Jameson (Chipata) – 1934

The A.M.E. Church at Fort Jameson was organized by Brother Elijah Chunga and his wife. This happened when the couple went on leave from Ndola where Mr. Chunga was a Clerk in the Government. He went with his brother-in-law Mr. Ted Mathongwe and his wife. These four met for their prayers in Mr. Kalongola Nkhosi's house. Mr. Kalongola and wife were the parents of Chunga's and Ted's wives. They converted their father and mother-in-law and some members of their families and relatives. They called Rev. Phiri, the then Presiding Elder of Northern Rhodesia and Nyasaland to Fort Jameson to organize them. Therefore, the beginning of the Church at Fort Jameson in Eastern Province in 1934 was spearheaded by the mission work from the Copperbelt.

The following were the first members of the A.M.E. Church at Fort Jameson: -
1. Kalongola Nkhosi
2. Zankosi Kalongola Nkhosi
3. Kefasi
4. H. Jumbe
5. J.D. Matola
6. Janet Nthawanga
7. Anna Daka
8. Abigail Daka, and many others.

Brother Kalongola Nkosi built a temporary church building at Fort Jameson at his own expense. He built it himself which was a great gift to the church from one person.

During 1934 to 1936, the Church was organized in Petauke and Lundazi Districts at the time of Rev. H.M. Phiri as Presiding Elder of Nyasaland District up to Chief Jumbe's area in Fort Jameson District. The first members of the A.M.E. Church at Jumbe were: -
1. Abel Chikulunitabantu
2. Mrs. Chikulunitabantu
3. Lucy Maumba, and then many others.

Rev. Langster D. Zulu, Presiding Elder (now retired, 2020) had worked with his grandson Langster Zulu, Jr., strengthening the Church in Eastern Province. Br. Langster Zulu, Jr., a former Senior Steward at St. David Simfukwe A.M.E. Church in Nyimba, had once been on the Finance Committee of the Chipata/Nyimba District. He helped in passing on of latest photos from Eastern Province.

Presiding Elder for Chipata/Nyimba District Rev. David Kaunda Phiri (left) with Bro. Matthews Nkhosi during the Pastors and Lay Meeting at Bethel A.M.E. Church in Chipata in 2019.

Presiding Elder Rev. David K. Phiri with his son at St. David Simfukwe A.M.E. Church in Nyimba. They stopped by at the church on their way to the District Conference in Chipata from Lusaka in 2019. Photos provided by Br. Langster Zulu, Jr., grandson of Rev. Langster Zulu, former P.E. of Nyimba.

For North Western Province, not much has been recorded on the work there. However, the Annual Conference held at Young's Chapel A.M.E. Church at Bulawayo from 27th February to 3rd March, 1933 which created two Presiding Elder Districts and had appointed Rev. David Dafite Khomela as Presiding Elder of Northern Rhodesia had recommended names. Bro. Nathan Soko was appointed to be Pastor at Solwezi. He likely was the first preacher for the A.M.E. Church in North Western Province. Also, records under my possession (Rev. Kapungwe) show that Rev. Henrique Matanda Lukamba had been appointed as Presiding Elder for Kasempa in 1945 under the auspices of the Zambezi Annual Conference, indicating that the A.M.E. Church had been active in the area. Rev. Manasae Siska was appointed Pastor to Solwezi on 5th January, 1939, where he was for two years and at Kasempa for a year in 1952 while Rev. Joel Perhaps Mumbili Kuyumba served at Kasempa in 1957 for a year.

On Friday, 8th May, 2020 after all efforts to get contacts in North Western Province failed, I decided to check online for any information. I came across some YPD postings which I pursued and found a contact, Br. Paul Mwango Kafusu who informed me that he was the YPD President of the Zambezi Conference (created in 2008)! Since his last name was familiar, I inquired if he knew Br. Louis Kafusu. He informed me he was his father! He also informed me his mother was a daughter of Sis. Regina Mwango. I immediately assumed he knew that his grandmother had served in my YPD executive about 32 years ago! When I began to tell him, I needed a photo from the region and began to explain who I was, the young man informed me that he already knew me! He has heard a lot about me from his father! Thank God I needed no introduction because his father passed on what we had imparted in him and to God be the glory! He had been in YPD at Bright Chapel, Kitwe.

Zambezi Conference YPD Convention participants in 2019 on a march-past going to Allen Temple in Solwezi photo by Paul Kafusu. Note: This Zambezi Conference is a newer Conference and must not be confused with the historic Zambezi Conference referenced to earlier!

Chapter 13
The A.M.E. Church in Southern, Central and Barotse (now Western) Provinces

The A.M.E. Church in Southern and Western Provinces was started by the Rev. David Dafite Khomela, Presiding Elder of Northern Rhodesia. He was appointed as the first Presiding Elder of Northern Rhodesia District at the Third Session of the Zambezi Annual Conference held in the Young's Chapel A.M.E. Church, Bulawayo in Southern Rhodesia in October 1931. Rev. Khomela was from Bechuanaland but he had been a Pastor in Southern Rhodesia before coming to Northern Rhodesia. Since his headquarters were at Livingstone, the Presiding Elder began the Church there making Livingstone the first town in Southern Province to have the A.M.E. Church. Northern Rhodesia was one Presiding Elder's District at the time and Rev. David D. Khomela (Southern and Western) and Rev. J.L.C. Membe (Central) would, therefore, be credited with pioneering of the work in these three provinces.

The A.M.E. Church in Zambia began at Broken Hill, (Kabwe). This, presently, is Central Province today and was known as Luangwa Province then. When Rev. Khomela visited Broken Hill, he brought with him Rev. Jonas Lesapi Honoko from Transvaal in South Africa. Rev. Honoko became the Pastor at Broken Hill in February 1932 and afterwards from here, the Church went into the Lenje Reserve in Chief Chipepo's area where Bro. Lester Somanje was elected a class leader and for Nine Native Farms. Rev. J.L.C. Membe who started the Church in Zambia began the Church in Central Province of Zambia before the official leader's visit.

Kabwe (Broken Hill), Provincial Headquarters for Central Province – the birthplace of the A.M.E. Church in Zambia in 1929. Photo: Chitanda House taken on 30th April, 2020.

The Annual Conference held at Young's Chapel A.M.E. Church at Bulawayo from 27th February to 3rd March, 1933 created two Presiding Elder Districts. They were Livingstone and Ndola. The Presiding Bishop was D.H. Sims. Rev. Johannes Marumo was appointed as Pastor of Choma, Rev. Phineas Nthoba as Pastor of Livingstone, Bro. David Njukwa as Pastor of Mazabuka, Bro. Isaac Simbeye as Pastor of Siyacitema while Bro. Benjamin West Chalomba was appointed as Pastor of Mapansa. However, only Rev. Marumo took up this appointment. Although not all appointments were likely taken up, evidence of church activities in diverse locations in Southern Province indicate that work had been started in many places.

Rev. Mack Basket Siduna, a Southern Rhodesian, joined the A.M.E. Church in 1932 in Southern Rhodesia. After being Pastor at Inkonyane, Selukwe and Fhlangano in Southern Rhodesia, he was transferred to Northern Rhodesia in 1937. He served as Pastor at Monze, Mazabuka, Livingstone, Choma, Namwala and Kabumbwe in Southern Province and was still in active ministry in 1962 there.

Rev. Joffrey Mangesana, who had been ordained in Salisbury, Southern Rhodesia on 24th July, 1949 by Bishop I.H. Bonner served in many places. He was from Southern Rhodesia. He once served as Presiding Elder of Fort Jameson District (now Chipata) for three years then returned to Southern Rhodesia at Wankie (now Hwange) as Pastor after which he was reappointed Presiding Elder of Fort Victoria District. He was again, sent back to Northern Rhodesia and stationed at Chitongo in Namwala District where he was still serving around 1962 as Presiding Elder.

Jordan Chapel A.M.E. Church, Libuyu Livingstone during the District Conference in March 2019. Jordan Chapel is the main church in Livingstone. From left to right: 1. Br. Chris Njekwa, 2. Sis. Phoebe Mungala, 3. Sis. Nsalamo Bwalya, 4. Sis. Florence Sana (District Secretary), 5. Sis. Chanida Mulonda, 6. Lucy Sibanda 7. Sis. Theresa Sunga (Trustee), 8. Sis. Elita Sibbili, 9. Sis. Monica Muzala, 10. Sis. Lister Mancishi, 11. Sis. Carol Magumesa, 12. Sis. Juliet Chilala (Lay President), 13. Br. Anderson Chilala (husband), 14. Br. Terry Sakala (1st Vice President on the District) and 15. Sis. Constance Sibbili (partially cut). Rev. Kutemwa Simuyemba is the Pastor (not in photo), April 2020.

Jordan Chapel A.M.E. Church, Libuyu Livingstone members in masks preparing to go to Old People's Home for distribution of hand sanitisers during the infamous Coronavirus (Covid-19) world pandemic that purportedly started in Wuhan, China and spread all over the world claiming thousands of lives. Photo April 2020. By this month the U.S. had surpassed Italy and China who had had the highest numbers of mortality rates due to the virus.

Beginning of the Church in Barotse Province (Western) – 1935

The A.M.E. Church in Barotse Province was started in 1935 by Rev. D.D. Khomela when he was Presiding Elder of the Livingstone District. He opened circuits at Lui and Mutondo as well as schools at both places. He also opened and organized the A.M.E. Church at Mulobezi, Lumbe and Ngwezi but the work of the Church there after sometime ceased temporarily. In 1935, Rev. D.D. Khomela organized the A.M.E. Church in Barotseland. He began the work in various villages and reported their respective membership: - S. Kalombe 197, Namengo 196, Kaulo 87, Kalandela 65 and Machile 21.

In the year 1949, as Presiding Elder of the Livingstone District then, Rev. M.K. Wakunguma, reopened Lui, Mutondo, Mulobezi and Lumbe. In the same year 1949, Rev. J. Marumo opened other points at Katima Mulilo and Nyamushakende. Rev. M.K. Wakunguma also reopened Ngwezi in 1949. In 1952, Rev. J.M. Mubita started the A.M.E. Church at Namitome and Mwekulipo. In 1956, Rev. D.D. Zimba started the Church at Machapa, and Brother L.T. Inambao organized at Matongo in 1955.

In 1957, the Rev. M.K. Wakunguma, P.E., organized the A.M.E. Church at Machile and Kabanga circuits. Rev. A.K. Matale and Brother J. Muyatwa organized the A.M.E. Church at Kataba in 1957. In 1960, Presiding Elder Wakunguma organized the Church at Mankoya and appointed Brother Albert Nawa Lutombi to Pastor the Mankoya circuit. After several months of trying to get latest information from Western Province failed, Rev. Kapungwe finally managed to get connected to Sister Inonge Banda who was in Mongu and was a member of St. Thomas A.M.E. Church there. She had been studying clinical medicine and offered us important photos. Rev. Kapungwe was able to get this connection through one of the old acquaintances of his in the Healthcare Christian Fellowship of Zambia (HCFZ) Sis. Linda Libingi who is based at Livingstone General Hospital.

Sis. Inonge Banda (former Church Secretary 2013-2015 and W.M.S. member) with St. Thomas Youth Choir in Mongu, Western Province. 16th April, 2020. Rev. Prince Tawila is the Pastor (not in the photo). Photo courtesy of Sis. Inonge.

St. Thomas A.M.E. Church, Mongu in Western Province.

St. Thomas A.M.E. Church, Board and Name.

Zambezi Conference Area 11 YPD (From North Western Province) outreach to Lukulu (in Western Province but has been incorporated into North Western Province due to proximity). Photo provided by Br. Paul Kafusu Zambezi Conference YPD President and son to one of our youths we had mentored in YPD in Kitwe Br. Louis Kafusu now Lay Organisation President in the Zambezi Conference. 1st Lukulu District YPD Seminar in 2019.

Chapter 14
Rev. David Dafite Khomela's Version – The First Presiding Elder of Northern Rhodesia in 1931

On 30th March, 1962, the Rev. J.L.C. Membe, in compiling the history of the A.M.E. Church in Zambia, stated that, "There are some people who claim to be the founders of the A.M.E. Church in this country." He was of the view that these people were doing so to mislead the people. He noted that because they were first official leaders of the Church, they were claiming to be founders without any proper evidence. Regardless, I was happy to lay hold of an old typewritten undated copy written by Rev. D.D. Khomela, P.E., titled, "African Methodist Episcopal Church Introduced in Northern Rhodesia 1929."

Interestingly, the Rev. David Dafite Khomela was acknowledged by Rev. J.L.C. Membe in his historical work as one of the members of the Historical Committee of the Zambezi Annual Conference of the A.M.E. Church. The Committee which started its work in 1936 had completed its compilation in 1938 and Rev. J.L.C. Membe had been its Secretary. It was chaired by Rev. J.A. Daniels. Other committee members he had named were Rev. S.N. Sangweni (Vice Chairman), Rev. D.D. Khomela, Rev. J. Tshaka, Brother E.M. Makghato (Vice Secretary), Rev. S.M. Kamdgshariwa and Rev. J. Marumo. Adding this information to our work proved valuable due to scarcity of historical documents in this part of the world, especially with failure to store such important historical works.

Mother Elizabeth Nelinya Lukamba Simyembe, widow of the Rev. Warren W.K. Simyembe was of great help in this feat. She retrieved the typewritten document from the church documents left by her late father, Rev. Henrique Lukamba, P.E., who passed away at my workplace (Kitwe Central Hospital), on July 14, 1992. This document was found in February, 2006. The old fonts depicting writings typical of an old typewriter was evident as was the old paper image of the background on which the words were. It read:

African Methodist Episcopal Church Introduced in Northern Rhodesia in 1929

There was once a certain Northern Rhodesia man, whose name was Paulos D. Zimba. While he was working in Bulawayo, he attended A.M.E. Church there. In 1929, he took his leave. There upon, he went to Ndola where he enthusiastically laid open to people the true facts about the doctrines of the A.M.E. Church, which had at its Head, Negro Bishops based in America. In Bulawayo where Mr. P.D. Zimba first identified himself with it, the A.M.E. Churches in different countries were mostly patronized by the African Ministers.

In Ndola, when they also heard of this Church, Messrs. E.A. Mwamba, E.E. Chunga, P. Phiri and some other 51 people, left London Missionary Society. They wrote to Rev. Z.C. Mtshwello, P.E., in Bulawayo, asking for permission to be received in the A.M.E. Church. In

1930, Revs. Z.C. Mtshwello, D.D. Khomela, S.N. Sangweni, C.H. Monne and J. Chingo came to Livingstone to request the Government to allow the A.M.E. Church to be founded in Northern Rhodesia. It was in that year the A.M.E. Church was recognized in Northern Rhodesia. In 1931, Rev. D.D. Khomela was the first Minister of the A.M.E. Church appointed alone to be Pastor and Presiding Elder in Northern Rhodesia as a whole, he then settled in Livingstone where the Government Headquarters were then situated.

In 1932, Rev. D.D. Khomela started his work for the first time by visiting Ndola where there were 51 people waiting to be received in A.M.E. Church. Here, in the course of his preaching 146 people joined the A.M.E. Church. These, together with the 51, raised the total A.M.E. Church membership in Ndola to 197. The following were elected the first A.M.E. Church officers: - E.A. Mwamba, P. Phiri, Circuit Stewards; E.H. Chunga Secretary, A. Kawala, Evangelist; J. Mumba, L. Kaluwa, A. Nsofu, L. Mukumbi, S. Banda, L. Mbiko, H. Mhango, T.K. Manda, H. Vachedwa. M. Mwase, I. Mporokoso, S. Ngulube, Local Preachers. Sisters, A.E. Mwamba was elected First Vice President, N.L. Mbiko, Second Vice President and E.E. Chunga as Secretary.

At Broken Hill, 78 people joined the A.M.E. Church. The first officers elected were A.B. Kazunga, Preacher and Circuit Steward, and Anderson Sakala, Steward. At Lusaka, 45 people joined the A.M.E. Church. The first officers elected were D.N. Banda, Preacher and Circuit Steward while at Choma, 27 people joined A.M.E. Church and the first officers elected were D.N. Moyo and H.K. Mangisana as Preacher and Circuit Stewards. At Livingstone, 68 people joined the A.M.E. Church. The first officers elected were T. Karenje, D.K. Chapenga and N.S. Mhango as Preacher and Stewards.

Rev. D.D. Khomela formed 5 Circuits the same year in Northern Rhodesia. They were: -

Livingstone, Rev. D.D. Khomela Pastor and Presiding Elder, Northern Rhodesia.
Ndola, Rev. J.R. Nkwayi Pastor.
Broken Hill, Bro. J.L. Honoko Pastor
Lusaka, Bro. N.S. Mhango Pastor
Choma, Bro. J. Marumo Pastor.

In 1933, Rev. J.R. Mkwayi returned to the Union of South Africa. This was because of the bad poverty and dreadful fever that blanketed the whole country of N. Rhodesia. As a result, ministers in Union and S. Rhodesia were afraid and refused to be appointed to Northern Rhodesia. However, Rev. D.D. Khomela remained in Northern Rhodesia, and while he was there, he encouraged all men and women of Northern Rhodesia to become Ministers of the A.M.E. Church, and work hard for their country.

Rev. D.D. Khomela oversaw the ministry. The first Local Preachers who were organized, prayed for and sent to towns and villages in Northern Rhodesia were as follows: -

Rev. D.D. Khomela, Livingstone. Bro. J.L. Honoko, Broken Hill. Bro. J. Marumo, Choma. Bro. S.N. Mohango, Lusaka. Bro. E.A. Mwamba, Ndola. Bro. D.N. Moyo, Mazabuka. Bro. A. Sakala, Fort Jameson. Bro. A.C. Nkhoma, Serenje. Bro. I. Banda, Namwala. Bro. M. Mbewe, Petauke. Bro. J. Kakonko, Kawambwa. Bro. D. Bangwe, Fort Rosebury. Bro. J.L.C.

Membe, Abercorn. A. Makalane, Siyacitema. Bro. S. Ngulube, Mapansa. Bro. B. Chalomba, Ayrser Mataka. Bro. D.N. Banda, Feira. Bro. B. Mwanza, Mkushi. Bro. J. Mumba, BIDIDI. Bro. P. Phiri, Mumba. Bro. N. Soko, Solwezi. Bro. A. Simwanza, Zimba.

In 1935, Rev. D.D. Khomela went to found A.M.E. Church in Barotseland. The following different villages had their respective converted membership as follows: - S. Kalombe 197 people, Namengo 196 people, Kaulo 87 people, Kalandela 65 people and Machile 21 people.

In 1937 Rev. D.D. Khomela was promoted Superintendent of A.M.E. Church and Schools in Northern Rhodesia. He was also tasked to go to Ndola to straighten the Congregation there which had lapsed into disregarding the laws of the A.M.E. Church and complete a Church Building which was left unfinished by Rev. H.M. Phiri. He erected a Ministers' House parsonage there.

In 1938, came Mother L.M. Hughes, President of W.H. & F.M. Society from America. She landed in Cape Town and soon thereafter got on a train which was bound for Ndola, the land which was remembered with fright by both Ministers and Bishops because of dreadful fever. Upon her arrival in Ndola, she proceeded to Sakania Station in Congo, and she returned to visit Southern Rhodesia and Union of South Africa.

In 1939, came Bishop B.R. Wright, Jr. to visit Ndola. In 1940, the first Annual Conference was held in Ndola. In 1944, the A.M.E. Church grew in size to 4 Districts: -

Ndola District under Rev. D.D. Khomela, P.E., with 9 pastors under him.
Lusaka District under Rev. J. Marumo, P.E., with 10 Pastors under him.
Abercorn District under Rev. J.L.C. Membe, P.E., with 5 Pastors under him.
Kawambwa District under Rev. J.H. Mabombo, P.E., with 7 Pastors under him.

In 1948 Rev. D.D. Khomela influenced and initiated the decision that Northern Rhodesia area should break ties with Southern Rhodesia area. This also meant that Northern Rhodesia was to be made the venue for all its Annual Conferences.

In 1949, Rev. D.D. Khomela was transferred to Salisbury in Southern Rhodesia. He left Northern Rhodesia quite firm and progressive. In his place, Rev. H. Ziyezwa was appointed P.E., Ndola and Superintendent in Northern Rhodesia.

The above short history made by Rev. D.D. Khomela P.E.

Note: This author decided to leave Rev. D.D. Khomela's writing almost the same way it was written to preserve originality. However, minimum editing deemed necessary, had to be done by the book author.

Chapter 15
The A.M.E. Church in Tanganyika Territory in 1933

The Rev. J.L.C. Membe went into Tanganyika Territory in 1933 to preach the gospel. He also wanted to extend the work of the A.M.E. Church into Tanganyika. He had not gotten a permit yet when he started going there accompanied by members from Northern Rhodesia. Opening up into Tanganyika gave him opportunity to explore advancement of the work into East Africa. He therefore, was kin to establish the work of the A.M.E. Church in Tanganyika Territory at any cost.

Since Chiyanga Mission in Abercorn in Northern Rhodesia was ideally located, Rev. Membe ventured into new missionary ground. He reached into Ufipa Province in southern part of Tanganyika Territory and the following is his account of his missionary trips: "In the Ufipa Province, Tanganyika Territory, I had many people who joined the A.M.E. Church. The following are some of the villages I went to preach to many times and had members as under:

Manda's village 88 members, Bro. Philemon Chipaila L., Leader.
Kasote village 98 members, Bro. James Namungolomwe, Leader.
Lyankaka village 120 members, Bro. John Matongo, Leader.
Kitwazi village 22 members, Bro. Muselepete Champuka, Leader.
Broli village 68 members, Bro. Izumeli Malamba, Leader.
Ngolotwa village 44 members, Bro. Stephen Mporokoso, Leader.
Tiswe village 48 members, Bro. Infant Puntu Chingala, Leader.
Kalangu village 52 members, Bro. Julius Kasakula, Leader.

At one time I went to visit the members and to preach to them as I had been doing in the past. One day, however, before I completed my tour at Kasote's village on 18th July, 1933, there came three policemen to arrest me and charged me with preaching in Tanganyika Territory without a permit by the Tanganyika Government. They took me to the District Commissioner at Sumbwanga on 21st July, 1933 in the afternoon and the District Commissioner ordered them to keep me in jail until the next morning. In the next morning, the District Commissioner told me that some Missionaries told me that you are preaching in this Province without a permit from the Tanganyika Government and that many of their Christians have joined your Church.

I produced the Holy Bible and told him that this is the permit I have been going about with. This annoyed the District Commissioner who sent me to jail again for another two days. Nevertheless, he took care of my two boys who came with me from Northern Rhodesia, Simon Sikazwe and Ferman James Sikazwe and twelve men from Kasote's village who came to see what would happen and then report back to my people. He gave them food and accommodation. The third day I was brought out and the District Commissioner told me to go back to Northern Rhodesia and apply for a permit to establish the A.M.E. Church in Tanganyika before anything else. I was sent back to Northern Rhodesia under escort by four policemen to the border of N. Rhodesia and Tanganyika and they went back.

When I went to Northern Rhodesia, I wrote an application to Chief James of Kasanga, Ufipa District, Sumbwanga, Tanganyika Territory. I asked for a special recommendation to the Government for it was in his area where I had members already numbering to 540. The following was the reply from Chief James:-

Kasanga
Ufipa Province,
Tanganyika Territory/
15-8-1933

Kwa Bwana (To Mr.) Lester Membe,
Chiyanga, Abercorn, N.R.

    I have received your letter and I am sorry to hear that your children are both ill, really, I am sorry. I pray that God heal them by his power and kindness.
    I went on tour visiting my area collecting Polio Tax from my people and I found your letter on my return.
    Concerning the Church matters I would like to see you here at Kasanga as soon as possible. I greet you and your wife. Stay well.

    I am Mwene (Chief) James Chinakila.

On 2nd September, 1933, I left Chiyanga to go to Kasanga with some members of the Church and a band of choir on foot. When we reached at Lyankaka, my wife sent a boy on a bicycle to tell me that my son had died the previous night. On September 3rd, I wrote a letter to the Chief from Lyankaka to tell him that I had been called back home where my youngest son died, and that afterward I would still come to Kasanga. I left with those who had accompanied me back to Abercorn.

On September 21, 1933, I left my place to go to Kasanga in Tanganyika. I was accompanied by my wife, Mr. Simpanya and wife Alice, Mr. Ben Chipungu and a band of choir. There was no other means of transport rather than to walk, so we walked for three days and reached Kasanga. When we were just about to enter the town, a group of Christians from the London Missionary Society came to meet us and started to mock on us and speaking all bad words against us without doing anything wrong to them and started to throw dust on us and making a lot of noise. However, the chief was aware of this, he sent his policemen to escort us until they got us through to the Chief's residence.

The Chief regretted the action taken by the members of the L.M.S. with their minister. He remarked that he wondered why Christians would fight each other and feel jealousy against one another. He thought such behaviour would discourage those who would want to become Christians and prevent them from coming to church.

The very day we arrived in the evening the Chief called for the local council to meet and discuss the A.M.E. Church in the area. After having explained about the A.M.E. Church history and its Constitution and about the countries in which the A.M.E. Church operates, the Chief asked his people's views on the matter and not to try and exercise denominational feelings. When this was put on vote 142 people voted in favour of having the A.M.E. Church established in their area, 6 voted against and a few abstained from voting.

On Sunday morning at 10:00 a.m., an open-air prayer meeting was held on the front of the Chief's Palace. Over 300 people attended the service including the chief himself. Brother Ben Chipungu and the choir rendered some selections and made the people very interested in their singing. Most of the people wanted the A.M.E. Church started right away there but I told them the permit is not yet granted. On Monday morning, a piece of land about 46 acres was given to the A.M.E. Church with 27 mango trees, 14 orange trees and 8 lemon trees inside the land for only £50. On Tuesday September 26, 1933, we left Kasanga by boat on Lake Tanganyika back to Northern Rhodesia via Chisanza.

I went to the Annual Conference and reported what I had done for the Church. I explained how far the Church has reached. Instead of thanking me for all these things, I was told there was no money to buy that land in Tanganyika, and they also blamed me for penetrating into the Tanganyika Territory at such a speed like that.

When I came back from the Conference in Southern Rhodesia, the Chief wrote to the District Commissioner of Sumbwanga to allow me to start the A.M.E. Church in his area. However, some Missionaries in that area had written to the Government there but the Chief told me that if your Church has been allowed to operate in many other countries by many other Governments, he wondered why others should try to persuade the Government to refuse it. The District Commissioner there encouraged me to only ask the Tanganyika Government for a permit. The Chief James wrote me the following letter: -

Kasanga, T.T.
10-10-33

Kwa Bwana Lester Membe,
Chiyanga, Abercorn, N.R.

Sir,

I am writing this letter to you if you are well, I am glad in the kindness of God of life, and Mama and children if they are well.

I have not many words to tell you. All the words which you told me and which you wrote to me in the previous letter from you I noted everything well. I wrote a letter to the District Commissioner of Sumbwanga, T.T. all about your application, he only questioned my clerk who took that letter to him of what kind of religion do you preach? My Clerk answered him that it was a Christian religion. I failed to answer one question on whether you want to start schools at the same time with evangelism? You did not tell me about this. Please let me know as soon as possible whether your Church do open schools for children of your Church.

I would like you to send me another copy of the photograph which you took me when you came here, I have received the one you sent me, but I want it enlarged. I will send you Sh.8/9 for the same. I have also received a pair of shoes which you sent me, thank you.

I understand you have many enemies in your country and here. Missionaries of many denominations do give you a lot of trouble for having many of their Christians join your Church. Would you please let me know everything about this rumour! It makes me feel sorry as a Christian to see Christians fight each other when they belong to one Lord, it is discouraging. But I still have much interest in your Church, and I know it is not you who cause all these troubles. Your co-workers in God's work are very jealous with your Church. Please let me know all about what is happening and about my photograph per my messenger to you on his return. Stay well.

      I am Chief James.

All the letters from Chief James are copied in the way they were written.

A.M.E. Church,
Chiyanga Mission
Abercorn, N.R.
October 15, 1933.

Chief James,
KASANGA, T.T.
Sir,

  I acknowledge the receipt of your letter of 10th October, 1933, per messenger which I read with interest.

  Regarding the accusation against me by many other missionaries and ministers of different churches in this country and in your country the Governments of both countries know well that it is only jealous and are no more listening to them.

  Concerning your request about the photograph I shall send you more than one copy at my expense, but this will take time for I have got to send them to the photo studio, Broken Hill to be enlarged. There are no photo studios near here.

  I want to assure you, Sir that I shall not stop to preach to my people in your area up to the time when I shall have the permit to do so by the Tanganyika Government. You have heard about what had happened upon me at Sumbwanga when I was arrested from your area. I wrote you all about this but there was no reply to my letter. What do you think about it, Sir?

  My best greetings to the Chief and the family, and to your people from me and family.

I have the honour to be,
Sir,
Your obedient servant.

J.L.C. MEMBE
<u>PASTOR IN CHARGE.</u>

A reply from the Chief: -

Kasanga, T.T.
20th December, 1933.

Bwana Membe, Minister,
Chiyanga, Abercorn, N.R.

    Greetings to you, Bwana Lester Membe, if you are well, I am glad and greetings to your wife and your only remaining child and your Church members. Bwana, I am also well with all my family and my people.

    I am pleased to have received your letter of October 15, 1933. I have heard all your words. Do you think I will receive all my photographs which you said you were going to send me? I have not many words to tell you Bwana Membe. I also want to know how far you have gone with the case between you and Rev. Henry Kasokolo? I also reported to the District Officer in Charge about the trouble Rev. Kasokolo did to you when you visited here in September.

    I understand that you want to establish your headquarters at Kasote here in Tanganyika after having received the permit, is that right? I shall be very pleased if this could be done provided a permit is granted by the Tanganyika Government. If so, why don't you want to have your headquarters here in Kasanga where I have already given you land which you should buy at a very cheaper price of only £50? You can pay this amount in installments if you cannot find the £50 at once.

    I am expecting to hear from you about what I have said in the letter.

<u>I am Mwene James Chinakila.</u>

After communicating several times with the Chief in letters and personal interviews, the chief had no objection to have the A.M.E. Church established in his area. The following were the copies of letters to the District Commissioner of Sumbwanga and from him to me: -

African Methodist Episcopal Church
Chiyanga Mission,
Abercorn, N.R.
4th August, 1934.

The District Officer in Charge,
Sumbwanga, Tanganyika Territory.

Sir,

    I have been instructed by the Presiding Elder Rev. H.M. Phiri of the A.M.E. Church, Northern Rhodesia to forward to you the Local Preachers Licenses for our Local Preachers in your area for indorsement and send them back to me for distribution to them.

    The same Local Preachers were elected by the Chiyanga Quarterly Conference of the A.M.E. Church held at Chiyanga, Abercorn, Northern Rhodesia, and were recommended to preach in your area there. Their names are as follows: -

    1. Philemon Chipaila, Manda, Chief James, Sumbwanga, T.T.
    2. Philemon Vyanda, Kasote,   "   "
    3. James Namungolomwe, Kasote   "   "

4. John Matongo, Lyankaka,	"	"
5. James Kayanga, Chipwa,	"	"
6. Izumeli Malamba, Ngoli,	"	"
7. Julius Kasakula, Kalangu,	"	"
8. Stefano Mpolokoso, Ngolotwa,	"	"
9. Muselepete Chapunka, Chitwazi,	"	"
10. Infant Pintu Chingala, Tiswa,	"	"

I shall esteem it a great favour if you will kindly have the above-mentioned men recommended.

I have the honour to be,
Sir,
Your obedient servant.
J.L.C. MEMBE
PASTOR IN CHARGE A.M.E. CHURCH
NORTHERN PROVINCE, N.R.
SUMBWANGA T.T.

Ref. No. K/5/47.

To L. Membe, Pastor,
African Methodist Episcopal Church,
Chiyanga Station,
<u>Abercorn, N.R.</u>

Sir,

I have the honour to refer to your letter dated 4th August, 1934.

This matter was spoken to you in person by my predecessor; sanction to preach in this District can be given neither to you nor to the Natives, named in the Local Preacher Licenses, forwarded under cover of your letter under acknowledgment.

3. These licenses are returned herewith.

4. Should you venture to come to this District, I would remind you that you are a prohibited immigrant, and the penalties of the Immigration Ordinance will be enforced against you.

I have the honour to be,
Sir,
Your obedient servant
C.D. POPPEWELL

GMP/PS.   A.G. DISTRICT OFFICER.

African Methodist Episcopal Church
Kalenda Mission,
Luapula District,
P.O. Kawambwa, N.R.
13th April, 1937.

The District Officer in Charge,
Sumbwanga,
<u>TANGANYIKA TERRITORY.</u>

Sir,

I have the honour and respect to address you this letter of introducing Pastor Jonas Hezron Sikalumbi to you who has been appointed Pastor in Charge of Ulungu District beyond the Kalambo River. He will be staying at Kasote village and build the Church there. That he may preach the Good News of our Lord Jesus Christ.

This African Methodist Episcopal Church is a well-recognized Church everywhere and its Discipline has been accepted all over. It was established in 1787 in America.

I trust that you will kindly give him the necessary assistance and advice regarding the Status of your Territory.

I have the honour to be,
Sir,
Your obedient servant.
J.L.C. MEMBE
PRESIDING ELDER
FOR BISHOP R.R. WRIGHT, Jr., A.M.E. CHURCH
SOUTH AFRICA.

<u>By hand per Pastor J.H. Sikalumbi.</u>

Ref. No. 251/111.

DISTRICT OFFICE
SUMBWANGA, UFIPA,
6th May, 1937.

Rev. J.L.C. Membe, Presiding Elder,
African Methodist Episcopal Church,
Kalenda Mission, Luapula District,
<u>P.O. Kawambwa, Northern Rhodesia.</u>

Reverend Sir,

I have the honour to acknowledge the receipt of your letter of communication to me dated 13th April, 1937. Pastor Jonas Hezron Sikalumbi arrived here today, and he is the bearer of this letter to you.

2. As your Mission has no land in Ufipa District, I must regret I cannot permit a Mission Station to be opened up here. You should first of all submit your application to me

for the right of occupancy over a piece of leasehold land in this District and the decision of the Tanganyika Government will then be conveyed to you in due course.

I have the honour to be,
Reverend Sir,
Your obedient servant.
M.A. CALLAGHAN
DISTRICT OFFICER.

MAC/ES.

African Methodist Episcopal Church
Kalenda Mission,
Luapula District,
P.O. Kawambwa, N.R.
1st November, 1937.

The District Officer in Charge,
Sumbwanga, Ufipa District,
<u>TANGANYIKA TERRITORY</u>.

Sir,

I have the honour to acknowledge the receipt of your letter, No. 251/111 dated 6th May, 1937. This letter has remained a long time unanswered. I went to Southern Rhodesia to attend the Annual Conference of our Church. I arrived here on 20th October, 1937.

2. Before I send in the application for the right of occupancy over a piece of land in your District, I shall be much pleased should you kindly outline for me some of the requirements concerning the matter, so that this would help me to put this case properly before the Bishop and the Annual Conference before the said application is made to you.

3. Could I be issued, if possible, with Tanganyika Government Gazette to have the above address?

Thanking you in anticipation.
I have the honour to be,
Sir,
Your obedient servant.
J.L.C. MEMBE
PRESIDING ELDER.

WESTERN PROVINCE   DISTRICT OFFICE
                                                    6th January, 1938.

Rev. J.L.C. Membe, Presiding Elder,
African Methodist Episcopal Church,
Kalenda Mission, Luapula District,
P.O. Kawambwa, Northern Rhodesia.

Reverend Sir,

    I have the honour to refer to your letter of 1st November, 1937, and I regret that I am unable to advice you in the matter and I would repeat that the result of your application depends on the decision of the Government, which I am unable to forecast.
    2. The Tanganyika Government Gazette can be obtained from Government Printer at Dar-es-Salaam at an annual cost of Sh.24/-.

I have the honour to be,
Sir,
Your obedient servant.
ALEX T. CURLE

ATC/HJM.   AG. DISTRICT OFFICER.

African Methodist Episcopal Church
Chiyanga Mission,
P.O. Abercorn, N.R.
1st March, 1944.

The District Commissioner,
SUMBWANGA, T.T.

Sir,

    I have been instructed by my Leaders to write you an application for a piece of land in Chief James Mutono's area in the neighborhood of Kasanga.
    I shall be pleased should you kindly set out for me some of the rules and ordinances relating to the owning of leasehold land on which to build our mission station in your country, Tanganyika.
    I shall be pleased should this application meet your favourable consideration of approval by your kindness by your recommendation to the Tanganyika Government.

I have the honour to be,
Sir,
Your obedient servant.
J.L.C. MEMBE
PRESIDING ELDER.

Ref. No. 1/12/34.

The District Officer,
Sumbwanga, Ufipa, T.T.
25th April, 1944.

To the Rev. J.L.C. Membe,
Missionary in Charge,
African Methodist Episcopal Church,
Chiyanga Mission,
<u>P.O. Abercorn, N. Rhodesia.</u>

Reverend Sir,

With reference to your letter of the 1st March, 1944, I should be glad if you should arrange to pay a personal visit to this office with the view to having a full discussion regarding your application to open up a mission in this District.

It would be appreciated if you would give me about ten days' notice of the date of your intended visit in order that I can arrange to be present in Sumbwanga.

Yours faithfully,
G. MITCHELL
DISTRICT COMMISSIONER.

<u>TELEGRAM DATED 10/5/44.</u>

POLITICAL SUMBWANGA
LETTER RECEIVED LEAVING MONDAY NEXT FOR SUMBWANGA – MEMBE.

On 20th May, 1944, after having spent two days and nights on the way to Sumbwanga, the District Commissioner of Sumbwanga sent a Government Driver to meet me on the way to bring me to Sumbwanga by vannet.

The discussion between me and the District Commissioner was very interesting. He asked me to go back to Northern Rhodesia and wait for the reply from Dar-es-Salaam. His driver also took me back to Abercorn in the vannet.

On 8th August, 1944, I wrote a letter to the District Commissioner of Sumbwanga and sent him a pamphlet I promised him. The following was the letter sent: -

African Methodist Episcopal Church
Chiyanga Mission,
P.O. Abercorn, N.R.
8th August, 1944.

The District Commissioner,
Western Province, Ufipa,
P.O. Sumbwanga, T.T.

Sir,

I promised to send you this little pamphlet of the Quadrennial report of our work in this country and other countries in Southern Africa, to show what the Church is doing for your information please.

I have just returned from Southern Rhodesia where I went to attend the Winter Rally Conference, Presiding Elders Council, and Missionary Board of Education held in Bulawayo, 8th to 13th July, 1944.

I have specially come back this time in order to collect the necessary information with regard to my application to open a mission field in that District and then be ready to report at the Joint Annual Conferences to be held in Bloemfontein, Orange Free State, in October.

We shall accept with thanks any place that can be given to us if there is not enough room for us in Kasanga. I would prefer to start our mission near the villages where we have members already such as Kasote, Mvundwi, Ngolotwa, and Kalangu to the direction of Kalambo River.

I have the honour to be,
Sir,
Your obedient servant.
J.L.C. MEMBE
<u>PRESIDING ELDER</u>.

Ref. No. 1/12/56.

From the District Commissioner,
Sumbwanga, Western Province, T.T.
15th August, 1944.

To the Rev. J.L.C. Membe,
Missionary in Charge,
African Methodist Episcopal Church,
Chiyanga Mission,
<u>Abercorn, N.R.</u>

Reverend Sir,

I have the honour to thank you for the Quadrennial Report which I have read with interest.

2. Your application is now in the hands of the Provincial Commissioner Western Province, as soon as his reply is received you will be duly notified of its contents.

9/LOM

G.O. MITCHELL
<u>DISTRICT COMMISSIONER</u>.

After some weeks, the following telegram was received dated 9th September, 1944: -

<u>T E L E G R A M</u>
REVEREND MEMBE CHIYANGA MISSION ABERCORN YOUR APPLICATION TO OPEN MISSION STATION KASANGA AREA APPROVED ACKNOWLEDGE – POLITICAL.

On the same day, 9/9/44, I replied by Telegram from Abercorn as under: -

TO POLITICAL SUMBWANGA
TELEGRAM RECEIVED APPROVING MY APPLICATION THANK YOU EXPECT ACKNOWLEDGEMENT AFTER VISITING KASANGA
– MEMBE.

I went to Kasanga to interview the Chief James and his Councilors on the subject of the approved application. The Chief and his people welcomed me. After some good talks with them the site was given to the A.M.E. Church. I went back to Northern Rhodesia and wrote to the District Commissioner of Sumbwanga as follows: -

African Methodist Episcopal Church
Chiyanga Mission,
P.O. Abercorn, N.R.
9th October, 1944.

The District Commissioner,
Sumbwanga, T.T.

Sir,

    I beg with honour to submit my report as follows: -

    1. I arrived in Kasanga on Thursday 5th October, 1944, the Mwene James and company welcomed me very well.

    2. The place was given to us on which to build our Church at the place where the old Dispensary was, between the Roman Catholic Church and the Dispensary.

    3. I have left the one Pastor Duncan Mpumpa of Chipwa village, Chief Zombe, Abercorn to take charge as an Itinerant Preacher of the A.M.E. Church here. Pastor Duncan Mpumpa has already served our Mission as an Itinerant Preacher for at least nine years in Northern Rhodesia and has rendered a good service to the Church.

    4. It has been suggested that before we find enough money to start building, we shall erect a temporary building for worship.

    5. I am leaving Kasanga for Chiyanga, Abercorn, this afternoon, and shall be going away from Abercorn to South Africa on 18th October, 1944 and shall probably be returning to Abercorn in December, 1944. Please, pass our gratefulness to the Tanganyika Government for allowing and accepting the A.M.E. Church in Tanganyika Territory, and particularly to yourself for having stood for us in everything. We are, with the Christian truth promised loyalty to the Government in every respect.

I have the honour to be,
Sir,
Your obedient servant.

J.L.C. MEMBE
<u>PRESIDING ELDER.</u>

TANGANYIKA TERRITORY HUKUMU YA WILAYA

Ref. No. 1/12/69.

From the District Commissioner,
Western Province,
Sumbwanga, T.T.
18th February, 1945.

To Rev. J.L.C. Membe,
A.M.E. Church,
Chiyanga Mission,
ABERCORN, N.R.

Rev. Sir,
I return herewith the Discipline Book which I have read with interest.
Yours faithfully,

1/3.

G.O. MITCHELL
DISTRICT COMMISSIONER.

Moto Moto Museum, Mbala. The building has been open since 1974. It has historical collections of cultural artifacts of the Bemba, art and slavery. Initial collections were started by a French-Canadian Catholic Priest Jean Jacques Corbel in 1950s in Northern Rhodesia's northern region after coming to Northern Rhodesia in 1943. The museum is named after a French Catholic Bishop Joseph Dupont who smoked a pipe and would ask for "moto" or fire and was thus nicknamed "Moto Moto!" He was the founder of the White Fathers missionary in Abercorn (1850 to 1930). He had been Chief of the Bemba in 1898. Photo by Everisto K. Kwesha, my former classmate at Chamboli Secondary School. 1st May, 2020.

In 1945, Rev. J.L.C. Membe was transferred to Nyasaland. All his successors never bothered to continue with the development, with the work of the Church that side of the Tanganyika Territory until the land that was granted to us was given to other people, which is a very discouraging thing indeed.

On his way to Nyasaland, Rev. J.L.C. Membe opened three more branches of the Church in the Southern Highlands Province of Tanganyika Territory. This was at Mbeya, Tukuyu and Nyela in December, 1945. The Church in all those three places is going on, and one of the three places, Mbeya is now a Presiding Elder's headquarters.

One Sunday at Mbeya in December 1945, a Minister of a Moravian Church invited Rev. Membe to preach in his Church. He was introduced as a Minister from the African Methodist Episcopal Church who was on his way to Nyasaland on transfer from Northern Rhodesia. After the sermon, some men went to the house where Rev. Membe stayed to inquire about the African Methodist Episcopal Church and the reason why they don't have it in their country! Rev. Membe explained to them more about the A.M.E. Church and that the Church has already been accepted into Tanganyika, and the Church has already been started in the Western Province, in Ufipa District.

They asked him to start one for them in Mbeya too. He assured them if they joined the Church, he could open for them. In the evening these men came with some other men. After evening prayers some of the brethren offered themselves to join the A.M.E. Church and their names were: -

1. Brother Philip Hlabati and wife
2. Brother William Kumwenda and wife
3. Brother G.E. Nyirenda and wife.

These and others whose names are not written asked Rev. Membe to spend a week with them before going to Nyasaland.

On Monday morning, Rev. Membe accompanied by P.H. Hara and Mr. William Kumwenda went to interview the District Commissioner concerning the Church matters. The District Commissioner assured them that there was no objection to opening a branch of their Church in his town, for the Tanganyika Government has already permitted the Church to operate in this country. Rev. Membe asked the District Commissioner to allow his followers to hold their Sunday church services in one of the Government School Rooms. The District Commissioner gave them a note to the Head teacher to allow them to do so. There were evening prayers every day during the week and the attendance was increasing daily.

On Sunday more than 60 people attended. After the service, more persons joined the Church and the number of members came to 26. The following brethren were elected as local Church leaders until proper ones are found and sent to them: -

1. Brother Philip Hlabati Hara, Evangelist.
2. Brother William Kumwenda, Steward and Treasurer.
3. Brother G.E. Nyirenda, Church Secretary.

On Monday morning, Rev. Membe left Mbeya for Tukuyu. At Tukuyu, he was a guest of Mr. Kawala, a Senior Government Clerk. The next morning Rev. Membe interviewed the District Commissioner for permission to hold a prayer service near the market place in the evening. However, the District Commissioner instructed his Senior Clerk to make some arrangement to meet in one of the school rooms. Brother Kawala invited as many people as he could. At this meeting four people joined the A.M.E. Church including Kawala who was at the same time elected by the other three members to lead them for the time being.

Rev. Membe continued his journey and arrived at Kyela. He spent 5 days at Kyela and 14 persons joined the A.M.E. Church there. He interviewed the Chief Mwangamilo of that area for permission to allow the 14 members to hold their prayer meetings freely until a proper leader is sent them.

The following were letters between Rev. J.L.C. Membe and the Government Authorities in the Southern Highlands Province of Tanganyika Territory: -

African Methodist Episcopal Church
Blantyre, Nyasaland,
9th February, 1946.

The District Commissioner,
<u>TUKUYU, TANGANYIKA TERRITORY.</u>

Sir,

I have the honour to introduce to you Jacob Burton Chalama Munthali, a member and Local Preacher of the African Methodist Episcopal Church, who has been sent to stay at Mwangamilo near Kyela in your District to preach to our Christians who are in that area. We have 45 members there without a Preacher; they sent us a petition to send them a Preacher who is the bearer of this letter.

Jacob Burton Chalama Munthali has been a member and a preacher in our mission for many years and is well trusted by us to be a good preacher.

Begging in anticipation.

I have the honour to be,
Sir,
Your obedient servant.
J.L.C. MEMBE
<u>PRESIDING ELDER</u>.

District Commissioner,
TUKUYU, T.T.
7/8/46.

Chief Mwangamilo,

Let me know as soon as possible whether you want this man to preach in his Church in your area. Let me know at once.

<u>DISTRICT COMMISSIONER.</u>

BALAKA LA IKOLO
RUNGWE, 8/8/46

The District Commissioner,
TUKUYU, T.T.

I thank you for your note. I would like to say that I have no room for this Church in my area. They should first go to other chiefs, areas who have room for them.
Greetings.
<u>CHIEF MWANGAMILO.</u>

Reply on the same paper: -

Chief Mwangamilo,

These people have Christians in your area, how can they go elsewhere where they have no Christians of their Church? Please allow them. The Tanganyika Government has accepted this Church and there is no need of fearing to give them a place. They have many members at Kyela in your area, why can't you let them stay at Kyela?
DISTRICT COMMISSIONER.

BALAKA LA IKOLO
RUNGWE, 8/8/46

The District Commissioner,
TUKUYU, T.T.

BARAKA LA IKOLO
9/8/46

The D.C.
<u>TUKUYU</u>.

Sir,

I will let them stay and preach at Kyela and in my District, but before this is done, I want to see their leader here to discuss personally with him concerning this Church. I am glad to hear that the Government knows the Church well.

Thanking you, Sir.
<u>CHIEF MWANGAMILO.</u>

TELEGRAM (DATED 13/8/46)
REVEREND MEMBE BLANTYRE NYASALAND
PLEASE COME TO KARONGA AND GO TO TUKUYU DC WANTS YOU
CHALAMA MUNTHALI

On 16th August I left Blantyre by boat on Lake Nyasa (Now Lake Malawi) and took brother Munthali with me to Ikolo. We had discussions with the Chief who granted permission for the Church to operate in his area, after which both myself and Brother Munthali went to Tukuyu to report this to the District Commissioner. We then came back to Kyela where we were welcomed by our members, and the work started. From this period the Church extended to Songwe River up to other places in the Nkonde tribe. After a few years, the Presiding Elder's headquarters of all these areas were at Mbeya, Tanganyika Territory.

In 1947, I went to visit these areas, Kyela, Tukuyu and Mbeya. At Mbeya, members asked me to apply for a land for them for Church and house buildings. The following was the letter of application to the Authorities: -

African Methodist Episcopal Church,
c/o Mr. P.H. Hara,
Public Works Department,
MBEYA, T.T.
16th August, 1947.

The District Commissioner,
<u>MBEYA, T.T.</u>

Sir,

In the name and on behalf of the African Methodist Episcopal Church, I beg with your honour to apply for two plots in your Township area on which to build our Church and house buildings in the African Township.

This Mission has its headquarters at 28 Walmer Road, Woodstock, Cape Town where the Presiding Bishop stays, and General Superintendent's Headquarters at Wilberforce Institute, Transvaal, South Africa, the Presiding Elder's headquarters at Kasungu, Nyasaland, Assistant General Superintendent's headquarters in Bulawayo, S. Rhodesia.

This application is being written in view of having the Presiding Elder's headquarters of our Church in this Province should it be favoured with approval for which I shall thank you very much.

I have the honour to be,
Sir,
Your obedient servant.

J.L.C. MEMBE
<u>PRESIDING ELDER.</u>

A.M.E. Church,
c/o Mr. P.H. Hara, P.W.D.
Mbeya, T.T. 19/1/48.

The District Commissioner,
MBEYA, T.T.

Sir,

I have the honour to send a copy of the Discipline Book of our Church to your office for your information please. Perhaps this will help you to know something about our Church.

2. With reference to my application of 16th August, 1947, for a plot on which to build our Church, and a house, I have heard no word about it. Would you please, Sir, let me know of what is going on about it.

3. If there is no place for us in the African Township area, could it not be possible for us to find a place somewhere outside the African Township area?

I beg to remain, Sir,

I have the honour to be,
Sir,
Your obedient servant.
J.L.C. MEMBE
PRESIDING ELDER.

Ref. No. 17/35/3.

From the District Commissioner,
Mbeya, Southern Highlands Province,
11th February, 1948.

Sir,

I regret the delay in replying to your letter of 19th January and in thanking you for the Discipline Book of your Church which you sent me.

2. Before your application is granted, I have been requested to ask for information on the following: -

(a) What kind of Missionary work do you propose to undertake, i.e., Spiritual instruction only or that and scholastic education as well?

(b) What are the funds available to undertake serious Missionary work, and their sources for your mission?

I am, Sir, Your Obedient Servant,
L.L. DE LESDEMOND. D.C.

African Methodist Episcopal Church
Mdabwi Mission,
P.O. Kasungu, Nyasaland,
5th March, 1948.

The District Commissioner,
MBEYA, TANGANYIKA TERRITORY.

Sir,

I thank you for the letter No. 17/35/3 of the 11th February, 1948, answering to my letter of 19th January, 1948.

2. With reference to para. 2 of your letter, the following is the answer: -

(a) The kind of Missionary work we propose to undertake just now is the Spiritual instructions only, and the scholastic education to follow should the government deem it fit to do so. In the Missionary work we do carry on with both Spiritual instruction and scholastic education as well.

(b) We have funds available in the Central Treasury in Bulawayo, Southern Rhodesia. We do get the money for Southern Africa by which we undertake the Missionary work with.

3. We have the work of our Church established in many countries under different systems of Governments or divisions. We have many schools of our own mission operating. We conduct the affairs of education of our mission schools according to the systems and educational Ordinance laid down by the Government of the country in which our missionary work is operating, for we go by the rule "Obedience to the Civil Government is one of the principal duties of all men."

I beg in anticipation.

I have the honour to be,
Sir,
Your obedient servant.

J.L.C. MEMBE
PRESIDING ELDER.

Ref. No. 17/35/3.

From the District Commissioner,
Mbeya, Southern Highlands Province,
13th March, 1948.

To the Presiding Elder,
African Methodist Episcopal Church,
c/o Mr. P.H. Hara, P.W.D.
Mbeya, T.T.

Sir,

May I remind you that before your application is granted information on the following points is required:

(a) What kind of Missionary work do you propose to undertake, i.e., Spiritual instruction only or that and scholastic education as well?

(b) What are the funds available, and their sources, for your mission to undertake serious missionary work?

I am Sir,
G. GLEY.

3/jfm.　　　　　　　　　　For DISTRICT COMMISSIONER.

African Methodist Episcopal Church,
c/o Mr. P.H. Hara,
Public Works Department,
MBEYA, T.T.
15th March, 1948.

The District Commissioner,
Mbeya, Southern Highlands Province,
<u>TANGANYIKA TERRITORY</u>.

Sir,

I acknowledge the receipt of your letter No. 17/35/6, dated 13th March, 1948, concerning my application for the land for our Church and mission house buildings.

2. If my letter of 5th March, 1948 cannot be understood, I too do not understand yours. Therefore, I think, it is better for me to see you personally and make each other understand by personal discussion on the subject.

3. I would like, before I go back to Nyasaland, to interview you at your Office tomorrow morning, if your duties permit you to exchange our views personally perhaps this will make me understand your questions on your two previous letters to me.

Thanking you, Sir,
Yours faithfully,
J.L.C. MEMBE
PRESIDING ELDER.

Mbeya, 15/3/48.

Reverend Father Membe,

Very many thanks for your suggestion of meeting personally and have a talk verbally on the application. The thing is, I wanted to know how much money you have deposited in the Bank here to carry on with your Missionary work within this District now. But we shall discuss this when we meet tomorrow. With many thanks.

L.L. DE LESDEMOND
<u>DISTRICT COMMISSIONER.</u>

In the next morning, after having a lengthy discussion for nearly one and half hours in friendly terms, the permission was granted. A note to the Township Authority for the land was also issued. After having drawn a rough building sketch plan by the help of the Township Officer, a land was given to us in the African Township area where the Church building stands now at Mbeya, Tanganyika Territory.

In 1949, I was transferred to Lusaka in Northern Rhodesia and left things as far as there."

Chapter 16
The A.M.E. Church in Belgian Congo in the Year 1957

Some of the members of the A.M.E. Church moved from the Luapula Valley in Kawambwa District and stayed on the other side of the River Luapula in Belgian Congo. These members asked Rev. Foodson Burton Shadreck Washiama to visit and preach to them there. Rev. Washiama tried hard to secure permission from the Congo Government to allow him to preach to those members there. After some struggle he was allowed to preach there from the other side of the Luapula and return, and was not allowed to stay in Congo. He tried all he could to gain some more members there. Subsequently, Rev. F.B.S. Washiama succeeded and organized the Church there, at three points: Chibambo, Nkambo and Kasenga in Belgian Congo.

Rev. Foodson Burton Shadreck Washiama in 1967.

Photo courtesy by Mother Diana Mapoma.

At the Annual Conference held in Livingstone, September 1959, Bishop V.F. Ball, appointed the following ministers as first ministers to carry on with the work of the Church in the Congo: -

1. Rev. Robert Kabala, first Presiding Elder in Congo
2. Rev. Elijah Mulenga Masongo, Pastor
3. Rev. Moses Makungu, Pastor
4. Rev. Donald Kapesa Katanga, Pastor.

This was a very great step forward as far as the work of the A.M.E. Church in Central Africa is concerned. Since the work of the A.M.E. Church started in Northern Rhodesia and other neighbouring countries there has been a great expansion and progress in ministry, membership and financially.

We will now give an overview of the bishops and missionaries who served the church in our region. This will be given in the next chapter. Some of the early history sketches of the first Bishops of the A.M.E. Church in South Africa here have been copied from the pamphlet published by the Rev. N.B. Tansi, of Pretoria in South Africa in 1940. I wish to thank him for this. Rev. Charles Kapungwe would also want to thank Mark Frazier on information on Bishop William T. Vernon and authors of "The Book Shelf" on information about the African Methodist Episcopal Church Historic Timeline 1703-1987.

Chapter 17
Bishops and Missionaries Who Served the A.M.E. Church in South Africa, Southern, East and Central Africa

The Ethiopian Church was the forerunner of the African Methodist Episcopal Church in South Africa. The Anglican, Wesleyans, Presbyterian, Dutch Reformed and Moravian Churches had been in existence for more than a century before the introduction of the African Methodist Episcopal Church in South Africa, Southern, East and Central Africa. The early Missionaries of the Church manifested no attitude of superiority, and a real fraternity existed. Later, as these missionaries were replaced, the African Preacher felt a change in attitude and a strong racial consciousness arose among them and their chiefs. This chapter shares pertinent records of Bishops from America and missionaries who served the Church in South Africa, Southern, East and Central Africa.

Racial consciousness and attitude of superiority by some in the Church created desire of independence in the subjugated. With this desire of an independent Church, Rev. Mangena M. Mokone and Jonas Goduka agreed to send their representatives to the United States of America to seek amalgamation with the African Methodist Episcopal Church. Rev. J.M. Dwane and Rev. J.G. Xaba were elected as delegates to the African Methodist Episcopal Church General Conference in America. The General Conference was held in Wilmington, North Carolina from May 4 to 22, 1896. Rev. Dwane went and the union was perfected between the two Churches. Bishop H.M. Turner, Dr. H.B. Parks, and Dr. J.S. Flipper received the delegates and perfected the union in Atlanta, Georgia.

This Church met great opposition in Africa and was the object of suspicion within and without.

1. Bishop Henry M. Turner came over in 1897 and held his first Annual Conference in Queenstown, South Africa. He organized the Cape and Transvaal Conferences. Bishop Turner made Rev. Dwane Vicar Bishop. Dwane then seceded to the Anglican Church (Ethiopian Order). Dwane's secession made it necessary to send another deputation to seek about the interest of the Church in South Africa. During this time of upheaval, Dr. F.M. Gow and Rev. J.E. Tansi wielded influence which greatly aided the new Church in stemming the tide. As a result of this deputation to Mother Church, Rev. I.N. Fitzpatrick was sent to South Africa to adjust the matter up. He gained favourable recognition from the Government on behalf of the A.M.E. Church.

2. In May 1900, Bishop Levi J. Coppin (1848-1924) was assigned to South Africa. He had been elected and consecrated Bishop at the General Conference convened in Columbus, Ohio in 1900. Bishop Levi Jenkins Coppin was born in Maryland and was editor of the

A.M.E. Review. The Rev. A.H. Attaway accompanied him. Subsequently, Revs. C.M. Turner, J.A. Gregg and H. Msikinya came to serve during Bishop Coppin's administration. Bishop Coppin left the work in a prosperous condition.

3. Bishop Charles Spencer Smith (1852-1922) succeeded Bishop Coppin in 1904. He had been elected and consecrated Bishop at the General Conference convened in Columbus, Ohio in 1900. Bishop Smith had been Secretary of the Sunday School Union and was Canadian. During internal strife, Bishop Smith was recalled to America. In the Cape, Father Gow, Revs. H.A. Fortune, D.D. Willenburg, A.W. Phigeland and D.P. Gordon held the doors of the Church open.

4. After the Church had suffered, Bishop William Benjamin Derrick (1843-1913) came in 1907. Bishop Derrick was elected and consecrated Bishop at the General Conference held in Wilmington, North Carolina in May 1896. He was born in West Indies and was a Missionary Secretary at the time (The Book Shelf, 1997). He succeeded in restoring peace.

5. Bishop James Albert Johnson (1857-1928) succeeded Bishop Derrick in 1908. Bishop Johnson was elected and consecrated Bishop at the General Conference held at Norfolk, Virginia in 1908. He was a Canadian and a pastor. He was the only Bishop to remain two quadrenniums leaving peace and prosperity (at the time) and extension of the work.

6. Bishop William Wesley Becket (1859-1925) followed in 1916. He was elected and consecrated Bishop at the General Conference convened in Philadelphia, Pennsylvania in 1916. However, the World War interrupted him while in America and could not bring his family over. He was born in South Carolina and was President of Allen University, Rev. Charles Kapungwe's alma mater.

7. Bishop William Tecumseh Vernon (1871-1944) succeeded Bishop Becket in 1920. Bishop Vernon was born in Lebanon, Missouri and was President of Western University (formerly Freedman's University) in Quindaro, Kansas. He had been appointed by President Theodore Roosevelt in 1906 as Register of the U.S. Treasury and was reappointed in the same capacity by President William Taft in 1912 (Frazier, 2010). This was the highest position at the time held by an African American. Bishop Vernon built Emily Vernon Institute in Basutoland.

8. Bishop John Andrew Gregg (1877-1953) was elected Bishop at the General Conference held in 1924 in Louisville, Kentucky. He was born in Kansas and was President of Wilberforce University at the time of his election. In 1924, Bishop Gregg succeeded Bishop Vernon. Bishop J.A. Gregg's administration was significantly blessed with Bethel Memorial Church, Cape Town, the Elisa Gregg Hall of Wilberforce Institute in Evaton, and the great expansion of the Church in Southern Rhodesia and to Nyasaland.

9. Bishop George Benjamin Young (1865-1950) was elected Bishop at the General Conference held in 1928 in Chicago, Illinois. He was a Pastor of Bethel Church in Texas where he was from. Bishop G.B. Young succeeded Bishop Gregg in 1928. Bishop Young's significant effort was to Gumtree Farm in Southern Rhodesia and the Young's Chapel in Bulawayo. It

was at the time of Bishop Young that the Church expanded across the Zambezi River into Northern Rhodesia.

10. Bishop David Henry Sims (1889-?) was elected Bishop at the General Conference held in 1932 in Cleveland, Ohio. He was born in Alabama and was President of Allen University in Columbia, South Carolina. In 1932, Bishop D.H. Sims succeeded Bishop Young. He brought new life to the work and made many friends among all racial groups for the A.M.E. Church. He built Sims Chapel in Salisbury (Now Harare), and by this time the Church extended to many parts of Northern Rhodesia and Tanganyika Territory.

11. Bishop Richard Robert Wright (1878-1967) was elected Bishop at the General Conference held in 1936 in New York City in New York. He was President of Wilberforce University and Editor of the Christian Recorder at the time. In 1936, Bishop R.R. Wright, Jr., succeeded Bishop Sims. He resurrected "The South African Christian Recorder" in his first year. He also built Mokone Gow Hall and the Normal Theological School and Clinic at Wilberforce and had the Catechism and Liturgy translated into Sesuto and Xhosa. During Bishop Wright's administration in South Africa, he was able to bring to South Africa from America in 1937 Dr. Andrew White who was appointed the Principal of Wilberforce Institute, and Mrs. Luella G. White as Secretary of Wilberforce Institute.

In 1938, Dr. J.R. Coan was appointed Dean of the Theological School at Wilberforce Institute in South Africa. Mrs. Lucy M. Hughes, Connectional Missionary President toured from Cape to the Zambezi in Northern Rhodesia and Belgian Congo in the interest of Missionary work. (Note: Ndola Circuit took its name from Mother Hughes).

Bishop Wright served worthily in a long line of distinguished predecessors from the great to the least. Only Bishop H.M. Turner to the eloquent and masterful D.H. Sims could be counted as equals. At the end of Bishop Wright's term in 1939, Dr. J.R. Coan succeeded him and became Superintendent of Wilberforce Institute in South Africa too due to the World War II situation.

12. Bishop Frank Madison Reid (1898-1962) was elected Bishop at the General Conference held in 1940 in Detroit, Michigan. He was born in Tennessee and was Pastor of St. Louis' St. Paul Church. Bishop F.M. Reid was assigned to South Africa, 15th Episcopal District in 1940, but as a result of the international situation which prevented the sailing of Bishop Reid, Dr. J.R. Coan was appointed General Superintendent and Bishop's representative in the 15th Episcopal District in November, 1940. Dr. Coan was the first to open schools of the A.M.E. Church in Southern Rhodesia and Nyasaland. Some of the schools he opened in Southern Rhodesia and Nyasaland are still operating except in Northern Rhodesia at Chilwa, Chiyanga, Chipwa, Mununshi and Solwezi. Also, Lyuchi, Karonga and Kaporo have all been closed down after he left.

13. Bishop George Wilbur Baber (1898-1972) was elected Bishop at the General Conference held in 1944 in Philadelphia, Pennsylvania. Bishop G.W. Baber was assigned to South Africa in 1944. Nevertheless, he could not come over to his District due to an international

situation, and Rev. Dr. Josephus Roosevelt Coan (1902-2004) continued as Bishop's representative in 1944.

14. Bishop Isaiah Hamilton Bonner (1890-1979) was elected Bishop at the General Conference held in 1948 in Kansas City, Kansas. Bishop I.H. Bonner was assigned to the 15th Episcopal District, South Africa in 1948, and made some improvements and progress. He built the Ebenezer A.M.E. Church at Lusaka in Northern Rhodesia and other buildings in Southern Rhodesia and South Africa.

15. Bishop Frederick Douglas Jordan (1901-1979) was elected Bishop at the General Conference held in 1952 in Chicago, Illinois. He was born in Georgia and he was from First A.M.E. Church in Los Angeles. Bishop F.D. Jordan was assigned to the 15th and 17th Episcopal District in South and Central Africa in 1952. Bishop Jordan completed many church buildings in South and Central Africa and built Jordan Chapel in Livingstone and one at Wusakile, Kitwe (Jordan Chapel) in Northern Rhodesia (where Rev. Charles Kapungwe was later to join the Church through Sunday school as a member at the age of 7 in 1969/1970). Bishop and Mother Jordan travelled extensively in the remotest areas in South Africa, Southern Rhodesia, Northern Rhodesia and Nyasaland up to Tanganyika Territory and Belgian Congo. He left the work of the Church in progress and in peaceful condition.

16. Bishop William F. Ball (1906-1984) was assigned to 17th and 18th Episcopal Districts in Central Africa and Bechuanaland Protectorate in 1956. He was elected at the General Conference held in Miami, Florida in 1956. It was at this time when the Nyasaland Conference was created from the Northern Rhodesia Annual Conference. Bishop Ball extended the work of the Church to Portuguese East Africa and Congo, built several church buildings in Southern Rhodesia and Northern Rhodesia, and went back to America in 1959.

17. Bishop Francis Herman Gow, (1896-2009) a South African-born preacher was assigned to the 15th Episcopal District in South Africa in 1956. He was elected and consecrated to the Bishopric at the General Conference in 1956 held in Miami, Florida. He had been the only African-born ever elevated to Bishopric since the establishment of the A.M.E. Church in Africa – in 1821 in West Africa and 1896 in the Union of South Africa. (Three other African-born preachers were elected 48 years later in 2004 at the General Conference in Indianapolis, Indiana U.S.A and were later consecrated as Bishops. This followed increased discontentment built over several decades among African churches over what they perceived as non-inclusion policy by top leadership of the Church in America). Bishop Gow stood in to preside on a number of Conferences when American bishops were unable to hold Conferences in South Africa.

18. Bishop John Douglas Bright, Sr., (1917-1972) was assigned to the 17th Episcopal District in Central Africa in 1960. He was elected Bishop at the 1960 General Conference convened in Los Angeles, California in 1960. He brought with him his family, composed of his wife, Mother V.M. Bright, his son, Mr. John D. Bright, Jr., his daughter Miss Gwendoline

Bright and his mother-in-law Essie Harris.

Like his name, Bishop Bright came to brighten the position and condition of the services of the Church generally. He created the Mashonaland Conference in Southern Rhodesia, and the North Zambia Annual Conference in Northern Rhodesia. Bishop Bright was the first Bishop to create the offices of the Director of Religious Education and General Superintendence as far as the 17th Episcopal District is concerned. Also, ministers received for the first time the yearly minimum salary. Many Church buildings were built and repaired and other churches were built at Matero in Lusaka (Bright Temple), Mufulira, Kitwe (Bright Chapel) at Kamitondo, and Kazembe. He did many great things but served only from 1960-1962 because he was recalled to the U.S.

During this time, Mother Annie E. Heath, Connectional President of the Women's Missionary Society visited the 17th Episcopal District in September and October, 1962. She travelled at large in Central Africa, and attended Annual Conferences in Nyasaland, Northern Rhodesia and Southern Rhodesia. She brought great spiritual inspiration and encouragement upon the work of the Church and ministry.

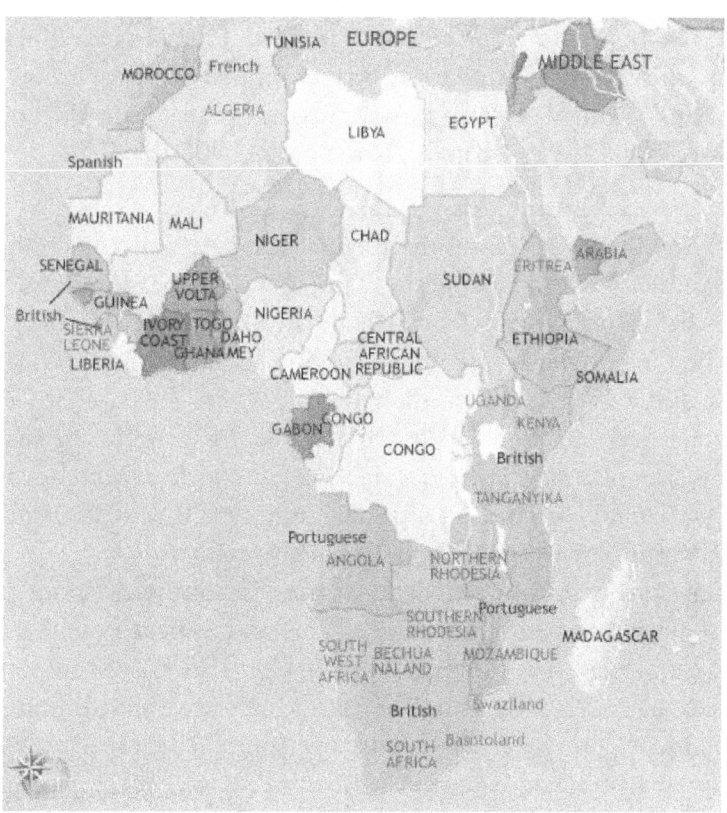

Map of Africa 1960 – Open source maps of Africa Yahoo Image Search 9-26-2018.

19. Bishop George Napoleon Collins (1896-1972) was assigned to the 18th Episcopal District in Bechuanaland and Basutoland Protectorates in 1960 in Southern Africa. He came

after Bishop Bright was called back to the United States in 1962 before his term was expired. The General Conference meeting in Los Angeles, California in 1960 elected Bishop G.N. Collins who was born in Florida and became a Pastor in New Orleans, Louisiana. He was assigned to the 18th Episcopal District from 1960-1963.

20. Bishop Harold Irwin Bearden (1910-1990) had been Pastor of Big Bethel A.M.E. Church in Atlanta, Georgia. He served the 17th Episcopal District between 1964 and 1968. Bishop Bearden was elected Bishop at the 37th Quadrennial Convention of the A.M.E. Church in Cincinnati, Ohio in May 1964. He was the pastor of Big Bethel in Atlanta, Georgia at the time of his election in his native state. The new bishops had been consecrated after a memorial service of President J.F. Kennedy.

21. Bishop Joseph Gomez (1889-1979) was elected Bishop at the General Conference held in 1948 in Kansas City, Kansas. He was born in Antigua, but moved to Trinidad as a boy then migrated to the U.S.A. He was assigned to the 17th Episcopal District from 1968-1972. He hardly served the 15th Episcopal District for two weeks in South Africa in 1948. (Previously, barely two weeks after the General Conference, Bishop Henry Y. Tookes who had been sent to the 10th Episcopal District in Texas passed away in 1948 following an illness. Bishop Gomez, who had even made the trip to South Africa, was reassigned to Texas following an Emergency meeting of the Bishops' Council. Bishop Bonner was assigned to the 15th in place of Gomez). Bishop Gomez served the 17th Episcopal District from 1968 to 1972.

22. Bishop Hartford H. Brookins (1925-2012) was elected 91st Bishop of the A.M.E. Church in Dallas, Texas in 1972. He was then sent to the 17th Episcopal District. The District, then comprised Zambia, Malawi, Rhodesia (Zimbabwe), Tanzania and Zaire (Congo DR). He served the 17th Episcopal District from 1972-1976. He is the first Bishop Rev. Kapungwe recalls seeing as a boy of 9. Charles had been singing in the Sunday School Choir at Jordan Chapel at Wusakile and had travelled to Allen Temple where the Annual Conference was held in 1972. The Sunday School Choir led by Bro. Lloyd M. Siwale, the teacher, sang in that Conference! Bishop Brookins had been escorted out of Rhodesia which was under Ian Smith who had declared Unilateral Declaration of Independence (UDI) from Britain in 1965 to lead a white minority government which denied blacks any rights.

During the time of his visit to Rhodesia (formerly, Southern Rhodesia), he had spoken against the white regime there. He had attacked the government's racist policies at a time of liberation struggle by blacks there, (Simmonds, 2012). This had prompted the government to ban him from staying in Rhodesia. Armed guards later escorted him out of the country, to Zambia, an independent country where he was welcomed. Bishop Brookins is well remembered as the Bishop who built the Chelston Housing Project, the Lusaka Farm and Episcopal Residence in Zambia. Before his election as Bishop, Brookins had built a church he had envisioned to cost a million dollars, First A.M.E. Church (FAME) in Los Angeles. Brookins founded Brookins Community A.M.E. Church in Los Angeles, California and appointed Rev. Larry T. Kirkland in 1977 who was Pastor there until Kirkland's election as Bishop in 1996.

Bishop Kirkland was later to appoint Rev. Kapungwe to Trinity in the same year and ordain him later both as Itinerant Deacon and Elder.

23. Bishop Cornelius Egbert Thomas (1917-2004) was elected Bishop at the General Conference which met in Atlanta, Georgia U.S.A. in 1976. He served two terms in the 17th Episcopal District from 1976 to 1984. Rev. Charles Kapungwe was in attendance at Thomas Chapel, Luanshya where Bishop Thomas preached in one of the Annual Conferences in 1982. Bishop Cornelius was born in Hamburg, Alabama. He was a former President of Wilberforce University. He raised money to build Thomas Chapel in Luanshya.

24. In 1984, Bishop Robert Lee Pruitt (1935-1997) was elected and consecrated as Bishop at the General Conference convened in Kansas City, Missouri from July 7 to 15. He was born in Greenville, South Carolina and served the 17th Episcopal District from 1984 to 1988. At the South Zambia Annual Conference held at Bright Chapel in Kitwe in 1986, Bishop Robert Pruitt, a great preacher gave a powerful sermon in a makeshift structure which had been erected on the church ground because the church was too small to accommodate worshipers. Bro. Charles Kapungwe was in attendance at this Conference too.

Rev. Paul Bupe, Rev. Wilson Mpundu, Bishop Robert L. Pruitt and Rev. Cuthbert Katebe at the South Zambia Annual Conference at Ebenezer in Lusaka in 1987.

25. One great gift the 17th Episcopal Church received in 1988 was Bishop Richard Allen Chappelle (1934-2012). He was elected and consecrated as the 108th Bishop of the A.M.E. Church in Dallas/Fort Worth, Texas in 1988. He served in Africa for 8 years, serving the 17th Episcopal District from 1988 to 1992 and then from 1992 to 1996 the 18th Episcopal District in Lesotho and Swaziland. He had been elected as the second General Secretary of the A.M.E. Church in 1976 in Atlanta, Georgia and had moved to St. Louis, Missouri in 1976 and established the General Secretary's Offices of the A.M.E. Church there. He modernised the office by installing electronic equipment which began the process of cataloging of records of the Church for the future generations. He served for 12 years as Secretary.

When he came to the 17th, he changed the Church and brought great enthusiasm in the members. This was because many had never seen a great administrator and preacher like Bishop Chappelle. He loved the people and showed great leadership skills spending nearly all his 8 years living on the continent of Africa. He brought robes for the clergy (many had difficulties in acquiring robes) and brought YPD T-shirts and the youths were very enthusiastic in them! I was in the YPD at the time and Bishop Chappelle had directed me in 1988 in Lusaka to become the YPD President of the newly formed North-West Zambia Annual Conference following the dissolution of the gigantic South Zambia Conference. I had been 1st Vice President of the then South Zambia Conference and Bro. Emmanuel Membe had been President. He was based in Lusaka and he was directed to be South East Zambia YPD President. Bishop Chappelle also brought literature with him, the first kind we had ever seen in our time. He also revived the Christian Education Congress in the 17th Episcopal Church where three countries of Zambia, Malawi and Zimbabwe congregated yearly.

Photo: Bishop Richard Allen Chappelle.

26. Bishop Robert V. Webster was elected as Bishop in 1992 in Orlando, Florida. He served the 17th Episcopal District from 1992 to 1996. He had been a longtime Pastor of St. Stephen A.M.E. Church in Jacksonville prior to his election. He was born in Arkansas. Bishop Webster served the Church in Africa greatly demonstrating the heart of a servant he is. His ability to resolve problems and love demonstrated the heart of the Shepherd. When the Church at Allen Temple in Mufulira had a nagging financial struggle with the lenders after they had borrowed money and bought a minibus but failed to repay the money, Bishop Webster intervened to resolve the problem. His heart of giving and care for the needs of his flock were unmatched.

When Rev. Paul Bupe, now Dr. Bupe was studying in the U.S.A., Bishop Webster appointed him as Pastor of St. Stephen A.M.E. Church in Sandusky, Ohio U.S.A. When Rev. Charles Kapungwe was having trouble paying in school in the U.S.A., Bishop Webster cleared the bill of $900.00! Many ministers lose their pastoral hearts once elevated to the Bishopric position but not the Rt. Rev. Bishop Webster, a great preacher and loving servant who served the 17th Episcopal District exceptionally well! He is a humble but powerful man of God! Rev. Wilson Mpundu calls him "A Father and a man with a big heart!" Once, Rev. Mpundu got an airline ticket on credit hoping to repay upon his return from the General

Conference since they had been promised refunds. He was given a check which could not be honored by one Bishop. However, Bishop Webster cleared many outstanding bills including this plane fare during his leadership!

Bishop Robert Webster wanted to take ministers he saw potential in to school. Among them was Rev. Wilson Mpundu but upon learning of the plans, the older ministers went and spoke "good" to the Bishop which made him change his mind! Bishop Webster was a very responsible, supportive and visionary leader. He was the first leader to reach a remote area of Kasompe in North Western Province of Zambia. He also helped many stranded students in the U.S. from the 17th Episcopal District. At the time Bishop Robert Webster helped me, I was in Maine and he was serving another District yet Bishop Preston Williams (17th Episcopal District Bishop) who I had met in Columbia, South Carolina before, told me not to call him, his office or bother his secretary!

My Note from Bishop Robert Webster then Bishop of the 3rd Episcopal District

Columbus, Ohio
20 October, 2006.

Dear Rev. Kapungwe,

It was nice talking to you on Thursday. I am praying that you will receive the money you need to continue your education. Enclosed is a check that I hope will help with your tuition. Praying for much success.
Sincerely,
Robert Webster

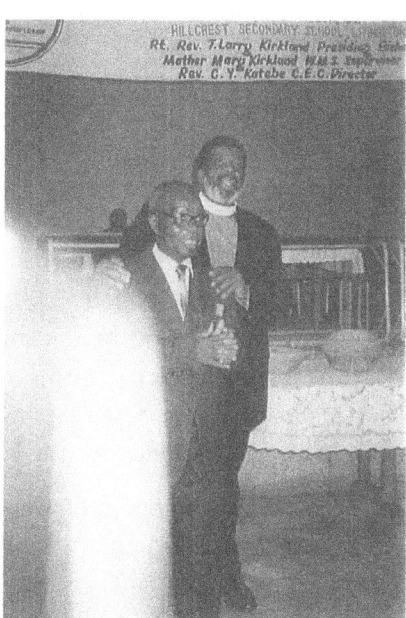

Photo: Presiding Elder Rev. Cuthbert Y. Katebe (left) with Bishop Larry T. Kirkland, 17th Episcopal District Prelate at the Christian Congress in Livingstone, Zambia in 1998.

27. Bishop Larry T. Kirkland was elected and consecrated as the 114th Bishop of the A.M.E. Church in 1996 in Louisville, Kentucky. He served the 17th Episcopal District from 1996 to 2000. He appointed Rev. Charles Kapungwe to the Pastoral Charge of Trinity A.M.E. Church, Garneton in Kitwe on December 1, 1996 at the Annual Conference held at the then Trans-Africa Bible College (now Trans-Africa Christian University) at Race Course, Kitwe, Zambia. He later ordained him as Deacon on Missionary Rule (which he stated that he too was ordained on that same Rule) on 5th October, 1997 at Holiness A.M.E. Church (now Kirkland A.M.E. Church) in Ndola and as Elder at The Trade Fair Grounds in Ndola hosted by Mother Hughes A.M.E. Church on 3rd October, 1999. Rev. Kapungwe served at Trinity from 1996-2000. He designed Trinity Church, paid off the land to the City using his personal funds and built the church.

28. Bishop Preston Williams was elected and consecrated as the 119th Bishop of the A.M.E. Church in 2000 in Cincinnati, Ohio. Rev. Charles Kapungwe was in attendance at this General Conference as an Alternate Delegate. Bishop Williams was sent to the 17th Episcopal District. He served from 2000 to 2004. Countries included the Democratic Republic of the Congo (Zaire), Zimbabwe, Zambia, Burundi, Tanzania, Rwanda and Malawi and the 17th District was split off to form a new 20th District. When he came, he found the African Jurisdiction Council in operation. It had been established before Bishop Williams came to Africa and had been pushing for ending disparities in representation in the Church.

When Rev. Kapungwe left Zambia in 2000, the African Jurisdiction Council was actively pushing for native-born Africans to be elected among the Bishops of the Church. The Church in Zambia lost the dynamic Preacher in Rev. Wilson Mpundu due to poor administration during this time. When Bishop Preston Williams left Zambia, he was brought to the 7th Episcopal Conference, South Carolina. During his time, seven congregations in South Carolina left the A.M.E. Church including my parent, Rev. Leroy Cannon in 2008! When I had no money for food in medical school and I had called the Bishop, he told me not to call his office or bother his secretary! Prior to this, I had met him in person when he came with Bishop Kawimbe in Columbia South Carolina in 2004.

29. Bishop Paul Kawimbe was one of the three indigenous African-born Bishops elected at the General Conference held in Indianapolis, Indiana in 2004. He served the 17th Episcopal Conference for two terms from 2004 to 2012 based in Zambia, his native country. After his term, Bishop Kawimbe was sent to the 19th District in South Africa in 2012. He served there for two terms too. In 2019, Bishop Paul Kawimbe was suspended for poor administration by the A.M.E. Church in the U.S. for matters pertinent to the 19th Episcopal District.

30. Bishop Wilfred Messiah was one of the three indigenous African-born Bishops elected at the General Conference held in Indianapolis, Indiana in 2004. (The third was Bishop David Daniels from Liberia). He served the 17th Episcopal Conference for two terms from 2012 to 2020. Initially, he stayed in Zambia but relocated to his native country of South Africa where he ran the Church from. A lot of discontentment from members characterized his tenure of

office and poor administration was evident. The A.M.E. Church in the U.S. had suspended Bishop Messiah in 2011 for poor administration in the 15th Episcopal District where he had previously served. In 2020, the world experienced an outbreak of Covid-19 which started in China and spread all over the world. The U.S. experienced the highest number of deaths due the disease. The General Conference of 2020 was cancelled, consequently.

Below is a list of Bishops and Missionaries from America who came to serve the Church in Southern, East and Central Africa. They include two South African-born bishops elected in 1956 and 2004 and one Zambian elected in 2004: -

1. Bishop Henry M. Turner — 1898-1899
   With Dr. I.N. Fitzpatrick — 1899
2. Bishop Levi J. Coppin — 1900-1903
   With Prof. A.H. Attaway — 1900
   Dr. C.M. Turner — 1902
3. Bishop Charles Spencer Smith — 1904-1906
   With Rev. J.J. Pearce — 1905
4. Bishop William Benjamin Derrick — 1907-, only.
5. Bishop James Albert Johnson — 1908-1915
   Bishop Johnson served for two terms.
6. Bishop William Wesley Becket — 1916-1919
7. Bishop William Tecumseh Vernon — 1920-1923
8. Bishop John Andrew Gregg — 1924-1927
9. Bishop George Benjamin Young — 1928-1931
10. Bishop David Henry Sims — 1932-1935
11. Bishop Richard Robert Wright — 1936-1939
    With Dr. A. White of Wilberforce Institute, South Africa — 1937
    Mrs. Luella G. White, Secretary of Wilberforce Institute, South Africa — 1937
    Dr. J.R. Coan as Dean of Theological School, Wilberforce Institute — 1938-1948
    Mrs. Lucy M. Hughes, Connectional President W.M.S. who
    toured from South Africa to Congo and went back to America — 1958
12. Bishop Frank Madison Reid (Did not come over) — 1940-1943
13. Bishop George Wilbur Baber (Did not come) — 1944-1947
14. Bishop Isaiah Hamilton Bonner — 1948-1951
15. Frederick Douglas Jordan — 1952-1955
16. Bishop William F. Ball — 1956-1959
17. Bishop Francis Herman Gow (15th Episcopal District) — 1956-1959
18. Bishop John Douglas Bright, Sr. — 1960-1962
    With him was Mother V.M. Bright, two children
    Mr. John D. Bright, Jr., and Miss Gwendoline Bright
    and Bishop's mother-in-law Mrs. Essie Harris.
19. Bishop George Napoleon Collins (18th Episcopal District) — 1960-1963.
20. Bishop Harold Irwin Bearden — 1964-1968
21. Bishop Joseph Gomez — 1968-1972
22. Bishop Hartford H. Brookins — 1972-1976

23.	Bishop Cornelius Egbert Thomas (served for two terms)	1976-1984
24.	Bishop Robert Lee Pruitt	1984-1988
25.	Bishop Richard Allen Chappelle, Sr.	1988-1992
	(18th Episcopal District)	1992-1996
26.	Bishop Robert V. Webster	1992-1996
27.	Bishop Larry T. Kirkland	1996-2000
	with Br. Cedrick who was later ordained Deacon in Zambia	
28.	Bishop Preston Williams	2000-2004
29.	Bishop Paul Kawimbe	2004-2012
	Bishop Kawimbe served for two terms with Dr. James Webb (served as Pastor of Bethel in Lusaka and planted a new church, Chrisma in Lusaka in 2005)	
30.	Bishop Wilfred Messiah	2012-2021
	Bishop Messiah served for two terms. Due to the Covid-19 worldwide pandemic the 2020 General Conference in the U.S.A. was rescheduled to July 6, 2021.	

Excerpts from the Book *"In Darkness with God – The Life of Joseph Gomez, a Bishop in the African Methodist Episcopal Church,"* by Annetta Louise Gomez-Jefferson

Pastor Kapungwe had a chance to explore the thoughts of Bishop Joseph Gomez (1889-1979). He was elected the 67th Bishop at the General Conference meeting in Kansas City, Kansas in 1948. Born in Antigua, moved to Trinidad with the family and came to the U.S. in 1908, Bishop Gomez gives us a glimpse of the mindset of Bishops who come to Africa. While this is not to be generalized, it gives us the insight into the experiences of those who do missionary work in developing countries. At the General Conference convened in Philadelphia, Pennsylvania, Bishop Gomez was assigned to the 17th Episcopal District from 1968-1972.

Bishop Gomez came at a unique time in history. It was at the turn of the political change in Africa. Reading the book, *"In Darkness with God – The Life of Joseph Gomez, a Bishop in the African Methodist Episcopal Church,"* Annetta Louise Gomez-Jefferson, the daughter, gives us the Bishop's mind while serving in Africa. The Bishop was well aware of the political role the Church had played as well. We got some excerpts for our readers! "Most of the influential African leaders involved in the liberation movements had belonged to the A.M.E. Church at one time or another: Kenneth Kaunda, Hastings Banda, John L. Dube, Justin Chimba, and W.K. Sikalumbi. Banda had been brought to America by Bishop John Gregg 'and received his first degree from Wilberforce University.' His uncle had founded the A.M.E. Church in Malawi.

For five years, Kaunda had been an active member of Ebenezer Church in Lusaka … He was a member of the Official Board, sang in the church choir, and had some of his children baptized in the church. He left the church in 1957 'After an argument on the conservatism of the church.' The presiding elder apparently said, 'People were using the A.M.E. Church as a platform for political purpose.' (Note from Author Kapungwe: Please note that President Kaunda's former Chilenje house, now a national monument, stands right opposite the Ebenezer

A.M.E. Church. Also, Honourable Wilson Chakulya, a former cabinet minister in the Kaunda government was a member of this church. When he retired, he became a member of Bright Chapel in Kitwe before he passed away).

Kaunda believed the church should be involved in liberation politics. Justin Chimba, 'an active and vociferous African National Congress leader in the anti-Federation campaign, Organizing Secretary of the Northern Rhodesia General Workers' Trade Union and later an executive member of the Northern Rhodesia African Trade Union Congress,' a coeditor of *Freedom Newsletter*, had once been a local preacher in the A.M.E. Church. (Note from Author Kapungwe: Please note that Mrs. Estina Daka Chimba, the widow of Honourable Justin Chimba was a member of Trinity A.M.E. Church at Garneton, Kitwe during the time Pastor Kapungwe was pastor from 1996 to 2000. She passed away when pastor Kapungwe was in the U.S.A.). W.K. Sikalumbi, former Trade Commissioner to Europe, Deputy General Secretary of the Zambia Africa Congress after the split with the ANC, and member of Kaunda's parliament, had also once been a minister in the church."

I read the book, "In Darkness with God – The Life of Joseph Gomez, a Bishop in the African Methodist Episcopal Church" with interest. I found that in 1972, at the Missionary Convention in Los Angeles, Bishop Joseph Gomez had been introduced to the Zambian delegation which included Mrs. Wakunguma *(wife to the Presiding Elder Rev. Mundia K. Wakunguma)*, Mrs. Nhekairo *(wife to Bro. Nhekairo, a prominent Lay Organisation member from Ndola)* and Princess Nakatindi, whom Joseph described as 'every bit royal personage.' [Note: Princess Nakatindi Wina (1945-2012) wife of Sikota Wina, a former minister, served as minister later in the Movement for Multi-Party Democracy (MMD) in the 1990s]. "It was at this time that Bishop Gomez chaired the trial involving Bishop William F. Ball of the 7th District," (Gomez-Jefferson, 1998 p 355).

I felt like including the Bishop's perception of Zambia during his visit in 1972. "Lusaka, the capital, was surprisingly modern – much more than the Gomez had been led to believe. They were impressed by the well-built highways, houses, business buildings (including the new Lusaka Trades Training Institute), and the supermarkets. Joseph was anxious to meet the progressive President Kaunda, who had led the Zambians to independence. He also wanted to see the A.M.E. Churches and schools," (Gomez-Jefferson, 1998 p 356).

"The Gomezes visited the A.M.E. churches in Lusaka, Mount Zion and Ebenezer, and learned that Zambia had over a hundred pastors and about nine thousand members. A few weeks later they were taken to the Copperbelt to visit the A.M.E. churches in Kitwe, Ndola, and Mufulira. During the long religious services, they were fascinated by the singing of the old hymns, which the Zambians had transformed and now sounded decidedly African. Hazel watched with wonder as each person in the audience swayed down the aisle to put her or his coin in the collection plate. The singing, hand clapping, drum beating, and body movement of each person were sheer artistry-together they were hypnotic. Every aspect of the service was entered into totally. Hazel thought about some of the lukewarm worshippers she had encountered in America.

The following week Joseph was taken to meet Kenneth Kaunda. He was impressed by the president's strong presence and sensitivity. Kaunda reiterated to Joseph what he had said at Kitwe in October 1963 at the Mindola Ecumenical Center, concerning his disappointment with the Christian church. He still believed that the Church should play a vital role in Zambia. If it was to do so it could not remain static and orthodox but had to be creative enough to attract the young. The Church should not separate itself from the social, economic, and political problems of the people, especially those that had to do with the independence and freedom of all Africa…," (Gomez-Jefferson, 1998 p 357).

"At the thirty-ninth Quadrennial of the A.M.E. Church convened in Dallas, June 21-July 3, 1972, the Gomezes had mixed feelings about returning to the state where Joseph had begun his episcopacy and had been accompanied by much pain. They were, however, delighted by the greetings they received from their Texas friends and the twenty-four delegates who had come all the way from Central Africa …

On Monday morning Joseph read a communication from the Honourable Dr. Kenneth David Kaunda, president of the Republic of Zambia. In it said, 'He valued the work of the Church in Zambia very much indeed. We believe that the teaching of Christ, that 'Man shall not live by bread alone,' is significant if we are to help lead our fellow human beings to enjoy a fuller life during their very short stay on this earth.' All the Christian churches were responding well in helping Zambia to develop; it was important that the A.M.E. Church participate. Kaunda stressed that the basic philosophy of Zambia was Humanism – and not the Humanism of Europeans. Zambians believed that man belonged to God, that he did not make himself. 'Whatever he is in terms of race, colour, or ethnic grouping is God's work and is not something that should lead us, humble beings, to differ and to quarrel among ourselves.'

Joseph asked the conference to respond to Kaunda's letter. Among those who seconded the motion was the Honourable Rev. Frederick Talbot of the 16th District, and a permanent delegate to the United Nations from Guyana. Joseph informed the conference that the Zambian government was prepared to furnish at least three quarters of the money needed to support the A.M.E. schools and hospitals in the area," (Gomez-Jefferson, 1998, p360, 361).

Americans dread the mentality of the African Church looking up to Americans for help. In my study of the book by Annetta Gomez, the daughter of Bishop Joseph Gomez, in which she writes, "As soon as the news of Joseph's appointment reached Central Africa, letters began to arrive petitioning the bishop for assistance," (Gomez-Jefferson, 1998 p352), the irritable atmosphere these requests for assistance produced was felt. It is indeed, hard to understand or conceptionalise the socio-economic, cultural, political and spiritual reasons behind those requests. Perhaps, reading the book, "The Cry of Mother Africa," by Charles Kapungwe may offer some answers to this complex question and its complex answer. It must also be noted that missionaries of other denominations have been building quality schools and churches in Africa which feeds into the expectations and anticipations by the people of these lands into similar beliefs that the A.M.E. Church would be expected do the same.

Mr. Finnbar Dunphy, a former resident of Zambia, Zambia's first Republic leader, President Kenneth David Kaunda and Rev. Charles Kapungwe at South Trust Building in Columbia, South Carolina, U.S.A. 20 March, 2003.

Society House on Cairo Road, Lusaka Zambia. Photo by Misheck Munsaka. 28th July, 2020.

Chapter 18
Rev. John Lester Coward Membe: Founder of the A.M.E. Church in Zambia

Rev. John Lester Coward Membe

When Rev. Charles Kapungwe began to investigate the history of the A.M.E. Church in Zambia, one name he had in mind was Rev. John Lester Coward Membe. To many who have been in this Church for many years in Zambia, the Membe family or "Membe," is a household name in the Church. Rev. Kapungwe sought for the help from Mother Elizabeth Nelinya Lukamba Simyembe for portions of relevant history. Portions of the following history on Rev. J.L.C. Membe were written based on the research work of Adrian Hastings, Research Officer, School of Oriental Studies in London, as recorded in his book, "Themes in the Christian History of Central Africa."

The book had also been based on interviews and discussions with the wife and children. Additional information had been extracted from the book "A Short History of the A.M.E. Church in Central Africa 1960-1962" by John Lester C. Membe, and various correspondences, certificates and notes from Rev. Dr. J.L.C. Membe's *(Honoris causa)* personal files.

Rev. Kapungwe reviewed some of these writings from available copies including Rev. David K. Simfukwe's work which guided him to come up with this writing. Rev. Simfukwe's work also included Rev. Membe's autobiography. Rev. Samson M. Kapufi was also a great resource because he provided the bulk of the writing in this work. Rev. Kapungwe then concluded with his short comments on the history of this pioneer of the work of the A.M.E. Church in Zambia. Mother Elizabeth N.L. Simyembe also provided materials and photos of this pioneer.

Rev. John Lester Coward Membe founded the African Methodist Episcopal Church at Broken Hill (Kabwe) in Northern Rhodesia (Zambia) in 1929. He was born on 2nd February, (between 1904 and 1910) at Ikawa Old Fife Village (Nakonde) in Isoka District, Northern Rhodesia. He was a son of Abraham Longa Mweni-Membe, who was a fifth-born son of Nchilinji with his wife Nampungwe. Rev. Membe's father, Longa Mweni-Membe was from a group of the Balombwa or Wa-Siwale, clan and Mwinamwanga ethnicity who were closely related to the Bemba who came from the Luba country. The ancestor of the Balombwa clan, Kapasa, came from the Congo and was a Muluba by ethnicity. He was a brother of Nkole (the then Chitimukulu, the paramount Chief of the Bemba). The father to Kapasa was Chief Mukulumpe (The Legend, 2016).

His mother was Rebecca Milundo Nakamba Membe, a daughter of Mweni-Mukone Siyame from Wiwa in Kafwimbi area. His grandmother from his mother's side was Nkweto Chibambamashi, daughter of the old Chief Nkweto Nalimbi of Chilinda in Chinsali District. Rev. Membe was born Longa Kapelembe in Isoka where his father was stationed at Ikawa. Longa Membe was the first African sergeant in the British South African Company (BSAC). He died in service in 1928 in Isoka, (The Legend, 2016).

Rev. Membe started school at the early age in 1916. This followed a recommendation by the late Rev. David Kaunda (father of the first President of Zambia, Dr. Kenneth D. Kaunda) of Lubwa Mission at Makoba's village. His teachers were Sandyford Shimwamba, Kosam Mfitula and Uria Shingoshe. When he got to Standard II, he went to Lubwa Mission in 1917 but he was refused boarding place because they thought he was too young to be a boarder. Rev. David Kaunda got him and stayed with him in his house till he was admitted into Standard III in 1918. He was a very bright student, therefore, authorities let him go and teach during holidays at Chibesakunda School. When he was in Standard IV, his older teachers turned him into their personal cook because they did not agree that he joins them in teaching. He was warned not to tell anyone that he was refused to teach. So, after three months, he returned to Lubwa Mission and he received his first pay of 4 Shillings 6 pence for three months he had worked.

In 1921, when his father was transferred to Isoka, Rev. J.L.C. Membe continued his school at Mwenzo in Standard V. Before completing Standard VI, he had been selected to train as a teacher while he was still doing his school. He would learn as Standard V and VI as a student from 08:00hrs to 12:00hrs and as a trainee teacher from 14:00hrs to 16:00hrs. He, thus, completed both Standard VI and teacher training course at the same time. He attended school at Lubwa Mission in Chinsali District up to Standard IV and Standard VI at Mwenzo Mission Boarding School in Isoka District, plus two years Teacher Training. He taught at two central schools for two years.

Rev. J.L.C. Membe was transferred to Livingstonia Mission for three months. This was for teaching methodologies. After completion he obtained a teaching certificate and went back to Mwenzo Mission. In the same year, he was sent to open a new school at Isoka as Head Teacher of the school. Rev. Membe was with three other teachers who were older than him. He was appointed at the same time Inspector of four schools including Isoka, Kafwimbi, Mweni-Malalale and Mweni-Chilanga. His salary was then 12 Shillings 6 pence per month.

Rev. J.L.C. Membe was baptized in the Presbyterian Church of Scotland by Rev. Dr. James Alexander Chisholm of Mwenzo Mission, Isoka in Northern Rhodesia on November 19, 1924. His faith was inspired by his mother who was teaching him about Jesus Christ from the time he was young. She planted a very strong Christian faith in him. She told him Bible stories and collected pictures of our Lord Jesus Christ to show him, whenever she had time.

As a teacher, during the holidays, he began bringing students and other people together for prayer meetings every Sunday morning. The Sunday prayer meetings encouraged him to become a self-styled preacher. He brought many to Christ by going around the villages every Sunday to preach the word of God to the people. He later built a small prayer meeting house at Isoka, Mweni-Chilanga and Kasimbi villages. The Missionary, Dr. Chisholm, elders and deacons from Mwenzo Mission, were then invited to come and baptize the converts.

After the school holidays, the Church Council at Mwenzo recognized the work of Rev. Membe. They suggested that he be accepted and recognized as a Local Preacher, despite his young age. At first, this request was turned down because of his age, but Rev. Membe was not discouraged. He continued going into the villages to preach and prepared the people for baptism. At this time, he received his calling but could not be a minister until after reaching forty years of age. However, through the Lord's wise providence and unfailing guidance, he became His servant. He owed his Christianity to his mother and education to his father. They both played very important roles in his life.

The Legacy of His Christian Life

Rev. Membe served as a teacher in the Presbyterian Church of Scotland for two years. He then left teaching. He left not because there was anything wrong but because he could not enjoy his rights in the teaching service accorded to his promotions because he was considered young. So, he left and travelled to towns along the line of rail. He could not find any Presbyterian Church in these areas so he would go to any church that was there. He visited Elizabethville (now Lubumbashi) in Belgian Congo where he met Mr. Nkhata, the Chief Clerk in British Council's Office who recognized him from Livingstonia Mission and at Mwenzo. He was a Presbyterian. He stayed with him for a few days and they went to American Methodist Episcopal Church which he had joined after he came back from Nyasaland. He is the one who talked to Rev. Membe about a Church in South Africa which is from America for black people only.

When he came back to Northern Rhodesia, he went to Livingstone. He joined the Government service as Clerk, Typist and Court Interpreter. There was no Presbyterian church in Livingstone so he started going to Paris Missionary Society Church. One day, he visited Victoria Falls Town in Southern Rhodesia and found members of the A.M.E. Church holding their

Sunday service under one big tree. He joined in their service and continued going there. Rev. Membe sent a letter to his Missionaries at home to report what he was doing. He requested that they send him a removal certificate to allow him to be received by the African Methodist Episcopal Church officially.

Dr. Chisholm of Mwenzo sent him a very good certificate of recommendation. It was sent to the Superintendent of the A.M.E. Church in Bulawayo. Rev. Membe joined the A.M.E. Church in June 1928 at Victoria Falls in Southern Rhodesia. Rev. J.R. Molefe, a South African minister, was the Pastor of the church at Victoria Falls Town. Rev. Membe rode his bicycle every Sunday from Livingstone for church. He spoke to Pengemali (Benjamin) Chanda of Chinsali, a Northern Rhodesia Policeman. He began going to church with him but the man later joined the Watch Tower Sect. Rev. Membe had been persuading Rev. Molefe to come to Livingstone to begin the Church. Rev. Molefe, however, declined stating that he had no permit to do so in Northern Rhodesia. He nevertheless, advised Rev. Membe to write to the Superintendent Rev. Z.C. Mtshwello of Bulawayo which he did in 1928 and before the response came, he was transferred to Broken Hill (now Kabwe) as a Clerk and Typist in the District Commissioner's Office. At that time the BOMA Headquarters were at Mutwewansofu.

Since there was no A.M.E. Church in Northern Rhodesia he attended services with the Wesleyan Methodist Church on Sundays. He seriously had been thinking about reasons why the A.M.E. Church had not been in Northern Rhodesia. He therefore, began to talk to friends about the A.M.E. Church. He converted first Mr. Aaron Mwenya and his wife Elizabeth from Kawambwa, Mr. and Mrs. John Mwila both from Serenje, Mr. Lazarus Besa and his wife from Luapula. All of them were mine employees living in mine houses. Prayer meetings were being held in Mr. and Mrs. Aaron Mwenya's house. These people also influenced their friends and brought them to the meetings. Thus, Rev. J.L.C. Membe started the A.M.E. Church in 1929 at Broken Hill in Northern Rhodesia without any appointment from the Annual Conference.

The first preaching permit was granted by the Magistrate on 18th March, 1930. He was received into full membership in the A.M.E. Church on 4th February, 1931 by Rev. David Dafite Khomela in Northern Rhodesia. Rev. Membe was appointed as the first Pastor of Broken Hill in October 1931, by Bishop G.B. Young under the Presiding Elder Rev. D.D. Khomela.

In 1931, Rev. Z.C. Mtshwello wrote Membe from Bulawayo to get ready to go to South Africa to train as a minister. This was to be done when the Bishop was expected in. That year, the Bishop was assigned to a different District and that delayed Membe going to South Africa. He was asked to study privately so that he could get ready to go to Kimberly to sit for the examinations together with the Bible students from Theological Schools of Wilberforce Institute in Transvaal and Cape Town. In 1931, he left the Government service on his own will but they were not happy with him leaving the service. He struggled hard with them until they let him go after three months' notice. He later joined Broken Hill Mine as a Clerk, Typist and Medical Orderly as the Church could not support him.

When Rev. David Dafite Khomela was appointed as first Presiding Elder of Northern Rhodesia District in October 1931, Bro. J.L.C. Membe had already been organizing the Church at Broken Hill. Rev. Khomela's headquarters were at Livingstone where he was also

Pastor of Livingstone after moving from Southern Rhodesia. Rev. Membe was recognized as a Part Time Minister at Broken Hill. Rev. Khomela's request to have Bishop G.B. Young bring a Supply Minister to Broken Hill was turned down in 1931 because the Bishop deemed Br. Membe capable of organizing the Church in spite of him being a Government employee who ran the Church on part time basis. In February 1932, Rev. D.D. Khomela the Presiding Elder, brought with him Rev. Jonas Lesapi Honoko from Transvaal, South Africa as full-time Pastor of Broken Hill, and Brother Membe became an assistant Pastor under Rev. J.L. Honoko. Rev. R.J. Mkwayi from Union of South Africa was appointed at Ndola.

Rev. Membe completed and passed his Third-Year studies. He was ordained Deacon by Bishop David Henry Sims on 3rd March, 1933 at the Joint Session of the Annual Conference held at the Young's Chapel A.M.E. Church in Bulawayo, Southern Rhodesia. Bishop Sims had been the Presiding Bishop in South Africa and Southern African Territories. Rev. Membe was posted to Abercorn (Mbala). In 1934, he was called to South Africa by Bishop Sims for the Fourth Year Theological Examinations at Wilberforce Institute in Transvaal for six months. This was before the exams and he did his practical helping out around Johannesburg District in preaching and learning other things including Presiding Elder's duties. He passed the exams and went back to Abercorn where he served from 1933 to 1944.

Late in September 1933, with colleagues, he went into Tanganyika where he began the Church. He faced hostilities from members of the London Missionary Society (L.M.S.) who were already in the area. Rev. Membe was ordained an Elder on 24th November, 1935 by Bishop D.H. Sims and appointed Presiding Elder at Bloemfontein in Orange Free State in South Africa. In September 1944, Rev. Membe obtained permission from District Commissioner G. Mitchell to open a Mission in Tanganyika.

Rev. J.L.C. Membe served as Presiding Elder in many places. He was Presiding Elder for Northern Province and Luapula Province from 1935 to 1944. He served as Presiding Elder for Nyasaland Protectorate and Eastern Province of Northern Rhodesia from 1945 to 1949. He was Presiding Elder of Lusaka District, Northern Rhodesia, from 1954 to 1960 and Luapula District again, from November of 1962 while still being Pastor in Kitwe.

There are several churches, the Rev. J.L.C. Membe pastored. He was Pastor of Broken Hill (now Brookins A.M.E. Church in Kabwe), 1931-1932, Chiyanga, Abercorn 1933 to 1944, Kalenda 1937, Kazembe 1938 to 1939, Blantyre, Nyasaland 1945 to 1946 and Kasungu, Nyasaland 1947 to 1949. He had been responsible for over five Districts, three in Nyasaland, one for Eastern Province of Northern Rhodesia and a fifth in Tanganyika Territory. He then became pastor in Lusaka, Northern Rhodesia from 1950 to 1953, Ndola 1954-1958 and Mufulira 1959 to 1960. He returned to Lusaka as Pastor in 1961, to Kitwe in 1962 and then to Kawambwa in 1963 at the time of writing his work.

There are several churches that the Rev. J.L.C. Membe built. He built the church at Chilenje, Lusaka (Ebenezer A.M.E. Church) and at Matero, Lusaka (Bright Temple A.M.E. Church). He also built Bright Chapel A.M.E. Church at Kamitondo, Kitwe and Jordan Chapel A.M.E. Church, Wusakile Kitwe (Rev. Charles Kapungwe's childhood church). He built Allen Temple at Mufulira, Kawambwa and many other temporary church buildings and parsonages at Chiyanga, Chipwa, Lusaka and many other places too numerous to mention. He worked and travelled to many countries and within Zambia, spreading the word of God, converting people to Christianity and building churches. Rev. Membe contributed also greatly to the publication of A.M.E. literature including translating and compilation of the A.M.E. Church Hymn Book in Chibemba in 1952. He contributed to the translation of Bibles from English into various languages, the legacy which all of us are proud of.

Rev. J.L.C. Membe served the Church in many other capacities besides ministerial duties. He served the Church as Annual Conference Secretary from 1936 to 1958 continuously. He was Superintendent of the Church from 1952 to around 1963 at the time of writing, Director of Religious Education for the 17th Episcopal District and Secretary/Treasurer 1954 to 1960. Besides the duties of the Church as a Minister of Religion, he was the first organizer and Chairman (first Chairman) of the African Hospital Advisory Committee at Lusaka, 1952-1953, and also first organizer and first Chairman of the African Hospital Advisory Committee at Ndola 1955-1958. Rev. Membe was Chairman of the Welfare Services Committee and member of Finance and General Committee. He was also member of the Housing Area Board and member of African Affairs Committee, all in the Municipal Council of Kitwe in 1962. In 1962, Rev. Membe was transferred to Kawambwa, and this was the end of all services with several memberships of the above-mentioned services with the Municipal Council of Kitwe in 1962.

Considering all records, Rev. J.L.C. Membe was thus reputed to be the first Zambian to worship as a member of the A.M.E. Church. Second, he was also thought to be the person responsible for first organizing the Church in Northern Rhodesia (Zambia). Third, he was also destined to be the first Zambian Minister to work inside the country. He was, however, preceded by Rev. Johannes Marumo as a member and minister. Rev. Marumo was a Pastor at Choma in 1933. He had been admitted to the Annual Conference in 1929, was first appointed Pastor to Shabani in Southern Rhodesia and was ordained Deacon in 1934. Consequently, for reasons stated above, and for his visionary and outstanding drive to extend the work of the A.M.E. Church both in Zambia and outside Zambia, Rev. J.L.C. Membe, is believed to be the founder of the A.M.E. Church in Zambia.

Eulogy Delivered at the Funeral of the Late Dr. J.L.C. Membe, D.D. (Honorary) Senior Presiding Elder and 17th Episcopal District Dean of Religious Education, Mbala 6th November, 1978 by W.K. Sikalumbi.

1. The Eulogy is delivered on behalf of the Church leaders and members of the African Methodist Episcopal Church which the late Rev. Dr. J.L.C. Membe, D.D., who died on Wednesday November 1, 1978, loved and loyally served for 50 years. I am greatly honoured and privileged to at least, say a few words about this great man.
2. The Rev. Dr. John Lester Coward Membe was born at Ikawa (Old Fife) near Nakonde in Isoka District between 1904 and 1910. A son of a Civil Servant known as Mweni-Membe Siwale, in and around the local men of the "Mweni," Membe is synonymous of owner or king of the Membe area.

3. Young John went to school at a Church of Scotland Mission Station. After graduating at Mwenzo Mission School, he later trained as a Teacher, then as Typist and Court Interpreter.
4. It was during the time he was working for the Government at Kabwe that he met Pastors and true friends of the A.M.E. Church in 1929. He became a strong believer in the Doctrine of the Church and thereafter, struggled hard to make himself relieved of the Northern Rhodesia Government services. He first established the Church at Kabwe, the place he worked. He also preached and established congregations at Ndola. In his endeavours to preach the Gospel, he chose Mbala District as a base for the Word of God in the year 1932. Chiyanga Mission was his first Mission Station that saw the timeless young Pastor who moved around the Lake shore villages including Kasanga in what was then called Tanganyika Territory and Sumbwanga where authorities arrested him for spreading the gospel. His choristers moved with the American Flag as he toured the areas and converted men and women to his beloved A.M.E. Church.
5. The Rev. John L.C. Membe became the first Zambian Presiding Elder in the year 1935. His charge covered the largest area of operation including Kasanga, Sumbwanga, Mbeya and Tukuyu Districts in Tanganyika. It also included Mbala, Mporokoso and Kawambwa Districts in Northern Rhodesia and Kasenga District in the present-day Zaire. He was using a bicycle as means of transport.
6. Between the years 1935 and 1945, his fame was such that the British Administrators were forced to recognize and respect him. Therefore, they extended invitations to him to attend important prayer meetings at Mbala and Kasama. In his humbleness, the student of African Theology preached and made the colonialists understand and appreciate what A.M.E.'s stand was in relation to its policies and objectives. It was during this time that American Bishops who sensed potential in this man recognized his services and loyalty to the Church and, consequently, offered him two intermittent scholarships to train as a Minister at established Theological Colleges in South Africa.
7. A strong believer in African Methodism and its self-reliance policies, he opened schools at Chiyanga, Chilwa in Mbala District and Nachula Mission in Southern Province.
8. The Rev. Dr. J.L.C. Membe now resting here built many church buildings with his own hands in Lusaka, Ndola, Kitwe, Kawambwa, Mporokoso, Nachula and many others in Northern and Southern Provinces of Malawi.
9. A gifted orator and multi-linguist, he spoke 14 native languages fluently. He spoke Namwanga, Mambwe, Chibemba, Chinyanja, Chitumbuka, Chitonga of Zambia, Chitonga of Malawi, Silozi, Chinyiha, Chinyakyusa, Sindebele, Kikaonde, Sizulu, Xhosa, etc. For being modest but very effective administrator and diplomat, Bishop Hartford H. Brookins chose him as emissary to go to Kinshasa, Zaire and represent the Church which was on the verge of being banned as a result of a decree pronounced by General Mobutu, President of Zaire. The late

Rev. Dr. J.L.C. Membe saved the Church from the total collapse by presenting A.M.E. Church Abridged Constitution (Discipline) which was among the required demands of the authorities of the land. A man with a vision chose Membe for this onerous task.

10. As a spiritual father of the A.M.E. Church, he was a humble man who worked day in and day out translating the Holy Bible with a group of those men who shall miss him greatly. As a lover of music and a singer himself, he has a Hymn Book to his credit. He had written and compiled a Chibemba A.M.E. Church Hymn Book which he treasured for 13 years until in 1973 when, with prayers and indeed incessant desire, he later found publishers. The Hymn Book is in circulation at present.

11. As a writer, one has to read "The History of the A.M.E. Church in Central Africa" which he wrote jointly with Father Hastings whom he befriended as a co-worker in the Bible translation bouts if one has to know this man. The Executive Committee of the Bible Society of Zambia will miss his fatherly advice immensely.

12. Father J.L.C. Membe's achievements cannot be counted in a short verse like this one. Those who knew him as a freedom fighter cannot fail to recollect that during the darkest days of struggle for independence of Zambia, especially, during the noteworthy National Days of Prayers, which were proposed by the leadership in this nation, Rev. J.L.C. Membe, fully aware of the consequences of associating himself with leaders in the forefront of the freedom struggle defied the intimidation by the British Administrators and openly demonstrated this defiance by ordering that the doors of A.M.E. Churches throughout Zambia should remain ajar when other imperialist oriented Churches shut theirs. He was later punished for conducting prayers at meetings and conferences held by nationalists. He was not daunted. He continued to associate and also invited leaders and also counseled them to pray for the coming independence to Zambia.

13. Most A.M.E. Church members loved him and this is true with other leaders and people of other Churches too. They all held fervent hope of his becoming Bishop of the African Methodist Episcopal Church. Alas, he was born too early for the occasion and it is a pity he passed away still leaving the Church being administered by the American brothers 12,000 miles away.

14. The Party and Government of the Republic of Zambia, in recognition of his services had in 1974 during the unique 10th Anniversary Independence Celebrations honoured him by inviting him specially to deliver a speech which left the new Ministers awestricken and wondering about him. We, as a Church, still congratulate the Party and Government for having remembered him every time.

15. It was in the year 1976 that through the contacts of Right Reverend Hartford H. Brookins, then Bishop of our area that Rev. J.L.C. Membe was conferred with an Honorary Doctorate Degree in Atlanta, Georgia U.S.A. The late Rev. Membe put it as "A rare honour given to the entire Church in Zambia and its true followers."

16. All in all, is it not true that secular leaders are not made but born leaders and is it not true that men of God are sent or given by God in order to serve mankind?

This man of God, started as a humble person when the whole of Zambia was looked upon as a Circuit. He and his few colleagues attended Annual Conferences either in Cape Town or Bloemfontein in South Africa. This man helped to see that another Annual Conference was created and named Zambezi Annual Conference to serve and cater for Southern Rhodesia, Northern Rhodesia and Nyasaland. He later saw to it that Northern Rhodesia had its own Annual Conference followed by Nyasaland having an Annual Conference of its own. A few years later, Zambia was able to boast a second Annual Conference, one for the southern and the other for the northern part of the country.

17. Yes, indeed, here lies a man who held firmly to his faith and worked hard to leave a legacy for all to see – dying a poor man without even a bicycle but going to his Christ holding the Bible and a Hymn Book in his hands saying to Him "Take me as I am, I have fought a good fight …" And as of now, it is for those who may be able to emulate him, that the doors of heaven are wide open for them to go and meet with him in his Master's bosom and glory but to those who have no faith, they may just as well say good-bye to Rev. Dr. J.L.C. Membe.

18. When we say "Good night, we know that we shall meet tomorrow."

W.K. Sikalumbi, (The Legend, 2016).

Rev. J.L.C. Membe was survived by a number of children. Among them were Webster, Beatrice, Justus, Frida, Elisha, Shorack, Rev. Suzanne Matale, Hilda, Rev. Frank Membe, Rhoda and Deborah

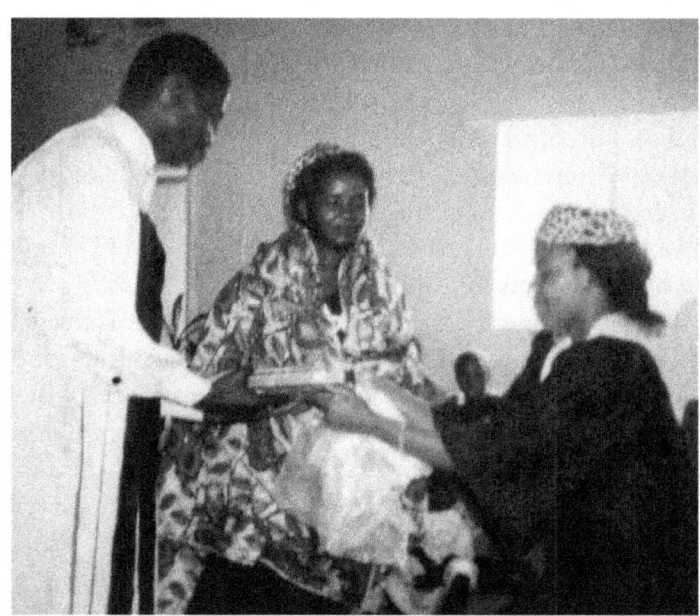

Pastor of Bright Chapel Rev. Wilson Mpundu and Mother Grace Mpundu handing out a gift to Sister Rhoda Membe (daughter of Rev. J.L.C. Membe) during the WMS' exchange of gifts with friends at Bright Chapel, Kitwe in 1990.

Sister, Hilda Membe, the daughter of Rev. Membe, now based in Florida informed me on 15th August, 2020 of how her father narrated to them how he met two lions on one of his trips. Going to another village while riding his bicycle, the sun was going down and just before 18:00 hrs., he had reached a peak of a mountain only to see a lion in front of him and a second one behind him on the dusty road that went to the second village. He stood still as the ferocious beasts stared at him and him at them! Rev. Membe then prayed to the Lord to save him aware of the work that still remained to be done. After a while he let go of a huge sound, a noise of "Wwwwww" which rattled not only the forest but the lions as well! When the lions heard the noise, they were terrified and ran away into the bush! Rev. Membe, then mounted on his bicycle and arrived at the next village! He fell down and collapsed upon arrival! The villagers knew why: The lions!

When I read a book by former President Kenneth Kaunda, Zambia Shall Be Free, I believe, I recalled his story of how he too survived meeting a lion in a similar manner in Northern Zambia in early hours of the morning! He had been organising people and used to ride a bicycle during colonialism. After a while, the lion had left the path for him to pass and it was a nerve-wrecking encounter. God's hand had been upon these servants! He had preserved them for a purpose. A day before the Rev. Membe went to be with the Lord, Sister Hilda told me he was telling her about the golden city and the beautiful chair of gold that he was seeing being giving to him as he lay in bed but her mother (wife) who was outside kept on telling her not to respond to what he was saying in his sickbed!

Perhaps, it is worth noting that Rev. J.L.C. Membe's contribution cannot just be limited to the A.M.E. Church. His contribution goes way beyond his denomination. It is his contribution to the Christian Faith in Africa and the world at large that is obviously remains an indisputable truth. Looking at the map of Africa, and observing how most parts of Africa in the north were subdued by Islam, makes us thank God for the missionaries who worked hard to curtail Islam's southward expansion.

The gospel which was spread by both foreign and local missionaries (Africans) was responsible for checking the spread of Islam southwards. Every believer must be thankful that Christian organizations, Churches and individual believers obeyed the Lord's command to go and preach the gospels to all nations as we see in this history. It is without doubt that Rev. Membe, Rev. David Kaunda, Rev. Johannes Mabombo, Rev. Hannington N. Ziyezwa, Rev. Henrique Matenda Lukamba, Rev. Foodson Burton Shadreck Washiama and many more who had worked to spread the gospel in Southern, East and Central Africa, led to our current map of preserving the region to the gospel.

Another most important piece of work that Rev. Membe left us was the A.M.E. Church Hymnal. Rev. J.L.C. Membe's translation and contribution to the Chibemba Hymnal left a rare jewel to believers across the nation of Zambia. The translation was chiefly from American Hymnal (A.H.), Sacred Songs and Solos (SSS), Child Songs [Bonner's Child Songs (C.S.)] and Church Hymnary (C.H.). There were additional hymns which included personal compositions derived either from Western hymns or were completely new with African melody to them, marked as (Afn. Mdy., or A.M.).

Rev. J.L.C. Membe's strong apostolic ministry was also expressed in songs. Many of his songs go a long way in showing us the mind of a genius he was. The songs, without doubt, show that they were drawn from Malawian, Zimbabwean, South African and Zambian experience. They were also enriched with a local Zambian culture and biblical experience which was a result of ministering in so many areas for years. This was coupled with Methodism experience which many are aware of the common adage that "Methodism was born in a song." Many of today's contemporary songs still fail to capture the spiritual touch of hymnal composers such as the Wesley brothers, John and Charles, and other American hymn writers including Membe's. "J.L.C.M.," are the initials he went by, to mark his composition. With him, were other great composers such as "H.M.L.," which stood for Henrique Matenda Lukamba. Rev. Lukamba's songs were just as inspired as Rev. J.L.C. Membe's.

Several songs stand out in the hymnal. It must be noted that nearly all songs are very powerful and each is meant to address specific needs such as, God's greatness and his works, Birth of Jesus, His works and reign, Jesus' death, His resurrection, The Holy Spirit, etc. Some of these songs include Rev. Membe's compositions while many others have no names of their writers but have the African melody or can synchronize even with certain English songs depending on tune used.

Some of these songs are gold to the believer's soul. You can check them out! Hymns number 20, 21 (with a South African tune), 67, 120, 122, 125 (J.L.C.M.), 126 (H.M.L.), 127, 136, 143, 160, 169 (Malawi), 173, 185, 253 (Zimbabwe) stand out. There is also one song, Hymn number 151, with the initials, of Mrs. R.M., who according to Mother Simyembe was the wife of Rev. Rowland Mwenyo. From the research, we concluded it is Mother Dofilia Kafeka Mwenyo. Rev. Jeremiah Mwenyo, the son, later confirmed our affirmation. Such, were the works of those who preceded us in ministry that we too may leave a legacy of impacting our generation for Jesus.

THE LEGEND

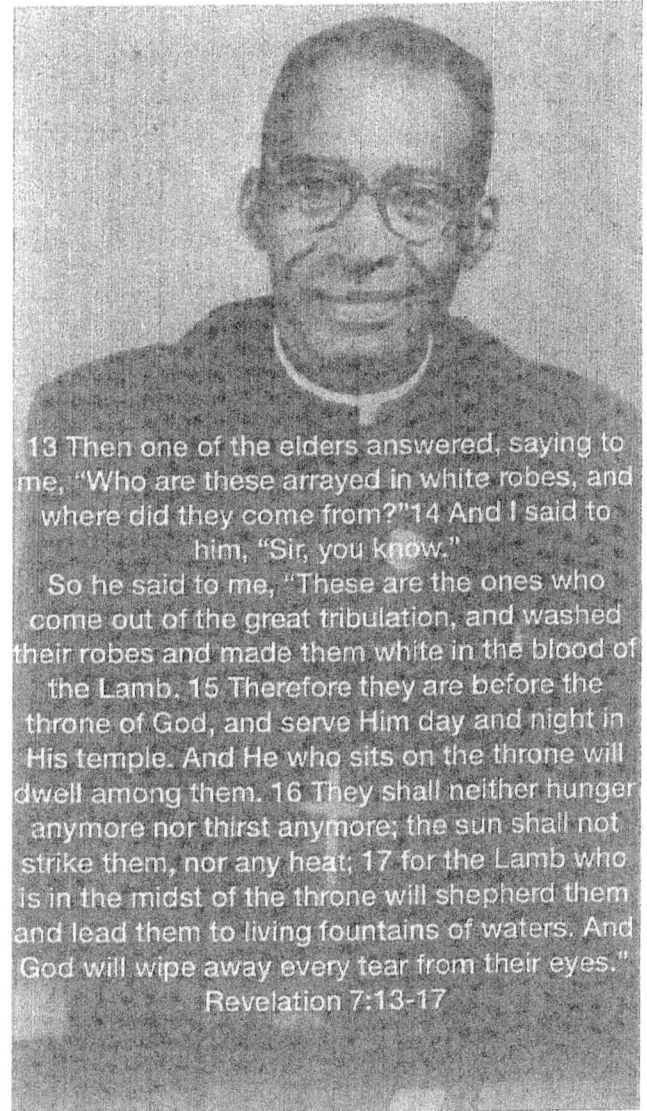

13 Then one of the elders answered, saying to me, "Who are these arrayed in white robes, and where did they come from?" 14 And I said to him, "Sir, you know."
So he said to me, "These are the ones who come out of the great tribulation, and washed their robes and made them white in the blood of the Lamb. 15 Therefore they are before the throne of God, and serve Him day and night in His temple. And He who sits on the throne will dwell among them. 16 They shall neither hunger anymore nor thirst anymore; the sun shall not strike them, nor any heat; 17 for the Lamb who is in the midst of the throne will shepherd them and lead them to living fountains of waters. And God will wipe away every tear from their eyes."
Revelation 7:13-17

Chapter 19
Rev. David K. Simfukwe – The Educator

Rev. David Kosam Simfukwe, a hard-working minister is a name that cannot be forgotten by many familiar with the A.M.E. Church in Zambia. He too, like many ministers who strived to make a difference by developing this Church, faced numerous setbacks through persecution and untold jealousies by both ministers and members because of his unwavering vision and burden to lift up the standards of this Church. He was fought against because he was an achiever who had strived to build and make a difference in the lives of his members and non-members, especially the poor. It is, however, his ministry of preaching, empowering the disadvantaged, humility and teaching that set him apart among many ministers in this Church.

I met Rev. Simfukwe in 1986 in Lusaka. I had paid a courtesy call on him at his mission house at Chilenje at Ebenezer A.M.E. Church. This was at the time I was studying clinical medicine at Chainama College of Health Sciences. As a young man of 23, I asked him a lot of questions about the A.M.E. Church and he produced printed booklets of his work on the History of the A.M.E. Church in Zambia. The booklets were done out of a stencil and had been type-written. I read the material with keen interest because it answered most of the questions I had about the Church. As a born again believer, I had carried a burden for this Church and had wanted to learn how this Church had been dragged into the state it was in. From his work which had also been sourced from the material the Historical Committee and Rev. J.L.C. Membe had written, I was equipped with important knowledge that was going to be crucial in the production of this history. I was also privileged to meet Rev. Simfukwe, Mother Rose Simfukwe and family in Jacksonville, Florida, U.S.A. 22 years later in 2008.

Photo: Mother Rose Simfukwe and Rev. David Simfukwe in Jacksonville, Florida in 2000.

Rev. David K. Simfukwe was born on 1st March, 1926 at Kawimbe, 12 miles East of Abercorn (Mbala) in Northern Rhodesia. He was born to Mr. Kosam Simfukwe and Mrs. Janet Nambeya. He married Miss Rose Mwambazi on 20th February, 1955, daughter of Mr. Lolo Mwambazi and Chitalu Nakazwe. Mother Rose Simfukwe was born in 1932 at Kambole Mission, 60 miles west of Abercorn in Northern Rhodesia. Kambole Mission was under the London Missionary Society and she was educated there too. Rev. Simfukwe, on the other hand, was educated at Kawimbe Mission of the London Missionary Society. He moved to Lusaka where he joined the A.M.E. Church through a friend. He attended Munali Secondary School in Lusaka, Zambia's prestigious and historical school which educated the bulk of many political leaders including Zambia's founding father of the nation President Kenneth Kaunda.

He trained as a photographer and found himself employed by the Northern Rhodesia Government. Rev. David Simfukwe worked at the Government Printers which was under the Information Department. One day, when the shift was ending and people were leaving the offices, Rev. Simfukwe came across a piece of paper he found on the floor which he picked up and subsequently read. He found disturbing news on it. It was an article that allegedly described how sugar could be used as a means of sterilization to control the population of Africans. The article described how fortifying sugar with some substance could help in reducing Africa's population. This surprised the young man who walked to his friend in the printing room to share the scary news he had just found. His friend like him, were the last persons on duty that day. (Rev. Kapungwe, in his masterpiece book *The Cry of Mother Africa* had heralded similar machinations to the world! In 2020, following the Covid-19 pandemic, Africans are now increasingly becoming aware of these covert operations to depopulate them which has been going on for centuries clandestinely carried out through vaccine programmes and other avenues).

Moved by anguish, the duo decided to publish their new-found news. Rev. Simfukwe's friend worked in the printing department and within minutes they began to run the machines to produce massive numbers of papers to distribute to their people informing them of their find. Unknown to them at the time, was the fact that the duo was not the last to be out of the building that day! They were shocked to see an "uninvited guest" enter their printing room! One white man, their senior, had not left and was still in the building! He had been startled by the sound of the printing machines running which he knew wouldn't have been that late. The sound of the machines reaching his office prompted him to go and investigate and his curiosity paid off! He caught his two African workers "red-handed" printing out "Illegal material" in bulk to distribute to their people! They didn't expect him to be around at that late hour!

The white boss asked the duo what was happening! Rev. Simfukwe then explained what he had found and the boss was furious. He ordered them to destroy the materials immediately. All the papers were bundled up and put out for disposal as trash. Rev. David Simfukwe, however, had managed to sneak a few copies out and presented them to the political leaders fighting for independence at the time. The African National Congress (ANC) was at its strongest at the time. He explained to them that if he gets killed this would be the reason since he expected severe retribution at the workplace the following day.

Rev. Simfukwe was picked up by police upon arrival at work the next day. He was handcuffed and led to jail. He was later sentenced to three years in prison in December 1952 "for spreading false information." Even though he was not into politics, he found himself in jail under the British Government of Northern Rhodesia. Rev. Simfukwe had just met his future wife to be Rose at the time. She was not sure if she was going to wait for him but Rose's cousin encouraged her to wait telling her "three years wasn't that long!" She was happy she waited and today she thanks God because many of her friends who had married at the time ended up divorced with the exception of one. Thankfully, Rev. Simfukwe's sentence received a commuted sentence later. He was released after serving two years and had a year suspended. Rev. Simfukwe was released in 1954.

In 1955, Rev. David K. Simfukwe moved from Lusaka to Masala, Ndola on the Copperbelt. He joined Ndola Circuit but later found a job at Luanshya. This is when the Mines were introducing schools. However, Mother Simfukwe worked for two years in Ndola with the Welfare before moving to Luanshya. She found Rev. Simfukwe had joined the Ministry as a Lay Pastor. He had earlier on, in Ndola, joined the Theological College of Central Africa but had stopped when he moved to Luanshya. Rev. Simfukwe had been among the first students to attend this College when it was opened in Zambia by the Baptists in the U.S.A. With him were Rev. Nimrod Simfukwe, a brother to Mrs. Eva Sanderson and Rev. Muzumala from Presbyterian Church.

In Luanshya, by the providence of God, the missionaries who had started the College in Ndola, somehow, had met Rev. Simfukwe again. They talked to him about resuming his studies in Ndola. Rev. Simfukwe resumed his theological studies and he was being driven to

Ndola and taken back to Luanshya by the founders. Rev. Simfukwe was ordained Deacon in 1961 by Bishop J.D. Bright at Bright Temple, Matero in Lusaka and Elder in 1964 at Ebenezer in Lusaka by the same Bishop.

In 1962, there was no Pastor and he became the Pastor of Bright Temple in Luanshya. This church had been built by the Mines. When Bishop Bright came and had appointed him as Pastor, the church was named after Bishop Bright. At this time, Rev. Simfukwe was working in the Mines in the school. The schools were enrolling students aged up to 12 years who began in Sub A because there was need to educate the populace. The students did very well since they were older and they used to learn very quickly. Mother Rose Simfukwe joined the Mines too as a teacher. When the Mines cut down on number of teachers, there was reduction in schools and Rev. Simfukwe who had been teaching Standard IV went to Lusaka to study Purchasing. Upon his return to Luanshya from training, he was employed in the Purchasing Department in the Mines. He was responsible for purchasing spare parts and other equipment for the Mines.

Roan was the base for the Simfukwe's at this time. The A.M.E. churches at Mpatamato and Mikomfwa were meeting in classrooms at this time. He used to go to Ibenga branch which he had organized and utilized the Mine's car as long as he did not go beyond the 10 miles-radius. The church at Mpatamato, Luanshya was built by Rev. David Simfukwe. He spent personal funds most of which the leaders would ask him to buy materials such as roofing sheets promising to reimburse him! He ended up completing the church this way and was never reimbursed! At the time, they hosted a Retreat. Before Bishop Brookins left in 1976, he promoted Rev. Simfukwe in 1975 as Presiding Elder and was moved to Kitwe as P.E., and Pastor. In 1975 he went to Kenya together with Rev. G.W. Kanyembo and Rev. Henry Alimasi for a short course.

In March of 1976, Rev. David Simfukwe came to the U.S.A. for studies in Chicago, Illinois U.S.A. He came to study Human Development. The course among other things was tailored to help them to be independent and learn how to raise funds and be successful in ministry. He was with Rev. Henry Alimasi and Rev. G.W. Kanyembo when he came to Chicago. When Rev. Simfukwe came for studies, he had quit his employment. It was at a time his children were in school and they wondered how they were going to complete their education but God took care of the family. Mother Simfukwe, on the other hand, was given a six-month unpaid leave from the school which enabled her to continue teaching upon her return to Zambia in 1976. They had no house in Luanshya and when they had moved to Kitwe, she began to teach at Mutende Primary School at Kwacha.

Rev. David Simfukwe in Chicago, Illinois in 1976.

Rev. David Simfukwe was a visionary man. During his time as Pastor of Bright Chapel in Kitwe he began plans to build a school at Blackmon at Kamfinsa. Blackmon, a white settler in Zambia, wanted to sell the land in the area which he owned. He was willing to offer concessions to the Church in 1976 but this failed to take off. Rev. Daniel Mkhwanazi who was a Principal at Northern Technical College, (NORTEC) in Ndola was also a Presiding Elder of Lusaka. He used to commute to Lusaka for Quarterly Conferences. Rev. David Simfukwe was Presiding Elder of the Copperbelt.

Members of the Church went and convinced the new Bishop, Cornelius Thomas to swap the two Presiding Elders. They informed him that "Rev. David Simfukwe does not have a job but Rev. Mkhwanazi does! Since Rev. Mkhwanazi is the head of the institution here in Ndola and he commutes to Lusaka, why wouldn't you let Rev. Simfukwe go to Lusaka and allow Rev. Mkhwanazi to come to the Copperbelt as Presiding Elder?" This made the Bishop to appoint Rev. Mkhwanazi as P.E. of the Copperbelt and had Rev. Simfukwe take up appointment as Pastor of Ebenezer and Presiding Elder of Lusaka in 1977. Ultimately, this killed the school plans at Blackmon in Kitwe.

During the time of Bishop Cornelius Thomas, scores of people and ministers had approached Bishop Thomas to have him transfer Rev. Simfukwe from Ebenezer. Bishop Thomas acted wisely and decisively against these advances. He told the people that Rev. Simfukwe has a vision and removing him would cost the church because not everyone was visionary and another person may not understand or pursue what he was doing. Nevertheless, Rev. Simfukwe ministry was not always cosy! Once, the Supervisor, Mother Thomas had summoned Mother Rose Simfukwe to her office. When Mother Simfukwe met her, the Supervisor complained that "I wanted to inform you about Simfukwe, the way he writes the Bishops' Council is not good!" This was in reference to a letter the Rev. David Simfukwe had written to the Bishops' Council in which he had highlighted an indiscriminate decision by Bishop Cornelius Thomas given as a directive to Presiding Elders to suspend all Pastors who had not gone to the General Conference in the U.S.A.

Mother Rose Simfukwe handled herself very well to the Supervisor Thomas. She told her, "If you are a teacher of a class and upon your return to the class, you ask, 'Who was making noise?' and the students point at one person as the one who was making noise, would you agree that, that was the person who was making noise?" The Supervisor had no answer! Mother Simfukwe then followed up. "Do you know that when a person is working hard, people would want to destroy that person?" It was obvious that the Supervisor didn't understand what had prompted the Rev. Simfukwe to write the Council of Bishops. During the Annual Conference of the South Zambia held at Libala Secondary School in Lusaka in 1988 presided by Bishop Richard Chappelle, Rev. Simfukwe was being grilled again before the Judicial Committee on matters of Ebenezer Secondary School and the Mechanical School in Lusaka.

"The four years of Bishop Robert Pruitt in Zambia were marked as the most peaceful period ever for Rev. David K. Simfukwe. Before this time, the Rev. Simfukwe was taken to the Judicial Committees yearly!" According to Mother Rose Simfukwe, "Bishop Pruitt knew who was a hardworking Pastor and who was not! Also, he had told every minister reporting to him and talking about their colleagues that he would bring out in public everything you told him in privacy! Therefore, this helped to cut down on those who went to speak ill of other ministers to him."

In 1991, at the Annual Conference held in Solwezi, members from the then Zaire had reported about a turbulent situation in Zaire (Congo DR). They had reported to the Annual Conference which was presided by Bishop Richard Allen Chappelle about the threat the Zairean government headed by dictator Mobutu Sese Seko had carried out against the A.M.E. Church in Zaire. The government had threatened to ban the Church in Zaire unless they presented proper documentation which was reportedly lacking. It appeared that the Bishop didn't show any commitment to go to Zaire. Rev. Simfukwe moved a motion in which he volunteered to go and speak to the officials which was accepted by the Bishop and the Conference. This Conference was attended by an official from the ruling Government of Zambia Honorable Alexander Kamalondo.

Rev. Simfukwe left for Lubumbashi in Katanga Province. He met the officials of that country and presented official paperwork and signed documentation which stopped the government of Zaire from banning the Church in that country. Upon his return, the Rev. Simfukwe reported to the Bishop his successful mission which pleased Bishop Chappelle. However, the success story soon became bitter news because some members went to complain to the Bishop that "Rev. Simfukwe posed as a Bishop in Zaire and signed papers in that country as though he were a Bishop," further attempting to estrange his relationship with the Bishop!

Unknown to these naysayers was the fact that history had repeated itself! Nearly two decades earlier, Bishop Hartford H. Brookins had chosen Rev. J.L.C. Membe as emissary to go to Kinshasa, Zaire and represent the Church which was on the verge of being banned as a result of a decree pronounced by the same dictator General Mobutu, President of Zaire. Rev. David Simfukwe, like Rev. J.L.C. Membe was also sent as an emissary to Zaire by Bishop Chappelle because of a similar situation which had happened earlier and the two ministers were, subsequently, used by God to remedy the situation. However, Satan in the members of the Church was not happy when Rev. Simfukwe did the same thing his senior minister had done about 18 years earlier! Did Rev. J.L.C. Membe pose as a Bishop earlier too?

When he built Ebenezer Secondary School in 1980 in Lusaka, he used to walk on foot galvanizing support. He reached out to Government offices and met Paul Doraisamy, an Indian Evangelist who was a friend to Rev. Mulimine, a Baptist Minister. Evangelist Doraisamy, a teacher at Kabulonga Boys Secondary School was introduced to Rev. Simfukwe by Rev. Mulimine who had a school. Rev. Mulimine's school was the first school to have computers and was being supported by the Baptist Church in the U.S. Evangelist Paul Doraisamy believed in Rev. Simfukwe's vision and passion and promised to be praying for him for the success and implementation of the school programme and he came every Wednesday at the home of the Simfukwes and prayed weekly for the project until bricks started to come! Later, roof materials followed! The prayer meeting became a source of concern by many too!

Rev. Simfukwe reached out to many organisations and well-wishers. He had been burdened by a high dropout rate of Grade 7 pupils in government schools. When the people he shared his vision with began to understand, they began to help by donating building materials and rendering help. He walked on foot to share this vision whenever the person who used to give him a ride was not available. Many members of Ebenezer were not concerned and used to discourage the Pastor by telling him that he just wanted to leave the church in problems later. The school he built received no money from the members and at the time, giving was very poor in the church! The contributions the church members ever made was towards the pews only. The Mennonites in the U.S. became the biggest supporters and they sent their missionary Mr. Thissin because they believed in community empowerment and organization. No A.M.E. Church abroad or locally ever funded Ebenezer Secondary School!

When the school began to be built, it began to receive some setbacks. Thieves began to break in and steal the frames. The Rev. Simfukwe decided to enlarge the church and built the school at the back which provided some security because it was in close proximity to the mission house. They made three classrooms in the church using boards as partitions and in 1980, Ebenezer Secondary School finally opened with three Grade 8 classes. The Pastor also got land at Katungu (where the Mechanic School was built) and added four classes. He received help from the Mennonites and the school never had any help from any A.M.E. Church. It was gratifying that when Rev. Charles Kapungwe attended Chainama College of Health Sciences in Lusaka in the 1980s, one of the students who had come there was a brother in the Lord who completed school at Ebenezer Secondary School in Lusaka. In 2008, Rev. Charles visited this brother in Delaware, U.S. where he had moved. Later around 2018, this brother obtained a PhD, showing that the investment the Simfukwes had done in the youths of Zambia as educators had borne fruit.

After the Simfukwes built the school in Lusaka, scores of members began to move to Ebenezer from other A.M.E. Churches in Lusaka. With this moving came more problems since many began to eye the school with motives of personal gain or as a means of profiteering from. During the time, Ebenezer A.M.E. Church had many prominent people including a then Cabinet Minister in the President Kenneth Kaunda's government, Honourable Wilson Chakulya. People would write letters to the Bishop complaining and instigating that the Bishop transfers the Pastor! Once, such a letter "from the Official Board" was written to Bishop Robert Pruitt copied to the Presiding Elder, Rev. Isaac C. Mumpanshya. It claimed, "We do not see all the money that Rev. Simfukwe makes and all our contributions to buy benches are not accounted for."

Rev. Cuthbert Katebe, Rev. Wilson Mpundu, Rev. Caleb Ngoma and Rev. Isaac Mumpanshya at Ebenezer A.M.E. Church just before Rev. Mumpanshya preached at the South Zambia Annual Conference in Lusaka in 1987.

One day, when Bishop Pruitt was leaving for the U.S., Rev. David Simfukwe went to bid farewell to him. Rev. Simfukwe found the P.E. with the Bishop and when he arrived, the Presiding Elder excused himself to leave. "Rev. Simfukwe," the Bishop motioned to him, "Did you receive the mail from the Official Board?" Rev. Simfukwe pleading ignorance asked the Bishop, "Which letter Bishop?" "The letter that was sent to the Bishop with a copy to the P.E., which the Pastor does not have," the Bishop replied. The Bishop then turned to the Presiding Elder and inquired, "By the way, Rev. Mumpanshya, have you given the letter from the Official Board to the Pastor?" "Which letter?" the Presiding Elder asked. "The letter that came to the Bishop and was received by the P.E.," Bishop Pruitt answered. "Yes! I remember!" the P.E. responded. "Will you give the Pastor a copy?" the Bishop directed.

The next Sunday, Rev. David Simfukwe spoke to the church after church service. He informed the people that the church had written a letter to the Bishop purportedly from the Official Board and since "I don't know when that Official Board which I did not chair was held; I will ask the Secretary to read the names of those who have contributed their monies." He then called the Church Secretary Sister Mabel Katongo to read the names of all who had contributed money earmarked for purchasing of benches. When the Secretary called the names, only two people had paid in full – the Secretary and the Pastor. The duo had contributed K500.00 (Five hundred Kwacha) or $34.00, each! He then asked the congregation which wrote the letter to the Bishop why it did so because "You normally ask about the money which you have given not which you have not!"

The church was stunned! Some members, however, were not happy that the Pastor had brought the matter to the congregation! They wished he had brought it to the leaders and not to the whole church! The Pastor, however, insisted that this was the right way to teach people faithfulness. Many who were instigators were ashamed. Rev. Simfukwe was Pastor of Ebenezer until 1991 when he was transferred to Allen Temple by Bishop Chappelle. Mother Simfukwe recalls informing Rev. Simfukwe to prepare himself to leave Ebenezer because she saw that there were many people who were against Rev. Simfukwe because of his trip to Congo DR that year. Rev. Simfukwe was Pastor of Allen Temple in Mufulira until he moved to the U.S.A. in September 1996 following his winning of the Green Card Lottery under the Department of State. "Many people misunderstood our migration to the U.S. as well because they never knew about this too," Mother Simfukwe informed me. Rev. Simfukwe had continued to run Ebenezer Secondary School until his departure.

Rev. and Mother Simfukwe had 7 children. They had 5 sons and 2 daughters with one medical doctor practicing in the U.S.A. Rev. Simfukwe moved to the U.S.A. as a permanent resident in 1996, ten years after I had paid a courtesy call on him at his home in Lusaka in 1986. The family lived in Jacksonville, Florida. The humble, strong leader, administrator and educator went to be with the Lord in Jacksonville, Florida on October 10, 2011. However, his legacy in Zambia and beyond, both in the Church and the field of education has never died! One great minister I have admired and loved passionately, the Rev. Wilson Mpundu described the man as follows: "The quietest man who never argued with any man was Rev. David Simfukwe! Accuse him of anything, he would just be working and smiling!"

Chapter 20
Ministers Who Have Served the A.M.E. Church Both in Northern Rhodesia and Zambia

In this chapter and the next, we share some of the names of ministers who have served the A.M.E. Church in our region. They include those who served as "missionaries" because they came from different countries to serve. This list is inexhaustible and not everyone who served could be listed because that task would be impossible. However, we list some of the ministers who served both in Northern Rhodesia and the present country of Zambia in these two Chapters 20 and 21.

Rev. David Dafite Khomela

Rev. David Dafite Khomela joined the A.M.E. Church in the early 1920s. He was first appointed Pastor of Francistown, Bechuanaland by the Zambezi Annual Conference, Bulawayo Southern Rhodesia and was ordained Deacon in 1929 by Bishop G.B. Young and Elder in 1931 by the same Bishop. Rev. Khomela came from Bechuanaland Protectorate, a Muchuana by ethnicity. He was appointed as the first Presiding Elder of Northern Rhodesia District in October 1931, with his headquarters at Livingstone. He first visited Broken Hill in February 1931. He first visited Ndola in 1932 and also visited Broken Hill, Lusaka and Choma.

Rev. Khomela was appointed Pastor of Lusaka in 1932 at the Annual Conference held in Bulawayo, Southern Rhodesia. Rev. Khomela was Pastor of Lusaka in 1933. He had been appointed P.E. of Livingstone District which included Lusaka and Rev. H.M. Phiri was P.E. of Ndola in 1932. In 1935, Rev. D.D. Khomela founded A.M.E. Church in Barotseland. Rev. D.D. Khomela was reappointed Presiding Elder of Ndola District in 1937-1949. In 1937, he was promoted as Superintendent of A.M.E. Church and Schools in Northern Rhodesia. He was transferred in 1949 to Salisbury in Southern Rhodesia and was replaced by Rev. H. Ziyezwa who was appointed P.E. of Ndola and Superintendent in Northern Rhodesia.

Rev. Benjamin Ben Chisela

Rev. Benjamin Ben Chisela joined the A.M.E. Church in November 1930. He was a bricklayer by profession and the first pastor at Ndola. Rev. Chisela was a Mutabwa by ethnicity of Chief Nsama, Mporokoso in Northern Rhodesia. He was transferred from Ndola to Southern Rhodesia in 1932 and was stationed at Matetsi. In 1933, he was appointed Pastor of Victoria Falls but was transferred back to Northern Rhodesia in 1934 and stationed at Kazembe. He served the Church at Ndola, Matetsi, Victoria Falls, Kazembe, Kalungwishi, Lukanga and many other places. Rev. Benjamin Chisela was ordained Deacon in 1939 and went to rest with the Lord up yonder in 1953. He was a faithful servant of the Lord Jesus Christ at the time when the Church was still under early organization. He learned how to endure many difficulties of the time. May he rest in the peace with the Lord and Saviour Jesus Christ to everlasting joy.

Rev. Johannes Marumo

Rev. Johannes Marumo joined the Church in early twenties in Southern Rhodesia. He was of Barotse ethnicity. He was a businessman and was first appointed Pastor to Shabani in 1929. He served in many places as Pastor in Southern Rhodesia. Rev. Marumo was admitted to the Annual Conference in 1929, ordained Deacon in 1934 and an Elder in 1936. Rev. Marumo was transferred to Northern Rhodesia and served the Church at Sesheke in 1937 and Luanshya in 1939. He also served as Presiding Elder of Lusaka 1941 to 1944, Barotseland District 1944 to 1949 and P.E. for Livingstone District 1954-1956. He was Presiding Elder of Fort Jameson District and Vice President of Nyasaland Annual Conference 1956 to 1958. He passed away to his Lord and Saviour Jesus Christ in 1958 at the Master's service to rest in the safe hands of the Lord and Saviour.

Rev. Thomas Mabula Bruce Mukamba

Rev. Thomas Mabula Bruce Mukamba was Bulima by ethnicity of the Ng'endwa clan. He was born at Ipeta, Chief Ndubeni, Luanshya in Northern Rhodesia on 19th November, 1907. His father's name was Lupumpaula Mukamba of Nsofu clan, of Kaluunda ethnicity while his mother was Mambwe Kanenga Ng'endwa, a Bulima by ethnicity of Lusengo's village, Chief Kaindu, Mumbwa, Northern Rhodesia. His father was a basket-maker and his mother a potter. He joined the A.M.E. Church on 24th April, 1931 at Ndola and was baptized by Rev. R.J. Mkwayi at Ndola on 21 December, 1931. He was received into full membership on January 12, 1933 by Rev. J.C. Dambuza at Ndola. He was first licensed as Local Preacher in 1936 by Rev. J.L.C. Membe at Mulundu and was first appointed to Kalenda as Pastor in November 1936 under Rev. J.L.C. Membe, Presiding Elder.

Rev. Mukamba was ordained Deacon on 25th September, 1939, and an Elder on 24th July, 1949. He served as Presiding Elder in the following Districts: North Nyasa District 1949 to 1952, Fort Roseberry District 1953 to 1954 and Kalenda District 1959 to 1960. He pastored at Kalenda, Kitwe, Luanshya, Solwezi, Karonga in Nyasaland, and Fort Roseberry in Northern Rhodesia. Rev. Mukamba attended school at Johnston Falls up to Standard II and Night School in Congo up to Standard IV. He was still serving in the Vineyard of the Master in 1962.

Rev. Andrew Lunkoto

Rev. Andrew Lunkoto of Mulwe's Village, Chief Kambwali, a Mutabwa by ethnicity, hailed from Kawambwa, Northern Rhodesia. He joined the A.M.E. Church in 1934 and was licensed to preach by Rev. J.L.C. Membe, P.E., in 1936. Rev. Lunkoto was ordained Deacon in 1939 and passed away on his way returning home from the Annual Conference where he had been ordained. He died in the Luapula Valley before he reached home. No information about his life was available at the time of his death because he passed away before he completed his "Information Sheet."

Rev. John C. Dambuza

Rev. John C. Dambuza came from South Africa on transfer to Ndola in Northern Rhodesia.

He came after having served the Church in South Africa for many years. He was appointed Presiding Elder of Ndola District for only one year in 1933 and went back to South Africa by the end of 1933. Rev. Dambuza was ordained Deacon in 1923 in South Africa.

Rev. John Richard Mkwayi

Rev. John Richard Mkwayi joined the A.M.E. Church from Wesleyan Methodist Church on Friday, October 2, 1931. Due to shortage of ministers to send to Northern Rhodesia, he was recommended by the Ministerial Efficiency to be ordained under Missionary Rule on 4th October, 1931, and appointed Pastor to Ndola in Northern Rhodesia to take the place of Brother Benjamin Ben Chisela. Rev. Mkwayi worked for only one year and went back to Southern Rhodesia by the end of 1932. He was ordained Elder in 1933 at Bulawayo by Bishop David Henry Sims.

Rev. Mack Basket Siduna

Rev. Mack Basket Siduna of the Mpofu clan was born at Mount Silinda, Zibonda's village, Chief Napungwana, Chipinga, Southern Rhodesia on 10th May 1902. He joined the A.M.E. in 1932 in Southern Rhodesia. Rev. Siduna attended Mount Silinda Mission School where he passed Standard V in 1920. He was baptized on 10th June, 1934 at Bulawayo by Rev. Z.C. Mtshwello and served as Pastor at Inkonyane, Selukwe and Fhlangano in Southern Rhodesia. He was transferred to Northern Rhodesia in 1937. Rev. Siduna was ordained Deacon in 1939 and Elder in 1950. He served as Pastor at Monze, Mazabuka, Livingstone, Choma, Namwala and Kabumbwe in Southern Province and was still in active ministry in 1962 there.

Rev. Benjamin West Chalomba

Rev. Benjamin West Chalomba was born in 1897 at Chitipa, Fort Hill, Chief Waitwika, Isoka, Northern Rhodesia. Rev. Chalomba, a Mwinamwanga by ethnicity of Wa-Sinkala clan, joined the A.M.E. Church at Mufulira Mine in 1931 from the Presbyterian Church of Scotland where he was baptized at Mwenzo Mission by Rev. Dr. James Alexander Chisholm in 1921. He attended school at Mwenzo Mission School and passed Standard V in 1924. He served as school teacher at several schools. Rev. Chalomba was first licensed to preach in A.M.E. Church at Nkana Mine, Kitwe in 1931. He was first appointed Pastor of Mufulira late in 1931, ordained Deacon on 13th November, 1949 and Elder the same day! He served as Pastor at Mufulira for eight years, at Lyuchi for ten years, and was appointed Presiding Elder for Abercorn District in 1955 to 1962. He opened a school at Lyuchi in 1945 which was closed down in 1948 due to lack of funds to run it. Rev. Chalomba was the first Pastor to organize the A.M.E. Church in Isoka District at Lyuchi, Chikawala and Nakonde under Rev. J.L.C. Membe as Presiding Elder.

Rev. Solomon Ngala Sangweni

Rev. Solomon Ngala Sangweni joined the A.M.E. Church in the early twenties. After having served the Church as Pastor in many places in Southern Rhodesia, he was transferred to Northern Rhodesia as Presiding Elder of Lusaka District in 1938 to 1940. He went back to Southern Rhodesia in 1941. Rev. Sangweni was ordained Deacon in 1929 by Bishop G.B.

Young and an Elder in 1931. He was one of the few senior ministers of the A.M.E. Church who served as Pastor and Presiding Elder in many places and countries. He was appointed General Superintendent of the A.M.E. Church in the 17th Episcopal District in Southern and Central Africa in 1961 by Bishop J.D. Bright, Sr., then Presiding Bishop of the 17th Episcopal District.

Rev. Hanock Msokera Chingo Phiri

Rev. Hanock Msokera Chingo Phiri, a Mchewa by ethnicity was from Kasungu, Nyasaland. His birth record was not available at the time of writing but he sometimes used to say he was old enough to work in 1899 and to travel at large during that period. He was educated in Free Church of Scotland at the Livingstonia Mission in Nyasaland where he passed his diploma. Rev. Phiri joined the A.M.E. Church in 1920, returned to Nyasaland in 1924 and founded the A.M.E. Church there. He was ordained Deacon under Missionary Rule at Bloemfontein, Orange Free State, Union of South Africa in 1925 and Elder in 1927. Rev. Phiri was appointed Presiding Elder of Northern Rhodesia and Nyasaland Districts in 1934 after having served as Presiding Elder of the Nyasaland District from 1927 to 1933. He was transferred back to Nyasaland District in 1937. His headquarters in Northern Rhodesia was at Ndola. There was no more record of his life after 1962.

Rev. Foodson Burton Shadrack Washiama

Rev. Foodson Burton Shadrack Washiama, a Chishinga by ethnicity was born at Tente's village, Chief Lubunda, Kawambwa Northern Rhodesia on 17th November, 1912. He joined the A.M.E. Church in October 1932, at Kalenda, Kawambwa in Luapula Province. He was baptized in the American Methodist Episcopal Church in Belgian Congo by the Rev. Dr. Sayers on 17th October, 1927. Rev. Washiama was first licensed as a Local Preacher by Rev. J.L.C. Membe, P.E. in 1937. He was first appointed Pastor to Mulundu in 1943. He was ordained Deacon on 24th July, 1949 in Salisbury and Elder on 11th November, 1950 in Bulawayo, Southern Rhodesia. Rev. Washiama was appointed for the first time as Presiding Elder of Kalenda District the same day on 11th November, 1950 to 1959, Kazembe District 1960 to 1961 and to Abercorn District in 1962.

Rev. Foodson Burton Shadreck Washiama in 1967. Founder of the A.M.E. Church in Congo DR.

He pastored at Mulundu nine years, Kalenda nine years and Kazembe two years. He is credited to have helped begin the Church in Belgian Congo across the Luapula River in 1957. Rev. F.B.S. Washiama organized the Church at Chibambo, Nkambo and Kasenga in Belgian Congo after some people from Northern Rhodesia (Luapula) had gone to settle across the river. Rev. Washiama was educated in the London Missionary Society at Mbereshi Mission where he passed Standard V. His father, Chikango Milimo, was a hunter and his mother was Mwila Walulumba; both were of Chishinga ethnicity. His father died in 1921 and his mother in 1922. I sought the help of Mother Diana Mapoma who was helpful on the history of Rev. Washiama. Mother Mapoma said that she was brought up in the home of the Rev. Washiama from childhood. She also indicated that the Rev. F.B.S. Washiama went to be with the Lord on 12th September, 1979 in Chililabombwe.

Rev. Aswell Filipu Chambwe Nkhoma

Rev. Aswell Filipu Chambwe Nkhoma, a Mchewa by ethnicity was a son of Chambwe Nkhoma and Zovwa of Kunda ethnicity. Rev. Chambwe was born in 1900 at Masumba's village, Chief Mwase, Lundazi in Northern Rhodesia. He joined the A.M.E. Church at Ndola in 1931 from the Dutch Reformed Church where he was baptized in 1924. He was licensed as a Local Preacher in 1932 and appointed for the first time as pastor to Broken Hill in 1939. After being at Broken Hill for 11 years he was transferred to Mufulira where he spent five years, Luanshya one year, Chanda and Mulundu two years. In 1958, he was appointed Presiding Elder of Mporokoso District. Later, he was transferred to Fort Roseberry District (now

Mansa) where he lost his sight and pensioned in January, 1961. Rev. Chambwe was educated at Bandawe Mission of the Church of Scotland where he passed Standard III.

Rev. Moses Wright Kaunda

Rev. Moses Wright Kaunda, a Mwina Chishinga by ethnicity of Balimbu or Bee clan, was born at Kapesha's village, Chief Kazembe, Kawambwa, Northern Rhodesia in 1898. He joined the A.M.E. Church in 1932. He was educated at Johnson Falls Mission School of the Christian Missions in Main Lands (CMML) where he passed Standard IV in 1925. Rev. Kaunda was baptized in 1926 in Congo at Jadotville by Bishop Springer of the American Methodist Episcopal Church. He was first licensed to preach by Rev. J.L.C. Membe, P.E. in 1936, ordained Deacon and Elder on 24th July, 1949 in Salisbury, Southern Rhodesia by Bishop I.H. Bonner! He was first appointed Pastor to Mulundu in 1937, to Kalenda in 1941, to Kapiri Mposhi in 1947, to Lukanga in 1948 and to Kalungwishi in 1949. Rev. Kaunda was appointed Presiding Elder of Kazembe District in 1951 to 1960, Pastor of Kalenda circuit in 1961 and to Kasenga, Congo, in 1962.

Rev. Silas Kapususu Chibwe

Rev. Silas Kapususu Chibwe, a Mutabwa by ethnicity was from Mporokoso District. He joined the A.M.E. Church in 1940 and was ordained Deacon in 1949 and an Elder in 1950. After serving the Church in many places he passed away in 1960. There was no record of his life available.

Rev. Henrique Matenda Lukamba

Rev. Henrique Matenda Lukamba, a Mbundu by ethnicity from Portuguese West Africa (now Angola), was born between 1910 and 1914 at Kipongo's Village, Chief Kanjundu, Bie, Portuguese West Africa. He attended school at Chiyuka School to Standard II and Chisamba Mission School to Standard IV. He joined the A.M.E. Church in 1935 at Nkana's village under Rev. Zakaria Kamanga at the time of Rev. Lumbo of Chisamba Mission of the United Church of P.E.A. on 10th March, 1928. He was first licensed to preach on 10th October, 1937 by Rev. S.N. Sangweni, P.E., at Nkana Mine. Rev. Lukamba was appointed as Pastor on 10th November, 1940 to Nkana. At the time of writing this he had served as Pastor in many places including Nkana Mine, Nkana village, Chapula and Mukutuma. He was first appointed Presiding Elder for Lambaland District and after some years, he was appointed Presiding Elder of Copperbelt District.

Presiding Elder Rev. Henrique M. Lukamba (Then Presiding Elder of Copperbelt District in 1950s) and Rev. Stephen Victor Chambata (seated) with YPDers.

Rev. Lukamba had been brought up in the Christian faith since childhood. He had been interested in singing as a church choir member and in Sunday school. He liked to travel with the preachers to sing for them wherever they preached. When he was 15 years of age, he was so active in the work of the church generally and was elected at an early age to preach and work as a sectional leader of the young people. "I was at the same time a leader of the Choir," said Rev. Lukamba. He had, on many occasions, taken a band of choir and go about to preach the Gospel. When he was at full age, he took a keen interest in farming. He grew vegetables and other plants, the job he loved doing everywhere he went to stay. He was doing garden work besides church work. Rev. Lukamba's parents were also interested in gardening, rearing pigs, sheep, goats and cattle as well as business, selling things like clothes and other materials. Rev. Lukamba's parents were both Mbundu.

In 2017, Rev. Charles Kapungwe reached out to Rev. Henrique Lukamba's daughter, Mother Elizabeth Nelinya Lukamba Simyembe now living in Kitwe, Zambia for additional information on her father. Mother Simyembe, a widow of Rev. Warren K. Simyembe, provided him with additional information on the life of this legend and early minister of the Word of God in the A.M.E. Church in Zambia. She sent him a number of his certificates of appointments, other important documents and Mother Beatrice Lusati Lukamba's history. She couldn't find all certificates of her father. However, she wrote that her father retired in 1986 at the Annual Conference held at Bright Chapel – Kamitondo, Kitwe Zambia.

Rev. Henrique Lukamba was admitted at Kitwe Central Hospital in July 1992. When Rev. Lukamba was admitted at this hospital where I worked, I reached out to this pioneer, introduced myself and wanted to be sure that this old minister, who I loved, was safe in the hands of Jesus. He told me he was, he had that assurance and was not afraid of anything. He was one of the ministers who used to come to Jordan Chapel to preach when I was young in the early 1970s, especially during Quarterly Conferences. We prayed together in the ward and on 14th July, 1992 he went to be with the Lord, just about three days after I had prayed with the minister.

Rev. Cuthbert Yoram Katebe later recounted about the Rev. Henrique M. Lukamba. "We have just lost a warrior," he told us. "With his going away, the Church has lost almost all the history he had and maybe with him as a custodian! He is the man who could have told you nearly everything about this Church from the time it had started! Sadly, he may have taken all that history with him, we did not get all of it!" the Presiding Elder Katebe lamented. Thankfully, Rev. Charles Kapungwe heard these words and reached out to Mother Elizabeth Nelinya Lukamba Simyembe. Rev. Kapungwe, while studying the works of this man, identified the initials of this preacher in the Hymn Book and inferred immediately, they belonged to this pioneer of the Church in Zambia!

Rev. Henrique M. Lukamba is a name that cannot be forgotten in the A.M.E. Church in Zambia. He is a composer and singer whose hymns are engraved in the melody of Methodism, the ministry which was born in a song. As we gave credit to the translator of the A.M.E. Church Hymnal, Rev. J.L.C. Membe who gave this Church a unique and highly spiritual Hymn Book that ushers the singer into the presence of God, contributions of Rev. Lukamba uniquely fit in our Hymnal just as other local contributors did. His compositions would be identified by the initials "H.M.L.," which are initials for his names. Hymns number 126 stands out as he calls to the Lord "To be with us as we worship and allow his power to be outpoured on us!" Another masterful song from H.M.L is Hymn number 183, which calls on "God to send a Friend to save me!" It also tells us to "Think about his mercy which outnumbers the sand!" His other contributions are Hymn numbers 23, 78, 79 and 152. This man was sent by the Lord to minister to his people!

Rev. Joel Perhaps Mumbili Kuyumba

Rev. Joel Perhaps Mumbili Kuyumba, a Lungu-Tabwa by ethnicity, of the Bwina-Bwali clan, was born at Munkanta's village, Chief Munkanta, Kawambwa on 10th January, 1909. He was educated at Mbereshi Mission of the London Missionary Society where he passed Standard V. He joined the A.M.E. Church on 24th October, 1932, at Nkana in Kitwe. He was baptized by the Rev. H.C. Nutter of the L.M.S., in 1920, received into full membership in the A.M.E. Church by Rev. J.L.C. Membe, P.E., at Chanda's village, Mununga, Mporokoso on 11th October, 1936. Rev. Kuyumba was first appointed pastor on 22nd September, 1937 to Chilwa circuit, Abercorn. He was ordained Deacon and Elder on 24th July, 1949 in Salisbury, Southern Rhodesia by Bishop I.H. Bonner! He served as Pastor at Chilwa for three years, Chienge one year, Lukenga three years, Kasempa one year, Mazabuka seven years and Shabani, Southern Rhodesia two years. He also served at Chingola, Northern Rhodesia three years, Kitwe one year, Kayezi one year, Mumana one year and at Chibuluma one year.

Rev. Kuyumba built churches at Mazabuka and Lukanga before he came into the Ministry of the A.M.E. Church. He served as a teacher in the L.M.S. schools from 1924 to 1928. He worked as a Clerk in the Rhokana Corporation 1931 to 1934 (Rhokana Mine, now Nkana Mine) and as a Postal Clerk in 1955. Rev. Kayumba's father was a Preacher for the London Missionary Society from 1902 to 1930. The father passed away on 17th January, 1931 while his mother died in September 1932. He was still in active ministry around 1962 at the time of this writing.

Rev. Joffrey Mangesana

There is no record about the life of Rev. Joffrey Mangesana at present. Nevertheless, he is known to have served the Church for a long time. He was ordained Deacon and Elder the same day in Salisbury, Southern Rhodesia on 24th July, 1949 by Bishop I.H. Bonner! After having served the Church in many places, he was appointed Presiding Elder of Fort Jameson District (now Chipata), for three years. Rev. Mangesana was transferred to Southern Rhodesia at Wankie (now Hwange), as Pastor after which he was reappointed Presiding Elder of Fort Victoria District. He was, again, sent back to Northern Rhodesia and stationed at Chitongo in Namwala District where he was still serving when this history was being written.

Rev. Amnon Katandwe Chirwa

Rev. Amnon Katandwe Chirwa was a Mtonga by ethnicity from Chinteche, Nyasaland. He was of Kapunda clan and was born at Kawiya's village, Chief Gulu, Nkhata Bay, Nyasaland on 15th February, 1915. Rev. Chirwa was educated at Bandawe Mission Church of Scotland where he passed Standard VI in 1932. He joined the A.M.E. Church on 6th June, 1933 at Luanshya, and was baptized by Rev. H.M.C. Phiri, P.E. Rev. Amnon Chirwa was received into full membership by Rev. John Tshaka in 1936 in Southern Rhodesia. He was first licensed in March 1937 to preach by Rev. R.I. Mkwayi and was first appointed as Pastor of Bubi circuit, Southern Rhodesia in 1944.

Rev. Chirwa was ordained Deacon on 24th July, 1949 in Salisbury Southern Rhodesia and an Elder in 1957 in Lusaka by Bishop W.F. Ball. He served at the following places: Bubi, Southern Rhodesia three years; Bindula two years, Wankie one year, Chombe, Nyasaland one year; Nachula, Northern Rhodesia two years; Broken Hill two years and Ndola. He passed away at the end of 1959 to rest with his Master and Lord Jesus Christ. He died after an operation in the Ndola African Hospital and was buried at Ndola.

Rev. Manasae Siska

Rev. Manasae Siska, a Tumbuka by ethnicity of Siska clan, was born at Kapika's village, Chief Mwafulirwa, Karonga, Nyasaland. He joined the A.M.E. Church from the Church of Scotland on 2nd February, 1932, at Ndola, Northern Rhodesia. He was baptized in the A.M.E. Church by Rev. H.M. Phiri, P.E., at Ndola and was received into full membership the same day on 16th June, 1932. He was licensed to preach on 6th May, 1937, by Rev. S.N. Sangweni, P.E., Ndola. Rev. Siska was appointed Pastor to Solwezi on 5th January, 1939, where he was for two years, Chingola ten years, Kasempa one year, Kapiri Mposhi one year and Florence in Nyasaland for six years. He was ordained Deacon on 24th July, 1949 in Salisbury and Elder on

13th November, 1949 at Ndola by Bishop I.H. Bonner! He was appointed Presiding Elder of North Nyasa District in Nyasaland Conference in 1957. Rev. Siska was still on active services when this history was being written.

Rev. Elias Aaron Mvula

Rev. Elias Aaron Mvula, a Tumbuka by ethnicity, from Mzimba, North Nyasa, had little record about his life at the time of writing. However, he was educated in the Free Church of Scotland and was baptised in the same Church. He joined the A.M.E. Church in later part of 1931 at Broken Hill. Rev. Mvula was first licensed to preach by Rev. D.D. Khomela, P.E., on June 12, 1932 at Broken Hill and his first appointment as Pastor was in 1934 to Kalungwishi in Mporokoso District, Northern Rhodesia at Chanda. In 1935, he was suspended by the Government and banned from staying in the District. He moved to Toka-Toka in Kawambwa District, but it was still known that he was in the Province and was forced to leave. He came back to his Presiding Elder at Ndola and was stationed at Kitwe in 1943. Rev. Mvula was transferred to Nyasaland District and got stationed at Chitimba in North Nyasa. He was appointed Presiding Elder of Zomba District in 1957 where he was still on active service at the time of writing. Rev. Mvula was ordained Deacon in 1949 and Elder in 1951.

Rev. Dixon David Zimba

Rev. Dixon David Zimba, was a Lungu-Tabwa by ethnicity, from Itabwa in Mporokoso District. He was educated in the London Missionary Society at Mbereshi Mission, Kawambwa where he passed Standard IV and was baptized in the same Church. Rev. Zimba was one of the first members of the A.M.E. Church in Northern Rhodesia on the Copperbelt in 1931. He left Ndola to his home in Kawambwa District in 1952 with a preaching license given him by Rev. R.J. Mkwayi who was then Presiding Elder of Ndola. Rev. Zimba helped greatly in organising the Church in Luapula Province. There is no proper record of his life and activities, except that he has served the Church as Pastor and Presiding Elder in many places. They include Chibilikila, Chingola, Solwezi and Chingola again. He had also worked as Presiding Elder of Barotse Province, Pastor of Isoka, Presiding Elder of Choma District, and Pastor of Mazabuka. Rev. Zimba then went to Bancroft (now Chililabombwe) where he passed away to him above the heavens.

Rev. Joshua Simeon Bota

There is no record on the life of Rev. Joshua Simeon Bota available at present. However, he joined the A.M.E. Church in 1943 from the Dutch Reformed Church and was admitted to the Annual Conference in 1945. He was ordained Deacon in 1949 and Elder in 1951. He served the Church as Pastor at Kitwe and Broken Hill. He was dropped from the ministry in 1957 as a result of domestic affairs.

Rev. Stephen Makani Dube

No proper record of information about Rev. Stephen Makani Dube was found. Nevertheless, he was found to have been a member of the Church for many years. He was ordained Deacon in 1949 and an Elder in 1951. He served the Church as Pastor at Mazabuka and

Nachula circuits, Presiding Elder of Central Nyasa District in Nyasaland stationed at Kasungu and later on he changed his headquarters from Kasungu to Chipili in Lilongwe District. Rev. Dube was transferred to Fort Jameson District (now Chipata), Northern Rhodesia as Presiding Elder. He was still on active service at the time of this writing.

Rev. Elijah John Jeya

Rev. Elijah John Jeya was one of the early members of the Church at Ndola in Northern Rhodesia. There was no record of information about him at the time of writing except that he served the A.M.E. Church as Pastor in many places. He served at Broken Hill, Luanshya, Kitwe and Mufulira. He was transferred to Nyasaland Conference where he was still on active service at the time of writing. Rev. Jeya was ordained Deacon and Elder the same day in 1949 before he was transferred to Nyasaland!

Rev. Edward Gerald James Payne

Rev. Edward Gerald James Payne of Yao ethnicity hailed from Nyasaland. There was no record of his life and information. Only available records state that he passed Standard II in Nyasaland and joined the A.M.E. Church in the later part of 1945. He was admitted to the Annual Conference membership in 1947. Rev. Payne was dropped from the Conference Roll on 27th January, 1949 but was readmitted on 13th November, 1949. He passed to second year class on 12th November, 1950. Rev. Payne was transferred from Zambezi Annual Conference to Northern Rhodesia Annual Conference in 1953 as Pastor of Choma. He later was transferred to Mufulira and was appointed Presiding Elder of Lusaka District in 1948 and to Barotseland District in 1961. He was still on active service when this information was being compiled.

Rev. Augustino Numa

Rev. Augustino Numa, a Mbundu by ethnicity was from Portuguese West Africa (now Angola). There was no record and information available at the moment about him except that he had been a Pastor for many years at Nkana Circuit. He was ordained Deacon (Local) in 1950 and Local Elder in 1957.

Rev. Yotamu Phiri

No proper record of information about Rev. Yotamu Phiri was found. However, this writer, (Rev. Kapungwe) recalls as a boy Rev. Yotamu Phiri as the first minister he knew who was pastor of Jordan Chapel at Wusakile in Kitwe in the early 1970s. He was the father of Mr. Gideon Y. Phiri the husband to Mrs. Minerva Phiri who both had held numerous positions at Jordan before they went to begin Calvary in 1994.

Rev. Ronald Richardson Kazoba Mkandawire

Rev. Ronald Richardson Kazoba Mkandawire, a Tumbuka by ethnicity, was from Karonga, Nyasaland. He was born at Mizimba, Nyasaland on 4th November, 1909 and joined the A.M.E. Church in July 1943 at Karonga, Nyasaland. He was educated at the Livingstonia Mission of the Church of Scotland where he passed Standard VI in 1920. Rev. Mkandawire was baptized by Rev. Dr. Mackenzie of the Church of Scotland in 1910. He was received into full membership by Rev. Dr. F.H. Gow at Karonga, Nyasaland, on 30th August, 1945. Rev.

R.R.K. Mkandawire was first licensed to preach by Rev. J.L.C. Membe, P.E., in January 1946 at Karonga, Nyasaland. He, thus, served the Church as Pastor at Karonga, Nyasaland 1946 to 1948, Nachula and Choma 1949 to 1950, Mazabuka 1950, transferred back to Karonga in Nyasaland in 1953, then to Luanshya in Northern Rhodesia again in 1955. Rev. Mkandawire was transferred back to Nyasaland in the same year on his request and was appointed Presiding Elder of West Nyasa District in 1958. In 1958, he left his appointment and went to work in the Mines at Bancroft in Northern Rhodesia.

Rev. Phillip Hlabati Hara

Rev. Phillip Hlabati Hara, of Ngoni ethnicity, was from Chief Mbelwa in Nyasaland. He was educated at the Livingstonia Mission School of the Church of Scotland in Nyasaland where he passed Standard VI. He joined the A.M.E. Church at Mbeya in Tanganyika Territory and was one of the first members of the A.M.E. Church at Mbeya. Before he joined the A.M.E. Church ministry, he had been working as an Instructor in Carpentry in the Public Works Department (P.W.D). at Mbeya. Rev. Hara was baptized in Free Church of Scotland and was admitted to the Annual Conference on 9th November, 1947. He was first appointed Pastor of Mbeya, T.T. in 1948, ordained Deacon in 1950, and Elder in 1954. Rev. Hara was appointed to Mzimba where he passed away a few months after the 1954 appointment to everlasting rest and joy. Rev. Hara was a humble and a good soldier of the Lord Jesus Christ.

Rev. Lazarus Samuel Sekandiyani Saka

Rev. Lazarus Samuel Sekandiyani Saka, a Mtonga by ethnicity, was from Chinteche, Nyasaland. He joined the A.M.E. Church in 1932 at Luanshya but after some time, he went back to his old ways. He, however, finally rejoined in 1938 and was licensed to preach in 1941. Rev. L.S.S. Saka was admitted to the Annual Conference membership on 13th November, 1949, ordained Deacon in 1951, and an Elder in 1957. Rev. Saka served as Pastor to many places including Kawambwa, Mindolo, Luanshya, Kitwe, Wusakile and Broken Hill. He was baptized in A.M.E. Church by Rev. D. Khomela. Rev. Saka did not return the completed form of Information Sheet from where to find proper information.

Rev. John Duncan Phiri

Rev. John Duncan Phiri, a Yao by ethnicity, was from Nyasaland. There is no record of his life and information available at present, except that he has been a Pastor of A.M.E. Church for a long time in Southern Rhodesia and also in Northern Rhodesia at Mulobezi and Bancroft. He was ordained Deacon in 1951 and an Elder in 1957. He had been transferred back to Southern Rhodesia.

Rev. Mafukeni Fungwe Mayeba

Rev. Mafukeni Fungwe Mayeba, a Lamba by ethnicity, of Bena Muti clan was from Congo. He was born at Chitambo, Chief Munene, Kasanga, Congo. He joined the A.M.E. Church in 1931 at Ndola and was received into full membership on 10th February, 1931 at Ndola by Rev. Z.C. Mtshwello. Rev. Mayeba was baptized by Rev. Moss of the Church of Scotland in 1924 and was first licensed to preach by Rev. J.L.C. Membe, P.E., on 20th

April, 1936 at Kalenda. He was first appointed Pastor to Lwamfwa on 5th November, 1936, ordained Deacon on 4th November, 1951 and an Elder in 1957. He was once a Presiding Elder for Isoka District for one year only. He pastored at Lwamfwa, Kalenda, Lukanga, Mulundu, Kazembe, Lubunda, Nkomba, Fort Roseberry (now Mansa) and Lyuchi. He attended school at Mubende Mission where he passed Standard III. Rev. Mayeba was still on active ministry at the time of this writing.

Rev. Constantino Segers

Rev. Constantino Segers, was a Eurafrican from Livingstone, Northern Rhodesia. No record about him was available at present, except that he was ordained a Local Deacon in 1951. He passed away some years ago on the Master's service.

Rev. Mundia Kabuyana Wakunguma

Rev. Mundia Kabuyana Wakunguma, a Mulozi by ethnicity of the Namate clan, was born at Mutindi, Chief Siambyana, Senanga, Barotse Province in August, 1917. He was educated at Barotse National School and at the Union College and at Helpmakar College where he passed his Matriculation in 1943. He was baptized in the Wesleyan Methodist Church at Broken Hill by Rev. James Mullala in June 1937. He joined the A.M.E. Church in 1941 at Ndola and was received into full membership by Rev. D.D. Khomela, P.E., in 1942.

Rev. Wakunguma was first licensed to preach by Rev. R.J. Mkwayi in 1946. He was first appointed to Ngwezi on 13th November, 1949 and was ordained Deacon on 24th January, 1954 and an Elder on 25th September, 1955. He pastored at Ngwezi from 1949 to 1956, Livingstone 1957 to 1961 and was appointed Presiding Elder of Barotseland District 1956 to 1961, Copperbelt District 1962, Assistant Conference Secretary 1956 to 1958, Chief Secretary 1958 to 1962 and Treasurer of the Northern Rhodesia Annual Conference from 1961 to 1962.

Before he joined the ministry of the A.M.E. Church, he was the first African Meteorological Officer. Rev. Wakunguma opened his own business as a trader. His father and mother where born in Barotse Province. They were of Basoto-Mbunda descendents from Basotoland, South Africa and East Africa, respectively. His father was a BOMA Messenger in the Northern Rhodesia Government. He was a great fisherman, hunter and a descendant of the royal family. His mother was of the a-Yeyi-alui descendant from Kaprivi Strip and Nglu now known as Barotseland.

Rev. Batwell Phiri

Rev. Batwell Phiri, a Tonga by ethnicity of the Phiri clan, was born at Kabunduli's village, Chief Kabunduli, Chinteche, Nyasaland. He was educated in Free Church of Scotland School at Bandawe Mission where he passed Standard III in 1928 and was baptized there in 1920. Rev. Phiri was born on 15th November, 1918 and joined the A.M.E. Church on 9th September, 1941 at Selukwe in Southern Rhodesia. He was first licensed to preach in June 1942 by Rev. S.M. Kamdgshariwa, P.E., at Gwelo and was first appointed Pastor to Victoria Falls in 1951. He was ordained Deacon on 7th February, 1955 and an Elder on 13th September, 1959. Rev. Phiri served as Pastor at Victoria Falls, Bubi, Livingstone, Chingola, Broken Hill, Lusaka and

Mumbwa. He has been located.

Rev. Jacob Pardon Kensington Masabi

Rev. Jacob Pardon Kensington Masabi, a Lungu-Tabwa by ethnicity, was from Mporokoso District, Northern Rhodesia. There is no personal record available at present except that he joined the A.M.E. Church from London Missionary Society in 1941 and was first licensed to preach at Chiyanga Mission in 1947. He was ordained Deacon in 1957 and Elder in 1959. Rev. Masabi was baptized in the London Missionary Society where he also passed Standard VI. He pastored at Chiyanga, Jordan circuit, Maluza, Chilwa and many other places. He was still on active service when this history was being written.

Rev. Thomas Chisulo Siyame

Rev. Thomas Chisulo Siyame, a Mwinamwanga by ethnicity of wa-Siwale clan, was from Isoka, Northern Rhodesia. He was educated in Free Church of Scotland where he passed Standard I. He joined the A.M.E. Church in 1932 at Ndola where he was also baptized by Rev. H.M.K. Phiri, P.E., in 1934. Rev. Siyame was first appointed and licensed to preach in 1935. He was admitted to the membership of the Annual Conference in 1952. Rev. Siyame was first appointed Pastor of Minsundu in 1958 was ordained Deacon in 1957 and an Elder in 1958. He has already pastored at Minsundu, Chipensu, Fort Roseberry (now Mansa) and Matipula. He was still on active service the time this work was being written.

Rev. Johannes Muyangwa Mubita

Rev. Johannes Muyangwa Mubita, a Mulozi by ethnicity of the Namate clan from Barotseland, was born at Namayula's village, Chief Munono, Mongu. He was educated in the Paris Evangelical Missionary Society where he passed Standard VI in 1946. He was baptised in the same Church on 5th April, 1942 by Rev. A. Jalla. He joined the A.M.E. Church on 25th May, 1950 at Mulobezi. Rev. Mubita was first licensed to preach the same year by Rev. J. Marumo, P.E., in Livingstone and appointed Pastor to Serondella the same year 1950. He was ordained Deacon on 20th October, 1957, and an Elder on 17th May, 1958. He pastored at Serondella, Namushakende, Mongu, Namitome, and other places. He was still on active service when this information was being written and there was no further record available on his personal life.

Rev. Jim Jacob Nyambe

Rev. Jim Jacob Nyambe, a Mulozi by ethnicity, was from Mongu in Barotse Province. There is no record about him at present except that he was ordained Deacon in 1957 and an Elder in 1961.

Rev. Luka Mwansa

Rev. Luka Mwansa, a Luunda by ethnicity of the Bena Mbushi clan, was from Chibwili's village, Chief Chiboshi, Kawambwa, Northern Rhodesia. He was born on 26th October, 1906 at Kazembe. He was educated in the London Missionary Society School at Mbereshi Mission where he passed Standard I in 1929. Rev. Mwansa was baptized in the same Mission of the L.M.S. in November 1921 by Rev. Turner. He was first licensed to preach by Rev. H.J. Mabombo, P.E., of the A.M.E. Church, at Kazembe in 1950 and was first appointed Pastor to Lwamfwe in 1950. Rev. Mwansa was ordained Deacon on 12th September, 1957 and an Elder on 20th October, 1959. He pastored at Lwamfwe, Lubunda, Kazembe, and many other places. He was still on active service when this material was being written.

Rev. David Bangwe

Rev. David Bangwe, a Chishinga by ethnicity, was from Chama's village, Kawambwa, Northern Rhodesia. He was educated at Kawama Mission School of the Christian Missions in Many Lands in Kawambwa District where he passed Standard I. He joined the A.M.E. Church on 20th September, 1931 at Mufulira. Before he came to the A.M.E. Church, he was baptized in the American Methodist Episcopal Church in Congo by Rev. Longfield in November, 1928. Rev. Bangwe was licensed to preach on 11th October, 1932 by Rev. D.D. Khomela, P.E., at Lusaka. He was first appointed Pastor on 5th January, 1946 to Mofwe, Kawambwa. He was ordained Deacon on 20th October, 1957 and Elder on 12th September, 1959. He pastored at Mofwe, Chipensu, Lwamfwe, Chituta, Lukanga and Fort Roseberry.

Rev. Moses Makungu

The Information Sheet on Rev. Moses Makungu had not been completed and returned to the writer at the time this material was being prepared. Therefore, there was no record available except that he was ordained Deacon in 1957 and an Elder in 1959. He, however, was still on active service at the time. He pastored Kabumbwe in Choma District, Lukanga in Kawambwa District, and many other places. He was still active at the time this information was being prepared.

Rev. Samson Kayabwe

No record on Rev. Samson Kayabwe's life was available at the time of this preparation. The only record available indicates that he was ordained Deacon in 1957 and Elder in 1959. He was once a Pastor at Kitwe, Wusakile Mine Compound, and at Kambwali. At the time of this writing, he was in Mporokoso District.

Rev. Robert Kabala

No record on Rev. Robert Kabala's life was available at the time of this preparation as well. He did not complete the Information Sheet and return it to the writer. Available record, however, indicated that he was ordained Deacon in 1957 and an Elder in 1959. He is the first Presiding Elder of Katanga District in Congo where he was still serving at the time of this preparation.

Rev. Moses Wilson Chola

Rev. Moses Wilson Chola, a Lungu-Tabwa by ethnicity of the Sichula clan, was born at Chabilikila's village, Chief Mununga, Kawambwa, Northern Rhodesia on 16th April, 1907. He was educated at Mbereshi Mission School of the London Missionary Society where he passed Standard III in 1926. He was baptized in the American Methodist Episcopal Church in Congo by the Rev. John Springer on 29th March, 1929. He joined the A.M.E. Church on 7th July, 1934 at Mufulira. He was first licensed to preach on 22nd March, 1936 by Rev. J.C. Dambusa at Mufulira. Rev. Chola was appointed Pastor on 27th February, 1955 to Kansuswa, in the Copperbelt District under the Rev. J.L.C. Membe, P.E. He was ordained Deacon on 20th October, 1957, and an Elder on 13th September, 1959. He pastored at Kansuswa for two years and was then appointed Presiding Elder of Lambaland District in 1959. He was transferred to Kazembe as Pastor in 1961 where he still was at the time of writing this information.

Rev. Isaac Chulu Mumpanshya

Rev. Isaac Chulu Mumpanshya, a Musoli by ethnicity, was from Lusaka District. He was educated in the Wesleyan Methodist Church where he passed Form IV and trained as Minister of Religion for five years in the Wesleyan Methodist Church. He was appointed Pastor of Kitwe (Bright Chapel) in 1957 to 1960. Rev. Mumpanshya was given a Bursary by the World Council of Churches to study in England. He left Africa in September 1960 and came back to his work as minister of the A.M.E. Church in 1962. He did not return the completed Information Sheet from where a proper record could be written in full. He resigned from the position of Presiding Elder and from the Church to form United Methodist Church after Bishop Richard Chappelle had differences with him in Lusaka in 1991 and Rev. David Simfukwe was appointed Presiding Elder. Mother Mumpanshya, however, remained worshiping in the A.M.E. Church. The Presiding Elder has since gone to be with the Lord.

Rev. Cuthbert Yoram Katebe

There was no detailed record available about the Rev. Cuthbert Yoram Katebe, P.E., in the works Rev. Charles Kapungwe looked at. He, therefore, contacted Mother Daisy Katebe, the surviving wife of the late Rev. Katebe and he received a full history on 15th November, 2018. Rev. Cuthbert Yoram Katebe was born on 24th April 1926 at Mukupo's Village, Chief Lubunda, Mwense District in Northern Rhodesia. He was born in the family of 4 boys and 1 girl. He did his primary education at Mambilima Primary School. Rev. Katebe completed Standerd VI (Grade 8) in 1946. He was baptized and received into full membership and then went to Munali Secondary School from 1946 to 1948 where he completed Form 2 (Grade 9). He went to Wilberforce Institute in Transvaal, South Africa for training as a Minister of Religion for three years and returned to Zambia. He was the first Northern Rhodesian (Zambian) to be trained there in 1948.

Photo: Rev. Cuthbert Y. Katebe, P.E., 2000.

Appointments

After completion he was appointed to be a Pastor at one of the churches in South Africa. However, members reportedly did not accept him because they felt he was too young to be their Minister. He then returned to Zambia and was appointed to go to Solwezi rural where the church failed to support him financially. Rev. Katebe then abandoned his ministry to look for employment in the Mines. After a very short period of serving the church at Chingola as Pastor, he got employed by the Mining Company at Nchanga. He was ordained Deacon at Lusaka in 1961.

In 1963, he got a Diploma in Journalism at Press Institute from Royal College, Nairobi, Kenya in East Africa. In April 1968 he furthered his journalism career at Thomson Foundation Editorial Center in Cardif, Britain. He worked for Nchanga Mines and Rhokana Mines as a Sub-Editor with Mining Mirror up to 1971. Rev. Katebe joined Mindolo Ecumenical Center 1972-1975 and then joined Times of Zambia as a Sub-Editor in 1975-1985. He returned into Ministry in Ndola in 1975 to pursue his calling and was ordained as an Itinerant Deacon and Elder by Bishop Cornelius E. Thomas in 1977. Rev. Daniel Mkhwanazi was the Presiding Elder at the time.

Rev. Cuthbert Katebe served the Church in various capacities. In 1961, he was appointed President of the Allen Christian Endeavor League (A.C.E. League) for Northern Rhodesia Annual Conference by Bishop John Douglas Bright, Sr. On 13th November, 1977, he was appointed as Pastor of Bright Chapel by Bishop Cornelius Thomas and from 26th November, 1978 to December 1981, he was Pastor of Chifubu Church (now Kirkland Church). From May 1981 to December 1982, he was appointed Presiding Elder of Lusaka District, South Zambia Annual Conference and from December 1982 to November 1984, he served as Presiding Elder of Copperbelt District. Rev. Katebe was also appointed as Pastor of Bright Chapel in Kitwe. From December 1985 – 1992, he served as Presiding Elder of Combined Copperbelt and Roan District, appointed by Bishop Robert Pruitt. He was reappointed as Presiding Elder of Lusaka District in October 1992 by Bishop Robert Webster. In April 1993, he was appointed Presiding Elder of Copperbelt East in the South West Zambia Annual Conference. From September 1996 to March 2001, he was appointed as Presiding Elder of Copperbelt East by Bishop Larry Kirkland.

Rev. Cuthbert Y. Katebe was also President of the Presiding Elders' Coordinating Committee (Council). He was the *second* Director of Christian Education in the 17th Episcopal District from 1989 to 2001. (Prior to this Rev. J.L.C. Membe had served as Director of Religious Education. The position had been dormant until now). He rendered faithful, dedicated and loyal service under the leadership of Bishops Robert Pruitt, Robert Webster and Larry Kirkland, a total of 12 years as a Director of Christian Education. He served as Ministerial Delegate to the General Conferences in the U.S.A. Rev. Katebe attended the General Conference in New Orleans, Louisiana in 1980, in Kansas City, Missouri in July 1984, in Fort Worth, Texas in 1988 and was an observer in Orlando, Florida U.S.A. in 1992. He was given a Leadership Award presented by the Association of Zambians living in Atlanta, U.S.A. in the same year. He had the interest of the youth at heart and was always with the smile on his face. He loved his Church and was always in God's Vineyard. He passed away on 20th March, 2001.

Speaking to Rev. Wilson Mpundu, a minister with great insight and knowledge of the A.M.E. Church in Zambia, he describes the Rev. Cuthbert Katebe as "the most intelligent person he came across in the 17th Episcopal District." He says, "He was followed by the Rev. Caleb Ngoma." He would address meetings in controversies in which leaders such as Rev. Clement Mkhwanazi were present defending his views concerning the Church in Zambia.

Rev. Henry C. Alimasi

Rev. Henry C. Alimasi was born in November 1935 at Chiwala on the Copperbelt Province in Northern Rhodesia. He was born to Mr. Kabati Alimasi and Mrs. Emeria Chintabamba. He grew up at Chiwala where he attended schools at Chiwala Primary and later he went to Standard II and pursued higher education including at Mindolo. In 1975, he went to Kenya with Rev. G.W. Kanyembo and Rev. David Simfukwe where they took a short course of study. In March 1976, together with Rev. David Simfukwe, he came to Chicago, Illinois in the U.S.A. where he studied Human Development.

Photo: Rev. Henry Alimasi, P.E.

Rev. Alimasi later took a course in Finland. He started his ministry in 1965 and was ordained Deacon in 1966 and Elder in 1967. He served 14 churches on the Copperbelt Province and Lusaka. He was pastor at Chapula, St. Phillip, Chibuluma, Brookins, Mother Hughes, Brookins – Kabwe, Quinns, Bethel – Lusaka, Bright Chapel, Ndeke – Ndola, St. Paul's – Kamuchanga and Thomas – Luanshya. He was appointed Presiding Elder of Copperbelt West District in 1990. Rev. Henry Alimasi served there for 10 years. He also served as Presiding Elder of Copperbelt Central for another 10 years and retired in 2011. He had worked in the Mines too. The Rev. Alimasi went to be with the Lord on 28th August, 2013 at the age of 78. He was survived by his wife Mother Damaless Alimasi. They had eight children three of whom are deceased. Rev. Alimasi's son Henry Alimasi, Jr., was a great singer and choir leader before he passed away. Rev. Baxter Alimasi helped with part of this history.

Rev. Nathan Joel Sichone

Rev. Nathan Joel Sichone, a Namwanga by ethnicity of the wa-Sichone clan, was born at Chitipa village, Chief Nyondo, Fort Hill, Karonga, Nyasaland on 10th December, 1910. He was educated at the Livingstonia Mission of the Church of Scotland at Kondowe in Nyasaland, where he passed Standard V in 1919. Rev. Sichone was baptized in Lusaka on 20th April, 1921 in the Presbyterian Church of Scotland by Rev. Nell of Dutch Reformed Church. He joined the A.M.E. Church at Luanshya in March 1931. He was first licensed to preach on 25th September, 1955, by Rev. H.J. Mabombo, P.E., at Chiyanga Mission, Abercorn, and first appointed Pastor to Kafukula the same month. Rev. Sichone was ordained Deacon on 17th May, 1958, and an Elder on 12th September, 1959. He pastored Kafukula, Kayizya and Chisanza. Before Rev. Sichone came to the ministry of the A.M.E. Church, he worked in the Northern Rhodesia Police as Clerk, Typist and Interpreter for many years and retired on pension. He was still on active service when this information was being written.

Rev. Henry Kachinda Chikoti

Rev. Henry Kachinda Chikoti, a Mushila by ethnicity, of the Bena Nkalamo clan, was born in the Luapula Valley in Kawambwa District. He was educated in the London Missionary Society school at Mbereshi Mission where he passed Standard II. He joined the A.M.E. Church in 1932. Having served as a Local Preacher for many years, he was first appointed Pastor to Kawambwa in 1935. He pastored at Kawambwa, Fort Roseberry, Lwamfwe and Mununshi. He was ordained Local Elder in 1961. Before he came to ministry, he worked as a Cook after which he worked as a Timekeeper in Congo. The full record of his life was not available at the time this preparation was being done.

Rev. Koweni Mwabu

No record about Rev. Koweni Mwabu was available at present except that he was one of the first members of the A.M.E. Church in Luapula Province. Rev. Koweni Mwabu served the Church as one of the Local Leaders of the Church for many years. His faithful service rendered to the Church in his area made his local congregation to recommend that he be ordained Local Deacon in 1957. Rev. Koweni Mwabu's service in the Vineyard of the Lord shall not be forgotten by those who knew him. He was a faithful Christian person, a humble man who never showed a rough face to anybody even if he was annoyed or wronged. He passed away peacefully in 1959 at Musangu's village, Chief Lukwesa, Kawambwa at the service of God our Father and our Lord Jesus Christ.

Rev. Elijah Mulenga Masongo

Rev. Elijah Mulenga Masongo, a Lungu by ethnicity of the Mbao clan, was born at Chama's village, Chief Kanyembo, Kawambwa, Northern Rhodesia. He was educated in the London Missionary Society school where he passed Standard I in 1919. Rev. Masongo was baptised in the Christian Missions in Many Lands by Rev. Cross on 10th August, 1930 at Ndola. He joined the A.M.E. Church on 28th May, 1933 at Kasumpa. He was first licensed to preach at Kazembe on 20th September, 1936 by Rev. J.L.C. Membe, P.E., and also appointed Pastor to Kalungwishi in 1936. Rev. Masongo pastored at Kalungwishi, Kasumpa, Mofwe, Kabimbi in Congo and many other places. He was ordained Deacon on 17th May, 1958, and Elder in 1959! Rev. Masongo's father was a blacksmith, a Lungu from Kaoma. His mother was Bemba from Chief Mwamba in Kasama District. Rev. Masongo was still on active service when this information was being prepared.

Rev. Thomas M. Siyame

Rev. Thomas M. Siyame, a Namwanga by ethnicity of the wa-Siyame clan, was born at Mbila's village, Chief Wayitwika, Isoka on 18th January, 1909. He joined the A.M.E. Church on 11th March, 1945 at Chiwale in Isoka District. He was educated in the Free Church of Scotland at Mwenzo Mission where he passed Standard III in 1924. He was baptized in the A.M.E. Church at Chiwale in 1945 by Rev. J.L.C. Membe, P.E., on 5th April, 1945, and was first licensed to preach by Rev. J.L.C. Membe in August, 1946. Rev. Siyame was appointed Pastor to Lyuchi in 1955 where he was still on active service at the time of this writing. He was ordained Local Deacon on 20th October, 1957 and an Elder on Itinerary on 17th May, 1958.

Rev. Samuel Mambwe

Rev. Samuel Mambwe, a Chishinga by ethnicity of the Mumba clan, was born at Mulundu's village, Kawambwa, Northern Rhodesia in 1909. He was educated in the London Missionary Society at Mbereshi Mission where he passed Standard I in 1914. He was baptized in the same Church at Mbereshi in 1921 by Rev. W. Freshwater. He joined the A.M.E. Church in 1932 at Musangu's village. He was licensed to preach at Musangu by Rev. J.L.C. Membe, P.E., in 1936. Rev. Mambwe was ordained Deacon in 1957 and an Elder in 1959 and was first appointed Pastor to Mofwe in 1948. He had served as Pastor at many places including, Mofwe, Mulundu, Kasama and many more. He was still in active service the time this writing was being done.

Rev. Stephen Mambwe

Rev. Stephen Mambwe, a Lunda by ethnicity of the Mfula clan, was born at Mwansabombwe, Chief Kazembe, Kawambwa, Northern Rhodesia. He was educated at Mbereshi Mission School (L.M.S.) where he passed Standard II. He joined the A.M.E. Church in 1936 at Lwamfwe where he was baptized by Rev. J.L.C. Membe, P.E., in 1937, who also licensed him to preach in 1939. He was first appointed Pastor in 1952 to Lundashi circuit in Luapula Valley, Kawambwa. Rev. Mambwe was ordained Deacon in 1957 and an Elder in 1961. He pastored at Lundashi, Chibwe, Chibambo and Kawambwa. He has now gone to rest with his Master beyond the universe.

Rev. Benjamin Brown Burton Siyame

Rev. Benjamin Brown Burton Siyame, a Mwinamwanga by ethnicity, of the Siyame clan, was born at Chisalala, Chief Wayitwika, Isoka Northern Rhodesia in 1920. He was educated at Mwenzo Mission in Isoka District where he passed Standard IV. He was baptized in the Free Church of Scotland by Rev. Jeremiah Sinyinza in 1937. He joined the A.M.E. Church at Chiyanga Mission, Abercorn (now Mbala) in 1944 and was first licensed to preach by Rev. J.L.C. Membe, P.E., in 1945 at Chipwa, Abercorn. Rev. Siyame was appointed Pastor to Nkanchilwa, Isoka, in 1947. He was ordained Deacon on 20th October, 1957 and Elder on 24th May, 1959. He pastored at Nkanchilwa, Isoka, Chikawala, Nachula, Lusaka, Chingola and Mufulira.

He was appointed Presiding Elder in 1958 and sent to Fort Jameson District (now Chipata). In 1961, he was transferred back to Mufulira on the Copperbelt Province as Pastor where he was still serving at the time of this recording. Before he came to ministry of the A.M.E. Church, Rev. Siyame worked as a teacher of the A.M.E. Church schools at Chiyanga, Chilwa and Chipwa schools in Abercorn District. When he left teaching-work, he went back to his home in Isoka District and opened Nkanchilwa circuit there, and greatly helped Rev. Benjamin W. Chalomba of Lyuchi to spread the work of the Church in Isoka District. He opened another school at Lyuchi with an enrollment of over 200 pupils and taught at that school for two years without a salary. The school was closed in 1951 due to lack of funds to run it, and he came back to pastoral work.

Rev. Willie K. Kasanda

Rev. Willie K. Kasanda, a Chishinga by tribe of Bakunda clan, was from Kabongo, Chief Kazembe, Kawambwa, Northern Rhodesia. He was educated at Congo Institute College of the American Methodist Episcopal Church in Congo where he passed Form 3 and obtained a Diploma. He was baptized in the same Church in Congo by Rev. John M. Springer on 10th October, 1920. He joined the A.M.E. Church on July 12th, 1954. He was already an ordained Deacon from Congo and was ordained an Elder by Bishop W.F. Ball in 1959. His first appointment as Pastor in the A.M.E. Church was made on the 9th December, 1956, to Chisenga in Luapula Valley. After Chisenga, he pastored at Lukanga and Kasumpa where he was still working when this information was being written. Rev. Kasanda's father was Matalicha Ombe, a Mutabwa by ethnicity and the mother was Yandwa Chisungu – a Chishinga by ethnicity. Rev. Kasanda was a well-trained Minister and was still on active service at the time of writing.

Rev. Amon Kambole Sikazwe

Rev. Amon Kambole Sikazwe, a Lungu by ethnicity of the Sikazwe clan of Isoka, hailed from Abercorn, Northern Rhodesia. He was born at Chituta, Chief Tafuna, Abercorn in 1891. He was educated at Kambole Mission of the London Missionary Society where he passed Standard IV in 1922. He was baptized at Kambole by Rev. D. Halkings on June 6, 1916. He joined the A.M.E. Church on 16th June, 1955 at Chiyanga Mission. Rev. Sikazwe was licensed to preach by Rev. H.J. Mabombo, P.E., in 1955, and appointed Pastor on 1st September, 1956 to Kazizya, later to Isoka where he passed away to rest with the Lord and Saviour Jesus Christ. Before he came to the ministry, he was a businessman. He left the business and became the Chief Councilor in the Ulungu Court under Chief Tafuna for many years at Isoka in Abercorn District. Rev. Sikazwe was ordained Deacon in 1957 and an Elder in 1959.

Rev. Abraham Phillip Chibwe Mapoma

Rev. Abraham Phillip Chibwe Mapoma was born on 27th August 1924 to Mr. Phillip Chungu Kapopo Mapoma and Mrs. Mulenga Kabusha, Luwingu at Ipusukilo Catholic Mission in Northern Rhodesia. He attended school there, at Ipusukilo where he reached Standard VI and went to Kapatu Mission at Mporokoso for seminary but left after spending 15 years with them wanting to become a Catholic Priest. He couldn't be allowed to be Father in part due to discrimination. Rev. Mapoma trained as a male nurse and had joined Ronald Ross at Mufulira in the Mines until his retirement in 1984. He then opened a shop at Chingola and later joined the ministry.

Rev. Abraham Phillip Mapoma in Lusaka in 2018.

He joined A.M.E. Church in 1977 at Bright Temple in Lusaka. Rev. Mapoma then moved to Mufulira in 1979 at Allen Temple under the Rev. M.P.P. Mwenya. He was ordained Deacon in 1991 by Bishop Richard Allen Chappelle and in 1993 as Elder by the Bishop Robert Webster. Rev. Mapoma was appointed to Quinns at Chingola as Pastor in 1991 by Bishop Chappelle. He was transferred to Nkana (Chief Nkana's village) in 1993 where he built a church which was named after him (Phillip Mapoma A.M.E. Church). He was pastor here until 1978 when he moved to Lusaka but poor health affected his ministry and caused him to take up the Associate pastoral role at Bethel until 2011. In 2011, he moved to Mother Lisabe at Chelston, Lusaka in the same capacity. Mother Diana Mapoma provided the history to Rev. Kapungwe.

Rev. Abraham Phillip Mapoma and Mother Diana Mapoma at Phillip Mapoma A.M.E. Church, Chief Nkana, Copperbelt Province in Lusaka in 2008.

Rev. Greenfel D. Kabwe

There was no detailed record available about the Rev. Greenfel D. Kabwe. I met him when I went to do my clinical rotations at Kasama General Hospital in 1986. He was Pastor of Solomon Temple in Kasama then. He has now retired from ministry. I used to go to this church during my two months' stay in Kasama.

Chapter 21
Ministers Who Have Served the A.M.E. Church Both in Northern Rhodesia and Zambia II

Rev. Joel E.S. Membe

No record about Rev. Joel E.S. Membe was available at present. However, he was a brother of the Rev. J.L.C. Membe. When Rev. David Simfukwe was Presiding Elder in Lusaka, he appointed him pastor in Kafue where he took the charge for a year only. He also served in Luanshya and was a very charming man with a great sense of humour. Rev. Joel Membe was the father of Emmanuel Membe, a great singer and choir conductor of Hosanna Choir of Bethel in Chililabombwe and Sarah Membe who worked with me at Kitwe Central Hospital as a nurse. She was a great singer as well and sang in the same choir and won a lot of trophies during Copperbelt Choir Competitions when I sang on the Jordan Chapel Choir in Kitwe.

Rev. Susanne Membe Matale

No record about Rev. Susanne Membe Matale was available at present. She is a daughter of the Rev. J.L.C. Membe and had once been a pastor of Bethel A.M.E. Church in Lusaka. She was one of the leaders who worked in the African Jurisdiction Council (AJC) to push for election of African-born Bishops before she became a minister. She served also as W.M.S. 17th Episcopal President and General Secretary of the Christian Council of Zambia (CCZ), later known as Council of Churches of Zambia.

Rev. Frank Membe

No record about Rev. Frank Membe was available at present. He is a son of the Rev. J.L.C. Membe and had once been a pastor of Brookins A.M.E. Church in Kabwe. He attended Morris Brown College in Atlanta, Georgia in the U.S.A. He had been a member of Bright Chapel in Kitwe before. Bishop Cornelius Thomas had hoped that grooming Rev. Membe was the best bet they had in preparing him for Bishopric. However, this did not materialize. He is back in the Church after a long absence ministering in Lusaka in 2020.

Rev. Stephen Victor Chambata

Rev. Stephen Victor Chambata, a Mbundu by ethnicity, was from Portuguese West Africa (now Angola). No record about him was available at present, except that he has been a member and minister in the A.M.E. Church for many years. After having served the Church as a Local Preacher for many years at Kalulushi, he was appointed Pastor of Chapula circuit. He was ordained a Local Deacon in 1957 and an Elder in 1959. (See photo above with Rev. Henrique M. Lukamba).

Rev. Samuel Komiha

Rev. Samuel Komiha, a Yao by ethnicity, hailed from Nyasaland. There is no record about him available at present, except that he first received a Pastoral appointment to Chiwala in 1954. He was ordained Deacon in 1957 and an Elder in 1959. He is now at his own business working for his living.

Rev. Jack Nyambo

No record about Rev. Jack Nyambo could be found at present. He, however, was one of the first members at Ndola. He was first appointed Pastor to Munkulungwe in 1954, and after two years, he was appointed to Minsundu. After serving at Minsundu, he went to Chembe in Luapula where he was still working when this documentation was being done.

Rev. George Green Mandah

Rev. George Green Mandah, a Mtonga by ethnicity and Mandah clan, was from Nyasaland. He was a member of the Presbyterian Church of Scotland for many years. He went to the First World War as a soldier from 1914 to 1919. Rev. Mandah was born at Kasingo's village, Chief Mankambila, Nkhata Bay, Chinteche, Nyasaland on 2nd February, 1896. He was baptized in the Presbyterian Church of Scotland by Rev. Y.Z. Mwase at Chinteche in 1911. He was educated at Bandawe Mission where he passed Standard VI and worked as a teacher for one year. He later went to Southern Rhodesia and got employed at Shamva Mine as a Clerk in the Mine for some years.

Rev. Mandah went to South Africa in 1920 where he worked as a Medical Orderly for fourteen years. After that, he was employed as Chef. During the time he stayed in South Africa, besides his daily work, he had been doing a part time ministry in the Church and got ordained as Deacon in 1957 by the Moderator Rev. D.M. Tembo. Rev. Mandah came to Northern Rhodesia in 1959 and joined the A.M.E. Church in 1959. He joined the Pastoral work and was ordained an Elder in 1961 and pastored at Wusakile, Kitwe up to 1962.

Rev. John Balika

No record about Rev. John Balika was available at present. However, available information shows that he was ordained Deacon in 1957 and Elder in 1959.

Rev. Jim Ndalusa

No record about Rev. Jim Ndalusa was available at present. He was ordained Deacon in 1957 and the writer could not trace his whereabouts.

Rev. Abner Bright Kazunga

Rev. Abner Bright Kazunga, a Mchewa by ethnicity, was from Fort Jameson (now Chipata) in Northern Rhodesia. The Information Sheet had not been returned to the writer. Records, however, indicate that he joined the A.M.E. Church in 1952. After having served the Church at Broken Hill for many years, as one of the faithful local church leaders, he went to Mkushi and stayed there on business for many years and adjoined himself to the Anglican Church in 1955. Rev. Kazunga was recommended by the Ndola Congregation for ordination as Local Deacon in 1957, and a Local Elder in 1961. He was still serving the Church at Ndola as a

Local Elder at the time of writing.

Rev. John Chinderema Chibvuri

Rev. John Chinderema Chibvuri, a Manyika by ethnicity, was from Southern Rhodesia. No full record was available at the time of writing. He joined the A.M.E. Church in 1936 at Kawambwa when he was a Driver for Messrs. Booth North Ltd., in the Luapula Province and Northern Rhodesia. He was baptized by Rev. J.L.C. Membe, P.E., at Ndola on 10th October, 1943 at the request of his Presiding Elder, Rev. D.D. Khomela. Rev. Chibvuri was first licensed to preach in 1945, ordained Local Deacon on 26th May, 1957 and Local Elder on 22nd January, 1961 at Mufulira. Rev. J. Chibvuri has always been one of the real and faithful Christian man, sober in his character and a peace-loving man.

Rev. John Bizali Phiri

Rev. John Bizali Phiri, a Mchewa by ethnicity, was from Malawi. There is no record about him at present except that he had been a minister of the A.M.E. Church for some years and had pastored at many places including Nachula and Kabumbwe. He was ordained Deacon in 1957 and an Elder in 1961. He went back to Malawi in 1962.

Rev. Amon Chanda

Rev. Amon Chanda, a Chishinga by ethnicity, of the Nsofu clan, was born at Chungu's village, Chief Chungu, Luwingu in 1907. He was baptized in the Christian Missions in Many Lands at Kawama Mission by Rev. C. Lammond in 1924. Rev. Chanda was educated at Mubende Mission where he passed Standard II. He joined the A.M.E. Church in 1932, was first licensed to preach in 1936 at Kalenda and first appointed to Lukanga in 1952. He was ordained Deacon on 24th May, 1959 and Elder on 22nd January, 1961. Before his retirement, he served as Pastor at Lukanga, Kawambwa and in the Katanga Province in Congo. His father, Kabinda, was a Mwaushi by ethnicity and his mother a Luunda. (The writer wonders how Rev. Chanda could himself be a Chishinga by ethnicity when the parents are not?). Nevertheless, he wrote all these with his own hand like all others in this book.

Rev. Loster Sempela

Rev. Loster Sempela, a Luunda by ethnicity, of the Kunda clan, was born at Waseba's village, Chief Kazembe, Kawambwa in Northern Rhodesia in 1912. He attended no school but taught himself to write and read in his own language. He joined the A.M.E. Church in 1932 at Lwamfwe and was baptized by Rev. H.M. Phiri, P.E., of the A.M.E. Church. He was first licensed to preach in 1938 at Lwamfwe by Rev. J.L.C. Membe, P.E. Rev. Sempela was first appointed Pastor in 1952 to Mununshi and was ordained Deacon on 13th September, 1959. He was still on active service at the time of this writing.

Rev. Reuben Sumba

Rev. Reuben Sumba, a Lungu-Tabwa by ethnicity of bena-Bwali clan, was born at Kalungwishi village, Chief Mununga on 19th May, 1910 in Northern Rhodesia. He was baptized in the London Missionary Society by Rev. H.C. Nutter on 10th June, 1929. He joined the A.M.E. Church on 1st October, 1931 at Ndola. Rev. Sumba was first licensed to preach on

15th November, 1931 and was first appointed Pastor on 14th December, 1958 to Mwanande. He was ordained Deacon on 13th September, 1959 and an Elder on 22nd January, 1961.

Rev. Sumba was educated at Mbereshi Mission of the London Missionary Society where he passed Standard IV. He is the person who started the A.M.E. Church in the Lukanga area of Chief Kambwali, Kawambwa. Rev. Sumba has now pastored at Kambwali, Kazembe and Chingola. His father Sumba Sichilima was a Mufipa by ethnicity from Chief Kapufi's area in Sumbwanga District, Tanganyika Territory and his work was a blacksmith. His mother, Mwali, came from Lupososhi in Chishinga to Kalungwishi where she got married to his father Sumba. Both his parents passed away in 1927 and 1929, respectively.

Rev. Herod Nonde

Rev. Herod Nonde, a Lungu by ethnicity, of the Sinyangwe clan, was born in August, 1922 at Chilwa, Chief Zombe, Abercorn in Northern Rhodesia. He was educated in the A.M.E. Church school at Chilwa, Abercorn, where he passed Standard III in 1947. He was baptized at Kawimbe Mission (London Missionary Society) in 1922 by Rev. E.H. Clark. Rev. Nonde joined the A.M.E. Church with his father Holland Nonde and his mother in 1933 at Chilwa, Abercorn, Northern Rhodesia. His father, Holland Nonde, was first appointed Pastor to Chilwa in 1936 where he passed away at his Master's Service in 1949. Rev. Herod Nonde was first licensed to preach on 13th March, 1949, and appointed Pastor in 1950. He was ordained Deacon in 1959 and an Elder in 1961.

Rev. Johannes Kabubi

No record about Rev. Johannes Kabubi was available at present. He was ordained Deacon in 1959 and an Elder in 1961. He has been a Pastor for some years and was now Presiding Elder in Barotse Province at the time of this writing around 1962.

Rev. Cheese S. Moyo

No record was available about Rev. Cheese S. Moyo. The only available information is that he was ordained a Local Deacon in 1959.

Rev. Alexander Kabuyana Matale

No record about Rev. Alexander Kabuyana Matale was available. He was ordained Deacon in 1959.

Rev. Daniel Madubango Mkhwanazi

Rev. Daniel Madubango Mkhwanazi, a Mundebele by ethnicity from Southern Rhodesia, came to work in Northern Rhodesia. He joined the A.M.E. Church at Ndola in 1957. He was first licensed to preach by Rev. J.L.C. Membe, P.E., of the Copperbelt District. He was also appointed a Chief Steward for the Ndola circuit where he rendered a very wonderful and faithful service. His first Pastoral appointment was in 1958 to Ndola. He was ordained Deacon in 1959 and an Elder in 1961. There is no record of his life available at present to give us details about his birth or educational background. He served as Principal of the Northern Technical College (NORTEC) in Ndola, Zambia.

Rev. Clement N. Mkhwanazi D.D. *(Honoris causa)*

Rev. Clement N. Mkhwanazi, a Mundebele by ethnicity from Southern Rhodesia was born in Bulawayo, Southern Rhodesia. He was a bother to Rev. Daniel Mkhwanazi. He was educated at Wright School of Religion in South Africa where he obtained a Diploma in Religion, University of Zimbabwe where he got a Diploma in Social Work, Morris Brown College in Atlanta, Georgia where he obtained a Bachelor of Arts Degree and Atlanta University where he got a Master of Social Work with concentration in Policy, Planning and Administration. He was awarded a Certificate of Recognition in Exemplary Leadership by the A.M.E. Church in 1964 and was given a Doctor of Divinity (honorary) degree by Lee Theological Seminary in Florida.

Rev. Clement Mkhwanazi served as a Presiding Elder for 43 years in Zimbabwe. He built three churches, six classrooms at Mpindo and Malope Elementary Schools. He wrote the History of the A.M.E. Church in Zimbabwe 1900-1995 and was employed as a District Officer for the Ministry of Public Services Labour and Social Welfare. Rev. Mkhwanazi was also a Professor at Paul Quinn College in Waco, Texas where he served as Director of Gerontology from 1980-1981. (This was before the campus moved to Dallas, Texas). Rev. Clement Mkhwanazi is the father of Rev. Jordan N. Mkhwanazi a minister in Dallas, Texas. (Once, in 2000, Rev. Jordan Mkhwanazi had hosted Rev. Charles Kapungwe at his church in Dallas, Texas).

Rev. Clement Mkhwanazi went to be with Lord on 25th December, 2003. To many members of the Church in Zambia who were part of the old 17th Episcopal District, Rev. Clement Mkhwanazi was a familiar man. (The 17th Episcopal District at one time comprised Zambia, Zimbabwe, Malawi, Congo DR). Rev. Dr. Clement Mkhwanazi, a brother to Rev. Daniel Mkhwanazi, P.E., was a familiar face even though he had not been serving in Zambia but ministered in Zambia during visits.

Rev. Samson Mulonga Kapufi

There was insufficient information on Rev. Samson Mulonga Kapufi when Rev. Charles Kapungwe was writing this book. Writings from the Rev. J.L.C. Membe and Rev. David Simfukwe indicated that there were no records available about his life but accurately gave his ordination dates both as Deacon and Elder. Rev. Charles Kapungwe reached out to Rev. Samson Mulonga Kapufi, who was living in Mansa (formerly, Fort Roseberry) in Luapula Province on phone from Maine, U.S.A. in 2017. They talked on more than four occasions and Rev. Kapufi, P.E., gave invaluable information not only about himself but about the Church both historical and in contemporary times. Rev. Kapungwe provided the finances to the P.E. in order to obtain postage of valuable materials, to which he is very grateful. The bulk of this writing was based on Rev. Kapufi's contribution.

Rev. Samson Mulonga Kapufi was born on 27th December, 1927, at Chanda's village, Chief Mununga, Chienge District in Northern Rhodesia. His parents were Kapufi Maingwe and Chongo Mwila. He was converted at an early age and joined the A.M.E. Church in 1936. He was baptized by Rev. J.L.C. Membe at Chanda A.M.E. Church, the place where his father was a Senior Steward and where the A.M.E. Church was started in Chief Mununga's area in

1933. "I did my primary education at Kafulwe Mission School and qualified to go to Mbereshi Boys Boarding School where I did my Standard VI in 1948," writes Rev. Kapufi.

Photo: Rev. Samson Kapufi.

Rev. Samson married on 6th October, 1952 to Maicah Mpundu. "Born to this union," he says, "are: Loveness Sume Kapufi, Jess Chongo Kapufi, Chalomba Samson Kapufi, Katebe Samson Kapufi, Suzan Mwila Kapufi, Josephine Mutakwa Kapufi, Chisala Samson Kapufi and Maicah Katayi Kapufi." He was received into full membership on 5th December, 1951 by the late Rev. M.W. Kaunda at Chanda A.M.E. Church. He served as a Local Preacher, Church Secretary, Senior Steward, Class Teacher and District Secretary before he became an Itinerant Preacher. Rev. Kapufi was admitted on 18th December, 1956 to South Zambia Annual Conference which was held in Livingstone and obtained his first Pastoral Appointment from Bishop William F. Ball. He was ordained Deacon on 22nd May, 1959 at Lusaka by Bishop William F. Ball and an Elder on 21st January, 1961 at Mufulira by Bishop J.D. Bright. He was appointed Presiding Elder at Kitwe on 9th September, 1964 by Bishop H.I. Bearden.

When the South Zambia Conference was split into two Conferences, North Zambia and South Zambia Conferences in 1972, Rev. Kapufi was elected North Zambia Conference Secretary. He served in this position until 1979. He was elected Conference Leader and Chairman of the Board of Examiners from 1979 to 1984. In 1984, North Zambia Conference was split into two Conferences, North-East and North-West Zambia Conferences. From 1984 to 1996, Rev. Kapufi continued to serve as a Conference Leader and Chairman of Board of Examiners for North-West Zambia Conference. From 1996 to 2000, he was elected on Coordinating Committee and Chairman of Board of Examiners. He was elected on "New Eyes to See," from 2000 to 2001 and from 2001 to 2002. He was also elected Bishop's Administrative Assistant for North West Zambia Conference.

Rev. Kapufi stepped down from Presiding Eldership due to illness in 2002. He however, was to be considered for Pastoral Appointment. He was appointed to pastoral charge of Dr. Membe A.M.E. Church in Mansa District from 2002 to 2005. He had pastored at Pansa,

Chanda, Kamekela/Senkwe, Kambwali, Chipipya, Kasumpa and Dr. Membe A.M.E. Church. He served as Presiding Elder for Mporokoso/Kaputa District, Nchelenge/Chienge District, Mansa/Mwense District and Kawambwa West District.

Rev. Kapufi was a ministerial delegate to the General Conferences of the A.M.E. Church held in New Orleans, Louisiana U.S.A. in 1980. He also was a delegate to the General Conference held in Fort Worth, Texas U.S.A. in 1988. He built St. Thomas A.M.E. Church in Mansa and Chanda A.M.E. Church in Chief Mununga's area. He praises the Lord for keeping his soul with a Psalm, Psalm 23 and a hymn, from the Bemba A.M.E. Hymnal #118 and American Hymnal (A.M.E. Church) 188, *"Leaning on the Everlasting Arms."* When Rev. Charles Kapungwe spoke to Rev. Kapufi on the phone on August 18, 2018, Rev. Kapufi recalled how the Church positioned itself during the struggle for independence. He recalled, "We supported the leaders who were fighting for independence by praying for them and offering encouragement that they remained strong."

Rev. Boniface Mulenga

No record or particulars about Rev. Boniface Mulenga were found. Information found about him indicated that he had been a Pastor at Wusakile (Jordan Chapel) in Kitwe and Nkana circuits. He was ordained Deacon in 1959. He left the Pastoral work in 1960 to an unknown place.

Rev. Friday Kawanda

No record or particulars on Rev. Friday Kawanda are available at present. Information found stated that he is still a Pastor in Solwezi District. He was ordained in 1959.

Rev. Kenneth Banda

Rev. Kenneth Banda, a Ngoni by ethnicity, of the Banda clan was from Fort Jameson (now Chipata), Northern Rhodesia. He was one of the first members of the A.M.E. Church at Ndola in 1931. He has been a faithful member of the A.M.E. Church all along and was ordained a Local Deacon in 1959 and an Elder (Local) in 1961. He was still an active member of the Church in the year 1962.

Rev. V. Peter Mumba

Rev. V. Peter Mumba, a Chishinga by ethnicity, of Zimba clan, was born at Lobola's village, Chief Kabanda, Kawambwa in 1910 in Northern Rhodesia. He attended no school anywhere, but he taught himself to write and read his own language. He joined the A.M.E. Church at Ndola in 1931 and was baptized by Rev. Z.C. Mtshwello in Ndola in 1931. He was a leader of the Choir for many years in Luapula Province at Kazembe. He was licensed to preach by Rev. J.L.C. Membe, P.E., in 1938, and appointed Pastor in 1950 to Mankanka. He has served the Church in many places. Rev. Mumba was ordained Deacon on 22nd January, 1961. He was still on active service in the ministry of the Church at the time of writing.

Rev. James C.K. Mukobe

Rev. James C.K. Mukobe, a Mutabwa by ethnicity of the Mbao clan, was born at Chibwe's village Chief Kazembe, Kawambwa in Northern Rhodesia in 1925. He was educated at

Mubende Mission where he passed Standard V. He joined the A.M.E. Church on 5th April, 1939 and was baptized by Rev. B.B. Chisela of the A.M.E. Church in 1946. Rev. Mukobe was licensed to preach in the same year in 1946. He was appointed Pastor in 1953 to Mutipula, then to James Chiwasha. He was still in active service at the time this information was collected.

Rev. Petro Chileshe

Rev. Petro Chileshe, a Tabwa-Lungu by ethnicity of the Bena-Bwali clan, was born at Lwali's village, Chief Lwali, Mporokoso in 1898. He attended school at Mbereshi Mission where he passed Standard III. He was baptized in the London Missionary Society at Mbereshi by Rev. H.C. Nutter in 1909. He joined the A.M.E. Church in 1932. Rev. Chileshe was licensed to preach in 1956, was appointed Pastor in 1957 and ordained Local Deacon in 1961. He is now retired from active service.

Rev. Stephen Bright Kopa

Rev. Stephen Bright Kopa, a Mambwe by ethnicity, hailed from Abercorn. No record or particulars were found, except that he had been a member of the A.M.E. Church for many years. He was ordained Deacon in 1961 and appointed to Isoka District as Pastor to Nakonde.

Rev. James Mwape

No record or particulars about Rev. James Mwape are available about him. However, the information holds that he had been a member of the A.M.E. Church for many years since 1934. He was ordained Deacon in 1961.

Rev. Donald Kapesa Katanga

There is no record or particulars about Rev. Donald Kapesa Katanga available at present. He is one of the first appointed Pastors to Katanga in Congo. He was ordained Deacon in 1961 by Bishop J.D. Bright, Sr.

Rev. Paulos Kamanga

Rev. Paulos Kamanga, a Mtumbuka by ethnicity, was from Nyasaland (now Malawi). He joined the A.M.E. Church in 1932 at Broken Hill and he has been a Local Preacher for many years. There is no record and particulars available about him at present. He was ordained Local Deacon at Mufulira in 1961 by Bishop J.D. Bright, Sr.

Rev. Matthew Silavwe

Rev. Matthew Silavwe, a Mwinamwanga by ethnicity of wa-Silavwe clan, was from Isoka District in Northern Rhodesia. There is no record and particulars about him at present, but he has been a member of the African Methodist Episcopal Church for many years. He was ordained Local Deacon for Mufulira circuit in 1961. He is a very efficient and active member of the Church in his area.

Rev. Godfrey Wilson Jere

Rev. Godfrey Wilson Jere, a Ngoni by ethnicity, was from Mzimba, Nyasaland. There is no record or particulars about him at present. He has been a member of the Church for a long time at Mufulira and Luanshya. After having served as Pastor at Mulungushi, Broken

Hill and Lwamfwe, he neglected his appointment due to some unavoidable circumstances in Luapula Valley and left everything. His whereabouts is not known. He was ordained in 1961 at Mufulira as Deacon by Bishop Bright, Sr.

Rev. Samuel B.K. Yanduli

Rev. Samuel Blackson K. Yanduli, a Chishinga by ethnicity, was born in Chief Mushota's village, Kawambwa, Northern Rhodesia. He was educated at Johnston Falls Mission School (C.M.M.L.), and at Mbereshi Mission (L.M.S.) where he passed Standard VI. He was baptized at Toka-Toka, Kawambwa in 1946 by Rev. H.J. Mabombo, P.E. He was licensed to preach in 1947. Rev. Yanduli was appointed Pastor of Kitwe in 1956 and Luanshya in 1961. He was ordained Deacon in 1961 and is a teacher by profession. He is now a full-time teacher at one of the schools on the Copperbelt Province.

Rev. Rowland Katemba Mwenyo

Rev. Rowland Katemba Mwenyo, a Mumbundu by ethnicity, was born at Ngamba Village in Portuguese West Africa (now Angola). Details about his life history were not available; therefore, Rev. Charles Kapungwe reached out to his son and minister Rev. Jeremiah Mwenyo who provided part of this important biography. Rev. Jeremiah, the son, was ordained on same dates with Rev. Kapungwe by Bishop Larry Kirkland. Rev. R.K. Mwenyo came to Northern Rhodesia in 1936 and settled at Chupa Village, Chief Nkana on the Copperbelt Province where he met Dofilia Kafeka and got married on 27th April, 1941. Rev. Rowland Mwenyo joined ministry in 1941. He was Pastor of various churches and planted churches in Chief Nkana's area on the Copperbelt. Rev. Mwenyo moved to Chibuluma Township where he came into contact with a politician, Timothy Kankasa, a member of the African National Congress (ANC). Here, he gave refuge to the freedom fighters such as Harry Nkumbula, David Kenneth Kaunda, Mainza Chona and others.

Rev. Mwenyo got transferred to Mufulira in 1963, a year before independence. He became Pastor at Allen Temple. He also planted St. Paul at Kamuchanga as a preaching point. Rev. Mwenyo was appointed Presiding Elder for Zambezi District where he traveled extensively opening churches in Solwezi, Kabompo, Kasempa and Zambezi. In 1971, he was sent back to Allen Temple. He later was appointed Pastor of Mother Hughes in Ndola, his final posting in the A.M.E. Church where he resigned in 1983.

Rev. Rowland Mwenyo and Mother Dofilia Kafeka Mwenyo in 1968 as Pastor of Mother Hughes in Ndola.

He faced a lot of opposition and persecution for his strong belief in the power of the Holy Spirit. He preceded the Rev. Peter M.P. Mwenya in wrestling this Church out of the jaws of Satan as one of the forerunners to birthing of a revival in the A.M.E. Church in Zambia. Rev. Mwenyo died in a road traffic accident on 6th December, 1983 and went to be with the Lord. Mother Dofilia Kafeka Mwenyo is the contributor of Hymn Number 151, *"Seni mutumfwe mwe Lesa"* with the initials "Mrs. R.M.," in the Bemba Hymnal. According to Rev. J.L.C. Membe, "Rev. R. Mwenyo has been a very faithful member of the A.M.E. Church for many years. He was one of the best bands of the Choir in the A.M.E. Church we have ever had in this particular area of the Copperbelt, and one of the best singers. He has been a Pastor at many places on the Copperbelt Province. He was ordained Deacon in 1961." Mother Elizabeth Simyembe and Rev. Jeremiah Mwenyo confirmed the initials of Mrs. R.M. as those of Mrs. Rowland Mwenyo, i.e., wife of Rev. Rowland Mwenyo.

Rev. Francis Chiku Paikua Banda

Rev. Francis Chiku Paikua Banda, a Musena by ethnicity was from Portuguese East Africa (now Mozambique). He was born at Mponda's village, Chief Mponda, Paikua Seana, Chipanga in Portuguese East Africa on 5th May, 1923. He joined the A.M.E. Church on 3rd October, 1959 at Kansunswa, Mufulira. He was converted by the Rev. J.L.C. Membe from where he had been a minister of the African Holy Spiritual Church where he was also baptized by the Rev. N.J. Ramoroesi on 3rd January, 1954. He was educated at Mathonga

Mission School, Beira, Portuguese East Africa where he passed Standard I. Rev. Banda was re-obligated to the ministry and admitted to the ministry of the A.M.E. Church by Bishop J.D. Bright, Sr., on 22nd January, 1961 and appointed Pastor of Lusaka at the same time. After Lusaka, he was appointed to Solwezi. He was still on active service in 1962 when this writing was being compiled.

Interestingly, Rev. Banda had served at Jordan Chapel, Wusakile in Kitwe in 1976. He had been Pastor to Bro. Charles Kapungwe at the time Charles was active in the youth and Sunday school. In 1994, the now retired Rev. Banda who had been approached to look for a Pastor to run a church which had been started by a missionary in Kitwe from the Korean Methodist Church and was still under construction reached out to Bro. Charles Kapungwe. Bro. Kapungwe at the time was Senior Steward at Calvary A.M.E. Church and two years later was to be appointed as Pastor of Trinity. Rev. Kapungwe, however, had declined the offer. Rev. Chiku Banda meant well and the new church building was on the property Rev. Banda was living on at a farm. The team had met with sponsors and some personal friends and believers from the A.M.E. Church too at Rev. Kapungwe's home in Parklands, Kitwe. Rev. Banda has now gone to be with the Lord.

Rev. J.M. Lukonga
There is no record or particulars available about Rev. J.M. Lukonga at present. However, he is known to have come from the New Apostolic Church as Deacon and joined the A.M.E. Church ministry in 1959. He was re-obligated in 1961 by Bishop Bright, Sr., at Mufulira. The Rev. J.L.C. Membe, at the time, wrote, "He is perhaps still on active service in Barotse Province."

Rev. Jonas Lesapi Honoko
There is no record or particulars available about Rev. Jonas Lesapi Honoko at present. Information available is that he was a Pastor for many years in Transvaal, South Africa, and was transferred to Northern Rhodesia to take the place of Rev. J.L.C. Membe at Broken Hill in 1932. He was ordained Deacon in 1933 and an Elder in 1935 in Bulawayo, Southern Rhodesia. He was transferred to Southern Rhodesia in 1936.

Rev. Johannes Mabombo
Rev. Johannes Mabombo, a Xhosa, was from South Africa. He had been a preacher in the Wesleyan Methodist Church in South Africa for many years where he was also ordained as Deacon in 1923 before he joined the A.M.E. Church. There is no record to give us his particulars to show the year he joined the A.M.E. Church or when he did come to Northern Rhodesia. He was ordained an Elder in the A.M.E. Church in Bulawayo. He was transferred to Mulobezi in Northern Rhodesia, and later to Machile in Livingstone District. Rev. Mabombo was appointed Presiding Elder of Kawambwa District in 1942. He was transferred to Abercorn District in 1946 and Mporokoso District in 1959 where he ended his earthly life. He died peacefully in the Mbereshi Mission Hospital, Kawambwa and was buried at Kazembe, seven miles away from Mbereshi Mission.

Rev. Mabombo was known by his love to everybody. He smiled anytime even if he is disappointed or annoyed. He was a very sincere servant of God. A few hours before his death he asked for the Holy Communion and Rev. M.W. Kaunda administered the Lord's Supper to him in Hospital at Mbereshi and said a few farewell words to those present and thanked Rev. Kaunda for the Holy Communion administered to him. An hour later, he breathed his last breath, and went to rest with his Master up yonder.

Rev. Robert Zuze Mpezeni

Rev. Robert Zuze Mpezeni, a Nsenga by ethnicity, was from Petauke, Northern Rhodesia. He, nevertheless, told people that he was Ngoni by ethnicity but those who knew him and his parents say he and his parents were Nsenga. There is no record and particulars about him available at present, except that he joined the A.M.E. Church in 1928 in Southern Rhodesia and served as Pastor in many places. He was transferred to Northern Rhodesia in 1940 as Presiding Elder of Lusaka District with his headquarters at Nachula in Choma District. He was transferred from Lusaka District to Luanshya as Pastor after which he was transferred to Nkana. After some years, Rev. Mpezeni was reappointed Presiding Elder to Fort Jameson (now Chipata). He was transferred again to Livingstone District in 1959. He was later expelled from the ministry and membership of the A.M.E. Church. Rev. Mpezeni was ordained Deacon in 1931 and an Elder in 1933.

Rev. Hannington N. Ziyezwa

No proper record or particulars about Rev. Hannington N. Ziyezwa could be found. However, he was a Mohangani by ethnicity from Southern Rhodesia. He was a member of the A.M.E. Church for many years in Bulawayo. Rev. Ziyezwa was sent by the Zambezi Annual Conference of the A.M.E. Church to Wilberforce Institute, Transvaal, South Africa, for Theological Seminary School in 1943. After his training, he came back to Southern Rhodesia and worked as pastor at one or two points in Southern Rhodesia. He was then transferred to Lusaka as Pastor and Presiding Elder of the Lusaka District in 1946. Rev. Ziyezwa was also transferred to Ndola as Presiding Elder of the Copperbelt District in 1948. During the time, he went to meet the Lord and Master beyond the sunset to the Glory of God, and to the everlasting life.

He was the first Assistant Superintendent of the A.M.E. Church in Northern Rhodesia until his death. Many who knew him and worked with him shall never forget his faithfulness, kindness, and sober life. Really, he was a faithful Christian and a good servant of God. He is commended to the "Safe arms of Jesus." Rev. Ziyezwa was ordained Deacon and Elder the same day by the visiting Bishop Gregg in 1944 in South Africa! Rev. Charles Kapungwe remembers the name of "Ziyezwa Choir" of Bright Chapel A.M.E. Church in Kitwe, Zambia which produced singles on wax in the 1980's as the group that was named after the first Assistant Superintendent of the A.M.E. Church in Zambia.

Rev. Dr. Samuel J.N. Tladi

No record or particulars about Rev. Dr. Samuel J.N. Tladi were available at present. However, he was a member of the A.M.E. Church for many years in South Africa and Southern

Rhodesia. He was transferred to Northern Rhodesia from Southern Rhodesia in 1954 as Presiding Elder and Pastor of Lusaka District. At the time of this documentation he was still on active service in Southern Rhodesia as Presiding Elder.

Rev. Ishack Basin Sithole

Rev. Ishack Basin Sithole, a Changani by ethnicity of the Sithole clan, was born at Magiyo's kraal, Chief Ndima, Chapinga, Gazaland, Southern Rhodesia in 1900. He was educated at Rusitu Mission School of the South African General Mission where he passed Standard VI in 1926. He was baptized there by Rev. John E. Hauch on 17th October, 1916. He joined the A.M.E. Church in 1931 at Salisbury. After having served as teacher at one of the schools in Southern Rhodesia, Rev. Sithole was appointed Pastor to Fort Victoria. He was ordained Deacon and an Elder in Salisbury on 24th July, 1949!

Rev. Warren W. Kalo Simyembe

I didn't have the name of Rev. Warren W.K. Simyembe in my historical "Q-source!" The expression is borrowed from Theologians who think that the synoptic gospels of Matthew, Mark and Luke are similar, therefore, they think that they may have copied from one another or that Matthew and Luke could have used Mark or another source called "Q source." I was blessed again to seek for the help of Mother Elizabeth Nelinya Lukamba Simyembe whose husband had passed away in 1971. Mother Simyembe was also a daughter of the greatly admired late former P.E., of the Copperbelt and one of the pioneers of the Church in Zambia, Rev. Henrique Lukamba. She gave me valuable history about her late husband.

Rev. Warren W. Kalo. Simyembe, a Lungu by ethnicity, was born at Isoko Village, Chief Tafuna at Abercorn (now Mbala) in Northern Rhodesia on 23rd February, 1932. When he was 12 years and being the last born in the family of three, two sons and one daughter, he was dedicated to the Church by his parents, the late Mr. and Mrs. Samuel Katako Simyembe while still at the same village in 1945.

Warren Kalo Simyembe was taken to Bulawayo, Southern Rhodesia (now Zimbabwe) by Rev. J.L.C. Membe to continue with his primary and secondary education. He was left there under the pastoral care of the late Rev. and Mama Lesabe of Young's Chapel A.M.E. Church, Bulawayo. The Lasabes played a role in sending Warren to Wilberforce Theological College in South Africa. His first appointment was at Gweru A.M.E. Church before he decided to come home to Northern Rhodesia in 1955. (The detailed history of how the A.M.E. Church came to the Union of South Africa in 1896 written in this book is credited to Rev. Simyembe who had written about this and Rev. Kapungwe had read through his paper).

He became Pastor of Buchi Circuit (now Bright Chapel) in Kitwe on the Copperbelt, the same year, 1955. The congregation used to meet at Buseko Primary School at Buchi, Kitwe and Bro. Gideon Miyanda was Senior Steward. The 1955 Annual Conference appointed him Pastor at Bancroft Circuit (now Chililabombwe, at Bethel). On July 28th, 1956, Rev. Warren Simyembe got married to a beautiful young lady named Elizabeth Lukamba, daughter of the Rev. Henrique Lukamba at Jordan Chapel, Wusakile, Kitwe.

At the Annual Conference of 1956, Rev. Simyembe was moved again to Chingola. He was appointed Pastor of Chingola Circuit. He built the church at Chingola Mine Township which he named Mt. Pisgar A.M.E. Church, and later it was changed to Brookins Chapel after his death. In 1958, Rev. Simyembe was promoted as Presiding Elder of Lusaka District and was stationed at Ebenezer. During this time, he decided to go to back to school for another career in East Africa. In September 1959, he left for East Africa and came back in October 1964. He rejoined Ministry in 1966 and took charge of Ndola's Masala A.M.E. Church, Zambia. Among his activities, he wrote a pamphlet called, "IMPUKA YA BA MANYANI" or "LESSONS FOR THE WOMEN'S MISSIONARY SOCIETY" in 1956 and others. He went to be with the Lord on 15th October, 1971 leaving behind a wife and five children. The cause of his death was Asthmatic bronchitis. He passed away at Kabwe General Hospital in Kabwe (formerly, Broken Hill), Zambia.

Rev. Kennedy Mazimba

Rev. Kennedy Mazimba was born at Mbala General Hospital on 2nd February, 1979. He is a son to Mr. Thomas Nondo Mazimba and Mrs. Beatrice Mwambazi Mazimba. He is of Lungu ethnicity from Mpulungu District, Senior Chief Tafuna. He is married to Yvonne Nayame Mazimba and they have a daughter, Serah Twiza and two sons, Timothy Lyapah and Favaur Nondo Mazimba. Rev. Mazimba, Presiding Elder, obtained an Advanced Diploma in Theology from Bible College of Western Australia and is now pursuing a degree at Logos University. Additionally, he has an Advanced Diploma in Logistics and Transport from the Zambia Institute of Management (ZAMIM) and National Institute of Public Administration (NIPA). He also has a Craft Certificate in Automotive Mechanics from Lukashya Trades Training Institute in Kasama. He joined the Church when he was a baby in 1979 and served in YPD as a youth.

Rev. Mazimba was admitted in ministry in 2006. This was at the Annual Conference hosted by Bethel at Mpulungu by North East Zambia Annual Conference. He was ordained Deacon in 2008 by Bishop Paul J.M. Kawimbe at St. Thomas at Nakonde by the North East Zambia Annual Conference and Elder in 2010 at Bethel at Mpulungu by Bishop Kawimbe. He was appointed as Pastor at Membe Temple in Kasama District in 2005. While working for the Government at Mungwi, Rev. Mazimba started a church there in 2005. He also was appointed Pastor of Solomon's Temple in Kasama District in 2008 and was Pastor at Bonner Chapel in Mbala South.

Bishop Wilfred J. Messiah appointed Rev. Kennedy Mazimba Presiding Elder for Mbala North in 2016. He served as Director for North East Zambia Conference Board of Christian Education, Secretary of the Board of Examiners and Coordinator of Kawimbe Theological School. Rev. Mazimba served as Secretary for the Conference for seven years and served in Kasama District as well. Rev. Kennedy Mazimba worked as Assistant Control Officer of Transport in the Zambian Government's Provincial Administration Northern Province (PANP) and as Chauffeur for Ministers and Permanent Secretaries. He was also a Mechanic at Water Affairs Department.

Bishop Paul Jones Mulenga Kawimbe

Bishop Paul Jones Mulenga Kawimbe was born to Mr. Kelvin Tandeo Mulenga Kawimbe and Mary Chanda Kawimbe. He is a former Pastor of Membe and Bethel A.M.E. Church in Lusaka, Zambia. He obtained a Diploma in Biblical Studies from Kaniki Bible College in Ndola and a Certificate in Evangelism from Haggai Institute in the UK. Full scholastic history was not available at the time of this preparation. He was a Secretary of the South-East Zambia Annual Conference, Dean of the South Zambia Annual Conference and former Presiding Elder of the Lusaka East District. He taught during the 17th Episcopal District Christian Education meetings and was the Vice Board Chair of Theological Education by Extension in Zambia (T.E.E.Z.) and Dean for His People Bible School International based at the University of Zambia, Lusaka where he also was once a Chaplain. He founded the A.M.E. Church in Kenya which is now a Conference on its own. He was elected as the 121st Bishop of the A.M.E. Church in Indianapolis, Indiana U.S.A. and was sent to the 17th Episcopal District in 2004. He served Zambia for 8 years and was transferred to the 19th Episcopal District in South Africa in 2012.

He is married to Episcopal Supervisor, Dr. Lister M. Kawimbe. The following are the children: Lethabo, Christopher, Emmanuel, Joshua, Paul Jr., Koketso, Damaris and Jemima Kawimbe. He is a grandfather to Paul, Kutlwano, Emmanuel, Kamogelo and Katlego. After the passing away of his first wife Yvonne Chinakila Kawimbe in 2010, Bishop Kawimbe remarried Dr. Lister M. Kawimbe who hails from South Africa.

Mother Carrie Nelson (wife of Presiding Elder Willie Nelson), Rev. Leroy Cannon (my Senior Pastor at White Hall A.M.E. Church in Jenkinsville South Carolina where I was Associate Pastor from 2000 to 2005), Rev. Charles Kapungwe and Bishop Paul Kawimbe. In front, Mother Helen Cannon (in a hat) and Supervisor Yvonne Chinakila Kawimbe at Allen University, Columbia, South Carolina U.S.A on 23rd July, 2004.

Rev. Dr. Stephen Chifunda

Rev. Stephen Chifunda was Pastor of St. Andrews and Richard Allen churches in Ndola. His father had been an A.M.E. Pastor. Rev. Dr. Chifunda had served in the Y.P.D. for a long time in the South Zambia Annual Conference before becoming a Pastor. He sourced about $7,000.00 which helped to build St. Andrews A.M.E. Church in Ndola, Zambia. He moved to the U.S.A. in 2004 and obtained a Doctor in Ministry. He has been Pastor of Reed's Chapel in Young's Town in Ohio since 2016.

Rev. Dr. Stephen Chifunda attended Kalonga Secondary School in Kabwe, Zambia where he obtained a School Certificate in 1979. He then studied at Zambia Industrial and Mining Corporation (ZIMCO) Institute of Management now called Zambia Institute of Management (ZAMIM) in Lusaka, Zambia. He obtained a Diploma in Marketing in 1982. He moved to the U.S.A. in 2004 and obtained an Associate in Biblical Studies degree from Andersonville Theological Seminary, Camila in Georgia in 2005. He obtained a Bachelor of Divinity in 2008, a Master of Divinity in 2010 and a Doctor of Ministry in 2011 from the same school.

Dr. Chifunda worked at the University Teaching Hospital, Lusaka Zambia as a Store's Manager from 1983 to 1986. He also worked at Ndola Central Hospital, Ndola from 1986 to 1994 in the same capacity. Rev. Chifunda worked at the Associated Chemicals Limited, Ndola, Zambia from 1995 to 2003 as a Sales and Marketing Manager. He was Pastor of Holiness Temple A.M.E. Church (now Kirkland), Richard Allen A.M.E. Church in Ndola from 2001 to 2002 and St. Andrew A.M.E. Church in Ndola from 2002 to 2003. He served as Associate Pastor at Lee Memorial A.M.E. Church in Cleveland, Ohio U.S.A. from 2005 until his appointment by Bishop McKinley Young as Pastor of Reeid's Chapel A.M.E. Church in Youngs Town, Ohio in the U.S.A in 2016. He joined two other Zambians as Pastors in the U.S., Rev. Nathan Mugala in Florida and Rev. Paul Mugala who had been a Senior Pastor together with Faith Mugala, Associate Minister in 2008 of Pleasant Valley A.M.E. Church in Detroit Michigan.

Rev. Chifunda served many Bishops while in Zambia. He used to drive the Bishops to the remotest parts of Zambia during his tenure in Zambia. Among those Bishops he served were Bishop Robert Lee Pruitt, Bishop Richard Allen Chappelle, Bishop Robert V. Webster, Bishop Larry T. Kirkland and Bishop Preston Williams.

Rev. Philemon Chakalipa Mumba

Rev. Philemon Chakalipa Mumba was born in 1928 at Nsakwa village, Puta, Chienge in Luapula in Northern Rhodesia. He completed primary school at Puta and went to Ponde Secondary School. Rev. Mumba was a Tailor by profession. He married Mellise Kafwanka in 1957 and they had 8 children, 2 boys and 6 girls. The family resided at Bulangililo Township in Kitwe and was congregating at Bright Chapel at Buchi under the leadership of Rev. J.L.C. Membe. When Rev. Membe left, Rev. David Simfukwe took over as Pastor of Bright Chapel. Br. Mumba was a very committed believer and was highly dedicated to the Lord's work.

In 1974, the family shifted to Twatasha Township in Kitwe. The family, however, continued to commute to Buchi for church. Rev. Philemon Mumba was received into Full Membership on 17th February, 1968. He was ordained a Local Deacon on 12th November 1977 by Bishop Cornelius Thomas and Local Elder on 30th November, 1979 by Bishop Thomas. Rev. Mumba was given his first appointment to open and run a church at Twatasha. There was no structure or building where they could meet at the time. Rev. Mumba, however, offered his residence, House No. 42 Twatasha for church services until 1977.

When the church acquired land to build the Lord's temple while still at Twatasha, he opened up two new points for prayers. They were one at Garneton, now known as Trinity and the other at Kawama/Kamatipa in 1979. Rev. Mumba was appointed Pastor to Jordan Chapel in Kitwe from 30th November, 1980 to 1985 by Bishop Thomas. He was Pastor to Charles Kapungwe at Wusakile. He was then transferred to Gethsemane (at Luangwa) in Kitwe from 22nd December, 1985 to 1988 by Bishop Robert Pruitt. From 9th October, 1988 to 1992 he was appointed to Quinns Chapel in Chingola by Bishop Richard Allen Chappelle.

Rev. Mumba was a faithful servant of God and served his God diligently. He was kind, served with honesty and love. His teachings focused mainly on hard-working, love and unity. He answered to the Lord's call on 9th November, 1992 after an illness at Wusakile Mine Hospital in Kitwe. A softly spoken man, Rev. Mumba is missed by many as he was a father and mentor to many. May he rest in peace till we meet again. "I always feel your presence dad!" – Vivian, his daughter writes. Hymn No. 37 was his favourite in the Bemba Hymnal. *"Nacetekela Yesu pantu enkwela yandi,"* i.e., "I trust in Jesus because he is my shield."

Rev. Kapungwe had reached out to Sis. Vivian Mumba Kaoma, the beautiful daughter of Rev. Mumba for this history. He is grateful that Sis. Vivian was of great help. Indeed, Rev. Mumba was a great minister of the Lord full of love and a hard-worker. There was no home he never knew and he did home visitations daily when he was our pastor at Jordan Chapel in Kitwe! If you came to Jordan Chapel in the 1980s 30 minutes' late, then you needed to be prepared to follow the services from the windows, outside, because you would find the church full! Such were the exploits of Rev. Philemon Mumba, a humble, loving and hardworking minister.

Rev. Theodore Kalumba
Rev. Theodore Kalumba was born in 1946 at Mununga in Nchelenge District in Northern Rhodesia. He was born to Mr. Thomas Kabole and Mrs. Angela Kalumba Sapi. He attended school at Mununga-Mbereshi up to Standard I. He was then taken by the Catholic Parish because they liked his humble spirit and hard work. They took him to Belgian Congo where he was enrolled in a Catholic Mission School at Mpweto Secondary School in Mpweto District where he completed Form IV in 1965. He was recommended to train as a Priest in the Roman Catholic Church but the parents refused to sanction him for that study. Instead, the Catholic Missionaries sent him to school where Rev. Kalumba studied bricklaying, plumbing and carpentry for three years at Mission Ngudia in Congo completing his training in 1969.

Rev. Theodore Kalumba was then sent to Lusaka in Congo near the Tanzanian border. He was there for a year studying the Bible. Rev. Kalumba was then recommended to be helping the Catholic Priests since his parents had refused him to become a priest. In 1973,

Rev. Kalumba decided to return home to Zambia. He moved to Mufulira and joined Allen Temple A.M.E. Church and began helping Rev. Rowland Mwenyo the Pastor. He met Rev. Cuthbert Katebe, Rev. Henry Alimasi and Rev. G.W. Kanyembo who recommended him to the Bishop to become Pastor and he was received into ministry.

Rev. Kalumba was ordained Deacon in 1975 by Bishop Cornelius Thomas and Elder in 1981 by the same Bishop. He was Pastor of Kansunswa (Mufulira) 1979 to 1985; Kamuchanga (St. Paul) 1985 to 1989; Jordan Chapel (Kitwe, was Pastor to Rev. Charles Kapungwe) and also served at Gethsemane in Kitwe from 1989 to 1991. He was Pastor 1991 to 1999 at Membe – Kitwe, 1999 to 2004 Judah (Mindolo) taking over from Rev. Elsie Musonda and 2004 to 2009 at Membe – Kitwe, again.

Between 2009 and 2011, Rev. Theodore Kalumba was sent to serve in Congo DR. He was asked to help Rev. Kabala, P.E., who was from Zambia and was serving at Likasi in Congo DR. Rev. Kalumba was accompanied by Rev. Jonas Musonda, Rev. Julius Musonda, Rev. Malaya, Rev. Kayabwe and Rev. Gift Kunda all from Zambia.

After serving in Congo DR for two years, Rev. Kalumba returned and was appointed in 2012 to 2016 as Pastor of Mumba in Kitwe. He was transferred to St. Peter in Kitwe from 2016 to 2018. He was appointed to Judah in Kitwe again in 2018 where he is currently the Pastor. He is married to Mother Maggie Kalumba. Rev. Kalumba worked for Reco in 1989, Lupungu Enterprises from 1990 to 1991 and Delecans 1994 to 1996 on Contract. He also worked at New Life Center in Garneton Kitwe making wheelchairs for the disabled in 2005. He returned there and worked for the same company after two years. He has now been working there for 16 years (in 2020).

Rev. Field Timu Sikazwe

Rev. Field Timu Sikazwe was born on 28th April, 1925 at Chipwa Village, Northern Province in Northern Rhodesia. There were no records or his name in the writings, therefore, Rev. Kapungwe reached out to his daughter Charity Nakazwe Chellah. This information was obtained from Sister Charity who was in YPD with Rev. Kapungwe in their younger years. Rev. Sikazwe was married to Enika Kasitu and they had 9 children, five boys and four girls. He was ordained and appointed Pastor of Bright Temple, Matero in Lusaka in the South Zambia Annual Conference by Bishop Hartford Brookins on 23rd November, 1975 where he served until 1990.

During that period, he set up Chunga, Naliyanda, Lilanda and Mandevu circuits. He served under various Bishops including Bishops Cornelius Thomas, Robert Pruitt, Richard Allen Chappelle, Sr., and Robert Webster. He served as Dean of Dr. Membe School of Religion which was offering training to those who were entering ministry. He was appointed Presiding Elder for Copperbelt East District in the South West Zambia Annual Conference on 12th August, 1990 by Bishop Richard Allen Chappelle, Sr. He served in this capacity until he went to be with the Lord on 18th February, 1993.

Rev. Elsie Musonda with Rev. Field T. Sikazwe, P.E. of Copperbelt East in Luanshya in 1992.

Rev. Elsie Musonda

Rev. Elsie Musonda was born on 28th October, 1932 at Nsholos village, Kazembe in Kawambwa District in Northern Rhodesia. She was born to Mr. George Mwango and Mrs. Mwansa Musonda. Rev. Musonda was born in a family of five children, four girls and one boy. She was educated at Mindolo Girls in Kitwe and then studied Social Work at National Institute of Public Administration (NIPA) College in Lusaka. She then worked for Nchanga Consolidated Copper Mines (NCCM) the forerunner to Zambia Consolidated Copper Mines (ZCCM) Nkana Division as a Community Development Officer until her retirement in 1976.

Rev. Charles Kapungwe recalls when he was in 6th grade, Rev. Elsie Musonda visiting their home in 1976. She was telling his parents that she was retiring and going into ministry. She also informed them that she was going to build a house at Ndeke Village, a place she had resided after her retirement. At the time, she used to live at Meshi-Ndeke and Ndeke Village was a new development then. There used to be an aerodrome before you reached Ndeke village just after Meshi Primary School. She went into full-time ministry in 1977 and served many churches within the A.M.E. Church until her retirement in 2006.

In 1976, Rev. Musonda served at Jordan Chapel, Wusakile Kitwe as a Deacon. She later that year served as a Pastor of Mindolo. From 1982 to 1988 after being ordained as Elder, she was appointed as Pastor for Brookins Chapel in Chingola. She embarked on a number of projects doing fundraising including a nursery for children. She was Pastor of Thomas Chapel in Luanshya from 1989 to 1999 and completed the church which was left uncompleted by her predecessor. Rev. Musonda was appointed Pastor to St. John's Chapel in Kitwe from 1998 to 2000. She was appointed to Judah at Mindolo from 2002 to 2004, a place she had been responsible for acquiring the land from the Mines over a decade earlier. Rev. Musonda was appointed Pastor at Calvary in 2005 in Kitwe and retired the following year from full-time ministry.

Rev. Elsie Musonda was a woman of extraordinary abilities and drive. After her retirement in 2006, she applied for a permit to preach the word of God at the Intercity Bus Terminus in the capital city of Lusaka. She introduced evangelism programmes in response to the command to go and spread the gospel to the ends of the earth with other pastors. During her preaching at the bus station she would buy food (a local food delicacy of nshima and beef) for destitute and homeless. When my niece (her daughter) residing in the United Kingdom, Mrs. Mildred Mutsvairo, would send her money, she would use the money not for herself but on the poor! She would buy second hand clothes, launder it and distribute it to widows and orphans, making her daughter Mildred to exclaim that she is her hero of faith!

Rev. Musonda also distributed tracts on the streets of Lusaka. My sister, Fridah Kapungwe, would tell me how she would meet her even when her age and health were not great, preaching! She would meet her sharing the gospel and handing over Christian literature to the people. Rev. Musonda used to cause laughter among gatherings in church or at the cemeteries whenever she preached in her matter-of-fact truths to her audiences. When she took long in preaching and people began to murmur at the graveyard, she would tell the mourners to keep quiet since she only was taking advantage of the occasion to share the word to them because "you don't come to church!" She went to be with the Lord on 9th March, 2019. The following were her children, Adam, George, Geoffrey, twins Mary and Margaret and Mildred. She is survived by Mildred in the U.K. and Mary in Lusaka, Zambia.

Rev. Alfred Mwika Kalobwe

There was no record or particulars about Rev. Alfred Mwika Kalobwe available at present. Rev. Kalobwe was ordained in Luapula reportedly on his sickbed. He attended Nkomba Circuit which was beyond Kazembe and had served as a Conference Secretary. He was immediately appointed Pastor of Jordan Chapel in Kitwe where he was pastor to Rev. Charles Kapungwe. He was transferred to Mother Hughes and then to Bright Chapel. Rev. Kalobwe had acted as Presiding Elder when there was a vacancy in the Copperbelt East District. He had improved himself educationally by going to school at Mindolo Ecumenical Foundation after coming from Luapula and this was a great success because it was seen in his messages. He became one of the most improved ministers. Rev. Kalobwe had been a policeman by profession before leaving Luapula. He went to be with the Lord in Kitwe in 2000.

Rev. Caleb Ngoma

Rev. Caleb Ngoma was born on 16th July, 1923 in Fort Jameson (Chipata) in Northern Rhodesia. He was baptized on 12th May, 1942 and was ordained by Bishop Joseph Gomez in 1971. He was first appointed as Pastor to Mboza A.M.E. Church in 1972 where he served until 1973. Rev. Ngoma was appointed Presiding Elder by Bishop Hartford Brookins in 1974, the position he held until 2000. He was appointed Bishop's Administrative Assistant (BAA) in 1981 and held this position until 2000. He was transferred from Chipata District to Lusaka North District in the South-East Zambia Annual Conference as Presiding Elder. He served as Pastor at Bethel in Lusaka and Mother Hughes in Ndola.

Bishop Preston Williams appointed Rev. Caleb Ngoma as General Bishop's Administrative Assistant (GBAA) in 2001, the position he held until his retirement in 2006. He attended many General Conferences in the U.S.A. Rev. Ngoma was elected Vice Chairman of the Bible Society of Zambia and he served eight Bishops as Bishop's Administrative Assistant in the 17th Episcopal District. The Bishops he served are: Bishop Hartford Brookins, Bishop Cornelius Thomas, Bishop Robert Pruitt, Bishop Richard Allen Chappelle, Bishop Robert Webster, Bishop Larry Kirkland, Bishop Preston Williams and Bishop Paul Kawimbe.

He passed away on 24th September, 2018 aged 95. Bishop Paul Kawimbe and Wilfred Messiah attended the funeral in Lusaka, Zambia. Rev. Michael Gondwe, a former Pastor of Ebenezer read the history at the funeral. Bishop Kawimbe gave a moving tribute while Bishop Messiah preached at the funeral held at Ebenezer A.M.E. Church in Lusaka. Rev. Ngoma was put to rest on 26th September, 2018 at Leopard's Hill Memorial Park. Rev. Michael Gondwe, Presiding Elder of Mongu/Akashi District in Western Province contributed part of this profile.

Rev. Caleb Ngoma was a very intelligent and accomplished minister. He spoke many languages and freely switched from one language to another as needed when translating in Conferences. He spoke many languages from Southern, East and Central Africa. He spoke Zulu, Xhosa, Tswana, Ndebele, Lozi, Nyanja, Bemba, Swahili, languages from North-Western Province among many others. He had worked in the Post Office as a Government worker and worked in many regions in Zambia before retirement.

From left: Bishop Larry T. Kirkland, Rev. Samuel Kapufi, P.E., and Rev. Caleb Ngoma, Bishop's Administrative Assistant at Mbereshi Mission Hospital, Mbereshi in 1999 for the North West Zambia Annual Conference.

Rev. G.W. Kanyembo

There was no record or detailed information available on Rev. G.W. Kanyembo at the time of writing. However, available information indicate that he was a prominent minister in the 1970s and beyond and was Pastor in many places. He had been one of the senior ministers Rev. Theodore Kalumba met when he returned to Zambia from Congo in 1973. Others were Rev. Cuthbert Katebe and Rev. Henry Alimasi. The trio recommended Rev. Kalumba to Bishop Cornelius Thomas in 1975 for ordination. Rev. Kanyembo went to Kenya in 1975 for a short course with Rev. Alimasi and Rev. David Simfukwe. They also came to the U.S. to study in Chicago, Illinois in 1976. Rev. Kanyembo was Pastor in Luanshya, Gethsemane in Kitwe and was once Presiding Elder of Roan District.

Rev. M.C. Chisamba Phiri

There was no record or detailed information available on Rev. M.C. Chisamba Phiri at the time of writing. He was a former Pastor to Charles Kapungwe in the early 1980s at Jordan, Kitwe. He had been Pastor in many places including Chambeshi, Bright Chapel – Kitwe and Ndola. Rev. Chisamba Phiri was a prominent figure with the Christian Council of Zambia and was a Pastor who was regularly invited to many political events and would offer prayers at Freedom Park in Kitwe. He has gone to be with the Lord.

Rev. Idah Simukwai

There was no record or particulars about Rev. Idah Simukwai available at present. However, Rev. Idah Simukwai was known to be a member of Mother Hughes as a youth in the Juvenile with Mother Rose Simfukwe when the latter joined the A.M.E. Church in Ndola in 1955. The two were friends and Rev. Simukwai played a role in Mother Rose Simfukwe, the future wife of Rev. David Simfukwe in joining the church. At the time, Rev. J.L.C. Membe was the Pastor and Presiding Elder at Mother Hughes in Ndola. Rev. Idah Simukwai was once an influential political leader in the Womens' League of the ruling party United National Independence Party (UNIP) and she served in many places. She had been Pastor in Ndola and Kitwe (Jordan Chapel) where she had been Pastor to Rev. Charles Kapungwe for a year. She was a born again minister and was instrumental in the revival of the A.M.E. Church in Zambia. She was not ashamed of her faith and used to stand firmly against spiritual opposition from leaders both in the local church and leaders above her. No mention of the revival in this Church could be spoken of without the name of Rev. Idah Simukwai. She went to be with the Lord in 2017.

Rev. Wilson Mpundu, Rev. Joel Mazimba, a Bro. Mulenga and Rev. Idah Simukwai at the welcoming service of Rev. Mazimba at Chifubu (Holiness) Church in 1986.

Rev. Joel Manda Mazimba

Rev. Joel Manda Mazimba was born on 10th March, 1938 in Kaizya Village, Mpulungu in Abercorn District in Northern Rhodesia. Rev. Mazimba joined International Red Locust Control Organisation for Central and Southern Africa (IRLCO-CSA) on 1st August, 1966 at its headquarters near Lake Chila in Mbala. He was an Aircraft Assistant until 1985. He was appointed Senior Aircraft Mechanic on 9th April, 1985. The same year, IRLCO-CSA, moved its headquarters and its operations by the Government of Zambia from Mbala to Ndola. He retired from his employment on 31st January, 1999. Rev. Mazimba was involved in God's work actively when he was in Mbala. He joined Ministry in 1973 and was ordained Deacon in 1975 by Bishop Hartford H. Brookins and Elder in 1980 by Bishop Cornelius E. Thomas.

He was appointed to Mapesa (Mbala) in 1973. Rev. Mazimba was later appointed to Makala and Chilwa (Mbala) in 1975, Bonner Chapel (Mbala) from 1978 to 1981, Bethlehem and Emmanuel in Ndola on the Copperbelt Province from 1983 to 1986, and Holiness (now Kirkland) 1986 to 2008. He was Located on request in September 2010 due to illness (after he had suffered a stroke). Rev. Joel Mazimba was transferred to Mpulungu (Musende Village) in Mbala District, North East Zambia Conference because of the same prolonged illness. He married Elizabeth Chifunda Mazimba (Mrs.) on 26th October, 1961 in Kaizya Village, Mpulungu and they had 9 children. Among the 9 are a set of twins, 3 are late and is survived by 6. He went to be with the Lord on Tuesday 19th October, 2010 at Musende Village in Mpulungu.

When he was a Pastor of Holiness in Ndola, Rev. Mazimba is fondly remembered by many for his laughter, joy, singing and dancing in conferences. He would also stump his feet joyously as he sang ministering to people who were in meetings. Rev. Mazimba had a good job with the IRLCO-CSA. He was a talented aircraft technician. When the company was resizing, Rev. Mazimba was not laid off because of his great skill. He thus, was retained until his retirement. He was paid a good pension by the company and he was at Holiness, a more appropriate name (which was changed to Kirkland in 1997) amidst promises from the Bishop to help in completion of the church building!

Rev. Joel Mazimba put in all his pension money into the church construction! This followed the understanding that the Bishop who had promised him reimbursement was going to do so. However, he was not reimbursed and he experienced great hardships financially before he went to be with the Lord. He made a lot of sacrifice and contribution to the gospel of our Lord and Saviour Jesus Christ. When Rev. Mazimba was sick and the leadership proposed that the church at Kirkland should be helping him with a small monthly stipend, a Pastor at the church had refused to sanction that! In spite of the leadership telling the Pastor the work Rev. Mazimba had done at the church, this pastor had refused! Presiding Elder Rev. Kennedy Mazimba of Kasama, contributed in part to this profile.

Rev. Dr. James Webb

Rev. Dr. James Webb was a gift to the A.M.E. Church in Zambia in 2004. I met him in Columbia, South Carolina with Bishop Paul Kawimbe soon after Kawimbe was elected in 2004. They proceeded to Zambia where he was appointed Pastor of Bethel A.M.E. Church in Lusaka. Rev. Webb was a former Executive Vice President and CEO of M.J. Associates LTD whose headquarters were in Cape Town, South Africa. He was also a visiting Professor of Southern History and Culture at Auburn University in Alabama, U.S.A. He helped in the negotiations that led to the release from prison of Nelson Mandela and had been involved in the work for Dr. Martin Luther King, Jr. United Nations Secretary General Ban Ki-moon appointed Dr. Webb as Special U.N. Envoy to African Union in June 2007.

He was stationed in Addis Ababa serving as a mediator to conflict resolutions in the Southern Africa Development Community (SADC) nations. The Church in Zambia, however, with poor leadership and poor visionary abilities failed to utilize the potential that Rev. Dr. Webb had brought to the 17th Episcopal District by sidelining him and not offering him the platform to help lead the Church in Zambia or connect it to those in the U.S. Zambia, therefore, missed the opportunity to develop the District. Dr. Webb is married to Myra Fields. He planted a new church, Chrisma in Lusaka in 2005.

Rev. Isaiah Phiri

Rev. Isaiah Phiri was born on 18th December, 1960 in Eastern Province in Northern Rhodesia. He attended Mutende Primary School and Kwacha Primary School in Kitwe. He then went to Luanshya Boys High School. He obtained a Diploma in Biblical Studies from All Africa School of Theology and was involved with Barnabas Ministry. Rev. Phiri was ordained Deacon in 1981 at Jordan in Livingstone by Bishop Cornelius Thomas and Elder in 1983 at Bright, Matero in Lusaka by the same Bishop. He was first appointed to St. Peter and then Gethsemane in Kitwe. He was transferred to St. James (Roan) in Luanshya and then to Thomas Chapel. Later in 2005, he was Pastor of both St. Mark – Mpatamato and Thomas Chapel in Luanshya. He is now Pastor of Brookins Chapel (2020). Rev. Isaiah Phiri wedded Fatness Phiri in 1984 at a wedding officiated by Rev. G.W. Kanyembo. They have a girl Inia Phiri and four boys Isaiah Phiri, Jr., Paul Phiri, John Phiri and Jeremiah Phiri. Rev. Isaiah helped with the 1981 Roll Call names of the former South Zambia Annual Conference to which I added many names of prior and future ministers. We are grateful for this contribution.

Rev. Alick Mulapwa

There was no detailed information available on Rev. Alick Mulapwa at the moment. However, available information indicates that Rev. Mulapwa was ordained Deacon in 1981 at Jordan in Livingstone by Bishop Cornelius Thomas and Elder in 1983 at Bright, Matero in Lusaka by the same Bishop. He was first appointed to Membe in 1981 after being ordained Deacon. He later was Pastor of St. Paul in Mufulira, Thomas in Luanshya and Bright Chapel in Kitwe. Currently, (2020), he is Presiding Elder of Copperbelt Central District.

Rev. Jonathan Silumbwe

No detailed information on Rev. Jonathan Silumbwe was available at the time of this writing. Rev. Silumbwe was Pastor of St. Peter in Kitwe and he worked for the Post Office as a government employee. He has gone to be with the Lord.

Rev. Godfrey Peter Mutembo

There is no record available about the life of Rev. Godfrey Peter Mutembo at the time of writing. However, Rev. Mutembo had been Pastor in Nkana/Kalulushi area and was a former Pastor of Jordan Chapel in Kitwe. He was a born again minister who was very zealous for his God and one of the ministers who helped in the revival of the Church in Zambia through prayer and teaching. He attended Kaniki Bible College in Ndola. Rev. Mutembo has gone to be with the Lord.

Rev. Samuel Mulapwa

There is no record available about the life of Rev. Samuel Mulapwa at the time of writing. However, his personal testimony when he was Pastor at Jordan Chapel in Kitwe where Charles Kapungwe was a member was that he got saved under the ministry of Rev. Peter M.P. Mwenya of Allen Temple in Mufulira. He then joined the ministry after receiving a calling. He was sent to Jordan Chapel at Wusakile in Kitwe and was later transferred to Luanshya. He was a school teacher and the father-in-law to Rev. Paul Bupe. Rev. Dr. Bupe's wife Catherine Mulapwa Bupe is a daughter of the late Rev. Samuel Mulapwa. Rev. Mulapwa preached salvation by faith and was very helpful to the ministry which was resisted highly by the older people of the Church during his time. He therefore, contributed to the revival of the Church in Zambia.

Rev. David Damus Musole

Rev. David Damus Musole was born on 6th June, 1959. His father was Kayombo Musole and mother Sofia Likumbi Musole. He attended Katendwa Primary in 1964 and Kabompo Aided Primary, Chiweza until 1970. He then went to Kitwe Boys Secondary School where he completed secondary education in 1975. Rev. Musole began his ministry in 1984 at Kabompo Katendwa Kasalya as a Lay Pastor. He then worked under Rev. Wilson Mpundu at Thomas Chapel in Luanshya and in 1986 he was ordained Deacon by Bishop Robert Lee Pruitt. Rev. Musole was ordained Elder at Mulungushi International Conference Center in 1988 in Lusaka by Bishop Richard Allen Chappelle. He was first appointed as Pastor to St. James at Roan in Luanshya in 1988 by Bishop Chappelle and in 1990, he was appointed Pastor to St. Paul at Mpatamatu in Luanshya. He was appointed as Pastor to Jordan Chapel from 1992 to 2000 (and was Pastor to Rev. Charles Kapungwe for two years) in Kitwe.

Rev. David Musole

During his tenure at Jordan Chapel in Kitwe, Rev. Musole opened Calvary A.M.E. Church in Kitwe in 1994. The meetings were held at Kitwe Primary School in Parklands initially, and then moved to Kitwe Main Primary School. Rev. Musole released some of his members which included Br. Kapungwe to begin Calvary. He later opened Covenant at Ndeke Village in 1998. He was one of the ministers who supported and baptized by immersion as opposed to sprinkling. Rev. Musole gave us a very supportive hand in ministry during the pinnacle of great opposition to the salvation by faith message we had been preaching at Jordan. He was a humble man of God but firm on the things of God. Rev. Charles Kapungwe spoke to him on phone in October 2018 and on November 8, 2018. He was now at Chilanga in Lusaka. He recalled the "Idol worship and worship of individuals" by the people as hindrances that made and still make this Church fail to progress. "A bishop is just like any person but this Church equates him to Jesus," he recalled!

Rev. Musole, during his time at Jordan, demonstrated a ministry of power over Satan. He never backed down to opposers of the word of God in spite of them having a mentality of "superiority complex" over him. Humble yet firm, Rev. Musole's passion for God made those who trusted in God refreshed because he stood on the word of God than on man's fantasies. Rev. Musole worked under Bishop Pruitt, Bishop Chappelle and Bishop Kirkland. He singles out Bishop Chappelle as a very good Bishop who was impartial. He was disappointed with one Bishop who he said showed a lot of favoritism. Rev. D.D. Musole can also be credited for helping with revival of this Church in Zambia.

Rev. Dr. Paul Bupe

Rev. Dr. Paul Bupe was educated at Chililabombwe Secondary School, Chililabombwe in Zambia. He later attended Theological College of Central Africa (TCCA) in Ndola, Zambia. He was Pastor of Bethel in Chililabombwe, Allen Temple in Mufulira and Mother Hughes in Ndola. Rev. Bupe was also Pastor of Crossroad A.M.E. Church in Saluda, South Carolina in 2001 and St. Stephen A.M.E. Church in Sandusky, Ohio U.S.A. He came to the U.S.A. in 2000 and enrolled at Allen University in Columbia, South Carolina where he graduated in 2002 with a Bachelor of Arts in Religion after transfer of credits from TCCA. He later obtained a Master's of Divinity at Payne Theological Seminary in Wilberforce, Ohio in 2007 and graduated with a Doctor of Ministry at Ashland Theological Seminary in Ohio in 2010.

He was consecrated Bishop by the Archbishop Elijah Mboho of the Goodnews Community International Church in Columbia, South Carolina in 2008. This followed his unsuccessful run for the Bishopric position in the A.M.E. Church in 2008 in the U.S.A. He returned to Zambia in 2010 and was appointed Pastor of Mother Hughes in Ndola. He later left the Church following some disagreements and joined Redeemed Methodist Church, an A.M.E. Church breakaway denomination of 2004. (Members who had been expelled by the then Presiding Elder Paul Kawimbe and had formed this Church). Rev. Dr. Bupe assumed the role of Bishop of this Church. He had been among those who had been a strong voice for preaching the salvation message in the Church during the contentious years when persecution was rife. He also advocated for the plight of the widow and orphan in Zambia. In 2019, Bishop Paul Bupe launched Revival Methodist Church after leaving Redeemed Methodist Church.

Rev. Wilson Mpundu

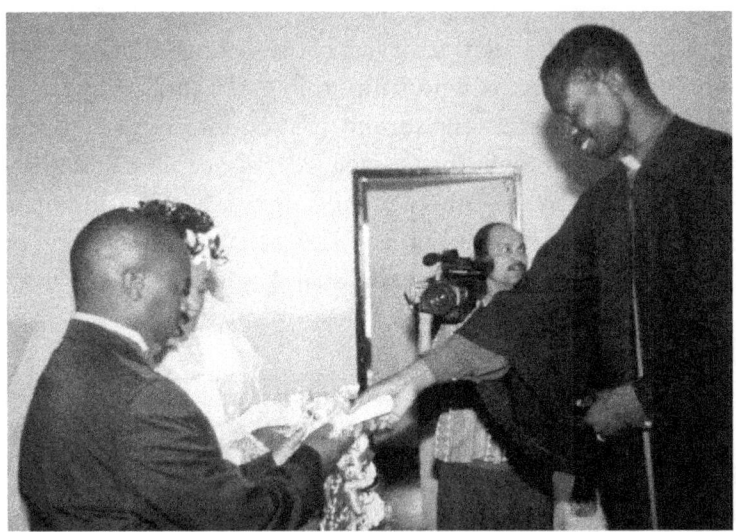

Rev. Wilson Mpundu officiating at the wedding of Sister Chanda Chibuta (daughter of Rev. Bernard Chibuta) to Br. Tembo at Mother Hughes in Ndola in 1996.

Rev. Wilson Mpundu, now Bishop Wilson Mpundu is the founder of Higher Dimensions Church in Zambia. "After serving 22 years, in our Mother Zion, African Methodist Episcopal Church," he writes, "I was found wanting over a very trivial issue, of the leopard's skin, used by women for their headdress in the Women Missionary Society (W.M.S.)." Here is his story in verbatim:

"In 1996, I was a minister in charge of Kabushi's Mother Hughes Church in Ndola, Zambia. On a special W.M.S. Area gathering, I was invited to teach about the 'History of the Leopard's Skin' which was and is still not well-known not only to the Women Missionary Society sisters but by most pastors. This, however, is known to a few people who are acquainted with the movement of Hopia (Ethiopian Church of the Mokone of the Ethiopian Royal Clan)."

[Book author's note: For readers unfamiliar with the issue, the A.M.E. Church in Africa, wearing of uniform is a tradition that has been practiced for decades. Women (W.M.S.) are clad in black and have leopard skin hats while girls in the youth (YPD), have black skirts, white shirts, black collars and black hats with three leopard skins on them. Boys wear black trousers and white shirts with a pocket size black and white badge piece of cloth adorning a leopard's skin. Prior to mid-1970s, boys used to wear a band across the chest with letters "A.E.L." which stood for Allen Endeavor League. As a boy of about 12, Rev. Kapungwe used to wear this too (the band). This, he believes, was a shortened form for Allen Christian Endeavor League (A.C.E. League). The band (sash) had one leopard's skin on the shoulder. Please note that this uniform is not a requirement in the U.S.A and other overseas A.M.E. Churches nor is it observed in the USA.[1] The story, "19th Episcopal District - Mangena Maake Mokone conference Women's Missionary Society" gives a narration on how the Church in South Africa incorporated African style in music and undoubtedly other ideas, following Charlotte Maxeke (nee Mannya) returned to South Africa to establish Wilberforce Institute with her husband].

"In that honourable session, I expanded on how Mangena Mokone embraced Ethiopianism in South Africa while preaching the gospel of Christ's redeeming grace. The message also incorporated emancipation from Arabian and European slavery along the Indian Ocean Coast and in South Africa. Being of royal descent, he used a leopard skin as a royal symbol of majesty. It was reckoned with higher dignity and honour by most African kingdoms.

The roots of A.M.E. Church in Southern Africa can be traced to the Ethiopian Church in South Africa. Also, this was a merger between the Ethiopian Church and the A.M.E. Church in the U.S. However, Mangena M. Mokone, a minister in the Wesleyan Methodist Church had broken away in 1892 principally due to segregation. The period from 1890 to 1920s had been punctuated with feelings of dissatisfaction and need for identity by Africans in their quest for God and worship. This quest for some led to what later was to be termed as 'Ethiopian movement.' The movement, (also known as Ethiopianism) widely incorporated all independent African churches or denominations which were not willing to identify themselves with the Western Protestant Churches which they viewed as being discriminatory. Therefore, Ethiopia or Cush became a common identity unifying them not just in their political struggle but in their search for God too.

Thus, for Mokone, seeing the South Africans using the leopard skin as a traditional dressing in the 1800s for war warriors mattered less. Amongst them were Christians who preached salvation in the name of Christ Jesus and liberation from apartheid. The two got together in the theme of freedom and Christian brotherhood. Later, at the peak of apartheid, slavery and segregation, the joint force of Mokone and the Freedom Warriors in the Church agreed to use the leopard skin as a symbol for ferociousness against the colonialist segregation and brutality in both the Church and social life. They said, 'We should be as ferocious as a leopard without fear or retreat in our faith and fight for freedom.'

Being a covenant theme, they allotted women to have their heads covered while men and boys were to put on a sash. The sash was to be worn across from the shoulder to the opposite side of the waist. Our forefathers having had no much theological understanding of scripture took at random Jeremiah 13:23 for scriptural support of the leopard skin. Looking at the entire chapter, I explained the validity of the same from the theological interpretation of the leopard – from Daniel 7:6 and Revelation 13:2. Then I brought in the usage of the leopard skin by historical figures like the South African warrior, Shaka the Zulu, who was not only king of the Zulu but a murderer as well. I then raised another contemporary leader Mobutu Sese Seko Wazabanga of Zaire (Congo DR), a well-documented dictator and murderer as well. To the list was added Idi Amin who was not only a murderer but was a cannibal who ate human flesh too!

We further agreed that most traditional healers adorned themselves in the leopard skin. It was a known fact these traditional healers who use the leopard skin are demonic consultants which many Africans were familiar with this truth. Upon learning these truths, some of the women stopped using the leopard skin not that I told them not to but because they discovered the truth and recovered from ignorance. It was this problem or say teaching that brought a lot of problems or chaos between me and the Presiding Elder and some other senior ministers and heads of the W.M.S. This problem lasted a long time! For six years, that is, down the line up to 2002, this problem was thorny and we continued to struggle over a simple issue of the leopard skin!

During the time of Bishop Preston Williams, the W.M.S. at the local church and District took to the Bishop false reports. These reports were not even authenticated by the local church or known by the church leadership, Quarterly Conference or even the District Conference except for a selected few who were in league with leaders of the Church to see me punished! Having been paraded before the Conference and castigated disrespectfully by the Bishop, some women and youth continued to shout, 'Shame! Shame!' I was then asked to apologise for all the accusations laid upon me! During the time, my wife was weeping. All I said was, 'I sincerely apologise for all the accusations laid upon me but we shall identify the sky when the clouds are cleared.'

Rev. Wilson Mpundu, a man full of wisdom beyond his age and one of the greatest preachers to ever come out of Zambia pictured with his loving wife, Mother Grace Mpundu, 2004.

I was demoted from a church of no less than 300 members in the town center, to one with no more than 20 in a shanty compound. I had children going to school and I had no house. The church had no capacity to support me as well. The late Bishop Richard Allen Chappelle, taught us not to embarrass the Bishop in public by going into a dispute with him in public. I took the disappointing appointment and then at the first Quarterly Conference presented a resignation letter while emphasizing to my Presiding Elder that 'I will still be coming to minister until the Bishop responds to my resignation.' However, the Presiding Elder came to church the following Sunday and asked me to hand over to him all the church property even though I had none! I tried to explain to him that I would be coming to the Annual Conference to present my credentials to the Bishop but to no avail. My Presiding Elder, Rev. Henry C. Alimasi, insisted that I stop coming to church.

In the two months I served at the church, membership improved. The member-pastor relationship was being stabilized. A sudden interruption caused some members to reach to the extent of harshly facing the P.E., and threatening violence. Others came to admonish me that I shouldn't have accepted the appointment, stating 'Why accept the appointment knowing you will resign? You took us from where we were because you came! Now why are you leaving us?' I could not answer all the people with different complaints and desperations.

My roots are connected to Mufulira's Allen Temple Church. I became a member through a Pastor's daughter, Christine Mwenyo and her friend Beatrice Chabala who had invited me to a Sunday service. Rev. Rowland Mwenyo was a highly-spirited old man with an 'Old Time

Religion's power.' He stood slender, dark and unpredictably proclaimed an evangelistic saving grace sermon that caused streams of tears in my eyes throughout his inspired sermon. I was not a good boy per se. Having been rejected by my father from childhood, I lived a lonely life. My father did not hide it from me that I was not his child even though people thought I was his nephew because I took on the face image of my father's sister.

I have come to understand that loneliness caused by rejection can breed violence in life. At school, I was a friend to almost everyone but I never took life cautiously. Any simple provocation would lead to a fight. This being the case, I avoided being in male groups because they easily provoked me than did the females. At one time, I beat a teacher up for slapping me twice. I broke his jaw and cut his lips that caused him to bleed profusely. When in his sermon, the Reverend had said, 'Come to Jesus, he loves you; you do what you do because you have not accepted his love for you,' I immediately thought, 'These girls must have told the Pastor,' 'Mpundu was going to come to church!'

I had nicknames which I had been given at school. Some called me 'Hitler' while others called me 'Jimi Hendrix!' They called me Hitler because of violence and Jimi Hendrix because of the guitar. When he made an altar call, even though I was among the first to answer the altar call, I did not know exactly what I wanted and what to do. However, the Reverend prayed for us and greeted us. At the end, he pronounced a fatherly, 'God bless you!' I left the church without talking to anyone as it was evident to everyone that I was crying in the church.

When I got home, I went straight into my small cabin. The words of the love of Jesus resounded in me. I closed the door behind me and wept the more. This time, loneliness grew even much more than ever before. I remembered my only and very loving mother who went to be with the Lord a year before. I wished she lived to see me go to church again. I missed her prayers for me. I missed her words of comfort. Here I am the lonely guy with only the open sky watching above. I wished I had gone with my late mother that very year. The prayer of the Pastor at the church haunted me. In a sense, it felt as though it was directed at me but it did not bear fruit – it still left a lonely and desperate poor young boy! I expected to see instant results of the unknown. There was a longing in me of some unknown fulfillment I could not share or desire.

The following day, I went to school. To my surprise, some classmates had heard about my church attendance! Entering my classroom, only to find words written in bold letters 'Hitler Goes to Church,' I was amused! Nevertheless, this at first, didn't make sense to me until Eunice, my friend asked me, 'Which church did you go to?' 'Who said I went to church?' I inquired. 'Who wrote there?' I asked her again while pointing to the board. 'That is about you! Don't you know?' she responded. I just smiled, took the eraser and wiped clean the blackboard.

From that day, I was nicknamed 'Priesty!' Fellow students spread the story of my Sunday service attendance. The Scripture Union Chairperson heard about it. He came to my class and congratulated me. Even though it was a serious and genuine gesture, I took it for a mockery and admonished him not to play me ridicule. Unwavering and being a mature Christian, he took my advice to him prudently and apologized. He then further said, 'Did you know we're glad to hear that you are not what many people think you are? We would love you to come and be a member of the Scripture Union! You know God loves you and salvation is yours!' Every word he said was familiar but meaningless to me. I considered him, however, to be serious and that he meant what he was communicating. I took him serious but I did not commit myself to the invitation.

Every time I remembered that preaching, I felt some surging unknown desires within. Without sharing to anyone, I planned to join the choir and stop playing the guitar. 'Playing the guitar would keep me away from the church,' I thought to myself. The following weekend, I got ready for Sunday. I did not know what time the service started because the other Sunday I had found the service on. Hence, I was at church before others came. When parishioners started coming at the church, no one seemed to have recognized me until Beatrice and Christine came. I felt at ease and at home when I saw them. They got me into the church and offered me a seat just in the first row. They then proceeded to the vestry to practice their chosen songs, choruses and hymns for the service. I was very expectant and I was looking forward to seeing and hearing the old time preacherman.

When the service began, I felt so challenged that I got involved in it! I participated in every activity with everyone else! We were singing, clapping and dancing! During the offering we continued to sing and dance and I followed the choir marching around in the church before giving the offering. I joined the choir from there and then. At the end of the year, we went to the Annual Conference. As pastors presented their Annual Reports, there came this handsome-looking Pastor in a white Safari suit. The very first time I saw him; I fell in love with him! The Spirit in me desired to have him for our Pastor there and then! Without a second thought, I loudly spoke, saying, 'This one is going to be our Pastor!' To our surprise, on Sunday, the day of appointments, Rev. M.P.P. Mwenya was pronounced Pastor of Allen Temple, Mufulira! We all responded with a standing ovation and great cheers!

Rev. M.P.P. Mwenya became our Pastor. He also became our teacher and parent in faith. He introduced prayers at the Church and those who regularly came to pray were called 'Prayer warriors!' Nevertheless, I did not see the need to join because I felt that just being a choir member was well enough. Days and weeks went by with no extended association with the pastor except during Sunday services.

One afternoon around 4:30 PM, I was coming from school escorting a friend. Ahead of us, I saw Rev. M.P.P. Mwenya with two girls and a boy from our choir and Y.P.D. with him. 'Where are you going?' I asked them. 'To fight the devil,' the Pastor replied. Upon hearing this, my heart was moved with inquisitiveness. 'Can I come with you?' I requested. 'Why not?' the Pastor responded. We then went to a home of one of the church stewards, a teacher at one of the schools in the compound. We found her mother deeply troubled.

The Reverend gave each one of us a passage of Scripture to read. All the Scriptures which were given to us were about the Jesus' healing the sick or casting out of demons. I read mine from Mark 9:20-27. When the last verse was read, we were told to lay hands on the oppressed mother. We in unison prayed casting the devils out of her in Jesus' name! To my surprise, the demonic mother cried out with an awkward voice and fell down to the floor. Rev. Mwenya then ordered her to get up in the name of Jesus. She got up from the floor sheepishly with the help of the Pastor who was holding her hand.

It was from that day that I came to learn and know about the power of the Lord in the Holy Spirit. The consecutive days and weeks saw me frequently visit the Pastor to ask questions. I asked him as many questions as I could. One of my questions was, 'People suffer from demonic oppression. Why can't we as well suffer from the Holy Spirit oppression?' The Pastor explained the difference between the Holy Spirit and evil spirits. He said the devil or evil spirits come to destroy everything God created meant for his goodness and glory. Hence, he comes by force to oppress and depress. He does not need invitation but opportunity while the Holy Spirit comes to save and maintain tranquility and order. Thus, he needs to be invited by a willing person. The Holy Spirit has principles of operation and does not defy them for any reason.

This made many people join the prayer warriors' group. As youths, we joined the group because of what we saw the Lord doing and were joined by eager women and men. It was during the prayer meetings and Bible study sessions that we learned much about the word of God, the Spiritual Kingdom and the call to serve the Lord was born in the Year of our Lord 1980. In 1981, I was admitted into the Itinerant Ministry. The following year, I left the National Service for College in Ndola. I went to Theological College of Central Africa (TCCA) where I got enrolled into a two-year Certificate Course. Later, I attended some other courses at Mindolo Ecumenical Foundation in Kitwe and South Africa for three years in leadership.

In 1982, I was attached to Rev. Best Kofi, a Local Deacon. He later became an Itinerant Elder without due ordination. I was encouraged to visit members and read Scriptures with them and exhorted them in the things of God and the Church. The old Pastor, Best Kofi, agreed with members that he would be paid K75.00 (Seventy-five Kwacha) or $65.00. However, there was no single month that the money was ever fully paid to him. At times, he was given half of the agreed-upon amount or even less. It was evident that the Pastor lived a sacrificial life in the church because he put in more than he received.

The following year, 1983, I was given my first appointment to Ndeke in Ndola on the Copperbelt Province of Zambia. I walked into a makeshift church structure built with timber and roofing iron sheets derived from drums. The first members I found on a Sunday were Mrs. Chiwele and her ten-year-old daughter. My heart sank! When the service of the three was over, I was challenged to evangelize and raise the membership.

I began with home visitation of former members. Many had gone to Mother Hughes at Kabushi in Ndola which was about 7 to 9 kilometers away while others had defected to other Churches. Within three months, membership was raised to 56, both young and old and it would come to no less than 90. In the second Quarterly Conference, I faced a Rock and Roll encounter! One of the stewards who had been a member before the church had been disbanded didn't like my administration. He was about five to six years older than me and was in secular employment. This man became antagonistic and began to disorganize the church by speaking ill of me and other members.

One fateful day, he organized a meeting where he presented malicious stories about me. One such tale went, 'Rev. Mpundu allows women attending monthly periods to prepare Holy

Communion and has destroyed the church!' Consequently, some people with simple minds sided with him and agreed that they would not be paying me the agreed amount of K44.00 (Forty-four Kwacha) or $33.85. Two weeks down the line, we convened an Official Board meeting. Strategically or intentionally, this man did not attend the meeting. In the meeting, the Secretary of the unscrupulous meeting asked if he could present the minutes. I asked him to explain which minutes and who the Chairperson was. 'The names of the participants are here and you will hear them at the end,' was the response. We unanimously accepted the request.

Upon hearing the accusations, I defended the Chairperson. I stated that, 'Number one, I don't think that these accusations are about me, because I don't have a wife who would help me prepare Holy Communion, whose period on the month I can know. Second, I found the church deserted when I came, now we are filling all the pews in here! How can that be me? Those accusations cannot be true.' However, the assembly disagreed with me. 'It is about you! If not, who else is the Pastor here?' they questioned me. Some honest people who had attended that meeting revealed that they had contested the accusations too even in the meeting in question. They suggested that the author of the same comes to explain. Nevertheless, I refused since I saw that most of the people disagreed with the accusation.

Regardless, a recommendation that I be moved from the church was mysteriously effected in the Quarterly Conference. This was being done against the backdrop of the new movement of the Holy Spirit (Charismatic) which scores of people vehemently were opposing. Rev. Rowland Mwenyo who was pastoring Kabushi's Mother Hughes Church in Ndola at the time, (1983) resigned. The Quarterly Conference advocated that I replace him. Rev. Cuthbert Yoram Katebe, Presiding Elder, however, refused strongly! Instead, he opted that I be his Assistant Pastor! This was graciously accepted.

The other problem that came up immediately concerned allowances. Rev. Mwenyo had been getting K220.00 (Two hundred and twenty Kwacha) or $169.00. The Quarterly Conference suggested that I, being in college, be getting K120.00 (One hundred and twenty Kwacha) or $92.31 and Rev. C.Y. Katebe, the Presiding Elder, getting K100.00 (One hundred and twenty Kwacha) or $76.92 since he was in full-time employment and part-time in pastoral work. I would need a witness to establish this truth. Why? I would because the issue about allowances protracted from about 13:00 hrs. to about 19:00 hrs. in the night. My P.E., asked the Quarterly Conference, 'Why should we give him that money?' The Conference responded by saying, 'Because he will be working for it and he needs it in school!' My honourable P.E., to say the least, was the most intelligent Pastor of his time. No Pastor or laity would battle with him in words over any subject.

I had to make a statement to end the conversation. I at last stood up and said, 'Give to Caesar what belongs to Caesar and God his dues!' The Rev. C.Y. Katebe boldly stood up and said, 'That is the word I was waiting for! That is my son!' I went to church from that Saturday for the next seven months, three times in a week from college (at Kansenshi) to Kabushi about seven to eight kilometers on foot, including Saturdays. Although the Presiding Elder had a car, he never offered me a lift. I ministered to the youths (YPDers) on Saturdays, went for Bible Studies on Wednesdays and for Sunday services but never got a quarter or a cent. Mind you,

Ndeke A.M.E. Church was merged with Mother Hughes at Kabushi like before, but some members had declined going to Kabushi's Mother Hughes because of the long distance to the church and opted to defect to other Churches within Ndeke locality.

At the Annual Conference, to everyone's surprise, the Rev. C.Y. Katebe recommended that I go back to the Ndeke deserted church! While everyone was surprised it did not surprise or shock my P.E., to make such a move! As per tradition, we do not contest with Elders. My heart was hurt but I took the disappointing appointment. I imagined how to plan the rebuilding strategy with tears in my eyes. This was during the era of Bishop Cornelius E. Thomas. He didn't know the church and its status at all.

The very first Sunday after the Conference, I did not go to the church I was appointed to. Meanwhile, the Rev. Best Kofi had gone to his Chifubu church in Ndola. In an unprecedented move, the unexpected took place! He announced that 'Everyone who meets with Rev. Rowland Mwenyo in prayers should leave the church.' At that very moment, more than half of the members left and joined Rev. Mwenyo. Rev. C.Y. Katebe, Presiding Elder, had no alternative but to reappoint me to Chifubu, with the view of bringing back the dispersed sheep. (This is the church that later was renamed Holiness A.M.E. Church and years later changed to Kirkland). I refused to accept the appointment with my whole heart and soul. The Presiding Elder, however, insisted that I did.

Photo: Rev. Cuthbert Katebe, P.E., in Atlanta, Georgia U.S.A. in 1999.

On Sunday morning, he (Rev. Cuthbert Katebe) came to get me for church. The first thing he asked for was to see the appointment which was given to me at the Annual Conference by the Bishop. Just there and then, when I presented it to him, with his pen, he squashed off Ndeke and wrote 'Chifubu' in its place and told me to get ready for introduction. That was the first time ever I drove in his car in the two years I was at college – about 250 meters away from his home.

Before we had even gotten to the church that Sunday, Rev. C.Y. Katebe, P.E., had shared my upcoming new appointment news to some church members during the week. He had informed them of his replacing of Rev. Kofi but most of the people detested the idea because they knew I was of the same breed of the Charismatic movement which they disliked. They associated me and Rowland Mwenyo who had resigned from Mother Hughes with it and we were both clustered into this group. In spite of this opposition, the Presiding Elder had to take me there.

A night before, I had a terrible spiritual attack. I fought with yellow, black and red demons in human form which appeared in my dream. They wanted to dash me on rocks in order to kill me but every time they threw me in the air, I shouted the name of Jesus whose power suspended me in the air and slowly descended me down. At times they tried to physically beat me but upon the mention of the name of Jesus, a line was drawn and they could not come closer. I struggled with these yellow, black and red creatures for a while in my dream that night.

The time came during the service for my introduction. This dark-skinned African, five feet six inches tall, stood up before the negative crowd of less than twenty both young and old parishioners who a year past were my fellow members in the same church but today have taken twisted stances. Even then, this intelligent P.E., was beyond their unrehearsed battle.

'Children of the Living God; my coming here is rather pitiful and mingled with delight. In a sense, some among us have defected but the one I have brought you does not equal them in any way! I understand quite well why some present here would like to stand toe to toe and shoulder to shoulder with me and contest about the coming of Rev. Wilson Mpundu but think again! You were with him some time back. What evil report did you have against him? Yes, he is of them but with a different degree of approach to religion and its practices. Bet me by allowing him to remain here for One Quarter. If you find him undesirable, I am coming to withdraw him. He has not come here for money; no, not for money! He has not come here for church or Christian fantasies but for what God called him and brought him this far to do. He is my son. He is my sacred cow! Allow him to stay with you from today. For there will come a day to withdraw him and every one of you will hate me for his transfer,' the P.E. spoke.

It was during the same introduction he presented me to preach. 'Now hear him do what he does best since he is still suckling, smell him even his mother's milk is fresh upon his lips and chest!' his words echoed. While people were still laughing and others giggling and smiling, the old man in his few words looked at me and said, 'I have brought you not to put me to shame, speak a word,' and he went to sit down.

I stood in the presence of God before his people. I spoke from Exodus about the very Exodus – 'The Gate from Slavery.' Truly it was in the presence of God before his people. Before I could hand over the pulpit to the senior Rev. to make an altar call, many times he shouted, 'Tell me to take him with me now and I will do just that!' The Lord's presence was so heavy that no single eye was dry including myself and the Presiding Elder's. When I pronounced 'May the GOOD gracious Lord God Almighty bless his living word,' there was sobbing, weeping and crying. The Senior Rev. couldn't stand to crown the sermon but just motioned me to continue which I did breaking the law of the Church, 'Calling people to be born again,' even though it was a taboo. Yet more than three quarters came to receive Christ as Lord and Savior.

Before this congregation was divided, we never gave more than K20.00 (Twenty Kwacha) or $15.38 as offering! The Rev. asked me to collect the offering in my own inspired style! Guess what? We collected K120.00 (One hundred and twenty Kwacha, i.e. or $92.31!) My Senior Rev. C.Y. Katebe (his soul rest in peace), stood up in tears or say with misted eyes as red as an aged African male. He uttered the words, 'Can I take him with me now?' The church grew hotter than an October day in Zambia (the hottest month in this Southern Hemisphere country) and colder than a June day (the coldest month here!). No one spoke a word. 'This is my son,' I told you. 'He stays! Support him and he will make you proud!'

I enjoyed serving this congregation. I visited them regularly. There was no house I didn't know and no child or person I didn't know by name. We started evangelizing and in less than three months, the church (classroom) we rented at Malasha Primary School was filled again. Within the same period, I had been contending with the Ndola City Council for a plot for the church. To the surprise of the members, on 18th March, 1984, I went to church and broke the news of the offer of a church plot. No one believed the explicit truth. I had not shared with anyone about my frequenting the City Council about the plot until this honourable day.

Although we used to have more than a thousand Kwacha a month in offering, the church paid me meagerly. I was given K100.00 ($41.84) allowance and K10.00 ($4.18) transport money weekly. At the First Quarterly Conference, our Presiding Elder was astounded to hear the Treasurer say, 'Total raised K3,780.00 ($1,581.59) plus!' The Presiding Elder's stipend was also paid in full. He used to have problems in the previous years when it came to financial reports and his stipend. Not now anymore!

However, the rejection was not over despite the positive results. They could not rent a house for me. By the grace of God, a friend of mine, a person I once had been with in the YPD had a sister who had a grocery store. While eating from his house, 120 meters away, he negotiated that I stay in a storeroom which the sister gladly offered me as my bedroom. There was no bed or mattress. I had a grass mattress, a blanket and a bedsheet to cover myself. No one dared to know where I stayed. One day, my Senior Steward, Mr. Sikapite visited me. When he saw where I lived, he was speechless. 'Do you live here?' he asked me. 'Yes Sir, I do!' I replied. 'Where do you sleep, Pastor?' he inquired. 'Just here,' I answered while pointing at the mat covered with a blanket and a bedsheet. 'You can sit here,' I told him pointing at a box full of my books and lecture handouts from college.

My Senior Steward could not believe or reconcile what he saw to how happy he had seen me go by. I had never complained of anything at all. I had told them during my first days that I would never complain about anything if they would not care for me, and I really never did. The Senior Steward, Mr. Sikapite, stayed but just a little while and pronounced his farewell, holding back his tears. I realized he had not been pleased with the condition in which I lived.

The following Sunday, he convened a special urgent meeting. He ordered the Trustees and Stewards to buy me a bed, mattress and a pair of bedsheets. Some leaders tried to oppose the idea but Mr. Sikapite challenged them saying, 'We have more money in our coffers since his (Pastor) coming than we ever had before. Why can't we appreciate and support him in this small way?' After a protracted contention, they voted and the proposal went through.

I was shifted from church to church around the Copperbelt District. Most of the times, my transfers were based on undue reports that came from some fellow Pastors. Most of the churches I went to, I was sent to either solve problems or rebuild membership. As hinted earlier on, in 1983, I went to Ndeke A.M.E. Church in Ndola because members had deserted. In 1983, (the same year) I went to Mother Hughes A.M.E. Church at Kabushi in Ndola as Associate Pastor to the Presiding Elder Rev. C.Y. Katebe because the Pastor had resigned. In 1984, I was sent to Chifubu A.M.E. Church because the Pastor had dispersed the members. In 1987, I went to Luanshya's Thomas because the Stewards were more powerful than the pastors before. Now, I was sent to Mufulira's St. Paul's A.M.E. Church in 1989. This time, the pastors there heard that I live in Low-Density Residential Housing or 'White man's area' so they went and spoke good to the Presiding Elder and the members who detested my intolerable leadership since they could not order me to follow their system. They opted for a senior Minister so we were swapped. After two years, I raised the membership, bought benches, or rather pews and put supports in the middle of the building since the roof was curving in.

In 1989, I was in Mufulira for only one year. I was transferred to Kitwe's Bright Chapel because there was a financial dispute between most members and the Pastor. The Pastor had been supporting the Senior Steward in organizing foreign support. The money was coming in but the church wanted to be monitoring and diverting some of the money to other projects which had not been intended for. This was 1990, and in 1994, I was sent back to Mother Hughes at Kabushi in Ndola because the Church was deserted. Out of 386 members, less than 100 members had remained.

In 2000, I was sent to Mufulira's Allen Temple. This was because Rev. Paul Bupe went for studies to the U.S.A. The big and advanced church could not be left without a capable Pastor. I went through a rough ride. Part of it was from my father in the faith and part of it from the District W.M.S. leadership and women members in general over the leopard skin.

I served six Bishops. I served under Bishop Cornelius E. Thomas for four years. I served under Bishop Robert Lee Pruitt from 1984 to 1988 and then Bishop Richard Allen Chappelle from 1988 to 1992. I also served under Bishop Robert Webster from 1992 to 1996 and under Bishop Larry Theodore Kirkland from 1996 to 2000. Lastly, I served under Bishop Preston Williams from 2000 to 2002 during which I resigned under duress and formed the growing Higher Dimensions Church. We now have seven established churches and have a community school called Human Concerns Community School – all under self-supporting basis."

Rev. Wilson Mpundu with President of Zambia, Dr. Kenneth D. Kaunda at State House in Lusaka for dinner after a Pastors and Church Leaders' consultation meeting at Mulungushi Hall, 1991.

Rev. Wilson Mpundu is a great preacher of the word. His messages are inspirational and he was powerfully used by the Holy Spirit. He was full of wisdom beyond his age and just a wonderful person you enjoyed being around. When you were in fellowship with him you wouldn't want to break whether in church or just visiting him or you. He exercised great restraint even under great persecution. However, like Jerusalem which our Lord Jesus Christ wept over, the Church failed to recognize a servant in Bishop Mpundu whom I loved greatly and God had sent them. His departure was a very painful experience not only for me but for many believers in this Church.

His ministry is a reflection of what an institutional church without Christ can do to its ministers. We have the body of Christ and the institutional church. This history is about the Institutional Church – the A.M.E. Church and the body of Christ waring against religion and non-believers influenced by demonic spirits. It is also about the power of God in the Church of God. Reminiscing of my discussions with the man of God who was one of my favourite preachers and colleagues I loved dearly in this Church, the persecution he had endured like many who preached salvation in Jesus was unimaginable. Once, around 1990 at Bright Chapel funeral service attended by many Pentecostal Churches who were related to the deceased, Rev. Wilson Mpundu preached a moving sermon in a packed church that left the hearers blessed and at the edge of their seats and the power of the Holy Spirit was intensely present touching and convicting every listener.

When Rev. Wilson Mpundu married Mother Grace Mpundu in July 1988 in Ndola, the wedding brought both joy and sorrow! It was an emotional occasion that further went on to reveal the hardships of an A.M.E. Church preacher of Christ in Zambia who had left everything for the cause of Christ. When the Rev. Mpundu was organising his wedding, he approached the Presiding Elder to inform him that all was set but he needed financial help so he could hold a wedding ceremony. The Presiding Elder, answered him instead by saying, *"Mukula mbulu uilange na maka, kosapo fye we mwine."* Basically, he was informing him that he had weighed himself for the occasion; therefore, he needed to show people that he was ready for it! The Presiding Elder, consequently, never offered any help to him!

Rev. Mpundu's father had retired. Besides, he had rejected him as a son; therefore, he couldn't go to ask for any help from him! He had, subsequently, decided to go to friends – his former schoolmates to solicit for help, and they did. "I went to my old friends from school and it was friends who paid for the wedding but on the day of the wedding, the bride had no shoes and the cake was not there either! The brothers and sisters of the bride held on to the cake because they didn't want their sister to get married to a preacher – and a poor A.M.E. Church pastor for that matter!" narrated the Rev. Mpundu.

It was now 12:00 PM, two hours after the time the wedding was supposed to be officially on! Word had now gone around that the wedding had been called off. The bride had a wedding dress but no shoes and was about to get it off as were the groom and his groomsmen. When Bro. Albeto Mwansa arrived from Lusaka, he was surprised that the wedding had not started. He immediately went and bought the shoes for the bride after learning of the predicament and everything was set. However, the team learned that the people who had brought food had dispersed and had taken sausages and chicken with them which they had distributed and had locked up the remainder! Rev. Wilson Mpundu was pastor at Thomas in Luanshya at the time.

Mother Grace Mpundu with Rev. Wilson Mpundu in Ndola, 2002.

The Rev. Caleb Ngoma officiated at this wedding. He married the couple and when the time came for the rings, they found that the rings were missing. Br. Bernard Chibuta lent the groom his ring and another person lent one to the bride and the vows were pronounced! "We had no bed and used to put clothes on the mat which we used as a bed," recalled the preacher to this writer. "Since I joined the ministry in 1980 and went into admission in 1981, this is the kind of life we lived."

At Mother Hughes A.M.E. Church, Rev. Wilson Mpundu was dragged to a local court by three church members. The members at Kabushi, Ronald Mwaba Pilikolo, a Mr. Banda and Deacon Mulenga (Rev.) had taken the Rev. Mpundu to court accusing him of insinuating that they were wizards! Rev. Mpundu had approached Ronald Mwaba Pilikolo and talked to him if what had just occurred (the death of his child) was the shock he had meant was to happen at the church or was he to expect a different incident? Mr. Pilikolo, in an apparent reference to the sudden death of Rev. Rowland Mwenyo who had died after being hit by a car just weeks after his resignation at the Church (Mother Hughes in Ndola) in 1983 had reportedly hinted on "another soon to be news of shock and taboo (*umupamba*) if Rev. Mpundu did not stop conducting prayers at the church or if he did not voluntarily depart."

Mr. Pilikolo had accused Rev. Mpundu of insinuating that he was a wizard. He requested the Pastor to apologise or else he was going to take him to court. The Pastor did not and he was taken to court by the trio, all members of Mother Hughes. After the Pastor explained what had transpired at the church to the local court, the three local court judges informed the plaintiff Pilikolo, Banda and Local Deacon Mulenga that, "You are wizards! You killed Pastor Mwenyo but you can't kill this one!" One judge said, "I will be praying for you," nevertheless, Rev. Wilson Mpundu in mitigation urged the trio that "We need to work together and stop all threats." The case was dismissed and closed but the court called them "wizards." The judge also told the Pastor on the team (Deacon Mulenga) "a wizard!" When his enemies told him, he was going to "cry" and wished him ill, he told them, "I was born in a family of 9 and I don't cry when it is painful, I cry when I am happy!"

Rev. Jeremiah Mwenyo

Rev. Jeremiah Mwenyo is a son of one of the pioneers of Revival in the A.M.E. Church in Zambia, the late Rev. Rowland Mwenyo. Rev. Jeremiah Mwenyo was born to Rev. Rowland Mwenyo and Mother Dofilia Kafeka Mwenyo on 27th May, 1949 at Chibanga village, Chief Nkana on the Copperbelt Province in Northern Rhodesia. He attended school at Chibuluma Primary School from Sub A to Standard IV then went to Kalulushi Primary School where he did his Upper Standard V and VI. He then went to Chifubu Secondary School following a 2-year break and completed secondary education there in 1971. Rev. Jeremiah Mwenyo obtained a Diploma in Theology from Western Cape University where he studied from 2001-2003.

Rev. Mwenyo began his ministry as a lay pastor in 1994 at Chibanga Circuit in rural Kalulushi. He was pastor here from 1994 to 1997. He was ordained Deacon by Bishop Larry Kirkland in the South-West Zambia Annual Conference on 5th October, 1997 in Ndola and Elder by the same Bishop on 3rd October, 1999 in Ndola. (Rev. Mwenyo was ordained on same dates with Rev. Charles Kapungwe. They were in the same class in the Annual Conference). He was appointed to Chapula Circuit from 1997 to 2001 and then was transferred to Calvary 2001 to 2002. Rev. Mwenyo was moved to Allen Temple in 2002 where he remained until 2009. Bishop Kawimbe moved him in 2009 to Brookins at Chingola where he was until 2013. In 2013, he became pastor of Mother Hughes in Ndola until 2015.

In 2015, Rev. Jeremiah Mwenyo was transferred to Thomas at Luanshya. He was there until 2016 when he was moved to Cummings Chapel at Chawama in Lusaka where he was still Pastor at the time I talked to him in July of 2019. Rev. Mwenyo was appointed Dean of the Episcopal Board of Examiners in 2003 and has been serving in this position ever since. He is married to Mother Beatrice Mwenyo who was born in 1952. They married in 1985 following the passing away of his first wife. They have seven children.

Rev. Jeremiah, a son of an A.M.E. Church pioneer in Zambia, Rev. Rowland Mwenyo who had suffered persecution greatly became another victim of Wilfred Messiah! Messiah, at what was to be his last Annual Conference in Lusaka, he reappointed Rev. Jeremiah to Cummings, a congregation with 700 members on 2nd September, 2019. However, three weeks later, Rev. Jeremiah was moved to another congregation, Thomas Chapel, a congregation with less than 100 members by Messiah effecting appointments outside the Conferences, a part of his legacy as a man who constituted illegal meetings to run the Church in Zambia. He would go into the annals of history as one of the worst leaders to ever run the 17th Episcopal District.

Although Thomas Chapel had an official membership of 100, only 50 people attended Sunday services! About two weeks later, Messiah called for a meeting of his cronies (he had appointed juniors who were drank with power and could not oppose his illegal activities) and some pastors to a "Mini-Post Annual Conference" to assemble at night at 22:00 hours (10:00 PM) where he made new appointments and changes again! Rev. Jeremiah Mwenyo was moved to Kabwe's Brookins Chapel, our "Mother Bethel," a church with no toilets and with a membership of 100!

Thus, Rev. Mwenyo was appointed to three congregations by Messiah in one month! Messiah was a law to himself and he seldom consulted senior Presiding Elders except for his appointed corrupt juniors. Brookins Chapel was even failing to pay Rev. Mwenyo who was demoted without an explanation, a fate several pastors have endured under Saul the king who Israel had asked God to rule over them so they could be like other nations!

According to the Discipline a minister cannot be moved from a "First Church" to a "Third Church" unless there was extenuating circumstances which may border on disciplinary reasons. Even in such circumstances the Minister has to be informed of the planned move at least three months in advance! Sadly, "briefcase appointments" had increased since Messiah came to Zambia and in the absence of an emergency, this was maladministration and basically signified corruption. As I talked to Rev. Jeremiah in May 2020, aware of what his father had endured in this Church, my heart bled because he was contemplating leaving. It was not surprising Messiah currently had an ongoing case in the High Court of Zambia from aggrieved members!

Rev. Aaron Siwale

Rev. Aaron Siwale (now Bishop Siwale) was born to Mr. Learnson Kalembe Siwale and Mrs. Beatrice Totamanga Siwale in Kitwe. He was a member of Jordan Chapel at Wusakile in Kitwe since childhood. His mother and siblings were also members of Jordan. He attended Sunday school regularly with Rev. Charles Kapungwe when they were young. They also sang in the choir, Jordan Chapel Choir and Great Pillars Double Quartet together. His older brother, Lloyd M. Siwale, taught us in Sunday school passionately in the early 1970s. Rev. Siwale attended Nkana Primary School from 1970 to 1976 and later Ndeke Secondary School. He married Elizabeth Simwanza of Judah A.M.E. Church (then Mindolo) in March 1990.

Mother Elizabeth and Rev. Aaron Siwale in Lusaka in 2013.

Rev. Aaron Siwale attended Theological College of Central Africa (TCCA) at Kansenshi in Ndola. He obtained a Diploma in Theology in 1988. He was ordained Deacon in 1986 by Bishop Robert L. Pruitt and Elder in 1988 by Bishop Richard Allen Chappelle. Rev. Siwale was first appointed to Gethsemane in Kitwe in 1988. In 1990, he was transferred from Kitwe to Lusaka and was appointed to St. Johns at Mandevu in Lusaka from 1990 until his transfer to Bethel, Lusaka in 1992. During the time he was in Lusaka, he taught at Ebenezer Secondary School.

Rev. Siwale was a courted speaker at the Christian Education meetings yearly and a great resource to the YPD. He was a great Teacher of the word with a powerful expository teaching ministry and greatly used by God in deliverance ministry. We worked together in this area and many people possessed with evil spirits or bound in witchcraft found deliverance through the Lord's ministry in him. Once, while praying for a woman in witchcraft in Kitwe in 1988, Rev. Siwale later teased me because the woman with demons had been pulling my shirt under demonic influence while saying "We will beat this little one!" At the time he was a Pastor of Gethsemane and I was a Conference YPD President! He also taught at His People Bible School hosted at the University of Zambia, Great East Road Campus when Rev. Paul Kawimbe was Dean at the time in the 1990s. We lived together from 1988 to 1990 in Parklands, Kitwe.

Rev. Siwale was among ministers who were highly persecuted for belief in the power of the Holy Spirit. Nevertheless, he was a bold believer who could not be intimidated! He pioneered the Charismatic movement in the capital City of Lusaka and was met with great resistance and persecution, especially at Bethel. He was instrumental to the revival in the Church in the Midlands. Nevertheless, in 1998, together with other ministers, Rev. Aaron Siwale pulled out of the A.M.E. Church to form Lift Him Up Church where he assumed the role of Bishop. It was the biggest exodus of believers from the A.M.E. Church at the time and many youths left at this time. Among the ministers who left were Rev. Richard Kasanda, Rev. Happy Mulwe, Rev. Samson Chalomba (son of Rev. Samson Mulonga Kapufi), Pastor Boyd Nkhoma, Pastor Benson Mashikini, Pastor Willie Kavungu, Pastor Mirriam Mwape and Pastor William Mwape (not related).

The word of God had spread in the A.M.E. Church by 1998 than at any period in the Church's history in Zambia. Copperbelt and Lusaka were the leading Provinces in this revival and seminars to empower believers were held yearly. Rev. Siwale nicknamed us "Commandos" because of the tenacity, non-compromising stance and steadfastness we had in sharing Jesus both in the Church and outside coupled with holding of prayer meetings including overnight prayer meetings frequently. In turn, we called him "General" because of his command of the Word of God and his fearlessness in battle. Rev. Siwale was a warrior who Satan fought relentlessly and the Church (A.M.E.) lost a great leader in him due failure by the leadership to recognize God's visitation. He was responsible for leading revival in Lusaka and was a courted speaker during Christian Education Congresses in the 17th Episcopal District. He is now leading a Church called "Tree of Life" as a Bishop in Lusaka.

Rev. Richard Kasanda

Rev. Richard Kasanda (now Bishop Dr. Richard Kasanda) was born in Chililabombwe (Bancroft) in Zambia. His father was Mr. John Kasanda. Mr. John Kasanda passed away in Ndola and was buried there on Thursday 15th August, 2019 and the mother is Mrs. Elizabeth Kasanda. He attended Nkana Primary School (the same school Rev. Charles Kapungwe attended in Kitwe) and Kitwe Boys Secondary School. Rev. Kasanda later obtained a Fabrication and Welding Diploma at Luanshya Craft Training School under the Mines Manpower Development School. He was employed by Zambia Consolidated Copper Mines Limited (ZCCM) Nkana Division in Kitwe. He attended Faith L.I.F.E. Ministries Bible School in Kitwe, Zambia from 1998 to 2000 and obtained a Diploma in Biblical Studies and Christian Education. (He was Rev. Kapungwe's classmate).

Photo: Rev. Richard Kasanda and Rev. Charles Kapungwe (Trinity) at their graduation ceremony (Deliverance & Counseling) at Destiny Christian Ministries & Bible School at Nkana Hotel in Kitwe on 6th February, 1999. The school was started by Pastor Matthews Mtonga, one of the brothers from our famous "nursery" of YMCA Wusakile Fellowship.

Rev. Richard Kasanda was ordained Deacon at the Annual Conference meeting at Holiness (now Kirkland) in Ndola. He was ordained Deacon by Bishop Larry Kirkland in the South-West Zambia Annual Conference on 5th October, 1997 and reappointed to Mindolo Circuit which he renamed Judah. Rev. Kasanda and I were first appointed on 1st December, 1996 to Mindolo and Trinity, respectively, by Bishop Larry Kirkland.

Rev. Kasanda was a gifted singer, praise and worship leader, Evangelist, Teacher and a great organizer. He was a very humorous Teacher of the word and a very hardworking brother. While at Jordan, we partnered in ministry together in youth groups and reached many churches and areas for Jesus. He travelled to every circuit on the Copperbelt including remote ones and beyond when we were in YPD. He was one of the pioneers of Calvary in Kitwe and we worked together effectively. As a Pastor, he turned around Judah and it became one of the fastest growing churches in Zambia.

Rev. Richard organized overnight prayer meetings regularly which we all gladly attended in Kitwe. He was a workhorse of a man among believers. Rev. Richard used to organize weekly Overnight Prayers every Fridays when he was Pastor of Judah and we attended these prayers without fail! They were very helpful to ministry! Rev. Kasanda was part of the joint Central Assembly of God and A.M.E. Church Bible Study Group that met at my home in Parklands, Kitwe from 1990 to about 1996. He left the Church in 1998 when they formed Lift Him Up Church.

He is now a consecrated Bishop. He was consecrated Bishop when he was pioneering a Church in Botswana. Bishop Kasanda has been empowering people in nations in Africa and running schools and ministries in Kenya and Uganda. He is also an author with a vision of strengthening the body of Christ. Among the books he has written are *"Lord Open My Eyes," "Back in the Race," "Everybody is Looking for You," "The Call of God," "Locating Your Spot," "Such As I Have," "The Mantle and the Blessing," and "Increasing Your Capacity."*

Bishop Kasanda is the founder and President of Kingdom Life Membership Institute. It provides leadership and mentorship to believers in Southern, East and Central Africa. The loss incurred by a visionless denomination in this man of God is enormous because he was a great organizer and a workhorse of a man in our fellowship and in our ministry. I frequently consult him and miss his ministry greatly. Revival in A.M.E. Church in Zambia, especially among the youth cannot be mentioned without him!

Rev. John Mukeya.

Rev. John Mukeya (now Bishop John Mukeya) was born on 27th July, 1956 in Elizabethville, (Lubumbashi) in Belgian Congo (Congo DR). He was born to Mr. Benoit Mukeya and Christine Ngoyi. He attended Saint Benoit Primary School and Secondary School of Kailima. He went to college and studied accounts in Lubumbashi, Congo. Rev. Mukeya was baptized on 10th May 1990 by late Rev. Richard Mwaba at St. Johns A.M.E. Church, Bulangililo Kitwe and was received into full membership in 1981. He was a Senior Trustee at St. John from 1985 to 1990 and in 1993 he moved to Trinity as Senior Evangelist. He got into Admission the same year at the Annual Conference held at Kabompo, North-Western Province under the South-West Zambia Conference.

Photo: Rev. John Mukeya. 8th May, 2020.

He was appointed to Membe before going into his second-year studies in 1994. Rev. John Mukeya was ordained Deacon by Bishop Robert Webster at Luanshya's Thomas on 15th May 1995 and as Elder on 5th October, 1997 by Bishop Larry T. Kirkland. He completed his Theological Education by Extension in Zambia (TEEZ) on 15th August, 1997. Rev. Mukeya opened Chimwemwe (Mumba Temple) while he was Pastor of Membe at Twatasha in Kitwe. The church used to meet at Mrs. Namuka's home as a cell group. He also opened Kawama in Kitwe. (Recall that these were points which Rev. Philemon Chakalipa Mumba had spearheaded).

Rev. John Mukeya was one of the most dynamic ministers of the Church. He was Pastor of a very closely-knit body of believers at Membe, Twatasha. A number of these members had their origins from Congo DR. The love for God the Church at Membe had was phenomenon! The church had a very strong praise and worship ministry. They regularly met for prayers at the church especially overnight prayer meetings and it attracted members and non-members from other denominations to these meetings for years. The people were drawn from far places including, Race Course, Kawama and Chimwemwe. This is what prompted the Pastor to open up two branches at Chimwemwe and Kawama because he felt that the distance was unbearable for those who came from distant areas.

Rev. John Mukeya is one of the ministers who helped A.M.E. Church in Zambia experience revival. Membe A.M.E. Church, which was a small church, was always full during worship services. It also enjoyed a membership that cut across age groups with both youth and adults well represented. In many other churches where revival had begun, many adults especially the older ones were resistant to change but at Membe, you saw older believers who had been equally zealous for the things of God. He understood the things of the Spirit and you could hold spiritual conversations with him unlike some who just were zealous for the traditions of their fathers.

Rev. Mukeya left the Church in 2000 and started Compassionate Pentecostal International following differences with the Presiding Elder. He had five churches but when he went to Congo DR for a while, two of the churches at Mufulira and Chingola which he had left behind were taken away. He currently has three churches now, two in Ndola and one in Kitwe. I talked to him over the phone on a number of occasions to get this history. On 8th November, 2018 I talked to him and praised the Lord for his love and dedication to the Lord's work. He had been instrumental in the revival of the A.M.E. Church in Zambia but sadly, again a visionless Church failed to see God's visitation in this servant of the Lord and saw him leave!

Rev. Joseph Sakwala

No detailed record or information was available on Rev. Joseph Sakwala's at the time of this writing. He was the Pastor of Trinity at Garneton and my predecessor. He had been Pastor at Trinity from 1991 to 1996 when he passed away at Kitwe Central Hospital where I worked. He hailed from Congo DR and was a brother of Rev. John Mukeya. He had a strong community church at Garneton comprising mostly immigrants who had come from Congo DR. He had just acquired the land from the City of Kitwe for Trinity before he went to be with the Lord and I paid for the land for Trinity in full using personal funds which was quite substantial at the time because the church was very poor. Rev. Sakwala worked as an architect at a private firm in downtown Kitwe. He was married to Mother Jane Sakwala and had a number of children.

Rev. Aram Mulwe

No detailed records or information was available on Rev. Aram Mulwe. He was married to Mirriam Mulwe and they had six children, three boys and three girls. Tupelo, Angel, the twins Kalande and Chibwe, Aram, Jr., and Chola. Two of the girls are married and Tupelo is a Pastor with Restoration Ministries. Rev. Mulwe was ordained Deacon at Allen Temple, Mufulira in 1998 by Bishop Larry Kirkland. He was ordained Elder in 2000 by Bishop Preston Williams. He was appointed to Chipulukusu A.M.E. Church in Ndola 2001 to 2002 by Presiding Elder Cuthbert Katebe and to Richard Allen in Ndola under the same P.E. His third and last appointment was to Holy Cross in Ndola. He went to be with the Lord in 2005. Rev. Mulwe left behind Eliashib Ministries for Orphans and Widows which the wife continued to run.

Rev. Happy Mulwe

No detailed records or information were available on Rev. Happy Mulwe. He was from Ndola where he went to school and was a younger brother to Rev. Aram Mulwe. He came from a family of singers and was a member of Mother Hughes in Ndola. Br. Happy was an influential YPD leader who taught salvation by faith in our time. Rev. Charles Kapungwe first met Brother Happy Mulwe in Kabwe in 1987 and they got acquainted at a choir concert at Membe A.M.E. Church. Rev. Mulwe later went to Lusaka and attended University of Zambia where he graduated with Bachelor of Science in Biology. He then became a teacher. He met Dr. Musenge Matibini who was to graduate later from the University of Zambia School of Medicine – Ridgeway Campus and got married. They were members of Maranatha A.M.E. Church in Lusaka and he organized yearly revival meetings in the Midlands which began to change many youths. He was ordained Deacon in 1997 by Bishop Larry Kirkland. He left the A.M.E. Church in 1998 when they formed Lift Him Up Ministries after what was seen as failure by the Church to change from traditions and poor leadership. Rev. Happy Mulwe is an author.

Rev. Royd Mwandu

No detailed information was available on Rev. Royd Mwandu at the time of this writing. However, Rev. Mwandu was ordained Deacon on 5th October, 1997 at Kirkland in Ndola and Elder on 3rd October, 1999 at the Trade Fair Show Grounds hosted by Rev. Wilson Mpundu's Mother Hughes in Ndola. He was ordained by Bishop Larry Kirkland during the South-West Zambia Annual Conferences. He is the Pastor of Downtown (Messiah) in Chingola, (2020).

Rev. Emmanuel Ngalala

Rev. Emmanuel Ngalala was born in 1974 at Mununga, Luapula Province in Zambia. He was born to Mr. William Ngalala and Mrs. Hildah Malangisha. He attended Nyamfwa Primary School at Mununga and John Bosco Secondary School in Mansa. He joined the A.M.E. Church in 1981 and was admitted in ministry in 2000. Rev. Emmanuel Ngalala was ordained Deacon in 2002 by Bishop Preston Williams and Elder in 2004 by Bishop Paul Kawimbe. He was pastor of Dr. Kawimbe (Puta), Mununga, Munkombwe, Chipipya, Samson Kapufi and Samfya. He is Pastor of Samfya A.M.E. Church (2020) which, currently, he said was the biggest A.M.E. Church in Luapula Province. He was appointed Presiding Elder for Mwense North District in September 2019. Presiding Elder Rev. Ngalala has been very helpful in collecting necessary materials for this writing. He has been the younger minister who was assisting Rev. Samson Kapufi pass important documents to my desk. This work could not have been adequately written without him and the senior minister Rev. Kapufi. I am thankful to God for them. He is now Pastor and Presiding Elder.

Rev. Emmanuel Ngalala, P.E., and Pastor of Samfya A.M.E. Church – 2019. (Photo 15th February, 2014 when he was Pastor of Samson Temple, Mansa).

Rev. Mirriam Nakapizye

No proper records were available on Rev. Mirriam Nakapizye. I first met her at Mufulira in about 1983 at a choir competition. She might have been 17 or 18 years then when I first knew her. She was from Chililabombwe where she probably had joined the Church. She had been in YPD there. Sister Mirriam Nakapizye worked for Zambia Railways. She came to Kitwe on transfer and later had worked at Kabwe Zambia Railways where she had been transferred to. We did a lot of ministry with Sister Mirriam at Jordan Chapel for over five years. She was a member of the Fellowship which we had started and used to meet after the main Church service at 14:00 PM every Sunday. This Fellowship came into being following a general discontentment by youths, especially the born again group with the nature of the services which hindered the work of the Holy Spirit and were seen to be rigid and traditional.

Rev. Nakapizye was also one of the founding members of Calvary A.M.E. Church in Kitwe. Sister Mirriam was part of the joint Central Assembly of God and A.M.E. Church Bible Study Group that met at my home in Parklands, Kitwe from 1990 to about 1996. She went to Zimbabwe early 2000s for school and attended United Theological College in Harare, Zimbabwe. She was appointed Pastor while there and was Pastor of Webster Temple A.M.E. Church in Harare in 2002. When she fell sick, she went to Zambia and went to be with the

Lord while in Zambia just days after she had preached at Trinity. She was ordained in ministry after I had left Zambia. Rev. Nakapizye had contributed greatly to the revival of the Church in Zambia through prayer and evangelism.

Pastor Bright Mumba

Pastor Bright Mumba was born in 1960 to Mr. Moses Chibale and Phoebe Mwelwa at Malele Village in Mwense in Northern Rhodesia. No detailed records or information was available on Pastor Mumba. He attended school at Buyantanshi in Mufulira and attended many A.M.E. Churches including Allen Temple in Mufulira, Bright Chapel, Jordan Chapel and Covenant in Kitwe. He was a great intercessor and a mighty man of valour or warrior for the Lord. He once accompanied me in 1994 when I went to organise the Healthcare Christian Fellowship (HCF) in Luapula Province visiting many hospitals there. We had shared the vision of HCF at the hospitals at Mansa, Samfya, Mambilima, Mwense, Mbereshi, Kawambwa and Nchelenge. He was instrumental in the revival of the A.M.E. Church as a Teacher and a great prayer warrior. He understood spiritual warfare a lot. He became a Lay Pastor at Covenant in Kitwe which was started by Rev. D.D. Musole in 1998. We worked together in the YPD ministering Jesus for years locally in Kitwe and on the Copperbelt Province. He went to be with the Lord in Kitwe in 2004.

Pastor Bright Mumba.

Chapter 22
The A.M.E. Church in Zambia and Congo DR Today

The A.M.E. Church in Zambia and Congo has expanded from what it was decades ago when it was planted in these two countries. The 21st Century has seen the growth in number of planted churches in these two countries and beyond. We have hundreds of churches today scattered all over Zambia and Congo DR. However, in Zambia, many of these churches lack basic amenities such as toilets, offices and are poorly built compared with many other progressive denominations in the country.

The biggest drawback to these churches is poor administration. Consecutive administrators emphasize on collecting what they call "The Budget" every six months from congregations as opposed to soul winning. Believers see this as "Taxation" and equivalent of "hut tax" or "forced taxes" (Chapter 3) that the British levied on Northern Rhodesians. This is not just for the Church in Zambia but is a part of the A.M.E. Church organization. Pastors failing to pay these budgets risk losing their appointments in spite of the fact that many of the churches they lead are very poor. As long as "taxes" are paid to support the Presiding Elder and the Bishop's Conference Claims, the "job" of the pastor would likely be "safe!" The second drawback is failure by administration to instill high standards. Therefore, in spite of the expansion of the church, the eyesore caused by poorly-constructed A.M.E. Church structures is endemically rampant today in these lands.

The A.M.E. Church in Congo DR has finally been embraced after many years of isolation. Consecutive Bishops have now regularly held Conferences there from 2000. Zambia has also enhanced contacts with the Church in Congo DR. For instance, Rev. Theodore Kalumba, (my former Pastor at Jordan Chapel in Kitwe from 1989 to 1991) was sent to serve in Congo DR between 2009 and 2011. He was asked to help Rev. Kabala, P.E., who was from Zambia and was serving at Likasi in Congo DR. Rev. Kalumba was accompanied by Rev. Jonas Musonda, Rev. Julius Musonda, Rev. Malaya, Rev. Kayabwe and Rev. Gift Kunda all from Zambia.

In 1991, Rev. David Simfukwe had been sanctioned by the Annual Conference presided by Bishop Richard Allen Chappelle at Solwezi to sort out uncertainties in Congo DR (Zaire). The delegation from Congo DR had reported that the Church was on a verge of being banned there. For some reason, Bishop Chappelle did not show willingness to go and Rev. Simfukwe offered to. He went two weeks after the Conference and met a Presiding Elder from Luapula, leaders from Congo DR and the Anglican Church leadership which had helped the Church to remain open because it had been speaking to the authorities on behalf of the A.M.E. Church.

Rev. Simfukwe registered the Church and signed documents on behalf of the Presiding Bishop of the 17th Episcopal District. He reported what he had done to the Bishop upon his return. This helped to lift the impending ban but he was to face wrath from his colleagues in Zambia who scorched him relentlessly for "posing as a Bishop in Congo and signing documents as though he were a Bishop!" The fallout was so bad that the political machinery of the Church ensured that he lost the first church Ebenezer in Lusaka and was transferred to Allen Temple in Mufulira in 1991! He remained there until his departure with his family to the U.S.A. in September 1996. He had however, not relinquished running of the school and a Mennonite missionary who had helped begin the mechanic school with Rev. Simfukwe had remained in Lusaka. The missionary left after four years. The departure of the Rev. Simfukwe marked the end of Ebenezer Secondary School as well! After Rev. Peter M.P. Mwenya had been at Ebenezer briefly, the same Church political machinery ousted him and was replaced with Rev. Banda!

We share names below of ministers from Zambia mostly drawn from the Roll Call of 1981. These names are from what used to be a very large South Zambia Conference which comprised North Western Province, Copperbelt Province, Western Province, Central Province (and Lusaka), Southern Province and Eastern Province before the Conference was split in 1988 by Bishop Richard Allen Chappelle. The former huge Conference became South East Zambia Conference and South West Zambia Conference following that split. We have also included a few ministers who were not present or were not ordained at the time as well. The Annual Conference Schedule of 2011/2012 is displayed after this listing of ministers and also covers Conferences in Zambia and Democratic Republic of Congo. South West Zambia Conference was later split during Bishop Paul Kawimbe's term in 2008. Zambezi Conference comprising North Western Province and part of Lukulu District (coopted in from Western Province, because of its proximity to North Western Province) was formed because of a large geographical area which disadvantaged rural areas in travelling to Copperbelt Province for meetings. Thus, Copperbelt Province became South West Zambia Conference taking the old name.

Former South Zambia Annual Conference 1981 Roll Call. Additional Names Prior and After Included.

Rev. J.L.C. Membe
Rev. Mundia K. Wakunguma
Rev. Foodson B.S. Washiama
Rev. Henrique M. Lukamba,
Rev. Caleb Ngoma
Rev. Cuthbert Yoram Katebe, P.E.
Rev. David K. Simfukwe,
Rev. Henry C. Alimasi, P.E.
Rev. Isaac C. Mumpanshya, P.E.
Rev. Dr. Daniel M. Mkhwanazi, P.E. 12th Nov., 1981 roll call
Rev. Samuel Blackson K. Yanduli, P.E.
Rev. R. Khumalo, P.E.
Rev. Ian Dusston R. Mawhaila, P.E.
Rev. Solomon Njolomba, P.E., North Western 1980/81
Rev. Nyambe S. Lifalile, P.E.
Rev. Julius Sakulanda, P.E.
Rev. Robert Mushaukwa, P.E.
Rev. Diamond. Z. Konde, P. E.
Rev. Geoffrey Manjisana 12th Nov., 1981 Roll call Livingstone
Rev. Happy Elias Chinula
Rev. Amon J. Chansa
Rev. Adam Banda
Rev. J.C. Banda
Rev. Edward L. Manjata
Rev. Nguvulu S. Kambeu
Rev. Elijah P. Banda
Rev. Field T. Sikazwe, P.E.
Rev. Jonathan Silumbwe (late).
Rev. Theresa Ngunga

Rev. Greenfel D. Kabwe (Kasama)
Rev. E. Viyela Katanya
Rev. David L. Hadebe
Rev. Coaster K. Kaunda
Rev. Henry K. Walizimba
Rev. Alick Sachipako
Rev. Chitungila Katoyo
Rev. Monica Ngosa, (Pastor, Roan)
Rev. Adam Banda
Rev. Mary Chipawa
Rev. Mayiles C. Phiri
Rev. C. Phiri
Rev. Rexta Banda
Rev. Joel E.S. Membe, (younger brother to Rev. J.L.C. Membe); also served in Luanshya
Rev. Makoloni Kachambalele
Rev. Y.K. Daka
Rev. Laston Mhango
Rev. P.S. Nkhuwa
Rev. Mateo Chibanga
Rev. E.D. Matebezi
Rev. Michael Simukonda
Rev. Winson Simukonda
Rev. Dhlakama
Rev. S. Saka
Rev. Kacencete
Rev. Stephen V. Chambata
Rev. Stanley Kunda
Rev. Baldwin N. Zulu (Was at Brookins then moved to Mother Hughes in 1979)
Rev. Brown C. Alumeta (Lusaka)
Rev. Richard Mwaba (St. Peter, Kitwe in 1985)
Rev. Laston Mhango
Rev. David Numa
Rev. Elijah N. Musonda
Rev. Philip Ondya
Rev. G.W. Kanyembo (Gethsemane A.M.E. once P.E., Roan District)
Rev. Levy Y. Kamanga
Rev. E.G. Matelevi
Rev. Samson H. Tembo
Rev. Obed Kombe
Rev. Kefasi R. Sichilongo, (Mother Hughes)
Rev. Samuel Musonda
Rev. Francis S.B. Kofi
Rev. Jamaica D. Ngosa
Rev. Dickson Kapepa, P.E.
Rev. Bedford Mwewa (Lusaka)
Rev. Theodore D. Kalumba, (former Pastor at Jordan, Kitwe)
Rev. Robertson Z. Chunda
Rev. Aaron J. Nkiwane
Rev. Philemon N. Shakange
Rev. Robert Tina
Rev. B.J. Phiri
Rev. Siusiku
Rev. M.P.P. Mwenya, P.E.
Rev. Rowland Mwenyo
Rev. Jeremiah Mwenyo (Son of Rev. Rowland)
Rev. Yotham Phiri (former Pastor at Jordan, Kitwe)
Rev. Isaiah Phiri
Rev. Philemon Mumba (former Pastor at Jordan, Kitwe)
Rev. Chalomba
Rev. Aaron Siwale
Rev. Richard Kasanda
Rev. Chisamba Phiri, (former Pastor at Jordan, Kitwe)
Rev. Susanne Matale (daughter of Rev. J.L.C. Membe)
Rev. Edith Mutale
Rev. Jones Sinyangwe
Rev. Edwin Fundi
Rev. Daniel Fundi, Gethsemane (Son of Rev. Edwin).
Rev. Ben Chiokola, Covenant A.M.E. Church
Rev. Enock Chipili Jordan
Rev. Chinyanta, (Judah A.M.E. Church)
Rev. Chabala (Mother Hughes)
Rev. Mabel Chanda (Allen, Ndola)
Rev. Sikapite
Rev. Idah Simukwai, (former Pastor at Jordan, Kitwe)
Rev. Wilson Mpundu
Rev. Paul Bupe
Rev. John Mukeya

Rev. Joseph Sakwala (Brother of Rev. John Mukeya above)
Rev. Senkwe (late April, 2011 – Jordan Chapel, Kitwe)
Rev. Enock Chipili (late 2016 – Jordan Chapel, Kitwe)
Rev. Samuel Mulapwa (former Pastor at Jordan, Kitwe)
Rev. Alick Mulapwa
Rev. Amon Chansa (Roan – Abigail Chansa's father)
Rev. Paul Kawimbe
Rev. Elasto Mwansa
Rev. Chalomba
Rev. Mirriam Nakapizye
Rev. Stephen Chifunda
Rev. Happy Mulwe
Rev. Alick Kapesa
Rev. Victor C. Sikazwe (Lusaka)
Rev. Charles Kapungwe
Rev. Hoppes Jacob Chiluba
Rev. D.D. Kunda
Rev. David D. Musole (former Pastor at Jordan, Kitwe)
Rev. Mwansa (Solwezi)
Rev. Phillip Mutalange
Rev. Joel Mazimba
Rev. Godfrey P. Mutembo (former Pastor at Jordan, Kitwe)
Rev. Elsie Musonda (Mindolo/Luanshya)
Rev. Alfred Mwika Kalobwe (former Pastor at Jordan, Kitwe)
Rev. Francis Chiku Paikua Banda (formerly, Jordan Chapel pastor, late)
Rev. G.S.S. Mulumbwa
Rev. Simbeye
Rev. Clement Chola
Rev. Stanley Kunda, late.
Rev. Benjamin Mugala
Rev. Frank Membe (Son of Rev. J.L.C. Membe)
Rev. Mackray Kaonga
Rev. Collins Kavuka
Rev. Anold Chipawa
Rev. Mbita Mbao (Lusaka)

Rev. Everisto Siulapwa
Rev. Khumalo (Kabwe)
Rev. Mulawo
Rev. Bernard Chibuta
Rev. Simuziya (Kabwe)
Rev. Kabaso (Lusaka)
Rev. Michael Gondwe (Lusaka/P.E. Mongu)
Rev. Richard Ngulube (Lusaka)
Rev. Laston Sichangwa (Lusaka)
Rev. Gilbert Masongo (Lusaka, late 2019)
Rev. Newton Masunga
Rev. Kaonga
Rev. Chapala Banda (Lusaka, retired)
Rev. Everisto Paul Kahenge (Queens)
Rev. J.J. Lukwesa (Bethel Church – Chililabombwe)
Rev. Mwewa (Light House, Kamenza)
Rev. Amigo Mwansa (Allen, Mufulira; Jordan, Kitwe)
Rev. Taylor Siulapwa (St. Paul – Kamuchanga, Mufulira)
Rev. Robinson Chileshe (St. Thomas-Chingola)
Rev. Albert Mwansa St. Stephen, Kalulushi
Rev. Royd Mwandu (Messiah Temple, Chingola)
Rev. Kennedy Mazimba, P.E.
Rev. Boyd Mazimba (Son of Rev. Joel Mazimba)
Rev. Walima
Rev. Samson S.K. Tembo (Chamba Valley – Lusaka, later P.E., Eastern Province)
Rev. Mayor Tembo (Thomas – Luanshya)
Rev. Kachusha
Rev. Dr. Bruce S. Gamakwenda
Rev. Pearson Chilukuta
Rev. Langster D. Zulu
Rev. Chansa K. Mulenga
Rev. Denovan L. Kaputula
Rev. Paul Shimunza
Rev. Kutemwa Simuyemba (Livingstone, 2020)
Rev. Prince Tawila (Mongu, 2020)
Rev. David Kaunda Phiri, P.E.

The A.M.E. Church in Zambia and Congo DR Today: Annual Conference Schedule – 2011/2012

South East Zambia Annual Conference

Lusaka District
Presiding Elder
Rev. P.M. Chilukuta
P.O. Box 31478, Lusaka

CHURCH	PASTOR
1. Ebenezer	M.Y. Gondwe
2. Membe	A. Sikapite
3. Mot. Lubemba	V.N. Sikazwe
4. Cummings	G.G. Ng'ambi
5. Bright	C.M. Masongo
6. Bethsaida	A.J. Sinyangwe
7. Mot. Lisabe	W. Chabala
8. Mot. Thomas	D.K. Phiri
9. Maranatha	S.G. Mutupa
10. St. Paul	T. Chishatama
11. Grace	E. Mwewa
12. St. Mark	D. Kazembe
13. Richard Allen	R.N. Kachusha
14. St. Joseph	H.K. Mumba
15. St. Luke	
16. Williams II	J. Zulu
17. Kawimbe Chapel	S. Lwimba
18. Chilambila	N. Phiri
19. Paul Kawimbe	J. Chinyemba
20. Mot. Yvonne	K. Kawimbe
21. Agape	J. Phiri
22. Mumbwa Town	B. Sampa
23. Emmanuel	B. Chabala
24. Siavonga	M. Kapwepwe
25. Keembe	V. Kamwendo
26. Kafue	N. Phiri
27. Mpatisha	D. Mungungu
28. Kirkland	E. Chiwala

Lukulu District
Presiding Elder
Rev. R. Kapeshi
P.O. Box 950002, Lukulu

CHURCH	PASTOR
1. Luachuma	K. Muke
2. Likomeno	P. Kachelewa
3. Jordan	A. Sawashipa
4. Bethsaida	C. Kasoka
5. Yvonne Kawimbe	R.C. Kaumba
6. Kawaya	F. M. Kangolo

Chipata District
Presiding Elder
Rev. C. Saizamba
P.O. Box 510165, Chipata

CHURCH	PASTOR
1. Bethel	J.M. Mbazima
2. St. Louis	C. Saizamba
3. New Jerusalem	R. Mwale
4. St. Thomas	
5. St. Peter	
6. Saineti	S. Banda
7. St. Matthews	L. Zulu
8. Ebenezer	E. Daka
9. St. Luka	E. Daka
10. Sinai	J.M. Mbazima
11. Bethrehem	R. Mwale
12. Mother Yvonne	M. Mbewe
13. Chama	
14. St. John	L.U. Banda

Nyimba District
Presiding Elder
Rev. Langster Daniel Zulu
P.O. Box, Nyimba

CHURCH	PASTOR
1. Petauke	
2. David Simfukwe	C. Mhango
3. St. Daniel	D. Daka

Mongu/Akashi District
Presiding Elder
Rev. G. Kambunda
P.O. Box 910050, Lukulu

CHURCH	PASTOR
1. St. Thomas	M. Limande
2. Bright Temple	J. Muka
3. St. Dorcas	M. Sepiso

Copperbelt West District
Presiding Elder
Rev. M.P.P. Mwenya
218 Jomo Kenyatta Ave, Mufulira

CHURCH	PASTOR
1. Allen Temple	A. Mwansa
2. Bethel	J.A.K. Lukwesa
3. Brookins	J.R. Mwenyo
4. Quinns	E.P. Kahenge
5. St. Paul	M. Chanda
6. Jordan	C. Ilunga
7. Kabundi	E. Mwansa
8. Emmanuel	K. Phiri
9. Chambishi	A. Lukwesa
10. Noah Temple	A. Chintala
11. St. Thomas	R. Chileshe
12. Paul Bupe	A. Mukuni
13. Down Town	R. Mwandu
14. Holy Temple	J. Lengwe
15. Bethel Lulamba	S. Kaile

<u>North West Zambia Annual Conference</u>

Nchelenge North District
Presiding Elder
Rev. M. Musangu
P.O. Box 750098, Kazembe

CHURCH	PASTOR
1. Rubber	R. Bwalya
2. Nchelenge	H. Makungo
3. Kashikishi	M. Muma
4. St. Bernard	
5. Ntonto	A. Chipili
6. Kenani A	
7. Kanakashi	J. Mulenga
8. Kafutuma	K. Chilupula
9. Bright	B. Manda
10. Muusa	
11. Kabuta	K. Chilupula
12. Lusha	J. Musonda
13. Mulanga	
14. Kenani B	
15. Mukwakwa	

Mwense North District
Presiding Elder
Rev. P. Mwaba
P.O. Box

CHURCH	PASTOR
1. Kapotwe	
2. Mulundu	
3. Dr. Kawimbe	D. Chomba
4. Nkomba	W. Seya
5. Kashiba	
6. Chitensha	
7. Kanyemba	S. Kanyembo
8. Bethel	A. Makwaza
9. Mwense BOMA	D. Chomba
10. Mwense Main	
11. Nyenjele	
12. Lubunda	E. Bwalya
13. Chibwe	
14. Musalanga	J.M. Chiwele

Chapter 22 • History of the A.M.E. Church in Zambia

Mporokoso District
Presiding Elder
Rev. C.K Mulenga
P.O. Box 470190, Mporokoso

CHURCH	PASTOR
1. Muombo	C.K. Mulenga
2. Mutamba	J. Kabwe
3. Njalamimba	F. Kalumba
4. Ching'onshi	F. Kalumba
5. Kashimba	

Kaputa District
Presiding Elder
Rev. J. Chiwele
P.O. Box 710548, Mansa

CHURCH	PASTOR
1. Lukwesa	D.B. Chanda
2. Mupandi	D.B. Chanda
3. Kasepa	
4. Kasongole	
5. Chiputu	D.B. Chanda
6. Nkosha	
7. James	W. Bwalya

Kawambwa East District
Presiding Elder
Rev. G.M. Mwenya
P.O. Box 730099, Kawambwa

CHURCH	PASTOR
1. Mbereshi	
2. St. Thomas	K. Bwali
3. Dr. Membe	C. Kawimbe
4. Kings	
5. Emmaus	
6. Jerusalem	D. Kabila
7. Kirkland	P. Chileshe
8. Mukobe	M. Pule
9. St. Matthew	G.M. Mwenya

North East Zambia Annual Conference

Mbala South District
Presiding Elder
Rev. C. Silupya
P.O. Box 420288, Mbala

CHURCH	PASTOR
1. Mt. Yvonne	C. Silupya
2. Mwiluzi	J.K. Sampa
3. Nondo	L. Lambwe
4. Kazembe	L. Kabwe
5. Masamba	G. Siulapwa
6. Kasulo	F. Walawala
7. Lukwesa	P. Chitambala
8. Kasozya	
9. Bethel	E. Kabwe
10. Bethsaida	G. Changala
11. Mpekesa	L. Kabwe
12. Emmanuel	B. Yamuseo
13. Nazareth	P. Kafuli
14. Mt. Sinai	
15. Paradise	E.C. Silumbwe
16. Reuben	J. Sinyangwe
17. Jerusalem	E. Sikazwe
18. Musafili	F. Kafuli

Dr. Membe District
Presiding Elder
Rev. S.K. Simuyemba
P.O. Box, Mbala

CHURCH	PASTOR
1. Niamukolo	A.B. Sikazwe
2. Bethel	C.D. Ng'ambi
3. Mpulungu Central	S.K. Simuyemba
4. Isoko	Kapindula
5. Sondwa	Sindano
6. Chitili	E.C. Simusokwe
7. Kapoko	E. Sikazwe
8. Chipwa	F. Sinyangwe
9. Muswilo	W. Maluti
10. St. Paul	J. Mayembe
11. Sumba	J. Mwinanzila

12. Mutondwe — K.N. Simfukwe
13. Membe Temple — E. Silwamba
14. Kasimango — B. Mushota
15. Kisutu — F. Sinyangwe
16. Namukale — N. Silondwa
17. Kapozwa — P. Simpokolwe

Nakonde District
Presiding Elder
Rev. B.K. Siyame
P.O. Box 430191, Nakonde

CHURCH	PASTOR
1. Lyuchi	C. Luyembe
2. Mother Dorcus	B.F.K. Siyame
3. Mwenzo Temple	O. Simfukwe
4. St. Thomas	P. Mwenya
5. King David	P. Sikaona
6. Sukwa	L.B. Chola
7. Kaku	J. Mukwasa
8. Mutowe	B.F.K. Siyame
9. Chilonga	C. Luembe
10. Bethsaida	P. Sikaona
11. St. Mary's	E.J.K. Sinkolongo

Zambezi Annual Conference

Mwinilunga District
Presiding Elder
Rev. C.H. Silongoti
Solwezi District
Solwezi

CHURCH	PASTOR
1. Mutumba	Rev. W. Kaumba
2. Chitambu	Rev. C. Kamba
3. Wamafa	Rev. J. Kabumba
4. Philadelphia	Rev. F. Ngolofwani
5. Kalitana	Rev. K. Kaumba
6. Kaisumba	Rev. W. Kandilo
7. Muzimbezi	Rev. G. Kapyasa
8. Tisasa	Rev. H. Kasoni

Chavuma East District
Presiding Elder
Rev. T. Kaika
P.O. Box Chavuma

CHURCH	PASTOR
1. Allen Temple Muyungwe	Rev. C.C.
2. Chiyeke	Rev. E. Mukoka
3. Kaundi	Rev. C. Chivweru
4. Siyolomba	Rev. Siyaulezo

Solwezi East District
Presiding Elder
Rev. D.S. Kapepa
P.O. Box 110124 Solwezi

CHURCH	PASTOR
1. Allen Temple	Rev. Sikula
2. Bethel	Rev. D. Kandilu
3. Bright	Rev. K. Kabambo
4. Emmaus	Rev. Samoma
5. Jordan	Rev. D. Kamponge
6. Bethsaida	Rev. C. Katiza
7. Katobo	Rev. Kapepa
8. Muselepete	Rev. Z. Muchova
9. Lwandamba	Rev. Chinyama
10. Wisdom	Rev. E. Sakwa
11. Sengelende	Rev. Kakese

Kabompo District
Presiding Elder
Rev. P.S. Sakuwaha
P.O. Box 130072, Mufumbwe

CHURCH	PASTOR
1. Allen	S. Masoya
2. Chatunga	M. Makalu
3. Emmaus	R. Chilemu
4. Chikata	N. Sachiyoya
5. Jordan	B. Musinda
6. Dorcus	W. Kawina
7. Kawina	
8. St. Thomas	M. Chinoya

9. St. Paul's	F. Kakema
10. Mirriams	H. Chilomba
11. Kawilo	
12. Kasalya	D. Samundengo
13. Robert	R. Njapau
14. Theresa Ngunga	G. Kamalamba
15. New Zion	T. Chipawa
16. Richard	R. Chiyesu
17. Ebeneza	H. Masoya
18. St. Peter	L. Malinda

Democratic Republic of Congo
Mbunjimayi West Annual Conference

Mbunjimayi West District
Presiding Elder
Rev. Jean Mubayi Kabundi
P.O. Box, Mbunjimayi Congo DR

CHURCH	PASTOR
1. Ditalala	Jean M. Kabundi
2. Ditekemena	Kalala Pierre
3. Siloe	Belelayi
4. Lubebue	Belebele
5. Lumiere	Pius Lukanga
6. Luhandu Lueta	Kabangu Mpinga
7. Bobumue	Tinta Jean Canon
8. Dibue D. Muditumba	Mbuyi Gilbert
9. Isalela (Mutoto)	Kabala Jean
10. Bunanukidi	Etienne Mabika
11. Bethnie	Celestin Kankonde
12. Kabondayi	Cisambu
13. Bobumue Miabi	Clement Mutombo II
14. Dipa Dia Nzambi	Kabeya M. Nzambi
15. Mutekemena	Kalonji Bayawaya
16. Lumu Luipe	Kabonga Tshiowa
17. Diyi Dia Moyo	Onemba Marcel
18. Masanka	Muzemba Stanis
19. Dibuluibua	Kabuebue
20. Filipoyi	Mukadi Nsenda
21. Yelushalema	Mualaba Biduaya
22. Mueleji	Ntumba B. Albert
23. Mpokolo	Mulemba Kalombo
24. Luse Lua Nzambi	Kamba Jifranc
25. Butumbi	Kabeya Likengu
26. Dinanga	Tshimuanga Katuwa
27. Mpokolo	Mukendi Synphorien
28. Bon Berger	Ntambua Tshiamua
29. Goshene	Honoure Mfunyi
30. Echelle De Bethel	Louis K. Mulumba
31. Luse Lua Nzambi	Jean Kashala
32. Kanana	Michael Lukusa
33. Dibwe	Augustin Tshisuaka
34. Diba	Mutombo Kadilu
35. Buakana	Bruno Kanyinda
36. Dibuluibua	Diamani Gaston
37. Dibuluibua	Kabuebua Andre
38. Bobumue	Mbuyi Jean Pierre
39. Bethel	Muepu Marcel
40. Ditekemena	Paul Mboyi
41. Terre Sainte	Kasonga Daniel
42. Bukola Buanzambi	Bondo Isidor
43. De la Grace	Dileji
44. Musungidi	Nyembua K.
45. Muena Bualu	Tshizubu
46. Saint Pierre	Balebela Jacque

Kolwezi District
Presiding Elder
Rev. Kalume Munjanilubita
P.O. Box, Congo DR.

CHURCH	PASTOR
1. Mwanga	Nsungu K
2. Jordan	Ilunga Kazadi

Lumbumbashi District
Presiding Elder
Rev. Chinyemba Kafwanda
P.O. Box, Congo

CHURCH	PASTOR
1. Sinai	Ame Mundeke
2. Kukovu	Kafwilo Pantini
3. Kasokota	Ngoyi Mayombo
4. Kalavya	Godo Kibwanga
5. Jordan	Ndulu

Kasenga District
Presiding Elder
Rev. Mulundu Kapanda
P.O. Box, Congo DR

CHURCH	PASTOR
1. Kibambo	Manita
2. Koilolelo	Zerimo
3. Kasolo	Kiola
4. Mubanga	Kasongo
5. Sebu	Kafrendwa
6. Beniyo	Michael Zongole
7. Kasenga	Lukwesa

Livingstone District
Presiding Elder
Rev. C. Wakunguma
P.O. Box 60839, Livingstone

CHURCH	PASTOR
1. St. Peter	J. Mwenya
2. Jordan	B. Kamakwenda
3. Mt. Olive	C. Wakunguma
4. Moonde	M. Siachikole
5. Chikole	M. Chibanga
6. Beautiful Gate	M. Chama
7. Monze	S. Muzungu
8. Calvary	B. Sepiso
9. Bethel Holy Temple	P. Mayamba
10. Mayoba	M. Muyunda

Lusaka North District
Presiding Elder
Rev. V.N. Sikazwe
Lusaka

CHURCH	PASTOR
1. Bethel – Lusaka	R.C. Ngulube
2. Jordan	E. Mayuya
3. Brookins	P. Chilukuta
4. St. Stephen	R. Kunda
5. Mulenge	C. Ndesaula
6. Lubuto	C. Ndesaula
7. Mulungushi	M. Mwanshi

8. Membe – Kapiri	R. Kunda
9. St. Matthews	S. Chakamba
10. St. Johns	W. Mwanza
11. Kapiri – Central	A.K. Chishala
12. St. Paul's	H. Nakazwe
13. Luanshimba	G.F. Mwale
14. St. Thomas	M. Mwashi
15. Likumbi	
16. Membe – Kabwe	S. Sinyangwe
17. Bethel – Kabwe	F.C. Chama
18. Chrisma	L. Kayando
19. Halumbwe	
20. Mother Yvonne	T. Ngosa

South West Zambia Annual Conference

Copperbelt East District
Presiding Elder
Rev. W. Walima
Luanshya

CHURCH	PASTOR
1. St. Mark	A.H. Simukoka
2. St. James	D. Kabika
3. Thomas Chapel	I. Phiri
4. Bathsaida	S. Feza
5. Holy Cross	M.R. Kaonga
6. St. Andrew	G. Chilekwa
7. Richard Allen	T.C. Siulapwa
8. Mother Hughes	Rev. Dr. Paul Bupe
9. Kirkland	
10. Emmanuel	B. Mazimba
11. Bethel	S. Feza
12. Mt. Sinai	
13. St. Paul	A. Kapesa
14. Bethrehem	T.C. Chilengwe

Copperbelt Central District
Presiding Elder
Rev.
P.O. Box 21678, Kitwe

CHURCH	PASTOR
1. Bright	A. Mulapwa
2. Trinity	
3. Judah	C. Chola
4. Membe	T.D. Kalumba
5. St. John	E. Mwansa
6. Jordan	E. Chipili
7. St. Philip	J. Kanungwe
8. St. Stephen	S.A. Mwansa
9. Bethsaida	J. Bwalya
10. Allen	A. Tembo
11. Calvary	E. Siulapwa
12. St. Peter	E.J. Fundi
13. St. Barnabas	B. Chiyokola
14. Covenant	S. Chinyanta
15. Kawimbe Temple	M. Sanjilu
16. Mumba Chapel	S.S.G. Mulumbwa
17. Gethsemane	Y. Chalwe
18. Bethel	Matafwali

Nchelenge South District
Presiding Elder
Rev. B. Musonda
P.O. Box 740021, Mununga

CHURCH	PASTOR
1. Toka	J. Mwila
2. Kanyembo	A.N. Mpemba
3. Mofwe	J. Lukwesa
4. Shimulundu	C. Chilambwe
5. Kapambwe	P. Mwewa
6. Chipashi	
7. Chawelwa	
8. Nshinda	M. Chimba
9. Kampampi	M. Swaba
10. Lukanga	N. Mpasa
11. Kasumpa	

Chienge District
Presiding Elder
Rev. J. Chiwele
P.O. Box

CHURCH	PASTOR
1. Allen	
2. Munkombwe	
3. Chanda	E. Ngalala
4. Chipipya	E. Ngalala
5. Florence	R. Kalwa
6. Dr. Kawimbe	A. Mbundu
7. Kelvin	A. Mpundu
8. Swali	
9. Mpapwa	R. Kalwa
10. Lupiya (St. Matthew)	A. Mpundu

Dr. Kawimbe District
Presiding Elder
Rev. Makwaza
P.O. Box

CHURCH	PASTOR
1. St. Thomas	K.M. Mwitwa
2. Dr. Membe	W.N. Sikazwe
3. Kalasa Mukoso	S. Kanyembo
4. Mother Yvonne	B. Chonde
5. Allen Temple	S.K. Mwenya
6. Chitamba	D. Chomba

Mwense South District
Presiding Elder
Rev. Dr. K.M. Mwitwa
P.O. Box

CHURCH	PASTOR
1. Ng'ona	P. Kasanda
2. Bunde Bunde	
3. Lwamfwe	P. Kasanda
4. Tondo	F. Mwelwa
5. Kapala	D. Kamuti
6. Chiwasha	D. Kapya
7. Mululu	A. Munkanta
8. Lukwesa	B. Mulunga

9. Kalenda	S. Chama
10. Kakusa	G. Mwandama
11. Musangu	B. Mulunga
12. Nkumbi	A. Munkanta
13. Loto	D. Kamuti
14. Kapamba	J. Kafubu
15. Chelekumbi	
16. Kanshimba	

Kawambwa West District
Presiding Elder
Rev. M. Bwalya
P.O. Box 730022, Kawambwa

CHURCH	PASTOR
1. Seesa	B. Mambwe
2. Salanga	L. Musonda
3. Katotoma	G. Kalipoma
4. Chituta	M. Pule
5. Chilange	
6. Senkwe	G. Kalipoma
7. St. Mark	W. Mwila
8. St. John	J. Chisenga
9. Nsholo	S. Chama
10. Mwanande	T. Chilengwe
11. Mukamba	B. Mambwe

Itimbwe District
Presiding Elder
Rev. M. Sichilima
P.O. Box, Mbala

CHURCH	PASTOR
1. St. Peter	H.N. Malunda
2. Mt. Sinai	M. Mwambazi
3. St. Paul	M. Mwambazi
4. Allen Temple	K. Sinyangwe
5. Bright Chapel	W.K. Mwambazi
6. Kings Chapel	W.K. Mwambazi
7. Jordan	H.N. Malunda
8. Brookins	N. Kapande
9. Mother Sarah	
10. Betenia	
11. Thomas Chapel	Z. Sinkonde

12. Mazimba Temple	Z. Sinkonde
13. Eden Temple	M. Mwambazi
14. Ebenezer	M. Mwambazi

Mbala North District
Presiding Elder
Rev. A.B. Sikazwe
P.O. Box, Mbala

CHURCH	PASTOR
1. Jordan	F. Sichilima
2. King David	W.M. Silupya
3. Ebenezer	G. Kambone
4. Nkonde	J. Nkonde
5. Lester	C. Sikazwe
6. Bethel	S. Bwelele
7. Wind Station	J. Sichilima
8. Ntenda	B. Simwanza
9. Mt. Zion	J. Simwanza
10. Chalomba	F. Phiri
11. Bathsaida	
12. St. Thomas	J. Simwanza
13. Shila	S. Simunyola
14. Kaluluzi	P. Simunyola
15. Allen	
16. Mt. Pisgah	B. Simwanza
17. Munyezi – Bernard	B. Simwanza
18. Safu-Isenga	P. Kamina

Kasama District
Presiding Elder
Rev. F. Sichilima
P.O. Box, Kasama

CHURCH	PASTOR
1. Solomon Temple	K. Mazimba
2. Mother Sarah	A. Kabuye
3. Stephen Temple	
4. Holy Temple	W. Wakunguma
5. Bethel	W. Wakunguma
6. Emmanuel	
7. Allen Temple	Kasonde
8. Membe	

9. Bethsaida — E. Mulenga

Isoka District
Presiding Elder
Rev. G. Nanyinza
P.O. Box 480236, Chinsali

CHURCH	PASTOR
1. Chinsali	G. Nanyinza
2. Chalomba	J. Simwanza
3. Mutunda	S. Simfukwe
4. Noah Temple	M. Simuyala
5. Kamekela	S. Simuyala
6. Lubuto	O. Sinkala
7. Dembe	M. Mulenga
8. Kalungu	S. Simfukwe
9. Mutukumbi	M. Mumba

Kawimbe District
Presiding Elder
Rev. P. Simuyemba
P.O. Box 420145, Mbala

CHURCH	PASTOR
1. David Chapel	P.K.J. Simuyemba
2. Mt. Sinai	O. Silumbwe
3. Wind Chapel	P. Sikazwe
4. Allen Temple	K. Mwila
5. St. James	C. Simbeya
6. St. Peter	
7. St. Ephraim	P. Sikazwe
8. Bethel	K. Mwila
9. St. Joseph	O. Silumbwe
10. Mabombo	
11. Paul Station	

Zambezi District
Presiding Elder
Rev. D.L. Kaputula
P.O. Box 130003, Mufumbwe

CHURCH	PASTOR
1. Ebenezer	Rev. Selwa
2. Mama Yvonne	Rev. N. Siyuka

3. Siyesonga
4. Chipalata — Rev. D. Muzungu
5. Sitiya — Rev. A. Chipoya
6. Thimwasu — Rev. Chitima
7. Lunyiwu — Rev. F.K. Kapalu
8. Musakana — Rev. Simbwambu
9. Chisamba — Rev. Kangungu
10. Nyakulenga
11. Katontu — Rev. C. Matinyi
12. Mumbezi — Rev. Mulumbankanyi
13. New Jerusalem — Rev. Chibunda
14. Kanyimbombu

Mufumbwe District
Presiding Elder
P.S. Sakuwaha
P.O. Box 130072 Mufumbwe

CHURCH	PASTOR
1. Quinns	Rev. D. Sikanya
2. Bright	Rev. Simasuwa
3. Lutoba	Rev. R. Sikanya
4. Bethel	Rev. C. Kamungulu
5. Mother Hughes	Rev. T. Peche
6. Sakuwaha	Rev. K. Sakai

Solwezi West District
Presiding Elder
J. Makina
P.O. Box 110139 Solwezi

CHURCH	PASTOR
1. New Jerusalem	Rev. C. Kapatamoyo
2. St. Thomas	Rev. W. Mutemwa
3. Bright Temple	Rev. K. Kachingwe
4. Ebenezer	Rev. D. Kaweze
5. Mother Yvonne	Rev. Kanyovu
6. St. Emmanuel	Rev. F.M. Kalulu
7. Malombo	Rev. K. Tisamu
8. New Paradise	Rev. Y. Eloma

Mbunjimayi South West Annual Conference

Kasenga District
Presiding Elder
Rev. Mulundu Kapanda
P.O. Box, Mbunjimayi Congo DR

CHURCH	PASTOR
1. Kibamba	Manita
2. Koilolelo	Verimo
3. Kasolo	Kiola
4. Mubanga	Kasongo
5. Sebu	Kafredue
6. Benlyo	Michael Zongole
7. Kasenga	Lukwesa

Katanga Annual Conference

Kipushi District
Presiding Elder
Rev. John Mukanda
P.O. Box, Congo DR

CHURCH	PASTOR
1. Jerusalem	Minikisa Ngweji
2. Allen Richard	Mumba Mwansa
3. Kawimbe	J. Mulano

Chapter 23
Obstacles and Challenges to Effective Ministry in the A.M.E. Church in Zambia

In Spiritual Warfare terms, believers are mandated to understand the battle they fight. They are required to know that they wrestle not against flesh and blood. Once they have grasped this, they will war with knowledge and understanding. Those who have been a part of ministry in the A.M.E. Church can identify issues which are tabulated here as being major battles they faced in ministry. Remember, Scripture says we wrestle not against flesh and blood. Therefore, allowing Satan to freely operate in the Church by inhibiting or rejecting the ministry and power of the Holy Spirit from doing his work has been a major obstacle to effective ministry in the A.M.E. Church in Zambia.

Paul, the servant of the Lord, had forewarned us. He said, *"Finally, my brethren, be strong in the Lord, and in the power of his might. Put on the whole armour of God, that ye may be able to stand against the wiles of the devil. For we wrestle not against flesh and blood, but against principalities, against powers, against the rulers of the darkness of this world, against spiritual wickedness in high places,"* Ephesians 6:10-12, (KJV). Learning history of the A.M.E. Church in this part of the world unveiled important facts or truths which are cardinal in overcoming Satan's deceptive bondages common not only in this Church but in many other traditional denominations. The issues below, consequently, formed major obstacles and challenges to effective ministry in the battle by believers in claiming the A.M.E. Church back to Jesus over several decades.

Iniquity-Related Battles in the Church

Iniquity is lawlessness. It is related to sin even though it may not be sin in itself but may predispose us to sin. It is also the same as generational curse. The battles believers are likely to war against in the A.M.E. Church in Zambia are related to iniquities or generational curses. These are found at local churches, District, Conference and Episcopal levels and you can identify them clearly because they run in the "bloodline of these institutions" and are inherited, passed on or acquired.

1. Failure to Progress

Failure to progress has been a traceable element in the Zambian A.M.E. Church for decades. Many neighbouring countries succeeded in building infrastructure (infrastructure with architectural beauty to it) such as schools, churches, parsonages, etc., but the Zambian experience has shown perpetual failure. South Africa and Southern Rhodesia (Zimbabwe) are prominent examples of successful infrastructure building including schools. Nevertheless, for Zambia, there has been a notable failure by each consecutive leadership to capture the vision, write it down and run with it. This problem may be coupled with regulatory institutions' failure to strictly regulate construction and infrastructure, poor education or exposure by the leadership, poverty or lack of money and misguided priorities.

We read earlier how through persistence and faith the Rev. J.L.C. Membe was finally able to get land in Tanganyika Territory. When the land was finally granted by the Colonial Government, lack of support from the Church made the deal to collapse. The Rev. Membe, with persistence amidst adversity, was able to convince the District Commissioner of Mbeya, L.L. De Lesdemond, in 1948 to offer land to build both a church and parsonage. Unfortunately, when Rev. Membe was transferred to Lusaka in 1949, the Church lost its hard-fought for land.

This pattern has been observed throughout Zambia. Leaderships' failures to pursue other people's hard-fought for victories has been an iniquity problem that has haunted the A.M.E. Church for decades in Zambia. Churches, such as Gethsemane, (Luangwa on the Kitwe-Ndola dual carriageway) Judah (formerly Mindolo, which acquired Mindolo Welfare Community Hall from the Mines) in Kitwe, and many other churches lost land in prime areas of cities in the 2000s to people who just came "from nowhere" and claimed and partitioned off land belonging to the Church while the leadership failed to act to prevent this! Calvary, a church I helped to be founded in 1994, lost its land in Kitwe after a pastor there sold part of the land! The same pastor had sold part of the land at Judah in Kitwe, yet the leadership (The Presiding Elder and the Bishop) gave him another appointment to Calvary! These are people a woman who wrote me a letter of ridicule stated "were led by God!" At Ebenezer, the land at Katungu at Libala in Lusaka has also been engrossed in a land controversy as well for a while now!

For years, the Church has repeatedly failed to purchase land or infrastructure offered to it! Affordable complexes no more than $100,000 with already built infrastructure have been offered to the Church on numerous occasions but the Church has failed to buy such buildings. In 1976, I am informed, Baluba Farm (Flamingo or Blackmon in the vicinity of Kamfinsa Prison) in a prime land on the Copperbelt was offered to the Church by a white settler who hinted he would help the Church acquire the farm which was just going at K2,000.00 ($759.20) at the time, but the leadership failed to take advantage of the offer. Today, this is an important prime land in the vicinity of a new Copperbelt International Airport being built.

When Rev. Mundia Wakunguma was once Pastor of Ebenezer in Lusaka, there was bare land adjacent to the church. The Pastor used to even grow vegetables on this land but the land was left to "rot" until someone else claimed this land. The person built a house right under the nose of the church which the church never saw any need to develop or claim! Other previous pastors such Rev. Siyame also never saw any need to claim that land! At the time, as read earlier, Ebenezer had influential members in the community and had a lot of money but lacked a vision and according to reliable sources, the leaders mainly spent the money on personal wants!

The same tragic news was experienced on the Copperbelt! We had members of the Church who held influential positions in the mining conglomerates and were in charge of facilities in mining communities but never saw any need to improve their churches in spite of their privileged positions. At the time, for instance, one Senior Steward at Jordan Chapel in Kitwe, Br. James Mschili who too was employed at Nkana Division of Zambia Consolidated Copper Mines (ZCCM) wondered why leaders who had a lot of influence in the Mines never utilized that power.

He was of the opinion that if the leaders who held prominent positions in the Mines had utilized their influence, our church building would have been better. Failure to approach management by these leaders led to failure from acquiring a lot of free building materials from the Mines! If you had an opportunity to follow up on such leaders and checked the churches they worshipped in and contrasted them with the places they lived or worked in, it would have shocked you! The type of structures they called their churches would definitely have broken your heart! Today, there are several locations with plots in cities which these leaders could have gotten which new and old denominations with similar connections to authorities have now gotten and developed!

When we (Rev. Charles Kapungwe and team) began a new church in the downtown City of Kitwe, a beautiful facility was on sale in the prime area of the city in 1994. It was going at about $30,000! Our leadership even took Bishop Larry Kirkland on tour of this facility to show him what could have been the best A.M.E. Church in Zambia at the time. If Calvary had obtained that facility, it would have been the first A.M.E. Church to own a church within the beautiful city center limits in Zambia in Nkana East. The Bishop never helped.

Another facility was on sale in Luanshya in the city center just near Thomas A.M.E. Church at around K40 million Kwacha ($36,463.08) in about 1996. It had several buildings ideal for a school. The Church failed to buy this property too! Our colleagues, the Baptist Church, however, later bought it and it became a school complex. Rev. Paul Bupe made concerted effort by gathering pertinent information and presenting it to the Church's administration but to no avail.

Kafakumba Farm and camping site was another facility this Church failed to purchase. Located on Luanshya turn-off, on a highway linking the cities of Ndola and Kitwe, Kafakumba Farm sits on a growing metropolitan land on the Copperbelt. It boasted of a farm and many facilities and was on sale at an affordable price. Although there has been no information found about the offer for sale to the A.M.E. Church, this farm was purchased by the United Methodist Church. The United Methodist Church who until now had their stronghold only in places such as Chipembi, Mindolo and Kembe consolidated their presence in 1995 in Kitwe. They bought this farm too and the A.M.E. Church now goes there to use the facilities at a fee! The Church also failed to buy a completed hospital building offered to it around 2005 in Ndola. At this time Bishop Paul Kawimbe had been talking to the owner of this facility at Itawa which had been earmarked to be a hospital. He even informed me he was interested in buying it! It never happened!

At this juncture, I presume, many would be wondering as to why the congregations themselves could not have bought these buildings. This will be answered this way: Most A.M.E. churches in Zambia are very poor! Many of the churches struggle or fail to pay even their pastors. Calvary A.M.E. Church which we planted in 1994 in Kitwe began with about 12 members. Of this number, maybe 6 people were employed at the time. Unlike in the U.S.A. where churches would get a mortgage to construct a church building, this practice and means are, or were almost non-existent at the time. Having been a Church Treasurer at Jordan Chapel A.M.E. Church in Kitwe for 5 years, from 1989 to 1994, I painfully observed how every month when I made expenditure for Pastor's support, or every 3 months P.E. Assessment, or every 6 months during Mid-year or Annual Conference budgets, the church's books were constantly in the red. This is the common story of nearly every A.M.E. Church in Zambia. Also, take note that our church, Jordan Chapel, was in a mining area which was by far better-placed than other rural churches.

The settling for mediocre-type of infrastructure has been the most painful part to the younger generation in this Church. You hardly would see a well-built A.M.E. Church in Zambia. If peradventure, you begin to dream of one, they will tell you, "It can't work!" Many would rather settle for the worst! I fought battles trying to make Trinity the best church. In spite of my regular guidance, the leadership (the Pastor, Presiding Elders including a Bishop) frustrated my plans and efforts! The Pastor would agree to my requests to follow my plans but constantly did the opposite! Several mistakes were made which I normally wouldn't have allowed if I were physically present! The denominational archaic structure and its poorly trained leadership trying overreach by continuously harvesting from local churches where they did not sow, hinders church growth by driving away new converts and educated youths!

In spite of giving directives to correct many of those mistakes and money available, ineptitude still overruled many of my suggestions! These came from a leadership used to mediocrity and selfishness. Many leaders are used to poorly constructed buildings and no standards or quality assurances in these processes are incorporated! This has been one of the contentions from the younger generation who prefer to leave than to stick around to fight incompetence. Remember, you cannot attract accomplished individuals to ramshackle buildings! That is just how life is! This in turn perpetuates poverty in the Church.

Photo: A construction of an A.M.E. Church in North East Zambia. Notice the bricks behind the shoulder of the third brother from left. If we can be erecting churches like this in 2018, the Egyptians who built the Pyramids between 2589 and 2504 BC (over a period of 85 years) would think we are a joke! I don't know how much a spirit level and a string cost in Zambia! This structure is not safe and can have people killed!

Fortunately, I designed Trinity around 1998 based on my desire to teach the Church importance of quality assurance and acceptable high standards. My church design which was done before I left Zambia already incorporated the Pastor's office, Stewards' office, Counseling room, Pastor's toilet, baptism pool, and men and women's toilets with showers. Trinity, I had conceptualized, was to be a model for other upcoming constructions of new church buildings in Zambia in this denomination. Even though these amenities were basic needs for any church, several church buildings in Zambia lacked them or had substandard amenities for them instead. With failure to understand the vision, one room was reassigned by the Pastor! Mother Rose Simfukwe told me that leaders at a church in Mufulira had forced the Pastor to cover the baptism pool up with earth, and they did!

When I was Pastor of Trinity A.M.E. Church at Garneton, Kitwe, I was the only person who had a job from 1996 to 2000. The church was extremely poor since it was located in an unplanned location, just at the end of a well-planned suburb of Garneton. Although after a crusade, I had two brothers who joined us and were employed, they did menial jobs for the city and this didn't change anything, financially. We had obtained a piece of land which had not been paid for. I used personal funds to pay for the land to the City of Kitwe. I also designed the church building and used personal funds to pay the architect. I lived in Parklands in Kitwe; therefore, I used public transport, three different bus rides to get to the church using personal funds too, for four years. I was aware that when time came for me to leave, my successor was going to have a difficult task considering the economics of the church and the area at the time.

On 3rd July, 2000, I moved to the U.S for studies. In 2001, after I had made a call, I learned that Pastor Elasto Mwansa who had taken over the church had been withdrawn by the Conference because the church was unable to support him. This was not surprising because I had known the economic problems of Trinity. By the grace, the Lord provided us sponsors who began to send money to Zambia. The New Covenant Presbyterian Church (NCPC) supported Rev. Elasto for 5 years, then, my adopting father, Mr. Robert Rabias and his wife Joellyn, took over supporting him for the next six years until Pastor Elasto was transferred to another church. The NCPC had also sent the initial $5,000.00 which was used to build the foundation.

I monitored the work and informed the team on the ground what needed to be done. I did this because I had designed the building and knew what needed to be done. From the beginning, I knew I was not going to make a structure that looked like the ones the Church had for most buildings. Even if this blessing had not come and I happened to have been in Zambia, I had it in mind to have an exceptional structure. Unlike, the time we fought running battles in the YPD or leadership; this was my first time to run a church independently with absolute powers to exercise without being sidetracked by naysayers in this Church. It is a Church in which I had spent most of my young adulthood fighting evil in leadership. I was appalled by poor workmanship of most of our buildings and I was not going to allow this to happen to a church I had taken control of (yet not I, but God who had it under his control).

When we learned that Trinity had no place of worship, a new structure was planned. They had been kicked out of a classroom where we used to meet at a government school. They then built a temporary makeshift structure for worship but whenever, Pastor Elasto would preach and it was raining, he had to reposition himself to avoid his Bible from getting wet! Finally, with the help of Mr. and Mrs. Robert Rabias, a new structure was planned. It was to be a cheaper one to be used before the one which was stalled at the foundation level was built. Members agreed to make bricks and burn them. Our partners then provided finances to begin constructing a smaller church that would help alleviate the problem of lack of a worship place.

Using burnt bricks, the church was able to put up a structure in a reasonable period of time. Trinity was able to have their first building. Water and power were connected to the building and a P.A. system, keyboard, speakers, communion table and benches were bought with help from our major sponsors Mr. and Mrs. Robert Rabias. Later, after several months, the family thought of revisiting the church I had designed. They picked up its construction from the "foundation box" where work had stalled. In spite of this grace, I was later to fight wolves which came against me in full force. Lord, have mercy upon us for this ungrateful attitude and our iniquity which we have committed against you as a Church.

The 17th Episcopal District (Zambia) has a budget or conference claims that each church is required to pay to the Annual Conferences yearly. This amount is determined by the Presiding Elder and Bishop or District. Failure to pay these monies by the Pastor may affect the Pastor's appointment. A local church pays budget at the District Conference and at the Annual Conference. In 2017, South East Zambia Annual Conference contributed the highest amount of K120,000.00 ($12,000.00) followed by South West Zambia Annual Conference K90,000.00 ($9,000.00). North East Annual Conference raised K60,000.00 ($6,000.00), Zambezi Annual Conference K50-60,000.00 ($5-6,000.00) and North East Zambia Annual Conference K20-30,000.00 ($2-3,000.00). Out of this, Zambia pays a meager $7,000.00 to the Connectional Church in the U.S.A. yearly. The rest of the money is used by the Bishop and or people close to him as personal funds while those who contributed the money are deep in sleep hoping that a Conference Center will be built for them by the selfish leadership!

The 17th Episcopal District receives about $45,000.00 in funds for "developmental projects" each year! The Bishop gets paid about $5,000.00/month. With this salary, it wouldn't be impossible for a Bishop to build one church just from his personal money in Africa and put his name on it! With the developmental funds, it wouldn't be impossible to build an office or a "Mother Bethel" church in Kabwe in one term of a Bishop, i.e., in four years! It would be weird not to do so in 8 years! The only reasons which would prevent you from doing so are either poor leadership, lack of a vision or misappropriation. In 2000, I watched in Dallas, Texas videos in which conferences had raised thousands of dollars for the "African District" (17th) under Bishop Larry Kirkland then but this District has remained the same: poor! Also, a stipend that never reaches Pastors is given by the Connectional Church in the U.S. but often ends up in the pockets of Bishops. Lord, have mercy upon us over this gross sin which we have committed.

2. Poor Leadership

Poor leadership in the Church in Zambia may be blamed for failure to progress. First, the leadership constantly fought against the message of salvation of sinners for years. For decades, they denounced or persecuted believers and pastors who were preaching the word that made people to be born again substituting it with a ministry of works to gain salvation. This killed the Church and made it fail to advance because only delivered people from power of sin and darkness can please God. These are the only kind of people who can allow the Holy Spirit to work in them and be led by Him. In turn, this invites God's presence to lead the Church, removing strife which had been common for decades.

Poor leadership had been observed at every level of this Church. This ranged from local to Episcopal level. Failure to have a vision, writing it down and running with it had caused the people to be going around and around in the wilderness like the Israelites. A knowledgeable leadership in the things of God would not allow mediocrity to be the defining word for all that it does either at a local church or regional. Many believers or educated youths ran away from the Church after noticing mediocre leadership, poor leadership or what they called "uneducated leadership!" Also, an educated leadership would stop a poorly constructed structure upon assessment and is likely to offer counsel or seek for resources from outside to offer help or guidance.

Deductively, it was not surprising that most of my friends who I had been with in Sunday school as a boy left the Church after reaching Form V (Grade 12). None remained in the Church after they went to College or University. Among them were my Sunday school teacher Lloyd M. Siwale (University of Zambia), Nathan Kawama (Evelyn Hone College), Dr. Noziac Chisenga (Russia) and his older brother Social Chisenga. Departure of Rev. Aaron Siwale in 1998 further proves this point. We had been in Sunday school together from early 1970s. (Please notice that this writer is not looking down on any person because in the sight of God the value of every person does not lie in what is obtained in school but from the Lord). These sentiments, however, are expressions given by many youths who keep leaving this Church.

Numerous failures in administration in the Church for decades point to unreadiness and inability of this Church to run any viable project. Unlike South Africa and Zimbabwe, Zambia or the 17th Episcopal District has consistently showed that it is not yet ripe to run any meaningful projects such as a farm, schools or even a hospital because of a number of reasons. From 1929 to 2020, i.e., for 91 years, (or for a century) the Church has not built an office for its Episcopacy, or for any of its Presiding Elders! Few pastors may boast of having an office and none may likely show the history of their local church or of their pastors from the time they were built!

All church administration is done in briefcases! This failure is embedded in mediocrity, resistance to the gospel of deliverance and of the Holy Spirit. It is further worsened by leaders with no vision, poor education and poverty. Many other denominations in Zambia do run hospitals and schools but the 17th Episcopal District has consistently showed that it is not yet fit for such works. Today, many denominations have even opened up studios and are broadcasting the word of God in Zambia! The story of leaders including Bishops acquiring land (attempts to extort Church land into personal land), misusing church funds and going into businesses at the expense of the church they lead brings shame and a bad omen for the Church than blessings.

All the meetings you will go to dubbed as "Conferences" are synagogues of Satan! There, debates are the norm and "intellectualism" is the operandi. Leaders who are supposed to meet separately or individually to seek the face of the Lord, alone to obtain guidance of how to run the church do so in meetings not suitable for such a serious operation. As a result, time needed to worship the Lord in such conferences is lost and inviting a non-believer to such meetings may be a mockery! Hurrying through the "spiritual portion of the programme" and spending a lot of time on "business portion of the programme" leaves worshipers dry. The spiritual portion involves a brief worship and preaching while the rest is dedicated to "business!" In this business portion, business is the "song," and money is the "chorus" of this song! To change this, we withdrew as believers and went to worship and honoured God especially in the evenings and not waste time in politicking in the Church. Lord have mercy upon us for this gross sin which we have committed.

3. Returning to Vomitus

Returning to vomitus has been another notable pattern in the Zambian Church. The Itinerant Preacher-nature of ministry in the A.M.E. Church and other Methodists, while offering the Church diverse opportunities for people to receive the Word from different preachers, on numerous occasions has been beset by the sin of taking the faithful back to the vomitus! Each time a new Preacher, who does not believe in the power of the Holy Spirit or does not embrace his power thereof comes on a new appointment, the congregation usually is steered back to traditions. This has made this Church to sit on revival. The A.M.E. Church, nevertheless, is one of the best Churches that offers its pulpit to many people to preach from, (including non-ordained preachers or leaders) which continues to grant it hope. Lord, have mercy upon us for this wickedness we have committed.

4. Covetousness

Covetousness by both the leadership and people for positions and churches has destroyed God's work in the 17th Episcopal District. When people, for instance, saw Rev. David K. Simfukwe build Ebenezer Secondary School at Ebenezer A.M.E. Church at Chilenje, Lusaka, and a Mechanical School, both the leadership at the church and some from outside tried to influence Bishops to have him transferred. Once, an unsigned letter by the "Official Board" which the Pastor had not officiated was written to the Bishop, Robert Lee Pruitt, claiming the Pastor benefits from the school financially! A school they NEVER built!

A copy was given to the then Presiding Elder, late Rev. Isaac Mumpanshya but not to the Pastor. The motivation for such behaviour was that they would begin to share the spoils once the Pastor was moved! Several members had moved from Bethel A.M.E. Church in Lusaka to join Ebenezer for the same reason. Bishop Pruitt instructed the P.E., to give a copy to the Rev. Simfukwe who had not even seen the letter!

Rev. Simfukwe had asked the Treasurer to read the names of those who had contributed money to buy benches. Only two people had paid in full to the fund! The rest, non-givers, were only interested in the money that was being generated by the school which on many instances was helping even the poor. These vultures, however, wanted to take over the running of the school for selfish motives. They were not even concerned that teachers needed to be paid as well and how that was being done, was not of their concern!

The same agitators had not even contributed anything to the projects which were going on at the church! When Rev. David Simfukwe who had also wanted to build a cathedral at the church moved to the U.S. as a Permanent Resident, all his work he had left collapsed! The school closed down and the Mechanical School was rented out! The people who were interested in "harvesting where they did not sow," failed to run the same programmes they had coveted for!

When school enrollment increased at Ebenezer in Lusaka, Rev. David Simfukwe began thinking of expansion. He frequented Lusaka City Council until he obtained land at Katungu where the Mechanical School was built. This offered additional three classrooms. It was also conceptualized that construction of a house at the site was going to be helpful in the long run. This was done and a three-bedroom house was built too. After this was done, the leadership informed Rev. Simfukwe that "This is your house! It is better you move in it and then we can renovate the Mission House or even demolish it and build a new one." Rev. Simfukwe had initially refused to move but the suggestion that this would be "the family house" made them to since they were told "Pastors in our Church never own homes!"

When Rev. Simfukwe moved, the Mission House at the church was never demolished or refurbished as had been hinted! When he went into the new house, he extended it at his own cost. He also built a garage but it was later used as an additional classroom. Many interested parties had been eyeing both the Mission House and the Katungu House! When the family left, the house was left under the care of a man from Ndola. Rev. Newton Masunga and Bro. Mwafulirwa had the knowledge and history of the same. When Rev. Masunga passed away and Br. Mwafulirwa moved who knew the history, the running of the property became a mystery to many. When I spoke to Mother Rose Simfukwe, she told me that the last time she heard of anything concerning the same was that someone had talked about a 25-year lease of the property!

At Ebenezer, Rev. Simfukwe had planned to build a Cathedral. He had talked about this for years. I heard that in Conferences! When former President Frederick Chiluba used to help churches, he gave a donation of K45 million Kwacha or about $35,046.73 at the time in 1997. However, the plans the Rev. Simfukwe did had been changed and the building remained uncompleted. When a minister came who was sent by the President in 1998, he was shocked that the building had not yet been completed. He gave about K8,000 ($5.35) and asked that individuals give at least K10,000 ($6.69) towards the completion. The building had been at the roof level and the President had wondered why it was still so!

At Thomas Chapel in Luanshya, a clique of leaders had become stronger than the Pastor in the 1980s. They refused to listen to ministers and controlled the Pastors! They thought because they contributed more money than anyone else, the Pastor was to listen to them and they needed to be consulted before any meeting or thing was done by the Pastor! They even controlled the finances and did not allow the Pastor to be a signatory to the bank! When Rev. Wilson Mpundu went there, replacing Rev. Mayor Tembo, he disbanded the clique which he found! They had lent church money to one another! When Rev. Elsie Musonda went there, she would let them know that "Witches you should stop pricking me at night you cannot kill me! You tried to kill my son Mpundu but you can't kill me, God will punish you if you don't change!"

At Jordan Chapel in Kitwe, it was disheartening to hear that the people we had left as young people have now taken over leadership positions. They have been persecuting pastors relentlessly and misusing church finances too! This is a common story in many churches! Rev. Musonda was right because witches use finances to control Pastors, especially via withdrawal of support and intimidation! This has been the iniquity passed on and inherited from leaders in these churches and they resist and oppose the Holy Spirit from breaking this iniquity or generational curse through the blood of Jesus.

It was painful to learn of a familiar fate take place in Kitwe, Zambia in 2004. Mrs. Minerva Phiri, a former W.M.S. leader at Jordan Chapel, my childhood church, ran a Non-Profit Organisation (NGO) called "C.A.R.E. Project" in Kitwe. She was one of the first members we had moved with from Jordan to begin a new church Calvary, in Parklands, Kitwe in 1994. Later, Calvary moved from Kitwe Primary School to Kitwe Main Primary School.

Mrs. Phiri was a highly gifted woman with years of experience as a Professional Secretary with Zambia Consolidated Copper Mines (ZCCM), Nkana Division. Using her skills, she began running C.A.R.E. Project which involved alleviating the distress of orphans. She operated under the Church's umbrella and for obvious reasons; several leaders became jealous and began to push for possession of the Project she had conceived.

C.A.R.E. Project received donor help from outside. The programme was being run at Bwafwano Community Center at Kamitondo, Kitwe. The Community Center was owned by the Kitwe City Council and the Council was at the verge of selling the facility to C.A.R.E. Project but the A.M.E. Church spearheaded by the same clique of people who were later to push for my removal from having contacts with Trinity after spending nearly U.S. $100,000.00 there, developing the church, forced the Church in a Conference to remove Mrs. Minerva Phiri! The clique comprised Lay Organisation leaders and Ministers with vetted interests, utter jealousies, men-pleasers and followers with no vision!

What the clique did not realise was that donors do not work with people they don't know or trust! The W.M.S. then started renting the building to the school after the removal of Mrs. Phiri. Later, Rev. Alick Mulapwa, then Bright Chapel Pastor in Kitwe, subleased the building to Destiny Church and when Destiny Church began to prevent the community from using the Center, it caused a lot of furor among the community. Rev. Alick Mulapwa had promised the Church that the Council was going to sell the property to AMEC but this was a pie in the sky!

Covetousness is a sinful trend in the 17th Episcopal Church. It is a common trend in the Church in Zambia and it emanates from selfishness, a phenomenon one person once described as "Kangaroo leadership." The decision to strip off the initiator of the project was done in the Annual Conference presided by Bishop Paul Kawimbe. Later, the project lost the vehicle, sewing machines, knitting machines and its computers which were grabbed for "safe-keeping" by individuals in the church and are not in use by the Church today. They took over C.A.R.E.

Project in 2004 upon Kawimbe's election and collected all office and other equipment in 2005.

When Bishop Hartford Brookins arrived in Zambia in 1972, he wanted to change the status quo by empowering the Church. He bought about 100 plots for houses at Chelston, Lusaka through a Bank loan for the Church. Only about 10 houses were done and around 90 plots remained to be developed, though some had foundations completed. Bishop Brookins also purchased a Farm where the only official residence of the 17th Episcopal District still stands today. The houses came to be known as the "Chelston Project." Today, the Chelston Project is no more! Before the project could be completed money disappeared! Zambia National Building Society repossessed the plots to recoup the money. When Bishop Robert Pruitt came in 1984, he resurrected the matter and engaged Robert Mumba, Attorney at Law, of Kitwe over the matter. Mr. Mumba was a Trustee and member of Bright Chapel in Kitwe and had helped in the refurbishing of the church too. The ruling, it was highly anticipated was going to be in favour of the Church and both the Attorney and Bishop had assured the Church of the pending favourable verdict.

Unfortunately, Attorney Mumba passed away before the case could be disposed of. Wolves then reappeared and devoured all documents related to the case. Someone in Lusaka (who I will not name), acting possibly with others, ensured that the Church would never hold on to the houses. This person never liked Bishop Pruitt because he knew the Bishop was tenacious and his departure was a joy for him. Nevertheless, this man (involved in the scandal) died soon after information of his involvement surfaced. You must remember that many appointed Bishops from America, chose to live in the U.S. and only came yearly to conduct Annual Conferences. This, consequently, deprived the Church which has had no Central Offices for decades of sustainable administration leading to a creation of a vacancy.

The Church Farm that Bishop Brookins had acquired in Lusaka had a tractor. The tractor suffered the same fate as well. A Presiding Elder was using the Church's tractor at his own farm and on other farms for personal gain. It hardly was used at the Church's farm! When the tractor broke down, the P.E., decided not to have it fixed but left it to "rot!" Also, in the recent past, (2017) there have been some powers who have suggested of selling off the Farm but the people have resisted such insinuations. However, latest reports according to the 2020 lawsuit to the High Court of Zambia by a Minister and the Lay Organisation against Bishop Wilfred Messiah argue that there are major violations about this land and other lands in the District which have been dubiously been passed on to individuals and the Church is now contending that. There are major land disputes in North Western Province and in Lusaka which had belonged to the Church. It also argues that the Bishop runs an account at the Episcopal District where his wife is a signatory to the Church Account. The matter is still ongoing. Lord, have mercy at these gross sins we have committed.

Infighting for top positions has occasionally led to people using the flesh and not the Spirit. Specific incidents which I cannot elaborate on in details have occurred where Pastors or members have coveted for higher positions using underhand methods of bribery (paying people) to influence decisions. This has occurred at every level of the Church. At one time, Bishop Larry Kirkland intervened and met senior leaders of the Church in Ndola after a woman had been paid to influence the Bishop so he could move a Pastor.

One pastor wanting to be appointed Presiding Elder after a vacancy had occurred was involved in this plan with some prominent members! A church was on the verge of receiving huge financial donation from the President and knowing that they could not manage to gain access to the money if the incumbent pastor had remained, they came up with a story to smear the Pastor to have him removed! Thankfully, the woman confessed before the Lord and the Bishop to what had been concocted. She presented cash to the leaders as evidence of the pay she had been given to implicate a Pastor! Lord, have mercy for these gross sins we have committed.

In Chingola, on the Copperbelt Province of Zambia, a Mrs. Molly Chilekwa of Chikola offered land to the Church in 2004. The leadership began plans to develop it and collected money from all churches. Bishop Paul Kawimbe roused the people to make contributions to build something on that land. A Presiding Elder working for the Bishop collected monies from people to build a "Conference Center" in Chingola! Churches throughout Zambia contributed money towards "this project."

When the Bishop was transferred to another District (19th District), the project "died" and the money which was collected "died" as well. It was not accounted for. At the time of writing this history in 2019, there was no activity that was going on the land and in the Annual Conference held in 2019 by the South West Zambia, the leadership failed to explain to the people who wanted to know where that money was now! In 2020, my further investigations found that the land acquired in North Western Province by the then WMS leader kicked out of the Church was being processed for personal businesses by one leader who was attempting to change titles or inherit the land into his name supported by corrupt little cronies who had been given positions close to him. They had been promised little shares in the ventures! Lord, have mercy upon us over this gross sin which we have committed.

As Bishop Wilfred Messiah's second term comes to closure in the 17th Episcopal District, he has been embroidered in many controversies and scandals. Upon realization that land offered to the Church at Mufumbwe and in Chingola was mineral-rich, attempts to change titles into his name were being made. He dropped all trustees familiar with cases and installed probishop elements. They began mining illegally. Authorities intervened and informed them to process papers but time was running out for the Bishop because his term was coming to an end in 2020. Also, Mapepe Farm was being dubiously being earmarked for some development without the full knowledge of the Church (Annual Conference). Details were scanty and it took the Lay Organisation to stop the project which was known to be a personal project shrouded in secrecy! Zambia National Broadcasting Corporation (ZNBC) filmed the failed launch which was stopped by the Lay Organisation at Ebenezer in Lusaka in 2019.

Another scandal involved the removal of a Pastor who was running a project in Livingstone. He was a recipient of money from the government for a school project. Attempts to get the money from him failed, therefore, the Bishop replaced him! The incident attracted ZNBC crew who filmed the fracas and was aired on TV in Zambia bringing shame upon the Church. Attempts to change Mufumbwe land as a personal property from the Church brought more troubles too. Sources in the Church are also aware that money which was collected for the conference center, which according to Bishop Kawimbe, was to be built in Chingola, now cannot be trace!

The Lord revealed details about this "disappearance" or embezzlement to Rev. Boyd Mazimba! He showed him in a dream who had taken this money. The Pastor saw two people one of which was a P.E. holding a bag. A third person then informed Rev. Mazimba that the money has been shared by these two while pointing at the P.E. who was holding a bag. Rev. Boyd Mazimba later consulted Rev. Idah Simukwai and shared God's revelation with her. Rev. Idah Simukwai confirmed the revelation and provided more insight into the cases to him. Like flies which are attracted to dirt, many ministers in this Church are attracted to money and for those responsible to keep it to misuse it! Lord, have mercy upon us for this gross sin we have committed.

5. Corruption

Corruption has been a major issue in the 17th Episcopal District especially in Zambia. This has been practiced by Pastors needing higher positions especially that of Presiding Elder or being appointed to First churches. Exchange of monies is the mode adopted by the corrupt and the corrupted. During vacancies of positions such as Presiding Elder this comes to play and Districts which have a lot of money, churches or people are targets. Also, some Presiding Elders in order to consolidate their positions, "bribe" Bishops or Pastors. A Presiding Elder using money raised by the District for a different cause spent money by buying and distributing shoes to Pastors in Districts without informing members on the committee or being sanctioned to do so! This was tantamount to bribery! Members of the Church have also been known to buy gifts including liquor for Presiding Elders to influence them to change a Pastor they don't want! Lord, have mercy upon us over this gross sin which we have committed.

6. Dependence on the Church by Ministers Financially

Dependence on the Church for finances by the ministers has been one major setback for ministers in discharging their ministry effectively. Ministers who are fully dependent upon the Church are more unlikely to stand up against wrongs the leadership makes for fear of losing their "jobs!" By jobs we mean, their positions which may come with glamour, for example, positions of a Presiding Elder or a Pastor holding a first church in the city. Unless such a minister is fully sold out to Jesus, the odds of seeing a minister fail to stand up against obvious violation of God's word or gross mistakes made by administrators or wrong judgments in carrying out of justice or decision-making process are high. For example, the violations that Bishop Messiah, a woman representing him and one ex-P.E. did in the case concerning Trinity was never challenged by any of the people at the church or entire Church leadership due to fear and intimidation from leaders even though the folly behind all their actions was evident.

Members are also more likely to intimidate a pastor making him see that it is them who provide for him. Some time back in 1990 when Rev. Wilson Mpundu was at Bright Chapel in Kitwe, members had informed him that "It is us who provide for you and feed you, so by not agreeing with us, it can affect your life if we don't give." Rev. Mpundu, in unequivocal terms, informed the woman and others that "God is the one who provides for me not you!" He told them, "I am not going to take a salary for a time and you will see that God, and not you, feeds me!" This was at the heightened time of opposition to the message of being born again. Rev. Mpundu could do this because he was not insecure and he knew his God. Other ministers could easily bend to the members' bullying, especially if they wanted to keep a big church or the appointment! Lord, have mercy upon us over this gross sin which we have committed.

7. Financial Dishonesty

As a youth, I had always wondered why the A.M.E. Church in Zambia inherently appeared poor. Very few churches in any city or town could boast of any quality building. After getting saved in 1985, I began my long journey of fighting the scourge through preaching and equipping of saints. My fight took me into the leadership positions so as to influence leaders. I found that the YPD leadership was supervised by directors who were appointed or elected by the W.M.S. Often, influential women who did not even know the Lord, were appointed as directors. They usually used to overrule the YPD leaderships or YPD Presidents who happened not to have a lot of say in major decisions.

Once, in 1988, I was 1st Vice President of YPD in a huge South Zambia Conference. It covered a large area from Mongu to Chipata and from Mwinilunga all the way through the whole Copperbelt to Livingstone. It was the richest Conference in Zambia at the time. When monies were given (as offerings or budgets), I learned, the Director had total control over the money and used it as she wished without any input from the YPD leadership at the Conference level! I was disheartened because it was a lot of money and the leadership had no concrete plans for its use. No wonder we hired schools to use their buildings because the leadership had no vision of coming up with lasting plans such as building a Center or something! (This included the Church leadership too!) I was also surprised that the YPD leadership was "paid" or given money after the Conference which made us fail to challenge the Director on how she used the Lord's money.

The same tale, I came to learn years later, happened (happens) at District Conferences and Annual Conferences. Some of the money churches work hard to bring to Conferences ended up being used up by leaders in "high places!" On the Copperbelt District, for example, before one minister became a Treasurer, the treasury for years was always in the red. The leadership had been helping itself to the account until he took over and grew the accounts to unprecedented levels. When he left for the U.S., the monies dwindled despite having left a fortune.

Another example on financial dishonesty involves the case of Thomas Chapel in Luanshya. Bishop Cornelius Thomas brought approximately $90,000 to build Thomas Chapel. However, the local leadership's poor accountability cost the Church in Zambia dearly – loss of trust! According to reliable sources, Thomas Chapel building would not to be the way it is now if donated money had been used appropriately! Scrounged for cement and other building materials from the Mines were used instead of purchasing building materials from reputable dealers in some instances by the leadership. This, therefore, showed in the poor quality of the building which could have been one of the best in Zambia – unfortunately, it is not! At Thomas

Chapel, the powerful lay leadership had inhibited the Pastor, Rev. Mayor Tembo from being a signatory to the church account! Rev. Wilson Mpundu changed that around 1986 when he went there. This further added to his woes in this Church! Lord, have mercy upon us over this gross sin which we have committed.

8. Desire for Self-Rule

Desire for self-rule has been upon the Church in Africa for years. This, while it must be noted, is not in any way sinful, parallel biblical lessons it draws, however, may be troublesome to those who have a sharp spiritual ear. It is every person's desire to have self-rule in the Church or in the political arena as we read earlier in Chapter 3. According to sources, the A.M.E. Church in Rwanda and Burundi had directed the 17th Episcopal District to find "local Bishops" to run the Church there but this was an insult to the "conglomerate" so the Bishop had to find another reason as to why he couldn't hold any Conferences there! Africans must learn that being ruled by others is retrogressive and perpetuates a superiority complex on them! However, the end product of that self-rule desire has not been as cosy as it had once been envisioned to be. When the Church in Africa began to push for having its own indigenous Bishops, few people were aware of the new troubles that realization was going to create.

Thus, for decades the African Church not only in Zambia but the all Southern and Central Africa had been demanding for indigenous leadership. The Church pushed for a new leadership that was indigenous to be elevated to the Bishopric level. Surprisingly, that self-rule and window of opportunity finally opened in 2004. Three indigenous African Bishops were elected for the first time in 48 years after Bishop Francis Herman Gow (1896-2009), a native of South Africa had been elected in 1956 in Miami, Florida.

As noble as the request for the Church to have its own Bishop (leader) appeared to be, the parallel it had with Israel's asking for a king was chilling! The African Jurisdiction Council (AJC) "innocently" pushed for the Church to have leaders (or kings) of their own from among their own installed. When a word came through one of the partners in ministry about the relationship between Israel asking for a king and the Church asking for one of them to be a leader as recorded in the book of Samuel, believers began to understand that this parallel was frighteningly similar to the Israelites!

Rejection of Samuel according to God meant rejection of God. God had been the leader of Israel but Israel had said, "They wanted to be like all other nations." The high expectations by members from the indigenous leadership which Zambia had been crying for sadly brought more misery and pain than hope and roses the Church had anticipated for. Of all African Bishops who were elected only Bishop David Daniels of the 14th Episcopal District equaled and exceeded the expectations of both the Africans and the Church in the United States. Bishop Daniels brought development to Liberia and his accountability exceeded the bar which the doubting Thomases had set for an African Bishop. He even extended the A.M.E. University in Liberia and his wife raising money too, adding more classrooms to the existing infrastructure there! Mrs. Daniels had been a professor at Allen University. The fears and the revelation which believers in Zambia had had through the word of knowledge were fulfilled for Zambia and for South Africa.

The Church in Zambia and Africa had missed it! It thought choosing of a leader among them was going to solve its problems! The problem was not about the leader solving its problems! The problem was about rejection of the Holy Spirit! It thought the solution lay in a Bishop, a Presiding Elder or in a Pastor! The solution for the Church was in the Holy Spirit whom it has been rejecting for years! When Mary was told by the angel that she was going to bear a Son, Mary asked the angel how this was going to be because she knew no man! The angel (God), said, "The Holy Spirit …!" When the Church was busy thinking "African-born Bishop" or "Leaders among our own," God was still thinking and saying, "The Holy Spirit!" However, none of the people would hear what God was telling them about the solution for the Church! Sadly, even today, many still think in the same way and do not hear God's response to their nagging misplaced question and demand!

Bishop Paul Kawimbe, Dr. George F. Flowers (Head of The Voice of Missions Magazine – Charleston, South Carolina, U.S.) and Bishop David Daniels of the 14th Episcopal District at Allen University in Columbia, SC. 23rd July, 2004. Rev. Charles wrote an article in the Voice of Missions Volume 140 Number 2 September-November 2006 Issue. Photo by Charles Kapungwe.

Following his election in 2004, Bishop Daniels organized all Africans he knew and called them to a meeting in Columbia, South Carolina. He also appealed to all the people he knew with any connections to Liberia to a strategic planning meeting. Rev. Charles Kapungwe was among those who had attended this meeting and saw how well-organised and transparent the Bishop's approach had been. Rev. Kapungwe immediately knew Bishop Daniels was going to be very successful. He had a well-done brochure in colour showing all checks he had received, $25,000, etc., from people such as Bishop John Adams, the then Senior Bishop of the Church and others.

Rev. Kapungwe immediately copied this model and took the brochure and shared it with Bishop Paul Kawimbe. He suggested to the Bishop from Zambia who he later met in 2004 in Columbia that if he could replicate this model, he too would be successful. The Bishop, however, informed him that his plans were far much better. Not surprising, sixteen years of indigenous leadership never produced an office building of the 17th Episcopal District nor any Presiding Elder's District! It was by the grace of God that the District did not lose the Farm and the Farm House Bishop Hartford Brookins had purchased which his successor Bishop Wilfred Messiah had wanted to sell. Having had a Farm that the leadership could not develop proved further incompetence in leadership. Bishop Kawimbe served from 2004 to 2012 (two terms) as did Bishop Messiah from 2012 to 2020. 16 years of indigenous leadership left no official offices of the 17th Episcopal District built but only a chain of stories of financial mismanagement and misappropriations!

Up until the year 2004, the A.M.E. Church had been a victim of its own past history. The Church which was born out of discrimination found itself fall into its own bitter past history of discrimination! The A.M.E. Church had fallen victim to its own past discontentment which it chose to propagate unconsciously or consciously. It continued to administer other Churches in foreign lands for several decades and deliberately refused to accept demands by those it ruled for participation in Church governance at the highest level of office.

While indisputably, a lot of factors influencing this deliberate denial were at play, the financial ramifications must have been on top of the list of such considerations. Understandably, overseas churches' financial contributions to the main Church in the U.S.A. has been negligible; such reasons need not to have hindered overseas believers from holding any top office in a so-called "spiritual organization!"

Undoubtedly, the Treasurer in the U.S.A. has been forced to subsidize Overseas Districts for decades. This subsidy involves running of Overseas Districts as well as funding of the Quadrennial Conferences in the U.S.A. Nevertheless, this scenario has not been dictated wholly by the Overseas Districts but by factors beyond the Overseas Districts' control. The Church holds its General Conferences every four years in the U.S.A. where delegates from all Overseas Districts are expected to attend. Many of these delegates depend on the Main Church in the U.S. to assist in travel, accommodation and food expenses.

It is at the General Conferences that new Bishops are elected and appointed. To the Overseas churches' sympathy, their financial strength which is dictated by international capital which disfavors them is not competitive enough to help support the Mother Body in America or its own delegates. Poor exchange rates in overseas nations' currencies also contribute to such disadvantages. Also, the Treasury supports Bishops' salaries as well as developmental funds to all Districts. Alas, not many Districts in many instances have seen such help reach them and comparisons to other non-A.M.E. Churches who have foreign ties have always been the contention to many an overseas' member or church!

Therefore, discontentment on either side of the aisle has been fueled by such misunderstandings. Observed failures, inconsistencies and sometimes selfishness have fueled mistrust. The wishes in overseas churches have been that the A.M.E. Church in America, instead of perpetuating a legacy of being a victim of its own past bitter history must emancipate overseas churches and unreservedly treat everyone as equals. Lord, have mercy upon us over this gross sin which we have committed.

9. Upholding to Observance of Formalism, Legalism, Rituals, and Traditions.

Believers who waged war to share Christ in the A.M.E. Church in Zambia, especially from the 1970s and on, faced great opposition from powers of darkness and religious leaders. Religious leaders resisted "A new teaching" which they claimed "Was foreign to the A.M.E. Church." The reason was simple. While it is true that for a Church, to have grown this big and reached many lands, God had been instrumental in its expansion, there must have been an era that allowed lukewarmness to creep in, like the Church of Laodicea in Revelation 3:14-22. The lukewarmness not surprising, took the form of upholding to observance of formalism, legalism, rituals, and traditions.

God had intended to reveal himself through Judaism. However, religious beliefs such as formalism, legalism, rituals, and traditions which were intended to be a shadow of things that were to come, became the quest by the A.M.E. Church rather than the reality which was to be Christ, Colossians 1:15-20; 2:6-14,16-19; Galatians 5:1-13. Missing Christ like the Pharisees did, and clinging on to the shadow of what was to come later, and is now here, yet failing to embrace it exposed worshipers to religious demons. Believers who were or have been at the frontline in claiming the A.M.E. Church in Zambia back to Jesus, would testify that they faced great opposition due to demonic spirits parading in the forms you will see below.

Religious Demons Believers Fought to Bring about a Mighty Deliverance

Formalism – Here, people put up a form or a front. They exhibited an outward appearance or formality which was unreal. This outward appearance differed from the state of the heart inside. Paul described it as having a form of godliness but denying its power, 2 Timothy 3:5. This was one problem Jesus had to deal with the teachers of the law and Pharisees, calling them hypocrites. They cleaned the outside of the cup and dish, but inside they were full of greed and self-indulgence. Jesus said, *"Blind Pharisees! First clean the inside of the cup and dish, and then the outside also will be clean,"* Matthew 23:26.

Formalism was not limited to the Pharisees alone. It is common even today in many of our churches. In Zambia, this was one of the spirits which presented itself as a form of religion and made people to appear very sanctimonious from outside but were empty inside. Religious demons are responsible for this deceit. Often, formalism is played around other people in settings such as church or gatherings but the worshipers remain detached from God. As you read the story of Rev. Wilson Mpundu, the Church's emphasis was, and in some still is on things like uniforms or fulfilling certain programmes which had or don't have any power over sin. Formalism cannot save anyone, instead it leads to death. "Gowning" or "uniform" became equated to salvation in many A.M.E. Churches (and most traditional denominations in Zambia) and preaching against this was met with great opposition.

Legalism – This involved use of laid down set of rules to follow. These are what many members think were stipulated rules which the authority or Church wanted people to strictly adhere to. Often, they cause people to miss the real thing which was truth even though they have an appearance of godliness by their harsh treatment of the body and may make you look "holy!" In legalism, people often miss the Spirit, and follow the letter, Galatians 3:1-14, 2 Corinthians 3:6. Remember, the letter kills but the Spirit gives life.

I, (Charles Kapungwe), laboured for years among people who were bound by these demons. Legalism forced people to wanting to follow laid down procedures or protocols. If by any chance you diverted from them, both the leadership and the people wanted to "stone" you for flouting the rules! Once, a pastor, Rev. Antoni Sinkfield, then Pastor of Bishops Memorial A.M.E. Church, in Columbia, South Carolina USA in 2001 took over such a church. He was a spiritual man and he started breaking these rules one after the other. One day he changed the programme deliberately but when he dismissed the people that the service was over, one leader told him "Pastor, we have not done doxology yet, you forgot about it!"

I used to attend Bible Studies at this Pastor's church which he conducted. He understood how enslaving legalism was and deliberately addressed it to help his flock. In Zambia, there were times the leadership would quote the Discipline as though they were quoting the Bible to make their point known! They would even, inadvertently, equate or zealously enforce a Conference Resolution, somehow, as though it carried the same authority as the word of God due to blindly adherence to legalism. Legalism which is or was just as enslaving as formalism still binds many A.M.E. Church congregations even today.

Rituals – This was the use of articles or things to worship God. Although, in the Scripture there are several semblances which provide divine truths, these articles which were not meant to be used to reach God, were utilised as important means to reach God. Satan had deceived many to borrow these rituals from Jewish traditions and from pagan worship and incorporated them into the worship. For example, the Holy Communion and the cross were and are often abused or misused as ritualistic tools of worship.

In Roman Catholicism, for instance, wine and bread are believed to be the real blood and body of Jesus, respectively, (instead of them being just symbols). The cross is made with the finger in a ritualistic performance that does not imply having any relationship with God. In the A.M.E. Church in Zambia, the uniform as a ritual was and has been a major stumbling block for many and has led many to miss Christ.

The Church may have some rituals which are neutral. There are rituals performed during the Holy Communion, weddings, and during burials. Some of the rituals performed at these functions, may be neutral in the sense that they neither enhance nor take away from the spiritual stand with the Lord. Other rituals, however, might be demonic in nature or work just as "pacifiers" to the worshipers giving them a sense of godliness but like formalism, just aid in trapping many and alienating them from Christ. The uniform would be a neutral ritual too if leaders stopped mimicking it to "salvation."

Traditions – This involves teachings of men added to Scripture. Tradition is another strong error that makes people miss the real thing or the reality, Christ. Many people or denominations majoring in formalism, legalism, rituals and traditions open themselves up to demonic influence. These practices take away, or as Paul put it in Timothy, deny the power of God. As a result, bondage ensues because only in Christ, are these spirits done away with. Although there may be traditions which are neutral and may not cause offense, those which go against God are always offensive to God.

When the Lord began to liberate people from the above bondages God brought about a revival to a once inert Church. Such a feat came about by combination of factors. First, God desired to heal his people and his Church. Through the Holy Spirit, he raised people who hungered for righteousness and for the "Real Thing" and not the counterfeit that had continued to be presented yet lacked power to restrain people from sin. The hunger for "the Real Thing" which was God or Jesus, the Son of God, drove many to prayer and fasting, reading and studying of the word and to fellowship. This led to God breaking the power of religion in the A.M.E. Church in Zambia and I will share a lot on that to give the historical account of God reviving this Church in Zambia.

Second, God used people he had set apart for himself. These were people who were willing to cooperate with God to fulfill his promise and work. They were a people who were willing to die to self and to be alive to God. They were a people who were willing to obey God and not man or the "Law" or the "Letter." They stood firm like what the disciples did in the midst of great opposition, they honoured God and not man. These were to be a few ministers and a few youths. Later some adults were saved.

Third, God was going to show a distinction between religion and life in Christ. This was going to honour him. It also was to take God to demonstrate his power and make the people to recognize the "Real Thing" – God or Christ through the power of the Holy Spirit. Since iniquity had been built up for a long time, it was going to take a long time to break this iniquity in diverse places. God, however, was going to begin breaking the power of counterfeit worship in leadership then extended it to worshipers. This was the process that was going to take a long time. Believers who were the forerunners to this revival were going to bear the brunt of Satan's attacks through persecution, like the Early Church. Many would eventually pull out and join other Churches. However, the light was finally going to be illuminated to those who once walked in darkness, and God was going to receive the glory for his work in the Church.

Several years ago, in the 1990s at the heightened period of battle to push for evangelism in the A.M.E. Church in Zambia, we faced a great deal of resistance and gross persecution. The resistance and persecution came from the older generation who were set in their ways. They viewed the message of salvation (being born again) as "Foreign to the A.M.E. Church!" Two common ridicules we received were: "You leave the Church and go and join those who chase out demons" or "You go to the U.S. and propose for a change of doctrine at the General Conference, then after the change in 'doctrine' you would be free to pursue your preaching!" Sadly, many of those who opposed us were unaware that in the U.S. there are hundreds of A.M.E. churches which are highly charismatic! Of course, there are hundreds which are traditional as well.

In 2001, touring the North East U.S. with the Allen University Concert Choir on which I sang, (and Rev. Paul Bupe), I was amazed at finding many A.M.E. Churches which were highly charismatic and "Pentecostal!" Bethel A.M.E. Church in Baltimore, Maryland a mega church where Rev. Dr. Frank Madison Reid III was Pastor then was among the churches we visited and sang in. Greater Allen A.M.E. Cathedral of New York in Jamaica, Queens, New York, is another mega church which has been led by the Rev. Floyd Flake. We had an opportunity to sing there with the Allen Choir again and the Church is "a very spiritual church" in all the sense of it!

On 21th June, 2015, I attended Bethel A.M.E. Church in Boston, Massachusetts. This was just a few days after the murder of nine people at Emmanuel A.M.E. Church in Charleston, South Carolina by a 21-year-old white male. I was also "shocked" to experience that the only "Traditional line" I heard in this service was during the offering when they sang "All things come of Thee O Lord!" The service had many young and middle-aged attendees and from beginning to end you hardly could tell you were in an A.M.E. Church service which mustn't be surprising at all. The church had two or so whites too.

The following Sunday, 28th June, I attended another church in Boston, The Historic Charles Street A.M.E. Church. In contrast, it had many elderly people. This service was different in the sense that it looked "traditional" in all aspects but the Pastor was still lively with the "Old Time Religion" message. It reminded me of other services at Paul Quinn Chapel at Paul Quinn College in Dallas, Texas where I had been attending briefly in July 2000. I learned that Satan is a deceiver and there mustn't be "A.M.E. Church services" and "Non-A.M.E. Church services" in our worship but only true worship by true worshipers! Lord, have mercy upon us over these gross sins which we have committed.

10. "The House of Saul."

"The House of Saul" as the name implies, is the presence of a group that continues to defy God. When God had rejected King Saul, he chose a man after the heart of God, David. However, there arose a battle between the house of Saul and the house of David which the Bible says lasted a long time. The house of Saul even though was destined to fail or lose continued to fight against God's will for Israel. The warning for the house of Saul is that you cannot win fighting God! It is a dreadful thing to fall in the hands of God. The house of Saul has been growing weaker and weaker and the house of David has been growing stronger and stronger! However, a few places where people are still set in their old ways have persistently remained. Many of them, due to ignorance while others due to the blind leading the blind. To the same, the Spirit of the Lord has been saying, "Repent or perish!"

Scores of leaders comprising Pastors, Presiding Elders and influential stewards had hindered the work of God for years in Zambia. They resisted the work of the Holy Spirit and persecuted believers relentlessly. We called them "Fire-quenchers," "Fire Fighters" or "Fire Brigade" because they loved to "pour water on the Fire" to quench the Spirit or the Fire of the Holy Spirit. Basically, they fought God in his Church whom they thought they represented! A little remnant continues to do the same, albeit, ignorantly. Paul calls this "Zeal without knowledge," Romans 10:1-3.

In mid-1970s to mid-1980s, the Lay Organisation in Zambia, especially on the Copperbelt Province and Midlands operated as "An opposition party!" It was a strong movement within the Church mostly comprising influential affluent leaders who targeted mostly Pastors who failed to tread their way! One minister, once made me hold back my sighs when he told me how they had proposed two or so "bad elements" he named to enter into ministry so as to quieten or calm them down! These were influential Lay Organisation leaders who were fighting pastors on the Copperbelt relentlessly. Their ministry, as you would guess, turned out to be an abomination to the Lord. Lord, have mercy upon us over this gross sin which we have committed.

11. Rejection of the Salvation Message.

The saddest news in the A.M.E. Church for years has been the rejection of the message of salvation due to ignorance! God intended to save sinful man through our Lord Jesus Christ. He sacrificed his Son so that we could be made the righteousness of God in Christ through his blood. There is no other way one can become a Christian except one repenting of his or her sins and accepting Jesus as Lord and Saviour, that is, to be born again! However, this Church has substituted this call by God with a righteousness of its own: Church membership! As a result, any preacher who had for years preached the whole counsel of God and the Holy Spirit's will, has been shunted to remote places by Presiding Elders or not appointed to First Churches. Also, the tragedy in this Church has been that many people who have joined this Church, especially in rural areas have joined with the notion of "So they could be given a good burial" or "So they could receive a good funeral service when they die!" It is a tragic belief common in many Traditional Churches and their blind leaders, just like their blind members, trod this same path! Lord, have mercy upon us over this gross sin which we have committed.

12. Failure to recognize God's visitation.

Perhaps the scariest part is the fact that many leaders and members failed or fail to recognize God's visitation. Talking to Revival pioneers in the Church like Rev. Peter M.P. Mwenya, on 2nd December, 2018, he bemoaned the downward spiral of the Church into the abyss of sin by the leadership. He equated the current leadership's selfishness to "wasted years" especially after having laboured for years preaching Jesus in this Church and now seeing everything being washed down the drain! Unlike the sons of Issachar who understood the times and knew what Israel was to do (recognized their time and acted upon the word God had wanted to be done in their time, 1 Chronicles 12:32), the A.M.E. Church in Zambia has, somehow, been in a laissez faire attitude or mood.

Failure by the Church to recognize God's timing and visitation led to a major exodus of Spirit-filled believers en masse in 1998. This large single exodus had never been seen before. Sadly, and to the ignorance of many, recognition that it takes a very long time or decades to make a man or a woman of God lacked, and still lacks in many. A man or a woman of God is not made in a popcorn-making machine or in a microwave. A real man or woman of God is made in the oven and it takes a long time for God to make one.

This failure is the catastrophe that led to mistreatment, unrecognition and lack of appreciation for servants of God who carried the message of salvation for this Church. It took a long time for God to bring them up and the leadership did not care to lose them in a single day!

They did not realize how long, hard or difficult it would take to have or raise or replace those rare jewels with great passion for God again! For years now, my brother-in-law has bemoaned the lack of young vibrant ministers who preach Jesus under the power of the Holy Spirit in the Church! "Many now," he said, "Were sleepy, old unenthusiastic pastors and Presiding Elders with no vision!" Lord have mercy on us for this gross sin we have committed. Like Israel, some ignorant Bishops, visionless Presiding Elders, sleepy Pastors and undiscerning members stone those who are sent to rescue them from sin – God's prophets but they know it not!

Jesus cried over Jerusalem. He said, *"O Jerusalem, Jerusalem, you who kill the prophets and stone those sent to you, how often I have longed to gather your children together, as a hen gathers her chicks under her wings, but you were not willing. Look, your house is left to you desolate. For I tell you, you will not see me again until you say, 'Blessed is he who comes in the name of the Lord,' "* Matthew 23:37-39. Please see Matthew 11:20-24 also. Lord, have mercy upon us over this gross sin which we have committed.

13. Blind Loyalty

The 17th Episcopal District has suffered underdevelopment chiefly due to the problem of what we may term as "Blind loyalty." Blind loyalty is the ability by members to follow their leaders especially the Bishops, Presiding Elders and Pastors without questioning them on matters requiring so. They follow like parrots or sheep to the slaughter without thinking independently using the word of God as standard in Church governance. In Zambia, this is inherently cultural. Many Zambians may unlikely question people holding influential posts because many are not proactive. This is even made worse if that leader is from outside, especially, a Bishop. However, I have been impressed by some young men who have decided to question the leadership including Messiah for the wrongs committed in the Church.

This trait of passivity is not as deeply embedded in other cultures such as the Tswana or South Africans. When Bishop Paul Kawimbe went to the 19th Episcopal District after serving for eight years in Zambia, his closest friend and advisor forewarned him that South Africans were not as inert as Zambians, therefore, he needed to be very careful. As predicted, the Bishop however, repeated the same behaviour he had demonstrated in Zambia and South Africans soon rose up against him demanding accountability on finances. The Church in the U.S. had to go to R.S.A. to sort out the mess. They also put the Bishop under supervision. Later, he was suspended! However, with the Church having new and upcoming ministers such as Rev. James Mwenya, Zambians are now beginning to question their Bishops who are making wrong decisions.

Previously, Zambians unlike South Africans, could not challenge Bishop Paul Kawimbe or Wilfred Messiah even when they observed obvious wrongs. Words spoken by the then Bishop Richard Allen Chappelle to the Rev. Peter M.P. Mwenya during the Bishop's tenure in Zambia in the late 1980s come to mind. "You cannot develop because you are too loyal!" The Bishop had bemoaned the backwardness of the Church in Zambia and the blind loyalty members gave the Bishops whom they addressed as "My lord Bishop." When you can't think freely and engage a leader on the basis of a brother-sister relationship but you worship him as a "lord" you sell your ability to question such a person or treat him as your equal. This is the biggest setback to the Church in Zambia and to an extent, the A.M.E. Church as a whole. Rev. David Musole noted the same which he called "Worship of a Bishop in the A.M.E. Church in Zambia!"

Most Pastors have no leverage against a Bishop. They also have no leverage against a Presiding Elder or churches they lead for two simple reasons: dependability on the church and lack of education. When as a Pastor you depend on the church solely for your survival, your ability to engage, question or challenge your superior or the church diminishes. Also, lack of education makes many people timid and the leadership is aware of this and takes advantage of it. A Pastor who has "financial independence," or holds a well-paying job secondary to his pastoral duties or is well-educated is unlikely to be bullied around by a Bishop, Presiding Elder or leaders of the church.

While these arguments may appear to be "worldly" or "earthly," they nevertheless, have contributed to stagnation and failure to challenge the leadership. Lastly, added to this is the undeniable need to be empowered by the Holy Spirit. Failure to being empowered by the Holy Spirit has led worshipers to timidity. Only the Holy Spirit can replace timidity with boldness. Of course, the Holy Spirit only indwells saved vessels! Lord, have mercy upon us over this gross sin which we have committed.

14. Magic arts or Charms

Many congregants who have been members of the A.M.E. Church for many years would tell you that there have been isolated cases in which some ministers have been associated with use of charms in the Church. Many of these incidents have been exposed at gatherings such as Annual Conferences where some senior ministers vying for senior positions or appointments to First Churches have been linked to use of such charms. One senior minister's wife informed me that once at an Annual Conference in Livingstone, one senior Presiding Elder (whom she named) had accidentally dropped a "small horn." Only ministers' wives who were seated in the front row had seen that. One other minister had picked it up and told the Presiding Elder about the horn he had dropped. The P.E. accepted and put it back in his pocket without saying a word. This is not an isolated incident because such talks are not uncommon in this Church.

When a son I had brought to the Lord was transferred to another church, he observed that ministry at that church was very difficult! In prayer, the Lord revealed to him that something was wrong at the church. When he began talking to the members who had now began to understand the things of the Spirit, they disclosed to the Pastor that "The previous Pastor who had built this church had buried some artifacts at the podium of the pulpit!" He allegedly had told them that "When we lay a foundation, we should put bones – human bones, a Bible, a Hymn Book and names of leaders." He informed them that "this is the normal way everywhere when a new church is built!" When the members confronted him as to where the human bones could be sourced from, the Pastor never said any word! Eventually, they buried a piece of paper with 13 names of the leaders of the church, the Bible and a Hymn book. When the new Pastor dug up the platform, only 3 members whose names were in the plastic bag were still living! Of course, I knew the man! He was one of the two men whom some Pastors had forced to join the ministry from the ferocious Lay Organisation in order to tame them and I guess they did! Lord, have mercy upon us over this gross sin which we have committed.

15. Iniquity-Prone Churches

Iniquity is a weakness or loophole acquired or inherited which acts as a doorway for demonic entry or activity that provides a foothold. (See the book *Ministry of Deliverance*, Chapter 11 by Charles Kapungwe). Iniquity is passed on from generation to generation. It is a weakness or bad habit that is inherited. It may not be sin in itself but it usually predisposes people to sin. Nearly all A.M.E. Churches in Zambia and outside, struggle with iniquity-related problems. Many churches inherit from their parents or their forefathers (people who began them), lawlessness, alcohol abuse, religious spirits, failure to progress, arguments, financial dishonesty (leaders sharing money from the Treasury), divorce, rebellion to authority (to Pastors), etc. Several churches such as Bethel in Chililabombwe, Bright Chapel, Jordan Chapel, St. Peter in Kitwe, Mother Hughes and Kirkland in Ndola, Thomas in Luanshya, Ebenezer and Bethel in Lusaka are among strong iniquity-prone churches. Pastors sent to these churches who fail to address such iniquities through God's prescribed ways of breaking of iniquities will unlikely be effective during their stay. In the late 1970s and early 1980s alcohol was what drew some Pastors and laymen together! They came to gatherings, especially to large events after drinking or would depart to drink! Many choirs did this too. Lord, have mercy upon us over these gross sins which we have committed.

Chapter 24
Obstacles and Challenges to Effective Ministry in the A.M.E. Church in Zambia: Leadership Crisis!

After leaving Zambia in 2000 with a relatively revived Church, two decades later, the A.M.E. Church in Zambia appeared to be in a shadow of that revived Church! For close to two decades from 1980 to 2000, believers had worked very hard preaching a gospel of repentance from sin which had impacted the Church with an obvious revival breaking through! Alas, with the coming of the "Local Leadership," in 2004, the Church began to drift into the abyss of uncertainty, deepening the obstacles and challenges to effective ministry in the A.M.E. Church in Zambia as a leadership crisis loomed!

What was happening to the Church in Zambia in 2019 and on must be viewed collectively within the context of the global A.M.E. Church as a whole. Speaking to senior ministers in Zambia brought a lot of sorrow as they narrated how they were being subjected to raise money at all costs to bring to the Conferences to the point of ignoring even the inability to pay by many churches. The ministers who I spoke to, were leading churches in poor communities but were expected to pay "Budgets" at all cost! Failure to provide the budget was not an option for them and they were constantly being bothered by the leadership to the point of weariness. The painful part was that the leadership never carried the same degree of concern about bringing souls to the Lord as they do about the money. Also, the budgets (conference claims) had sharply increased in recent years.

Although, this unfolding Zambian leadership crisis was not anticipated by many, the wise had feared of its looming. Those who could discern the times, like the sons of Issachar, understood the times they were living in. They were able to read the writing on the wall just as Daniel had because they saw that what had been achieved by God through prayer to dislodge the spirit of religion in the Church was now being trashed by the House of Saul. The A.M.E. Church in Zambia, like the Galatians church was being bewitched just as the Apostle Paul put it in Galatians 3:1-3. In v 3 he tells them, *"Are you so foolish? After beginning by means of the Spirit, are you now trying to finish by means of the flesh?"*

This was due to the fact that the new leadership was now forsaking answered prayers of the saints. What God had done through the Holy Spirit was now being replaced with a righteousness of its own: Leading a Church by the flesh. It was a painful experience to all those who had labored and witnessed what had been a spiritual transformation regressing to what the enemy of souls has always desired to see – a debacle of Satan's reign! This failure was also as a result of individual local churches' authority to manage their local churches being supped by the organization. Any time a church grows bigger than the local church, leaders must always check for and guard against the "yeast of Pharisees."

Witnessing the despondency by the remnant was heartbreaking. Undoubtedly, they were witnessing the Church being steered back to the enemy – being taken to the traditions again. Thus, to many who have invested a lot of time for years, agonising in prayers, fasting and preaching, this was a traumatizing development. Subsequently, this historian was of the opinion that ignoring the bus driver and the bus which are the means by which the passengers are carried on to their destination, wouldn't do justice to our history if we do not truthfully inform both the Church and those who watch the "traffic" daily. When observers see the bus and its passengers with the bus driver pass by, the observers have to discern what the actions of the bus driver have on the passengers and the bus, that is, their safety and lives which were placed in the driver's hands.

Many a member familiar with this Church would point out that money is the Achilles' heel of the A.M.E. Church. The hierarchy of the Church has been set in such a way that leaders, such as Bishops are responsible in conducting Annual Conferences. Here, Pastors are ordained and other deliberations of the Church in the District are done. Nevertheless, money is at the center of "Ministry" and Presiding Elders are mandated to collect "cash" at the District Conferences and at the Annual Conferences. Although leaders have to report conversions, more emphasis, sadly, is placed on money than is on souls!

This trend is also true at the General Conference. At General Conferences held in the U.S.A. every four years, Bishops are elected but again, "money" more than "ministry," appears to be the "Chorus!" While this is true for many other denominations and is not just limited to the A.M.E. Church, the enemy's trap in this Church has been to make leaders "hunt or look for money" and "not for souls" a distraction that makes evangelism a secondary pursuant in the Church. Although the Church would be happy to see numerical growth, the emphasis often is "money first" and membership second, at least for most part.

I read an article by Frank Langfitt in the *Baltimore Sun* with great interest and it did not shock me. The article, titled, "A.M.E. faithful ponder Reid's words" published on July 12, 2004 made sad reading but spoke what many members of this Church know to be true. The article about Rev. Frank M. Reid III, a serious and devout minister of the word who I have seen twice at his Church in Baltimore, Maryland in 2001 and at Allen University in Columbia, South Carolina when he addressed us as students there, the Rev. Reid, whose father and grandfather had been bishops of this Church understands the system which he called, "Satanic!" Rev. Reid is one of the Church's ministers who preach salvation in a manner that the word of God demands us to.

Langfitt of *Baltimore Sun* had this to say: "At the group's convention in Indianapolis last week, the charismatic leader of Baltimore's Bethel A.M.E. Church and one of the nation's most prominent black pastors hammered a church electoral system that he said has been marked by back-stabbing, betrayal and money passed out in envelopes. He also criticized a church bureaucracy that he said values career advancement over ministering to the needy. In a 24-page booklet sold at the convention for $7 a copy, he called the A.M.E. Church bureaucracy a "satanic system." As the document spreads online, it is provoking strong reaction in Baltimore and around the country.

Reid said he wrote the pamphlet as an act of conscience after again witnessing a corrosive electoral process in a recent campaign for bishop. In the introduction, Reid recalls how, as a college student, he helped his father pass out money to defray the cost of delegates' lunches during the elder Reid's race for bishop at the 1972 General Conference in Dallas. 'My father sent me to give a Presiding Elder from another Episcopal District a group of envelopes with five dollars in each one,' Reid wrote. When he learned that the leader had pocketed the money, Reid was furious. But he recalled his father telling him to let it go, saying, 'It's the system, son. It's the system,' " (Langfitt, 2004). (Author's note: Rev. Reid was finally elected as the 138th Bishop of the A.M.E. Church in July of 2016 and assigned as an Ecumenical Officer and Endorsing Agent of the A.M.E. Church).

During the run-up to the General Conference of 2004, the A.M.E. Church in Zambia was dragged to court by discontented members. At the time, Bishop Preston Williams was at the helm of the 17th Episcopal District. Also, Bishop Wilfred Messiah was taken to Court by the Church through the lawyers representing twelve widows and their families from the North-West Annual Conference (Luapula). The widows were spouses of the late ministers who were demanding to be given money due to hardship they were experiencing following the demise of their husbands in a road traffic accident. With news that money had been sent to them through his Office that ran the affairs of the District, the widows were surprised that they were in the dark about that money. The Connectional District had to send a representative to the 17th to see the developments. Consequently, the District was reprimanded and lost the case in the Zambian Court. Bishop Messiah was ordered to pay the widows and their families.

While, the unfolding Zambian leadership crisis was not anticipated by many, to the wise and discerning believers this senseless misconduct was not surprising. Thus, the current debacle stands as the most poignant experience to believers who had laboured tirelessly in this Church for decades because it translates to "lost years of investment!" They had witnessed a once upon a time traditional-leaning Church undergo a spiritual transformation but now were seeing it go down the tubes, again! Consequently, for many who have invested a lot in terms of time for years through agonising in praying, fasting and preaching, this was a traumatizing development to experience.

Subsequently, this historian was of the opinion that readers must be made aware so they would pay a lot of attention to both the bus driver and the bus that passengers ride on. Ignoring the bus driver and the bus which are the means by which the passengers are carried on to their destination, wouldn't do justice to our story – our history. Therefore, if the truth is to be told to those inside and outside, the bus drivers' impact on the passengers they carry and the state of the bus itself will ultimately determine the fate of the passengers they carry, we hypothesized.

The story of Trinity A.M.E. Church at Garneton, Kitwe where I served for four years, I felt would serve as an example of a leadership crisis we want to share. Following my departure from Zambia in 2000, God had put a burden on my heart to help me build the church I had laboured for with no pay for four years. He made a way to help me build what I desired to be the best church building in Zambia in the A.M.E. Church. After supporting Trinity financially for 17 years, I was not shocked that none of the consecutive leaders ever engaged the supporters with a message of goodwill besides those whom I had chosen to receive the money. When the building was nearing completion, word came to me through the Pastor, Salome Mangwende that "The Bishop wanted to say 'Thank you' to the sponsors so he needed to be furnished with the names and addresses of the sponsors!"

When this news reached me, I was deeply distressed in the spirit. There is a parallel to this in Scripture to what had happened to our Lord Jesus Christ just before Judas betrayed him, John 13:18-30. Please see v 21 again. (This is just a comparison!). I called a friend who was also a minister from Zambia based in the U.S. and like me, confirmed my fears. We knew that the letter was not about being grateful but it also bore more than what was expressed in the letter. We dissected the email and immediately "prophesied" a gloomy cascade of events soon to come. It was disheartening. We also knew that it was about the glory being taken from the initiator of the project and I predicted that time had come for people to carve their names on stone! This, I knew was the reason they were "thanking" us. I had informed the pastor that I needed not to be written a letter of thanks and instead gave the Pastor parties who the Bishop was to thank.

The following monies had been sent to Trinity prior to the South West Zambia Annual Conference of 2017 and after:

MONEY SENT TO PASTOR SALOME MANGWENDE & REV. LEONARD CHOLA.

Money sent to Trinity A.M.E. Church between January 2012 and June 2018 during Pastor Salome Mangwende's Time. All moneys were sent through Rev. Leonard Chola's Account. This includes money to install power and water in the smaller church built under Pastor Elasto's charge of 11 Years from 2000 to 2011. The rest was for building the church Rev. Kapungwe designed. This list does not include Pastor Elasto's stipend that was paid to him for 11 years and money sent to build the smaller church for the previous 11 years including the $5,000.00 sent to begin building the current church's foundation in 2003.

$450.00		23rd January, 2012
$1,000.00		26th March, 2012
$300.00	(For Pastor Elasto Mwansa)	" " "
$550.00	($340 to install electricity & $200 to install water)	5th July, 2013
$954.00		2nd October, 2014
$3,000.00		12th March, 2015
$3,000.00		22nd August, 2015
$7,000.00		19th January 2016
$10,000.00		31st May, 2016

$10,000.00	27th October, 2016
$12,000.00	10th February, 2017
+ $8,000.00	24th July, 2017
$30,000.00	[Money Messiah thanked the sponsors for but erroneously referred to it as $29,241.30, provided to him by an irresponsible Pastor who ignored the $17,000.00 given to the church earlier, and the other amounts above and the moneys sent 11 years earlier! Not shown here!] Or was the other money, $758.70 stolen?

MONEY SENT TO PASTOR ELASTO MWANSA AFTER RETIREMENT OF PASTOR CHOLA

$6,000.00   31st January, 2018
   $5,000.00   [I instructed Pastor Mwansa not to use this money]   19th June, 2018

Charles Kapungwe
Auburn, Maine U.S.A.
26th December, 2019.

Note: The Bishop's mail of thanks only showed money sent from 27th October, 2016 to 24th July, 2017! The three figures' total amount was $30,000.00! However, the figure quoted in the correspondence to the sponsors was wrong and was undervalued too! Also, note that prior to 27th October, 2016, more than $17,000.00 shown above was sent to Trinity! The figures shown above are just to help our readers see sense of my contention with these stubborn corrupt unqualified disparaging religious leaders who have been destroying the Church of God! Please note that this is just an extract because we started sending money in 2001!

On 27th October, 2016 $10,000.00 was sent and on 10th February, 2017, $12,000.00 was wired for Trinity. On 24th July, 2017 $8,000.00 was sent. Later, in January 2018, just to have our readers make sense of my correspondence; $6,000.00 was sent on 31st January, 2018. Therefore, the mails that the Bishop had written which should have acknowledged receiving of at least $30,000.00 cash (excluding the last $6,000.00 and $5,000.00 of 2018), failed enormously to live to that expectation! Even if all this had been based on the Annual Conference Report of 2017, they still disappointingly fell short. I later asked Pastor Mwansa to surrender the $5,000.00 meant to complete the water tank.

The letters from the Bishop thanking the sponsors, however, erroneously reported a figure of $29,241.30! (I don't know how Pastor Salome Mangwende, an enrolled nurse and Pastor Leonard Chola, a retired administrator in the Mines arrived at this figure!). Also, since this was a first correspondence of conveying thanks, failure to acknowledge monies sent prior to this year showed poor leadership in my view. Writing to a Church which was a non-A.M.E. Church which would never even have made sense that you were "thanking them for what they did for the year and not what they have been doing for the past 17 years" made my heart to cringe in pain! I was also aware that the Pastor too had demonstrated poor judgment in spite of having been guided by me as well on whom they were to thank! She had the spillover of the poor habits she had been doing in all of her financial reports in this.

Bishop Wilfred Messiah's Letters to Trinity A.M.E. Church's Sponsors in the U.S.A.

Office of the Bishop

African Methodist Episcopal Church
17th Episcopal District

God Our Father   Christ Our Redeemer   Spirit Our Comforter   Humankind Our Family

The Rt. Rev. Wilfred J. Messiah
Presiding Bishop
Tel: - +260 211 237533
Fax: +260 211 237 533
Email: bishopmessiahJ20@yahoo.com

Episcopal Residence Address
411A Long Ridge – Mapepe Chilanga, Lusaka
Mailing Address
P.O. Box 36628, Lusaka
amec17thdistrict@yahoo.com

REF: AMEC/SED/WJM/09/17
Date: 25th August, 2017

Mr. & Mrs. Steve Marbert
Mr. & Mrs. Bob Rabias
<u>United States of America</u>

Dear Mr. Mrs. Steve Marbert,
Mr. & Mrs. Bob Rabias,

<u>RE: GRATITUDE FOR THE ASSISTANCE RENDERED IN CONSTRUCTING/ BUILDING OF TRINITY AFRICAN METHODIST EPISCOPAL CHURCH (AMEC) IN KITWE TOWN – REPUBLIC OF ZAMBIA</u>

We extend warm and tender greetings to you in the mighty precious name of the Lord and Saviour Jesus Christ.

During the 27th Session of the South West Zambia Annual Conference, of the African Methodist Episcopal Church (AMEC) held in Kitwe, Republic of Zambia, my office through the Pastor in Charge, Rev. Salome Mangwende, received a very progressive and heart touching report about your contributions to building of God's kingdom at Trinity African Methodist Episcopal Church/(AMEC), which is based in Kitwe – Zambia.

As the Bishop of the African Methodist Episcopal Church (AMEC) in the 17th Episcopal District, I and the Episcopal Supervisor, Mrs. Carol I. Messiah, and on behalf of Trinity AME Church Congregation in Kitwe, we wish to express our sincere gratitude to your office for the assistance rendered on the following contributions:

- ❖ Your generous Financial Assistance estimated in the sum of US **$29,241.30**, equivalent to Zambia Kwacha (ZMK) **248,551.00** donated to the Construction and erecting a Church Building at Trinity AME Church (AMEC).

Kindly receive our utmost gratitude and thanks to you for these very valuable and generous contributions, which we don't take for granted. We wish you God's blessings in all your endeavours.

Yours for Christ, Church and Community

AFRICAN METHODIST EPISCOPAL CHURCH
<u>The Rt. Rev. Dr. Wilfred J. Messiah</u>
    BISHOP

www.amecdistrict17.org

Burundi   Congo Brazzaville   Congo DR   Kenya   Rwanda   Zambia

After these two letters were sent to the two families who had been supporting the construction of Trinity, I decided to talk to the Pastor by phone in August, 2017. I pointed out to her not only how wrong the information on the letter was but how embarrassing the two letters had put me in with the sponsors. I informed the pastor that "Just this year (2017) you have received two amounts of $12,000.00 on February 10 and $8,000.00 on July 22, respectively. You also received $10,000.00 on 27th October, 2016, $10,000.00 on May 31, 2016 and $7,000.00 in January 2016! What the Bishop mentioned in the letter," I informed the Pastor, "was just for the year 2017 plus a last instalment in 2016! Notice how the dollar amount has cents too!" This had not been the first time the Pastor's report has had such anomalies in the cents' figures!

"Stating to the sponsors that this is what they have given was very embarrassing to us!" I informed the Pastor. I reminded her how I had informed her of the need to have a list that should tabulate amounts of money sent to the church which she could easily consult from, but she had ignored that repeatedly. She indicated that she was going to inform the Bishop and a letter of rectification was going to be written but three months passed and nothing came! I had immediately apologized to our supporters.

A few months later, I received a report from non-members of Trinity that the Bishop, the Presiding Elder and the Pastor had officially opened the church without informing us! Without informing the sponsors and me, the team, I was also informed, went to have a feast after the "Official opening!" The leadership in Zambia, I presumed was of the view that informing me and the sponsors who had put up two buildings at Trinity and supported the church for the past 17 years was uncalled for! I didn't know how to break the news to the sponsors. For years, they had indicated that they would love to see us go to Zambia and see me preach during the church's Official Opening Day! Alas, no leader in the 17th Episcopal District could discern that this was utterly wrong and embarrassing!

Chapter 24 • History of the A.M.E. Church in Zambia

My Letter to Bishop Wilfred Messiah after the Bishop, the Presiding Elder and the Pastor "Officially Opened Trinity A.M.E. Church" Without Informing Us!

December 22, 2017
121 Spring St Apt 9
Auburn, ME 04210
USA
1-207 330 9944
charliekaps@hotmail.com

Bishop Wilfred J. Messiah
Presiding Bishop
17th Episcopal District
AME Church
+260 221 237533
Bishopmessiah120@yahoo.com

Dear Bishop Messiah

<u>RE: Embarrassing & Poor Leadership – Trinity AME Church</u>

It is with great sorrow and pain that I write this letter to you. I have endured the pain and embarrassment for a while now but I can no longer contain my disappointment and wish to inform you of my displeasure with the leadership at Trinity.

I was the second pastor of Trinity A.M.E. Church from 1996 to 2000. At the time, we used to meet in a classroom at a primary school in Garneton in Kitwe, Zambia. I was the only person with gainful employment at the time. When I did a crusade, I got two more souls who had been employed but they did menial jobs which were insignificant to support the church, therefore, the church remained poor financially. I was not receiving any salary but provided for my needs. I paid for the plot out of my pocket (God's) and I designed and paid for the church's blueprint – again out of my personal funds for the love of God since the poverty levels in the area were high.

I was aware that after I left, a pastor appointed to Trinity would unlikely be sustained. My fears were confirmed as Rev. Elasto Mwansa, my son in the Lord, who had been appointed to be pastor, was prematurely withdrawn by the conference after Trinity Church was unable to support him. While in the U.S., I never forgot about Trinity, a place where I had laboured for four years. I had spoken about it to an AME Church where I was associate Pastor for four years but they could not help. The church, at this time, had been kicked out of the school and was now meeting in a makeshift structure. By the providence of God, I met believers at the New Covenant Presbyterian Church in Aiken, South Carolina who listened to my plight and testimony. This church through its mission's committee unanimously agreed to begin supporting Pastor Elasto Mwansa in 2001, subsequently, led to the reinstatement of the pastor to the church. Pastor Elasto received support for about four years from the New Covenant Presbyterian Church of South Carolina as upkeep. They also gave us about $4,000 to begin the foundation of the current new church after I had shown them the blueprints and explained the inability of the church to do so in about the same year. I had put in checks and balances which involved use of the former Presiding Elder Rev. Leonard Chola to receive all finances.

The New Covenant Presbyterian Church stopped sending help around 2005 and Mr. and Mrs. Bob Rabias took over. The couple is like a family to me. They built a new smaller structure, paid for water and electricity connections to the church including the Public Address system and speakers. They later resumed giving to the main church, which I had designed, since work had stalled because it was too costly. Pastor Elasto had introduced Rev. Salome Mangwende to the couple and I had mentioned to them of the change of leadership. Pastor Elasto had informed the incoming pastor of my preferred builder who had done the initial settings for Trinity and foundation because in my view was an expert and as a former choir mate from Jordan Chapel AME Church in Kitwe, Bro. Feckson Simukoko was deemed as the best person to help Trinity. However, the pastor had continued to sideline Br. Feckson for several years even though most of the major work of the church has been done by him often, disregarding my directives. I was aware that the pastor had no experience in building and her numerous mistakes displayed to our sponsors left me bewildered. When work had become enormous for a single family to do, the Rabias family was joined in by the Steve Marbert family who too has given generously for over three years now.

The following issues are not only disturbing but show gross disrespect and lack of appreciation for both this servant and the sponsors of the project.

1. For years in spite of being told that a member of our church was qualified enough and must be utilized unreservedly, she continued to sideline him/them (with Pastor Elasto) who were my contacts on the ground only when forced by this servant to use him/them or asked to correct mistakes made did she grudgingly allow them.
2. Although the pastor is a novice at building, she became the sole controller of the funds paying those she contracted void of checks and balances. The church, unlike at my time, has now capable men who run businesses and are a powerful resource but she continued to frustrate them and at one time everyone did as they pleased because they were not aware how much had been given to the church. She allowed only a few women to go with her to get the money from the Presiding Elder Rev. Leonard Chola. After that, she was in control. This was unacceptable.
3. In spite of being told that Br. Simukoko was an expert in sewer and water pipes installation and was asked by this servant to have him do the work, she allowed him to just show them where the man holes were to be made and she went and found a group of men from the Nkana Water and Sewerage Company who knew nothing about installation of the water pipes and the sewer systems. She had given them the money in advance and in full. She had accepted that these people were to come and work on the system once a week and they came as they pleased sometimes missing weeks which turned to be about six months. When I came to learn about it was too late. The sewer lines together with the pipes had been messed up – wrongly installed. Br. Feckson, thankfully, corrected the wrong installation at a great cost and man hours.
4. I informed her at this juncture that she was not to pay people in advance because she had lost this money. However, in spite of agreeing, she went ahead and paid thousands of dollars to another company to make 35 benches. It has taken over seven months now with Pastor Elasto left to struggle to get the remainder of the benches since not all the benches have been delivered and the pastor had gone against our discussion not to pay anyone in advance. In addition, the benches which supposedly were to be painted with vanish were painted with a brown paint. She could not do anything about it and has not been proactive leaving most of the work to Pastor Elasto to follow up.
5. The design of the building required windows to open double-sided. This, my colleagues (Elasto and Feckson) were aware since I had told them how the windows were to be made but to my dismay, I discovered she had allowed the windows to be installed opening only one side. This was at the time she was sidelining my experts and as pastor she shares the blame.

We just finished redoing the windows all over again – again at a great cost this November 2017.

6. The spoon drain was also poorly done and I, consequently, ordered them to demolish it and rebuild it. They rebuilt an apron which is better by far, and by Br. Feckson, even though, admittedly, he had a hand in the first. This was done under her eye, however.
7. The door at the back was poorly fixed. See the photo. It narrows from top to bottom. She has no idea that this is unacceptable especially that this church has been blessed with thousands of dollars and no other church can be compared to it in Zambia in our denomination with such a blessing. This was done by people who never cared.
8. Our sponsors always ask for photos and she is aware of this but we always have to ask for photos or plead for them to be sent. She put up a makeshift structure on the back of the church knowing too well that this would ruin the beauty of the building and photos which the sponsors need. I have asked for it to be removed but it has been months and the structure still stands to date.
9. Less than two months after the sponsors had sent $10,000, they followed up with a request of putting up the ceiling. Br. Feckson was tasked by me to do the job. As an expert, he informed her that she needed to pay the welders (because he is not a welder) to put up bars to attach timber to and to pay the electricians to put up the lines for lights. She told Pastor Elasto there was no money for the electrician! (She likely had spent it on benches without informing any of us). This surprised me and shocked the Rev. Chola months later who later said, "Did she say that?" I did not want the matter to take time, I decided to send Pastor Elasto money to pay the electrician without letting my sponsors aware but she appeared to be asking for additional expenditure for other related work!
10. She was directed by this servant that all the bathrooms needed to be lined up with tiles from bottom to top. She asked people of her choice to put up the tiles (but came out badly, were not well-aligned horizontally) and put plaster above contrary to my instructions. When asked for photos she sent only one and for over one year no photos were sent for the bathrooms which I had directed to be completed. Thankfully, as I write this Br. Feckson has been correcting the tiles which demanded removal and reapplying, again at a great cost! He would sleep at the church to avoid travelling expenses but for four days ending up doing nothing because there was no water there and she offered little assistance.
11. About a year ago, this servant finally decided that Feckson and Pastor Elasto where to be in charge until the building was completed. She was, however, left with the control of finances out of courtesy and she had specifically asked, "What about the finances," to which this servant had told her, "You are the pastor, you will be in charge of that." However, the events of her paying in advance on the benches and not letting this pastor and the sponsors aware of her expenditure at the time or disclosing it as needed on time together with failure to paying the electrician led to the decision of striping her of the control of finances – and this happened just early this year.
12. I had several positive plans for the church and her behaviour made me quash a lot of these plans off. All print-outs for stuff that is required to be done at the church have been sent to her but she never informs her members or ignores the advice, repeatedly. While, this servant respects the charge, no other church in Zambia has had such a blessing. Requests to plant trees with other stuff have stayed without being attended to for more than two years.
13. This servant sent her beautiful wall clocks, photo frames, Words for the name of church to put on the church and other stuff but these have not even been shown to those who are

supposed to help her and they are in her home for the past two years.

14. When the sponsors decided to strip her of the right to handle cash, she stopped reporting on what has been going on at the church preferring non-church members to report when the church is benefitting from thousands of dollars received with her not working for it in spite of it being her responsibility to do so!

15. How a pastor receiving money to build a church could hold a ceremony to officially open the church without the knowledge of the people who have sacrificed so much defies logic.

16. How a person helping build the church has to be put in a position of begging for photos and frequent progress updates when this should be the responsibility of those who are recipients of help is disturbing and startling.

17. The prolonged slow work has gobbled huge amounts of money, in part due to incompetence and irresponsibility. The church had informed the sponsors that if all the money were available the church could be completed in three months. This has not been the case!

18. When the request came that the Bishop wanted to say, "Thank you" to the sponsors, this servant declined to be thanked. Instead he explained that The New Covenant Presbyterian Church, Mr. Robert and Mrs. Joellyn Rabias and Mr. Steve and Kathy Marbert were to be thanked. Surprisingly, only the two families were thanked, leaving out the NCPC, sixteen years after the high offices have been receiving the reports of this unmatched benevolence to our church.

19. The discrepancy from the Bishop's letters of thanks to the two families was again an embarrassment to this servant. The New Covenant Presbyterian Church, the Rabias and Marbert families in supporting Pastor Elasto Mwansa, building the first church and the second church have spent way over $100,000.00. The figure of US $29,241.30, cited in the letter from the Bishop as the total money our sponsors have spent on Trinity, I had informed the Presiding Elder Rev. Leonard Chola who had been the person through whom all the moneys were sent and Pastor Salome that this too was an embarrassment to me. I had apologized to the sponsors and sought for an apology from the Pastor as well. She informed me she was going to correct this discrepancy while acknowledging that the mentioned figure was for just the year under review. It is now over three months and that correction has never been done! The pastor had been informed on more than two occasions to keep a record of all the moneys this church has spent on the projects for easy reference when needed but has not! If a thank you letter were to be written, either it was to cover the all works our sponsors have done or nothing needed to be written at all! Also, the accurate record of the amount was to be reflected or better if it had been left out, and not undervaluing the help!

20. Some of the concerns here were passed on to the former Presiding Elder, Rev. Chola, by myself and the sponsors but it is of my view that this did not warrant his serious consideration.

I hereby, would love to inform the bishop, that servanthood leadership demands honest and integrity. What I have seen in the past years through the Rev. Salome Mangwende is grossly embarrassing for me. In spite of being helpful to her and on many occasions, being there for her, she keeps on showing poor judgment repeatedly. The Lord had revealed to me by revelation what was spoken as they made a costly mistake of "Dedication of the Church," in this, her latest mishap, without informing those who have laboured tirelessly for the project. The words spoken by the two leaders were revealed to me by the Lord (The same way Samuel heard the bleating of the sheep in his ears – and remember, Saul had had gone to Carmel and had set up a monument in his own honour, 1 Samuel 15:12-23 because they deliberately chose to do it in secrecy!) In this same way, the word of the Lord had come to me and none from the church had revealed this to me but the LORD and he did it audibly! The LORD had shown me exactly why she (or they) chose not to inform this writer or the sponsors. Nearly everything and the beauty you see at Trinity (construction) have been directed from here but people in Zambia chose to erect monuments in their honour without even having the courtesy of informing the people behind the projects!

I know I am not the current pastor (as the Lord revealed to me was their discussion point) but a wise person should look above and discern if his or her actions are in order. Scripture says, "Blessed are those who die in the Lord and their deeds follow them." Servanthood leadership is not about building castles or monuments or putting up our names on marble when we know for sure we contributed nothing to the structure! Simple consultation would have had this matter handled very well and would have prevented people from conducting themselves like non-believers. Suppose the sponsors had wanted to travel for the dedication? This servant has paid money out of his pocket and designed Calvary AME Church in Kitwe as well at the request of the brother-in-law at the church there. This servant was one of the founding members of Calvary church in 1994. Calvary and Trinity are destined to be the best in Zambia of all AME churches if they follow the plan, nevertheless, selfishness by leaders as observed above makes it hard for this church to find genuine partners for the work of the Lord. What a shame! How many bishops or pastors in this church have ever done such work before? Persons spoken to at the church later have confirmed informing the pastor or asking her if she had informed the sponsors or this brother of the upcoming events but the pastor kept dodging that question, an indication that what was being done was not an oversight but a deliberate decision made with impure motives and out of immaturity.

May the bishop consider this in his future work because several times this servant has been forced to backpedal on plans for Trinity because such poor leadership in the church stands in the way of the Lord's work.

Blessings.
Charles Kapungwe (Rev.).
Former Pastor Trinity AME Church.
1996-2000.

cc. Rev. Salome Mangwende, Pastor Trinity AME Church
    Mr. Robert & Mrs. Joellyn Rabias, Sponsor, Aiken, SC USA
    Mr. Steve & Mrs. Kathy Marbert, Sponsor, Aiken, SC USA
    Rev. Elasto Mwansa, Current Administrator.
    Br. Feckson Simukoko, Builder
    Br. Joseph Mapila, Interim Consultant
    Davidson Sinyangwe, Leader
    Stewards & Trustees Board Trinity AME Church.

The Bishop did not respond to my letter. About five months later, our sponsors wrote the Bishop.

The Sponsor's Mail to Bishop Wilfred Messiah

Dear Rt. Rev. Wilfred Messiah
Presiding Bishop
African Methodist Episcopal Church
17th Episcopal District
Lusaka,
Zambia.
Date 5/12/18

<u>**Subject:**</u> Trinity AME Church Construction

    Greetings to you in the name of our Lord and Savior Jesus Christ. I hope that all is well with you and family, and that the Holy Spirit of God is working in the hearts and minds of many in your part of the world to hear the Word of God and learn and accept His plan of salvation, His free gift for all who believe in his Son.

    I am not quite sure I know where to begin this letter especially since we have never had any kind of prior contact or communication. Until now, most of my communication has been with Pastor Charles Kapungwe, and also with Pastor Elasto Mwansa. There has been very little interaction of any kind with Pastor Salome.

    I first met Pastor Kapungwe in the summer of 2002. He visited New Covenant Presbyterian Church in Aiken SC. while attending school. Since then we have become more than just acquaintances. He explained his desire for a medical education with wish to return to Zambia to help his people medically and also spiritually through the Word of God and his education. In the process, he also made some of us at NCPC aware of Pastor Elasto at Trinity AME, and his dream of building a new church on property that was purchased prior to his departure to America some 18 to 20 years ago.

    Pastor Charles preached at NCPC on 2 or 3 occasions and prayed in front of our congregation with a powerful heart moving many with a desire to financially assist in some small way. Charles was attending a church in Columbia SC, and on two occasions the choir of approximately 20 people from his church traveled 60 miles one way to sing at our evening service when he preached. A "Love Offering" was taken each time and $2,500.00 was offered by the congregation at each service. This $5,000.00 was sent to Pastor Elasto and a footprint foundation was built by church members with blocks made by church members from property ground.

    This was just the beginning of realizing a dream. NCPC had a men's Bible Study that met then every Saturday morning, and every man without exception would contribute money to a Fund for Trinity AME, and once or so a quarter I would wire money to Pastor Elasto for his support and incremental church building. This money would be wired to Pastor Leonard Chola's bank account. This wiring of funds from the men's Bible group continued for approximately 5 years from 2002 to 2007 and involved many men, all eager to help.

    Over the course of the last 16 years between the two "Love Offerings," the men's Bible group, and the last 10 years, approximately $66,000.00 has been wired to Zambia for the construction of and Trinity AME Church and it still is not complete but is almost finished. A major piece of construction remains that includes a well for water that has already been dug but the plumbing to the church and construction of a water tank still remains. This well is an added asset to the church that was not part of the original plan.

The primary purpose of my informing you of all that has transpired so far to date is so that you are personally aware that the major contribution to the building so far has been accomplished by Pastors Elasto Mwansa, brothers Feckson Simukoko, Davidson Sinyangwe, Joseph Mapila, John Musukwa, Webby Phiri all of whom were on site, and Pastor Charles Kapungwe who is temporally living in America but has communicated over and over again over these many years with his instruction and vision.

I must include Pastor Salome's time and contribution but, it was very limited because of her full time job as a nurse. Because of her full-time job, she was not available when needed and as a result a decision was made to ask Pastor Elasto to assume the responsibility of handling all finances and communication with others. This he has accomplished at a high level even though he is a Pastor of his own church and has other demands on his time.

Over the course of the last 18 months or so two very important issues involving the church construction were discussed with Pastor Salome. The first item involved the need to identify on a blueprint a footprint of all electrical and plumbing and sewer lines and pipes before the concrete floor was laid and finished for future reference, and the need to discuss with church members the need for a security fence of some kind.

Over a year has passed and when Pastor Elasto brought the subject up with church members they said the matter has never been discussed. For whatever reason, Pastor Salome totally forgot her responsibility. I do not intend to be unkind but matters of this importance demand attention and action from a leader greater than what Pastor Salome has displayed. In addition to the deficiency in communication she has also exercised poor judgment in handling finances. When purchasing benches for the church which cost $200.00 each. She paid for them before they were even manufactured. Needless to say, there was some serious difficulty in getting all the benches made correctly. She chose to make decisions on matters she was not experienced with without consulting people who are experienced.

In my opinion the major errors in judgment that I just highlighted should never have happened by a person in a Pastoral leadership capacity. Additionally, we had a major problem much earlier in construction involving the windows that were purchased and installed. The wrong style of window was ordered and installed and the serious error involving air ventilation had to be corrected. Not to mention the door that was installed that was of a different width at the top than at the bottom. Pastor Charles noticed this from a picture that that was submitted.

Bishop Messiah, I bring this matter to your attention because much has been accomplished over the years with the hope and aspiration that Trinity AME will be a fountain of hope and salvation for many who have never been drawn to Jesus Christ but strong leadership is necessary and it cannot be done by someone who has a full time job as a nurse. It demands 100% energy and attention and someone with good leadership skills! Too much has been accomplished to not have the right person assigned.

I respect your position and responsibility and hope I have not offended you with my comments but do hope and pray that you give serious thought to some of what I say.

I remain Respectfully Yours;
Robert J Rabias.

Like to my first mail, the Bishop did not acknowledge receiving this mail from our sponsors too. He also did not respond to them either. Instead, after seven months from the day of my first mail, the Bishop delegated the response to my letter and that of the sponsors' mail to an incoming person who had no thorough knowledge of the intricate details of this work! Our sponsors who have been supporting Trinity A.M.E. Church for 17 years and bought speakers for St. John A.M.E. Church in Kitwe too (another A.M.E. Church where Pastor Elasto Mwansa had been transferred to from Trinity) and had supported an A.M.E. Church Pastor monthly pay for eleven years at Trinity were treated with contempt to my dismay!

Here is the response from Bishop Wilfred Messiah through a second party:

**AFRICAN METHODIST
EPISCOPAL CHURCH**

**17TH EPISCOPAL DISTRICT
SOUTHWEST ZAMBIA CONFERENCE**
OFFICE OF THE PRESIDING ELDER
COPPERBELT CENTRAL DISTRICT
P.O. BOX 240325
NDOLA
ZAMBIA
CENTRAL AFRICA

Email: margaretmwanza@gmail.com   mobile: 0977-776406

REF: AMEC /SWZC / MNM / 01 /18
Date: 09th July, 2018

Mr. Robert Rabias
New Covenant Presbyterian Church in Aiken SC. (NCPC)
…… Blvd
…… City MI
<u>United States of America</u>

Dear Mr. Robert Rabias,

RE: SPONSORSHIP SUPPORT TO THE WORK OF TRINITY CHURCH OF THE AFRICAN METHODIST EPISCOPAL CHURCH (AMEC) IN GARNATONE –KITWE – REPUBLIC OF ZAMBIA

Greetings to you in the joy of the Lord. It is my prayer that you, family and the NCPC ministry are doing well through the grace of God.

1. I make reference to your letter, dated 5th May, 2018 in connection with the above captioned subject matter. Before I specifically respond to your letter, I wish to make reference to Rev. Charles Kapungwe's earlier eight-page letter, dated December 22, 2017; which he entitled: "Embarrassing and Poor Leadership – Trinity Church". Just like your recent letter, Rev.

Charles Kapungwe's letter was also addressed to the Bishop of the Church, The Rt. Rev. Dr. Wilfred J. Messiah respectively. The same was copied to yourself and Pastor Elasto Mwansa, who was addressed as administrator, and other four lay persons, including Rev. Salome Mangwende herself.

2. In the first place, I wish on behalf of the Bishop of the African Methodist Episcopal Church thank you and other partners you work with for the Financial Assistance rendered to Trinity AME Church in Kitwe – Zambia. I say we are grateful and still ask you to receive our most sincere gratitude for your kind gesture and shall always cherish that spirit of love.

3. The Rt. Rev. Dr. Wilfred J. Messiah is the overall superintendent of the African Methodist Episcopal Church in the 17th Episcopal District, comprising of six (06) Countries; Kenya, Burundi, Rwanda, Congo DR, Congo Brazzaville and Zambia. As such, the Bishop Wilfred J. Messiah does not handle matters at the level you are trying to engage with him. Matters of this nature are usually handled firstly, at District level by the Presiding Elder, and secondly, at the Conference level by the Bishop's Administrative Assistant. In fact, Rev. Charles Kapungwe, knows this fact clearly, and if he had indeed obediently and honestly cared to follow the Doctrine and Discipline of the African Methodist Episcopal Church (AMEC), out of which he had received his pastoral ordination, he could have guided you on how the AME Church operates.

4. In Rev. Kapungwe's earlier communication, he had inadvertently and unfairly entitled his letter, and referred to Rev. Salome Mangwende as: "Embarrassing and Poor Leadership at Trinity AME Church". To say the least, Rev. Kapungwe's letter was downright unethically, unchristian, unprofessional and mostly insulting to the leadership of the AME Church, especially the office of the Bishop who is the Appointing authority responsible for placement of pastors as he sees fit through godly judgement for the following reasons among others: -

   (i) Rev Kapungwe is not the appointing authority for Rev. Salome Mangwende for him to refer to her leadership as embarrassing and poor. He is not entitled to use the derogatory words towards a fellow minister. (unethical)
   (ii) He is not present at the Church to see or appreciate or disapprove of Rev Mangwende's work culture.
   (iii) The fact that he is the one who made contact with you for the financial sponsorship does not make him an overall overseer of the AME Church, let alone Trinity Congregation.
   (iv) He has no right to judge someone based on unfounded reports received from an illegally constituted committee to supervise a substantively appointed minister at will and conduct himself as though he is an authority,

   It was as though Rev Charles Kapungwe was addressing kindergarten kids on how to run a church, yet he was addressing somebody whom he calls his Bishop. This is most unfortunate and very embarrassing, especially from someone like him who claims to be well taught in the culture and tradition of the African Methodist Episcopal Church.

5. In short, the actions of Rev. Kapungwe of appointing an ad hoc committee that included Rev Elasto Mwansa constitutes a serious breach of the Doctrine and Discipline of the AME Church, which is the supreme constitution of the AME Church in the Connection.

In fact, the Rev Mangwende has just been very tolerant due to the love of having continuity of the development of the Church, otherwise, she could have raised disciplinary Charges against Pastor Elasto Mwansa for Pastoral interference in her congregation.

6. In his letter Rev. Kapungwe went at length talking history and addressing issues he considered to be shortcomings of Rev. Mangwende, but one thing he forgot was that he was actually committing an offence and a breach of Maladministration himself. The reason being that Rev. Kapungwe, for God's sake, had no right whatsoever to appoint an illegal committee to supervise an appointed minister in the AME Church. The AME Church has a procedure in which it handles its projects and other works through the Board of Trustees and Stewards, who are under the supervision of the Pastor in Charge, in this case the Rev. Salome Mangwende. While we may appreciate Rev Kapungwe's concern for the construction of the Church, his style, strategy and approach lack procedure and replete of any guidelines as per AME Church constitution, of which he is very much aware of, needless to remind him about it.

7. Secondly, may I now address the concerns of your letter as follows: -   We still want to thank you for the financial assistance and your love for overseas ministry, out of which you have made such great sacrifices, we are really indebted and ever thanking God for you. However, after reading your letter, it appears to be a replica of Rev Charles Kapungwe's letter to the Bishop as indicated above. After scrutiny of your letter, what came out was that, you were prompted to write to the Bishop, probably (may be) after pressure from Rev. Charles Kapungwe as his letter did not receive the due attention from the AME leadership of the Church as he had expected. The reason why his letter was not responded to is that it was wrongly addressed to the Bishop instead of the Rev. Margaret N. Mwanza (myself), who is Presiding Elder and Bishop's Administrative Assistant in the District in whose jurisdiction Pastor Mangwende and the Trinity Church under discussion fall under.

8. Further, you seem to have been prompted and compelled to replicate Rev. Kapungwe's letter because his idea of Regime change at Trinity church did not receive any response. I have taken note of the positive points you raised in your letter and do appreciate the observations made. We may address some of them that are completely outside the realm of interference with Rev. Salome Mangwende' performance at Trinity Church. I still wish to reinstate that the evaluation of Rev. Mangwende's performance is the preserve of her supervisor and appointing authority; that's the Presiding Elder, the Bishop's Administrative Assistant (BAA) and finally the Bishop; of course not from any outsider, regardless whether they be sponsors or not, including yourselves.

9. It is also noted that there was a very serious anomaly perpetuated by Rev. Kapungwe, after the retirement of Rev. Leonard Chola who was the Presiding Elder and Bishop's Administrative Assistant (BAA) then. It is that he deliberately misled you to believe that there was no one to succeed Rev. Chola, when in actual fact I was there. Therefore, instead of giving you correct guidance in terms of remittance of the donations to my office as Presiding Elder and BAA, he instead misled you and gave the responsibility to Pastor Elasto Mwansa who is actually under my supervision too. This was deliberately putting things upside down which is a recipe for the current confusion and lack of progress you are trying to blame on Rev. Mangwende.

10. Further in, in your letter you highlighted that Rev. Salome Mangwende is not performing well just because she has a fulltime job, to the contrary, it's the frustration caused by Rev Kapungwe's illegally imposed Committee which is confusing itself in the discharge of duties. There is nowhere, even in your church at NCPC where the lay persons supervise an ordained Minister- it is strange. The rest of your letter is exactly like Kapungwe's ideas, but what must be made clear is that, in the AME Church, part time pastors are allowed and Female pastors have an equal standing as their male counterparts. I know the other reason why you have issues with Rev. Mangwende is because may be in your church the doctrine does not allow female ministers to pastor.

11. In conclusion, while we appreciate the financial support that you rendered to the AME Church, Trinity Congregation in particular, we wish to make ourselves clear and state as follows: -

    (a) All futures correspondences regarding Trinity AME Church should not be addressed to the Bishop of the Church, but through my office.
    (b) All goodwill donations or contributions from local or abroad shall be channeled to the Pastor in Charge, Rev. Salome Mangwende. My office shall ensure that she accounts for every coin remitted and periodic reports sent to you our sponsors. While Rev Mangwende is answerable to you through my office, not Rev. Kapungwe and Mwansa.
    (c) Rev. Elasto Mwansa and his illegal committee which Rev. Kapungwe imposed on the church shall be disbanded immediately, and will have nothing to do with Trinity Church anymore, unless otherwise invited by Rev. Salome Mangwende through my office.
    (d) The recent email letter written by Rev. Charles Kapungwe instructing the Rev. Salome Mangwende to make duplicate Keys for handing over to Br Joseph Mapila one of the lay persons from another church is misplaced and inconceivable, therefore shall not be honoured.
    (e) A new committee to oversee the works shall be constituted in accordance with the rules, guidelines and procedures as per the Doctrine and Discipline of the AME Church. Progress reports shall be submitted to you periodically, and you shall be at liberty to seek any clarifications should need be, as you are aware that no contract was signed between AMEC and NCPC.
    (f) All donations, gifts, financial or materials shall be directed and received through the Presiding Elder or the Pastor in Charge, Rev Salome Mangwende.
    (g) All committees and works shall be supervised by Rev Salome Mangwende, who is the Pastor in charge, who shall be required to account for all funds remitted to her charge in a transparent manner to you through my office.
    (h) Rev Elasto Mwansa is subsequently withdrawn from all the affairs and activities at Trinity AME Church, unless otherwise so invited by Rev. Salome Mangwende through my office. This will give him sufficient time to concentrate on building his Church spiritually which is the core reason for his appointment as a Pastor in the AME Church.
    (i) Rev. Charles Kapungwe must desist from directing issues at Trinity church using unorthodox methods. He should instead learn to be humble, obedient and deal directly with the authority in the office, the Presiding Elder and BAA
    (j) The Bishop shall never remove an officially appointed Pastor based on external pressure

and recommendations, as the situation seems to be now as every Pastor in the AME Church is protected under the Bill of Rights.

It is my hope and prayer that most issues you raised have been tackled and that you now have an idea of how the AME Church operates. I therefore pray that all parties will abide to the above stated points, for the smooth running of the Church.

In the Lord's Service
Rev Margaret Nkana Mwanza
Presiding Elder & Bishop's Administrative Assistant
SOUTH WEST ZAMBIA CONFERENCE
Cc: The Rt. Rev. Dr. Wilfred J. Messiah – 17th Episcopal District Presiding Bishop
 The Rev. Salome Mangwende – Pastor in Charge Trinity AME Church
 The Rev. Elasto Mwansa – Pastor in Charge Kirkland AME Church
 Trustees and Stewards Board – Trinity Congregation
 The Rev. Cosmas Wakunguma – President – Presiding Elders' Council
 The Rev Charles Kapungwe - U.S.A

5 | Page

My Second Letter to Bishop Wilfred Messiah, the Council of Bishops, Bishop McKinley Young, Senior Bishop and the General Secretary:

November 12, 2018

121 Spring Street
Apt 9
Auburn, ME 04210
USA
charliekaps@hotmail.com
+ 1 207 330 9944

Bishop Wilfred Messiah
17th Episcopal District
411 A Longridge
Mapepe, Chilanga 10101
P.O. Box 36628
Lusaka, Zambia
011-260-1225967

UFS: Rev. Dr. Jeff Cooper
General Secretary A.M.E. Church
500 8th Avenue South
Nashville, TN 37203
Phone (615) 254-0911
cio@ame-church.com

UFS: Bishop McKinley Young
Senior Bishop
& The Bishop's Council
A.M.E. Church
288 South Hamilton Road
Columbus, OH 43213-2034
(614) 575-2279

UFS: Rev. Salome Mangwende
Trinity A.M.E. Church
Garneton, Kitwe Zambia
Phone: +260 966 749 629

Dear Bishop Messiah, Bishop McKinley Young, Senior Bishop, the Bishop's Council & The General Secretary,

<u>DISAPPOINTING AND INCOMPETENT LEADERSHIP IN THE CHURCH IN ZAMBIA</u>

This is to introduce to you Charles Kapungwe, a former Pastor of Trinity A.M.E. Church at Garneton Kitwe, Zambia from 1996 to 2000. This is an appeal letter to the global A.M.E. Church in the U.S.A. contesting to what I perceive to be a poor judgment and response to my letter (enclosed) written to Bishop Wilfred Messiah but responded to by one of his leaders in Zambia. During my time as Pastor at Trinity, we met in a classroom at a school! The community was very poor, therefore, I supported myself since I worked for the Government. To reach Garneton, I paid my way to and fro using three public transports one way. Since the community was poor, no one considered Trinity as a place that could host even a District Conference or any meetings involving other Churches in the District because it lacked basic infrastructure!

The land had just been gotten but was unpaid for so I used my money to pay for it in full to the City of Kitwe. Since no one could afford the architectural fees and design, I did the design and paid the architect – again out of my pocket. When I left Zambia in 2000, the Church was still meeting at a school and they were later kicked out. I knew there was no way that Church was going to be built and I prayed for the opportunity to find money to construct a building.

Pastor Elasto Mwansa had been a person I had led to the Lord when I was at Jordan Chapel A.M.E. Church in Kitwe. He had become a Pastor in the Church, and by the providence of God, he had been appointed to Trinity. Also, by the providence of God I attended a Bible School in Kitwe run by a white American Missionary, Rev. Sue McDermott. Rev. McDermott was so happy with me that she had asked me to bring a member of my Church to attend her Bible School for free! Since, Garneton was far, and I had only two women who could have been eligible, I asked her if it were fine for me to bring a person from another Church. When she said it was okay, I asked Pastor Elasto who was from Jordan Chapel A.M.E. Church, my childhood church. He went to the Bible School for four years for free at a time I had not even been aware he was going to take over from me at Trinity after I departed in 2000.

In about 2001, I learned that Pastor Elasto had just been withdrawn from Trinity

Church. The reason was that Trinity was unable to support him; therefore, the Church was put on a Supply Pastor. It was at this time that I met members of the Presbyterian Church in Aiken, South Carolina where I was attending Summer School. (I had been an Associate pastor at White Hall A.M.E. Church at the time in Jenkinsville, South Carolina, over 60 miles away). The Missions Committee agreed that they could help my Church in Zambia as long as the Church was willing to reinstate Pastor Elasto. Since I needed to show trust, I gave them the number of Rev. Sue McDermott who knew both Elasto and I. She gave a very good recommendation to the Missions Committee and they told me they were very happy from what they heard from Rev. Sue McDermott about both Rev. Elasto and me. Also, I could have informed the Presbyterian Church to send the money directly to Pastor Elasto but I thought of sending it through a Pastor of Calvary A.M.E. Church who I had known for several years and I had served there as a Senior Steward before I had moved to Trinity as Pastor. This was BEFORE he had EVEN BEEN A PRESIDING ELDER!

I want the CHURCH to understand that sending money through Rev. LEONARD CHOLA was my IDEA and NOT THE IDEA OF ANYONE! IT WAS MY PREROGATIVE. The woman who wrote the letter to me had NO IDEA ABOUT THIS just like she has no idea about many things which transpired in the last 17 YEARS nor DOES THE BISHOP! For your information, Rev. Chola was not a Presiding Elder at the time and there was no need for me to even have involved him if I had wanted. This was a TRINITY project, a local church but because I had wanted to win trust and put in accountability, **I chose NOT TO SEND MONEY DIRECTLY to TRINITY and opted that he received this money. When he became a Presiding Elder years later, he just continued to receive the money and nothing ever came up to force me to alter that arrangement.**

The New Covenant Presbyterian Church (NCPC) raised about $900 for me when I graduated in 2004 from Allen University. They had invited my Church from Jenkinsville, White Hall A.M.E. Church and the choir came together with my Pastor Rev. Leroy Cannon. The Church also raised $5,000.00 which they sent to begin the construction of Trinity. I had asked Pastor Elasto to send me the copies of the drawings which I had left in Zambia. I showed them to my Church but White Hall A.M.E. Church could not afford to render any help. **I had asked Pastor Elasto to split the $5,000.00 so that they could lay a foundation and put the rest into an income generating project to help build the CHURH but the project TRINITY had started was botched and consequently, TRINITY lost all the money around 2003. This was my initial setback with my zeal to help a Church I loved!** It took several months before this problem was resolved. Mr. Rabias had a discussion with Pastor Elasto, forgave the Church and the hatchet was buried. The woman who wrote that letter to me and her BISHOP HAVE NO IDEA OF THIS HISTORY AS WELL.

Regardless, our sponsors who were already supporting Pastor Elasto with monthly pay decided to help the Church build a smaller structure to help them have a place to meet. They were meeting in a makeshift structure at this time. Members made bricks but Mr. and Mrs. Rabias, at this time used their personal money to pay for the construction of the first Church building and put in power, water, a communion table and PA system. NCPC also supported Elasto for five years as Pastor of Trinity. After five years, NCPC stopped supporting Pastor Elasto. However, my adopting family, the Rabias family took over and supported him for the next 6 more years – a total of 11 years. When former Presiding Elder

Rev. Leonard Chola came to the U.S., I took him to this Church in Aiken, South Carolina and I facilitated for him to preach in the Church. When Bishop Paul Kawimbe was elected Bishop, I took him too and the Zambian delegation to the home of Mr. Rabias and we sang and praised God in his house with many members from the Presbyterian Church who had funded TRINITY, present. I have preached in this Church representing A.M.E. Church and God who I have served too.

When the leadership changed, Pastor Elasto had informed the incoming Pastor what had been happening. I did as well. We were not sure if the same was going to continue. After some months, we discussed with Mr. Rabias and he was willing to go it alone and build the Church. At the time Pastor Elasto had informed her of my choice of the man I knew could help in the construction. He is Bro. Feckson Simukoko who was a member of Jordan Chapel A.M.E. Church where I grew up in Kitwe and we sang in the same choir at Jordan. Bro. Feckson had a ton of experience in construction and I had personally talked to the Pastor telling her of many buildings he had been a part of building in Zambia, all quality structures under the Mining Company. **Br. Feckson, actually, together with my former Senior Steward's husband, had laid the foundation of this structure at TRINITY in 2003 including the initial settings before the current Pastor had come to Trinity. He also had called on the City to inspect the foundation. Again, the woman who wrote me the letter had NO IDEA ABOUT THIS ARRANGEMENT because I don't know her personally and she never lived in the City of Kitwe!**

Respectfully, the first person the new Pastor had contracted did a good job. The person did a good job on the slab with the walls. However, after his demise the Pastor began to engage people who began to do substandard works. **Nevertheless, it was again Bro. Feckson's advice to put up a ring beam in the structure and his insistence in going up higher that made this building what it is now. When the building had reached the window level the Pastor had insisted on putting up the roof after two courses on top and I had to stop her! If it had not been for my continuous monitoring of the work, which many people both in the Church and outside are proud of and see as a marvel, it could NOT have been what it is today!** (KINDLY SEE A PHOTO OF A DIFFERENT CHURCH BUILDING IN ONE RURAL AREA AND SEE HOW SOME BUILDINGS ARE DONE. THE PHOTO YOU SEE IS AN A.M.E. CHURCH UNDER CONSTRUCTION and I never wanted to have a similar tragedy from the outset. **Once again, the woman who wrote me the letter you see HAD NO IDEA THAT THIS HAD BEEN GOING ON FOR YEARS! Poverty is a disease and when one is aware of its presence one will take advantage of it to exploit the disadvantaged and the ignorant unqualified leadership to what he wants.**

I must state that the Pastor is a woman and depended a lot on the men who had supported her in the construction. These men who the writer of the letter barring me from completing the Church which I had conceived and directed for years and sourced funds for indicated in letter that I was collaborating with the "lay" an indication of lack of understanding of ministry. **The Pastor of Trinity did well during the first half of the construction but I began to notice poor techniques in construction after the demise of the initial bricklayer who she had hired. I began to see construction being done without a spirit level, poor workmanship and poor accountability in finances. In spite of raising these concerns to her, it appeared she never cared.** I had constantly been reminding them of poorly constructed A.M.E. Churches in Zambia and I never wanted Trinity to have the same fate especially that Trinity had enough money to complete the Church without any problems. I also kept reminding her how some Africans have broken trust in America due to insincerity. There are so many things I could itemize that could have been even worse with the Church which many people in Zambia are now proud of but are not aware that I had kept on insisting on how the construction was to be done:

1. If I never intervened, the roof could have been fixed wrongly! The Pastor thought after reaching the window level, she needed to put up the roof. I insisted not to! She had to change her mind and I told the person I had appointed earlier to ensure that they go up at least 5 courses even though I am aware the building had the measurements but they never stated anything to that effect.

2. I was surprised to hear that they were installing the power lines on the surface of the building instead of inside the walls in spite of me having given those directives and specifications to the people she was sidelining! I stopped them from doing that otherwise today, power lines would have been on the surface and not inside the walls. Thank God I have been constantly on the phone giving guidance! **The woman who wrote me the letter is ignorant of this fact yet she chose to indulge in matters she has no clue about!**

3. I told them how the ceiling was to be installed otherwise it would not have been what it is now. I gave Pastor Elasto and Bro. Feckson guidelines and we had discussed on the phone extensively before arriving at our choice. They sent me sample photos with Bro. Feckson because I had earlier on told them they needed to put up a suspended ceiling. We finally settled for what is now installed including the type of lights which I specifically had ordered to be installed! She had a different idea from what is in the Church now! Pastor Elasto then, informed the pastor what to buy and that is how the ceiling was done. **The author of the letter to me is unaware of this information too. Br. Feckson and Elasto then put up the ceiling with the help of another individual.**

4. I told them to put up an apron in a certain way but I was surprised it was badly done in spite of the fact that I had asked the sponsors for the money specifically for it and we were given $5,000.00. This was to help the walls which had been stained. **Poor quality of paint had been used earlier in spite of my directives and this time I asked them to get it from specific stores and I sent them specific colors from Lowe's Store in the U.S.A. this time as samples. The woman who wrote me the letter, I am sure, had no knowledge about this too.**

5. I had asked them to be using a Bro. who had been with me at Jordan Chapel A.M.E. Church because I knew he was good at the sewer lines' installation but the Pastor, singlehandedly sourced and chose people who worked for a Water and Sewerage Company who never knew how to install the lines or plumbing works. She lost the money and that took about 6 months. The Brother who was not given the job corrected the works. **The woman who lives in another city and has chosen to supervise the construction whose vision she did not conceive and has no idea about its beginning, and progress of this church ignorantly decided to lecture me on matters she has no understanding on or the history thereof!**

6. It must be noted that I have spent a lot of money for the past 17 to 18 years calling Zambia because I had to be updating our supporters. Sometimes (on many occasions) they could not get or understand fully what the people or the Pastor meant so I had to get details. I found out that they had installed the windows in the church wrongly in a country with a tropical climate. The windows opening one side was unacceptable because the ventilation

was going to be extremely compromised and any gathering was going to be affected badly! This was worsened by the fact that the design I did incorporated toilets and offices to the main sanctuary and had led to deficit in number of windows required. When I learned about this, I was left with no choice but to ask that they uninstall the windows last year and redo them costing more money again. If this were not done, the all construction of the Church was going to be a mockery because poor air circulation was going to impact worshipers negatively. It must be noted that this mistake had to be communicated to the sponsors and was only discovered after the church was coming to completion. **The WRITER OF THIS LETTER KNEW NOTHING ABOUT THIS TOO AND HER IGNORANCE IS NOTICEABLE IN HER MAIL SINCE SHE WAS NOT A PART OF THIS PROJECT!**

7. When some changes were made to the bathroom doors to be installed outside, I advised them to make an incline (ramp) for wheelchair accessibility and steps on the opposite side. Sadly, while I am appreciative for the hard work the volunteers did, the incline was out of proportion, so I gave them a mathematical formula to use and made corrections. I explained to the pastor asking her to give an engineer who would interpret my sketch and he was one of the members of the church, a part of the group which has worked so hard to build this church and one of the recipients of my first letter which this woman author calls "LAY PERSONS" as though they are less special than her! Thankfully, this was corrected. (See my ramp calculations and the poor ramp which had been made before!)

8. During construction, the team came up with adding an extra door to the main sanctuary. I had no objection with it but I noticed they had compromised the architectural design and beauty; therefore, I made a design that corrected this fault and explained the rationale. It took over a year to make that correction which they have acknowledged correcting **but we have not seen any photos of the corrections. (See my designs).**

9. I had sent photos to the Pastor of how the tiles were to be installed and this was clearly explained and the money was sent. However, to build the tiles has taken what I may refer to as "robbing Peter to pay Paul," through taking monies from three other instalments which were earmarked for something else due to selfishness, controlling and lack of transparency. The money which had been budgeted for never served the purpose that it was meant to. When I followed up repeatedly, she deliberately left the bathrooms locked up to keep people out and when I insisted trying to know if tiles had been put up, she sent us only one photo showing tiles and that remained so for over a year! (Note: The Church has three bathrooms with showers). After a year I discovered that the tiles had been given to another person to install (**only done because I wanted to see the photos**) and were not aligned and contrary to my advice of putting tiles from bottom to top, plaster was put on top and still were incomplete. I asked them to use the Brother from Jordan Chapel A.M.E. Church who removed the plaster and the tiles and with the help of other four people who we paid again, new tiles were reapplied even though the bathrooms are still incomplete, to date! Bro. Feckson also discovered that the walls were not perpendicular in the bathrooms and had to redo portions to make the tiles align smoothly. **(THE WRITER OF THE LETTER TO ME AND HER BISHOP ARE INCONGRUOUS WITH THIS FACT TOO!)**

10. You may wish to know also that before money was sent at each juncture, a budget which stipulated needs and estimates was requested first. I have all the information to that effect which even the BISHOP does not because I have been running this work from inception. I had informed the Pastor that they NEEDED to buy benches made of **HARDWOOD** and the quotation we received stipulated so! It was marked at $200/bench and the money

which was sent was based on that. Alas, to my dismay, the Pastor bought benches made out of **SOFTWOOD** and of low-quality contrary to our expectation and my instruction. After seeing the benches on the photos, I had noted immediately that they likely will be affected by those with a heavy weight and will definitely sag and may not last long. In addition, she never even stated to us about that change and it took me to notice when I saw the benches on the photos! Also, it took one year to deliver 35 benches which the Pastor had already paid for in full without informing us! This was again contrary to my discussion with her. An independent person who looked at the benches was agreeable with me and lamented that there are better hardwood benches they could have bought at nearly the same price that they had informed me they had gotten these benches. **Although I had stated this in my first letter, the woman who wrote me a letter and our sponsors chose to ignore these facts. She has never spoken to me and I have never spoken to her and I do not know her personally!**

11. You must also be interested to know that as a person who ran this project from the first day, I have documentation of every transaction that was done. I understand the project better because I am the person who has been the conduit between the sponsors and the Church. I have provided the same to independent persons who reevaluated the costs. I am aware that in building, especially in a developing country like ours, construction materials vary, however, large discrepancies are not acceptable and **this woman author of a letter who does not understand or is unaware of the intricate details I know, decided to throw herself into the matter she hardly has all the facts on hand, making herself a joke to those who have all documentation about this project!**

12. Once, when the spoon drain was poorly done, I asked them to demolish it and to redo it. I have the photos of this poorly done work. This author woman doesn't have and she had no idea why I asked them to demolish it! **All she has seen is the final product which they are made to believe the Pastor did and are very happy and are patting her on the back!** Certainly, the final product is good but for those who do not understand details, those who have been used to poor structures, this is the best they have ever seen in this denomination and give the Pastor all the credit forgetting the so-called "LAY" like Brother **Davidson Sinyangwe** or Brother **John Musukwa** who volunteered relentlessly and sacrificed a lot to make this Church building become what it is today! Without the duo, TRINITY would not have been the marvel it is today as well! **The Pastor also took advantage of the two who paid money out of pocket in spite of having sufficient money from our Sponsors to do all the projects! I am also aware that the Pastor was NEVER informing the Conferences yearly that Rev. Charles Kapungwe and the New Covenant Presbyterian Church in Aiken, South Carolina were responsible for the construction of the Church at TRINITY but alluded all the work to "The hardworking people of Trinity," the folly caused by greed and self-praise that will now take us into another phase resulting from selfishness!**

13. The writer of the letter is unaware that I had designed a block of apartments for this Church to help it stand on its feet financially and the current pastor is not suitable to manage this, I had come to learn. I cannot relinquish control to any person other than a person of my choice on financial matters because I have learned a great deal dealing with this Pastor and everyone in Zambia. If I had been aware from the beginning of this problem this is what I could have done and would have freed the CHURCH from any obligations of the moneys sent and construction could have been done by the team outside the Church. I could not have appointed Rev. Leonard Chola, a man with corporate experience yet he failed lamentably to supervise his erring minister. My sincere desire to help the poor and my

trust in the CHURCH I have laboured in since I was a youth blinded my judgment. I have learned a lot and I know more about this Church than what some people may think.

14. I was aware that I needed to help the church on evangelism too. I had thought of buying a **projector and projector screen** which I had explained to the Pastor of its importance. I bought them movies such as "The Passions of Christ" and shipped them at my cost. When they failed to find a right projector in Zambia, I purchased a projector in South Africa using my friends there at the cost of $2,000 purchased with the money from our sponsors. The projector was transported to Zambia by a friend who we started Calvary A.M.E. Church with but had left the Church because of the same irresponsible behaviour like we see in this case. The Pastor acknowledged receipt but our supporters have not been briefed about what has been happening for a year now to this projector. I do know how it is being used and I fail to give answers when asked. The problem I made, it appears, was my approaching the sponsors and informing them of the importance of this evangelistic tool for the CHURCH. I also bought a **large projector screen** for the Church, courtesy from our sponsors for about $279 on Amazon and our Sponsors paid for shipping to Zambia. I shipped the projector screen together with other items I had put in as gifts for the Church which came to about $1,000.00 to ship with a few of personal belongings. I transported two large glass tables which I bought as gift and shipped at my cost for Trinity. The items took four months and when they arrived in Zambia, this letter informed me I had a **"RESTRAINING ORDER slapped upon me against TRINITY CHURCH"** appeared! It was sent three months earlier, apparently sent purposely to an obscure email address which I concluded perhaps was not intended for me to see and was meant to "frighten" the "LAY PEOPLE" and show them who was in "CHARGE," a foolish notion to do. In addition to these items, I had bought several more picture frames and photos (14) for the Church to honour the so-called "LAY PEOPLE" and all the Pastors who had laboured to build this Church but **ignorance** has made me to hold on until normal behaviour – **Christian behaviour** returns to the Church of God if I am to hand over these items, I spent about $700.00 to get. (This is a second bunch of photo frames I sent to this Pastor).

15. When I observed problems in accounting and financial reports which were of concern to our sponsors, I informed the Presiding Elder Rev. Chola about it. **The problems they raised were delays in sending financial reports, irregularities, poor communication, or updates and poor images. Also, they mentioned that Elasto's reports and information had been clearer and better compared to Salome's. I was, therefore, always being forced to give updates needing a lot of explanations every time Pastor Salome sent information because it was not clear, shoddy or was very brief. Sadly, the Pastor was doing most of the financial reports by herself, because she was the custodian of the money and sole controller!** She was also not conversant with conversions since the money had to be reported in dollars. This was surprising to me because the Church had a lot of educated people and my initial inquiry into this received a cover up by a trusted person at the church who told me that the money is put in the open and everyone is aware about it. I had erroneously informed the supporters of the same but it was about several months later that I began to question the initial report. On many occasions I had asked her that at least three names must be a part of the financial report, alas, only Pastor Elasto came to her rescue and helped her. It was at this time that the financial reports improved! At one time there were three decimal points in the dollar amount and clearly, she had issues with conversions and this was very embarrassing on my part. **When I told the Presiding Elder, Rev. Leonard Chola that our sponsors were now happy**

with the reports after Rev. Elasto's regular help because all the queries have gone down, Rev. Chola informed me that I should let them know that she now has improved! I told him I couldn't say that. This is the Pastor (Elasto) that this woman (writer) was castigating me for using as Administrator for the Project which Rev. Chola himself had suggested as the person to be receiving money when he retired because he was intrinsically aware of the problem. (See the email from Rev. Chola to the sponsors). This woman was not aware of this but ignorantly accused me of installing an Administrator and answering mail she was not addressed to nor was she a part of when I was doing the best to develop the church! On this, I am willing to fly to any destination in the U.S. to come and discuss this issue with the Council if the Bishops' Council or the General Secretary so chooses.

16. When the Pastor told me that the Bishop wanted to say "thank you," I was surprised because it took 17 years for the office of the Bishop to finally write our sponsors. In my conversation with the Pastor, I informed her that the Bishop must thank:

    (i) The New Covenant Presbyterian Church that helped support Pastor Elasto for five years and gave us money to begin building the Church. (Please notice that members of **NEW COVENANT PRESBYTERIAN CHURCH** and NOT A.M.E., in SOUTH CAROLINA raised the money and it did not just come directly from the Church).

    (ii) The Bishop should also thank Mr. and Mrs. Rabias who supported Pastor Elasto for the next 6 years (a total of 11 years). He also built the first Church and connected power and water plus musical equipment and a PA system and a Communion Table.

    (iii) When the work of Trinity Church became huge Mr. Rabias was joined by another family the Marbert family. These are the people who I had informed the Pastor that the Bishop needed to thank.

17. Sadly, only two families were thanked excluding the **NCPC**. Also, the amount of money which was quoted by the Bishop $29,241.30, as the monies the two families had sent for the construction of TRINITY was NOT FACTUAL because this amount was **just for the year 2017**! At this juncture, I had informed the Pastor that this was embarrassing to me. She told me she was going to correct the mistakes but three months passed without any word either from the Bishop, the Presiding Elder Chola (who had preached in the NCPC when he came to the U.S.A. for the General Conference because of my introducing him to the Church before and was paid for that ministry) or from the Pastor herself. When I saw the discrepancy, I had apologized to our brethren, the New Covenant Presbyterian Church. **This woman who wrote this letter must be ashamed of further painting ourselves as being an insensitive and unappreciative Church to the outsiders!**

18. I had made Pastor Elasto and Br. Feckson to be in Charge of the completion of the building after a series of mistakes the Pastor had demonstrated **ONLY** less than three years ago. I had, however, left her with the control of the money. As I had stated in the letter, she had asked me, "How about the money?" I had informed her that she was the Pastor and she was going to be in charge of that!" PLEASE NOTICE THAT, AGAIN IT WAS MY PREROGATIVE TO ASSIGN A PERSON WHO I THOUGHT WAS RELIABLE TO HANDLE THE FINANCES. NO ONE CAN INFORM ME THAT THIS MONEY SHOULD BE GIVEN TO PEOPLE OF HER CHOICE WHEN THEY HAVE NO IDEA HOW THIS HELP CAME ABOUT AND WHO WAS SENDING IT! THAT IS THE WORST REQUEST I HAVE EVER HEARD FROM A PERSON IN LEADERSHIP, especially

taking into account of the aforementioned. Also, the Pastor failed to understand that by being in charge of finances also meant being accountable. TO MAKE ABITRATRY DECISIONS AFTER THE COMPLETIONS OF TWO MAJOR BUILDINGS AGAINST A PEOPLE WHO HAVE SACRIFICED A LOT AND ENTRUSTED ME WITH THE MONEY AND THE PEOPLE I KNEW IN ZAMBIA IS INSULTING TO THE PEOPLE WHO TRUSTED ME AND ENTRUSTED ME WITH THE MONIES AND RESPONSIBILITY TO EXECUTE OUR PROJECT. **PLEASE NOTE THAT THE MONEY WILL NEVER BE GIVEN TO ANY OTHER PERSON I CANNOT APPOINT.**

19. At this time, we had raised concerns over the 35 benches which were purchased by the Pastor and she had never told anyone of us about her purchase. Procurement took one year but the Pastor had paid the company in full. She had gone against her word and our agreement following a similar mistake she had made before when she gave the plumbers money and the people who did not know how to install water pipes and sewer lines. We had discussed that matter thoroughly and she had agreed she would not pay the people in advance! In spite of this fiasco, our sponsors were kind enough and sent more money and we bought an additional 100 chairs with steel frames.

20. At this time, I thought of involving the church members who had not been involved except the "Trustees." The Church Treasurer, the Senior Steward and the Financial Secretary had not been a part of all her financial reports. I informed them they were to buy a book and record all the moneys and Pastor Elasto was going to supervise the transactions and write the report. This was done because we desperately wanted to finish the Church building and the Pastor never raised any dust then because she knew she had not been compliant and this was done **only around 2017**. However, once the building was nearing completion, all hell broke loose! The Pastor stopped answering questions or giving reports to the sponsors and began to act like a heathen.

21. The Presiding Elder Leonard Chola, aware of the mess, informed us hardly a month before his departure that he was going on retirement and he would stop receiving the money! The Sponsors never responded for weeks! He had to send another email to which Mr. MARBERT responded to, because in my view, it did not look right to inform the people who had supported the Church for 17 years a month's notice, and ONLY as a response to the mail they had sent money to complete the well (borehole) which initially, had not been in the plans and Pastor Salome had indicated they were going to do it but never communicated to any of us such plans. Rev. Leonard Chola, the outgoing P.E., had proposed the name of **Rev. Elasto Mwansa** to the two families as the person who could continue to receive the money because the recommendation stated **"he was honest"** (Kindly see the email!) **The writer of the mail to me obviously, as I have stated all along was not aware of all the correspondence which I have over Trinity both from Zambia and from the sponsors.** She lives 60 kilometers away and has scanty knowledge on details of this work for her to inform me how a project I had conceived must be run!

REV. LEONARD CHOLA (FORMER P.E.'s EMAIL ACKNOWLEDGING RECEIPT OF MESSAGE ON $8,000.00 & BREAKING OF NEWS OF RETIREMENT 7/24/2017)

Rev. Leonard Chola <leodor2003@yahoo.com>
Mon 7/24/2017, 12:07 PM

jobob409@.....net;
Steve Marbert

Hi Bob and Steve

Calvary greetings in the name of our Lord Jesus Christ.

Have received the message regarding wire transfer of $8000. I will check with the bank on Thursday to allow for transfer to be cleared.

I have no words enough to thank you for your continued assistance to Trinity Church. May the Almighty God richly bless you and your families.

I chaired a District Sunday School Convention from 1st to 4th of this month at Trinity. We used the new building for the first time. It was captivating to be in the magnificent sanctuary. Pleased that you saw some pictures of the Convention.

I wish to let you know that I am retiring from ministry at end of August this year. I am now 75 years-old which is the retirement age in our Church. The implication of this is that I will no longer be handling funds for the Church or on behalf of the Church after retirement. **Therefore, we have to discuss, yourselves, Pastor Charles, Pastor Elasto and Trinity Building Committee, to find out how best the funds will be handled after my retirement.**

Best regards Joellyn and Kathy

Leonard

Sent from Yahoo Mail on Android

MR. ROBERT RABIAS MAIL TO PRESIDING ELDER LEONARD CHOLA REMITTANCE OF $8,000.00 July 22, 2017

On Sat, Jul 22, 2017 at 10:23 PM, Bob Rabias <jobob@...com> wrote:

Sent from Mail for Windows 10

Hello Pastor Leonard Chola!

Blessings to you & family & greetings from Mr. & Mrs. Steve Marbert as well as from my wife Joellyn & I.

I hope & trust that all is well with you & your wife Dorcas.

It is indeed exciting for us all to read Pastor Elasto's e-mail notes as well as having conversations with Pastor Charles Kapungwe of the work being completed in the building of Trinity AME church. The pictures that Charles' nephew takes & sends us also contribute to our looking forward to the day when the building is basically complete & church services begin.

Based on the last report received from Elasto & information from Charles, I would say we are 75% to 80% complete.

I cannot say enough about how much of value the volunteer work of brothers Feckson & Davidson & Pastors Elasto & Kapungwe have meant toward this construction. This of course does not exclude whatever others have contributed that I know nothing about; such as young people who have slept in the building at various evenings protecting the unused materials from being stolen. This gratitude of course also includes Pastor Salome's contribution although she has a full-time job as a nurse & only had limited time & energy available for this construction.

I write this note to advise you that Steve Marbert has wired to your account as in the past $8,000.00 & it should be available sometime early next week. It is my understanding that there is approximately $2,100.00 remaining in the bank which is set aside for the purchase of the projector & screen. After reviewing the last two summaries of materials required as submitted by Pastor Elasto which sub totaled $3,440.00, $1,738.29, & $8,391.16 for a total of $13,569.45, it appears to me that if they deferred the purchase of the 15 benches, the sofa, and the floor tiles for the porch, there would be enough funds for the purchase of all other materials listed on these last two summaries.

This of course is only my opinion & not necessarily etched in stone. Brothers Feckson, Davidson & Pastor Elasto know best. In closing please advise when these funds become available.

Yours in Christ:

Robert Rabias

PS: It certainly was a blessing to hear that the church building has already been used for a conference for young people. It is our prayer that many will come to know Christ or know Him better through the Word that will be taught in the walls of Trinity AME church.

PPS: Also, a decision must be made as to what will become of the building that has been used for church services till now.

(REV. LEONARD CHOLA (FORMER P.E.'s EMAIL RECOMMENDATION OF PASTOR ELASTO AS THE HONEST PERSON TO HANDLE THE MONEY AS A REPLACEMENT NOV 23, 2017)

From: Rev. Leonard Chola <leodor2003@yahoo.com>
Sent: Thursday, November 23, 2017 6:32 PM
To: bobjob@att.com
Cc: Steve Marbert
Subject: Fw: CUSTODIAN OF FUNDS
<u>Sent from Yahoo Mail on Android</u>

On Thu, Nov 23, 2017 at 8:01 PM, Rev. Leonard Chola <leodor2003@yahoo.com> wrote:
Hello Bob and Steve

Greetings in the mighty name of our Lord Jesus Christ. Hope and pray our God is keeping you and the families well.

I write reference to my earlier communication to you informing you about my retirement from active ministry as I have reached retirement age of 75 years and therefore cannot handle any funds on behalf of the Church as per our Church rules. I had suggested in the earlier message that we should agree on someone who should now receive and keep the money we receive from you. I have so far not received response from you concerning this matter. **My humble suggestion and recommendation is that Pastor Elasto is most suitable to replace me. For the many years we have worked with him on the Trinity project he has proved to be honest and trustworthy.** Let me express my heartfelt appreciation for the trust you had in me for many years to be custodian of the funds you send for Trinity. May the Almighty God richly bless you. Pray for me as I start new life of retirement.

Best regards to the family.

Leonard

(**N.B.** THIS IS MY NOTE HERE: WAS THE EMOTIONAL & UNQUALIFIED ROOKIE WOMAN WHO WROTE ME A HIGHLY DISPARAGING MAIL AWARE OR WAS SHE INFORMED THAT THE OUTGOING P.E. CHOLA HAD SUGGESTED PASTOR ELASTO TO BE THE BEST PERSON TO BE RECEIVING MONEY BECAUSE HE WAS **"HONEST & TRUSTWORTHY?"** OR WAS THIS JUST PRETENSE FOR THE CHURCH TO CONTINUE RECEIVING MONEY BECAUSE YOU KNEW THAT SIDE THAT WE HAD MADE UP OUR MIND THAT PASTOR SALOME WAS **NEVER** GOING TO BE IN CHARGE OF THE MONEY AGAIN BECAUSE OF HER IRRESPONSIBLE FINANCIAL MANAGEMENT?)

22. Unaware that the Pastor had planned for an OFFICIAL OPENING of the Church which was being officiated by BISHOP WILFRED MESSIAH, THE PRESIDING ELDER LEONARD CHOLA and PASTOR SALOME MANGWENDE in OCTOBER 2017, I was shocked at the insensitiveness and poor leadership displayed at every level and faulted the Pastor in the matter. However, since this was a **collaborative effort,** looking back to what I see as gross failure and lack of genuine appreciation as observed in the letter of response by the Church, I can see a **very serious leadership crisis** at every level of our Church in the 17th Episcopal District in Zambia. This hurts because this is just one of the many failures that I have learned have been going on in the Church in Zambia. I found fault in the Pastor the very essence I decided to call and discuss with the Pastor and the Church over the issue. Sadly, the Church seemed not to see anything wrong with their decisions. I had by now come to a conclusion that the Church was aware that there would NEVER be any consequences for any decision they would make no matter how wrong that decision was because they thought **"The rich fools in America and their little clueless donkey will continue to send money regardless of what wrong we do here!"** Therefore, I thought of writing a letter to the Bishop who sadly chose not to respond to me either! I am of the opinion that just as the Church and the Pastor had shown no sense of remorse, the Bishop alike, reacted the same. Mr. Rabias then decided to write the Bishop. Unfortunately, Bishop Messiah again, chose both not to acknowledge receipt of the mail and to reply to it for several months. It is in this vein, therefore, that I came to the realization that my kindness and support for this Church and that of our sponsors were being repaid with a cantankerous attitude not befitting coming from a Church, both from the grassroots up to the highest office of the 17th Episcopal District there was no display of any Christian's etiquette expected from believers!

23. This is heartbreaking to me having worked very hard bringing people to the Lord for years in this Church. Looking back, as a young boy in the Church, I remember attending a Conference presided over by Bishop Hartford Brookins. I never heard or saw the District that was being run by Episcopal Supervisors. This trend in this Church now is frightening and it is no wonder unqualified women are being made to run the Church at the expense of qualified Pastors who are being sidelined, as a result these women are making similar questionable decisions which they do not understand were detrimental to the Church.

24. Kindly, take note that my communication with **Pastor Salome Mangwende** had been cordial before. However, I had noticed that familiarity had set in and she had taken things for granted knowing that there was nothing I could do if she did anything wrong. At one time I stopped communicating to her for weeks but resumed because I knew the work belonged to God and we needed to complete the task. She fell back on the same attitude, however, in spite of me guiding her how to win favor from sponsors citing to her examples of many Africans I personally know and countries that have been unfaithful to American sponsors here. **However, I sensed that she had developed a familiarity spirit where she took our kindness and warm gesture for granted and became unaccountable. Receiving such huge amounts of money NEVER just happened!** There were regular discussions by this writer with our sponsors and the people in Zambia. As you can see, I still have a lot of information that I can show but I am aware too that I am a minister of the word of God and I trust that this information can be enough for you to make a well-informed judgment.

25. My decision to make Pastor Elasto and Feckson to be in charge of the construction was based on numerous failures in observance of construction codes or guidelines. It was not based on vindictiveness. I never wanted the building to have the same fate I have seen in our churches in Zambia – poor unsightly structures. That is why I left her to be in charge of the money! Today, I regret being that lenient. However, I am of the opinion that, that decision was the one that vindicated me in my judgment. Kindly, notice that even the $8,000.00 sent to do the well (borehole) failed to complete the well because more money had to be taken from this amount to try and complete the bathrooms!

26. The selfishness, greed and insensitiveness of this leadership is appalling! I can cite a different example here! For several years a Pastor's wife who I talked to regularly was living in the U.S. She worked very hard and regularly sent money to Zambia to build her home church she loved. When the church was "officially opened" by the same team [Bishop Messiah and Presiding Elder Chola on the same day they "officially opened" Trinity, the lady who had worked very hard to build her church (NOT Trinity and was in Zambia now) and another man who had sacrificed a lot were not even mentioned! The other person quit!] **However, the team went on to have a party after "officially opening" churches they had not built, appreciated or acknowledged those who had put up huge amounts of money on them! I do not need to be appreciated because I know that the work was done to the glory of God but I am doing this to enforce accountability and responsibility and I promise you, I will!** I am made to think retrospectively (which I actually had foreseen the moment the impending request for thanking the sponsors came), that the Church leadership in Zambia was trying to seize an opportunity for self-promotion! **Even people I had introduced to the sponsors began to act as though they were the ones who had negotiated for help!**

CONCLUSION

The author of these two letters demonstrates lack of analytical and critical thinking skills that this office requires to discharge reasonable decisions that reflect basic Christian etiquette, values and wisdom. The letters go a long way in denting the image of our Church which already has been by the Pastor for the past six years. Writing to the USA, outside your country, to persons who belong to a different denomination, of Presbyterian faith, who paid one of your itinerant ministers a salary for eleven years, built for you two church buildings, gave money to buy a communion table, bought public address system with speakers and a keyboard, benches and chairs in both churches and are now putting up a well (borehole) [which you have halted and whose warm gesture towards its construction has taken no less than $8,000.00, because of love, yet rewarded with disrespectful mails show poor judgement and leadership flaws.] Rewarding people who have spent nearly $100,000.00 on your Church they know nothing about except through one of your ministers who has had a burden for his people and Church and because of asking of questions, such unfortunate correspondence was sent, definitely indicates that the writer is not qualified to hold such a position.

This kind of leadership makes this Church a laughingstock to the outsiders. The writer of the letters to me and to the sponsors had the audacity to write this baseless "authoritative letter" to show the members of Trinity her seemingly "powers" she holds over me when my letter was addressed to the Bishop and not to her is to say the least ridiculous! I doubt if she even ever thought through as to why the Bishop never replied to my mail but instead she was asked to reply to mails she had no idea about! Did she? If this were done within A.M.E. Church, it was going to be fine but we have members of another denomination involved and we are not even embarrassed to parade our ignorance before them? Please note also that Pastor Elasto had asked to be excused after the completion of the current construction of the borehole but I, consequently, prematurely released him and asked him to transfer the money which had just been sent to a new account in Kitwe specifically for the project before the project was completed. **The sponsors have that communication and details of why I did this and she doesn't have the reasons and details why this was done by me either!**

I do not even know who she is! No one told me who she was or ever introduced herself to me! The work that has been done at Trinity for the past 17 years, Churches with great leadership could have taken an initiative to find out who are the people who have done this, call them and thank them! This has NEVER happened and instead this is what the leadership would allow an individual to write such a letter against the aforementioned? According to this woman, **"The Bishop does not deal with or talk to Pastors"** making me to infer **"He only robs their achievements to make them his own!"**

For your information, I have no desire to be a pastor at Trinity! In case that is their fear! I just want the best for that Church and for it to be a model for other churches. Unfortunately, the Church has made a terrible mistake of failing to separate sense from nonsense and right from wrong. It has done what I told the pastor in the congregation (I have only spoken to her, if I can recall, twice in the congregation with her permission). The first was to offer advice on how they could increase membership because I foresaw that once the church was completed, the next phase our sponsors were going to be looking at was church growth. It was done in a loving way. The second time is when they had dedicated the church without informing us and I had told them after they began going into circles playing me, basically telling me that they had expected Pastor Elasto to have reported about the dedication of the church as though he were the Pastor and began to inform me that it was my mistake because I had installed "two heads" ignoring what had transpired and had led to the removal of the pastor from handling cash!

This is the same attitude the author of the letter to me and copied to the Church has shown: great ignorance! When the church had seen that the building was nearing completion, they began to display an attitude of not caring, never reported on what was going on or sent any photos and I told the Church you are saying to us *"Mwapezula Ilofwa,"* meaning "What are you going to do about it, we already have a completed church building?" It is the same behaviour I had observed which prompted me to write a letter to the Bishop and the same that has made me write this to you, now. What a shame! I have seen how this Church, A.M.E. Church, has built poor structures before and I had insisted on quality work and they were in a hurry to putting up a house and I told them there will be a block of apartments or flats which would help the church raise money and I had those plans sent to Pastor Elasto and Bro. Joseph Mapila **because I have been in this Church a long time and seen the level of ignorance of the leadership in that part of the world.** This is what you see being paraded to me now!

Initially, I had thought of building a school at the church and I did the plans for it. When I saw the same ignorance being paraded including unfaithfulness, I changed and thought of just putting up a block of apartments. I informed them to do a metal fence, and they never came back to me it is over two years ago now. If it had not been to enforcing accountability and helping of a visionless people, I could have quit a long time ago. The Bishop comes from a country with much better infrastructure and he may even be laughing at their ignorance and level of immaturity when he sees them failing to recognize God's blessings and opportunity – gross failure to discern nonsense from sense and allowing him to take advantage of their ignorance! Lord, have mercy on us!

Writing the History of this Church in Zambia, I see the same heart-breaking news repeat itself over and over! I see the same pattern of poor leadership like this writer who does not know what she is doing destroy this Church. When Rev. J.L.C. Membe began some projects in Tanganyika people like this woman who wrote me a letter failed to carry on with the vision of the person who had initiated the work after his transfer led to the work to suffer and stop because they didn't conceive the vision! You may wish also to know that a certain member of the WMS in our Church in Zambia had conceived an idea of running an Orphanage. She received support from outside and the same people trying to kill the vision at TRINITY were in the forefront of killing the orphanage and rounded up the assets! Where are the computers and the vehicle now? Who owns them now? Similarly, the same vultures are now ready to take a sumptuous meal where they did not sow! I will not allow them to! I will close the program if they so want. **Do loud-mouthed people wish me to send a record of all monies sent since** we began sending monies 17 years ago to Zambia? Would they want me to tabulate it and send it to all the District? Yes, I can! I have all the records "The Chosen and Highly Qualified Noise-Makers" do not have!

When Bishop Brookins built houses for the Church, "Chelston Project," someone sold them! **I have studied this Church's iniquity for years and its administration is one I am well-familiar with, the same reason it keeps losing young visionary leaders because of people with poor administration skills, lack of the fear of the Lord and lack of wisdom.** When the Farm was started some people began using the tractor for personal use and some wanted to sell the farm and even today some people want to sell the farm not for good intentions but for selfish reasons. They also want to borrow money and leave the Church in debt! When Rev. David K. Simfukwe began a school, some people were after the school! The Mechanic School is no more. People love to jump into visions they never conceived to destroy or to hijack for personal glory.

The level of ignorance and lack of discernment in our people is appalling. Someone wants to flex their muscles and show that they are in control because they feel as though their power or authority is being threatened! I grew up at Jordan Chapel where we had been building toilets and it has taken over 30 years to build them and they are still incomplete today. I was one of the founders of Calvary A.M.E. Church in Kitwe. We assembled a team of great believers and the Church was promising. The same conduct you see here made everyone leave, and today, Calvary still meets in a classroom, 24 years after we started that Church! I sent them a design and paid the architect who I had used for Trinity and paid him using my money to make perhaps what I thought was going to be the best A.M.E. Church in Zambia. I have sent money to Jordan Chapel and contributed towards their building to help this Church but I am afraid Africans have a long way to go and feel embarrassed I have to defend myself in such a manner. **The scariest and painful part to all this fiasco is the fact that the writer of the letter to me seems not to understand the spiritual ramifications of such a document to both Trinity and the A.M.E. Church in Zambia or even to the global Church. It is possible for a Church to remain with a beautiful sanctuary with no Holy Spirit's presence.**

This is a typical example in the Scriptures of what happens when the blind leads the blind. I learned a long time ago about leadership. I learned that leadership is not position. I also learned that leadership is not management. You can win an argument and lose the person. The blunder this Church has been perpetuating is comparable to what the Prophet Samuel had assumed when God sent him to anoint a leader over Israel. This Church has been suffering because, like Samuel the prophet, it has been choosing people based on outward appearance and not upon God's will. As a result, these are the people we are seeing who are willing to please their appointing authorities rather than God quoting written stuff from men by men as though they were quoting Scripture from God, matters they do not even understand. **The leadership is committing a spiritual offense that will affect the Church long after they are gone and none has the understanding of the consequences they are placing the Church in!** If the Church chooses not to deal with the house of Saul's iniquity, God himself will. This is the appeal I make to the Council of Bishops and the General Secretary of the Church today. I also appeal to the Church that in future we choose leaders who will not disgrace the Church.

I am embarrassed to even write this letter to explain my seemingly assailing the incompetence of the highest office in the Episcopal District. The rookie author of the letters before you and the pastor who has run the church are a reflection of gross failure in leadership to understand things of the Spirit. Nevertheless, I kindly ask the General Secretary of the Church and the Council of Bishops to carefully look into this dereliction of duty and poor administration of the Church in the 17th Episcopal District before we put both the name of the Lord in disrepute and become a byword of a failed Church to both the people in and outside of this Church. Perhaps it is important as ministers to remind ourselves of the scriptures. When King Ahab let his wife run Israel the end was not endearing. I pray that the Lord grants us the Spirit of wisdom and understanding. May he give us the Spirit of discerning right from wrong, truth from a lie and sense from nonsense and help this Church from a free fall into the abyss of Satan.

As I was writing this letter, (this last week of November, 2018), I received an email from Zambia from someone asking me to urgently provide them a phone number of my architect. The person requesting the number was from Calvary A.M.E. Church, in Kitwe the same church I had helped plant in 1994 and I had designed a 1,000-seating capacity sanctuary and a 300-seating capacity Fellowship Hall and I had paid the architect money out of my pocket in February of 2017. I asked the person the reason he needed the number for but he never responded. I then informed him that if he didn't let me know of the reason why, I was not going to provide him with my architect's number. I was now informed that the church wants to reduce the size of the plan because a former Pastor had sold part of the land! This pastor had done the same to another church (Judah A.M.E. Church) in Kitwe which had a huge land prior to him being appointed to Calvary! **YET, THIS LEADERSHIP HAS GIVEN HIM ANOTHER CHURCH!** You may wish to note that the former P.E., Rev. Leonard Chola is a member of Calvary in Kitwe and had overseen the appointments of the same Pastor before! I sought to confirm this matter through a second party and here is the email correspondence to the same:

On Friday, 7 December 2018, 20:52, Charles Kapungwe <charliekaps@hotmail.com> wrote:
Hello NAME WITHELD,

Grace and peace. I trust the Lord that you are fine. I learned a few days ago that the former pastor of Calvary had sold part of the land at Calvary and they were asking for a phone number to our architect and I refused to provide them. They never mentioned at first until I told them that without explanation as to why you need the number, I will not give it to you. I sent this twice. It was then that I was told about it. It appears the man did the same to Mindolo land again. It is sad because the design I paid for had 1,000 seating capacity for the sanctuary and 300 for the fellowship hall. PLEASE DO NOT GIVE them the number if you have it! This Church is a disgrace. I have included this in my letter to the CHURCH.

DELETED PARAGRAPH.

Blessings.

Charles.

From: NAME WITHELD <email address removed>
Sent: Saturday, December 8, 2018 10:06 AM
To: Charles Kapungwe
Subject: Re: HISTORY

Good morning Reverend.

> It's great to hear from you.
> Indeed, yes, that is the position on the church plot. Really sad and disappointing.
> We lack good leadership. Very few people have a vision of what the church should be in the next say, ten years. It seems no one is prepared to think that far.
> I guess the same can be said about most African governments. Absolutely no clear vision other than lining their pockets with ill-gotten gold and silver. All at the expense of the suffering majority. The church (not only AMEC) is no different.
> PARAGRAPH REMOVED.
> May God bless you.

NAME WITHELD.

I immediately remembered the words I had written to Bishop Messiah in my first letter! I had stated that **"Calvary and Trinity are destined to be the best in Zambia of all A.M.E. Churches if they follow the plan, nevertheless, selfishness by leaders as observed here makes it hard for this Church to find genuine partners for the work of the Lord."** I am vindicated by those words! I have been writing a book, *History of the A.M.E. Church in Zambia* which is close to completion. If the leadership of the Church cannot make sense of this, then I think the readers of my book will make sense out of it and will be left to judge who was right and who was wrong. They will also be able to distinguish sense from nonsense and truth from a lie.

I hereby, therefore, humbly appeal to the Global A.M.E. Church through the General Secretary and the Bishops' Council:

1. **To reverse the irresponsible and myopic arbitrary decision from the author of the attached letter who impulsively and inappropriately responded to a letter which had not been written to her and does not have all the facts which I have.** The Catholic Church thinks that the Pope is infallible. Similarly, this deception by Satan makes many A.M.E. Church members to think the same about their Bishops. Some in leadership erroneously believe that their role is to shield colleagues from sinful ideations, the same they cannot do to God who knows all things and watches all that we do.

2. I am requesting the Global Church to write a letter of apology to our Supporters Mr. Robert Rabias and Mrs. Joellyn Rabias and Mr. Steve Marbert and Mrs. Kathy Marbert who have sacrificed so much and sent thousands of dollars and are being smacked in the face by an irresponsible and uncaring Church's political machinery which they are not a part to. Their service is a demonstration of love of God, the people of Zambia, the A.M.E. Church and

I, as a friend, and minister of this Church. Their service is also embedded in the desire to see people come to the saving knowledge of Jesus, that is, to be born again and not to play church. I am also kindly requesting that your letter should indicate the true thanks from an appreciating Church and not one covered in the cobwebs of personal vendettas, deceit and stained with failure to perceive what is at stake.

3. I am requesting that the New Covenant Presbyterian Church which supported one of our ministers for five years and raised money that was used to make the foundation of the Church at Trinity be thanked too. Their member also supported an A.M.E. Church Pastor for 6 more years a total of 11 years, built the first Church building and the second. You may wish to know that photos are displayed in the U.S. to show the work of a caring Church to personally unknown people which we, as a Church can hardly do to a people we never knew personally judging by this myopic leadership's conduct I see here!

4. I am also asking this Church to consider carefully that any inert response to this issue, risks putting the A.M.E. Church on a list of Churches with a poor reputation to those who render help from outside should the ill-advised letters be allowed to stand. Kindly note that an orphanage by a member of this Church which was supported by funds from outside had been abruptly halted by another administration. The persons involved in that abolition are the same clique of people now seeking to destroy Trinity's blessings. They had ransacked the assets of that orphanage.

5. There is money in Zambia in the amount that is close to $5,000 awaiting the team I had appointed to complete building of the water tank. I have instructed them not to be answerable to anyone who wants to assume control and was not there when the project started! This woman, without my knowledge, had gone to see my consultant for the project who has tons of experience, worked in the Mines and was involved in huge mining projects so that she could be in control. Rev. Leonard was aware of my appointing him and he immediately had noted "Is he there to monitor them?" To which I had said "Yes!" He had found a lot of discrepancies and she was not happy that he had told her that everything was under control and he was going to complete this project without her involvement, **she then, in retribution came up with trumped-up charges against me! "Unorthodox methods being perpetrated by me and need for me to humble myself?" Someone must be unhinged!** My Consultant had been a member of Jordan A.M.E. Church, my childhood church. **In the event the team is prevented from completing the installation of the water tank and plumbing required, (the borehole has already been dug), I will instruct them to return the money and wind up the work at Trinity and I and our sponsors will disgracefully let go because I will not allow selfish, corrupt people get credit for a project they had not conceived. I will leave this to posterity to judge us and to God who weighs motives of men.**

6. I am requesting that you review the competence of the woman who wrote the attached letter to me and to the sponsors. I am asking that you evaluate her competence to hold such a position she has just been given. I am also requesting that you kindly review the competence of the woman Pastor who runs Trinity as well. I am saddened that there is an outcry in the Church in Zambia. Sadly, the Church in Zambia cannot listen to any voice of reason and I am ashamed that it is only able to listen to a Judge or an Attorney, a trend we have observed there. With this kind of incompetent leadership, it is not surprising that this Church is repeatedly being dragged to the courts of law for arbitration in Zambia. This Church must precisely deal with the spirit of Herodias before it destroys the Church.

7. I am also asking that **THE GLOBAL CHURCH AUDITS THE ACCOUNT OF**

TRINITY CHURCH. CONCURRENTLY, I WILL CONSTITUTE AND COMMENCE AN INDEPENDENT AUDIT MYSELF THAT MAY INVOLVE A COURT ORDER. I ALSO RESERVE THE RIGHT TO: (A). FILE FOR CRIMINAL INVESTIGATION AND PROSECUTION IN THE EVENT FINANCIAL MISCONDUCT OR FRAUD ARE PROVEN. (B). Obstruction and intent to shield such financial misconduct by the author of the letter to me. (C). Obstruction and accessory to such by the Bishop should item (A)., be proved.

8. Kindly read my first letter I sent to Bishop Wilfred Messiah and Trinity A.M.E. Church's all-weather sponsor Mr. Robert Rabias' mail to him. Kindly note that the Rabias' family has spearheaded erection of two buildings at Trinity and was instrumental in the support rendered to an A.M.E. Church minister of Trinity's monthly compensation for 11 years from 2001 to 2012. Kindly rule on my inference that the current Bishop of the 17th Episcopal District has demonstrated gross incompetence in discharging duties expected of him at the Episcopal District's level. **Therefore, it is my opinion that he is unfit for such a task, and as an institution charged with Administration of the Church I beseech you to fairly and justly offer me and the Bishop counsel and direction on the above matter, since Scripture says "In the multitude of counsellors there is safety,"** Proverbs 11:14 (KJV). I further advise that the Bishops' Council reviews the performance of this Bishop in the District vis-à-vis, sidelining of senior ministers who have God's wisdom and abilities fit to run this Church for mediocre ones. You may also wish to know that the Government of the Republic of Zambia found Bishop Wilfred Messiah liable in a case that the Church took to court in Zambia. However, this appeal is not based on that totally unrelated case.

9. Kindly investigate how such incompetence has affected the Church in Zambia and killed the enthusiasm of many worshipers.

When I got the letter three months after it had deliberately been sent to a wrong email address, I replied to the Bishop immediately and all the contacts they had put who knew nothing about this work, informing them that I was very disappointed with their response! I promised to reply thoroughly to the mail and this is that response. I want to categorically state that if the Church still fails to make sense of the aforementioned, **involvement of a second government which our Discipline Book acknowledges as being supreme and was quoted by the author of the despicable letter may be the ultimate step to take.**

Thanking you in anticipation.

Yours sincerely,

Charles Kapungwe,
Former Pastor of Trinity A.M.E. Church 1996-2000.

NB: KINDLY SEE THE ADDENDUM TO THIS LETTER. IT NULLIFIES THE KIND OF REASONING WHICH CAME FROM A LEADERSHIP THAT I DEEM TO BE INSENSITIVE AND UNQUALIFIED AND IS THE VIEW OF MANY PERSONS I HAVE SPOKEN TO IN ZAMBIA. IT ALSO CONFIRMS THAT THE JUDGEMENT MADE CONCERNING TRINITY A.M.E. CHURCH WAS MADE BY AN INDIVIDUAL WHO WANTED TO PLEASE HER MASTER AND NOT GOD.

I am also taking this opportunity to thank Bishop McKinley Young, (Senior Bishop) for the help rendered to me in 2006 ($200.00) when I was in Medical School. Thank you

Bishop Young! I also extend my thanks to the retired Bishop Robert Webster.

    Cc. 1. The General Secretary A.M.E. Church
        2. Bishop McKinley Young, (Senior Bishop) and the Bishop's Council
        3. Rev. Salome Mangwende, Pastor Trinity A.M.E. Church, Kitwe Zambia
        4. Rev. Elasto Mwansa, former Pastor Trinity A.M.E. Church, Kitwe Zambia
        5. Stewards Trinity A.M.E. Church, Garneton, Kitwe Zambia.
        6. To all interested parties.

December 10, 2018   <u>ADDENDUM</u>

Dear Bishop Messiah, Bishop McKinley Young, Senior Bishop, the Bishop's Council & The General Secretary,

DISAPPOINTING AND INCOMPETENT LEADERSHIP IN THE CHURCH IN ZAMBIA – ADDENDUM

This is in response to the mail dated July 9, 2018 which I came to see on October 12, 2018 because it was deliberately sent to a wrong email address. When I read it, the first thing that came into my spirit was "No OIL!" It was a Scripture from Matthew 5:2. I have never had any conversation with this woman and I do not even know her personally. Neither did the outgoing Presiding Elder Rev. Chola ever mention about her! When exactly did I begin installing an illegal leadership and begin the so-called "Unorthodox methods which demanded that I humble myself and to whom?" is the question that perplexed me! After having been involved in helping Trinity for the past 17 years, the writer took me off-guard with an unsubstantiated letter! Who told her that I had told the sponsors that there was no one to replace Rev. Chola? Am I that dull to say that? These questions are being directed at Bishop Messiah who authorized her to write a letter to me and to our sponsors in spite of being aware that my letter was addressed to him. Also, I am addressing it to the General Secretary and the Global A.M.E. Church so that you can see the record of what we have done for this Church in Zambia! When did I begin to put the illegal committee and begin unorthodox methods at TRINITY:

When I paid my way to and from Trinity using personal money for four years on three different public buses from home from 1996 to 2000?

Or when I supported the Church because all my members were not employed?

Or when out of my personal funds I paid for the plot in full where the two Church buildings now stand?

Or when I designed and paid for the blueprints out of my pocket to build a Church because we were meeting in a classroom?

Or was it when I sent to school one of the members who was an orphan to train as a teacher and today, she is a secondary school teacher? (The time I was a Pastor there).

Or when I learned from Rev. Leonard Chola when I had called him in 2001 on the phone and he told me, "We are all fine except your Church, Pastor Elasto was withdrawn by the Conference two weeks ago because Trinity was unable to support him and you know your Church!" The same day by the providence of God New Covenant Presbyterian Church Missions Committee began sending money to Pastor Elasto through Rev. Chola who I had proposed before he was even P.E.! They did this for about 5 years and then Mr. and Mrs. Bob Rabias began sending him for the next 6 more years – a total of 11 years?

Or was it when I asked White Hall A.M.E. Church in South Carolina where I was Associate Pastor for 4 years to help with clothes after they had asked me "What can we do to help our brothers in Africa?" but when they collected 4 large bundles, the Pastor told me, "Charles, we cannot send the clothes to Zambia because it was very expensive to send?"

Or was it when I heard Pastor Elasto and the church had been kicked out of the classroom and they were meeting in a makeshift structure, whenever he preached and it was raining, he was being soaked with rain and had to find a better position to stand on so as not to get wet with his Bible; then I had asked him to send me the copy of the blueprints which I had done but White Hall A.M.E. Church put them in the drawer for six months?

Or was it when I took the blueprints and asked for favour to the same people who had supported Pastor Elasto for 11 years and they sent $5,000.00 to begin the foundation of the Church I had designed?

Or was it when some money was lost because I had told pastor Elasto to begin a project and use the rest on the foundation? Mr. Robert Rabias, later spoke about the issue and resolved it since all the money which had been put into the project was lost?

Or was it when I gave counsel to the Church repeatedly so as to avoid the tragedy that Africa has had, a bad name among Americans helping Africans on misuse of funds – that is use of unorthodox methods to the A.M.E. Church leaders in Zambia? Or because I gave them examples of people repeatedly who had messed up in Africa and never wanted us to be embarrassed?

Or was it when I lobbied to my retired adopting parents for the church to construct a smaller structure before they could erect the expensive one which now stands and I found favour in their eyes and the people there made bricks and my people here paid for the construction of the building which helped them from being soaked in rain? The people who sent money there didn't just dream that some people in Africa had the needs but someone told them about it, right? They connected water at the Church and power and made a Holy Communion Table and bought PA system and speakers and this was use of unorthodox methods by me, right?

Or was it because of the directive I had given to use someone from Jordan A.M.E. Church who was a builder and a former choir member of mine but was repeatedly ignored after the sponsors resumed supporting the Church to begin building the big sanctuary again? The sponsors had stopped after half of the first donated money had been wasted on the project and only a foundation box had been done!

Or was it because the Church told me of a young woman who had completed school and had been my member in Sunday school at age 10 and God was using her greatly but had no father and I talked to the people here when she was 19 and they sent her money to train in computers because that is what she had wanted, that is being arrogant by me and need to humble myself, right? And to whom?

Or was it because I told the people who were volunteering in construction not to build without a spirit level, a major violation in construction as I saw? That is use of unorthodox method to them?

Or was it because I told the people who were constructing that the windows needed to open both sides as I had designed it because the toilets and office took away a lot of window space and making only one window to open meant loss of a total of 11 double windows leading to poor air circulation and already the building was uncomfortably hot? I had already told those I knew how the windows were to be. This was unorthodox method, right?

Or was it because I told the pastor who was excited that the building was now "completed" and had wanted to put the roof after reaching the top of the windows with two courses on top and I had insisted that they go up five courses even though I believe the height must have been on the drawing? This would have been another major disaster. This was unorthodox methods, right?

Or is it because I had insisted that the windows in the corridor were to be sliding doors? I did design that if I were not around, they had no idea what was to be there! This is unorthodox method and who needs to humble himself or herself?

Or is it because I insisted they needed to buy hardwood doors for the exterior doors and hardwood benches and they did? Or is because I had told them to buy benches made of hardwood but I was cheated on the benches because the calculated price had gone up from $130/bench to $200/ bench in the space of 2 years but when money was given softwood was bought which took 1 year to deliver 35 benches giving us an expenditure of $7,000.00. That is use of unorthodox methods from a person who made it possible to have a church of this make, right?

Or was it because after this we told the pastor not to handle the money because she had paid the money in full and had lost more money on pipes and sewer lines which had been wrongly done? Or because the people who were sending money were fools and they had never worked for it? They had a Dollar Tree where they plucked the dollars to send some Africans of the A.M.E. Church and the money was going to continue to flow regardless of poor accountability for it? Or was it because I sent money to pay the electrician out of my own pocket when the Pastor had said she had no money less than 2 months when she was sent $10,000.00? This was unorthodox methods, right?

Or is it when I saw the stains on the walls from the rain water and I requested for money to build an apron and were sent about $8,000, I think, but made a mess of the spoon drain and I consequently, told them to demolish it? They had made a small apron that could serve no purpose when money was specifically asked for that work? To date, we have not received the photos of the completed apron which we were told has been done! Neither have we received the photos of the Church after repainting. The paint was very expensive! They were informed to make corrections before they painted but they painted anyhow! These were unorthodox methods from me, right?

Or was it because the sponsors wanted to hear how the Church was doing spiritually? Or did you think they were just throwing away money and were not interested in soul winning which was the purpose for the help?

Or did she think if money was sent for one purpose or specified purposes and she was told about those expectations, she could do whatever she wanted and not abide by those expectations?

Or was it because once photos were taken and the place was overgrown with grass and the sponsors asked to clean up the place, that was unorthodox method? (I am sure you are not aware that photos are displayed to the congregation members which comprise different professionals who understand construction as well!)

Or was it because the recipients were asked to tabulate moneys spent on the whole project for easier reference to in the future, yet they chose to ignore the instructions?

Or was it when I corrected the poor construction of the back door which was made like a funnel and burglar bars were put without realizing how foolish this was? Or was it when I repeatedly informed the Church that the window angles below and sides were out of shape and needed to be corrected?

Or was it because I intend to use Trinity A.M.E. Church on a front cover of my soon to be published book "The History of the A.M.E. Church in Zambia" which shall highlight poor and ungrateful leadership such as this as well?

Or is it because I informed the builders to send us the estimate for the borehole and how long the work was to be done. They sent the amount and said the work will take 7 days to complete. BUT IT TAKES 21 DAYS FOR CONCRETE TO CURE!

Or is it because the estimate to make a borehole was given at $1,200 but ended up costing $2,530.99, (just for drilling?)

Or was it because when I gave appropriate technical requirements for making the foundations for the tank, my instructions which were clearly given both orally and in writing were not followed and the bars were being scrounged for in the compound instead of buying them from engineering companies and money was available but they chose to bring in deformed bars bought from second hand metal dealers? My Consultant, she was disparaging (as an illegal group) is the one who went and spotted this after I had begged him to go and check! This was unorthodox method, right?

Or is it because I used to help the pastor to avoid embarrassing ourselves until I proposed Pastor Elasto to be helping her with the financial report even though he (Elasto) had not been there when she used to spend money, sometimes by herself? Which church on the Copperbelt or elsewhere could receive such huge amounts of money and the Financial Secretary, the Church Treasurer, the Senior Steward or educated and talented men who have businesses would have no idea how much money had come into the Church except for two to three women she took with her to the P.E., to get the money? (The women could not question her because their literacy levels were lower than hers).

Or was it when I shared about the poverty in the area and how poor the people were and the friends here sent money to the Church and Rev. Chola officiated and foodstuffs including cooking oil, mealie meal, etc., were distributed to the needy in the Church? That was when I began unorthodox methods, right?

Or was it when I shared about Pastor Elasto ministry at St. Jones A.M.E. Church and they asked me to ask him what he needed and he said to build a wall around the Church but because he thought they were still helping Trinity, he asked for a laptop and it was the time he got a transfer to Ndola. They sent him a laptop. That was unorthodox method to you, right?

Or was it the time I told them of the death of a Mr. Phiri who had been helping Bro. Feckson Simukoko to put up the tiles in the bathrooms (which have swallowed up thousands of dollars in spite of being given adequate money to complete them, twice we had to fall back on money sent for other purposes) and the sponsors asked that $100.00 be given to the family of late Mr. Phiri. Those were unorthodox methods on my part, right?

Or was it a few months ago when I learned that Bro. Feckson Simukoko while working on the bathrooms and spending nights there and his wife had gone to Church, thieves broke into his house in Ndeke and store items including a flat screen TV and when I informed the sponsors, they asked that $200.00 be released for him? Unorthodox methods?

Or was it because after a brother (Davidson Sinyangwe) had hired a grader which leveled the ground at the Church and I had explained to the sponsors and the sponsors had informed me to refund the brother $200.00 he had used? Unorthodox methods?

Or was it when I directed that you can use the youth of the Church to help you with small jobs at the Church and then pay them from the money we had sent since many are very poor? They used them but did a poor job even though they were paid and that was installing an illegal committee at the Church, right?

Or was it because the Pastor had wanted the side to the Church (next to the wall see photo where you see opened windows) be a parking lot for the Pastor right where the shade is but I refused and instructed that they put up concrete slab because the place was an ideal spot for fellowship and I had a different area designated as a parking lot?

Or was it because I spoke against the obvious wrongs including putting up of a structure which was unsightly near the building, unkempt building surroundings, demanded to make corrections to mistakes, requesting for photos to be sent, or making of a cornerstone in the name of the Bishop, the P.E. and the pastor without the input of this brother who has sacrificed for the work and put his name in ridicule without consideration of those who have supported the Church, built 2 buildings, supported (paid) a pastor for 11 years monthly?

Or is it because for over 2 years I had spoken and written the Pastor for the need to do drawings for the sewer lines, water pipes, drainages and electricity cables but in spite of being given the name of the person who could do this and the money she just could not do even with reminders until the sponsors began to think either she was not interested or she was too busy with work and these were unorthodox methods because this was being told to her like a song until all the lines were covered and now it might take a miracle to spot or recall where the lines passed through! That is a very responsible leader, right?

Or was it because I was in touch frequently to ensure that the money was used appropriately as it had been intended and, on some occasions, this was not the case?

Or was it because one of our sponsors who had been co-opted in to help had had received a soliciting mail for funds by a person who could have gotten email address from only two people there and I had addressed that? That was unorthodox method?

Or was it when I purchased the Projector from South Africa at a cost of $2,000 plus, because in Zambia they couldn't find one and I had told the Church this was needed as an evangelistic tool? I also sought for people to transport it to Trinity. This is still with the Pastor, I think, and no word has been given to the sponsors over it in spite of questions which have been asked to her concerning its use! These were unorthodox methods right?

Or was it when I bought a huge 148 Inch – Projector Screen at a cost of $279.00 on Amazon and arranged for it to ship to Zambia together with two used glass tables for the Church and 14 picture frames to honour those who had built the church and enlarged photos of 4 pastors who had been at Trinity or the books I wrote which I sent to the Church for free or the 4 clocks I bought and shipped to Zambia to install in the Church at my cost or the computer-generated letters and names to the rooms, offices, blackboard and toilets for the Church I had paid for and shipped them to Trinity, at my cost? Those are unorthodox methods to you? Shipment and the cost of the Projector screen were paid for by the sponsors whom we have let down and the two glass tables and other new 14 photos/frames were paid for by me and shipping costs to a Church I love. Unorthodox methods?

Or was it when I bought a camera and sent it to the Pastor of Trinity through a friend who came to Zambia so that she could be sending photos regularly?

Or was it last May, 2018, when I informed the Pastor and Pastor Elasto that someone from America was visiting Zambia and will also be visiting Trinity and got no response and were reminded of the dates and the person arrived at Ndola Airport and called everyone and there was no response, therefore, he was forced to hire a taxi to Kitwe, a distance of 30 miles and came back to the U.S.A. without worshiping in the Church?

Or was it when I was offering help on how to report on finances that someone had spent and the report was embarrassing and I put in measures to avoid that? (SEE ONE OF MY CORRECTIONS). The writer of the mail has no idea of what has been going on, nor has she had any information for the past 17 years. I have the documentation and so are the sponsors. This is really embarrassing. Before the sponsors would send any money, they first would ask for estimates. After that, they would send the money. By this we could tell any discrepancies but she has no idea! Besides, this project was a local project and I am surprised how people have gotten interested in it now and want to hijack the glory meant to go to God when they don't even live is the city where we have been building this church!

Or is it because I questioned about the Pastor's failure to inform us about the "Official Opening of the Church" but informed those who never even put a cent on the building? Or was it because I informed her that putting the names of the people on the cornerstone who never contributed any money at the expense of those who had sent thousands of dollars to build two structures you are now proud of means unorthodox method to the Church in Zambia? For years, the sponsors had planned to go to Zambia for an official opening but the Pastor chose to do it secretively and my questioning this wrong has led to the CHURCH to bar me from doing the work and complete what I had started and you see this as being right in the eyes of the Lord?

When the Bible talks about deceit in the heart of man, it means it! I received the photos from the friend in the U.S.A. who had told me he had received photos of the official opening of the Church from the woman who wrote me the letters you see! I was informed later that the people who had wanted it to be a secret blamed her for sending us the photos! The Lord is a good God! Today she is defending the same folly!

The last Scripture that came to me was Jude 17-18.

"But, dear friends, remember what the apostles of our Lord Jesus Christ foretold. They said to you, 'In the last times there will be scoffers who will follow their own ungodly desires.' These are the people who divide you, who follow mere natural instincts and do not have the Spirit," (NIV).

"THE WORK OF JEZEBEL AND HERODIAS IS TO KILL THE PROPHETS OF GOD OR MAKE THEM FLEE," Charles Kapungwe.

May God the Father and our Lord Jesus Christ who judge motives of men be the judge in this matter and I pray and wish you all the best in all your endeavours.

Yours in His Vineyard,

Charles Kapungwe,

2nd Pastor Trinity A.M.E. Church (1996-2000).

Cc 1. The General Secretary AME Church
    2. Bishop McKinley Young, (Senior Bishop) and the Bishop's Council
    3. Rev. Salome Mangwende, Pastor Trinity A.M.E. Church, Kitwe Zambia
    4. Rev. Elasto Mwansa, former Pastor Trinity A.M.E. Church, Kitwe Zambia
    5. Stewards Trinity A.M.E. Church, Garneton, Kitwe Zambia.
    6. All interested parties.

My Letter to the President of the Bishop's Council

After sending the above mails, I learned of the passing away of the Senior Bishop, Bishop McKinley Young. This, was a blow to the case, I felt. Nevertheless, I continued to call the General Secretary for days and left messages on his voice mail. He never responded. I called the President of the Bishop's Council. I had a chat with him in February 2019. He informed me that it is unlikely they would discuss the mail without the invitation of the Bishop of the 17th District. I informed him of a case in 1972 which he recalled immediately and discussed with me. He then told me if that were to happen it were in June of 2019 and there was going to be a new President of the Council and advised that I write him too! The President of the Council of Bishops had not received my letter because I had erroneously sent it to Nashville, Tennessee and not to Atlanta, Georgia where he resided.

For several months the Pastor of Trinity had not communicated to the sponsors. We had no idea of what had been done nor did we receive any photos after the painting of the Church or if the name had been put. I had sent this over two years ago. On April 6, 2019 I got an email from the Pastor thanking me for what I had done at Trinity and mentioning that she had not received the projector screen! I informed her that you missed the point! "I think you missed the seriousness of the matter highlighted in the letter and this shows me that you missed the weight of the whole letter and its intents. This is a very sad episode in the congregation when leadership cannot weigh what is at stake." She responded that she wrote that because of the "inventory." A few weeks later, I heard from one of the Pastors I had called, that "The Pastor at Trinity has been transferred." The Bishop, the woman who wrote me the letter and the pastor herself never informed us about the issue and we waited for months.

In April 2019, the Pastor of Trinity was "quietly" transferred to another church. There was no word about the transfer given to Rev. Charles Kapungwe or to the sponsors who have built and supported Trinity. There had been no official communication for two years to the sponsors or any updates. Rev. Kapungwe learned about the transfer from non-Trinity members after a routine telephone call to Zambia. Meanwhile he continued to carry out everything he had indicated in his second mail to the Global A.M.E. Church in the U.S.A. and to Trinity.

Suspension of Bishop Paul Kawimbe and Bishop Wilfred Messiah

In June 2019, we heard of the suspension of Bishop Paul Kawimbe of 19th Episcopal District and Bishop Wilfred Messiah of the 17th Episcopal District. However, the duo was given opportunity to appeal and in August, due to a short period between the Conferences, they were asked to continue with the Conferences. In September, 2019 the suspension of Bishop Paul Kawimbe was finalized and announced. Bishop Wilfred Messiah conducted his last round of Conferences in Zambia to worshipers who were dissatisfied with the financial reports in conferences in South West Zambia. His suspension was lifted following an appeal on November 22, 2019 by the Judicial Council. Meanwhile, the church (Trinity) which has been helped with monies to build stopped communicating with sponsors or giving of updates of the state of the church for two years prompting one believer in Zambia burdened with the whole fiasco to term it a "robbery!"

According to The Christian Recorder Online Edition of 1 December, 2011, Bishop Wilfred Messiah had been suspended by the A.M.E. Church in October, 2011. He was suspended by the Judicial Council for maladministration until the ensuing Forty-Ninth Quadrennial Session of the General Conference. The matter involved his poor administration when he was Bishop of 15th Episcopal District.

In March 2020, a few months before ending his term, Bishop Wilfred Messiah was taken to Lusaka High Court in Lusaka, Zambia. Christine Chihane in an article in Zambia Daily Mail on 20th March, 2020 titled "Reverend, congregants sue bishop" made sad readings both for the A.M.E. Church and Christianity again. The suit demanded that Bishop Messiah pays back all the money he did not account for. The congregants were also seeking for an order for the defendant to disclose bank accounts held by the church both locally and abroad. "Also sued are Reverends Cosmas Wakunguma, Martin Chama and Nathan Phiri. Rev. James Mwenya claimed that the defendants have continued to use the church to raise money for their personal gain, a practice the church forbids. They also sought for an order that Bishop Messiah should account for all the money handled by him on behalf of Lusaka District for the period of 2012-2020. The suit also asked for auditing of all finances for the same period." Sadly, to this writer, this appears to be the only possible way to deal with matters involving a Bishop because there is almost no other appropriate Christian way of resolving conflicts involving a Bishop within an Episcopal District in the A.M.E. Church.

Sadly, the world was hit with a pandemic in 2020. Covid-19, a viral disease which started in Wuhan, China spread to the whole world prompting the A.M.E. Church to cancel the General Conference of 2020. This meant that Bishops in respective Districts were going to oversee the work in 2020. This was bad news for the 17th Episcopal District which was going to suffer another year of being led by an incompetent and corrupt Bishop. He was given an extended stay in which he began to intimidate the people behind the lawsuit through dividing and conquering methods.

My Letter to the Judicial Council
In September 2020, I wrote the Judicial Council of the A.M.E. Church over my Trinity case.

Chapter 25
Regression

In nearly every country, when a president of a country speaks, his word becomes policy. Understandably, there is a constitution as well but speeches which are made by presidents do translate into policy. For this reason, advisors of Presidents are weary if a President has an "out of control" personality! They have to keep up with the Press, other concerned citizens and international observers because they have to explain the President's pronouncements. Similarly, Presidents' wives are not elected officials meant to be stand-ins for their husbands! As a result, they are to detest from making pronouncements which likely would send mixed signals which may run a risk of being interpreted as policy. Therefore, sane Presidents understand their role and consequences of their speeches and those of their spouses just like sane Bishops do unless there has been regression as unfortunately has been the case in Zambia after 2004!

However, insane Presidents and their insane spouses have no understanding of these rules. The A.M.E. Church's structure has a Bishop at the helm of an Episcopal District. The Supervisor, a Bishop's wife, is by virtue of her position, a W.M.S. Episcopal Supervisor. They are not supervisors of Pastors! Sadly, ministers and worshipers in countries in Africa, may likely be taken advantage of easily. When the discontentment of "being led" by "Foreign Bishops" in the Church in Africa reached a boiling point, the desire for "Self-rule" became pronounced. However, a word of knowledge had come to the brethren in Zambia from God in 1997 of what "Self-rule" meant in the Scriptures.

The words of Samuel were revealed to brethren in the run-up to the self-rule demands. The scripture revealed says, *"But when they said, "Give us a king to lead us," this displeased Samuel; so he prayed to the LORD. And the LORD told him: "Listen to all that the people are saying to you; it is not you they have rejected, but they have rejected me as their king. As they have done from the day I brought them up out of Egypt until this day, forsaking me and serving other gods, so they are doing to you. Now listen to them; but warn them solemnly and let them know what the king who will reign over them will claim as his rights,"* 1 Samuel 8:6-9.

Reports of Supervisors addressing Conferences became rife in the African Districts! The Supervisors castigating Ministers who they are not supposed to "supervise" became a heart-breaking occurrence among the timid ministers. This was not limited to one Supervisor's tenure but was observed in the District by consecutive administrations from 2004 to 2020. The "Presidents" did nothing to stop their "First ladies" from issuing policy; a deed which was not their mandate. Once, one source informed me that supervisor had castigated a senior minister, a Presiding Elder in the Conference for using the Budget money for a funeral. The Presiding Elder lived in a rural area and had no income. At another time another Supervisor told off ministers and warned them that she had power over appointments! In both cases the "Presidents" said nothing!

The exodus of the young and youthful ministers in the A.M.E. Church in Zambia in late

1980s and 1990s began to show its negative effects within two decades of their departure. It was the effect that many believers who had survived the exodus feared would soon happen. The tenacity and steady growth in numbers of believers in a predominantly traditional Church had reached a pinnacle and began to exhibit signs of a new life (new wine) in the Church that had thrived on old wine for decades. Alas! It was now on a brink of taking itself back to Egypt once more – thanks to the "House of Saul." Sadly, the achievement which had taken decades to build, and that through the sweat of the youth and the visionary born again ministers through persistent prayer and fasting, evangelism and discipleship risked going down the tubes of mediocrity once again beyond the year 1998. Admittedly, the revival had been the work of God through the Holy Spirit.

The regression, if it were to come, was to be a self-inflicted wound by the blind who were leading the blind. Having seen numerical growth and a somewhat spiritual growth, Satan craftily began to use the leadership to fight the success that the Lord had brought about! Ignorantly, the Church's leadership in the 1990s began putting pressure on the leadership in the youth, forcing the mature youth who had led the Church to revival to retire! Those who were pushing for this were mostly women. The Young People's and Children's Division (Y.P.D.) was by constitution supervised by *women*. The W.M.S. appoints Y.P.D. Directors who are *women*. They in turn supervise Y.P.D. leadership. Isaiah states, *"Youths oppress my people, women rule over them. O my people, your guides lead you astray; they turn you from the path,"* Isaiah 3:12.

Wherever these *women* (W.M.S) wielded power, they used it inappropriately to drive out those who had brought about spiritual awakening. "Retirement mantra" was the most befitting phrase they would come up with in their bid to quench the Spirit or to stop the salvation message that now had become ingrained in most churches on the Copperbelt and the Midlands. Years later, the Supervisor Messiah was to ask the older Y.P.D. leaders in North East Conference to retire. This was around 2015 unknown to her that this is what Satan had used to kill Revival in the Church on the Copperbelt and Lusaka by attacking the root of change in the 1990s. Older Y.P.D. members had remained and thrived in North East Zambia Conference unlike on the Copperbelt Province and the Midlands where they had been chopped! "Constitutionally," their call was prudent but spiritually it was ungodly!

The push to have the born again youth leadership to retire was to be a self-inflicted wound that the Church was going to suffer dire consequences for. The W.M.S. supervised Y.P.D. Presidents and their leadership at the local church, District, Conference, and Episcopal levels. Their push for retirement of the born again youth leadership showed that they were unmindful of the contribution to the revival in the Church that these "older youths" had done. Many such directors were not saved and were blinded into believing that numbers in the youth would remain high after pushing out those who had laboured tirelessly with passion and vision!

Alas, the new leadership was likely to be doomed as was the Church! However, where the directors knew the Lord as their personal Saviour, the YPD ministry thrived. During our time, we had evangelised the Districts by the grace of God and the spiritual awakening became huge. Nevertheless, non-believers began to put pressure on the Directors to have us "graduate" because we had reached the age of 26.

Unknown to many of these leaders was the fact that a Church without a strong youth base was doomed to die! This is the fate that haunts many congregations in the U.S. which hardly have any youths in church! Also, unknown to them was the fact that after graduation, these youths had to fit in either the Men's Fellowship or W.M.S. The Men's Fellowship was also known as the Sons of Allen by different churches or circuits. The tenacity, vision or organization in these secondary bodies were lacking and could not be compared to the Y.P.D. which had been organized for a long time. Thus, the forcing of retirement of the visionary, spiritually driven and highly burdened leadership from the youth was the grave that the Church ultimately dug itself in!

In 2015, at a Women's Retreat in Mpulungu, Supervisor Messiah disrespectfully addressed the gathering with disparaging overtones. My mature daughter in the Lord, Alice Manase who had moved to the North East Zambia Conference was a YPD Conference Director at the time. When she arrived, she found the Supervisor castigating YPDers during the elections. She demanded that everyone presents National Registration Cards (NRC), i.e., official national I.D.s, for her to check before anyone would be allowed to stand on any position! "You want to take advantage and be impregnating the young ones!" she told them. "She was shouting at us like we don't think!" Sister Alice informed me. "Mupelwa Chama, the President was ordered out by the Episcopal Supervisor and 2nd Vice President Obed Mwape was asked to continue because his age was accepted!" she told me. "I quit the position of Conference Director on that day! You could clearly see how she wanted to be worshiped but I was taught not to worship human beings!" she said.

On Sunday 15th March, 2020, I spoke to my daughter in the Lord Alice Manase on phone. She was living in Kasama now. I informed her that I have photos of Older YPDers taken on an Older YPDers' Day at Solomon Temple in Kasama in 2018. She informed me of what I already understood was to be a consequence to arbitrary stopping youths who wanted to serve – death of the groups! "That meeting was organized to revamp the YPD," she informed me! "The Presiding Elder and other leaders had observed that following Supervisor Messiah's sentiments and departure of the older mature organisers she had kicked out, the youth groups in churches had died! I had also been invited to that YPDers' Day but I never went," Alice told me.

Consequence to forced retirement, numbers of the youth dwindled over the years after the departure of the mature and visionary leaders in our time in the 1990s. Building of a successful Church depends on the youth and lack of the enthusiastic youths translates to death of any denomination. This "forced graduation" coupled with the exodus of believers over the years was enough to bring the Church back to a state of dryness – an unforeseen circumstance by the blind leadership and Satan's subtle attack on the Church to take it back into mediocrity.

Kitwe District YPD President and South West Zambia Conference YPD President Charles Kapungwe in 1989 in a pensive mood in a religious ceremony of "gowning" which he was at odds with because he always had to explain that "The uniform was not Salvation but repentance and receiving Jesus was!"

During the early 1980s, Y.P.D. conventions were vibrant. The attendance in local churches, District meetings (E.g., Kitwe District where Pastor Charles Kapungwe was once a YPD President comprising 8 churches in the City was phenomenon). Kitwe District *"Yesu Akabwela Cincileni"* (Jesus is Coming Back Be Vigilant) would boast of attendances of around 200 or more youths in some meetings. The self-afflicted wounds soon began to show with dwindling numbers in attendances in Y.P.D. seminars and conferences. To be fair, YPD gatherings even in the late 1970s, (between 1978 and 1980) had gone up. This was during the Conferences or Retreats which involved three countries Zambia, Malawi and Rhodesia (Zimbabwe). At the time, though only a few believers were known. Such Retreats could boast of huge numbers of up to 500, 1,000 or more attendees.

Although scores of youths who had come to know the Lord Jesus Christ (saved) had steadily been leaving the Church for years, the 1998 exodus was by far the biggest to hit the A.M.E. Church in Zambia. With it came the regression in that the cream or most ambitious believers left the Church en masse. However, the effects of that exodus were going to take long to be felt. When the Zambia National Soccer Team lost its top footballers in the Gabon Air Disaster aboard a Buffalo Military Plane while on their way to Senegal in a World Cup qualifier match in April 1993, Zambia's soccer was negatively impacted for years. The nation, therefore, galvanized its resources and rebuilt a new team which even reached the African Cup of Nations (AFCON) final against Nigeria and narrowly lost 1-2 to Nigeria in 1994.

Nevertheless, the effects of that loss of players in the air disaster took a while to be felt by the nation. Years later, the effects of that loss of the cream of the Zambian footballers began to impact the nation. Falling standards in games in a manner never envisioned before began to show even though other factors undoubtedly, had contributed to low standards as well. It was only in 2012, 19 years later, that Zambia managed to win their maiden Africa Cup which many soccer fans would still admit that the high standards of soccer the nation once boasted of was long gone! Please note that hundreds of A.M.E. Churches if not thousands in the U.S.A. do not even have Y.P.D. meetings! Many of them have no youths in their churches! The ones you may commonly see in photos are mostly found in mega churches. Yet, Africans would want to be instructed on how to run their youth departments by people who have failed to bring the youth in America to Christ or to church!

Although I had been living in the U.S.A. for two decades, I had still constantly been in touch with the Church in Zambia. Building Trinity Church from around 2001 to around 2018 ensured that I was in constant touch with members and understood what was at play. During the latter half of this period, the A.M.E. Church in Zambia lost more senior ministers too. These ministers opted to leave the Church than to continue serving under a visionless leadership. Among those who left were Rev. Dr. Paul Bupe and Rev. Wilson Mpundu. Dr. Bupe left the Church after returning to Zambia from the U.S.A. where he had been with me for studies while Rev. Wilson Mpundu left earlier during the reign of one Bishop who was very arrogant and proud!

When this Bishop was in one Episcopal District in the U.S., about 7 churches left the A.M.E. Church. This included my Pastor who I had served as his Associate Pastor! (My pastor in Columbia, South Carolina left the church with his wife. Nevertheless, everyone's departure was attributed to this Bishop who I had even visited in his home). Both senior leaders (Rev. Mpundu and Rev. Bupe) had faced the political system or machinery that systematically kills prophets, supervised by incompetent Episcopal leaders. This is the time the Connectional Church instructed all churches to ensure that they had titles to their churches because in South Carolina, churches who had chosen to operate under the A.M.E. Church umbrella pulled out with their buildings. Other senior ministers who had left were the Rev. John Mukeya and the Rev. David D. Musole. New and younger ministers like Rev. Everisto Siulapwa also left.

When a friend asked me to read the book of Nehemiah in February 2019, the full picture of the current status of the A.M.E. Church in Zambia was unveiled before me again. The book reminded me of what I had come to know and learn in the last two decades. The Lord showed me how the Church had regressed. It was comparable to the disgrace Israel suffered when the walls of Jerusalem had been broken and had been set on fire. The parallels with the story in the book of Nehemiah to the surviving remnants in the A.M.E. Church in Zambia caused a lot of pain because the picture looked so real to me. Also, I was clearly able to see the spirits of Sanballat the Horonite, Tobiah the Ammonite and Geshem the Arab at work! Remember us with favour, O our God, for all we have done for these people. Remember Tobiah and Sanballat, O my God, because of what they have done.

The painful story is narrated here of what had become of the Church hardly two decades of my departure from Zambia. After a protracted observance of the failure to follow instructions on a project that I had started and at one time I had desired to build a school on the property, I changed my mind! I already had the drawings of the school on scores of papers utilizing my Technical Drawing and Geometrical and Mechanical Drawing skills from secondary school. However, trust issues prompted me to change my mind. I finally settled for building just a block of apartments in a bid to help the church raise money for itself through rent and for the purpose of provision of accommodation to future Pastors. However, this too came to a halt because I still hit against another political machinery of the Church that is known for killing progress and prophets!

I had already designed the apartment building of 6 units with four bedrooms each when the restraining orders against me came! I had sent the drawings to Zambia and had asked the individual overseeing the work to take them to the architect and like the designs I did for Calvary, I was going to pay the architect! However, I was given an embargo by an incoming incompetent leader masquerading as a "Presiding Elder," directed by an incompetent Prelate taking instructions from an outgoing incompetent Presiding Elder as narrated in the mail earlier! I considered the letter sent to me an expulsion letter in all sense of it but I had to wait for an opportune time before leaving – handling of Messiah's case to the end. Seeing eyesore of structures called "churches or missions" had been very distressing to me and I had planned to design better buildings in all historical places in Zambia to replace the archaic structures. However, Satan, through the letter and behaviour of Messiah and his incompetent cronies altered everything for good. In my mind, this was childish leadership in all sense of it!

This woman acting under the instruction of a Bishop and an outgoing P.E., misstated facts and brought me to a state of surprise and shock. I was also aware that she was acting under instruction of the two leaders besides the Pastor who I had relinquished of power to handle finances. The story of shame and demise is narrated in the history which you have already followed from my testimonies above. I was of the opinion that my secular employers would have handled this issue differently and possibly wisely than the way the Church had handled it. It is also important for readers to be made aware that while revival had come to the A.M.E. Church in Zambia, there were known A.M.E. churches in Zambia which never participated in revival meetings regularly. Such churches usually had one or two saved people who participated. They therefore, remained as "Satanic strongholds" which continued to produce leaders for the house of Saul as evidently seen above. As the wise, we would often predict the behaviour of any leader based on where they came from – which church they had been members of!

In African traditions and culture, there is a tale that simulates what had become of the A.M.E. Church in 2019 and lately. Africans in Zambia have traditionally taught their children or shared words of wisdom in gatherings, special meetings, at school or in homes. There is a story set in a village where a young man has succeeded his late father and becomes a king. A group of young advisers soon approach the king informing him that he should kill all elderly people in the village because they would bewitch him and take over his kingship; therefore, he follows their advice! However, one young man hid his aged parents and spared their lives. When a challenging event later came, requiring the wisdom of the elders, the young king was at a loss because he had no reservoir of knowledge from the experienced elders whom he had systematically wiped out!

A snake had come and coiled itself around the neck of a king! This brought about panic in both the palace and kingdom! When help could not be found, the king was reminded of how foolish a decision of getting rid of the older people had been! In distress, he asked that they would search for any old man who would provide them with counsel! A young man, after making them swear that they would not kill his parents whom he had hid, informed his father who advised that a rat tied to a string be brought. When the snake saw the rat, it began to uncoil and it went for the rat! It was then unanimously agreed that the wiser older man deserves to be the king and so it was! The "child childish king" stepped down.

In the run-up to the elections of the first indigenous African Bishop elected in Zambia, the Church got divided. In Lusaka, Zambia, two factions began to spar with each other. Ebenezer was at the center of the controversy with Rev. Edith Mutale, pastor of the church leading one faction and the then Presiding Elder, Rev. Paul Kawimbe, candidate for the Office of the Bishop, the other. One faction doubted the qualification of the person the Church was advancing for the post of a Bishop while another convincingly advanced the idea. The former, presented reasons why they felt so, citing numerous incidents that made them believe the Church was going in a wrong direction. The other group, however, stood by their convictions and was being supported by the then incumbent Bishop Preston Williams who was merely a visitor to Zambia.

In 2003, the faction led by the Pastor of Ebenezer Rev. Edith Mutale and 70 members were expelled from the Church. According to "The Post Newspaper" of 21st November, 2003 written by Noel Sichalwe, the expelled group appeared before Lusaka High Court Judge Anthony Nyangulu. The Judge ruled that "There is too much politics in Churches." He said this during the hearing of the contempt of court case in which African Methodist Episcopal Church Rev. Edith Mutale and seventy (70) others were contesting expulsion from the Church. The expulsion was sanctioned by the Presiding Elder Paul Kawimbe.

Judge Anthony Nyangulu lectured the Church. "I don't understand why children of God are busy quarrelling in the synagogue. This is very unfortunate indeed. There is so much politics in the church but we shall end it. God can't be happy with the quarrels in the church," he said. "You should ask for forgiveness all of you in here while awaiting judgment from this court." Rev. Mutale, 55, said in her evidence led by lawyer Kelvin Bwalya that she was surprised that the Church had decided to expel her together with 70 others when another case was awaiting judgment before judge Nyangulu's court. She said in the main case awaiting judgment, A.M.E. Bishop Williams had sued her with other church members for disobeying the doctrine of the church. Rev. Mutale said on November 5 this year, she heard on Radio Phoenix that she had been expelled from the church together with 70 other church members with immediate effect without any given reason.

She said the news item on radio stated that the expelled church members were advocating for a local indigenous leadership for the A.M.E. Church in Zambia. Rev. Mutale, a day later on November 6, said there was another news item on Zambia National Broadcasting Corporation (ZNBC), which was attributed to Rev. Michael Gondwe insisting that she was expelled from the church. "On the same day, I received a letter signed by Rev. Newton Masunga that was addressed to me stating that I was expelled from the church," she said. At this stage, A.M.E. Church lawyer Sachika Sitwala wanted to object to the tendering in as evidence the expulsion letter and the press release that was sent to the media, nevertheless, Judge Nyangulu told

Sitwala: "We have not reached that stage of producing these documents. So, shut up!" "My lord, I would like the court to withdraw the words, 'shut up'," Sitwala demanded. "Withdrawn and let's proceed," Judge Nyangulu responded.

Times of Zambia newspaper of Tuesday, 11th May, 2004 reported that there was a near punch-up by the two groups! The paper reported that "Ebenezer African Methodist Episcopal Church (AMEC) Pastor-in-Charge Edith Mutale has clarified that there was no meeting called at the weekend to reconcile rival factions as claimed by some members. She explained in Lusaka yesterday that the faction led by Paul Kawimbe (Candidate for Episcopal Office) had no right to disrupt the church service on Sunday because she and her group were still in charge by way of a court injunction. Rev. Mutale said there was no way a reconciliatory service could have been convened when the matter was still in court and also refuted reports that there was an announcement in church that those who belonged to the Kawimbe group should leave the building."

Meanwhile Judge Nyangulu had on May 3 ruled a stay of execution granted to the A.M.E. Church in Zambia. According to the Times of Zambia, the Lusaka High Court had discharged the stay of execution granted to African Methodist Episcopal Church (AMEC) Reverend Edith Mutale in the matter involving a leadership wrangle in the church. Judge Anthony Nyangulu in his order said there were no grounds to vary or alter his judgment of May 3 as requested by Rev. Mutale who is AMEC Ebenezer pastor-in-charge. Rev. Mutale had obtained a stay of execution to seek clarification on the judgment after Judge Nyangulu's earlier ruling that the two parties should go and reconcile outside court.

Reverends Josephat Siyomunji, Edith Mutale and 49 others were expelled for being against the church doctrine. The court, in its May 3, judgment ruled that the church should reconcile and further restrained the Rev. Edith Mutale committee from interfering with the AMEC operations. In his order upon review to clarify his judgment, Judge Nyangulu advised the AMEC members to reconcile and live in peace. The judge said the wrangles in the church were worrying and urged the church to live as one. Judge Nyangulu said he, however, agreed with Rev. Mutale's cry for a local bishop for the church and that it was a genuine call.

Nevertheless, he said the court was not asked to make a decision on how to elect a bishop in Zambia. This was based on the view that the doctrine did not state that. He advised Rev. Mutale to float a candidate and campaign for the person of her choice in the forthcoming AMEC July 2004 elections if she and her supporters wanted a local bishop. The judge reiterated that the court wanted to promote and preserve peace in the church and advised Rev. Mutale to desist from bringing confusion in the church. There had been disturbances at AMEC (Ebenezer) at Chilenje in Lusaka at the weekend when the two groups clashed.

Tragic Deaths of Ministers in North West Zambia Conference in 2012

On September 16, 2012 nine people, members of the A.M.E. Church died in a road traffic accident at Mwense in Zambia. The accident involved a Mitsubishi Canter light truck which had 31 passengers on board. The accident allegedly occurred after a tyre burst. The truck had careered off the road, hit a tree and overturned. The passengers had been returning home from the North West Zambia Annual Conference in Mansa to Mwense. Those who died were four Itinerant Elders, three Licentiates (and were Pastors) and two Stewards. Three members reported to be in critical condition were in hospital and eighteen people with injuries were treated at Mambilima Hospital. Those who passed away were Rev. James Mwila, Rev. Muyambo Chimba, Rev. Patson Mwewa, Rev. Jackson Ng'onga, Licentiate Kasongo Lumbwe, Licentiate Morgan Chipasha, Lazarus Mungo and Musonda Chinyangwa. Messiah invited every Conference in Zambia to attend unveiling of the tombstone. Alas! Everyone was disappointed when they saw a single tiny tombstone put at the center of all the tombs meant to honour his ministers – Messiah's ministers!

This case also ended up in court. Following the demise of the members of the Church, the Church kept dragging its feet in helping the widows and families who had lost their loved ones. By the "Church" this writer means the leadership of Wilfred Messiah. Members in North West Zambia Conference, consequently, had to hire an Attorney and took the Bishop to court. The members contended that they had information that money had been donated by well-wishers but it had not reached the intended people. In 2015, Lusaka Voice reported that Paul Kalwa, widow's spokesman informed the Press that Bishop Wilfred Messiah allegedly received money from the W.M.S. in America, South Africa and Zambia but did not deliver it to the intended beneficiaries. He released 23% of the money after being questioned at Police Force Headquarters, (Lusaka Voice, 2015).

According to a W.M.S. report to the General Board dated June 23-26, 2013 hosted in Kingston, Jamaica, $12,500 had been donated to the 17th Episcopal District presided over by Bishop Messiah. The women group contributed this towards the families of the deceased. Also, people present in South Africa I spoke to, confirmed money being given to the Bishop towards the same. This case was finally taken to court in Zambia for settlement. The Bishop's Administrative Assistant Cosmas Wakunguma when asked by the reporter about the case was quoted as saying, "There was no such a case and that Mr. Kalwa was just inviting problems upon himself and the widows. If it is about that issue (money for the widows) there is no story there, those people don't know what they are talking about," (Lusaka Voice, 2015). The Bishop is said to have told the court that he thought that the money which was given to him in South Africa was his honorarium.

Chapter 26
God's Powerful Hand in the Revival of A Traditional Church to His Glory & The Rev. Peter Mfula Pious Mwenya's Story

Without doubt, the A.M.E. Church has been classified as one of the Traditional Churches by many authorities in Zambia. Traditional Churches, by and large, are identified by their rigid structures and mode of worship which traditionally has not been accommodating to "the move of the Spirit!" While this definition may be subjective, the A.M.E. Church may not be likened to the Catholic or Anglican Church if the strictest sense of a "Traditional Church" per se, were to be applied. The A.M.E. Church both abroad (in the U.S.A. and in Africa) has had a mixture of both traditional and contemporary services for centuries. Nevertheless, the "Spiritual services" are the very traditional ones which emanated from its founders such as John and Charles Wesley – founders of Methodism but Rev. Peter M.P. Mwenya may undoubtedly be dubbed as the father of revival in the A.M.E. Church in Zambia.

Several denominations enjoy the spiritual grace from God which has been demonstrated worldwide. However, the repression of the Holy Spirit's work and deliberate inhibition of teaching of the born again experience was what the Lord began to change in the Zambian Church and by his grace brought back a revival to yearning and thirsty souls. While many

Pastors including the Rev. Rowland Mwenyo and others can be counted among revivalists, the Rev. Peter M.P. Mwenya, by virtue of outliving many and being amongst the earliest recognizable ministers who produced several preachers by the grace of God over many years, may arguably be regarded as the man who helped the A.M.E. Church in Zambia greatly and to some extent be numbered among Zambia's early revivalists. He helped the Church and the nation learn about the power of the Holy Spirit and the Lord Jesus Christ.

This grace of change came by the mighty hand of God. Since there were countless deliberate incidents in which the leadership had been systematically opposing a certain way of worship which it deemed to be "foreign" or "Not Methodist," including holding of prayer meetings, the revival of this Church was slow but timely. Through his grace, the Lord began raising up believers in the Church and he began using them to preach a gospel of separation from sin. These believers did not endear themselves with those who had for years adhered to the importance of the "Uniform," "Belief in salvation by works," "Not casting out demons," and so on, even though the Doctrine of the Church as espoused by the Discipline Book of the A.M.E. Church doesn't hold to such or disavow such beliefs! In this chapter, we will see how the Lord began to raise ministers and young believers who began to preach the gospel under the power of the Holy Spirit to liberate the A.M.E. Church in Zambia.

Today, with all honour given to God, there is hardly any congregation that would stop you from casting out demons. Decades ago, this was so contentious an issue that it could have you be brought before the "Sanhedrin" (as we called it) or "Official Board." While the revival of this Church is an ongoing process, it can be noted that churches which had ministers who were born again or were actively participating in revival meetings with other equally saved believers exhibited and continue to exhibit that change even today. However, A.M.E. churches (congregations) which neglected such important meetings which unleashed spiritual impartation continue to lag behind. Ministers who came or come from such congregations usually exhibit odd or unspiritual behaviours which can easily be spotted by their poor decision-making processes. Nevertheless, it is the general change in the nation and to a large extent in the A.M.E. Church that the Lord brought about this transformation which he is being praised and thanked for, for helping this Church to embrace the things of the Spirit.

Rev. Peter Mfula Pious Mwenya – Undisputed A.M.E. Church and One of Zambia's Bearers of the Revival in the Nation

Rev. Peter Mfula Pious Mwenya, now Presiding Elder of the Copperbelt West District, is perhaps the undisputed man the Lord used as the "Father of Revival" in the A.M.E. Church in Zambia. (This writer is also mindful of the Rev. Rowland Mwenyo's great contribution to revival in this once upon a time purely traditional Church). Rev. Peter Mfula Pious Mwenya's credentials, however, cannot be limited to the A.M.E. Church alone but must be numbered among many saints God used to bring about Revival in the nation. He is the unsung hero of the Cross who for years has preached Jesus under the power of the Holy Spirit before the current Pentecostal and Charismatic movement had taken root nationwide. He is also one of the most persecuted ministers in this Church I have ever known. Nevertheless, he has been the torch-bearer of the love of God to many and his persistence in faith brought scores of people to the Lord and thousands experienced deliverance from powers of darkness through his powerful ministry.

In spite of his great ministry which has brought thousands of people to the Lord, he remained relatively unknown to many for a number of reasons. First, his ministry was not broadcasted on television or radio as is for many well-known televangelists of today. Second, the A.M.E. Church was by and large regarded as a Traditional Church; therefore, it did not command a lot of following or attention by outsiders. Third, his ministry was at "the corner," in a small Copperbelt town of Mufulira near the border with Congo DR (then Zaire). Fourth, he bore the scars of persecution in a Church that resisted change for years and did a lot to stop his influence.

My older sister, Mrs. Mary Kapungwe Musonda, for instance, found deliverance in 1982 under the Rev. Mwenya's ministry. She had suffered greatly from demon possession and oppression for a long time. Although she was a member of the Choir in latter years, no one helped her in the church at Jordan Chapel in Kitwe, in part due to lack of knowledge of the power of God over demons or because of the deceitful covert operations of Satan in the Church. As observed from our testimonies and ministry, you would realize that there were actually many people in the Church who were possessed or oppressed by powers of darkness but because the knowledge of the grace of God was lacking, the ministry of deliverance was not exercised nor was there any preaching of a gospel of salvation. As a result, Satan continued to have people bound and he vigorously fought any ministry which tried to expose him or have people preach salvation. He did this through use of religious leaders and unsaved members. Between 2000 and 2019, some unsaved junior ministers were elevated and put in influential positions for the purpose of thwarting what God had been doing earlier.

My sister found the grace when she went to live with our cousin Patrick C. Musonda in Mufulira. At Allen Temple A.M.E. Church, she came face to face with the power of the Holy Spirit through the Rev. M.P.P. Mwenya's ministry. She now serves the Lord in the women's ministry and she is a coveted speaker in many of the women's gatherings in the Church. Any mention of Rev. Mwenya, in the mid-and late 1970s was often rebuffed by the larger Church community or dismissed with the words "The ones who evoke evil spirits" which literally implied "The ones or groups of people who prayed to Satan or to evil spirits!"

Please note that believers who cast out demons under the power of God were erroneously dubbed as "The ones who evoked evil spirits!" By smearing this preacher even by people who never had sat under his ministry, the hearsay propaganda of Satan and his demons had continued to dismiss the powerful work this servant had done in the Church for years. Not surprisingly, one was erroneously made to believe the hearsays until one was able to hear in person the Rev. Mwenya speak, pray or preach to appreciate the great grace and power of the Holy Spirit which was upon this great man of God.

In 1991, he was transferred from Allen Temple, Mufulira to Ebenezer A.M.E. Church in Lusaka. It was, in fact, a swap which saw the Rev. David K. Simfukwe be transferred to Allen Temple in Mufulira. Rev. Mwenya, for a number of reasons, decided to be commuting from

Mufulira to Lusaka, which obviously was a costly venture. Understandably, he had a beautiful house in the suburbs of Mufulira which had been granted to him by the Mines and relocating at this stage in his ministry as a sitting tenant, likely would have led to the loss of his house which was being earmarked for sale to sitting tenants. It is important that you are made aware that ministers in the A.M.E. Church hardly have any pension! Also, by and large, they are not able to purchase any house from the meager income they receive! Of course, not everyone was supportive and this too became a distraction to many. When Rev. Mwenya reported to Ebenezer, the Lay organization spearheaded by the Mulolo's and others informed Bishop Chappelle that "Ebenezer has rejected Rev. Mwenya!" This made the Bishop to transfer him just weeks after that appointment in 1991 to Jordan A.M.E. Church at Wusakile in Kitwe.

This was the most exciting news for believers at Jordan! Having spent many years battling religious leaders with their traditions, we were excited that the Lord had answered our prayers! Alas, as soon as the appointment had been announced at a Planning Meeting held at Bethel in Lusaka in 1991, some of the leaders from Jordan had secretly met and word had reached us that they had hatched out a plan and had written the Bishop that the church at Jordan had rejected Rev. Mwenya! This had been before he even had stepped his foot at Jordan. It was one of the most trying periods of my ministry in this Church! The Bishop, however, held on to his decision and when Rev. Mwenya arrived at Jordan on Sunday, the "leadership" called for a meeting in which they subtly delivered the "leadership decision" of which my fellow born again believers and I were not aware of – "He was not welcome at Jordan!"

They began arguing and were completely in the flesh. Rev. Mwenya never said a word! Mother Grace Mwenya was also present! We began to debate the other group and I was so upset and angry at Satan and his people that I stood firm denouncing Satan's insinuations through them! I gave them a history of Jordan Chapel to as far back as I could remember how hard-hearted these people had been and how they had been rejecting every godly servant from the time I was young until now mentioning all the Pastors one by one by name! I did this in a similar way Stephen had done before he was stoned. I also informed them that there had been no meeting of leaders at the church which constituted an official agreement concerning the fate of the Pastor because as a leader I could have attended that meeting, but I never did!

One leader was so angry with me that he gnashed his teeth at me but I stood by my words. You clearly, would see the two factions at Jordan at play and the ones who had spearheaded this unfortunate rejection. (Thankfully, years later, God saved some of these leaders!). The transfer of Rev. Simfukwe from Ebenezer to Allen Temple was also as a result of influential laymen working with some clergy behind the scenes. They claimed Rev. Simfukwe "posed as a Bishop and signed documents to register the Church in Congo in 1991!" In spite of Bishop Richard Chappelle having authorized Rev. Simfukwe, he listened to the pressure group and transferred him to Allen, and Rev. Mwenya to Lusaka. However, The Laymen at Ebenezer, again had pushed for Rev. Mwenya to leave through the Bishop and at a Planning Meeting in Lusaka the same year, he ended up at Jordan but only for a year!

God was gracious to us that Rev. Mwenya became our Pastor after everything had been said and done. He however, remained at Jordan only for a year. My immediate older sister,

Foster, still recalls with excitement of the ministry she witnessed from the Rev. M.P.P. Mwenya. Foster had been waylaid by the Jehovah's Witnesses but through prayer and God's grace, the Lord snatched her out of that cult. She recalls with amusement as she imitates the man of God praying in the church and how great power of the Holy Spirit would manifest in the congregation as people who were possessed would scream and manifest with evil spirits. This would just be an opening prayer of the service! "Satan, I bind you in the name of Jesus," Foster would recollect amidst some laughter as she imitated the Rev. Mwenya's prayers!

For many people unfamiliar with Presiding Elder Rev. Peter Mfula Pious Mwenya, the question "Who is M.P.P. Mwenya?" would frequently be asked. Rev. M.P.P. Mwenya was born on 2nd February, 1946 at Broken Hill, Northern Rhodesia (now Kabwe, in Central Province of Zambia). He was born to Mr. Mfula P. Mwenya and Zedia Nanyangwe. Both parents are deceased. Rev. Mwenya began his primary education at Kaloko School in Ndola (Sub A). He then went to Kambole Mission, Fundi Yamali, Mpulungu Boarding School and Mungwi Secondary School in Northern Province of Zambia. When he was unable to continue school at Mungwi due to failure to pay school fees, he went to Luanshya where years later completed his General Certificate of Education (G.C.E.) "O" Level Exams.

Rev. Mwenya studied Theology at Theological College of Central Africa in Ndola where he enrolled in 1976. He did several short courses in Nairobi, Kenya, Zimbabwe Bible College in Zimbabwe and ITI in Chicago, U.S.A. He also attended Mindolo Ecumenical Foundation in Kitwe and Teamwork College in Nashville, Tennessee where he obtained a BA in Theology in 2019. Rev. Mwenya had been a member of the Church of Scotland, (now United Church of Zambia) from childhood but he joined the African Methodist Episcopal Church in 1963 in Kabwe where he received the call into ministry in 1971.

God's dealings with Rev. M.P.P. Mwenya began during his childhood years. Rev. Mwenya's early supernatural experiences as a boy were the initial preparations that God had instituted in him to show him the calling that he had placed upon him. That calling was later to be revealed to him and it was a preparation that involved supernatural experiences with God through encounters with the Holy Spirit. He began his Sub A at Kaloko School in Ndola in 1953 and then went up to Standard IV at Kambole Mission (London Missionary Society) in 1958 in Northern Province. Rev. Mwenya then went to Fundi Yamali for Standard V and eventually to Mpulungu Boarding for Standard VI in 1960. He later studied Form I and Form II at Mungwi Secondary School from 1961 to 1962 aged 15 and 16, respectively.

One day, in 1958 when Rev. M.P.P. Mwenya was a border at Kambole Mission School situated about 60 miles (96.6 km) west of Abercorn, he met a pride of lions! The school was about 15 miles (24.1 km) from his home at Kaula Village. He would therefore, leave for school on Sundays with friends and returned on Fridays. He was about 12 years-old at the time doing Standard IV (Grade 6). "One day during my school days I met a pride of lions! I used to walk to school a distance of 15 miles. I lived in the village called Kaula. We often trekked up and down through the hills in groups with friends on a track that passed through the thick forests. I had never seen a lion before.

After school, I trailed my friends who had left me behind hours earlier. As I walked through the hills and made a turn, I found myself staring at what I presumed were a group of baboons or gorillas! As stunned as I was, the beasts too looked at me for what appeared to be an eternity to me. With great interest, they wondered and gazed at my motionless figure of mine that had remained fixated at their grayish-brown hue of a pride of about 12 'baboons' that stood in my way just about 6 meters in front of me. Then, unannounced, the 'baboons' slowly and majestically trod away into the bush leaving the path clear for me to pass!

About 500 meters in front of me was an old man standing still off his bicycle. He had been standing a little ahead, beyond my scene of encounter with the beasts. He had been observing the entire scenario at a distance when our world and time had come to a halt. He apparently, had patiently been observing what would happen to me and spoke no word. As soon as he saw me resume my trek, and I got closer to him, he engaged me in a conversation asking me to get on his bicycle. He had been riding a bicycle going in the opposite direction but had stopped to see my encounter with the animals. He offered me a ride home deciding to return to the village and not to proceed to his destination which was in the direction I was coming from.

The old man did not want to alert me and induce fear in me about what the animals we had met were until we had gotten to the village. When we got to the village, he asked me if I knew the animals I had encountered and I told him ignorantly, 'Yes! I know them! They are monkeys! They are baboons!' He then responded: 'Go and celebrate! Those are the famous lions you hear about!' My heart sank within me and I got shaky! When the parents were told, they informed me not to trek alone. It was a great encounter that I later attributed to God's miraculous hand of saving me from a pride of about 12 lions with cubs!

I was later transferred from Kambole Mission School to Fundi Yamali School in Northern Province in 1959. The school was near Nsumbu Game Reserve where the famous Kasaba Bay, a place laden with lions and other cannibals in northern Zambia is located. The area is just a few miles south of Lake Tanganyika. The school was about 5 miles from my village, therefore, was closer than my first school. I went from lower to upper primary school doing Standard V (Grade 7). I still continued to go to school on Sundays and returned home on Fridays.

One day, on a midmonth break, the school had closed at 10 o'clock. I had to walk back home, a distance of about 5 miles (8.1 km) through the thick forest of the game reserve. Fortunately, two men from the same village had come for some business at our school. They offered that I would ride with them going back home on one of their bicycles. I therefore, decided to go and sing in the choir before we would leave together. To my dismay, the duo didn't come the time they had said they would. Consequently, I felt let down and deceived, so I decided to go back with a little boy of about 5 years. (I came to learn later that they had come at school at 4 o'clock!). I was about 13 years-old at the time. We thus, ran at the pace small boys would. We ran for almost two hours but we were still far away from getting home as dusk began to set in. Soon, the darkness set in and the forest became awfully darker and darker but I was still in the forest with the little boy – on our way home!

We pressed on and on through the dark forest. Glittering insects shone around us but we pushed through the dark heading home. We then saw a pair of glittering insects just at a short distance, few meters from us. What we thought to be glittering insects, we noticed grew bigger and bigger. A pair of glowing insects in the dark, we thought, grew wider and wider with blue, red and green hues and what we had thought to be glowing insects in the dark, we came to learn were actually eyes of a huge lion standing before us! We found ourselves staring at the beast speechless and highly apprehensive! We all took a moment apparently sizing ourselves up face to face with the lion, the king of the African jungle! The lion was staring at us and us at the lion! Motionless, indecisive and glancing at the beast and the beast at us for what appeared to be half an hour, we wondered what our fate was soon to be!

Suddenly, a miracle from the Most High God, in an unexplained turn of events happened! With what appeared to be God's righteous hand descending from above, we were scooped and lifted high up above the beast and I felt as though my head was touching the clouds in the skies. As I looked down, I noticed below us that the beast was following in our direction too. We had been moved by the gracious mighty and most powerful hand of God for what looked like a mile away from our original position where we had been and landed us or placed us safely on the same track upfront towards the direction of our home! I was still holding the hand of the boy the entire period. After landing on the path, we started running and saw that the lion was coming after us! I was surprised that I was taking very huge strides which looked like exaggerated wide or gigantic leaps and I felt as though I was so tall that my legs were also long that each step was like a huge leap or step.

To our surprise, when I looked behind, I saw the men who I had thought had left us earlier cycling behind us! The lion, having seen the lights from their touches, got distracted and no longer thought of pursuing after us! The men had seen the lion coming after us and had begun to jeer and shout at the lion hoping to frighten and distract it with their noise and lights of their torches. We took to our heels running faster! When we arrived at the village, we pushed through heading to our home. I was still outside an opened door standing when the boy passed by me and went into the house. The older ones came and looked at me and from my gaze and appearance they suspected something strange must have happened to us.

I was still by the door and felt that my soul had left me. I was listening but not responding – I had fainted! When they pulled me inside and sat me down, I was still speechless for minutes. I now felt as though my soul had returned! When they looked at me, all I uttered was 'Lion!' Soon the two men on bicycles arrived and explained what they had seen confirming that we had met a lion! May praise, honour and glory be to the Most High God, the Father of our Lord Jesus Christ who saved us from the paws of the lion by his outstretched and powerful hand so we would give a testimony of his marvelous deeds and wonders of his grace!"

In 1961, Rev. Mwenya went to Mungwi where he attended Form I and Form II. After failing to pay school fees in 1963, he left for Kabwe. He was 17 years old now. It is here where he joined the A.M.E. Church at Brookins, the place where the A.M.E. Church began in Zambia in 1929. "Needing funds to further my education, I decided to look for a job. This, I thought, was going to help me raise school fees. I joined the Department of Game and Fisheries. One day we were sailing on Lake Tanganyika on our way to a place called Kabyolwe in Yendwe area near Kasaba Bay. Without warning, six of us were caught in a furor of an angry lake and our boat was battered by the storm. In spite of being a good swimmer, I couldn't make it to the shore!

I saw four of my friends caught up by the wave and appeared to be drowning. I was trying to swim but was overpowered by the fierce storm. I could only see one friend near me who was trying to swim and stay afloat. I then prayed, 'Father, if you do not have a mission for me, let this sea take my life!' In answer to that prayer, the Lord commanded three huge waves to blow us to the shore! When we hit the shore, I was conscious but four of my friends had been unconscious. I am not sure how the other friend made it too to the shore. Like me, he had not drowned! Soon, the fishermen who were nearby came and resuscitated the four. Yet again, I witnessed God spare my life in a miraculous way." [Note: Lake Tanganyika is the longest freshwater lake in the world (677 km or 420 miles) and the second deepest lake after Lake Balkal in Russia. It is 1,433 m (4,700 ft.) deep – an incredible 642 m below sea level! Its width spans about 50 km, i.e., 31 miles. Its borders are shared by Zambia, Tanzania, Congo DR and Burundi.]

Rev. Mwenya married Mother Grace Mwenya in 1970. He continued to receive great revelations and wonders from God which further kept on revealing God's call upon his life. He was a member of Brookins Chapel at Kabwe at the time. Rev. Mwenya was working for a contracting firm in 1971 when he went to see a workmate who was very sick. He prayed for him and the man recovered! A Mr. Kaspar, a steward at the church, came looking for him because he thought he had taken longer to return. When he found them and began to reprimand him, Rev. Mwenya saw heaven open up and a bright light shine on him. The experience was exhilarating but his colleagues never saw it. He kept showing them the bright light but they could not see it. When he got home, the wife was also asking him why he had taken long to get home. He explained it to her but she seemed not to understand or believe him!

He began experiencing visitations of God's glory. This was similar to what we read about in the Bible where God's glory was manifested. The Israelites, for instance, witnessed God's glory descending in a form of a pillar of cloud at Etham on the edge of the desert as they trekked in the wilderness soon after departing from Succoth, Exodus 13:20-22; Exodus 33. The Rev. Mwenya had again seen heaven open and a bright cloud descend from heaven through an open window directly upon his face at around 21:00 hrs. "Instantly, an indescribable joy filled my soul! Surprisingly, the two colleagues who had been with me did not see what I had seen nor did they experience anything! When I asked them if they had seen what I had seen they pleaded ignorance to anything that I told them had occurred," Rev. Mwenya recalled.

"Later, I explained this to my wife at home. She, however, could not believe me! Two days later, my wife and I were in small room having dinner at 20:00 hours. Suddenly, a bright light covered me and the phenomenon was so overwhelming that my wife remained still and speechless because of the awe and presence of God. The bright light could only be described as a 'Transformation' which humanly speaking could only be explained as to what we read in Scripture and is described of our Lord Jesus Christ at the Mountain of Transfiguration in Luke 9:28-36. Jesus accompanied by Peter, John and James had been transfigured by a flash of lightning in the presence of his disciples and Moses and Elijah had appeared. A similar splendor of glory had appeared and changed my countenance in the presence of my wife who remained speechless and overwhelmed because great fear had come upon her."

"Similar events of great proportion in unexplained fashion continued to happen to me. Once, I saw heaven open and an exceeding fury of fire poured down from heaven consuming the inhabitants of the earth. Many people died from that fury and when I lifted up my eyes again, I saw the Lord Jesus Christ! He had a crown and I asked him a question! 'My Lord, my Lord! Are you Jesus of Nazareth, the God I worship?' The Lord answered me saying, 'Yes!' I then inquired, 'Lord, if you are the One, then bid me to come!' The Lord interestingly responded: 'Come!' When I went up to him, I looked at the few people who had survived the fiery fire that had been poured out of heaven. I then asked him: 'My Lord Jesus, are these the only people who have been saved from the fiery fire?' 'Yes, they are,' the Lord answered me. I then, filled with sorrow, told the Lord, 'You are a merciful God, my Lord! How would you let so many people perish like this, my Lord?'

The Lord then, with an extended hand invited me to go to him! I went up to him. When I was with him, I was able to look down the earth below and I saw an island. The Lord then commanded me saying, 'Go and preach repentance to those,' showing me the inhabitants of the island. Agreeable to his command, I left his presence to go and do his ministry. Nevertheless, out of fear, I deviated to another island. I went into a ship because I was fearful of witches and wizards in the land the Lord had sent me to. While in the ship, a terrible storm came and the owner of the ship began to inquire about the cause of this problem and to my dismay they found out who was responsible for the fury – me!

They asked me, 'Who are you?' I informed them who I was and told them that I was running away from the Lord, by not obeying God's commission that he has commanded me to preach. They further asked me, 'What do you want us to do to you?' 'Throw me in the water to save yourselves and all that you have,' I told them. They mercilessly approved of my ruthless offer and threw me down into the open sea! In what looked like a rehearsed Jonah story of the Bible, soon, a huge fish appeared and swallowed me up! In its spacious belly, I cried to the Lord for mercy! I cried and despaired for life noting that this was a horrible death to experience! Therefore, I begged the Lord to take me back! To my surprise, after being in the belly of the fish for a day only, I was cast out of the belly of the fish to the same island I had refused to go! When I rolled around, I found I was in bed! My 'Jonah journey' had been only a dream!

Once in 1972, I had gone to Mansa with a friend on vacation. It was the period I had received the call. One day I left for Mulundu and planned to return the following day. My friend, however, remained behind in our rented home and I had planned to rejoin him the next day. Being alone, my friend hooked on a married woman whose husband was a bridge-builder and had been away at Musonda Falls. Upon my return, I was surprised to find my friend on our bed with the woman and I immediately reprimanded him severely. Later, an appealing desire gripped me. I then let go of the thoughts choosing not to further entertain the desires. I decided to switch positions and slept on the bed while they slept on the floor.

While in sleep, I heard a very strong voice speak to me. The voice was so strong that it could not be missed or ignored, 'Mwenya,' the voice called my name! 'Yes, Lord,' I responded. 'Speak my Lord, your servant is listening!' I said. 'Are you aware that Sodom and Gomorrah have come?' the voice questioned me. 'Why have you forsaken the Lord?' the voice reprimanded me. 'Forsaking the Lord Jesus Christ?' my response came, albeit in a way that sounded like a statement than a question. Upon the mention of the name of Jesus, great overwhelming grief flooded my heart and tears flooded my eyes and flowed uncontrollably for over three hours. I sobbed from 20:00 hrs. till the early hours of the morning.

In hardness of heart, I had struggled with the Lord's voice in me. The struggle prompted me to go and seek counsel and clarity about my ministerial calling from my elderly mentor, the late Rev. Steven Simuyemba. I wanted to know if this was the nature or way which happens to all the servants which God calls to serve him. 'Yours is a special one,' he told me, 'God has a mission yet to be revealed to you. Just be patient,' he informed me.

I lived under great fear of the Lord in the aftermath of this. This happened before I went to college and an unmistakable unction was upon me which both elders and members of the Church confirmed or testified to it that it was the hand of God that was upon me. I received the call to join the ministry while at Kabwe in 1971. In 1972, I went to Mansa and planted a church there. I was ordained Deacon in 1973 by Bishop Hartford H. Brookins at Mpulungu and sent to Mulundu. The same year I was transferred to Mansa then to Chingola by the Bishop (a total of three appointments to different churches in a single year!) I was ordained Elder in 1975 by Bishop Brookins at Nchanga A.M.E. Church (Brookins). When I was Pastor of this church, I was also overseeing Chikola A.M.E. Church (Quinns). My epiphany moment occurred in 1975. Although I had known that God had called me from the time I was young, it was in 1975, however, that I experienced his power come into my life.

I was in my room one day when a very large figure came upon me. It was a huge figure that almost filled the room. It was an evil presence that wanted to harm me. I rebuked it and began to pray to God. The power of the Lord came upon me and the oppressing spirit left. I was then led by the Lord to begin commanding the evil to leave. I also prayed for myself and saw that I was delivered. I continued to pray from 02:00 hours up to 05:00 hours alone and the Holy Spirit came upon me in power. When I went to church at Chingola, everyone who was possessed would fall down and had demonic manifestation. This continued to the time I went to college and whenever I went to a place where people were possessed, evil spirits would manifest and they would fall down. I began to understand the grace of the Lord that he had put on me and it helped me to help those who were under the powers of darkness. I would pray for them and lead them to Christ.

Bishop Brookins had come with a Dr. Quinns. I had asked the Bishop to help in the building of the church and when he did, it was named after him. I also had asked Dr. Quinns to assist at Chikola. He bought pews for the church and it was named after him. This was just before I left for training at the Theological College of Central Africa (TCCA) in 1976 in Ndola. While in college in Ndola, I did my preaching practical in Chingola. In a Church that had been steeped in traditions for years and was grossly opposed to change, I constantly fought battles in ministry. Many were unfamiliar with the liberating power of the gospel; therefore, persecution was the order of the day. However, in spite of me facing numerous battles with the leadership and groups of people who opposed this powerful ministry of the Holy Spirit, thousands of people found Jesus and freedom from oppression and possession.

In 1976, I was sponsored to college by the A.M.E. Church. I opted to go to Theological College of Central Africa at Kansenshi in Ndola. My study was a three-year Diploma in Biblical Instruction. At the time, I served in Chingola under the able leadership of Rt. Rev. Bishop Cornelius Thomas. In the process of sponsoring me to go out for studies in the U.S.A., rumours of false accusation against me impregnating a girl spread like a wild fire in the District. The rumours whose source was traced to a senior minister, was the initial major battle that continued to beleaguer my ministry in the Church throughout my contentions with powers of darkness. At the time, the Church was deeply steeped in traditions and a strong highly sophisticated antispiritual, anti-God and antirevival movement was in operation in the Church. It was spearheaded by influential laity – men and women. They were supported by a few clergy, especially some Presiding Elders. Some Bishops were also pandering to the same machinations.

The gruesome accusation robed me of an opportunity to be a candidate to the General Conference in the U.S.A. It simultaneously affected my chances of going for further education in the U.S.A. as well where I was earmarked to go for theological studies. The Lord, however, moved in a mysterious way during the Conference. The Bishop had summoned my church leadership to inquire about the accusation. Mother Diana Mapoma, a delegate to the General Conference stood up to present the astounding truth that crushed the Bishop's spirit! He heard that my church members and leadership had had no record of that accusation and needed their Pastor back! This news shocked the Bishop! It was my first setback in ministry in this Church that moved me to a point of resigning and leaving the Church due to a sense of frustration.

Mother Diana Mapoma

I had just graduated from college and was moved from Brookins A.M.E. Church to Quinns A.M.E. Church within Chingola. However, I did not stay long there and was moved to Allen Temple in Mufulira in 1979. It was at Allen Temple that we began to see the power and work of the Holy Spirit in the ministry. Here, demons were cast out, the dying restored to life, the good news preached and hundreds of people saved. I vividly recall an incident one Saturday morning when we were at a Prayer Warriors' meeting when I was summoned to go and baptize a dying child at Ronald Ross Hospital. I took with me a young man by the name of Wilson Mpundu to accompany me.

At the hospital, (Ronald Ross) we found that the boy has just passed away! I took the baby in my arms and prayed! I told the Lord that through the commission invested in me to preach and baptize, sanctify this water for this peculiar service Lord to your glory in Jesus' name! Nurses were waiting to take the child to the mortuary at this moment and I scooped some water from the bowl that was in Wilson's hands and sprinkled the water over the child. Bro. Wilson was interceding in prayer at this time. The child inhaled and exhaled! I handed the child to the mother who had been weeping. The incident amazed many with awe including the nurses and the doctor. When the news of this testimony of the miraculous work of God reached the ears of those at the church some got apprehensive while some were overwhelmed with joy and many joined the Prayer group, most of which were young people.

Allen Temple Church was built in the 1930s. At the time, the size was adequate for the small number of Africans who were in the area. When the Lord began to bring souls to himself, the number of people coming outgrew the building. We witnessed the healing of the deaf and the dumb, people who never used to hear began to hear and those who could not speak began to speak! The old structure could not handle the increased numbers which we began to see. I therefore, decided to demolish the building and build a better and bigger one. Meanwhile, young men and women from other Churches began to come in large numbers to Allen because they gravitated towards what the Lord through the Holy Spirit was doing in his church. Scores of people attended prayer meetings and Sunday services inducing more and more opposition from the A.M.E. Church circles in the District against what the Lord was doing!

When Bishop Robert Lee Pruitt came in 1984, many of my young men, stewards and trustees had become Pastors from my church. Many more had become Pastors outside the A.M.E. Church. The antispiritual movement or say the antirevival spirit continued to sweep across the Copperbelt Province and throughout the 17th Episcopal District because of the unction of the Holy Spirit in my pulpit and church. I was repeatedly accused of having destabilized the Church with wrong and unethical doctrines. If we looked at, or examined critically the allegations leveled against me, the 'wrong unethical doctrines' they claimed, were nothing but 'casting out of evil spirits, deliverance from all kinds of bondages, preaching salvation through the new birth or being born again!' This is what was termed as 'wrong doctrines!' "

From left to right: Rev. Paul Bupe and Rev. Wilson Mpundu and their father in ministry Rev. Peter Mfula Pious Mwenya at the Annual Conference at Mother Hughes, Ndola in 1985.

"My name went wildly famous and this offended many senior ministers and laity. If my ministry had been telecasted it would have brought the evidence in public and perhaps many of these moral accusations, I battled for years could have been addressed differently. Many who heard of this work of the Holy Spirit heard it in the negative which continued to fuel rumours of unbelief and misinformation by Satan because his kingdom was being destroyed. The late Bishop Robert Pruitt was among the leaders who the enemy had instigated to do something to me and he had vowed to stamp me out of the A.M.E. Church, purporting that 'You have become a stumbling block and obstacle and a threat to the entire Church!'

My home and church became a shelter for the suffering both spiritually and physically. Being so receptive and approachable, I accommodated two girls whose father had accused them of being confused because of the charismatic prayers. Later, the parents complained to Bishop Pruitt alleging that I had impregnated his two daughters. God was good to me again because he held my head above the storms of my life. This parent, under the influence of some church members, was advised to circulate a document that brought my name into disrepute to bring about character assassination and to hurt the church's reputation. Copies of the document were handed over to the police, the Presiding Elder and other concerned community citizens. To their amazement, the girls explained to the higher authorities how their father had been ill-treating them and how they had become destitute and that they had found refuge and solace at the church which they call their home!

The A.M.E. Church's trend in Zambia has been like a denomination stricken by poverty from its inception. When Bishop Hartford Brookins came in 1972, many people saw it as the redeeming era that was going to change the trajectory of this Church in Zambia.

However, selfishness by men and women turned his great efforts into mediocrity, a curse that has hovered around the A.M.E. Church in Zambia for decades. Bishop Brookins initiated a housing project and bought 100 units of housing plots in the capital, City of Lusaka with the view of building those houses for rental purposes to benefit the Church. He further got a loan of K250,000.00, at the time ($349,993.00) from Zambia National Building Society so that he could complete the project. This was done with the help of the President of Zambia, Godwin Yoram Mumba, who was a Director of some company and Mr. W.K. Sikalumbi who once had been a minister in the United National Independence Party (UNIP) Government. Mr. Sikalumbi, Mr. Nekhairo and others were among the people who had been assigned to manage this project.

Alas! Mr. Sikalumbi out of selfish reasons contracted his brother-in-law for a builder. This was devoid of checks and balances and lacked close supervision. After a while, some houses were built up to the window level while others remained at the slab level at which the contractor was reportedly to have vanished! Money, it was discovered had been misappropriated. Later, Mr. G.Y. Mumba who had facilitated for the church in getting a loan was assigned to negotiate the buying of Mapepe Farm with the view of raising money. (Mapepe Farm is the farm on which the current 17th Episcopal Residency now sits). Bishop Brookins had been asked to officially wed Mr. Mumba to a prominent lady in the church but the Bishop had turned down that request and suggested that Rev. David Simfukwe, a pastor should instead. Rev. Simfukwe wedded the couple.

While the Bishop was in the U.S.A. and was planning to come and repay the loan, they learned that the Construction Company responsible had filed for bankruptcy. This led the Bishop to back off on plans of raising money to repay the loan. When Bishop Brookin's term came to an end in the 17th Episcopal District, Bishop Cornelius Thomas succeeded him. However, Bishop Thomas showed no interest in pursuing the case of the hundred houses which had been started by his predecessor. He chose to have nothing to do with them for reasons best known to himself.

In a struggle to recover the money in order to continue the housing project, the Church hired Barrister Robert Mumba. However, Mr. Mumba died while the case was in the process of being finalized. Subsequently, Mwanawasa and Company was contracted to complete the task that Mr. Mumba had started. Sadly, being politically inclined, the case delved into further disarray since it was discovered that the management team had helped themselves with goods and funds and no other person outside the group knew the inventory and the case remained unresolved for years.

Since the farm had no one living on it, Mr. Godwin Yoram Mumba and his wife asked that they move into the farm house. Later, there was a claim made for the farm house possibly linking it to being a form of payment connected to the loan but the A.M.E. Church contested that and the matter ended up in court where Mr. G.Y. Mumba lost the case and he and his wife vacated the farm house. This was the time of Bishop Robert Pruitt and Rev. David Simfukwe, as Presiding Elder of Lusaka, was contesting the matter on behalf of the Church. He saved the loss of the farm and the farm house.

The coming of the late Bishop Richard Allen Chappelle in 1988 brought relief into my ministry. He reconciled many things and appointed me 17th Episcopal District Treasurer. Bishop Chappelle was a great administrator and his vision for the Church was sound. He supported the work of the Church and streamlined the work in the 17th Episcopal District. He brought a lot of literature materials, clothing including the robes for clergy, youth and revitalized the Farm and Episcopal Residence of the 17th Episcopal District in Lusaka where he spent considerable period of time within the District unlike many of his predecessors.

Bishop Preston Williams succeeded Bishop Larry T. Kirkland in 2000. Bishop Kirkland had replaced Bishop Robert Webster in 1996. Bishop Preston Williams came at the heightened period of the struggles in the Church when the Church in Africa through the African Jurisdiction Council (AJC) was pushing for election of native-born Africans to the Episcopal position. This push being at its peak led to the Bishop being incapable and visionless in what he could do in the District. The District was marred with a lot of confusion, thus the Bishop started with battles and ended with battles and surely accomplished nothing. During his tenure of office Rev. Wilson Mpundu left the African Methodist Episcopal Church and started Higher Dimensions Church. It was another painful loss of a great man of God by this Church which chose to elect (appoint) juniors to supervise a visionary leader by people who had made the Church spiritually stagnant for years.

Bishop Paul Jones Kawimbe succeeded Bishop Preston Williams in 2004. The words of the Lord were fulfilled. It is true, 'A prophet is not honoured in his homeland.' He tried to bring development to the District but the Bishop who succeeded him shot down everything he did or attempted to do.

(i) He received a farm of 200 hectares on which he intended to build a Conference Center
(ii) He obtained land at Kambalange Settlement Center for farming and a housing project iii. Bought a boat for water transport on Lake Mweru
(iii) Constructed a Refrigeration Facility at Mpulungu, Northern Province
(iv) Started a Guest House at Nakonde
(v) Obtained a farm and title deed in North Western Province
(vi) He established a 17th Episcopal District Headquarters in Lusaka which was disbanded by Bishop Messiah

viii. He started a Theological School for ministers. He travelled extensively in the Districts and went to countries other Bishops never attempted to and started A.M.E. Churches in those countries. He went to Rwanda, Burundi, Congo Brazzaville, Congo DR and Kenya. However, everything that had Bishop Kawimbe's signature was watered down by Bishop Wilfred Messiah.

When Bishop Paul Kawimbe left in 2012, he was replaced by Bishop Wilfred Messiah. Bishop Kawimbe had left me as the President of the Presiding Elders' Council. When Bishop Messiah came to the 17th Episcopal District, unfortunately, I had been invited by Bishop Kawimbe to South Africa where Bishop Kawimbe was hosting his first Annual Conference there. My absence and being in Bishop Kawimbe's Conference cost me the Presiding Elders' Presidency of the Council! I was replaced with Rev. Cosmas Wakunguma. Not only was I replaced, my two sons Rev. Peter Mwenya, Jr., and Rev. James Mwenya, because of our relationship with Bishop Kawimbe were transferred from a good city church to a small village church that was incapable of supporting them! Rev. James Mwenya complained to the Connectional General Secretary in the U.S.A. but no action was done!

As I was penning this in 2019, I felt disheartened to see the Church go this downhill. From the day and year Bishop Wilfred Messiah came, my two sons and I have never seen good days in this Church again! I was the Dean of Christian Education, Chairman of the Board of Examiners, member of the Episcopal Committee, member of the Revisions Committee and a member of the Elections Committee. As of 2019, I have had 48 year-unbroken service in the A.M.E. Church and in all the years, I have never been so frustrated and pushed around as I have been serving under Bishop Messiah.

I was moved from a well-supporting District to a very small District. I was demoted in order to make me frustrated and leave the Church. To my dismay, my juniors were elevated to the position of Bishop's Assistant and another person who hardly had served as a P.E. for a year was elevated without giving me a notice or even a reason why! I have often been forced to wonder as to whether the victimizations of my family and I were related to my connection to the previous Bishop! If one analyses what has happened to me and to my two sons who are also ministers in this Church, one is made to think that this Church lacks godly leadership.

At one time Bishop Messiah had transferred my son Rev. Peter Mwenya to another Conference! The transfer letter had Bishop Messiah's name and signature on it. However, when my son reported in the Conference he was transferred to and had presented the credentials to that effect, a transfer letter bearing the Bishop's own signature, the Bishop became abusive to my son for reporting to a Conference he had assigned him to! In spite of the evidence that my son produced, Bishop Messiah in full view of the Conference and in rage tore to pieces the transfer letter he had himself written for Rev. Peter Mwenya! It was embarrassing to see a Bishop tear the evidence he signed for Rev. Peter Mwenya's transfer in public!

My two sons have been put out of ministry for years now. They have been living without support and have been frustrated by the leadership that is supposedly appointed to serve God and administer justice to those who are called to preach the word. They have repeatedly seen evil in the House of their Heavenly Father from a vengeful and vindictive treatment from my supervisor Bishop Messiah. Nevertheless, the Lord had graciously granted me strength to stand firm as I serve my last three years remaining to my retirement."

This story makes my heart bleed as I write to highlight this unheralded soldier of the cross in this Church of Natives. Rev. M.P.P Mwenya is one of the very few ministers ever whose churches attracted scores of believers from other A.M.E. churches and denominations on Sunday services! It must be understood that the Church of God is the body of Christ. It is not A.M.E. Church, Baptist, Methodist, Anglican, Nazarene, Catholic, Pentecostal, etc. As some persons have put it, there are no Methodists, Baptists or Pentecostals in heaven, only believers in Jesus. Our experience showed that many ministers who failed to cut through denominational barriers were likely either pandering to traditions or were not preaching the word that brings about salvation of souls.

Rev. Peter Mwenya, one of Zambia's greatest preachers and revivalist preaching at the Annual Conference at Mother Hughes, Ndola during Bishop Robert Pruitt's tenure in 1985.

It was preaching the message of the cross, we were aware, which was offensive to the natural man. However, to those who were spiritual this word attracted them to God or to godly gatherings because it was not about a denomination but about Jesus. Believers who had realized and stood for this belief were the ones God used to turn around this Church which had been steeped deep in traditions of men for decades. Scores of believers traveled from other towns including other A.M.E. churches to go and hear Rev. Mwenya preach at his church. Few preachers would boast of this experience in this denomination.

Rev. Peter M.P. Mwenya, however, is a minister we would undisputedly credit with the revival in the A.M.E. Church in Zambia. He was one of the earliest ministers who preached salvation by faith when many others did not! He has had a strong apostolic ministry which has been characterized by signs and wonders just as our Lord Jesus Christ entailed. As an unsung hero and my former Pastor, I wanted to herald this story so that this Church may recognize that a Prophet is without honour in his home town just as our Lord Jesus Christ once said.

Presiding Elder Mwenya is a man who has led thousands of people to the Lord Jesus. He has brought into ministry over a hundred ministers both in and outside the A.M.E. Church. What a man of God he has been – a man who has been bruised for decades by Satan and his agents for standing true to God's calling of leading many to Jesus! It is a shame that a person who calls himself a Bishop could fail to recognize a servant of God with such a ministry! It is a shame that a person who calls himself a Bishop could choose a junior or juniors to supervise preachers who have served in this Church for decades simply because you want to control and manipulate them! When I talked to the Rev. Mwenya, he bemoaned the state of affairs in the Church in Zambia stating that "The current Bishop never consulted Presiding Elders in major decisions! He would make pastoral appointments indiscriminately, without their input, choosing to make them at Planning Meetings as opposed to the Annual Conferences!"

When I talked to other Presiding Elders, I was shocked how Messiah had appointed them to distant regions of Zambia to preside! Some of these areas take six hours or more to reach and the churches there are too poor to support them! I knew of at least three of such Presiding Elders! With my experience in ministering in Zambia, I found such appointments an indication of poor leadership and gross incompetence! Appointing a person who lives in Lusaka as P.E. of Mongu, another who lives in Lusaka as P.E. in Chipata or one who lives in Samfya to Mwense shows lack of judgment or empathy for those ministers since they would be too timid to decline! I looked at 1 Kings 12:8. It read: *"But Rehoboam rejected the advice the elders gave him and consulted the young men who had grown up with him and were serving him."* Filled with great sorrow and anguish, I laughed at the wisdom of the simple.

On Monday December 2, 2019, I talked on phone with Mother Diana Mapoma in Zambia. I asked her about how she viewed the Church and reminded her of her testimony to the Bishop, Cornelius Thomas when the Church (By this I meant leaders mostly outside the local church) had risen up against Rev. Mwenya. She gave a laughter and then said, "That had been a problem for years in our Church. This had to do with the foundation! Many of our founding fathers of the church were not educated and were not saved. As a result, they could not stand on truth. Many were even afraid to stand up and speak the truth even when they knew that the accusations which were being paraded were unsubstantiated and utterly untrue! The Church was steeped in traditions at the time and lacked sound teaching!" We both laughed at the failed machinations of the enemy, yet it was painful to see that many people had failed to honour this God's prophet who had been among them and sadly missed the visitation of God to them through him!

From Left to right: An unidentified Zimbabwean delegate, Rev. M.P.P. Mwenya and Rev. Wilson Mpundu at the General Conference in Cincinnati, Ohio which I also attended in July 2000. At the time, the 17th Episcopal District comprised Zimbabwe, Zambia, Malawi, Tanzania and Congo DR.

Chapter 27
Called, Committed and Compelled to Serve: The Story of Charles Kapungwe

My "First" Calling

As unorthodox as the term "First Calling" may appear to be, the truth it represents justifies its use for me. While theologians would cast a shadow of doubt on the use of words of "first," "second," "third" or even "fourth" calling, the circumstances applicable to them all warrant their use! Thus, the "First calling" takes place at a tender age of 7 in an unplanned fashion that points to the divine than to that of man's instigation.

We lived in the mining City of Kitwe, Zambia's second largest city on the Copperbelt Province. As boys, we loved to play with toy cars which we made out of clay, wires (including copper wires), plastic or metal ones if we came across them. We would go down our section to the banks of a huge drain that constantly had water flowing from the smelter of Rokana Division of Nchanga Consolidated Copper Mines (NCCM). The drain went into Kamatemate Stream then into the Kafue River. The drain separated B from C section and E from F Section.

City of Kitwe, the Hub of the Copperbelt Province and Zambia's second biggest city. In the background is Hotel Edinburgh and Zambia National Provident Fund (ZNPF) building. Photo taken on 8th May, 2020 by Robert Moyo.

We would take a 10 to 15 minutes' walk, cross the main road, Church Road in Wusakile that separated B from F Section. From B and F Section, Church Road crossed the bridge going to join Kitwe-Ndola Road, just in the vicinity of a narrow bridge, we would go under to scoop clay. "F Sectioners" or "Children of F Section," as we would call them were notorious for causing trouble. They would descend upon you and beat you up, so we made sure we ran away whenever they appeared. Once, one had put my shirt in human excreta because we used to put them on the bank to avoid them getting dirty!

We posted a sentry or two above on a mound. They would signal to us if "F Sectioners" were coming and we would immediately get our clay and shirts and run across the main paved road that divided the two sections to our side, B Section. Once on our side, we would evaluate if we needed to call it a day! In latter years, these boys began to fall into the hands of the law. They would beat up people who passed through their section which had about two routes and a main road popularly used by football fans going home to Chamboli after watching matches at Scrivener Stadium (Now Nkana Stadium). It was only after we had grown up that we came to learn many of the boys from this section abused drugs and were under influence of marijuana. Knowledge of this helped me to make up my mind as a child never ever to indulge in this evil! I had observed marijuana destroy friends as a youth.

One day, we had been in the ditch for just a few minutes when our sentry up signaled to us to come out quickly! "Children of F Section!" he had exclaimed. As we made our way out of the ditch heading to the road just a few meters away, we heard a voice of one of them urging us not to run! "We are friendly! Please don't run!" he calmly kept shouting! We crossed the road and stood about 30 meters away. The older boy who appeared to be the leader of the group of 5 boys was about 12 years-old. He had a great personality and beaconed to us to go to them emphasizing that they were friendly. This was unimaginable! We quickly gained their trust and crossed the road back. We introduced ourselves to one another. Our group comprised five boys. He told us his name was "Fighton Sikanyika." (Even though he was "Fighton" he never engaged in fights!).

Fighton then invited us to come to Sunday school "This coming Sunday morning." "Where?" we had asked. "At Methodist, there," he told us pointing in the direction. The Church was less than half a mile from where we were standing. We were on Church Road which had many churches on it. An extension of the road on the end of F Section had another line of churches. The churches lined up, were thus, Jehovah's Witnesses' Kingdom Hall, African National Church, Presbyterian Church, a Mosque, Jordan Chapel A.M.E. Church and United Church of Zambia (UCZ) [formerly Free Church of Scotland]. Next to UCZ was a huge concrete water reservoir for the mining townships and the engine building. Close to this was then a public mine's swimming pool, New Apostolic Church and then the drain where we had been scooping the clay from. Across the drain the road began to ascend and there was C7 Clinic, for miners, an open area (later a Pentecostal Church was built here in the 1980s), then a Catholic Church, Reformed Church in Zambia (formerly Dutch Reformed Church) and Anglican Church.

As a boy, we used to follow our older sister Mary to a Wusakile Catholic Church. We were young and my two older sisters were 11 and 9 and my younger brother 4. We went possibly out of curiosity to watch the white Father who spoke a local language. We were welcomed at the Methodist Church with my immediate younger brother Amos, Jr., and my two friends Andrew Chibuta, Brighton Musukwa and his younger brother Geoffrey Musukwa, and there began my long journey of learning about God. Those who had brought friends were asked to stand up and so were the visitors.

We were welcomed by the teacher Lloyd Morris Siwale. He soon became my mentor and for the next few years, I learned how to memorise Scripture and was a part of our learning of the Word. There was a huge calendar-like picture brochure or catalog of about 86.5 cm by 61 cm (approximately 34 inches by 24 inches). It nearly covered the entire front of the pulpit and had pictures of "Jesus" and many other Biblical characters in colour. They were my favourite visual stories which connected me to "heaven!" This must have been around 1969 or 1970.

I later joined Allen Endeavor League (A.E.L.), a precursor to Young People's and Children's Division (YPD). This is also known as Allen Christian Endeavor League (A.C.E. League). Wearing black shorts or trousers and white shirts and a black sash across the chest adorning white letters A.E.L., for boys, we visited the sick in hospital or did home-visiting. I was hardly 11. My teacher liked me and we competed in memorising Scriptures and the Christian Bookstores provided assorted study materials. There was one at Wusakile near the smelter and one at Chamboli Shopping Center. In early 1970s, YPD was known as "Juvenile!" So, we went to Juvenile on Saturdays and Br. Lloyd M. Siwale was our teacher. Often, I would go with him, both of us dressed in uniform to visit the sick in hospital or homes.

We then joined the Sunday School Choir. My first memorable trip was in 1972 when we went to Allen Temple A.M.E. Church in Mufulira. I was just 9. It was an Annual Conference, we were told, and Bishop Hartford H. Brookins, a new Bishop who had just been assigned to Zambia was at this Conference. I remember going to Mufulira driven on beautiful well-marked clean roads. We sang at that Conference. Three years later, I was "baptized," i.e., sprinkled. I was also elected Sunday school teacher at age 12, in 1975! Fighton Sikanyika's father retired from the mines (Nchanga Consolidated Copper Mines, Rokana Division) in 1974. They left for the village in Isoka and I never saw him again.

I enrolled in two Bible Schools in 1976 at the age of 13! At the time, whenever word went around about a new thing happening in our community, we would jump in! We had learned about Bible Way Correspondence School in Ndola and Emmaus Bible School in Luanshya from peers. The two schools were offering Bible School education via correspondence. They sent us beautiful lessons and booklets. Each lesson came with questions and once you answered all and finished that booklet you mailed your answers. It only cost 3 ngwee (approximately 3 cents) for postage and we mailed extra for return postage but the lessons were free! We boasted to one another as we showed the beautiful certificates (especially from Emmaus) and their beautiful study materials. We studied the Books of John, Romans, etc. I did most of the work myself and if I found a word or two in English difficult, I asked my dad or my cousin whenever he returned on holiday from boarding school. I did this for two years until I passed 7th Grade to go to Form I (now, Grade 8). Taking 9 classes made me stop my Bible Correspondence classes at the age of 15 in 1978.

My dad loved newspapers. He bought newspapers daily! Often, I would go ridding his 3-Speed bicycle in the morning and brought him the paper. He would ask me about the heading of the day and I had to explain! If I failed, it became a teaching moment! As I got older, I was amazed to learn that my grandmother and grandfather on my dad's side and my grandmother on my mother's side were "Natives," i.e., they belonged to the A.M.E. Church in Luapula Province! The Church, (African Methodist Episcopal Church or A.M.E. Church in Luapula where my dad hailed from and had trekked to the Copperbelt to look for employment, in 1953 was a well-known Church there, and their parents attended that Church! It was sometimes referred to as the "Native Church" and worshippers were sometimes referred to as "Natives!").

I called this my "First Calling!" Joining a Church "at random" I was not aware was a Church of my grandparents in the Village hundreds of miles away, I came to realise was orchestrated by God and not by man! When I thought through that there were nine churches close to our home but I was only led by the Lord to go to a church of my grandparents must have been directed by God. This, I figured, was never coincidental but consequential. We later moved to T Section and then to B Road near the Flats, Scrivener Stadium or Wusakile Hospital where dad retired from in 1991.

I was born on 27th September, 1963 in Kitwe in Northern Rhodesia! (I have always said Zambia but I would love to fit into the narration in this book! Northern Rhodesia gained her independence a year later, on 24th October, 1964 and became Zambia). I was born to Mr. Amos Kapungwe, Sr., and Mrs. Nancy Mulenga Kapungwe. Mr. Amos Kapungwe, Sr., was born on 6th June, 1935 to Jacob N. Kapungwe and Mrs. Fanny Mwape Kapungwe at Mwanda's Village, Chief Lubunda in Mwense District in Northern Rhodesia. He was a first-born son in a family of 9 children, 4 boys and 5 girls. My grandfather, Jacob, was born in 1914. He had named his sons Amos, Joshua, Aaron and Enoch (the last born). The girls were Nancy, Robinah, Manasseh, Jane and Elinah. He was an amazing man! At around age 73 in 1987, he could ask me to open the Bible, gave a Chapter and verse. When I opened there, he could start speaking the Scripture word for word without looking at it since his sight was not very sharp at the time. We could go through a number of Scriptures while he laughed, showing me what he was made of! He had passed on that "gene" to me!

My mother, Nancy Mulenga Kapungwe was born in 1940 at Ndaso's Village, Chief Kazembe in Kawambwa District. Mam was born to a chief and to Leah Chanda. Due to traditional disputes grandmother Leah separated with grandfather when mam was young. She was taken by her uncle Morgan who raised her up until she got married. Mr. and Mrs. Kapungwe had had 10 children, 6 girls and 4 boys.

I was a third born son. With 6 sisters, Mary, Foster, Mabel, Fridah, Gift and Cecilia and 3 brothers, Amos, Jr., Emmanuel and Bernard, we were children of a miner. My father Amos, Sr., went to Nsakaluba for school and attained Standard IV. He passed to Standard V but had no money so he went to Kitwe on the Copperbelt in 1953 to see his father who was working for the mines then. His father, however, was not very supportive because of lifestyle problems. My dad then got employed as a Garden boy to a white miner and when his boss saw that he was very intelligent he found him a job at the Mine Club, Nkana Mine Mess. He pursued his classes until he reached Standard VI. He married Nancy Mulenga Kapungwe on 27th June 1958.

Mr. Amos Kapungwe, Sr., Rev. Kapungwe's father, a Locomotive Driver, ZCCM Nkana Division, Kitwe 1980.

Mrs. Nancy Kapungwe, Rev. Kapungwe's mother at the wedding of her last-born Cecilia to Jonathan Mwale on 16th May, 2009 at Nkana East in Kitwe. With my mother is my aunt Mrs. Manasseh Chanda (fourth-born in dad's family). Sadly, Mr. Mwale passed away on 23rd July, 2020.

Mr. Kapungwe was later employed by the mines at Rokana Division of Nchanga Consolidated Copper Mines. NCCM later merged with Roan Copper Mines (RCM) to form Zambia Consolidated Copper Mines (ZCCM). He worked as a shunter then successfully completed his training as a locomotive driver. He worked as a locomotive driver for the mines hauling copper ore, concentrates and other goods for the mines until his retirement in 1991. He resettled at Mulungushi Agro Scheme Farm with his wife in Kabwe, Zambia. He fell sick for a few weeks and was taken to Kitwe Central Hospital admitted Friday September 20, 2013 and passed away on Monday September 23, 2013 at the age of 78 of pneumonia. He was buried in Kitwe on Thursday September 26, 2013. At the time of his death he was a Church Treasurer at his local church of United Church of Zambia having been converted to the Christian faith following his retirement. Mam passed away over two years later on 25th June, 2016.

Rev. Charles Kapungwe attended Nkana Primary School from 1971 to 1977 and Chamboli Secondary School from 1978 to 1982. From 1984 to 1987 he attended Chainama College of Health Sciences in Lusaka where he studied as a Clinical Officer (equivalent to Physician's Assistant). He obtained a Diploma in Clinical Medical Sciences. He was registered by the Medical Council of Zambia to practice medicine. He worked at Kitwe Central Hospital, Zambia's third largest hospital from 1987 to 1999. Pastor Charles trained as a Psychosocial Counselor dealing with HIV/AIDS patients in 1990 but continued to practice medicine concurrently.

Rev. Charles joined Jordan Chapel A.M.E. Church at the age of 7. He became a Sunday school teacher at the age of 12 and served there as Church Treasurer for 5 years from 1989 to 1994. He, with 12 other members from Jordan A.M.E. Church, with the blessings of Rev. David D. Musole of Jordan planted a new church, Calvary A.M.E. Church in 1994 (where he served as Pro Term). Then in 1996, exactly 100 years after the A.M.E. Church had reached South Africa and 67 years of its existence in Zambia, Bishop Larry T. Kirkland of the then 17th Episcopal District appointed him to be pastor of Trinity A.M.E. Church in Kitwe. He was ordained Itinerant Deacon in 1997 and Itinerant Elder in 1999 by Bishop Kirkland. Rev. Charles had preached at Brookins in Kabwe the birthplace of the A.M.E. Church in Zambia in 1987, exactly 200 years after the A.M.E. Church was founded in the U.S.A. This was when the Bicentennial Celebrations were being held and it was 58 years after the Church had been established at Kabwe. This is the same year he first got employed by Ministry of Health in Zambia on 1st October, 1987.

Rev. Charles served as Pastor of Trinity A.M.E. Church from 1996 to 2000. He attended Faith L.I.F.E. Ministries Bible School in Kitwe, Zambia from 1998 to 2000 and obtained a Diploma in Biblical Studies and Christian Education. Pastor Kapungwe was Associate Pastor to Rev. Leroy Cannon at White Hall A.M.E. Church from 2000 to 2004 while studying at Allen University. He obtained a B.Sc. Degree in Biology in May 2004 from Allen University and enrolled in the Doctor of Medicine/graduate dual degree programme with St. Matthew's University School of Medicine of Grand Cayman, Cayman Islands and St. Joseph's College of Maine, Standish, Maine, respectively. Charles completed Basic Science training in medicine in 2006 and took leave of absence waiting to finish his one and half years of clinical rotations to complete his medical education.

He obtained a Master's in Health Services Administration from St. Joseph's College of Maine in May 2008. He also obtained four Associate Degrees in Maine; U.S.A. Rev. Charles got born again in May 1985 while in his first year in the College of Health Sciences in Lusaka, Zambia. He got baptized in the Holy Spirit in 1987 and became greatly involved in the YPD and Youth Fellowships in Zambia. Charles was the National Chairman of the Healthcare Christian Fellowship of Zambia, (HCFZ) and national leader from 1991 to 1999. Rev. Charles Kapungwe's desire was to be involved in medical missions and share the saving power and knowledge of our Lord and Savior Jesus Christ. He is grateful to God and to all who have made it possible for him to be where he is.

I had desired to become a medical doctor. When I completed secondary school in 1982, I had not gone to the University. The economy began to go down in the 1980s and going into college became highly competitive. I began praying that "Lord if you make this possible, I will work for you!" Miraculously, I did apply and was called for written tests at the only school offering clinical medicine studies in Lusaka, Zambia. After passing written tests, I was shortlisted for personal interviews which I passed too! 200 students had come vying for only 40 positions! I began training in September, 1984. I also obtained GCE "O" Level Certificates in Physics with Chemistry in 1984 and Mathematics in 1985 from University of London.

Distressed in spirit, I began searching for God for two weeks. I had a strong conviction that I had walked away from the Lord I had known as a boy. Thankfully, Chainama College of Health Sciences Christian Fellowship, a member of Zambia Fellowship of Evangelical Students

(ZAFES), an affiliate with the International Fellowship of Evangelical Students (IFES), organised a week-long Revival Meeting at the College. It was held in the Double Classroom, one of our lecture rooms. The first day, I failed to respond to the invitation even though I had gone there with the view of doing so. "You are already a Christian! You have been a preacher, a teacher in Sunday school and a Choir member! Why should you disgrace yourself when you are already a Christian? Besides, these guys will be blocking your freedom," a voice kept telling me. I listened to it and never responded to that invitation the first day.

The second night, the voice kept on saying the same words to me. A very powerful word, delivered by, I think Brother Lubinda Sitali (now Rev. Lubinda Sitali in the United Church of Zambia in Southern Province), came on this night. I still did not go upfront when the invitation was done. Brother Dygate Thindwa, my former classmate and a believer in the Scripture Union at Chamboli Secondary School in Kitwe, now a schoolmate at Chainama College of Health Sciences was in the meeting as well. He was 9 months ahead of me. He stood up and spoke in front that "God was calling someone here! You need to come in front and you know who you are! Just come and give your life to Jesus!"

I knew it was me! I stood up and went in front. With tears I knelt down. A second student followed me behind. We were led into a sinner's prayer and I got saved! It was the "Second calling!" About 40 students were present. If you call it a first calling, I still wouldn't blame you! The transformation was evident. I became a member of the Fellowship and we had regular meetings every week. Every Wednesdays, we met for evangelistic meetings. One of the leaders of the fellowship or an invited guest from outside came to preach. We met from 18:00hrs to 20:00hrs. On Fridays, we had prayer meetings. We prayed as individuals or corporately and we took prayer requests or generally prayed for specific items. The testimonies of answered prayers in consecutive meetings were phenomenon and real! We then met for Bible studies every Sundays at the same time. The Fellowship personified God and presented him in the "Now" as opposed to my Church which presented him in stories and in the "Past."

Within a few months I was selected by the leaders to attend Discipleship Training (DT 100). It was held at the neighbouring Natural Resources Development College (NRDC) on Great East Road, Lusaka. The training, among other things, taught us how to target people we were to reach out to. We were to love them genuinely, befriend them and regularly pray for them. After a while, when opportunity arose, we were to share the gospel to them, and God was going to do the rest! Through this approach, I soon won my first soul to the Lord in 1985, Martin Makweti, a classmate. We were on our way to Chama, Eastern Province, for our first practical training and on a United Bus Company of Zambia (UBZ) bus, I began sharing the word of God to him. When we reached Luangwa Bridge, Martin was ready to receive the Lord. He accepted him!

After spending two days at Chipata General Hospital we headed for Chama Rural Hospital in November, 1985. We had a very beautiful newly completed hostel at Chipata with warm water and new beds! At Chama, I found a Fellowship which met at a Primary School. The school was less than a kilometer from a nearby Secondary School. The fellowship was amazingly powerful and unbelievably great for a rural setting and I was amazed to see how vibrant and powerful the saints there were! About 30 years later, one of the brothers from that Fellowship, Br. Joseph Kansema (now a Pastor in South Africa) who I was aware was in Botswana found my book on the Internet and located me via an email. He was now a pastor in South Africa. We also talked on phone!

The power of God at work which I witnessed at Chama has never left my memory! One testimony I remember from there, shared with excitement, and brethren after brethren, chipping in, described a day when one of the brothers was standing under a tree and right above his head was a snake! The brethren told him not to move and he didn't! They then commanded the snake to leave in the name of Jesus! The snake obeyed and left going higher away from the brother! The joy among the brethren was contagious and so was their love for one another! Two twin sisters there were singers and they were marvelous, full of the Spirit of God. In fact, I was told a crusade had just ended at Lundazi, a closest town few weeks earlier.

Another testimony involved my personal encounter with God while at Chama Rural Hospital. It became a life-changing encounter for me. As students, we were required to bring to College two short case histories and one long case history. It was our first clinical experience in which we screened and treated patients. Synthesizing, medical knowledge from theoretical class work into practical real-life situation was exciting but challenging as well. We could consult one another or the Clinical Instructor at the Hospital but for unexplained reason I decided to keep to myself one very challenging case I had chosen for my long case. I chose a Mr. Mumba, for two reasons: First, he was a retired miner from neighbouring Chingola town on the Copperbelt Province where I grew up and I could speak in a language he understood without any problem. Second, I felt compassion for him laying down in a rural hospital being attended to by students and wished he were in the city where the mines provided excellent free medical care. For these two reasons I, endeavoured to do the best for him.

The presenting complaints of Mr. Mumba were challenging to this new student. He had heart palpitations, delirium (some episodes of confusion), diarrhea, swelling of legs and tiredness. As I wrote the symptoms, I knew how difficult this was but I had correctly identified the systems involved and correctly inquired and wrote down reviews of those systems involved. I then had examined them (the patient) and came up with a provisional diagnosis. I was afraid it was not the real diagnosis I had wanted, therefore, I needed to find out more. I however, gave the provisional treatment which too, was of symptomatic in nature than a curative one. Nevertheless, I never forgot about my patient since I was thinking about him constantly.

During lunch hour, we sat in the large spacious living room which also doubled as a dining place. After the meal, I debated within my mind as to what book I would read before returning for work at 14:00 hrs. Our hostel was just across the hospital. I picked up the Holy Bible and a medical text book, Davidson's Principles and Practice of Medicine, which was our standard textbook of choice in Internal Medicine. When I sat down, for unknown reason, I put the Bible on the side and took the medical book instead and unpremeditatedly opened to a page which I never flipped after I was on it. I began to read that page without any cause for it! The book had over 1,000 pages and the page I had opened had not been read by me perhaps in months after we had learned about this condition in class.

I read the definition of the disease with its introduction. I then came to the paragraph on signs and symptoms. As I read the symptoms and was about to finish, the Spirit spoke to me audibly in my mind, (the same way Satan had been telling me not give my life to God because I was a "good person!") This time, the words came with my name, *"Charles, Don't you think your patient in the ward has this kind of disease?"* As soon as I heard that in my head, my eyes were opened and I recognised the symptoms and they matched my patient's complaints, exactly! (My four friends were having a conversation and were right in front of me in the dining area and I was on the sofa but they never heard that voice!).

I was reading on the chapter on Nutritional Disorders. I was reading on a condition called *"Beriberi."* It was Vitamin B-1 Deficiency also known as Thiamine Deficiency. Before we came to Chama, we were warned of the starvation in the area because of the drought that had devastated the area. We therefore, had to buy our food supplies ahead of time at Chipata to avoid starvation. We also had seen a truck from the World Food Programme distributing food in the area. I quickly went to the treatment portion of the narration. To date, I still remember what Davidson's read: "One of the great advances of medicine," it narrated, "is that once it has been ascertained that the patient is suffering from Beriberi and is put on thiamine, within two days his heart palpitations go away, his diarrhea stops and delirium disappears too. Edema subsides and the patient begins to feel stronger." It was my first time I had experienced God speak to me so "audibly" in my spirit following my salvation and I put to rest my questions of "How do they know God said this or that to them?"

In the afternoon, I changed or added to the treatment plan thiamine which fortunately, was available at the hospital. Within two days, my patient improved and he smiled at me when I went to see him during morning ward rounds! I gave him a piece of paper on which I described the condition and how to avoid it in future. He was so excited that he invited me to his home but I couldn't make it. This is the Lord I knew I was going to carry to the world. He had been faithful.

When I returned to Lusaka, I began to be hurt each time I went to church. I attended Chamba Valley (now Mother Lubemba A.M.E. Church) at Kaunda Square Stage I which was across the Great East Road from our Chainama Complex (College and Hospital) and it was about a 40-minute walk. I also attended Mother Thomas Temple at Mtendere from time to time, especially for youth meetings. It was only 15 minutes' walk from our College. I began to get the fire inside me to share the true God because it was painful to me to sit listening to the so-called "parables and tales" void of the power of God or of the Holy Spirit in church.

I purposed to make my Jesus known. I applied to be a preacher at Chamba Valley in 1986, but the pastor, Rev. Laston Sichangwa asked me a number of questions as to why I wanted to be a preacher. (Rev. Sichangwa had replaced Rev. Samson S.K. Tembo who had been appointed Presiding Elder for Eastern Province and had moved to Chipata). I told him why and he asked me to write a letter to the Official Board which I did. I attended the meeting and after some deliberations, my letter was considered and I began to preach the gospel in Lusaka. I also shared Jesus in the YPD every Saturdays either at Mother Thomas or at Mother Lubemba. From time to time I would take the team from the College Fellowship to my church. Once,

I took the fire baptized, Spirit-filled zealous brethren to a YPD meeting at Mother Thomas at Mtendere in Lusaka! They set the place on fire and prayed for people with all power and love and seriousness! Thank God we were not banned!

In 1986, I had the opportunity to meet Rev. David K. Simfukwe at Ebenezer A.M.E. Church in Lusaka. I had known him for years but we never ever sat down to talk about the Church. I had introduced myself and we sat in his house. He showed me his work and it was at this meeting that I had learned more about the history of the A.M.E. Church in Zambia. I learned that it had started in Zambia at Kabwe in 1929, Ndola 1930 and so forth. We discussed what he was doing and he shared with me that he saw hope in the Church in the youth like me. There was a meeting at Ebenezer at the time and as usual I took opportunity to share the word to as many people as was possible. I was not aware at the time that I was going to need the Rev. David Simfukwe's work which together with Rev. J.L.C. Membe's, were going to be valuable for me in the future. Their work was done on stencil paper, an old method or technology that hindered its worldwide distribution. God was going to change this, just over three decades later.

I did my clinical practical at Kasama General Hospital in Kasama for two months in 1986. I had a privilege of meeting Rev. Greenfel D. Kabwe at the A.M.E. Church there. I had recalled from my reading that the Church had reached Kasama I think in 1932 but I found a new church building under construction using concrete blocks. This was at Solomon's Temple. To their credit, the structure looked better than some church buildings I had seen in some towns on the Copperbelt Province. Nevertheless, when I received photos for this work in September 2018 from the Presiding Elder and Pastor, Rev. Mazimba, I noticed that 32 years later this building was still under construction!

My daughter in the Lord in 2020 has been attending this church after moving back to Kasama. She is a school teacher and she gave the building a failing grade – the agony of many A.M.E. church buildings in Zambia! I began attending YPD meetings and began to share the word of God and the grace of the Lord was present. When I returned to Lusaka, I continued with the ministry at both Chamba Valley (now Mother Lubemba) at Kaunda Square and at Mother Thomas (Mtendere) sharing Jesus mostly to the youth and to the congregations.

I had a stint at Samfya Rural Hospital the same year. We continued with the "order" or advice of declaring who we were each time we went out from the Fellowship in Lusaka to any practical area within Zambia. We had been trained to inform those we met that "We were born again Christians." We then lived to defend that confession devotedly via a lifestyle that demonstrated that confession! This had been the grace the Lord had cultivated in me and was the grace I had been called to: to share even in the A.M.E. Church when the Lord called me. It came from God and not from man.

After arriving at Samfya, I went to look for an A.M.E. Church the following day. While pointing for me in the direction, my guide told me, "They used to meet there but their pastor had some problems and they do not meet anymore!" It saddened my heart. As I was walking, I found myself following a group of youths just in front of me and when I drew closer; I heard them discussing the word of God passionately! When I caught up with them, we greeted one another and I introduced myself. I learned they were members of a Pentecostal Church which used to meet at one of the nearby schools. We became friends! I attended their Church and I was with them for two months. They too had a very powerful fellowship and one song I learned there still helps my faith to surge each time I sing it. It reminds me of the faithful saints whom God has scattered all over the world.

Later in the year, I was attached at the Liteta Leprosium for a month. It was several kilometers away from Kabwe. I returned to Lusaka and continued to learn and do the work of God with great passion testifying to the Lordship of Jesus in the A.M.E. and outside. In early 1987, Pastor Joe Simfukwe, a Baptist Minister and theologian, a lecturer at a Bible school came as a guest speaker to our College Fellowship on a Wednesday night. He was a well-respected Teacher of the word in Lusaka and beyond. He spoke about the Holy Spirit so effectively that this day marked another milestone in my Christian faith. He told us that he had been skeptical on the topic of Baptism in the Holy Spirit for years and took several years to study this subject until God showed him its importance. It was a different experience from salvation, he had indicated and in nearly all cases in the New Testament, he said, "There was evidence of speaking in new tongues by those who received the baptism."

When he ended the teaching, he told us that he was not going to call people in front to be prayed for to receive the Holy Spirit. He however, instructed us to go and pray when we went to our rooms and urged us to go and ask God in prayer to fill us with the Holy Spirit, that is, to be baptized! That day, in my room I asked God to baptize me in the Holy Spirit and he did! As I prayed, the Holy Spirit came on me and I started praying in a new language that I didn't understand! This experience, therefore, changed my ministry and prayer life!

Later that year, I bade farewell to Mother Lubemba A.M.E. Church at Kaunda Square Stage I one Sunday morning in April 1987. I was going out for Obstetrics and Gynaecology practical at Kabwe General Hospital in Kabwe (formerly Broken Hill), Central Province for six weeks. I had been praying to share Christ wherever I went and I knew it was my opportunity to share Christ at Brookins A.M.E. Church, the place where the A.M.E. Church had been planted first in 1929 in Zambia.

This meant a lot spiritually for me and in the spiritual realm, I had thought. I needed to claim the Church from where the roots began. After a week of being at the hospital, I visited Brookins on a Saturday afternoon around 13:30 hrs., 58 years after the Church was first planted here. I was highly expectant of seeing a great "Mother Bethel" of Zambia. I had asked for directions and I found it was just a few minutes' walk from the hospital. To my shock and disappointment, the church was a small structure that could possibly hold only about 100 people or less and I think was made of clay, maybe plastered. My heart sank within me!

I was the first to arrive. I noticed that less than 10 meters from the old church, a new foundation of a new church had been laid. It had about one-course of concrete blocks completed. The structure, I estimated could hold maybe 250 or so people. There were a few concrete blocks stuck nearby. I sat down on the new foundation's one-course concrete block and broke down. I wept for the Church with tears flowing amidst great sorrow and pain. I was there for about fifteen minutes repenting of our sins as a Church and deeply overwhelmed with a sense of failure to progress prevalent in the Church.

When I looked up, I saw a man seated about 100 meters away at a house. I walked to the man and introduced myself. He offered me a chair. He was Rev. Khumalo, the Pastor, I learned. He was outside the mission house. We then had a conversation and talked about a lot of issues to do with faith. We talked about "New Churches which are coming up," as he put it, and Christianity. I explained the concepts of salvation and he told me that there had been a crusade just a week ago across the main road (Lusaka Road). He was an open-minded man and we shared out of respect for each other. When the youth finally came, I went in and we had our YPD meeting. I learned later that the City had ordered the church to demolish the new church building after it had reached the window level. The inspectors found the construction faulty. After the demolition, some bricks had been stolen and construction stalled for two years. This news was painful to listen to as well.

The following day, a Sunday, I stood up when they called for visitors. We all walked in front and the Secretary took our names. She then introduced us one by one. When she came to me, I was surprised by her unexpected comments to the congregation! "This is Bro. Charles Kapungwe! He is from Chamba Valley (now Mother Lubemba) A.M.E. Church in Lusaka and he is a very powerful preacher!" She then mentioned a lady who had told her about my coming for a while to Kabwe! "He is a great preacher!" she told the church.

The comments caught me off-guard! Of course, the praise was a little embarrassing for me and I never expected or anticipated such an introduction! I didn't come with a letter from the church nor did I anticipate such an introduction, therefore, I was genuinely surprised! I also had not expected to be known by anyone here! I nevertheless, spoke no word. There were no cell phones, text messages or emails in the year 1987 as it is today! She must have heard it possibly in person in the course of the week by either being in Lusaka or somebody from Lusaka who must have visited Kabwe. Perhaps, it could have been by phone – maybe by a landline phone but it still was a surprise!

After a couple of weeks or so, Rev. Khumalo gave me an opportunity to preach at Brookins Chapel! In those days, I never mounted the podium to preach without fasting and praying. It was a deed I had practiced for years. When the day came, the Lord spoke so powerfully that the church was electrified by the power of the Lord. When I ended the message, I asked Rev. Khumalo to make an invitation but he told me to continue and invite people to Christ. The people came in front. One of the people responding to receive Jesus was a lady I had recognized who had been a churchmate at Jordan Chapel A.M.E. Church at Wusakile in Kitwe on the Copperbelt Province.

She must have been as surprised as I was to meet each other in such a manner! She must also have been amazed to hear me preach in a manner I had not been when we were together on the Copperbelt. It must have been a great shock indeed to her, I thought! As she came to answer to the Lord's call, she fell down powerfully and demons manifested. Everyone was just observing. No one had touched her. As I moved towards her, I felt as though I was floating! The power of the Holy Spirit was so overwhelmingly great that you would notice and feel. I commanded the demons to go even though it was my first experience. Other people responding received the Lord as well.

I thanked God for what he had done. There was no indifference shown to the gospel and people welcomed the grace of God enthusiastically. It was several years later that I came to learn that the lady who had welcomed and introduced me at Brookins was Mother Elizabeth Nelinya Lukamba Simyembe! I had recognized her when I saw her in Kitwe. She now was a member of Bright Chapel where, unknown to me then, her husband had been a Pastor here several years earlier! She was, a daughter of one of the pioneering fathers of the work in Zambia, the Rev. Henrique M. Lukamba, P.E., who passed away a few days after I had prayed with him in the hospital I worked on 14th July, 1992.

The Rev. Lukamba had been one of my favourite ministers who added a mood of expectation every time he came to Jordan. I was young then and I had never known that her daughter and now a widow of Rev. Warren Simyembe who passed away in 1971 (when I was in first grade) would play a role in my writing this work 30 years later, in 2017! She contributed significantly to this writing when I was gathering my material! Her wedding to Rev. Warren Simyembe in 1956, I came to learn, had actually taken place at Jordan Chapel, my childhood church! What a God of miracles we serve!

Two weeks or so later, I attended an overnight Choir Competition at Membe A.M.E. Church in Kabwe, (formerly, Broken Hill). Several choirs were in attendance including those from Ndola. I went seeking to have an opportunity to share the gospel with many. It is here that I met a young believer by the name of Happy Mulwe from Mother Hughes in Ndola. He had travelled with the choir and had an older brother and sister who sang in the choir. They were YPDers too. Another, older brother of his Aram Mulwe was later to be ordained as a Pastor. Bro. Happy Mulwe was also later to be Rev. Happy Mulwe. He was a born again believer and it was exciting to share and find common ground. Unknown at the time, he was going to be a partner in ministry in igniting the Fire of the Holy Spirit in the lives of the youth and in our churches later.

While in Kabwe, I was invited to attend a National Conference of the Hospital Christian Fellowship, (HCF). It is also known as Healthcare Christian Fellowship. The Conference was held at Jim Ford's Farm, a well-known farm in Kabwe. The owner was a white believer who had helped impart the word in many who were hosted at this farm for years. The National Scripture Union Camp meetings used to take place here and Zambia's revival in Schools cannot be mentioned without attributing it to the work of this servant of the Lord at this farm. It is here that my "Third calling," which was into the Healthcare field came to me. I was to share the gospel to patients, members of the healthcare team and their families.

There were a lot of uncertainties on our postings as we came towards the end of our training. I began to pray that God would send me to Kitwe Central Hospital. I had a burden for Jordan Chapel, my childhood church and I had wanted to share Jesus there. Three people chose Kitwe Central Hospital and two (a man and a woman) did not pass the final exams. They repeated for six months. I was the only one who passed of the three and I was sent to Kitwe Central Hospital! I began work on 1st October, 1987 under the Ministry of Health. I stayed with my parents and siblings for a year and began the ministry of proclaiming Jesus as Lord and Saviour at Jordan under the power of the Holy Spirit. We faced great opposition from those who thought we were bringing a foreign doctrine but we stayed on course, declaring Jesus as Lord urging people to believe in him to be saved and not trusting in the Church system.

When I arrived at Jordan, I began with the youth, the YPD. I also preached to the congregation on Sundays when opportunity availed. I made it clear in my preaching that people needed to be born again. This message I declared without wavering from it. I had identified a team and worked with it. I was glad my childhood friend and Sunday school peer Aaron Siwale had gone to Theological College of Central Africa (TCCA) to train in Ministry. He was going to be a partner in ministry too. His younger brother Shadreck Siwale was saved too and he was to be another coworker. The two were younger brothers of my mentor and former Sunday school teacher Lloyd Morris Siwale who now was not a member of the A.M.E. Church. He had gone to the University of Zambia and like many educated youths at the time, had left the Church.

As we continued to minister, we found that God had begun saving a number of youths at the church. I met Bro. Richard Kasanda who had left for Ndola. He had met the Lord there and when he returned to Jordan, he brought strength to our Fellowship. Others were Loveness Chewe and her Sister Kampamba Mwango, Sandra Nanyinza and his brother, Sunday Sinyinza. Bro. Shadreck led one sister to the Lord. She had been troubled by evil spirits. She was delivered at her home and she became an integral member of the growing fellowship of believers. Nearly all were youths. We had Sisters Threasa Namfukwe, Mirriam Mwape, Mirriam Nakapizye, Rose Mwape, and Br. Bernard Mwape, to name a few. I had found Elasto Mwansa at home and shared the gospel. He received the Lord and was a great resource to this Fellowship. Years later, he was to replace me as a Pastor at Trinity in Kitwe after my departure for the U.S.

Dissatisfied with the way of worship, we formed a Fellowship at the church. It was meant to help share the word without any hindrance. We met after the main Sunday service at 14:00 hrs. The spiritual fervency was great and I was elected Chairman. We formed a choir whose songs radiated power because all the singers were born again, prayerful and the message they presented bore testimony of their lives. This began to impact the church. We now began person to person evangelism reaching out to church members who we knew were not saved. We went in their homes and shared Jesus with them!

One day, we were to visit one of the women in the church at Chamboli Township. We knew she did not know the Lord. Shadreck, Mirriam Nakapizye and I planned to meet Saturday at the church then go to visit those we had in mind. We were to meet on a Saturday at 9:00 hrs. After waiting for Sister Mirriam for an hour, we left word at the Mission House informing them to let Mirriam know where she would find us. We were welcomed by the woman at her house in H Section. She had a daughter of about 3. "My husband," she told us, "Has just left for a walk." He was not a member of our church therefore, we hardly knew him.

We soon began to share the gospel to the lady. After a while, she was ready to accept Jesus. We were just the two men with her and as soon as we began to lead her into a sinner's prayer, suddenly, without warning, the demons manifested powerfully! She fell down and began to sprawl around uncontrollably. For a second, we were speechless, stunned and just looked at each other with Shadreck. The dress began to expose her body and immediately, the little girl began to cry. Without being directed, Bro. Shadreck promptly, began to cover the woman and within a minute there was a knock at the door! As I went to answer the call, to my relief, Sister Mirriam was at the door! She immediately understood what had transpired and took over the role of Shadreck while I ordered the demons to leave in the name of Jesus!

Jordan Chapel A.M.E. Church Wusakile, Kitwe 1990 Fellowship members. Charles Kapungwe, Silvier Nachalwe, Misozi Witi, Mirriam Nakapizye and Shadreck Siwale (Rev. Aaron Siwale's brother) and two children squatting.

Two or so minutes later, another knock was heard on the door. It was the husband with a cigarette in his hand! I politely asked him to stop smoking and he did. He left the house and went away leaving us behind helping his wife. After the demons had left, we led her to the Lord! It was a victory that I have cherished for years. I was thankful to the Lord because that incident could have brought a lot of darts on us from the enemy at the church but our God is a Man of War! He granted us victory over Satan and we continued to testify about his power!

I continued to pray for those who I was to reach out to weekly. This Sunday, after church service, I was to speak to a young man, in 12th grade, Moses Kapembwa. Moses had grown up in the church but he had not known Jesus, I was aware. After the service, I approached him and began a conversation about his relationship with the Lord. He told me he was better than some of the people in the church! We began to walk as he headed home, a 40 minutes' walk on the road from Wusakile to Chamboli. I had studied a book on Soul Winning and had read about the excuses people gave on not wanting to receive Jesus. I therefore, had a Scripture to provide Moses with, to all the excuses he gave me and the Lord began to minister to him. When we were 5 minutes' walk away from his home, still on the main road, Moses was ready to accept Jesus! We stopped on the side of the road about a meter away from the tarmac and led him in a sinner's prayer. I encouraged him to pray and read the Bible asking him to specifically read the book of John. I then returned to the church thanking God for his wonders.

It was, however, Moses' testimony the following Sunday that left the Fellowship dumbfounded! Moses attended our Fellowship for the first time after Sunday service in the afternoon and gave a very moving testimony. After parting with me, he had gone home to his room and began to pray. He had prayed for a long time and something had happened to him which he had never experienced or seen before! He had begun to speak in tongues, a thing that surprised his mother! (Her mother was a member of our church as well). She had come to check on him but Moses had continued to pray for hours even though he had noticed her! We gave God the glory and explained to him what being baptised in the Holy Spirit was all about! What a wonder-working God we serve!

We had Kitwe District Young People's and Children's Division (YPD) meetings regularly. The Church had somehow many programmes which drew the A.M.E. churches in Kitwe together either monthly or bimonthly. The Women Missionary Society (W.M.S.) also met at their local churches or held joint meetings within the city. In order to reach out to the rest of the churches in Kitwe, I ran for the Presidency of the YPD and after being elected Kitwe District YPD President, we put in, by the grace of God, a formidable team which began to reach out to other circuits. Our meetings were often fully packed and had at least a minimum of 200 youths on many occasions. Different circuits hosted us according to our calendar. Jesus was preached and our emphasis was on getting saved, praise and worship, evangelism and discipleship. The churches in Kitwe participating were Jordan Chapel, Bright Chapel, Gethsemane, St. Peter, Mindolo (later changed to Judah by our brother Richard Kasanda when he assumed the role of Pastor in latter years), Membe, Trinity and St. John. This was before Mumba, Calvary and Covenant were established.

Scores of youths gave their lives to Jesus. A memorable name is Sister Elizabeth Simwanza Siwale from Mindolo, the future wife of Rev. Aaron Siwale and Pamela Muyemba Kasanda, the future wife of Rev. Richard Kasanda. In order to help churches, we came up with visitation programmes of churches, similar to the one we were doing at Jordan to share Jesus to individuals. This wouldn't have been viable if we were pastors at the time but as youths we could "Go in any territory and share Jesus!"

Once, we did home visitations at Bright Chapel in Kitwe! Bright Chapel was a very resistant ground to the work of the Spirit! We had visited many people including the home of the Br. Charles Chibwe, a senior leader, before his wife Sis. Ruth had passed away. We had prayed with them. Several years later, (maybe two decades later) I heard of a moving testimony that Bro. Chibwe was a well-known evangelist at the prison (the biggest prison on the Copperbelt, Kamfinsa Prison). He leads prisoners to Christ there. He had mentioned to people that he had thought Bro. Bright Mumba and I had been destroying the Church until he found the Lord! He mentioned what a great work we had been doing. I talked to him on phone in 2017! What a joy it was!

Pastor Bright Mumba. One of the greatest revivalists of our time, a great prayer warrior and intercessor who brought many souls to the Lord especially among the youth. He was a great partner in ministry.

I also contested for the position of 1st Vice President of the South Zambia Annual Conference. Bro. Emmanuel Membe became the President. By getting into leadership, we thought it was going to provide us with opportunity to share Jesus and not be spectators. It was the biggest Conference and it stretched from Mongu to Chipata and from Livingstone to Mwinilunga. With Brethren such as Richard Kasanda, we explored all opportunities to share Jesus. In 1988, we met at the Northern Technical College (NORTEC) in Ndola and found that God had been converting scores of youths in our Church across the nation. We had a memorable fellowship and sung throughout the night at that Conference which had hundreds if not a thousand youths at this meeting. (After the main event, believers remained behind with a warm fellowship).

We sang the all night with praise and worship. We were with Br. Bright Mumba, Richard Kasanda and many from the Copperbelt and our brethren from Lusaka Charity Nakazwe, Vera Nachilima, Irene Nakazwe, Yvonne Chinakila and many more. This was the last YPD South Zambia Convention in which the team led by Bro. Abraham Sachikola and had the likes of Bro. Stephen Chifunda, Ojoni Gondwe, Deborah Membe, Alberto Mwansa, and others retired. When the W.M.S. leadership was intimidating us, we stood united and sung joyously, "They cannot separate us, we are one family!"

A similar gathering, a Retreaty had been held at Chalimbana in Lusaka in 1988 under the auspices of the 17th Episcopal District, then comprising Malawi, Zambia and Zimbabwe. Bro. George Mwambazi, a businessman of Lusaka had given us a cow for food. The other YPD huge South Zambia Convention took place in Livingstone in 1988. Sharing the name of Jesus at these meetings was our goal and if we did not speak to the Convention directly, we did individual outreaches, carrying out person to person evangelism and hundreds of youths were in attendance in these gatherings.

Once, we had planned for a Seminar at Jordan Chapel at Wusakile in Kitwe. It came hardly two or so months after a meeting in Ndola where the South Zambia Annual Conference YPD Convention had been held at NORTEC in 1988. We held a Seminar at Jordan Chapel organized by our local leadership. We invited our brethren from Lusaka A.M.E. Churches. They had been as enthusiastic as us and were burning with the zeal of the Lord. Our brethren in Lusaka had been doing similar works there like us on the Copperbelt, spearheaded by Bro. Happy Mulwe who now had moved to Lusaka from Ndola.

We however, were taken aback to hear that our Seminar had been canceled by the authorities! The cancellation came at a short notice just about three days or so before the YPD Seminar! The YPD Director had talked to the Copperbelt District Presiding Elder urging him to cancel the meeting, "since we just finished attending another Conference in Ndola!" The letter reached me at the 11th hour and by this time our brethren from far places such as Lusaka were already in Kitwe.

We tabled the matter with Rev. Samuel Mulapwa, himself a born-again believer and son in the Lord of Rev. M.P.P. Mwenya from Mufulira. He now was our Pastor at Jordan at this time. He gave us authority to continue because "Prayers cannot be stopped by any person," he ruled. We had also reached at this conclusion that they cannot stop us preaching the word. The South Zambia YPD Director Mrs. Victoria Samuchapi who was a member of Bright Chapel in Kitwe at the time, had passed through to see if there was any activity going on. Sadly, our attendance had dropped to just around 30 because of that "cancellation" letter which had been distributed. Months later, I worked under this YPD Director as 1st Vice President of YPD of South Zambia and she did provide me with great respect and we worked well together! Also, years later, the Presiding Elder, Rev. Cuthbert Katebe who had been influenced to cancel our YPD Seminar, was the man who recommended me for appointment to Trinity A.M.E. Church as Pastor! We worked together amicably and by the grace of God, he offered me the respect after finding out that we really meant well for the Church! To God be the glory!

Copperbelt District was strategic to us in reaching out to as many youths and churches as possible. It was the richest, biggest and most influential District besides Lusaka. In 1988, I contested for Copperbelt District YPD Presidency. At the time the District had not been divided. Sister Rodah Membe beat me in the election in Ndola. She had all the numbers with her with a large following of girls behind her and the name! Sister Rodah was a daughter of Rev. J.L.C. Membe. Nevertheless, Bro. Richard Kasanda, our partner in ministry, went through into the executive and carried out our mission of making Jesus known. Several believers we knew from different churches on the Copperbelt had been present. The then Rev. Paul Kawimbe, now Bishop Kawimbe was present too.

In 1988, the last South Zambia Annual Conference was held in Lusaka at Libala Secondary School. It was presided by Bishop Richard Allen Chappelle. The Conference divided the huge South Zambia Annual Conference into two Conferences. At the time, I was 1st Vice President of YPD while Bro. Emmanuel Membe was the President. Bro. Membe was a nephew to Rev. J.L.C. Membe. Bishop Chappelle made us to stand before the Conference. He directed Br. Emmanuel Membe to assume the role of YPD Presidency of the newly formed South-East Zambia Conference since he was based in Lusaka while I became the YPD President of South West Zambia Conference, and I was based in Kitwe. This, by the grace of God, was an answer to our prayers because Copperbelt District fell under our jurisdiction and the mission of evangelism was going to be carried out without hindrance.

With other believers, we began to reach out to youths beyond Kitwe District. Brother Richard Kasanda, was among many warriors God had raised for our time. He made more impact than any single one of us by reaching out to every corner and remotest place of Copperbelt. He had charismatic endowments from the Lord, was a great Teacher of the word and a strong Evangelistic ministry as well. Added to the grace, he was a gifted singer too! We toured Kalulushi with him and encouraged the brethren there, doing home visitations and sharing Christ! With him, we also went to Chief Nkana's area and St. Joseph in Kalulushi region where we taught the word of God during a YPD Seminar there. There were many brothers who had given their lives to the cause of Christ. Bro. Bright Mumba was a soldier and he too traveled with us to many places. He was a strong intercessor and had great understanding of the spiritual world and taught demonology with great grace.

We were aware that reaching out to the YPD was the quickest and best way to reach out to the Church. "If you were confined to a single church, for example, as a Pastor, it was going to take a long time to change the A.M.E. Church," we were aware. To influence change to the whole denomination which at the time, was steeped in traditions and was resistant to the things of the Spirit, the YPD ministry offered us a unique opportunity. Also, we were aware that the youth were quick to learn and were genuinely seeking for the truth. Often, the gatherings involved youths from many circuits. Therefore, this was ideal to our ministry and the burden of sharing Christ we had was being addressed in this way.

Our older folks, on the other hand, had their minds made! Many of them were set in their ways and change took a long time to come. In spite of this, we still enjoyed the support of a few elderly leaders who saw our sacrifice and desire to see change. We were supported, for example, at Jordan Chapel by the Senior Steward, Bro. James Msichili, Rev. Samuel Mulapwa,

Rev. Idah Simukwai, Rev. M.P.P. Mwenya, Rev. David D. Musole, to name a few. (These pastors came to Jordan on transfer at different times. They stood by us and supported our cause without fear of those who opposed our ministry). Sharing Jesus to youths from different churches in one setting was instrumental in winning the A.M.E. Church back to Jesus in Zambia. The Copperbelt Province being the most developed with more churches and towns than any other region (besides Lusaka and a few towns along the line of rail) was ideal for such a cause and strategy.

In 1989, the First Session of South-West Zambia Annual Conference presided by Bishop Richard Allen Chappelle, Sr. was held at Helen Kaunda Secondary School in Kitwe. I was a leader of the YPD both at the Conference and Kitwe District level. Our mission at such meetings was clear: evangelism! This was accomplished through person to person evangelism. We learned later from those who had given their lives through our ministry that they used to run away from us each time they saw us approach them! "Born Agains," they called us. They avoided us because we used to engage them in conversations and we had to establish if they were born again or not. We then ministered to them. At this conference we ran into a group on break and shared Jesus. The group accepted Jesus but two special sisters from that group stood out because we became acquainted in a very special way.

Sister Joyce (not her real name) lived close to my home in Parklands, Kitwe. It was just four-minutes' walk away. Her friend Maggie (not her real name) lived in Bulangililo (Township changed for privacy). After the duo had accepted Jesus, they began coming home for counsel. I lived with Rev. Aaron Siwale, my childhood friend from Sunday school days. When he had graduated from Theological College of Central Africa, he was appointed to Pastor Gethsemane A.M.E. Church at Luangwa in Kitwe. He requested that we live together and for two years, we did. This was also a blessing because we did ministry together. Maggie was a very beautiful girl. Unaware at the time that she was only fourteen; scores of men would waylay her, sometimes even picking her up from church in their posh cars.

Maggie was a girl from single parenthood. She was living with her grandparents. Each time she asked for money for books, her mother would inform her that she was a woman like her as well, she could find the money. This led to men to take advantage of her but God had put that to the end. The two girls began to grow in the Lord and each time they came home they came together and we offered them help for a while. One day, we had a day seminar at the YMCA at Wusakile in Kitwe. This Fellowship was interdenominational in nature and it comprised believers who were very powerful in word and deed. As was our custom we invited our new converts to this meeting. About 20 or so youths from A.M.E. churches including Moses Kapembwa, Joyce and Maggie were in attendance.

We had a great Fellowship. After the meeting, we decided to walk from Wusakile to the downtown Kitwe an hour's walk or so. The Chamboli and Wusakile groups had remained in their area. Pastor Siwale was with our group of about 10. Moses was with us since he was living in Nkana East at the time. We escorted Maggie to the Bus Station and she boarded a mini bus to Bulangililo. It was around 19:00 hrs. We were very happy the youths had been blessed and were very excited!

Sadly, I was shocked to hear, the following day upon my return from work that Maggie had come to our apartment crying. "Oh boy! The devil has risen!" Rev. Siwale informed me. "Maggie's parents want to see you! They want you to go to their home! They want to know where she had been the all day yesterday! Her aunt told her, 'You always say,' 'I went to see Kapungwe; I went to see Kapungwe, one day from Ba Kapungwe, will come ChiChipungwe!' " Rev. Aaron told me. Her aunt was a YPD member at the same church Joyce and Maggie attended and she knew us well but chose to scandalize our names. She was actually telling her that one day you will come with a baby or "ChiChipungwe!"

Rev. Aaron and I went to see Maggie's guardians. We found that she lived with her grandparents. Her auntie who was in her twenties, like us, saw us and used the rear door to bolt out! Maggie had told her "Ba Kapungwe" or "Mr. Kapungwe is here!" She never came to welcome us! We sat in the living room and Maggie's grandfather sat next to Rev. Siwale. You could tell he was very angry. Rev. Siwale introduced himself and me. He was a Pastor of Gethsemane, "and this one," looking at me, "is the YPD President of Kitwe District. He is a leader of the youth of all our churches in Kitwe. We do our best to help our youth who we regard as our sisters and brothers so that they can know Jesus and grow in the Lord. We would never do anything to jeopardise that trust given to us. Yes, it is true Maggie has been coming home but each time she came, she came with her friend Joyce who lives near us. I have always been around each time she came. We were concerned and have been offering her help with her friend. I believe you must have noticed change in her life ever since we came to know her!" Rev. Aaron concluded with a statement.

The grandfather was now more relaxed and the Holy Spirit had taken control! He acknowledged that they had seen a great change in Maggie and had observed her read her Bible a lot. Rev. Siwale then explained how we helped the youth grow by taking them to special meetings which we thought were helpful and we had just done the same to Maggie and she was not the only one present. That is all it needed for God to put Satan where he belonged: under the feet of Jesus! As we trekked to the station to catch a minibus for home, Rev. Siwale burst into laughter of scorn at me! "Oh boy! You were in a lot of trouble there!"

A few months later, I was on call in the Emergency Room (ER) or Casualty Department as we called it, in the Out Patients Department (OPD) at the hospital I worked. I received a patient who was in breathing distress and after confirming it was acute severe bronchial asthmatic attack, I ordered for IV aminophylline to help relieve the patient from severe respiratory distress. This medicine is administered for about 10 minutes and as you're doing so you can talk to the patient. Wait a minute! As I was treating the patient, his face looked familiar but I could not pick up where I had seen him before. I looked at the card and I had a clue! Maggie! Maggie's grandfather! I asked him and he confirmed! He was so much overwhelmed with embarrassment but I reassured him. From that day on, we would often meet at the hospital and he showed me great respect that is only accorded to an in-law! He would squat whenever we met but I would let him feel relaxed! Those were the exploits of the Man from Galilee in his children in claiming the Church to Jesus!

Months later, I arrived home from work one day only to be greeted by a distressed-looking man of God, Siwale. Rev. Aaron Siwale was laying down on the floor praying. When asked what the matter was, he gave his usual expression whenever Satan had attacked, "The devil has arisen!" He then explained that "Helen" (not her real name), "was here! She told me that I was needed by her mother. Thinking there was an emergency; I took my Bible and went to Luangwa. While on the way to the station, she was acting weird and I kept asking her what the matter was but apprehensively she kept telling me, 'I told them it is not him, but they (with her grandmother) kept on insisting that he is!' I told her, 'Satan is under the feet of Jesus!' When we got home her mother informed me that 'Your friend is not alright!' (A common expression the elderly used if a girl was pregnant). 'Therefore, we called you so that we can discuss the matter privately and resolve it faster knowing that you are a Pastor before news would get out!' "

The surprised Rev. Siwale pleaded ignorant to the matter. He told the mother and the grandmother that he had nothing to do with the case and asked them to sit down with her and patiently find out from her. When the Pastor asked her, she was equivocal about it. Rev. Aaron prayed for them promising to see them in three days' time or so, thinking by then Helen would let the family know the truth! He was wrong! She didn't.

Helen had been one of the promising youths in the church where Rev. Siwale was Pastor. He had helped her spiritually and she was showing potential signs of being groomed to become the YPD leader. At the same time, Rev. Siwale was aware of desire in young women for marriage. He had seen also that the mother would give some produce to her daughter to give the Pastor whenever he did home visitations. The pastor would end all visitations at Helen's home and Helen would often escort him to the bus station and he would take a minibus to the city center in Kitwe. She then would walk back home. Pastor Siwale ensured that no woman from his church ever visited our home. As a matter of fact, only two Stewards from his church had ever come to our place.

When Rev. Siwale had returned to Helen's family, he was shocked that the status remained the same! The family still thought or insisted it was the pastor who was responsible. I saw the Rev. Aaron distressed. I had never seen him like this before! He would lay down on the floor praying, "Vindicate me, Oh Lord!" I informed him that on Friday, when I returned from work, we were going to see the family and we continued to pray over the matter. When we arrived at Luangwa Township, we found Helen, the mother and the grandmother home. Rev. Siwale introduced me and the family was introduced to me. We then sat down in a circle with the mother in the doorway, the grandmother to her right followed by Helen, Rev. Siwale and I.

I went to work immediately. "Helen," I began, "We are in the presence of God and the pastor. I want you to say the truth without any fear. This is very important." When I caught the attention of everyone and Helen was ready, I asked her a question. "Helen," while pointing at Rev. Siwale, "Do you know this man?" "Yes," she responded. "How do you know him?" I asked. "He is our Pastor," she replied. "Now I hear that you are pregnant and you are saying it is him who is responsible?" I asked her. "It is not me who said that," she answered, "It is my mother!" I told her that I thought you are the right person to answer that question and not your mother! She was silent.

Then I questioned her, "Has the Pastor ever proposed to you or ever slept with you?" "No!" she retorted. "But how come you said he is responsible for the pregnancy?" I asked her. Agitated she answered, "I told you it is my mother who said that and not me!" I then asked her what had made her fail to correct that wrong impression. She kept quiet and later said "He can forgive me!" I asked her to ask for forgiveness from him. She looked at him and asked him to forgive her! "God has forgiven me of my sins, so I also forgive you," Rev. Aaron responded. It is at this stage that the demons manifested!

Photo: Rev. Aaron Siwale preaching in Lusaka, Zambia in 2014.

"Boo, boo, our plans have been thwarted! Our plans have been destroyed!" the demons kept on sighing. It was no longer Helen talking but a different voice in her! My friend who is quick in discerning spirits, jumped on the occasion immediately, "Satan, I knew it was you! You are under the feet of Jesus!" The demons begged us not to harm her stating, "Leave her alone. It is not her but us! She is innocent!" Rev. Aaron commanded them to explain what they meant by that. The demons repeated that she was innocent and should not be accused of anything since it was them who had planned all this! They promised they would explain what had transpired. Rev. Siwale then commanded them to explain.

"It was not her who did this but us. You were so persistent on us! You chased all my friends out and I am the only one left! Even me, I am outside! We let her go to the home of "Patrick." "Which Patrick?" I interjected. "Patrick H…, they responded. She had come from escorting you (Pastor Aaron) at the bus station and we made her go to the home of Patrick. If it were not for us, it would not have happened!" Rev. Aaron asked them, "Satan, why did you do that?" "We wanted the church to suspend you! You have been very persistent on us! But boo, boo, our plans are thwarted! Leave her alone please, she is innocent!" they narrated. It is at this time that Rev. Siwale commanded the demon to go in the name of Jesus! "Satan, I command you to go out in the name of Jesus!" It agonised in pain saying, "I am the only one left and I am outside!" He still commanded it to go and within a minute there was silence. Helen was still in her sitting position the whole time the incident was happening.

She then came back to herself as though one coming out of sleep. She surveyed the area and saw us waiting on her and she asked us what was going on. We explained. We also asked her if she knew "Patrick." She said, "Yes." When asked about him, she informed us he was the man responsible for her pregnancy! Asked as to where he was, she informed us that he had left for Livingstone, Southern Province. We concluded that Satan had engineered an affair which resulted in Helen's pregnancy and then made Patrick (not his real name) to leave the city and go some 926 km (574.1 miles) away leaving the girl in the red! Pastor Siwale then began to encourage the family with the words of the Lord. They had been so stunned by the power of God that they remained mute!

As we trekked back home going to the bus station, I knew my time to revenge had come! "God is a very fair God," I told the preacher! "What do you mean?" Rev. Aaron asked. "When we were coming from Bulangililo concerning my matter with Maggie, you had exclaimed that, 'Oh boy, you were in some hot soup there!' I think, oh boy, you were in much hotter soup here!" What a day it had been! He could now afford to laugh because the God of the armies of Israel is a Man of War.

About three years had passed. We had gone to the graveyard to bury a church member. Several A.M.E. congregations in the city were present including members of the church my friend had been a pastor of. Rev. Aaron was a pastor in Lusaka now and was not in attendance. After the burial, we were walking out of the graveyard to go and board waiting buses outside when a woman from the late Helen's church asked me if I ever knew where Helen lay. I told her, "No!" "What? Was Helen dead?" The way she had asked me made me become aware that she, somehow, must have gotten wind of the story. We had been walking back in Chamboli Cemetery passing through numerous graves until we had walked within reach of the grave. "Here is the place where Helen lies," the woman told me, pointing to the grave. Fresh memories of that deliverance episode gripped me and I wondered just what had transpired!

"Helen died in your hospital," the woman explained. "She never had been sick or anything like that but she just woke up complaining of a headache. The headache persisted that day and became severe. So, they took her to your hospital (where I worked). She was admitted and the following day she passed away!" "Just like that?" I asked. "Just like that!" she replied. "It was a very shocking, sudden, and unexpected death," narrated the woman. It was a sad experience for me in that God by his outstretched hand allowed Helen and his family to witness the miraculous hand of God but Helen had lapsed into unbelief again. After giving birth, people in the area could ask her to show them "the Pastor's baby" and amidst some laughter she could show the baby without correcting the misconception. To date, I have no doubt in my mind that Helen's death was connected to the Judgment of God.

I shared this testimony for the first time at our Camp Meeting held at Zambia Institute of Business Studies and Industrial Practice (ZIBSIP) in Kitwe in 1997. Calvary A.M.E. Church had hosted the Camp Meeting in the downtown City of Kitwe. Rev. Siwale who was now in Lusaka was present as well as many brethren from other parts of Zambia. By Mid-1990s there had been great awareness on the things of the Spirit and I felt compelled to share that testimony to help believers understand the battle that goes on but many older leaders were still ignorant of! We still continued to experience poor representation from some "hardcore" churches which had been resisting change. Nevertheless, the youth had made a great progress in turning around the Church, and to God be the glory!

In 1990, we were invited to attend Copperbelt West District YPD Conference held at a School at Mufulira. This was at the height of the major revival then sweeping through the Church. I was South-West Zambia Conference YPD President then. I was the first person to hold this position since the creation of the Conference. We were invited by our counterparts from the Copperbelt West District. Bro. Richard Kasanda, Bright Mumba and I lived in the City of Kitwe and were from the Copperbelt East District; nevertheless, both Districts fell under the South-West Zambia Conference. (South West Zambia Conference at the time comprised North Western and Copperbelt Provinces).

The YPD Director for the Copperbelt West District at the time was Ms. Florence Chileshe. Although the YPD President was in charge of the meeting, by protocol she was answerable to the YPD Director. Ms. Florence Chileshe was a very influential beautiful woman who did not believe in the things of the Spirit. She had connections to the higher hierarchy of the Church that made her "a powerful woman in the Church!" She vehemently used to oppose the Copperbelt West District YPD leadership and our team was aware of it but wouldn't openly confront her.

We had just met the Presiding Elder, Rev. Henry Alimasi on the first day of the meeting. He was the P.E. of the area. He talked to us of how proud he was of us (i.e., Bro. Bright Mumba, Br. Richard Kasanda and I) especially the work we were doing in the Lord in the Church. He blessed us with kind words. Later, late afternoon, Rev. M.P.P. Mwenya was the preacher in the Conference. The Secondary School Hall was packed with the youth and the man of God ministered the word very powerfully! He spoke on issues to deal with deliverance. When he made an invitation, scores of youths stepped forward to receive the Lord. With time constraint, (we were preparing to go for supper), he did not pray for those who had come in front but had led them to the Lord, regardless. He then gave a directive that we (my leadership) should meet later after supper and pray for all those who had come in front to accept Jesus.

We met the group at 21:00hrs in one of the classrooms. About 20 souls which had given themselves to the Lord had come. YPD leaders from the host Copperbelt West District had come as well and Bro. Richard Kasanda, Bright Mumba and I (from Copperbelt East) were present. My older Sister, Mary Kapungwe who had been delivered from evil spirits in the 1980s which had troubled her for decades was also in the room. I asked the people what they wanted God do for them and why they had come. One by one each told us their story. "When Pastor Mwenya was preaching, something was telling me to leave the Hall, 'Leave the meeting and go out!' " Another told us, "When he was preaching, I was experiencing heart palpitations and restlessness." Yet, another person told us that, "I do not talk to my sister-in-law and would want to harm her." More and more youths spoke unashamedly giving reasons why they had stepped forward and wanted to be prayed for because of what they perceived as something being wrong with them.

I then told them that "We are going to worship Jesus in here! Whatever the issue you have, God is going to set you free! All you need to do is to surrender to Jesus!" I then called on my ministry partner Br. Richard Kasanda to lead us in a worship song. As soon as we began worshiping God with a powerful worship song, the power of God came down in the room and without warning scores of those who had come to confess the name of Jesus violently fell down and evil spirits manifested with screaming and shouting. I was unaware at the time that the local (host) leadership had fled the room, only the three of us, (leaders who had come from another District) had remained. My back was facing the door and since we were in a mood of prayer, I had not noticed their departure immediately.

The suffering of the people sprawling on the ground appalled me. I was filled with pain and anger against the devil so I stepped forward, squatted near one person and I commanded the demons to go in the name of Jesus! As soon as I had done that, a person touched my shoulder from behind and I opened my eyes only to find myself face to face with an angry-looking YPD Director Florence Chileshe. (Note: Sometimes we can command the demons to leave while looking and this usually is the case in deliverances of this kind. I did this for the most part but the time she came I had closed my eyes briefly).

She immediately spoke to me in anger, asking a barrage of questions! "Are you the President?" I responded, "Yes!" "And you are doing this?" she followed up. I again said, "Yes!" "Is it allowed?" she asked again. I again answered, "Yes!" She then left the room immediately with fury. Regardless, we continued the work of God! All the people were delivered and there was so much rejoicing among the group that they sang praises to God and many gave the testimonies of how light they felt. It was a night of victory!

However, there was a lot of commotion the following day! The Copperbelt West District YPD Director Florence Chileshe, convened a leadership meeting to discuss the events of the previous night. The Presiding Elder, Rev. Henry Alimasi, Mother Grace Mwenya, wife to the preacher, the local YPD leadership and our team (Bro. Richard Kasanda, Br. Bright Mumba and I) were present. We came from the Copperbelt East District but I was the South West Zambia Conference YPD President. The Conference I was President in comprised the Districts mentioned above. It also included Copperbelt Central District, Solwezi District, Solwezi East District, Solwezi West District, Mufumbwe District, Kabompo District, Chavuma District, Zambezi District and Mwinilunga District. She accused me of having been in a "trance" when she had spoken to me! She wanted the Presiding Elder to rule if what she had "seen happen last night; Was it A.M.E., or not?" The P.E., informed the gathered leaders that, "I too have seen that happen but whether it was A.M.E. or not, I cannot tell!" He carefully trod the middle ground!

Mother Mwenya, then, full of wisdom and the Spirit of God asked if praying for people who had problems and felt better in the end was a problem. The Director then accused us of going outside "this hall" to conduct other prayers! Mother Mwenya, then said, "What I hear here is that if the prayers were done here, there wouldn't have been a problem, right?" She was getting worked out and brought up another issue. As I was writing this story, a text message came from Rev. Richard Kasanda from Zambia and I told him what I just finished writing! He sent another text stating, "I can't forget the boldness and wisdom of Rev. Grace

Chapter 27 • History of the A.M.E. Church in Zambia

Mwenya on that day!"

We are thankful to God for the souls who were delivered. We are thankful to God that he showed himself strong. As you can see, this was a hot issue, decades ago before God had softened the hearts of those who were hardened by the deceitfulness of Satan. Instead of rejoicing that souls which had come to church seeking help from the Lord were delivered, some people in leadership chose to gnash their teeth at those who were offering help to the oppressed! They must have been in the same tank as it were, with Satan! Today, as I pen this, you may unlikely ever find this reaction by any Director or members of the A.M.E. Church in Zambia. God has graciously been able to educate many on the issue and this has been done through men and women whom God raised to teach the unadulterated word of God and it is my prayer that the Church of the future will never forget and be trapped into religion again like the Church at Laodicea. (I am thankful to the Lord that Rev. Wilson Mpundu informed me that years later, he had led Ms. Florence Chileshe to the Lord!)

There were opposing groups in the Church at the time. There were some who believed in deliverance from demons through prayer and the power of the Holy Spirit and those who opposed such prayers, vehemently. Through deceit, Satan would identify or classify ministers or churches which believed in praying for the sick or the possessed into one group. He called it "People who invoked evil spirits or prayed to spirits!" Those who didn't expel the demons were seen as "True or Normal" or as the "Right way to worship!" As you can tell, our ministry emphasized greatly on need to be born again and not Church affiliation. This was the sword that Jesus brought to separate right from wrong or brother from sister or from parent if any chose not to accept the Lord. Therefore, by misnaming believers or Pastors who cast out demons which Jesus had commanded us to do, Satan had blinded many. They consequently, entertained his demons which, as you know, had a purpose – to lead many to hell with them.

During the mid-1980s, similar works by the Holy Spirit were being done in many so-called "Traditional Churches." Neighbouring United Church of Zambia (UCZ, formerly Free Church of Scotland now an amalgamation of several Churches after Zambia's independence in 1964 and one of the biggest Churches in Zambia), had its born again youths constantly persecuted. This was at Wusakile in Kitwe. Thankfully, they received an older Pastor who at the time was one of the few who embraced the work of the Holy Spirit. The elders were against the "Fellowship" which was operating at the Church. Rev. Chumya, however, their first Central Africa Evangelist in the denomination, stood for the right cause.

UCZ which was just across the road from Jordan grew exponentially in numbers! Their church demolished and expanded their building three times in a period of about ten years. They had 120 deacons and 80 elders! Meanwhile, Jordan Chapel, a stone's throw away from UCZ, still remained the same! The youths from UCZ began a Fellowship at the YMCA Wusakile and several of them were leaders from the Scripture Union in Secondary Schools. Many believers from other churches became a part of them. At least 75% to 80% of members of this Fellowship became pastors. This is an interdenominational Fellowship meeting on Sunday afternoons that we found helpful to young converts in our Church. Therefore, we took them there to help them grow spiritually.

I ministered a lot to youths who had come out of powers of darkness. Naturally, after leading them to Jesus, many had wanted to come to "my Church!" Unfortunately, depending on case, I would not permit them and instead would refer them to my friends' Churches (other denominations) which did not deal with highly divisive faith-based or doctrinal conflicts and were not as worse off as ours! Pastor Harrison Chileshe in Kitwe (now leading a very big Church in Lusaka), was among the believers I would refer delivered young converts to. If you prayed for an individual who had been possessed and was delivered, the person expected to find more people at your church who would help him or her to grow there! Alas! Would it not be shocking to them if all they found in your church were people who were devouring one another? Wouldn't that be a surprise? We therefore, out of caution and safety for our converts referred them to Churches where we were sure they were going to sprout.

Meanwhile, other denominations were also being challenged with the word of God. Earliest localised ministry was by Rev. Magowan at Maranatha Assembly of God in Kitwe, Rev. David Way of Eastlea Assembly of God in Mufulira and Rev. Tisdale at Northmead Assembly of God, all in the mid 1970s. Bro. Callaghan and later Bro. Bob helped in ministry at Kitwe's Maranatha. In 1981, Evangelist Reinhard Bonnke came to Kitwe and held open air crusades in other parts of Zambia too. Other notable ministers were Pastor Garry Skinner and Marylin who had been running a church in Lusaka around 1982. They moved to Uganda and are the brains behind Watoto's Children's singing ministry. Evangelist Peter Pretorius from South Africa was another touch bearer to Zambia's revival with Jesus Alive Ministries' crusades and teachings in the 1980s. Bonnke's crusades unleashed a lot of excitement among youths even with those we knew as "sinners!" Meanwhile, Secondary schools like my school, Chamboli, were burning with the word. The deputy head got born again following the impact by the Scripture Union there. One of my former classmates in Kitwe Bro. Gift Siwila had come to know the Lord in 1977 in Mufulira (at a Youth Camp). He was a member of the neighbouring United Church of Zambia in Kitwe. One of the pioneers of the Revival in Zambia Rev. Dr. Winston Brooms had preached the word that led him to Jesus.

Br. Gift Siwila got saved during early revival trendsetters in Zambia. He was my classmate in Form I (Grade 8) in 1978. Rev. Dr. Winston Brooms from Trinidad and Tobago, West Indies a missionary to Zambia from 1976 to 1980 and a former pastor of Maranatha Assembly of God in Kitwe, had shared the word at a school in Mufulira which set forth a chain of events. When Dr. Brooms had arrived in Zambia, he had stayed in Lusaka for weeks where his preaching impacted people at Northmead Assembly of God before he took up the work in Kitwe. Maranatha was set on fire too! Mr. Peter Matoka, a former Cabinet Minister, had two children a boy and a girl. They got saved when Dr. Brooms stayed at Northmead briefly before proceeding to Kitwe. During his time in Lusaka, Lusaka got electrified. It was this time that Honourable Matoka's children got saved. Their father was upset that his children who he wanted to continue in Catholic church could not be dissuaded. He therefore, left for Kitwe with intents of harming Rev. Brooms!

When he found him at Maranatha, he had not even been spoken to but the power of God touched him. He ended up giving his life to Jesus and disclosed his ill intentions he had come with to do to Rev. Brooms. Bro. Gift Siwila who was a member of UCZ at Wusakile was also a regular member of Maranatha at the time. The same fire was brought to UCZ – Wusakile where many born again youths mostly from the Scripture Unions began to impact their church. This church was our neighbour at Jordan A.M.E. Church. When the elders later banned the Fellowship, many at the church had already been born again! They started a Fellowship at Y.M.C.A. Wusakile but by this time St. Margaret UCZ in downtown Kitwe had gotten the fire too. Later, the fire got to UCZ churches in Luanshya, Ndola, Mufulira and the all Copperbelt. Secondary schools also got affected.

Brother Gift Siwila used to fast and pray near the school playground (Chamboli). There, they counseled and led many to Christ, Students who attended Scripture Union began to return the books they had stolen confessing the name of Jesus! Their testimonies touched the deputy head whose daughter had been one of the converted at Chamboli Secondary School: He gave his life to Jesus! This made the nearby Ndeke Secondary School to invite the brother and the Fellowship. Ndeke Secondary School experienced the same: converts confessing and returning stolen textbooks. Word went around and other secondary schools in Kitwe got similar experiences.

Two students at Chamboli confessed participating in magic arts and study of the same. They brought the books and Bro. Gift burned them. In the Scripture Union at the time were Br. Bernard Nwaka, Andrew Mwaipopo, David Lusale, Joel Mhango, Erick Mwambelo, Dygate Thindwa, Chabs Sibale and many more. When Br. Gift Siwila went to preach at the Baptist church at Chamboli Township, scores of friends, many from the Catholic church of Chamboli came to the meeting. He spoke on "But you shall receive power after the Holy Spirit has come on you," from Acts 1:8. The power of God was so heavy in the meeting that nearly everyone was weeping even before the alter call was done! Many gave their lives at the end of the meeting.

They voluntarily asked that they go the following day to preach at Luangwa Township! The group included new converts! The same fire made the brethren to go into the community (Luangwa) and began preaching and to visit all surrounding churches to start Fellowships. They planted new Fellowship meetings in many churches including Chamboli Catholic, the Nazarene and Baptist. Many girls who were possessed at school (Chamboli) would experience demonic manifestations especially during Prep Time and the Scripture Union was always asked to help these students. However, the Fellowship at Wusakile Catholic church lasted only two weeks. It was stopped!

Chamboli Secondary School had a large S.U. group. It was disliked by groups which harboured evil intentions especially towards the girls since the Fellowship was winning them to Jesus! Bro. Gift Siwila informed me that he had a list of 200 students which he was doing follow-up on! Chamboli Secondary School had a student body of about 1,000. The Deputy Head also became a member of the Scripture Union. He shed tears when Br. Gift Siwila and the Scripture Union presented him several stolen text books which converted students had returned to the Scripture Union Fellowship. He recalls the power of God present in meetings as well as the joy of the Lord when they met even strangers who were believers but they would easily connect spiritually!

This excitement evolved into early trends of revival in Zambia in 1982. During this period, Wendy Kruger, a white sister in the Lord began to share her popular song in a Zambian language of Bemba in Kitwe and around the Copperbelt. The song titled *"Ninsanga,"* translated "I have found," talked about a personal testimony of the singer having found Jesus. This began to set the tone of a wider spread of the born again experience in Zambia. These were among the early Pentecostal-Charismatic movements that began to influence the City of Kitwe and Zambia. Rev. Dr. Brooms became a pastor at Maranatha Assembly of God in Kitwe around 1977. Br. Nevers Mumba had been a member of this church. He had interpreted for Reinhard Bonnke during the Crusades in 1981. Bonnke had seen potential in him and had sent him to the U.S.A. to study. When they were students at Hillcrest Secondary School in Livingstone, Br. Dan Pule (Pastor) had influenced Br. Nevers Mumba (Pastor) to come to the Lord!

Before the time of the Rev. Nevers Mumba, many unsung heroes were involved in the spread of the word of God in Zambia. Among them are Bro. Christopher Ngoma and Mrs. Pamela Ngoma. Bro. Ngoma worked for Stanbic Bank, Ndola in the late 1970s and late 1980s. Bro. Christopher was a son of former Posts and Telecommunications Corporation (PTC) General Manager, Mr. Philemon Ngoma. He was a young and vibrant believer in the Lord who was a highly sought-after speaker in Scripture Unions all over the schools on the Copperbelt Province and later the all Zambia. He was a former Baptist brother transformed by the power of the Holy Spirit. Br. Ngoma also led Mr. Frederick Chiluba to the Lord and later became a Senior Private Secretary of the President when Chiluba became President. Br. Ngoma travelled extensively throughout Zambia preaching the word in the 1980s.

When Pastor Mumba came back, he launched Victory Ministries and Victory Bible Church in Kitwe. Evangelist Nevers Mumba helped to unify the Church (the body of Christ) in Zambia and created a strong voice for the Church in Zambia. He also added a voice to other televangelists of the mid-1980s such as Evangelist Jimmy Swaggart. Swaggart Ministries opened a bookstore with music and Christian Literature in 1985 in Lusaka. Rev. Kapungwe recalls buying tapes and a book there. Christian Bookstores including Father Whitehead, an Anglican Priest in Livingstone, the father of a friend, Peter Whitehead and fellow National HCF leader, distributed important Christian literature which helped in spreading the word of God in Zambia.

Jim Ford, a believer in Kabwe is also among the revivalists in Zambia. Jim provided a farm (Jim Ford's Farm) for various Christian groups for camping. Among the groups included Scripture Union groups drawn from across Zambia. They camped here during holidays and this was among the earliest outreach groups in Zambia from the late 1970s. It was at this farm that I got acquainted with the Hospital Christian Fellowship (incorporating Healthcare Christian Fellowship or HCF) in 1987. Jim Ford Farm hosted the HCFZ National Conference and I was doing my Obstetrics and Gynaecology practical at Kabwe General Hospital when I first attended the conference here.

Scripture Union (SU) in Zambia must also be listed among those who contributed to revival in Zambia. In additional to them are Bible Schools such as Kaniki Bible College and

Theological College of Central Africa in Ndola. Bible Correspondence Schools e.g., Bible Way Correspondence School and Emmaus Bible School in Ndola and Luanshya, respectively, in the 1970s as well as many Christian Book Stores helped the word to get root in Zambia. Brothers Mpundu Mutala and Sister Seko Phiri, the General Secretary of S.U. were among early believers who contributed to the word of God to spread in Zambia.

Zambia Fellowship of Evangelical Students (ZAFES), an affiliate with the International Fellowship of Evangelical Students (IFES) was another parachurch organization which helped in the revival of Zambia. ZAFES had tremendously been used by God in colleges and universities in Zambia to bring about revival. It was our lifeline in schools of higher learning during our time. Christian Literature Press in Chingola had also contributed to the edification of the body of Christ through songs of inspiration and the word of God.

Soon, the word of God began to be accessible to many people conspicuously than at any point in the history of Zambia. What was often seen as localized activity of the word of God in various isolated parts of Zambia began to be a unified movement, thanks to the radio and television broadcasts. These ministries began to impact many denominations and some of the members joined these new ministries. Victory Ministries, for example, though based in Kitwe held yearly Conferences in Lusaka and attracted people from all denominations and international speakers mostly from the U.S. or West Africa. It was now evident that the A.M.E. Church was not going to remain the same because those who listened or looked around found that what we were preaching was agreeable with the message that was constantly being presented around us. God began to save the youths whose parents used to oppose us constantly and through these youths some of the parents were later won to Jesus!

Evangelist Ernest Angley, an American Televangelist, played a role in ministering to Frederick Jacob Titus Chiluba when he got born again. Chiluba, then Zambia Congress of Trade Union (ZCTU) Chairman, had been imprisoned during the presidency of Dr. Kenneth Kaunda. He was being accused of agitating trouble and while in prison, he got born again through the ministry of Br. Chris Ngoma. The TV ministry of Br. Angley was helpful as well to Chiluba. (My immediate younger brother Amos Kapungwe, Jr., got born again under the Evangelist Angley at Nkana Stadium in 1994 before he went to be with the Lord. President Chiluba had invited the Evangelist Angley to do crusades in Zambia at this time).

When Chiluba became President in Zambia after 27 years of one-Party rule, he declared Zambia a Christian Nation in 1991. This declaration also had an impact upon the Church (the body of Christ) in Zambia. Satan, through some denominations, fought this declaration but the declaration prevailed and it was later incorporated in the preamble of the Zambian constitution. Without doubt this declaration had impacted the A.M.E. Church as well. In 1994, the Healthcare Christian Fellowship of Zambia (HCFZ), of which I was one of the National Leaders, invited the President to officially launch the Fellowship in Zambia. He came and did so at Ndola's Savoy Hotel. Although the Fellowship had been in existence in Zambia since the early 1970s, (1972), we felt it was important to have a public launch to help publicise its work in the hospitals of Zambia.

With the declaration of Zambia as a Christian Nation, the country opened itself up to believers outside. Trinity Broadcasting Network (TBN) opened a Television Station in Zambia and Radio Christian Voice came into operation in the early 1990s. Many international evangelists such as Benny Hinn and other pastors came to hold crusades or were courted speakers in Christian Conferences. When Benny Hinn came for example, he would send advance parties for training and believers from different churches worked together regardless of denominations. Pastors would then form committees, months before crusade days coordinating logistics, training counselors and ushers.

When the crusades were over, Benny Hinn Ministry donated food packages (bags of mealie meal) to hundreds of volunteers in amounts never seen before in Kitwe and Ndola. The recipients were organisers and counsellors who had spent months in planning and helping thousands of people who were coming to Jesus. The volunteers were not even aware this was going to happen! They did it out of love and excitement of serving God. The interdenominational spirit and awareness of God in the nation had reached an all-time high and it was a revival that began to impact families, churches and the nation itself.

From the 1980s Interdenominational Fellowships had been formed in many parts of Zambia. In Kitwe, for instance, Wusakile YMCA was a powerful influential Fellowship which drew believers from many denominations. Over 75% of members here became Pastors who have been very influential in ministry in Zambia including Pastor Harrison Sakala, Pastor Sylvester Daka, Bishop Bernard Nwaka, Pastor Harrison Chileshe, Pastor Maybin Sichangwa, Pastor Chabs Sibale, Pastor Watson Kondowe, Pastor Pythias Chabala, Pastor Steve Mwakibinga, Pastor Eric Mwambelo, Humphrey Gondwe, Pastor Matthews Mtonga, Pastor Joel Mhango, Pastor Jonathan Malaika and many more. We were also a part of this fellowship since Jordan Chapel was in the area. Rev. Aaron Siwale, Rev. Richard Kasanda and I were a part of this. We eagerly looked forward to meeting in the next fellowship and there was great joy and love in these meetings!

There were other similar Fellowships in Kitwe. At YMCA Town Center, Kitwe, people who worked in the area could attend the lunch hour fellowship there and souls were being won to Jesus. Other meetings were held at Mindolo YMCA, Richmond Gardens YMCA in Parklands (which I also attended, as Mighty Men and Women of Valour) and even some hospitals had very powerful fellowships. Scripture Union in Secondary Schools and later Primary Schools began to influence people with the word of God. Rev. Sky Banda of Maranatha Assembly of God in Kitwe was one of the men from early converts of the 1970s spreading the word at this time. He had taken over from Rev. Brooms as Pastor.

By 1990, the word of God (sound teaching) was common in many denominations. Bishop Joe Imakando who had been a Baptist Minister and lecturer at TCCA in Ndola became a leader of Bread of Life Church which grew enormously. The spiritual awakening began to be felt across denominations and the A.M.E. Church was not to be an exception. In spite of the few pockets of resistance in isolated places, you hardly now could find any church where the leadership would resist or persecute you for praying for people who were demon possessed/ or for casting out demons. This was a great doing by the Lord which came through a combination of factors. Nevertheless, it was the light that the believers who had remained in the

A.M.E. Church and had kept on emitting to everyone that was instrumental in changing the Church which had been steeped in traditions and believed in salvation by works for decades.

These believers, in spite of great persecution, acted like how the sons of Issachar did! They interpreted the times which they were in and knew what they were to do. They did not follow what their religious leaders ordered them to despite undergoing great persecution. Undoubtedly, these remnants became a catalyst to this revival of the A.M.E. Church in Zambia. My recommendation later in 1996 by the Presiding Elder who had been influenced to cancel the YPD seminar we had organized at Jordan Chapel several years earlier was an indication of the power and grace of God at work in the Church at this time!

In 1988, I was the Kitwe District YPD President of *"Yesu Akabwela Cincileni."* We organized believers and ensured that only those with a testimony of having been born again were put in the leadership. This was important to us to induce evangelism and help erase the attitude of playing church which many youths and congregations kept on inheriting for years. This also helped us focus on praise and worship, ministry of the word, testimonies and preaching of the salvation message. We rotated church to church in Kitwe and held very spiritual meetings in the 8 churches monthly in the District. Memorable names are Br. Davy Kavungu, Br. Elijah Chansa, Sis. Mirriam Mwape, Sis. Regina Mwango, Br. Bright Mumba, Br. John Mwamba, Sis. Loveness Chewe, Br. John Mpundu and many more.

Charles Kapungwe and Rev. Wilson Mpundu at Mother Hughes in Ndola at the wedding of Bro. Peter Kavungu, 1996.

We formed an Evangelism Committee in 1993. It was under the auspices of Copperbelt East District. Initially, it was chaired by Rev. Wilson Mpundu. Later, I became the Programme Committee Chairman but I worked with Rev. Mpundu as a Co-leader. We had Br. Siwell Mpundu as Secretary and Br. Christopher Chikulungu as Vice, Br. Emmanuel Chibwe,

Treasurer, Sis. Mirriam Mwape, Financial Secretary, Music – Bro. Elasto Mwansa, Worship Committee – Br. Bright Mumba, Br. John Mpundu, Sis. Pamela Katebe, Fanwell Mubanga and Kennedy Chinyama. Other leaders involved in this were Frederick Kabwe, Omega Ilunga, Maggie Chansa, Threasa Namfukwe and Grace Phiri.

The team was to do outreach in circuits. It was subdivided and tasked to reach specific circuits and share the word there. This programme ran through 1994. On Tuesday 21st April, 2020, reminiscing this ministry, I spoke to Sister Threasa Namfukwe Musonda on phone! She recalled with joy how we went about in churches and homes doing good and preaching the good news. She had been converted to the Lord at Jordan in 1991.

The Church, (A.M.E.), began to realize that it was losing many youths to the new Churches. Many English-speaking youths were more comfortable with those they could relate to and listening to messages which were applicable to their lives. They gravitated to what they saw was relevant to them than listening to what they termed as "parables and tales" at their bases. The A.M.E. Church realized that most of its churches were located in high density areas. They never catered for a certain category of people such as the educated.

Educated youths, for example, were unlikely to continue attending A.M.E. churches. This was noticeably common. The debate to begin planting churches in low density areas, thus, was aroused. This led to new churches being planted such as Maranatha A.M.E. Church in Lusaka meeting at Evelyn Hone College, Calvary A.M.E. Church (launched from Jordan Chapel), meeting at Kitwe Primary School in Parklands and later moved to Kitwe Main Primary School, Richard Allen A.M.E. Church in Ndola and Downtown A.M.E. Church in Chingola, (now Messiah).

Alas! For Calvary, the Pastor there didn't understand the vision of the new church! It was not just about coming into the downtown areas of the cities that we were after! We still needed to preach the unadulterated gospel that changed lives. This disconnection made the church begin to wander into oblivion and he perceived it not! For instance, Calvary in Kitwe has been meeting at a school since 1994, i.e., for 26 years in 2020! One member informed me a medical doctor came to church around 2017. It was apparent from the beginning that he was not going to return due to the obvious disconnection of ministers from the congregation and presence of "old unenthusiastic sleepy ministers prevalent in many churches including P.E.s!" To run these new churches in the downtown areas also required born again Pastors with a vision – not staunch traditionalists.

Rev. David D. Musole was very gracious. Many Pastors would hold on to members but he gave his blessings to us to begin a new work. I therefore, would say he is the one who started Calvary A.M.E. Church in 1994 where I had served as Senior Steward. Later, Rev. Musole from Jordan, again, launched another new church, Covenant A.M.E. Church at Ndeke Village in Kitwe. Bro. Bright Mumba helped this Church. We were geared to launch a church (Calvary) which reflected the spiritual ministry that God required in setting captives free. We therefore, assembled a powerful group of believers which among many included believers who had come from Bright Chapel to meet that task.

It was a joy to experience a largest constituent of believers gathering together. This had been a rare occurrence in the past. We had Bro. Richard Kasanda, Br. Bright Mumba, Bro. Kennedy Chinyama, Bro. Christopher Chikulungu, Sister Mirriam Mwape, Sister Threasa Namfukwe Musonda, Sister Mary Kapungwe and Sis. Fridah Kapungwe (my sisters). Others were Sister Musonda Phiri, Mother Dorcas Chola and many more. Brother Elijah Simulunga and his wife transferred from Bright Chapel. Many souls and households were converted to Jesus including the Phiri family and the Katilungu family.

Although we generally did well, we were unhappy by the tendency of one leader trying to hinder the work of the Spirit of God. The house of Saul had been warring against the house of David. Prophetically, God will make Abner to die, to pave way for the establishment of the house of the Lord or the Church of God. (He who has ears let him hear). This team, if it had not been hindered, would have made Calvary a great church and would have had a building by 2000 but the "spirit of religion began to hinder the work" because of a pastor. Calvary was never to be the same afterward. Victory Bible Church was just a stone-throw away from us and was meeting at Kitwe Little Theater. It was at this time that Brother Richard Kasanda and I went there and got "immersed" (baptized).

Calvary began to grow spiritually even though as believers, we were not happy with the presence of the house of Saul. A hindrance spirit from a leader who was working against what we knew God wanted to do was frustrating progress at Calvary. Regardless, we held two Camp Meetings in 1995, 1996 and 1997. These were Conferences organized by the local team of believers and where held at Zambia Institute of Business Studies and Industrial Practice (ZIBSIP formerly, MIMSU), a Mines Training Center in the City of Kitwe town center area.

Our friends from Lusaka attended both meetings. They were believers who had been expanding similar works at Maranatha A.M.E. Church and other A.M.E. Churches in Lusaka. Brother Happy Mulwe led the team in Lusaka and they began to publish a magazine called "ABLAZE" which highlighted the spiritual breakthroughs at the time. It also provided articles which gave spiritual insights to the lost generation. The meetings in Kitwe and Lusaka added great impetus to the growing movement of those who were born again and genuinely wanted the Church to be steered away from traditions which it had been steeped in for decades. In Kitwe, brethren from Mufulira, and other Copperbelt towns attended the Camp Meetings and were also a source of strength.

Rev. Paul Bupe was among our speakers at the Camp Meetings. Rev. Aaron Siwale was another. We also had the local speakers such as Brother Richard Kasanda and I. Brother Happy Mulwe had went through Admission at the Annual Conference and was ordained Deacon in Lusaka in 1997. Their Conference in Lusaka, which was equivalent to the Camp Meeting organized by Calvary A.M.E. Church in Kitwe, was called the National Convention. They held conferences too in 1995 and 1996. Speakers there included Rev. Paul Kawimbe, Rev. M.P.P. Mwenya, Dr. Musenge Matibini, (now wife to Rev. Happy Mulwe), Rev. Happy Mulwe, Brother Richard Kasanda and I, to name a few.

I spoke on "Servanthood Leadership" on 5th April, 1996 in Lusaka at the National Convention. Dr. Musenge Matibini spoke on "Breaking of Soul-ties." Bro. Happy Mulwe spoke on "Meaning and Method of Spiritual Warfare" while Rev. Aaron Siwale taught from Mark

5:1-5 about the "Demon of Gaderenes." Bro. Richard Kasanda taught on "Believer's Authority" and on 6th April, 1996, Rev. Paul Bupe taught on "Spiritual Gifts." Reading from 1 John 2:15, Rev. M.P.P. Mwenya taught on "Natural and Spiritual World." On the same day, Rev. Aaron Siwale who was living in Lusaka at this time and was teaching at Ebenezer Secondary School under the Rev. David K. Simfukwe who was running the school, taught on "Setting the Captives Free." Rev. Siwale was Pastor of Bethel A.M.E. Church in Lusaka at this time. Rev. Idah Simukwai, a spiritual woman of God, taught on "Friendship, Courtship and Marriage." Rev. Paul Kawimbe taught on "Spiritual Healing" on 7th April, 1996 and on 8th April, 1996, the Rev. M.P.P Mwenya taught very powerfully on "Discipleship."

Sadly, this was the last National Convention that was to be held! Many leaders of the Convention dissatisfied with the leadership and the state of the Church decided to pull out of the A.M.E. Church and form a new ministry called "Lift Him Up." This happened in 1998 and Calvary A.M.E. Church lost some believers because the hindrance spirit there from the pastor had continued to frustrate believers. When Rev. Richard Kasanda and I had left Calvary to be pastors of Mindolo (Judah) and Trinity, respectively, Calvary believers felt dissatisfied.

The pullout from the A.M.E. Church in September 1998 by believers was to be the biggest exodus ever recorded since the spiritual battle of trying to evangelise or change the Church's tradition-leaning stance. There had been a few members who had left and started new ministries in Chililabombwe, Mufulira, and elsewhere but this was the biggest ever recorded departure and it involved the young, elite, energetic believers who loved God. The following were the ministers who left: Rev. Aaron Siwale, who became the leader in Lusaka, Rev. Samson Chalomba (son of Rev. Samson Kapufi, P.E.), Rev. Happy Mulwe, a graduate from the University of Zambia Biology programme and teacher (with his wife Dr. Musenge Matibini, a medical doctor from University of Zambia School of Medicine). Others were Benson Mashini, Mirriam Mwape and many more.

In Kitwe, Judah A.M.E. Church lost the charismatic leadership of Rev. Richard Kasanda. He was an artisan in the mines, at Nkana Division of ZCCM. We also lost the young and budding believers who went to form a new church under Lift Him Up Ministries at Chimwemwe. It was a testimony to the resistance to change by many adults and this news shook the Church to the core. It was now that some people who had been at the forefront providing resistance to the things of the Spirit realized they had hindered the work of God for years. We thought the people were now learning that it was not just about going into downtown perimeters of towns or cities that those who were seeking for change in the Church were looking for but it was repentance and genuine change. Leaders had been happy or contented with wearing phylacteries and sitting in positions of honour in the Church (Matthew 23:5) to be noticed by people and chose religion rather than to obey God and to honour his word.

Calvary in Kitwe lost the elite and faithful in the Lord. Br. Kennedy Chinyama and Br. Christopher Chikulungu who were very faithful brothers left. They had been at Copperbelt University in Kitwe where they had been studying land economy and accountancy, respectively. Others were Mirriam Mwape, Threasa Namfukwe, my sister Fridah Kapungwe and many more. From Bright Chapel were the likes of Bro. Willie Kavungu who became a co-leader with Mirriam Mwape at Chimwemwe's new church.

News of this breakaway sent shockwaves in the A.M.E. Church in Zambia. It was a wake-up call for leaders and members alike that prompted them to carry out an introspection to understand how their dealings with God and response to his work in the Church had been over the years. A meeting was organized in October 1998 at Jordan Chapel. The Presiding Elder, Rev. Cuthbert Katebe, his wife Mother Katebe and many local and outside leaders including those who had vehemently opposed believers in the past were present. One after the other, many of them broken, leaders confessed at the night of prayer and rededication to God. I sobbed. I saw a number of leaders including the Rev. Cuthbert Katebe and his wife shed tears when in turns people went to the front at the pulpit to pray. Lord, remember our repentance and forgive us of all our sins.

Many people remained weary for months. They kept on speculating that I was the next person who was to follow. I had not been aware of the impending departure until a close brother had hinted to me about plans which he had heard were being discussed, I still did not get a release in my spirit to go. One other brother came home in the run up to the departure and engaged me indirectly. He didn't mention about their impending departure but had just been asking me how I was seeing the Church and I kept saying "A lot of progress has been made!" He gave me reasons which could make people leave but I told him that the reasons given were genuine and I agreed with him but I never had peace which was determinant for any major decision for me. I am glad that the Rev. Aaron Siwale was not among those who had spoken to me about the issue. He preferred to be silent about it.

Two years before the breakaway, we had been co-opted into ministry. (Bro. Richard Kasanda, Bro. Happy Mulwe, Br. Samson Chalomba and I were just entering the ministry). Bro. Richard Kasanda had gotten into Admission at the Annual Conference in 1995. While meeting at the Annual Conference held at Trans-Africa Bible College (now Trans-Africa Christian University) in Kitwe in 1996, I was called to Pastor Trinity A.M.E. Church in Garneton. Rev. Joseph Sakwala, the first Pastor of Trinity from 1991, had passed away at the hospital I was working in a few months earlier in 1996. (Trinity had been started by Rev. Philemon Chakalipa Mumba as a point). The Presiding Elder, Rev. Cuthbert Katebe had met me and we had discussed the vacancy. When I was agreeable, he recommended my name to the Bishop. This Presiding Elder was the preacher who had been influenced to cancel our YPD meeting a number of years ago at Jordan Chapel. We had been getting closer, working with the Presiding Elder over the years and I am thankful to God for his grace! This was my "Fourth Calling!"

South West Zambia Annual Conference Ordination Ceremony of Itinerant Deacons at Holiness A.M.E. Church (now Kirkland) by Bishop Larry Theodore Kirkland, not in the picture, on 5th October, 1997 in Ndola hosted by Rev. Joel Mazimba, Pastor. From right to left Rev. Charles Kapungwe, Rev. Joseph Chinyanta, Rev. Richard Kasanda, Rev. Jeremiah Mwenyo ....

On 1st December, 1996, I was appointed Pastor to Trinity A.M.E. Church at Garneton in Kitwe by Bishop Larry Theodore Kirkland. This was at the South-West Zambia Annual Conference (comprising North Western and Copperbelt Provinces) meeting at Trans-Africa Bible College in Kitwe. After having been Pastor for a year, the South-West Zambia Annual Conference meeting at Holiness (now Kirkland) A.M.E. Church in Ndola proposed that I be ordained Itinerant Deacon under Missionary Rule since I had been a Pastor for a year, following a motion raised by the late Rev. Godfrey P. Mutembo of Jordan Chapel, Kitwe. Bishop Kirkland informed the Conference that he too, had been ordained under Missionary Rule and on 5th October, 1997, Rev. Richard Kasanda and I were ordained Itinerant Deacons and reappointed to Judah A.M.E. Church and to Trinity, respectively, by Bishop Kirkland. Rev. Kasanda had been appointed also on 1st December, 1996 as Pastor of Mindolo (which he renamed Judah). I was ordained Itinerant Elder on 3rd October, 1999 by Bishop Larry Kirkland at the South-West Zambia Annual Conference meeting at the Trade Fair Show Grounds hosted by Rev. Wilson Mpundu's Mother Hughes. I was reappointed to Trinity, the fourth year.

South West Zambia Annual Conference Ordination Ceremony of Itinerant Elders at the Trade Fair Grounds hosted by Mother Hughes A.M.E. Church (Rev. Wilson Mpundu, Pastor) on 3rd October, 1999 in Ndola. Standing from left to right: Rev. Paul Bupe, Rev. Paul Sakuwaha, Rev. Peter M.P. Mwenya, Rev. Godfrey Mutembo, Rev. Alfred Kalobwe, Bishop Larry Theodore Kirkland partially obscured and Rev. Caleb Ngoma. Kneeling from left: Rev. Joseph Chinyanta, Rev. Charles Kapungwe and Rev. Royd Mwandu. Rev. Samuel Mulapwa is seated in the background in the front row seat.

Trinity A.M.E. Church was on the outskirts of the City of Kitwe. When I first arrived there in 1996, I was welcomed by Rev. John Mukeya of neighbouring Membe A.M.E. Church at Twatasha, which was just about 5 kilometers away. At the time, we were meeting at Mwambashi Primary School. The school was at the boundary of Garneton and a shanty compound known as "Zambia Compound." The beautiful Garneton houses used to be occupied mostly by whites before independence.

Rev. Mukeya, a brother to the late Trinity church pastor Rev. Joseph Sakwala told me, "Rev. Kapungwe, welcome to Garneton! Garneton is the headquarters of demons in Kitwe!" At the time, I felt as though my senior Minister was not aware of what he was talking about! However, Rev. Mukeya was one of the great spiritual leaders of our Church. He was one of the few ministers who ran a vibrant church which had members who hailed from Congo DR but spoke Bemba (Just as Trinity had been under late Rev. Sakwala). His Church (Rev. Mukeya's) was one of the few if not the only two (with Rev. M.P.P. Mwenya's Allen Temple) which attracted Churches of other denominations to prayers. He loved the Lord and had a very strong well-knit community of believers.

Within one month of my arrival at Trinity, I lost a young woman who passed away at Kitwe Central Hospital. I decided to visit the funeral home to see how I was going to arrange for the burial. I was surprised that the minibus I had boarded with about 18 passengers on it, careered off the road and almost had us all killed! We were on the main highway (before the dual-carriage was built). The driver was driving at a speed of possibly 40 miles an hour (64.4 km/hour) and without slowing down began to take a turn into the road that went to Garneton and joins the highway making a "T" intersection.

He couldn't negotiate the corner! Therefore, the minibus began to go into the grass along the main road missing the intersection. "If he turns the steering wheel again," I began to think, "We are going to overturn!" At this point everyone on the minibus was screaming. There were about four or five primary school going children and they were calling on their mums! The driver turned the wheel to the right again trying to get on the road that joined from the right and we began to roll over to the left side. Everything happened very fast as though it was in a movie! I then shouted at the top of my voice the name of Jesus with all my might! "J-E-S-U-S!"

The vehicle immediately came to a standstill! It came to rest at almost 45 degrees' angle tilting towards the left and had found itself in a small ditch away from the main branch of the road we were to go in. How the ditch had been there, no one would know because it was covered with grass and it had not been visible. With relief, we began getting out one by one with hardly any injuries. Taller ones, like me, had minor bruises on the knees. We talked to the driver asking him what he was thinking and he looked as stunned as many of us around him. We then pulled the bus out of the ditch and miraculously, it was still able to run and it took us to our destination which was just about 10 minutes away. I immediately, knew, Garneton was going to be a frontline for my spiritual battle. I had to trust God to prevail and I did!

Ministering at Trinity soon proved to be a challenge. I got to the church by boarding three separate modes of public transportation. Returning home was by two or three as well. In the church, there was no person who had a job besides me and that meant that I provided for the ministry and received no financial payment. This, was no problem for me because I had learned over the years not to depend on people, nevertheless, the cost of transportation began to get high. I was also a national leader in the Healthcare Christian Fellowship of Zambia (HCFZ), which demanded a lot of sacrifice since it involved traveling across Zambia. We supported ourselves individually for such work. Additionally, I came to learn that poverty was a biggest challenge in the area and being far away from the town center of Kitwe made life difficult for many.

One member, for example, used to brew illicit beer at home to make ends meet. She understood the requirements of the word but she had no other means of supporting her family. She quit church! I soon found myself in a difficult situation of teaching people to stop other behaviours which were their only source of income! Also, I noticed when I taught the word, many in the congregation, I could tell, had had no meals! They were not following when I taught! At first, this was very hard to bear! By the grace of God, I was able to connect and began to help the people. Mother Jane Sakwala, the widow of the founding Pastor, now late Rev. Joseph Sakwala, later confessed to me when I returned for my second year in 1997 stating, "Pastor, I thought you were going to run away! Now I know you are for real! The first year, we were testing you!"

I began teaching and preaching to ground the people in the word. No more than one or so was ever born again in the congregation. Nevertheless, the team sang with passion and cultivating on the strength they had, the Holy Spirit helped me to teach. I had to be lively to help them not to sleep or switch off. My theme for my first year, 1996 to 1997 was borrowed from the Bishop who had ordained me, "Called, Committed and Compelled to Serve." I then prayed and the Lord gave me specific topics for the whole year. The topics where, Salvation, Prayer, The Holy Spirit, Baptism, Evangelism, etc.

I spoke every week and taught in Sunday school. We began to have overnight prayer meetings at the church. We also began to invite other denominations to these prayers and by the end of the year the Lord had given me souls! I also would invite close friends of mine who had been in my inner circle either from other A.M.E. Churches, such as Rev. Richard Kasanda or other denominations. After a while, the spiritual growth demonstrated by believers at Trinity was phenomenon! It nevertheless, came at a great cost and sacrifice.

I remember when the brethren were planning to leave the Church one brother had raised this point. He had said, "Normally, the setup of ministry has to be that the sheep must be providing for their Shepherd and the sheep looking to you for everything was not in the will of God." I had informed my brother that I also do not see it wrong for me to share the blessings with those who had nothing. Other leaders from Calvary A.M.E. Church where I had come from, would also bemoan or sympathise with me that I had to provide where necessary for my members and not vice versa.

Two denominations enjoyed better numbers in Garneton. They were the Catholic Church and the United Church of Zambia. The former, had a white Father who owned a van, and he could easily transport the sick in the community to a hospital approximately 10 kilometers away. Sometimes, when I was on call at this hospital, I would see the Catholic priest bring his people even after midnight! The latter, has and is known to have a strong helps ministry and cell groups which help members. Therefore, the rest of the denominations in the community couldn't attract large membership.

My second year, 1997 to 1998 I had a theme, "From Membership to Discipleship." It must have been from my Bishop as well. I conducted an open-air Crusade and I got two precious souls, both were males. Nevertheless, they did menial jobs for the City Council and they did not change the financial situation of the church. However, transformation began to be noticed even by neighbouring Churches especially in joint overnight prayer meetings and the community began to notice too. The Lord gave me souls which got the passion for souls and Soul-Winning was one of the topics I had taken. Since I was working for the Government, my interaction with the members was limited. Usually, it was over the weekends only. However, those who hungered for fellowship or the word would come to the hospital I worked and when I was done, we would walk, go to a grocery store, buy food and sit under a tree. I would have them open the Bible and teach. The hunger for the word of God was unimaginable, and I passed on the grace of the Lord he had given me in this way.

I sang on the choir and taught many songs. This could only be done on Sundays! Therefore, after church service, we did Choir rehearsals, prayed together and then went on home visitation. Sometimes I made it on Saturday afternoons and did ministry. The third year, 1998 to 1999, our theme was "Called to Make a Difference" and my fourth and last year, 1999 to 2000 was a prophetic theme which said "Completing the Task!" When we sang in meetings the power that was emitted was amazing. The reason was simple. The singers had a personal relationship with Jesus. They were born again and spent time in prayer and in the word. This is not a bragging right but is true.

After four years, the spiritual growth that occurred at Trinity was astounding! When you talked to several believers who had committed their lives to Jesus, you would think they had been in the Lord for at least 10 years! For sisters, men with evil intentions who never knew who they were would back off immediately after engaging them! Every person they saw was seen as a "soul," that is, a potential soul to be won for Jesus but was on its way to hell. Evangelism was therefore, being exercised by believers! To God be the glory!

I cannot exhaust sharing all the testimonies the Lord did at Trinity. Regardless, it is important to share a part of the work of the ministry of the Holy Spirit to provoke a Church that has sat on the demands and commands of God and settled for mediocrity and traditions of men. By so-doing, we have sent scores to hell because we have believed in our own agenda and not God's! We have hindered the work of the Holy Spirit and trashed Jesus' command to go to all the world and preach the good news, drive out demons and baptize those who believe. When we abscond from God's call, we invite demonic spirits to imprison souls. I have shared a lot in other books concerning this but I will share the following testimony to have this denomination and many other denominations which hold on to traditions of men so they can see how they support Satan to hold people captive. They have "Full Members" or "Sprinkled Sinners" or just members of their Churches, yet they have prevented them from experiencing an encounter with the power of the Holy Spirit that sets sinners free.

God's Miraculous Works in His Church – A Case of Prisca

As I walked into church one Sunday morning everything looked usual. It was in 1997. After putting down my brief case and prayer a trusted sister walked to me that she wanted to share something with me. Sister Alice Manase was my church treasurer and was among a group of sisters in the church whose spiritual growth had amazed many. She told me that I needed to see Prisca (not her real name) and speak to her after service. When asked as what it was pertaining to, Alice just said, "No pastor, you just talk to her. I think she will tell you herself."

I had three of my stewards remain behind after church service. They were Sister Elizabeth Lubozya who was the pro term, Sister Alice Manase, church treasurer and Sister Cynthia Mwelwa, church secretary. Prisca was a beautiful young girl of 18, dark in complexion and one of the members who had not been very consistent in attending church. I started by finding out how she was doing spiritually after a formal greeting. Shyly, she said she was fine and then as she warmed up, she narrated one of the most disturbing stories a young girl of 18 could be subjected to.

Prisca's parents had divorced and her mother let her go to live with her uncle at Garneton. Her uncle was a polygamist, a relatively uncommon situation in many parts of Zambia. Her uncle, 48 had two girls who were around 18-years-old too. At night Prisca would dream of the uncle coming to her in a form of a large snake. She would distinctly recognize his face as he appeared and clouds would form the background to his face. He would then come and have sex with her in sleep.

What surprised her each time was the aftermath of every episode. Whenever, the uncle slept with her, she would start her menstrual periods. The uncle would now knock at the bedroom door of his niece and two daughters, inquiring as to how Prisca was feeling. This now would be in the physical and Prisca said she would tell him that she was fine to which he would persistently insist to be told the truth. He would say, "I know you are not feeling well, tell me!" "When I concurred that indeed I was not alright, he would immediately give me some medicines to take informing me that I would be well soon. Bleeding would cease always as soon as I took his medicines and this had been going on for a long time," narrated Prisca.

I inquired if ever she had slept with him physically. Prisca denied it. Asked about if ever he had made any physical advances to her, Prisca said, it does appear that if he had had any chances, she was without any doubt he could. "His behaviour shows it all. He often buys me more stuff than his girls and he would enter our bathroom when we are naked under a guise of bringing us soap or something," Prisca explained. At this juncture, I asked her how she felt about this against the backdrop of our African culture which regarded any mature girl as your "mother" in terms of respect and keeping of distance by fathers or father figures. Prisca did not see this behaviour as normal or acceptable.

I also referred to the Bible especially from Leviticus 18. A man of his status was not to see the nakedness of his daughters or that of her niece. It was at this point that demons manifested and took over her mind. They were so mad at Alice for disclosing what had happened that they started chasing her around the room accusing her of being the cause of all this. I commanded them to be quiet and to leave. They said they were not leaving because this (Prisca's body) was their house. I told them it was God's house and that Jesus was taking over now!

They were upset and told us that the uncle was actually present! He knows about this (about the deliverance that was ongoing) and that they were not going to leave! (In deliverance of people from demons it is always common to hear demons always say they were not going to go! They may even cry for loss of a home as they did here but we had to drive them out!) After a while, all the demons left and Prisca came back to her normal self. She opened her eyes and looked at us like someone coming out of a deep sleep. She surveyed her surrounding and looked at each one of us as we all had surrounded her. She then noticed that her dress was covered with dust so she started dusting it off. She also noticed that she was not at the spot where she had been before when we had started talking to her and she inquired as to what had happened to her.

I gave her a briefing of the entire episode. I informed her also of how God loves her and how he had delivered her from demons. I shared to her the importance of accepting Jesus. After a while Prisca confessed her sins and accepted Jesus Christ as her personal Savior. I shared assurance of salvation as I always do to all new converts and counseled her about the long and difficult spiritual battle for her that I foresaw but I told her not to worry but to trust God in it all. I however, emphasized the need for prayer, the word and fellowship for her.

As we walked home, I told my leaders of the need to visit her home. They all never said a word at this but I told them that we needed to begin praying because I foresaw a difficult battle for the young girl. I needed to talk to the uncle about Jesus. We set the time and gave ourselves two weeks. We prayed and fasted and the hour finally came.

I was with more troops when we visited Prisca's home. We already had sent word about our proposed visit. About eight praying warriors were with me when we "invaded" Satan's hideout. We found the first wife present (Prisca's aunt) but not the uncle and the second wife. This disturbed me but we all continued interceding while we talked to the aunt. Prisca was present too. Our intercession was done quietly and you wouldn't know the saints were praying even while they were in the conversation unless you had been trained in Special Forces or as a commando who was well-versed in spiritual warfare. To our delight, the Lord brought the uncle in within 10 minutes and we knew it had to be the Lord!

The man became very restless and jittery at our sight! He greeted us quickly but failed to sit down in his own house! He was like in an acute panic attack mood! He tried to sit on two or three places but each time got up and went to the bedroom. He couldn't stay there longer too, so he came back into the sitting room. I then decided to talk to him, introducing the group and tried to make him feel as comfortable as possible – in his own home! The troops were waging warfare through the blood of the Lamb and such a situation was to be anticipated.

I informed Prisca's uncle that we primarily visited to share the word of God with the family. He surprisingly said that was okay with him! I asked again how he felt about our sharing he repeated the same words saying, "Who could refuse people sharing the word of God?" I then went into sharing the word and the need to give ourselves to Jesus. I thought of it as an introduction and hoped to come later going into specifics because of the large group although I mentioned the need to give up all and follow Jesus. We prayed and left promising to come again next time.

It was after we had left his house that my sisters informed me of God's breakthrough. They told me that when I had suggested about the need of visiting that home, we had thought to ourselves, "O Lord! The reason was that, that man never allowed any person from any church to enter his yard! He has chased and cursed many who had attempted to visit him. He called them prostitutes and other unprintable words after them! As a result, no church has dared to step in his yard, let alone in his house." They mentioned different denominations by name and I immediately concluded that it had to be the Lord! We didn't go in the *name of our church but in the name of Jesus!*

Sister Irene Mushinge invited Prisca to stay with her for a week at our apartment. Sister Irene, like me, worked at the hospital. She was a nurse tutor at Kitwe Central Hospital School of Nursing and lived on the first floor of St. Fergus Court while I was on the ground floor. Gladly, Prisca's uncle accepted and this was used to disciple her and praying for her. It was not the first time we had done this in cases of this magnitude. "Pastor Morgan Bwalya" and his wife had also stayed with another girl I had led to the Lord who had had a strong spiritual battle with mind-binding evil spirits. The Lord had used them too for that girl.

Prisca's exponential spiritual growth left me dumbfounded. The Lord quickly transformed this shy, timid, and quiet-looking young girl into an imposing spiritual girl whose impact soon began to bear fruit even at her home. The testimony she came to share with us one day left us speechless but we were thankful to the Lord for his grace.

Her uncle had gotten very ill in the night one day. His condition had deteriorated to the extent that the family gave up all hope of him recovering at all. Garneton was far away from the downtown area and transportation was always a big problem and I am sure they had ruled out of any possibility of getting any vehicle to take him to the hospital. As the night deepened, the wives decided to call their daughters to the bedroom to come and see their father die and to possibly get any last words from him.

"When we entered the bedroom, my uncle was so sick that he hardly could move. Everybody was overwhelmed by the impending death. We waited for a few minutes and nothing was going on except to watch him die. Then all of a sudden, I got so much power in me and felt the urge that God was telling me to pray!" Prisca informed us. "I told the family that, 'Let us pray!' They looked at me in amazement but I had really meant what I had said. It was around 01:00 hr. in the morning. I started praying as the power of God was all over me. I rebuked the sickness and commanded Satan to go! What followed pastor left everybody in awe!" a soft spoken but authoritative Prisca explained.

"We suddenly saw a small human being in a form of a small baby all in blood! This was over my uncle's body and everyone saw it! The baby was all bloody and after a while, it just disappeared by melting away! My uncle moved a bit and power was still over me in a way I have never experienced! The Lord told me to go into the wardrobes and cupboards. I opened them and found a lot of herbal medicines and fetishes. I grabbed them while still praying! Family members were all looking at me and none of them ever said a word," Prisca narrated.

"Garneton is very dark at night, pastor! I was not afraid as a girl! I got out and went into the pit latrines outside and threw these herbs in there. I came inside and the Lord told me there were still more, I searched every area in the bedroom and house and again I went outside and threw them in the same place. I then came to the uncle and prayed over him again and all of a sudden, the man came back! He moved his body and I continued to pray and we made him to sit up! It was such an overwhelming experience for everyone. The Lord had given me this anger in my spirit that I continued to pray and dedicated the house and everybody into the hands of the Lord. When everybody went to sleep, I remained praying until morning and the Lord had healed my uncle!" Prisca told us.

"I was called by my aunts in the morning. They gave me strict orders not to say or tell anyone about the experiences that we had witnessed that night," Prisca narrated to us. I had witnessed yet another of my babies in the Lord being transformed and empowered by the Holy Spirit for signs and wonders which Jesus had promised were to follow those who believed in him. We had no word but to give God all the praise! Prisca became one of the powerful children in the Lord who the Lord had given me at the church. Our fellowship one with the other was always lively as everyone exhibited the joy and love of the Lord. Testimonies of what God was doing were one of the driving works of the Holy Spirit that knit us together and we were all aware of the constant spiritual warfare we all faced as saints daily and the victory that God grants us.

This is the ministry that God has called us to execute. It is the ministry we knew God had told us to do – to set captives free. We therefore, preached that people should repent from sin. We preached that everyone must be born again. Unless you were born again, you were not a Christian! We preached that faith comes by hearing and hearing the word of God. We preached that church membership was not Christianity and would not save a person. Jesus would! We preached that the uniform wouldn't save anyone, faith in Jesus would. We preached that everyone needed to be baptized in water following salvation and there were no multiple answers to a single question of what must we do to be saved?

The answer was to believe and be baptized in the name of Jesus for forgiveness of sins! We preached that we needed to go in the water and die with Jesus (get immersed and come out as new creatures – die with him and be alive with him!) We then needed to be baptized in the Holy Spirit to do ministry and to overcome Satan! This is the whole will and counsel of God! This is the message of the Cross and we were determined to preach it and not what man wanted us do or say and we chose to obey God and not man.

I had undergone "Military training," so I thought! I was a "Soldier" – a Soldier of the Cross! I had been trained to obey the commander! My training also had taught me to obey the King. I had been trained to know and distinguish between the word of the King from that of the commander. I had been trained to be in the presence of the King and to hear what the King said. I was trained to see if what the King said differed from what the commander said. I was trained to honour the King and obey him if the words of the commander differed from what the King said. Like the young man in 2 Samuel 18:5; 10-14, who had heard the King say, *"Be gentle with the young man Absalom for my sake,"* in the presence of the commanders Joab, Abishai, and Ittai and the troops, I was to honour the King's word. I was trained to honour the King.

The commander, Joab, had not been willing to obey the King. His words differed from the King. This was our message to our troops. To honour God and not commanders who misrepresent God! However, if you, as a Commander, honoured the word of the King, we would honour and obey your word as well. This was not too complicated not to be understood. Rev. J.L.C. Membe was right when they arrested him in Tanganyika Territory and accused of "Preaching in this Province without a permit from the Tanganyika Government (Now Tanzania) and that many of their Christians have joined your Church." He showed the District Commissioner the Holy Bible as his permit. He was put in jail two more days!

I was aware that Roman Catholicism had corrupted Christianity. Many Protestants including Methodism erroneously retained infant baptism and sprinkling in their doctrine after the Reformation. I was also aware that doctrinally, the A.M.E. Church was sound in its Articles of Faith except where it retained the baptism of infants and sprinkling, therefore, the problem lay in the commanders by and large, and not the doctrine. To its credit, it also accepted immersion. Men (Preachers), therefore, often said it was up to the individual to choose whether to be immersed or sprinkled! The teacher in a school *NEVER* tells his student to choose what they *want* for an answer before teaching them *TRUTH!*

This is why Jesus told his disciples to go and make disciples of all nations! He told them to go, baptizing them in the name of the Father and of the Son and of the Holy Spirit and teaching them to obey everything he had commanded us! Also, when Jesus was baptised, *he went up out of the water*, and at that moment heaven was opened and he saw the Spirit of God descending like a dove and lighting upon him. Then a voice said, *"This is my Son, whom I love: with him I am well-pleased!"* Matthew 3:16-17. Baptism, by immersion, is what the Church should have been practicing if to see the Spirit it has.

Two souls were added to the church after the open-air Crusade we conducted. They were Bro. Patrick Mbao and Br. John Kaluba. Bro. Patrick was soon transformed by the power of God and he loved to dance and to praise God. When I baptized him, he experienced deliverance! He came to testify in church that, "When I came out of the water, I felt as though something got lifted off me! I got delivered! I never used to see a 'dress' pass without pursuing it!" He spoke with great joy and his wife was in the meeting! Baptism in water is important and Jesus knew why he commanded us to undergo it unless we were like a thief at the cross who did not have the opportunity to do so before he died, we must be immersed! We obeyed it to fulfill all righteousness and never substituted it for our convenience!

I was aware that after I left, salvage wolves were going to come to steer the sheep back to religion so I warned the saints just like Paul, the apostle, and Jesus himself did. When Rev. Joseph Sakwala, my predecessor who had been the Pastor at Trinity from 1991 went to be with the Lord in 1996, he had just acquired the land but had not paid for it. The members showed me the land but they could not afford to pay for it! By the grace of God, I paid for it using God's money out of my pocket. I gave the money to the City of Kitwe. At the time, no one thought of Trinity as anything but a remote and poor place. We called it our "Nazareth" and we knew something good, was going to come out of it despite being looked down upon! Once, an African-American missionary, Bishop Lavinia Williams who had been seeing me in meetings in the City at the YMCA Richmond's Gardens' Mighty Women and Men of Valour visited Trinity. She informed me that they had wanted to put me in a remote place but God was going to bless me and "this place!"

A.M.E. Church, we had observed as youths, pushed the young and budding ministers in poor distant communities. While, there was nothing wrong to have an upcoming minister learn ministry in such areas, however, the practice appeared odd to the young believers. For example, when Rev. Aaron Siwale, whom we called, "A General," (he called us "Commandos"), graduated from Theological College of Central Africa (TCCA), he was sent to a small poor church in a shanty compound in Kitwe. Although we were not despising the poor, we just thought that the practice was not just.

We had very few Pastors with his qualification at the time. Only three other ministers, Rev. M.P.P. Mwenya, Rev. Paul Bupe and Rev. Wilson Mpundu had attended that prestigious and well-respected institution, besides Rev. David Simfukwe. Rev. Paul Kawimbe and Rev. Godfrey Mutembo had attended Kaniki Bible College. In our view, if Rev. Siwale in whom the Church had invested a lot by sending him to school had been given, for example, Bright

Chapel or Jordan, he could have doubled or tripled the membership there! Probably, I believe, he could not have left the Church too. Since the Gethsemane could not support him, he chose to live with me and we stayed together for two years.

On the other hand, for me, I had welcomed my Trinity appointment. (I am sharing this against the backdrop of the feelings of dissatisfaction and how the youth felt about the leadership in the Church over what they perceived as mistreatment of the upcoming vibrant young ministers). I had a mindset that believed that I was a soldier and as a soldier, I was made to survive in any unfavourable circumstances. That said, I too believed if I had a more prosperous church, or a church within the city, the outcome would have been different, i.e., a larger number would have been brought to the Lord and the impact would have spread to other churches faster. However, I was content and I loved the church I was sent to. I might not have been happier anywhere else as I was at Trinity where I saw the grace of God demonstrated in power and in signs and wonders.

My ministry partner, Rev. Richard Kasanda, for example, had been sent to Judah. (Judah was at Mindolo – a mining community. He only had a small community hall, a building which was acquired from the mines by Rev. Elsie Musonda when she had been a Pastor there, years back. Rev. Musonda had worked for the Mines in Community Development Department and had retired from the Mines in Kitwe in 1976. Judah met in this building). Rev. Kasanda had the fasted growing church, only matched by St. Andrews where Rev. Stephen Chifunda was in Ndola at the time. Rev. Richard had a different audience but also was a great minister and an unmatched organiser of our time. We were of the view that if the Church had appointed ministers like him to the first churches, this Church (A.M.E.) would not have been the same. Smaller churches would have been influenced by such arrangements but the leadership remained behind failing to catch the vision due to selfishness and need to inhibit the work of the Holy Spirit.

Another example was on the then Rev. Paul Kawimbe. When Rev. Kawimbe graduated from Kaniki Bible School in Ndola, he was sent to Kalilo Ipafu, a place which was in the "middle of nowhere!" He didn't go, and he opted for going to school. He went to the UK instead, for a year to do a course in Evangelism. Rev. Alick Kapesa, the former Pastor of St. Paul in Ndola attended school with him there and shared what had transpired in UK indicating the poor choice that Zambia made for Bishopric. Of course, the fear of "spirituality" taking over the Church or the dreaded "born again" experience by some in leadership appeared to be the mitigating factor in many such appointments which involved young ministers at the time.

I designed Trinity Church building and paid the architect out of my pocket using God's money. The design had the Pastor's Office and toilet, the Vestry, Counseling Room, Steward's Office, Men and Women Toilets and the main sanctuary. I put in a baptism pool for a reason too. Before that, we were using the nearby Mwambashi River to baptize converts.

The toilets were part of the church building. I had observed with dismay that Jordan Chapel, my childhood church had had no church toilets for decades and worshipers used one toilet in the mission house! I had also painfully observed that when we began building the two toilets at Jordan in 1979, they took more than 30 years to complete and to date, they have not been completed! I was, therefore, going to make toilets a part of the building to avoid making them become another new project! I was going to have shower rooms incorporated into them too in the event we hosted Conferences – and this I did! I often paid budget at Conferences out of my pocket, and if you never had been there, (at Trinity), you would never understand why this was so!

Many people would ask me how I managed to stay in what was known as a "Traditional Church" but still kept the fervency. I told them, "God!" God was the one who did it! Remember, I mentioned earlier that you have to be in the presence of the King yourself and hear what the King says for God to do his work. Your commanders may say something different but if you spend time with the King you will do what he says and not what they say. We prayed a lot as well! I remember, periods we had overnight prayer meetings every Friday. There were also periods we had overnight prayer meetings every month or scheduled as deemed necessary.

We did this with Rev. Richard Kasanda and the team. We did this too when we were at Calvary before we became ministers. The combined fellowship (A.M.E. Church and Central Assembly of God) in Parklands, Kitwe, regularly went to the mountain on designated Saturdays for prayer and fasting. It was while there that a Sister in the Lord had told me to write a book and I had dismissed the suggestion but the conviction came after a year and my first book "Soldiers of the Cross" was written!

We stayed in touch with other believers in different A.M.E. Churches too. We also remained constantly in touch with believers outside this denomination. Through this, we knew it was not about "Richard Allen" but about Jesus! It was also not about the Bishop but about the Holy Spirit and not about the A.M.E. Church but about the Church – the body of Christ which Jesus said, *"And I say also unto thee. That thou art Peter, and upon this rock I will build my church; and the gates of hell shall not prevail against it,"* Matthew 16:18 (KJV). We also knew it was not about the Uniform but about being marked with the seal of approval of the Holy Spirit, (Ephesians 1:13-14).

It was about putting on the whole armour of God so we could stand against the wiles of the devil, (Ephesians 6:11, KJV). Fellowship with the body of Christ was important in ministry. My Healthcare Christian Fellowship (HCF) ministry was also helpful. I was fed there and I did ministry there as well. We would often joke with my Bro. Kasanda that "If you don't go out you will be content and stunted in your spiritual growth and you will never see the best unless you went out!"

I had co-values which helped my drive. Often, I wrote them down and ran with them. I wrote in my song book several of these revelations. "Trained to Survive in Hostile Environment." The other read, "The Soldier is made to Survive in Unfavourable Environment." Another one said, "I AM A SOLDIER." I also had this one which was a stand not to compromise against what Jesus had called me to preach about. It read:

> *"Br. Charles, Do not preach what man tells you and do not be zealous for the traditions of your fathers: Preach what Jesus tells you."*

Another one was simply from a song we used to sing and it said,

"I have anchored my faith, LORD in you."

The Ephesians' Scripture to believers from Paul, the apostle, was important in my ministry. He told us to be strong in the Lord and in the power of his might, Ephesians 6:18, KJV. To fight off the spirits of religion, deception, old wine, etc., demanded to have a resolve or stand and then to be dependent upon the Holy Spirit. Without them, it meant being set up to courting or embracing failure. On 28/8/1997, I wrote:

"Respect your constitution and miss God's visitation
Respect your law and miss the Messiah
Respect your programme and miss the visitation of the Holy Spirit."

In 2017, at the request of my brother-in-law I designed Calvary A.M.E. Church in Kitwe. I was in the U.S. then. I sent my drawings to the same architect who had done Trinity and paid for it with God's money. It included all the amenities that were at Trinity, but I added a floor up, to serve as the Upper Room for prayers and a Fellowship Hall with Storage Room, Kitchen and Food Store. The main sanctuary was to have a 1,000-seating capacity while the Fellowship Hall was to have 300. Calvary was like an unfinished project for me, a church whose potential had been hindered by man – a pastor, who had continued to fight the word of salvation. God have mercy for all we have done and for our sins.

When my departure for the U.S. was coming close, the local Healthcare Christian Fellowship (HCF) threw a farewell party for me in June 2000. It was held in the Staff Clinic on the first floor of Kitwe Central Hospital where I had worked for 12 years. I became a Vice Chairman in 1987 when I first got employed there. Bro. David Katongo had been the Chairman and after his transfer to the Pneumoconiosis Bureau in Kitwe in 1988, I had assumed the role of Chairman for the Fellowship for about five years. I became one of the National Leaders in 1991 consequently relinquishing the role of a local chairman in 1993 to Brother Lumba Kazembe. By 1992, Kitwe Central Hospital Healthcare Christian Fellowship had become the biggest lunch-hour fellowship in our hospitals in Zambia. The average attendance had reached 30 and for a busy hospital like ours, that was a remarkable feat! In 1993, I had come to Dallas, Texas as a study exchange student and returned to Zambia the same year.

From Left: Mrs. Fernandez, Charles Kapungwe (Vice National Chairman – from Kitwe Central Hospital), Rev. Gervas Tembo [National Coordinator, a Lab Technician at the Tropical Diseases Research Center (TDRC) in Ndola] and Dr. Oscar Fernandez [National Chairman of the Healthcare Christian Fellowship of Zambia (HCFZ) from Nchanga Hospital in Chingola] at the Victoria Falls, Livingstone Zambia, August 1993. (Dry Season).

I served at the national level as a leader for eight years from 1991 to 1999. I served as Vice National Chairman for four years from 1993 to 1997 and for two years as National Chairman of the Healthcare Christian Fellowship of Zambia from 1997 to 1999. In 1993, we represented Zambia at the Southern Africa Healthcare Christian Fellowship International (HCFI) Conference at Victoria Falls Town in Zimbabwe. We also represented Zambia in 1995 at the World Conference of the Healthcare Christian Fellowship International (HCFI) in Johannesburg, South Africa. About 300 delegates from all over the world were present. We represented Zambia at the Southern Africa Healthcare Christian Fellowship International (HCFI) Conference too in 1996 in Windhoek, Namibia.

We planted fellowships in many parts of Zambia. In 1994, I took with me Bro. Bright Mumba (and my one month's salary to pay for the trip. Only Sister Christine Temba, a nurse and "my seer," at the hospital, contributed to my trip as well). We visited Mansa General Hospital and attended St. Thomas A.M.E. Church in Mansa with Bro. Shadreck Siwale from Jordan Chapel who was now in school at Mansa Trades. We also visited Samfya Hospital (where

I had done practical in 1986), Mambilima Hospital, Mwense District Hospital, Kawambwa District Hospital, Mbereshi District Hospital and St. Paul Hospital at Nchelenge sharing the vision of HCF of what we believed was the work Jesus wanted us to do in our hospitals. We also talked about the soon to be held Provincial Conference at Mbereshi. Three months later, we returned with leaders of HCFZ, Irene Mushinge and Rev. Gervas Tembo but I took Bro. Bright Mumba with me also. We had organized a Three-day Provincial H.C.F. Conference where I was one of the speakers at Mabel Shaw Secondary School at Mbereshi.

We had planted other fellowships across the nation. I had been a part to the ones at Nchanga North and South Hospitals in Chingola. I had visited Mufulira Mine Hospitals as well and we had planted Kabwe General Hospital Christian Fellowship too. Livingstone General Hospital and Kapiri Mposhi were also among the fellowships we planted. My friends had visited more hospitals when time and finances proved to be a constraint for me at times but we met for national leadership frequently and visited many hospitals throughout Zambia. When I became a Pastor for Trinity, I could not fulfill some obligations and later stepped down as National Chairman but remained active with the ministry in the healthcare field. Many great testimonies the Lord did are shared in my other book, "Soldiers of the Cross."

In 1994, I had also done some missionary work which took me to Lusaka. I reached out to believers in Lusaka and I spoke at the University Teaching Hospital (U.T.H.), Maina Soko Military Hospital, Chainama College of Health Sciences, Evelyn Hone College (made contacts here only) and the University of Zambia, School of Medicine at Ridgeway Campus, sharing the vision of H.C.F. Brother Shadreck Siwale was in Lusaka at this time and he accompanied me to the School of Medicine where I spoke to medical students.

At the farewell party organized for me at Kitwe Central Hospital in 2000, we shared a lot of what had been done in ministry in our hospitals. Brethren spoke kind words of encouragement and I also thanked them for having been great partners in ministry. When the meeting was over, Sister Regina Mwasulama, the younger sister to Sister Dorothy Onesi, spoke to me the prophetic revelation the Lord had shown to her in a dream. Sister Regina was a part of a combined A.M.E. Church and Central Assembly of God Cell Group which met at my home. I was teacher of the group, courtesy of their Pastor who had agreed that I could. She had a prophetic ministry. She informed me that God had revealed to her through a dream that I was going to face great hardships in America.

After that, God was going to send someone who was going to offer me help. She described the person and it came to pass just as the Lord had spoken. Sister Dorothy Onesi, a nurse at our hospital and neighbour, had also spoken to me after the meeting that I was not to fear anything, "The Lord owned everything and what is there belongs to our Father. In fact, you are going there to get what was taken away or what we sent ahead of you." We lived in the same apartments which were owned by the hospital. She, in fact, had been the person who the Lord had used to communicate to me about writing a book! Ten years earlier, while on the mountain praying and fasting in 1990, Sister Dorothy had told me "Br. Charles, you must write a book!" I had dismissed the suggestion but she seriously told me I have a lot to pass on to the Church. One year later, my first book title was revealed to me by the Lord and it was released in the U.S. years later!

Leaving Trinity was not easy. Ministry was a blessing. To see the level of growth and maturity of the saints at Trinity was a joy. We often spoke in parables using the word, a deed I had carried from our Jordan Chapel Fellowship. We would engage a person when we saw them holding a conversation with a friend. "Do you have a Son?" we would ask. This would put off many, especially if they were young, or a young woman! "No! I don't!" a person would answer. Then, we would say, "You should because if you don't you do not have life!"

When they looked perplexed, we could clarify by using Scripture. *"And this is the testimony: God has given us eternal life, and this life is in his Son. He who has the Son has life; he who does not have the Son of God does not have life,"* 1 John 5:11-12. We would then open up and share Jesus. At other times, we just would use contextual conversation using the word! "He has gone back to Egypt," we would say, meaning "He has backslidden." We may ask someone, "How many children do you have?" The person, if young, would look surprised, but this, if directed at a believer, was the best way to provoke them to have children – spiritual children.

We prayed regularly together too. We held our last Overnight Prayer Meeting at Mrs. Estina Daka Chimba's home, the widow of Mr. Justin Chimba, Zambia's freedom fighter and member of the first cabinet in 1964 under President Dr. Kenneth Kaunda. Mr. Chimba had been the Minister of Labour and Mines. Mrs. Estina Daka Chimba had been a member of Trinity and she lived in Garneton. I blessed the team and they blessed me. It was a very humbling, yet tremendous occasion where the presence of God was evidently present. A farewell card was presented to me in June of 2000! It read:

The front's caption had the words:

****

It's Farewell to you Pastor – Deuteronomy 28:6

****

God bless your journey and make you fruitful in all aspects of your life.

****

Cheerio
Being with you for 4 years Pastor brought a great change in our lives at
Trinity Church.
I appreciate so much to God for who you were to us, a man of passion, compassion, mercy and love over souls. A man full of tears for the lost souls and with a heart of concern over God's Church. How hard it has become to believe that you are leaving us behind but it is God's timing and there is nothing to say apart from lifting up his Holy Name. May he bless your going and coming back to Zambia.
Deuteronomy 28:6

Bye – byeeee!!

****

How God has brought promotion to you Pastor! Leaving this country also is promotion. Surely, promotion does not come neither from the East, West nor South but from the One above the heavens. May he finish what he has started doing for your leaving which shall bless many of us, although we will miss you for some years.

****

WITH SORROW!!

With great sorrow! When you pronounced a word of farewell to us as a church, I felt how sorrowful it was for the disciples when it was time for Jesus to go back to his Father. Quite alright, disciples knew how beneficial or profitable it was for Jesus to go but the presence, not being with him for coming days, made them to feel sorrow. Same applies to us at Trinity, Pastor. You will greatly be missed in what you have done to us in Jesus' name.

May the faithful Father in heaven remember your good works you have done to him and to us. Nehemiah 5:19.

MISSING YOU!

****

I speak God's protection, guidance and care upon your ministry. May the Lord let it be known even in that Land that you are His and use you mightily because every place is for the Lord. Possess every land your foot shall step on in Jesus' name.

****

YOUR MINISTRY

How you have influenced many people with your ministry! Your Garneton Ministry meant and revealed a lot about you that you are a chosen man of God called to make a difference despite the hardships. But not many, can sacrifice the way you sacrificed yourself to be at Trinity – *Twalimonamo ubukulu bwakwa Lesa.* (i.e., "We have seen, in it, the greatness of God"). Reap in abundance, Ecclesiastes 11:1, because it wasn't a waste for you to be at Trinity and worthy to God and it is my prayer that God can raise other Ministers in churches with patience and serious attitude towards God's mission like you.

God's grace and favour goes with you and the people in that land which the Lord has given you to acknowledge how God works in you and the wisdom he has given you, 2 Chronicles

9.

****

When You Face Uncertainty

The Lord said, "I know the plans I have for you ... plans to prosper your Pastor Charles and not to harm you, plans to give you hope and a future," Jeremiah 29:11.

Praise be to the Lord who shall be your refuge even in the land and taking care of your life whenever you face uncertainty.

If God be for you, what kind of mountain can stand your way? Zechariah 4:7.

****

There is enough light for every step taken by faith to succeed in life.
****

GOD'S BLESSINGS

As you were a blessing to us, I pronounce a word of blessing upon your life in everything including the people you are going to be with. Be a blessing and lack nothing in the Lord as it was to our father, Abraham, Genesis 13:2.

TO OVERTAKE YOU

****

The Lord shall take care of your family.
Psalms 145:15-17.

****

PERSONAL THANKS

Personally, I am so much thankful to the Lord that you have let me to be at a place which was supposed to be done by my parents as their responsibility. When I remember the things I passed through, just since I lost my beloved parents, I don't help crying for the great kindness the Lord revealed to me through you. The Lord be mindful of his covenant in Proverbs 19:17 and pay you, who gives in abundance for the sponsorship I am receiving from you.
Taking me to college is not a waste and God shall reward you over it.

Wherever I shall be, I would never forget this great thing you have done to me in Jesus' name! It will stand as a great remembrance in my life for what the Lord has done to let me to have you as my spiritual father with a merciful and lovely heart. It wasn't my choice but by his grace that I can be at Trinity and be your disciple. The Lord is so gracious to me and to the house of my father because I am not worthy to find God's favour in your eyes. How I pray that for remembering me, may the Father of the fatherless remember you and your family and bless you.

See You by God's Grace,
Sis. Alice.

****

You will be greatly missed!!!
Byee! And thank God for the work you have done to us. Happy stay and God's mercy and love be upon you all the time.

****

The back's caption:
Cheerio bye-bye!!!

The Lord shall continue taking care of the Church. Your labouring at Trinity was not in vain.

Philippians 1:6   1 Corinthians 3:9

****

A short note was attached in the card. It read:

Pastor,
So, Sunday was the last day to see you? *Aweee!* (i.e., Nooo!)
Just one more time to pay a visit for us! *Tulemifuluka, katwishi uko mukaila!* (i.e., "We are missing you already, it will be worse when you leave!") Its only transport money I would have come as well.
Sis. Alice

****

Note: A group from the church had come to my home in Parklands, Kitwe just days before my departure for the U.S.A. Sister Alice Manase didn't make the trip because she didn't have money to pay for the bus ride. This is the day they handed me this farewell card.

I had informed the Presiding Elder Rev. Henry Alimasi to be considerate when doing appointments on Trinity. I politely had informed him that the level of growth of individual believers was relatively too high to be disturbed by bringing in a minister who would take them back to the vomitus. I did not hide him what I had heard them say during my departure. "Pastor, if they bring us people who speak 'parables and tales,' it would be better for us to leave; we will go!" they had told me. I wouldn't blame them! They had seen and witnessed a lot of it before. Thankfully, Pastor Elasto Mwansa, my son in the Lord, who had been a part of our ministry for years at Jordan Chapel was appointed to Trinity and there was no disruption in ministry as I had feared when I had left for the U.S.A. in July of 2000. To God be the glory!

When we did ministry, we always thought of empowering people. Rev. Richard Kasanda and I believed we needed to do so and this was important. Ministry was not theoretical but involved practical work. This is what even the Apostle Paul called for in Philippians 4:9, to put into practice what we have heard from him or from Jesus. When I saw a daughter in the Lord whose spiritual growth was phenomenon and both her parents were deceased, I thought of helping her go to school. Besides, she had finished secondary school but had had no means of support.

Her younger brother, Dickson Manase, visited us for a while at Garneton from home. He too, got born again and became zealous for the Lord! Sadly, he died of malaria, I presume, at a very young age of 20 when he returned home to Kasama where he had begun to share the good news about Jesus. Nevertheless, the investment in our sister was done by the Lord and because of that decision, God raised people in America in my darkest hours to send me to school for years and support me. It was also in answer to the prophetic words and uttered prayers you read from the card. God also raised people who blessed Trinity in a manner never seen in Zambia before in this Church.

From 1998 to 2000, I attended Faith L.I.F.E. Ministries Bible School which was started by an American Missionary to Zambia. While there, the Founder asked me if I could bring any member of my church to her school for free for two years! What a miracle! When I looked at the church I was in at the time, only two, I thought could have been eligible and were women. I was concerned that they lived far since the school was in Parklands. We met twice a week from 17:00 hrs. to 20:00 hrs. I suggested a name from my previous church and our Teacher, Rev. Sue McDermott was agreeable. Bro. Elasto Mwansa, my son in the Lord, therefore, went to the school by God's providence. He told me the school later had extended the training to four-years. Unknown to me at the time, the Lord had prepared it in such a way that he was going to take over the church after my departure! He was Pastor of Trinity for 11 years! To God be the glory!

Rev. Charles Kapungwe with the Allen University Concert Choir "Tour of the East Coast." Here, the choir is getting ready to go to the stage to sing at Bethel A.M.E. Church in Baltimore, Maryland, a mega church where Rev. Dr. Frank Madison Reid III was Pastor then. 2001.

Rev. Charles Kapungwe with the youth he used to teach at White Hall A.M.E. Church in Jenkinsville, South Carolina U.S.A. 25th December, 2005.

Rev. Charles Kapungwe with Sister (Mrs. Veronica Rabb) and Sister Sandra Bell at White Hall A.M.E. Church in Jenkinsville, South Carolina U.S.A. 25th December, 2005.

Trinity Miracle Unfolds

I had been in the U.S. for only 11 months when the Lord began to do the greatest blessing we had ever seen for our church in Zambia. I was a student at Allen University in Columbia, South Carolina studying for a B.Sc. degree in Biology. After my first year, I attended Summer School at the University of South Carolina (USC) – Aiken in Aiken, South Carolina where I was studying Environmental Health, Environmental Chemistry and Soils and Hydrology. I had been an Associate Pastor at White Hall A.M.E. Church in Jenkinsville, SC about 35 miles from Columbia. The Rev. Leroy Cannon and Mother Helen Cannon were of great help to me and it is with their help that I went to Medical School. They did a lot for me! May the Lord remember them for all their sacrifice.

Rev. Charles Kapungwe in the Pastor's Office at White Hall A.M.E. Church in Jenkinsville, South Carolina. March 2002.

Before I went to Aiken, we had begun our summer break at Allen University. I had taken time to pray that God would show me which Church I was going to be attending while in Aiken in May of 2001. This was a very agonising prayer because there were specific requests I had made. I had also asked God that I had wanted to reconnect with a similar ministry I had been a part while in Zambia for years.

I saw someone sharing the word of God at the USC – Aiken Campus. This was a strange occurrence taking place in America as far as I could tell! However, seeing all my classmates avoiding the man who was sharing the word to them was hurting! I felt touched by the behaviour showed towards him and wanted to tell him what a wonderful work he was doing. For some reason I said to myself, "It is fine, let him continue." In the afternoon, after lunch, I still saw him again and I felt that it was not right as a believer not to introduce myself so I walked to him and introduced myself. I praised him for his courage and ministry. He was from New Covenant Presbyterian Church (NCPC).

In my heart, I kept battling, "No God! It was not a Presbyterian Church that I had prayed for!" I was wrong! God wanted me to go there! The man, I came to know, was Pastor Wesley Holland, an Assistant Pastor of NCPC. He gave me a card and told me if I needed him to pick me up for church on Sunday, I could call him. "Definitely, that was not the Church I had prayed for, I kept thinking," but when Saturday was approaching, I knew I had to call him and I did.

It was a dynamic church with about 300-membership. I was the only black person but I didn't feel lost. The members were welcoming and very good. Many talked to me and asked where I was from. After the service, a man walked to me and asked me if I had anything planned for the afternoon and I said "No!" He introduced himself as Robert Rabias and showed me his wife Mrs. Joellyn Rabias who played the piano in the church. The couple invited me for lunch. We went to eat lunch and when we got home, many leaders from the church were present including the Pastor, the Chairman of the Missions' Committee Mr. George Brodie and a few other members.

Mr. Rabias asked me if I had spoken to the people home lately. I told him, "No! It has been a while." He gave me the phone and told me to call and never mind on number of minutes I took! At the time, cell phones were not common as they are today, so I called one of the leaders since I knew his home phone number by heart. He told me, "We are all fine except your church, Trinity! Pastor Elasto Mwansa was withdrawn from the church by the Conference two weeks ago because the church cannot support him – you know your church!" Rev. Theodore Kalumba has been asked as a supply Pastor. I was moved in the spirit. When the phone call was over, Mr. Rabias asked me how the people were and I told him they were fine except a Pastor who took over the church I had has been withdrawn and it was not surprising because when I was there, I supported myself throughout. I gave them the overall picture and I was asked how much it takes to support a Pastor and I gave them a minimum basic amount that could help.

They immediately, consulted one another within the house. (A friendly rebuke to the A.M.E. Church and other bureaucratic-prone Churches – our supporters from the Presbyterian Church NEVER waited for a matter to be discussed in the Official Board! They made a decision right there and then, in the house of Mr. Rabias to begin supporting Pastor Elasto! Their Pastor was there but the leaders took the initiative and offered to help!). When they asked the Missions' Committee Chairman, Mr. George Brodie, he responded, "Yah, we can do that!" The group unanimously agreed to begin supporting the Pastor and asked for details. I was aware that I needed to show maturity, responsibility, integrity and honesty. Trustworthiness is the virtue I tried also to let the recipients show throughout the course of this benevolence to our Church, However, years later this disappointingly waned.

I had immediately thought of contacting Rev. Sue McDermott in Kitwe to vouch for us. She was an American missionary who had been my former teacher for two years. I gave the Chairman of the Missions' Committee her details. When they had talked, later, Mr. George Brodie confirmed details from her and told me, "Charles, we talked to the lady! She said nice things about you! She knows Elasto too." Having confirmed knowing both Pastor Elasto Mwansa and I, Rev. Sue gave Mr. Brodie a very strong recommendation. I then provided them a name of a pastor through whom moneys would be sent for accountability's sake.

New Covenant Presbyterian Church supported Pastor Elasto for 5 years. Mr. and Mrs. Bob Rabias then took over and supported him for the next 6 years, a total of eleven years. By all accounts this has never happened in the history of this Church, confirming to us that this was an act of God. I later asked Pastor Elasto to send me the drawings I had done and had paid for when I was Pastor. When he did, I showed them to the A.M.E. Church and they were put in the drawers for 6 months. I consequently, explained about the project I had in mind to the NCPC and informed our supporters that I had paid for the land and the drawings. They invited our Church Choir (White Hall A.M.E. Church) from Jenkinsville, South Carolina. My Pastor, Rev. Leroy Cannon, together with our church drove about an hour to Aiken, South Carolina. New Covenant Presbyterian Church raised $5,000.00 which they sent to Zambia to begin the foundation of Trinity in 2003.

Since I was aware of the financial uncertainties, I advised the pastor to split the money. $2,500.00 was spent on the foundation box and the other $2,500.00 on a project. I saw an opportunity for them to engage in an income-generating project which would be used to help fund the building program. I also instructed them to begin the foundation as well. That way, I thought, was going to sustain the construction. I was wrong! This became our first mistake! They finished the box foundation for the church but the whole $2,500.00 invested into the project got lost! The produce in which the investment was done got wasted. It was an agonising pain for me! Mr. Rabias addressed this with the Pastor and there was a breakthrough concerning building fund after some years. Ahab, Jezebel and Herodias (you will learn about them later), did not know about this history.

At this time, the church got kicked out of the school classroom where we used to meet. They built a makeshift structure where they met for church services. There were Sundays the Pastor would get soaked by the dripping from the rain as he preached and had to reposition himself frequently to avoid the leaking roof. Since the planned church was costly, a plan to build a smaller structure was hatched. Members were going to make bricks using mud and burn them. The Rabias' family provided the finances and soon a new church at Trinity was erected alongside a foundation for my dream church. The Rabias' family paid for the Holy Communion table, public address system, keyboard, and all the required amenities. They put power into the church and brought water connections to the church while still supporting Pastor Elasto monthly financially as a family. Mr. Bob and Joellyn Rabias had adopted me as their son. While at their home, one day, they informed me of their desire to do so. It was a humbling experience.

In about 2012, the family was concerned about the abandoned work and began sending money in order to complete the church. This time, there was a new Pastor and I had explained the requirements and pitfalls to avoid. For years, things went on well and I kept on giving guidance on how to run projects coming from donors. The previous Pastor had also instructed the incoming Pastor about my preference of a named person who was to lead the construction. This person was from a church I had been a member when I was a youth because the man had been in the construction sector before. However, this request was not honoured wholeheartedly.

My expectation was that the person who had the vision needed to be consulted repeatedly. My expectation was that the person, who did the drawings, paid for everything and sourced for funding was to be asked, informed or be consulted regularly. My expectation was that the Pastor was going to involve everyone, that is, the Senior Steward, the Church Treasurer, the Financial Secretary and prominent leaders, not just a few – people of her choice – called "Trustees!" Nearly all of them with basic education and females! My expectation was that leaders were also expected to know that an individual, who came up with such a project, obviously knew what was to be put on the cornerstone! I don't know about you what your expectations would have been if you had come up with such a work? Lord, forgive us of our trespasses as we forgive those who trespass against us.

Nevertheless, I gave instructions on what to do at every juncture. I advised them that the outside doors needed to be made out of hardwood and so were the benches. (However, the pastor made the benches out of softwood!) I also ordered the redoing of the ramp to the toilets because the slope was wrong. I gave them a mathematical formula to use to calculate the slope and measurements and it was corrected. When I noticed construction being done without a spirit level, on minor works, I informed them it was a major violation. They began to getting worked out! I was only able to tell wrongs from photos and I noticed they sent us purposely selected photos only. I asked that the spoon drain be demolished because it was badly done and was not straight. I also asked that windows be removed because they opened one side and not both sides. They had been fitted for over a year and glasses had been put in place but I was not aware they opened one side in the main sanctuary.

I decided to reorganise the team. I asked that Pastor Elasto Mwansa be a part of the financial report because multiple mistakes which were embarrassing kept coming up! Remember, I had been a Church Treasurer for 5 years at Jordan Chapel before! Also, the sewer lines and water pipes, I had discovered were wrongly done and later were corrected by the man I had told them was to lead construction but was being sidelined! I asked that tiles be removed in the bathrooms and corrected as well since the Pastor had given inexperienced personnel to do them. Instructions had not been followed on how they were to be fitted! I had wanted all the bathrooms to have tiles from bottom to top, however, plaster was put on top instead and tiles below, not the right way, were not well-aligned and contrary to my instructions!

That said, there were great works which were done by the team. The trusses were well done and so was the roof. The roof was done by a professional who had joined the church, sadly such qualified persons remained as outsiders in this work! The tile decorations below the windows outside walls were fine only I insisted needed to show symmetry. The foundation and the walls were also well done by the person the pastor had contracted. Sadly, after his passing away, the people who did the work afterwards became shoddy on many occasions.

I still wanted the best done for the church. However, I noted with dismay that I was battling the same spirits I used to contend with since I was a youth. I had determined to change that. Trinity, I had planned from the beginning, was going to be a model for other all A.M.E. Churches in Zambia to follow and emulate. Overall, I was happy that the threshold of quality had at least exceeded the average since the people now in charge had never envisioned running such a project or handling such huge cash before! When the work had become too expensive for a single family to do, the Rabias family was joined by Mr. Steve and Kathy Marbert family. They too gave generously to the work of God.

I decided to make changes. This came as a result of failure to honour directives. The people who had done the sewer lines had been paid in advance and took six months to complete. They did the work wrongly! We agreed immediately after learning of the matter that money was not going to be paid in advance. However, to my surprise the same thing happened when 35 benches were bought. Money was paid for in full in spite of a consensus that it was not going to happen again. The 35 benches took one year to be delivered (the last bunch). In my new changes the leaders (Trustees and Stewards) were going to administer the funds with Pastor Elasto Mwansa who was no longer at the church. During this time, a dedication of the church was done without the knowledge of the sponsors and me. I knew why this was done. I decided to talk to the church but I was not given a satisfactory answer. This was very embarrassing to me since the sponsors had always wanted to attend the dedication service and had told me that they would want to see me preach during the occasion!

I made changes again after a verbal talk couldn't work. The funds were going to be run by Pastor Elasto Mwansa. The sponsors decided to help putting up the borehole after I had informed them of the water blues which were being experienced at the church. The money was sent for this purpose. However, since the bathrooms were still incomplete in spite of having been budgeted for and on two occasions we had been forced to "rob Peter and pay Paul," we asked that part of this money be allocated to the completion of the tiles in the toilets.

We needed more money to finish this! Sadly, when they sent more money again and the instructions for putting up the borehole, this time under Pastor Mwansa, instructions were not followed again! I decided to put a stop order on the money and constituted a new team from outside the church to finish the project. For historical record, I had planned to put up a school at this church and had even done draft drawings for this! However, seeing poor compliance and unprofessional manner on how the project was being run, I had dropped that idea about two years earlier.

I had decided I was going to construct an apartment building at Trinity instead. I was aware of the needs of the community and how needy the church was. A block or blocks of apartments was going to be helpful to this church I had envisioned. My sponsors were very happy to see my plans but my people wanted a house built instead! I was aware that a house was going to benefit one person only! I was also aware through experience with Jordan where building of a toilet took over 30 years that building of a house could take several years and would mean that a three-storey 4-bedroom block of 6 apartments would never materialise with the mindset of the people I was dealing with.

When this was shared with other professionals in Zambia, they saw the potential and were enthusiastic. One of those friends, offered to help in putting up a borehole. We worked hard but never met our expectations. I made another change. I constituted a board from outside to run and administer the funds and direct the building of the tank, do the architectural drawings which I had already sketched and begin the initial metal fence which they were to be forced to follow because the response had been cold. However, every effort crumbled! God have mercy for all our failures and bless those who have worked hard for your kingdom.

I continued to receive requests from many churches requiring help to build their churches. These were both A.M.E. Churches and non-A.M.E. Churches! I began to think that "people who want their names engraved on marble had a great opportunity to do so since there were countless lists of churches needing to be built!" "Why couldn't they build one or two of these churches and put their names on them? It was all that simple! Instead they decided to hijack someone's project and made it appear to be theirs!" I thought to myself. I wrote, *"Blessed are the dead who die in the Lord from now on, 'Yes,' says the Spirit, they will rest from their labour, for their deeds follow them,"* Rev. 14:13. Good deeds which will be our testimony will follow those who labour for the Lord and they need no names to be engraved on stone.

Trinity A.M.E. Church under construction at Garneton in Kitwe, Zambia, 2016 right side elevation. Rev. Charles Kapungwe designed the church around 1998 when he was pastor from 1996-2000. He paid the architect and for the land out of pocket with no single contribution from any church member. The church was designed with a Pastor's office with toilet and shower, men and women's toilets with showers, vestry/conference room, stewards' office and counseling room. When the church was completed, Bishop Wilfred Messiah, his presiding elder and the pastor put their names on the cornerstone without informing the person who was raising the money or built the church!

Trinity A.M.E. Church, Kitwe. Vestry, 18th May, 2017. Three years later, no latest photos had ever been sent in spite of requests made!

Trinity A.M.E. Church main entrance. Rev. Charles Kapungwe continued to direct construction from the U.S. where he was sourcing money to build Trinity. He had directed that the front door be fitted with double doors made of hardwood, 6th July, 2017.

Trinity A.M.E. Church right side anterior 1/3 of the church with pouch. This was after Rev. Charles Kapungwe directed that the windows be redone so they can open both sides and the photos showing the same be sent. The spoon drain on the side had been poorly done (was irregular!). He ordered that it be demolished too and was replaced ideally with the apron. 6th July, 2017.

Trinity A.M.E. Church left side and front. Earlier, the elevation to the ramp and steps to the men and women's toilets had been wrongly done. After the demise of the builder Webby Phiri, errors became common. Rev. Charles Kapungwe gave them diagrams and calculations to follow to do the incline and steps. Br. Davison Sinyangwe corrected the errors and put up the front and side canopies. Working with Bro. John Musukwa, their roofing was impeccable. The late Webby Phiri did a great work on the erection of the building too while Bro. Feckson Simukoko and Mr. Gift Lubozya did great foundation settings. 6th August, 2017.

Trinity A.M.E. Church, Kitwe left side. These are the redone works following Rev. Kapungwe's directives! Please compare this with the photo of the side below which I ordered to be redone! 7th September, 2018.

Trinity A.M.E. Church, Kitwe. Poorly done ramp and steps. Rev. Charles Kapungwe drew for them a diagram with a mathematical formula to use to calculate the angle of elevation and other dimensions. This ramp was greater than the standard elevation of 30 degrees. Please compare with the redone works above after the corrections were made. Originally, doors were designed to be inside but the team agreed to put them outside. Rev. Kapungwe supported them and gave them advice. Messiah and his staff inferred that Rev. Kapungwe was putting up "illegal committees" when the foul loud-mouthed people he had appointed had no idea about construction yet they still wanted to be in charge – because of money! There are several things that I could put down in this work which were wrong (including Financial Reports) but I trust the Lord that our readers will understand the setbacks and pain of this servant of the Lord trying to lead the blind. 30th January, 2017.

Trinity A.M.E. Church, Kitwe. Leveling of the ground, 9th January, 2017. The pastor had wanted this slot to be a parking spot for her car but Rev. Kapungwe informed her it was ideal for fellowship! A landscaping design which included road, parking lot, walkways and fruit trees' planting had been given to the Pastor and she did nothing about it for years! According to the Bible, it is easier to lead sheep than goats. That is why Jesus is called the Lamb of God.

Trinity A.M.E. Church, Kitwe, rear view showing stewards office (partially), counseling room, vestry and Pastor's office. Leveling of ground, 9th January, 2017.

One of the toilets/shower rooms at Trinity A.M.E. Church, Kitwe. This was after Rev. Charles Kapungwe had ordered for the removal of poorly done tiles and plaster following failure to follow instructions by the Pastor. Bro. Feckson Simukoko (silhouette image in mirror), was asked to correct the anomalies and he did. Rev. Kapungwe ordered them to put a stone platform (and large mirrors you see which the Pastor had no idea about!). They could not even put cupboards under the sinks/platform which he had designed for them due to poor financial management! For over a year, images of the toilets were not sent in spite of numerous requests to do so. 21st June, 2018.

Trinity A.M.E. Church, Kitwe. Shoddy works done by the Pastor. Compare and contrast the tiles in this photo with the one above. The pastor was sent sample photos of how she was to put up the tiles and given instructions before installation! She was spoken to on the phone by Rev. Kapungwe and written to but she ignored both the samples and instructions which were given. She put plaster on top and small tiles which she had clearly been told not to use! She had also been instructed to use the man who put up the tiles you see above but she sidelined him. After seeing this mess, Rev. Kapungwe ordered them to remove everything – again at a great cost. Since removal was taking months, we finally got four men from Jordan Chapel to remove the tiles and plaster and were paid! 6th July, 2017.

Trinity A.M.E. Church, Kitwe. Corrected shoddy works! 14th April, 2018.

Poorly done spoon drain. 17th August, 2017. Consequently, Rev. Kapungwe ordered them to demolish it too.

An apron was built instead and was far much better than the "dugout canoe" done earlier masquerading as a "spoon drain!" 29th November, 2017.

Trinity A.M.E. Church, Kitwe – baptism pool under construction. 28th December, 2017.

Trinity A.M.E. Church's shoddy work by the Pastor as she continued sidelining people Rev. Kapungwe had instructed to do the work. Rev. Kapungwe asked them to redo this door. (The top is longer than the bottom!). Bishop Messiah and his incompetent crew saw nothing wrong with this! 28th December, 2017. Also, it took about 6 months of persistent requests for them to remove the algae from the wall! Paul in Philippians 3 called them "Those dogs – those who do evil" and I haven't called any of them that yet. Jude called them "Shepherds who feed only themselves. They are clouds without rain, blown along by the wind, autumn trees, without fruit and uprooted – twice dead." I haven't called any of them that too.

Trinity A.M.E. Church, Kitwe. Vestry, Pastor's office and toilet with shower room. 28th January, 2017.

Trinity A.M.E. Church, Kitwe – Unkempt surroundings. Photo was sent by a non-Trinity member. The sponsors were not happy and told me to inform the Pastor about this! 28th January, 2017. ("Good work culture by the Pastor" according to ignorance and Miss Ignorant!)

Trinity unkempt surroundings by the "hard-working Pastor" and her ignorant Presiding Elders! The Pastor and her now retired unethical corrupt incompetent supervisor – recipients of thousands of U.S. dollars in cash instructed Miss Corrupt Ignorant to write a letter to a person who designed this building, paid for the land out of pocket, sourced for money to construct it and facilitated for a previous Pastor's monthly support for 11 years and to the people who made this possible a senseless letter without any sense of remorse! Ignorant says "You cannot judge another Pastor's work culture even if you have been doing a project there for 17 years! You cannot be embarrassed by that Pastor too! You cannot even tell by reading Financial Reports because you are not qualified to do so! I am a new Supervisor too of the person you brought to Jesus, a former Pastor of this church! However, send us more money because my ignorant Ahab who asked me to write you a letter of rebuke hears from God and you don't!" Photo: 28th January, 2017.

Trinity A.M.E. Church, Kitwe – Time to clean up following instructions from sponsors! 8th February, 2017. Please note that Rev. Kapungwe donated computer-generated name for the church in April, 2016 and for four years those letters have still not been put in front of the church by the "hard-working Pastor." Rev. Kapungwe also sent them tags with names to put on doors for all offices and toilets and beautiful wall clocks which he shipped to Zambia at his cost but has never seen them displayed!

Trinity poorly-done apron around the building. Rev. Kapungwe had asked for $5,000.00 from the sponsors to put this slab because rain water was staining the walls. This money was sent specifically for the apron. He instructed the builders to make at least 1-meter (3.3 ft.) concrete slab from the wall. This picture shows what was done at the back of the church. When Rev. Kapungwe asked the person who did this if they had run out of money, he was told "No!" When he asked if they had run out of sand or cement, he was told "No!" Miss Ignorant then wrote Rev. Kapungwe informing him not to be embarrassed because even her two ignorant supervisors (Ahab and one retired unethical incompetent informer) were not embarrassed at all (since they were not dealing with the sponsors directly!). He was also told not to judge a book by its cover because he was not qualified to do so. They had promised to rectify this and in 2020 there has been no photos sent from Trinity since 2017.

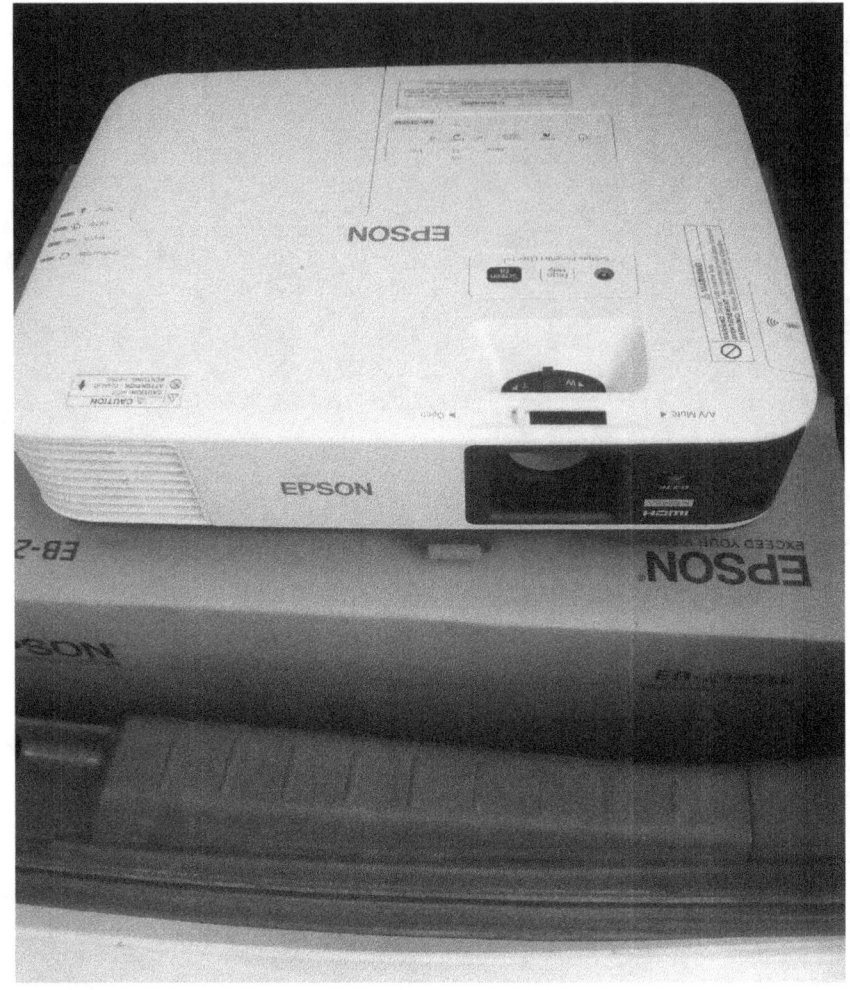

When Ahab refused to remove Herodias from Trinity and instructed Jezebel to write Elijah the Tishibite a letter of contempt so that he could be forced to flee, Elijah decided to report the matter to the Police before fleeing. Ahab then hurriedly and quietly transferred Herodias to another church, arrogantly, without informing the people who had been sending money to build the church about the transfer! Herodias had acknowledged receiving this Projector in September 2017 which was purchased by Elijah in South Africa at the cost of $2,000.00. She moved without installing the projector at Trinity and took it with her! Herodias had asked Ahab to give her the head of John the Baptist on a platter because she had been dancing to his tune. John the Baptist called them "Brood of Vipers." The Apostle Paul called them "Foolish Galatians, who has bewitched you?" *Elijah* calls them "Corrupt foolish AMEC officials" because he doesn't know who has bewitched them either. Ahab called Elijah "the trouble maker of Israel" through Jezebel, the witch, while Jezebel, Herodias, one now retired unethical incompetent informer, and Ahab himself have no understanding of who really the real trouble makers of Trinity and the 17th Episcopal District were.

One of the 35 "Hardwood" benches quoted at $200/bench that turned out to be softwood benches purchased by the hardworking Messiah's Pastor (according to Jezebel) which took one year to complete and had been paid for in full! Notice the thickness of the wood! They were painted with a brown paint afterwards which I asked them to scrape off and use varnish instead! 17th July, 2017. Note: Before any purchase of such items, thorough discussions were made among sponsors, Trinity and Rev. Kapungwe. A budget of estimates was given. Rev. Kapungwe would then inform them what was to be done! Here, he had directed them to buy hardwood benches and had told the Pastor "like the ones you had at Bright Chapel" and she had said "Yes!"

"Where there is no vision, the people perish," Proverbs 29:18 (KJV).

Trinity A.M.E. Church, Kitwe. Passage between the vestry and the partition wall of the stage. When I gave directives about the sliding doors to be installed, the Pastor had no idea this was what was to be installed! Thank God, I raised it up before they put in windows of her choice! 6th May, 2018.

Trinity A.M.E. Church completed ceiling done by Br. Feckson Simukoko, 6th January, 2017. All specifications were discussed and Br. Feckson was informed on what to use on lights and overhead fans by Rev. Kapungwe. One day when Rev. Kapungwe had made a call, he was told by the Pastor's team, (Br. Feckson had not been consulted) that they were beginning to install power lines on wall surfaces in the church! Rev. Kapungwe was furious and stopped them immediately! Br. Feckson had been told how and he was to do it, but had been sidelined again! He consequently, put the lines inside the walls!

Trinity A.M.E. Church, Kitwe. Borehole Drilling 24th April, 2018.

Borehole Drilling 24th April, 2018.

Proposed 6 Unit – 4-bedroom Flats at Trinity designed by Rev. Charles Kapungwe and sent to the "Illegal Committee" at Trinity! Here, only one view is shown. (Note: Space cannot allow us to show all the evidence this writer has including Financial Reports. In spite of warning Messiah about this writing and overwhelming evidence to come, he still stubbornly ignored this writer and his sense of reason!). These apartments were meant to help Trinity become financially independent and to have one unit become a mission house.

However, a visionless and selfish Pastor was insisting on building a house instead! Various landscaping designs sent to her with road, parking lot, metal fence, specific trees to be planted remained unattended to for nearly three years in spite of verbal and email reminders! Jezebel, Ahab, one now retired double-tongued unethical incompetent informer and Herodias (a woman incompetent Pastor) who obviously could NOT lead a construction of a two-storey building when she has no idea about construction and failed on the church project as evidence above shows, still was being courted by the corrupt leadership as seen from the letter where the pathetic informer, Ahab and Jezebel were ignorantly directing Rev. Kapungwe that Herodias should not be instructed on what to do because he was not a supervisor of her but was told to continue sending her money! When they come to America, they write reports of "churches they have built in Africa" with their names on them! Churches they never put even a cent on! No wonder, educated and visionary people can't stay in this Church to be led by uncircumcised corrupt foolish visionless incompetent thieves who are a joke! Design: 18th May, 2018.

Some of the partners in ministry to the great work done at Trinity A.M.E. Church in Kitwe. From left: Pastor Wesley Holland, Associate Pastor; Rev. Charles Kapungwe, Pastor Mike Phillips and Mr. Robert Rabias. New Covenant Presbyterian Church, Aiken, South Carolina, U.S.A. 18th December, 2005.

My caring mom Mrs. Joellyn Rabias. She played the piano at the church. New Covenant Presbyterian Church, Aiken, South Carolina, U.S.A. 18th December, 2005.

In the U.S. and the Grand Cayman, Cayman Islands, I did what the Lord had called me to do. I was a missionary. At Allen University in Columbia, I taught the word to students in Bible Study while at White Hall A.M.E. Church in Jenkinsville, South Carolina I was Associate Pastor to Rev. Leroy Cannon and taught the youth and the church God's word. I also preached around South Carolina including a non-A.M.E. Church (Christian Methodist Episcopal Church – CME). In Maine, we ran a church for about 7 years in Portland before I moved to Lewiston-Auburn where we planted a church under Bethel Christian Center. This we did with Rev. Etienne Nahimana and when he went to be with the Lord in July 2019, I helped as a caretaker Pastor. In Cayman Islands and in Maine (while in medical school) I continued to spread the word of God to students. May the Lord be glorified because everything was done to his glory!

Some of my classmates at St. Matthew's University School of Medicine (medical students) in Scarborough, Maine U.S.A. with me (third from right) 2005.

Rev. Charles Kapungwe in Columbia, South Carolina U.S.A. preaching the word at the Goodnews Community International Church Conference, May 2008. (Praying).

Chapter 28
The Legends

The work of the A.M.E. Church in Zambia can be credited to thousands of people. God had raised many people in different locations and at different times to help establish this Church in Zambia. However, not all people could be mentioned in this work due to logistical and poor data storage problems. It must also be noted that the clergy were not the only persons who built or contributed to the establishment of this Church in Zambia and many other regions discussed in this work. Although the clergy provided leadership in the work shared in this history, achievement of success in this enormous task would not have been possible too without the work of the "laity" whom we dedicate this chapter to as "Legends in Ministry!"

Mother Lusati Lukamba

Mother Beatrice Lusati Lukamba, a Mbundu by ethnicity was born in Portuguese West Africa (now Angola) in 1914. She was the last-born daughter of Paramount Chief Kanjundu Hosi of the biggest Mbundu ethnic group in Angola. She was married to Mr. Henrique Matenda Lukamba while in Angola and they had their first girl child in Angola named Esther Ngeve Lukamba, born in 1934. In 1935, Mr. Lukamba and family migrated from Portuguese West Africa by foot into Chief Nkana's kingdom in Northern Rhodesia to look for big monies they had heard about while in Portuguese West Africa.

After their first-born daughter, they got two more daughters. They were Elizabeth Nelinya Lukamba, now called Mother E.N. Simyembe and Lucy Njamba Lukamba Malama. Lucy is late as well as the first-born girl child, Esther.

In 1945, father Lukamba was given a certificate of appointment as Pastor of Nkana Circuit. Meanwhile, the circuit was being assisted in Church Doctrine by some senior leaders of the A.M.E. Church of Wusakile Mine (Jordan Chapel) and one of them was Mr. Paul and Mrs. Mary Gwamba who were very close to the Lukamba's family. "The Women Missionary Society in the 1940s was just beginning to be active with the help of some senior Church leaders from Southern Rhodesia, particularly, Mother L. Lisabe of Bulawayo. It was during this period that Mother Lukamba and few other women were gowned with the W.M.S. uniform by Mother Lisabe who used to come and stay with us in our village occasionally," writes Mother E.N. Simyembe.

Northern Rhodesia and Southern Rhodesia used to hold joint Annual Conferences at the time. The Conferences were usually held at Bulawayo, Southern Rhodesia. Very few members from Northern Rhodesia attended these Annual Conferences. Gradually, the W.M.S. in Northern Rhodesia started to grow in the 1950s with more appointments of Pastors and Presiding Elders. This meant that the Pastor's wife automatically became the W.M.S. Local President and the Presiding Elder's wife became a District W.M.S. President just as it is today that the Bishop's wife becomes the W.M.S. Episcopal Supervisor.

Later on, the W.M.S. Constitution kept on changing the rules. Most officers were now being elected. Mother Beatrice Lisati Lukamba held several offices before they retired in 1986. These were as follows: -

1945 – 1950 W.M.S. President Nkana Circuit
1955 – 1958 W.M.S. President Lambaland District
1958 –   Acting President – Northern Rhodesia Conference Branch
1971 – 1973 W.M.S. 2nd Vice President Zambezi Conference
1973 – 1975 W.M.S. South Zambia Parliamentarian
1975 – 1986 W.M.S. President Copperbelt District.

They retired at the Annual Conference held at Bright Chapel, Kitwe in 1986. Mother Lukamba died on 8th April, 2007 at Kitwe Central Hospital. Both my parents and two sisters are late. May the Lord bless you all! Amen.

Written by Mother E.N. Simyembe, daughter of Rev. Henrique Matenda Lukamba and Beatrice Lusati Lukamba. 13th May, 2017.

Mother Elizabeth Nelinya Lukamba Simyembe

Mother Elizabeth Nelinya Lukamba Simyembe is a daughter of Rev. Henrique Matenda Lukamba and Mother Beatrice Lusati Lukamba. Rev. Henrique Matenda Lukamba and family migrated from Portuguese West Africa on foot into Chief Nkana's kingdom in Northern Rhodesia in 1935. Rev. Lukamba and Mother Lukamba had their first-born daughter in Angola in 1934 and they had two more daughters, Elizabeth Nelinya Lukamba, now called Mother E.N. Simyembe, and Lucy Njamba Lukamba Malama. Lucy is late as well as the first-born girl child, Esther. Mother Elizabeth was born in 1936. I spoke to her on phone on 28th March, 2020 to obtain more information.

Mother Elizabeth Lukamba married Rev. Warren Simyembe on 28th July, 1956 at Jordan Chapel, Wusakile Kitwe my childhood church. Rev. Warren Simyembe passed away in 1971 in Kabwe. When Rev. Warren passed away, they had five children. Rev. Charles Kapungwe met Mother E.N. Simyembe at Brookins Chapel in Kabwe in 1987 unknown to him then that she was going to be of great help to this work. She provided a lot of literature from her father and information on Rev. J.L.C. Membe, the founder of this church in Zambia including photos.

Mother E.N. Simyembe started school in Sub A in Chief Nkana's area. This was the time they were writing on the ground and on slates. After completing Sub B, she began Standards I and then II which was at Chibuluma. She walked on foot to go to school at Chibuluma. When she got to Standards III and IV, she began walking to Kitwe Main Bus Station (KMB) to Kitwe Primary School since there was no school in Chief Nkana's area offering higher education. When the parents went to Angola, three children remained including Mother Simyembe to continue schooling. Br. Gideon Miyanda who was working for the BOMA as a Messenger, kept them.

She then went to Mindolo for Standards V to VI. After passing Standard VI at Mindolo Secondary school, she went to Chipembi to do Form I and Form II. When she completed

Form II, she was forced to get married. She married Rev. Warren Simyembe on 28th July, 1956 at Jordan Chapel, Wusakile Kitwe. After she had three children, she went back to school to train as a Domestic Science Teacher at Kitwe Teachers College (KTC). Mindolo was also offering part of this training so this was combined with Mindolo which had a Tailoring School. Mother E.N. Simyembe graduated as a Domestic Science Teacher and went to teach at Kalulushi Primary School. She only taught for eight months and went to Headquarters at Kitwe Ministry of Education in 1964. Mother E.N. Simyembe also worked in Kabwe at the Ministry of Education as a Homecraft Organizer in Homecraft Department. She retired from the Ministry of Education at the age of 50 in 1986.

Mother E.N. Simyembe was gowned in the W.M.S. in Livingstone in November 1956. The following are the works she did:

1956 – 1959 Local W.M.S. President, Bancroft (Chililabombwe)
1958 – Director of Promotions and Missionary Education, W.M.S. South Zambia Annual Conference
1971 – 1975 W.M.S. Treasurer, Copperbelt District; 17th Episcopal District W.M.S. President. She held this position for a short period due to pressure of work at her workplace at State House, Lusaka
1979 – 1983 Exhorter, Brookins Chapel, Kabwe
1983 – 1987 W.M.S. President South Zambia Annual Conference
1987 – 1989 Senior Steward Brookins Chapel, Kabwe
1992 – 1993 W.M.S. Local President Bright Chapel, Kitwe
1994 – 2005 Recording Secretary – Pastors' Wives Alliance – Copperbelt East District.
1995 – 1997 W.M.S. Chairperson Affiliated Group – Standing Committee – Bright Chapel, Kitwe
1997 – 2001 Chairperson of Christian Council of Zambia – Buchi Branch – Kitwe District
2000 Life Member.

Mother Daisy Katebe

Mother Daisy Katebe was the wife of Rev. Cuthbert Yoram Katebe, former Copperbelt Province Presiding Elder. Rev. Katebe was married to Daisy Katebe and the couple was blessed with 6 children, 4 boys and 2 girls and many grandchildren. Mother Daisy Katebe was a secondary school teacher who served the Ministry of Education for 37 years. She retired in 1999. She was a hard worker and is now a senior citizen. She too had a history of committed service in God's work, especially in the Women's Missionary Society. She was received into full membership in 1977 and was gowned the same time. She served as a Local President, Recording Secretary at Area and Conference level for many years. She was a W.M.S. Chairperson for the Copperbelt and Lusaka District and was the Episcopal 2nd Vice President in the 17th Episcopal District.

Photo: Sharon Katebe (daughter-in-law) and Mother Daisy Katebe with Presiding Elder Rev. Cuthbert Yoram Katebe in Atlanta, Georgia, U.S.A. at home in 1999.

Mother Katebe was appointed and elected as W.M.S. Conference President in the South West Zambia Conference from 1993 to 1995. She was W.M.S. Episcopal Editor of Missionary Magazine. She was also gowned as a Silver Sister at the Conference and Episcopal Level. In 2013, she was honoured as the Life Member in the W.M.S. She was the President of the Pastors' Wives Alliance (PWA) which later became MSWAWO. Mother Daisy also held offices at local circuit as a Trustee, Steward, Class leader and Director of B.O.C.E. In 2001, Bishop Preston Williams appointed her as Episcopal Director of Christian Education for 4 years. In 2004, Bishop Paul Kawimbe reappointed her to the same office for 8 years since he served as Bishop for 8 years. Mother Katebe, therefore, served for 12 years in this position. Take note that this is the same position that the late Presiding Elder Cuthbert Katebe had held for 12 years until his passing away in 2001.

Mother Daisy Katebe was a delegate to the W.M.S. Quadrennial Conventions in the U.S.A. on many occasions. She attended the conventions of 1983, 1995, 1998, 2003 and 2006. She has continued to serve in the church faithfully as a widow at the age of 76 years (submitted this story in November, 2018).

Mrs. Minerva Mulenga Phiri

Mrs. Minerva Mulenga Phiri is a committed Christian with a passion for the vulnerable in society. She was born as Minerva Musonda Mulenga on 10th December 1951 in Kabwe District (formerly Broken Hill). Her father was the late Mr. Peter Chilamo Mwansa Mulenga and her mother is Mrs. Phoebe Makumba Mulenga who both hailed from Mporokoso in the Northern Province of Zambia.

Mrs. Phiri attended Mindolo Girls Secondary School from 1966 to 1969. After that, she joined Rhokana Corporation Typist Training School, a mining conglomerate training Centre as a Trainee Typist. She moved up the ladder and acquired professional certificates. Mrs. Phiri is a full-fledged Professional Management Secretary having attained the highest Pitman's Certificates in both Typing and Shorthand from Pitman's College and The Royal Society of Arts Institute in the United Kingdom.

Miss Minerva Mulenga got married to Mr. Gideon Yotamu Phiri, a son of an A.M.E. Church minister Rev. Yotamu Phiri on 11 April 1970. Rev. Yotamu Phiri was once a Pastor at Jordan Chapel at Wusakile in Kitwe. The couple has five children, 4 girls and 1 boy. They are also foster parents to 7 children, making a total of 12 of their larger family, 6 girls and 6 boys. Five of which have given them 9 grandchildren, that is, 5 boys and 4 girls.

The urge to get involved in working with the vulnerable in society became strong in 1991. Coincidentally, it was the period Southern Africa and Zambia, in particular, was losing so many parents due to HIV/AIDS. She felt the need to do something about it, but how? The urge to serve as Conference Branch President of the Women's Missionary Society of the South West Zambia Conference became so strong that she could not push it away! She stood for election during the 1991 Annual Convention held at Bethel A.M.E. Church in Lusaka but was not successful. She made a second attempt again in 1993 in Chililabombwe but could not make it again! From this, she learned that God's time is the best and that losing an election is not the end. She also wants to encourage those in similar circumstances that if God has spoken to you, just continue to try again and again until the right time comes because the God who knows your motives will continue to stand with you!

In 1995, during the Annual Convention held at Allen Temple A.M.E. Church in Mufulira, Mrs. Phiri was elected unopposed to the position of South West Zambia Conference Branch President. Bishop Robert Webster, the then presiding prelate of the 17th Episcopal District immediately declared her winner and mandated her to conduct the election of the other positions in conjunction with the Nominations Committee. A very good team was elected to take office, some for the first time to serve at Conference level. Her immediate task was to share her Vision and to ask every elected and appointed officer to walk the talk with her to fulfil a very hard task. They were to be exploring new avenues in the area of mission work and revitalizing the Conference Branch of the Women's Missionary Society with prayers as never seen before. During the time she served at Episcopal level, they were nicknamed *"Born Agains"* because of the early morning rise and shine prayers and night vigils they regularly conducted!

Mrs. Minerva Phiri was amused by the nickname! She notes, "The surprising thing was that those calling us such a name were very senior leaders in the Women's Missionary

Society!" The Lord blessed her with a dedicated team of both old and young women leaders and together they dedicated their time to serving their God in very diverse ways. The Lord started opening new doors and nearly every member, officer or not, started to experience the blessings of God in their lives. Testimonies about God's greatness and power began to flow, and they began to exploit what had never been done before. What they were reading in the Connectional Missionary Magazine began to be a reality in their Conference. It was still very hard to convince everyone about the Vision but they laid out their plan and people started buying into the programme and slowly the long journey started.

Positions Held in the A.M.E. Church

Mrs. Minerva Phiri was a member of Bright Chapel A.M.E. Church in Kitwe from 1967 to 1970. She then moved to Jordan Chapel A.M.E. Church in Kitwe in 1970 up to 1994 when she was among the founding members of a new point, Calvary Temple A.M.E. Church in town. Mrs. Phiri held various positions from local, District (Area for YPD and Women), Conference and even Episcopal level. Some of the major positions held were: -

Young People's Division:

1. She served as local President and later local YPD Director.
2. She was among the founding YPDers to start *"Yesu Akabwela Cincileni"* in Kitwe between 1972 and 1973 as a way of fundraising for local churches in Kitwe as well as Bible Study.
3. She served in the YPD in various positions rising to South Zambia Conference Vice President and briefly as Conference President from 1973-1976. She was elected in absentia taking over from Mrs. Diana Mapoma at the Annual Convention in Lusaka while Mrs. Martha Mulobeka became YPD Director. Later, a team playing "Church politics" replaced Mrs. Phiri. Mrs. Phiri became YPD South Zambia President in 1976 for merely three months. When she could not attend one meeting in Lusaka because she could not obtain leave at the workplace, she was replaced by a person who had never been involved in YPD at Area or Conference, William Mutale, a friend to one of the influential women in the church dynasty!

Main Church Positions Served

1. Mrs. Minerva Phiri served as Church Secretary, Steward Member, and Board of Trustees at Jordan Chapel in Kitwe. She was part of the team that organized two golf tournaments to raise money for the building and rehabilitation of the toilet block and church at Jordan.
2. She became the first lay person and woman to be South West Zambia Conference Secretary when Bishop Richard Allen Chappelle took up his appointment as the 17th District Presiding Prelate. This was during a Conference held at Bright Temple in Lusaka in 1988 and she served in this position up to 1995 when she became the Conference W.M.S. President for South West Zambia. During this time, she produced minute books and updated Pastor's personal records and generally applied

her secretarial skills to her work.

3. Later, she was also given the position of Episcopal District Secretary and started working hand in hand with Conference Secretaries in the 17th District helping them to produce minutes and keeping proper records. Mrs. Phiri served in this capacity during the tenure of Bishops Richard Chappelle, Larry Kirkland and Robert Webster. She served as a Board Member of the Council of Churches in Zambia (CCZ) representing the A.M.E. Church from 2000 to 2004.

Women's Missionary Society
1. Mrs. Minerva Phiri served as Copperbelt District W.M.S. Treasurer under the Area Chairmanship of Mrs. Daisy Katebe around 1985 to 1987. During the period, she spearheaded the buying of Canvas Shoes and garbs for Deaconesses. She also served as Vice Area Chairperson under late Mrs. Ruth Chibwe.
2. She became the Corresponding Secretary for the 17th Episcopal District W.M.S. 1988 – 1990 and introduced an Episcopal Directory for all officers.
3. In 1990 to 1994, she served as the first Promotion and Missionary Education Director (PME) of W.M.S. in the 17th Episcopal District. During this time, she printed a W.M.S. Desk Calendar and also produced a local Missionary Prayer Book out of which two (2) contributions were included in the Connectional W.M.S. Prayer Calendar. She used the position to teach the W.M.S. to understand the Constitution and their role in the Church, to know the different roles played by the P.E.'s wife and the President or Area Chairperson and how to embrace the YPD in their structure.
4. Mrs. Phiri was elected as the only delegate to the W.M.S. Quadrennial Convention from South West Zambia Conference in 1991, held in Baltimore, Maryland in the USA. This was under the leadership of Bishop Richard Allen Chappelle and Mother Barbara Chappelle. Thereafter, she was privileged to represent South West Zambia in 1995, 1999 and 2003. These visits exposed her to institutions in the US which were providing assistance to the elderly like the Breeze Acres and day care centres providing help to children whose parents were drug addicts and clinics providing health care to those suffering from HIV/AIDS and Drug Abuse.
5. In 1994 to 1995, she served as the first Local W.M.S. President at Calvary Temple A.M.E. Church where they donated foodstuffs to Kitwe Central Hospital patients coming outside Kitwe. They also taught widows in Nkana West their basic legal rights in view of rampant property grabbing by relatives at the time and linked them to a female lawyer for assistance. They also paid for medical scheme for widows and orphans.
6. In 1995, Mrs. Phiri became the W.M.S. South West Zambia Conference Secretary. At this time, the Conference catered for Copperbelt and North Western Provinces. She introduced Prayer Breakfast every April and Annual Retreat every long July holiday. The first Retreat was held in Zambezi in 1997.
7. In 1999, she founded the W.M.S. C.A.R.E. Project. The acronym stood for (**C**onnect with **A**ct for/with them **R**espond to their needs and **E**xperience God's

blessings. The W.M.S. through this project supported 3,147 Orphans and Vulnerable Children (OVCs) in the entire Conference from Grade one to tertiary level with school requisites and user fees. Fifty households in Kitwe were beneficiaries of monthly foodstuffs, 200 adults and 2,000 children received blankets. All this was achieved through the support of The Irish Embassy in Zambia. They even bought a small mini-bus for the Project, the first ever vehicle for the entire A.M.E. Church in the 17th Episcopal District.

8. A community school was started at Bwafwano Centre in Kamitondo Township near Bright Chapel A.M.E. Church. Here, children from pre-school up to Grade 4 were being provided with an education. They were sent to Government Schools when they reached Grade 5. A feeding programme was introduced to encourage school attendance. All this was with the help of The Irish Embassy again.

9. When the project came to an end, 185 students in Grades 9 and 12 in the two Provinces risked not writing their qualifying examinations. Mrs. Phiri negotiated with the Examinations Council of Zambia to allow them to do so using the name of another organization while explaining the dilemma the children had found themselves in. Fortunately, they were all allowed and even other students countrywide benefited. The condition was that they would not collect their results until they settled their arrears and up to now some children have not collected their results!

10. When Mrs. Phiri's term of office as Conference President came to an end in 2003, she was relieved of her position as Coordinator of the C.A.R.E. Project. She utilized her positions in the Church – the African Methodist Episcopal Church (AMEC) from local to Episcopal level and advocated for the rights of the widows and orphans and vulnerable children. Later, in 2005, she started Bwafwano Care Project which changed its name to Bwafwano Care Providers in August 2011.

11. Mrs. Phiri was recognised for her work by the U.S. Embassy. In 2013, she was honoured by The U.S. Embassy in Zambia as one of the first U.S. President's Emergency Plan for AIDS Relief (PEPFAR) Champions in recognition of her contribution to the welfare of OVCs in Zambia from 1997 to 2013. She is thankful to God for the opportunity to serve him in this Ministry. She finds great satisfaction reaching out to the orphans and vulnerable children, senior citizens, widows and widowers, children and youths with special needs, and the neglected. She gives glory to God for her journey in which she learned to depend on God and has seen his hand.

Mother Edith Norongwa Lubemba

Mother Edith Norongwa Lubemba is a well-known name in the Midlands of Zambia. No biographical information was available on her life but she is known to have contributed immensely to the building of the present Mother Lubemba A.M.E. Church at Kaunda Square Stage I in Lusaka. The church, formerly known as Chamba Valley where Rev. Charles Kapungwe was an affiliate member during his college years in Lusaka in mid-1980s was meeting at a

Primary School at Kaunda Square Stage I at the time. They began construction of a large church around 1987. At Kaunda Square, the classroom was often full during Sunday services. With the help of Mother Lubemba's financial contributions and connections, Chamba Valley A.M.E. Church was able to complete this sanctuary. Subsequently, the church was named after her. She was a dedicated W.M.S. member who attended many meetings inside and outside Zambia. She hailed from South Africa. Mother Lubemba was not a Pastor's wife but the title was given to her because it was befitting her motherly role to many.

Mrs. Joyce Mukupo

No detailed information was available on Sister Joyce Mukupo at the time of writing. She was a well-known W.M.S. member in the Church. She travelled extensively to many meetings during her time including Malawi, Zimbabwe and others. She was the first person to become YPD Director in the 17th Episcopal District. She was married to Mr. Titus Mukupo, the father of Ms. Florence Chileshe, a former Copperbelt West YPD Director.

Mother Rose Simfukwe

Mother Rose Simfukwe was born in 1932 at Kambole Mission, 60 miles west of Abercorn in Northern Rhodesia. She is a daughter of Mr. Lolo Mwambazi and Chitalu Nakazwe. She was educated at Kambole Mission under the London Missionary Society Church. Mother Simfukwe was taken from Kambole to Ndola by her brother Bernard Mwambazi. She then went to a boarding school at Mindolo in Kitwe. When she completed Standard VI at Mindolo, she attended Mindolo Girls Boarding School. This was popularly known as (Kwa Nakatuntulu, named after the first principal). The school was changed to Mindolo Secondary School after independence.

At the time, there were only two secondary schools for women in Zambia. They were Mindolo Girls Boarding School in Kitwe and Chipembi Mission under the United Methodist Church at Chisamba outside Lusaka. Mother Diana Mapoma later came to the school (Mindolo) years after Mother Simfukwe had left. Mother Simfukwe completed school in 1951 and her brother who was now a Headmaster suggested that she joined him at Nkambo Native Authority School at Chief Nkambo in Mwinilunga. She taught Standard II (Grade 4) in the morning and Sub A (Grade 1) in the evening there.

Mother Simfukwe left Mwinilunga for Ndola to get married. She married Rev. David K. Simfukwe on 20th February, 1955. She began to work as a Social Worker in Ndola and later returned to teaching in 1960 there. When Rev. Simfukwe found a job in the Mines in Luanshya, the couple moved to Luanshya from Ndola. Mother Simfukwe also joined the Mines which had begun introducing schools in their communities. Since miners' children had had no schools before, the programme enrolled teens into Sub A and they did very well! They were fast learners because of the age. She taught from 1961 to 1965 until the time the Mines began to implement changes in the schools. Rev. David Simfukwe had in 1962 become the Pastor of Bright Temple in Luanshya.

She returned to the Government to teach. After independence in 1964, the Government changed from Standards to Grades and Forms. The old grades were Sub A (Grade 1), Sub B

(Grade 2), Standard I (Grade 3), Standard II (Grade 4), Standard III (Grade 5), Standard IV (Grade 6), Standard V (Grade 7) and Standard VI (Grade 8). Some schools (not boarding schools) had Standard VI (Lower and Upper). Secondary School got Form I to Form V. Teachers were trained for a year and the demand for teachers was very high since now they had more schools but fewer teachers. She completed Form II in the 1960s via night school. Mother Rose Simfukwe joined the A.M.E. Church in Ndola in 1955. She was a friend to the late Rev. Idah Simukwai who was President of YPD at the time and was instrumental in making Mother Simfukwe to join. At the time, Rev. J.L.C. Membe was the Pastor and Presiding Elder at Mother Hughes in Ndola.

Mother Simfukwe held many positions. She had been a Local W.M.S. President. She also served as Secretary of the Conference when Zambia had one Annual Conference. Once, when Mother Diana Mapoma was Episcopal President and Zimbabwe was not doing very well because of the political situation in Southern Rhodesia, Mother Simfukwe travelled extensively to encourage the churches in Zimbabwe and Malawi. She recalls being at Kasungu, Malawi where the church slaughtered a cow for them at a Conference. Mother Rose has been a strong mother in faith who we looked to for support at the time of persecution in the youth. She had been a faithful woman of God who had also battled persecution in this Church for decades but stood firm because of her love for Jesus.

The family emigrated to the U.S.A. in 1996. They had been at the Quadrennial Conference in July 1995 in Detroit, Michigan when she learned that Rev. Simfukwe had been selected for the Green Card programme. She is a mother seven children with the Rev. David K. Simfukwe, 5 boys and 2 girls. They are Dr. Maybin Simfukwe, MD., Faith Simfukwe Mugala, Chansa Simfukwe, Chisha Namfukwe, David Simfukwe, Jr., Philip Simfukwe and late Samuel Simfukwe who went to be with the Lord at the age of 28 in 1999.

Mother Diana Chungu Mapoma

Mother Diana Chungu Mapoma was born in 1940 in Chingola in Northern Rhodesia. She was born to Mr. Simon Chungu and Mrs. Elizabeth Mwila Chungu. She is a niece to Rev. Foodson B.S. Washiama. She went home to Luapula and attended Lukwesa Local Education School Authority. Mother Diana then returned to the Copperbelt and attended Nchanga Primary School. She was educated at Mabel Shaw at Mbereshi and completed Standard V and VI. This was the last grade students would reach at the time. There were only three schools of higher learning in Northern Rhodesia for girls: Mbereshi, Chipembi (Chisamba in Lusaka) and Mindolo in Kitwe. Mother Mapoma then studied by correspondence to further her education. She got employed at Mufulira's Ronald Ross Hospital as a nurse. She worked here on Job Training. She worked at this hospital for 7 years and went to Mindolo Ecumenical Foundation in Kitwe from 1960 to 1962. Mother Diana trained in Christian Leadership, Youth and Women Organisation, and Home Economics.

Mother Diana Mapoma at Ebenezer, Lusaka at Ministers' Spouses, Widows, Widowers and Pastor's Kids Retreaty in June, 2018.

Mother Diana Mapoma joined the Mines in 1963. Her job involved teaching women Home Economics that is, knitting, cooking, etc. She stopped work and went back to school to train as a teacher at Mufulira Teachers Training College from 1968 to 1970. After completion, she taught at Mufulira Central School in lower primary grades, teaching First Graders. She then went to Mary Moffat to teach Grades 6 and 7s. This was a mixed-race school with whites and blacks. When the husband, Abraham Phillip Chibwe Mapoma stopped work after his pension from Mufulira's Ronald Ross Hospital in 1973, the family moved to Chingola where they had been running a business – Dairy Ben Café dealing in ice cream and other products. She began to teach at Hellen Walter School, which was a mixed school (now renamed Nakatindi Primary School, after Princess Nakatindi Wina, a former minister).

At this time, there was a change in teaching methodologies. There was a change from Traditional to English. Teaching had to be done in English and she became an English Supervisor of Teachers and also taught Grades 6 and 7 English Language. Mother Mapoma was later sent to Chalimbana College in Lusaka in 1979 to upgrade teaching methods in Upper Primary and teach in Secondary Schools. She was promoted as Deputy Head at Maiteneke Primary School in Chingola in 1978 to 1979. She was promoted to another school – a Grade 1 School as Head Mistress in Chingola until 1990 where she retired.

Mother Mapoma joined the A.M.E. Church as a child. She was living with her uncle Rev. Washiama; therefore, she attended church with him. She later joined the Youth which was known as Juvenile, a precursor to the YPD. When Mother Mapoma attended an Annual Convention in Washington DC in 1975 (women and men, unlike today, never used to meet together) she was asked to adopt the name of YPD and to unify the Juveniles together both males and females. Men had bands with letters A.E.L. (Allen Endeavor League). She continued to work with YPD and became South Zambia Annual Conference YPD Director. This was the time Bro. Abraham Sachikola was YPD President and the time of Alberto Mwansa were in Y.P.D. Mother Mapoma was YPD Director of this Conference for 8 years.

The legendary Mother Mapoma held several positions during her time. She served as W.M.S. Conference Assistant Corresponding Secretary from 1983 to 1984. She later became W.M.S. Conference Worship Director in 1984. She succeeded Mother Phelly Mumpanshya who was W.M.S. South Zambia Conference Branch President at the time South Zambia Conference was divided in 1988. She became the first W.M.S. President of the newly formed South West Zambia Conference from 1988 to 1995. She held this position prior to Mrs. Minerva Phiri holding it in 1995. Mother Mapoma became W.M.S. Episcopal Director in 1997 under Bishop Larry Kirkland. She made several trips to the U.S. to Conferences. She attended the General Conferences in 1980 as YPD Director in Louisiana and 1984 in Kansas, Missouri. She also attended Quadrennial in 1991 in Baltimore, Maryland and the General Conference in Orlando, Florida in 1992.

Mother Mapoma attended the General Conference in Michigan in 1996. She attended the Convocation in 2006 with Bishop Gregory G.M. Ingram who was at the meeting with the W.M.S. in Dallas, Texas. The meeting was organized by Mrs. Ingram, the Supervisor, and was for prayers. In 2008 she was at the General Conference in St. Louis, Missouri. At this Conference, the then U.S. Senator (later) President Barack Obama addressed the Conference. Mother Mapoma also attended the General Conference in Nashville, Tennessee in 2012. She attended all Conferences in Zambia, Malawi, Zimbabwe, Congo Brazzaville and Congo Kinshasa (Congo DR). She served as a Historiographer for 8 years and served under many bishops.

There are several other positions Mother Diana held. She was appointed as Episcopal President of Ministers Spouses, Widows, Widowers and PKs (Pastors Kids). She was first appointed to this position by Bishop Paul Kawimbe from 2005 to 2013 and worked with Bishop Messiah for a year. She worked in Rwanda, Burundi and Kenya. Mother Mapoma also served many other organisations including the Christian Council of Zambia (CCZ) as Family Life Member Chairperson 1989 to 2002 and worked with Rev. Violet Sampa Bredt, Rev. Susanne Matale and Rev. Edith Mutale. She is a recipient of many awards.

Mother Mapoma is a recipient of a Certificate of Life Member from the Connectional W.M.S. of the Meritorious Service. She serviced for 25 years and on 24th February 2017, Dr. Shirley Cason Reed, W.M.S. Connectional President awarded her the Life Member Certificate. She was awarded the Sara Allen Award for serving faithfully in missions by the same Connectional W.M.S. President Dr. Reed on 7th July, 1916 at the 50th Session of the General Conference in the U.S.A. She also got a Certificate of Achievement from the 17th Episcopal District for serving for 8 years as a Historiographer at the Episcopal level by Bishop Paul Kawimbe on 20th April, 2012. She obtained another award for serving the Ministers, Spouses, Widows, Widowers and Pastors' Kids for 8 years and being the first person to hold this position. Mother Mapoma is also a recipient of Women Aglow award for serving the ministry for 10 years. She was awarded the Certificate by Ruth Daka, the National President at the Women Aglow International Conference held in Zambia in 2002.

Mother Daphine Mutalange

Mrs. Daphine Mutalange, a former nurse for Kalulushi Division of Zambia Consolidated Copper Mines is a wife of Rev. Phillip Mutalange. She is a dedicated W.M.S. member who served the church at Kalulushi on the Copperbelt Province for many years. No biographical history was available but she was known to clean the classroom every week where St. Stephen A.M.E. Church used to meet before they built the current church. The classroom used to be soiled with human excreta weekly but Mrs. Mutalange would be the first person to be at the church every Sunday since she lived close to the school. Mrs. Mutalange would clean the room thoroughly and used ash to kill the scent of human waste before congregants arrived. Once, Rev. Henry Alimasi, P.E., who had come early for a Quarterly Conference observed her hard work and gave her a word that God was going to reward her for her hard work.

Later, she helped bring her husband who had been Catholic to the Lord and he joined A.M.E. ministry. Mother Mutalange came to Indiana in the U.S.A. upon her retirement from the Mines in 2004. She worked very hard sending money to build the church at Kalulushi. Although many other people contributed to the building, she provided the bulk of the money to build the church in Kalulushi before she returned to Zambia. When Bishop Wilfred Messiah "officially opened" or "Dedicated" the church, the same day he "officially opened" Trinity on 29 October, 2017, there was no mention or recognition of the person who had sacrificed a lot by sending money from the U.S. to Zambia from 2004 to 2017 to build St. Stephen A.M.E. Church.

Mother Catherine Bupe

No detailed information was available on Mother Catherine Bupe at the time of this writing. However, those who know her are aware that she is the wife of Rev. Dr. Paul Bupe, a former minister in the A.M.E. Church. She hails from Mufulira where she attended school and then went to the University of Zambia Great East Road Campus. She didn't complete her studies there but years later enrolled at Allen University in Columbia, South Carolina in U.S.A. She graduated with a B.A. in Social Sciences in 2005. She has four children with Rev. Bupe – Faith, Hope, Paul, Jr., and David. All the children live in the U.S. Mother Bupe was among the group who brought about the revival at Allen Temple in Mufulira through prayers of intercession and evangelism. She lived through the persecution era of believers in the late 1970s through 1990s. She is a daughter of Rev. Samuel Mulapwa.

Mother Catherine Bupe with her youngest son David, Rev. Charles Kapungwe and Professor Campbell at the Graduation Ceremony of Mother Bupe (with a BA in Social Sciences) on 30th April, 2005 at Allen University, Columbia S.C. USA.

Brother Westone Mutale Bowa

Brother Westone Mutale Bowa was born on 8th June, 1954 in Luanshya on the Copperbelt Province, Northern Rhodesia. He was born to Mr. Moses Bwalya Mbula and Mrs. Leah Mwansa. His parents are Bemba from Chinsali now Provincial Headquarters of Muchinga Province. He attended Kampemba Primary School at Chimwemwe in Kitwe and Kitwe Boys Secondary School. He studied Personnel Management with University of Zambia Distance Learning Programme and obtained a Certificate. He trained in Zimbabwe as a Stepping Stone and REFLECT Trainer. Brother Bowa also studied Journalism at Mindolo Ecumenical Foundation (MEF) in Kitwe where he graduated with a distinction. He worked for Kitwe City Council as Public Relations Officer. He later left and joined a Non-Governmental Organisation (NGO) Copperbelt Health Education Project (CHEP) as a Community Programme Coordinator. He left in 2007 and joined AFYA MZURI, another NGO where he has risen to become the Executive Director. He is married to Annie Chanda.

His ministry had been in the Lay Organisation where he has held many positions in the Church. Below is a list of positions, achievements and church activities Brother Bowa has held: President – 17th Episcopal District Lay Organisation (2010-2015), Lay President – South West Zambia Conference (2006-2010), Recording Secretary – South West Zambia Conference (2001-2003), Local Director of Lay Activities – South West Zambia Conference (2004-2005), Lay Organisation, member (1987-2008) and Lay Organisation Africa Development Initiative (LOADI) Chairperson (2016-2018). This is a group which was formed by the Episcopal District Lay Organisations of the 15th, 17th, 18th and 19th Districts to look at the developmental issues of their Districts and to encourage participation of the Lay Organisation in church programmes. Brother Bowa hosted the Connectional Lay Organisation Summit in Livingstone, Zambia from 5th to 11th December, 2011 at Sun Hotels attended by Episcopal Districts 1-13 and 14-20.

Brother Westone has held many local church positions. He was at Bright Chapel in Kitwe on the Copperbelt Province from 1980-2007. While there, he was a Lay Preacher, Church Secretary (1992-2007), Member of Board of Stewards and Senior Steward (1988-2007). He was Chief Class Leader (1989-2007), Baptism and Full Membership Trainer (1987-2007), Lay Organisation member (1993-2007), and Sons of Allen member (2001-2002). Br. Bowa had been a member of St. Thomas Church (Nakonde – Muchinga Province from 2007-2009). While there, he was a Lay Preacher (2007-2009), Assistant Pro tem (2007-2009), Director of Christian Education (2007-2009), Assistant Choir Director (2007-2009), and Lay Organisation member (2007-2009).

Brother Bowa has been a member of Ebenezer Church in Lusaka since 2011. While at Ebenezer, he has been a Lay Preacher and Pro tem (2017/2018). He has also been a Sunday School Superintendent (2017/2018), member of the Board of Directors for the Affairs of Ebenezer Church Mechanical Institute that was developed by Rev. David K. Simfukwe, (2013/2014), Lay Organisation member (2011-todate) and Director of Christian Education (2018/2020). He served at Mother Lubemba in Lusaka from 2009-2010. He was a Lay Preacher (2009/2010), Steward (2009/2010), and a Lay Organisation member (2009/2010).

Sister Hilda Membe

No record about Sister Hilda Membe was available at present. However, those who remember her know that Sister Hilda Membe is a daughter of Rev. J.L.C. Membe. She served the Church faithfully at Bright Chapel in Kitwe for years and was appointed Episcopal Secretary by Bishop Richard Allen Chappelle when he came to the 17th Episcopal District in 1988 to 1992. She served the Church in this capacity for four years. When Bishop Chappelle was transferred to the 18th Episcopal District in Lesotho and Swaziland from 1992 to 1996, Sister Hilda moved with the Bishop and served the Church in the same capacity in Lesotho. She came to the U.S.A. after Bishop's tenure in Africa ended and she now lives in Florida. Rev. Charles Kapungwe spoke to her on phone in 2019 a few times.

Other People Worth Mentioning

There are several people who worked hard in this Church to sustain it. Many of them we will never know. Besides the Pastors and women mentioned in this book, there are several lay people in different provinces who served the Church in various capacities. Poor records are the reason that many of them could not be mentioned. For the Copperbelt Province where I was a part in the 1970s until 2000, several names which were household names come to mind.

The A.M.E. Church ranks among the elite denominations known for music in Zambia. This became so because the leadership in the 1970s promoted choir competitions among the churches on the Copperbelt. Winners were presented with trophies and I had joined the choir around 1980. This made us to go to many towns and cities and participated in choir competitions. Household names were Hosanna Choir led by Bro. Emmanuel Membe a great choir conductor and singer with his sister Sarah Membe. They were from Bethel A.M.E. Church in Chililabombwe. They won a lot of trophies and were great singers. They were children of Pastor Joel Membe, a younger brother to Rev. J.L.C. Membe.

Several names can be remembered from Bethel in Chililabombwe. Notable names from there in 1990s were Br. Charles Mulenga, Senior Steward, Br. Jason Miyambo (Treasurer), Br. Cephas Kapalala (Trustee), Mrs. Chitenge, Christine Kopa and Chanda. Minister Sanjilu was the Associate Pastor to the then Rev. Paul Bupe.

Melodies of Allen Temple, Mufulira was another force to reckon with in music circles. Their conductor was Gilbert Mwansa but had great singers such as the Rev. Paul Bupe, Mother Catherine Mulapwa Bupe, Bro. Gilbert Mwansa and others. They too won a lot of trophies. Later, Bro. Albert Chanda, Bro. Paul Bupe and Morgan Chola became choir conductors. Allen Temple was among churches which helped to revive the A.M.E. Church in Zambia. They persistently offered prayers of intercession to God about this Church which had been steeped deep in religion.

Thank God for great efforts and leadership of Rev. Rowland Mwenyo and later Rev. M.P.P. Mwenya. Among those who petitioned God for mercy led by Rev. Rowland Mwenyo and later Rev. Peter M.P. Mwenya were Brother Nathan Mugala (Now Rev. Nathan Mugala, Pastor in Florida, U.S.A.), Leah Mugala, Joyce Mulapwa, Christine Kopa, Catherine Mulapwa, Br. Katele, Ackson Lukwesa (now Rev. Lukwesa), Br. Benjamin Mugala, Paul Bupe and Wilson Mpundu (now all ministers). Others are Samuel Mulapwa (later a minister), Sister Beatrice Chabala and Br. James Mwape who now is in the U.S. These were vibrant believers who carried the banner of Christ from late 1970s into the 1990s. Their ministry in prayer and the word helped change the trajectory of this Church.

Br. Benjamin Mugala served as Senior Steward at Allen Temple for many years. He was very helpful in ministry and supported Rev. Peter M.P. Mwenya whole-heartedly. He was the father of three committed children who sang in Melodies Choir, Nathan Mugala, Leah Alice Mugala and Sara Mugala. They were also committed prayer warriors at the church who helped in the revival of this church. Bro. Nathan Mugala was a great conductor and teacher of music. He is a Pastor in Florida today (2020). When Br. Benjamin Mugala retired, he settled at Nakonde where he joined the ministry and is now Rev. Benjamin Mugala.

Allen Temple youths: Harry Simbeya (late), William Mwape (now Pastor in Lift Him Up Ministries in Lusaka) and Nathan Mugala (Now Rev. Nathan Mugala in Florida U.S.A.) at Butondo Secondary School in Mufulira in 1979.

The other great choir on the Copperbelt Province known for music in the 1980s was Bright Choir of Roan, Luanshya. Their Choir Conductor was Br. Emmanuel Chansa, a son of Rev. Amon Chansa. They produced an album *Searching the Scriptures*. They had many family members in the choir too. Memorable names are Lilian Chansa, Annie Musepa, Majory Chansa, Mirriam Chansa, Doreen and Faith, Elizabeth Chansa, Christine Chansa, Osward, Chris Nyungu, George Chilekwa (Now Rev. Chilekwa in Luanshya), to name but a few. They produced an album on wax (LP) just like the Hosanna (Bethel, Chililabombwe) and Ziyezwa Quartet of Bright Chapel in Kitwe which produced two singles on wax. St. James Luanshya had Br. John Mwansa and Sis. Annie Mwansa. Bright Chapel Choir (Kitwe) was good at singing. Ziyezwa Quartet, at Bright Chapel had the likes of Bro. Gift Kaunda, Boyd Chanda, Bro. Patrick Moyo and many more.

Jordan Chapel Choir was led by Bro. Aaron Siwale. He was our choir conductor. We did well even though we were not among the top. We sang live in 1980 at the then Zambia Broadcasting Services (ZBS) Kitwe TV studios, the precursor to Zambia National Broadcasting Corporation (ZNBC). Memorable names were Queen Mwamuleshi and her sister Judy Mwamuleshi, Esther Nambela, Charity Nsama Musonda and her Sister Rose Musonda. We also had Loveness Nyirongo, Jack Mapila, Jr., Loveness Chewe and her Sister Alice Chileshe Mwango. We had my sister Mary Kapungwe, Steven K. Ngosa, Jones Mhango, Feckson Simukoko, Reuben Kayombo, Gabby Ntanga, Elijah Sichone and Rev. Philemon Mumba's daughters who sang in the choir in the 1980s. They are Sisters Vivian Mumba, Jacqueline Mumba, Felistas Mumba and Aggie Mumba. Bro. James Chama was a gifted conductor who had come from Chingola. In the late 1970s the choir had Br. Albert Mulenga, Br. Felix Chilimboyi and Jacob Chilimboyi.

Jordan Chapel A.M.E. Church Wusakile, Kitwe 1981 combined YPD, choir and members. Standing from left: Julius Tembo, Loveness Nyirongo, Charles Kapungwe, (Abel Siwale, younger brother to Aaron), Monica Kishombe, Aaron Siwale (now Bishop), Esther Nambela, Stephen K.T. Ngosa (now Pastor). Seated/squatting: Baby Kishombe (younger sister to Monica), Jones Mhango, Alice Chileshe, Nathan Kawama and James Banda.

Jordan Chapel had many leaders who must be remembered. Mr. Gideon Yotham Phiri, the husband to Mrs. Minerva Phiri held various positions including Senior Steward, Chief Trustee and Choir Director. His father had been a Pastor in early 1970s at Jordan. Other men are Br. Nason Kawama, Br. P.J. Bwalya, Br. James Mschili, Br. Stephen Chishimba, Br. Jack Mapila, Sr., and his wife Mrs. Mwape Mapila, a former YPD Director and Mother Dorcas Chola. Ms. Loyce Phiri, Gertrude Munyinda, Mrs. Mary Hlabangana from Zimbabwe and Mr. Frank, a Eurafrican and his wife Senefa Samoa, Br. Cosam Nyirongo, an Evangelist and Mrs. Leah Nyirongo were household names at Jordan from the 1970s on. Mrs. Beatrice Totamanga Siwale, mother to Rev. Aaron Siwale, Shadreck Siwale and their oldest brother Lloyd M. Siwale my first Sunday school teacher in 1970 were household names. Br. Washington Kombe and I were Sunday school teachers. Once in a while, Bro. Gershom Siyame would visit and teach too. Mr. Paul Gwamba was a well-known steward from Jordan Chapel who organized the church from 1932 at Wusakile and helped strengthen Nkana Circuit too. He was the father of Sister Martha Mulobeka who was 17th Episcopal District W.M.S., 1st Vice President in 2000. At the time Sister Fashion Musa was the President. Jordan was the first church to be established in Kitwe before Bright Chapel.

In the 1980s we had Br. Alex Simulunga and Philip Simulunga. Others who were prominent at Jordan are Br. Godwin Kasoka, Julius Tembo and James Banda. Bro. Moses Phiri was a choir conductor in the 1990s and was later helped by Br. Geoffrey Mumba who I had led to the Lord and to this Church. Bro. Richard Kasanda was also a great choir conductor. Beatrice Mwitwa, Happy Mwitwa, Godfrey Kaunda, Monica Kishombe, Moses Kapembwa, Miriam Nakapizye, Kampamba Mwango and Threasa Namfukwe were also some notable names. Jack Mapila, Jr., Joseph Mapila, Ann Mapila, Chungu Mapila and their older sister Mrs. Chilemba and my younger sister Mabel Kapungwe who also sang in the choir are other names to recall.

Mother Hughes had a great choir as well. It was among the top competitors too. At Mother Hughes in Ndola prominent laymen included Br. Mbita, Br. Michael Chibvuri and Br. Nekhairo. Br. Chibvuri owned a fleet of buses and was in transportation business. Nekhairo was the other prominent name in the 1970s and beyond. He was a prominent 17th Episcopal Lay Organisation President and was a delegate to the 1984 General Conference in Kansas, Missouri U.S.A.

Calvary was started in 1994 in Kitwe. It was started by Rev. David D. Musole who launched it out from Jordan. I was among the founding members along with Mother Dorcas Chola, Bro. Gideon Y. Phiri and his wife Mrs. Minerva Phiri. Others were Bro. Elijah Simulunga and Mrs. Simulunga who came from Bright. We also had Ngawa Katilungu, Bwalya Katilungu, Chileshe Katilungu and Nzali Katilungu. Other members were Musonda Phiri, Gwenn Phiri, Lilian Chanda, Kennedy Chinyama, Christopher Chikulungu, Threasa Namfukwe, Mirriam Mwape, Julian Kafusha, Catherine Bwalya, Hope Muluka, Mary Kapungwe, Fridah Kapungwe, Gift Kapungwe and Cecilia Kapungwe. Br. Richard Kasanda was among the founders as well.

Calvary A.M.E. Church, Kitwe at ZIBSIP Camp Meeting 1997. Standing from left Bwalya Katilungu, Ngawa Katilungu, Hope Muluka, Mirriam Mwape, Kennedy Chinyama, Rev. Charles Kapungwe, Aginess Chifita, Julian Kafusha, Catherine Bwalya and Nzali Katilungu. Seated: Gift Kapungwe, Lilian Chanda, Fridah Kapungwe and Musonda Phiri. Br. Christopher Chikulungu (not in photo) was a great organizer of these meetings. This was the last Camp Meeting.

Bright Chapel has had many prominent men and women. Br. Charles Chibwe has served in leadership for many years there. He now leads an outreach ministry to prisoners in Kitwe. He is a well-known person within the Kamfinsa Prison circles. Bro. Bernard Chibuta (now Rev. Chibuta) was a member of Bright before moving to Ndola. Bro. Jim Chumbu was a prominent Lay Organisation member while Br. Chilangisha was a Steward. Rev. Edwin J. Fundi was also a Lay Organisation member for years before becoming a minister. Bro. Patrick Moyo was Choir Conductor and Director for years. Bro. Davies Musonda, Sr., was another Bright Chapel prominent leader who later moved to Calvary. He is married to my older sister Mary Kapungwe Musonda. Other renowned people at Bright Chapel were Br. Gift Kaunda, Br. Boyd Chanda (Choir Conductor/Ziyezwa), Br. Emmanuel Kaunda and Br. Davies Musonda, all members of Ziyezwa.

There are many names too numerous to mention from the 1980s at Bright Chapel. Among them are Mercy Kavungo, Peter Kavungu, Davy Kavungu, Willie Kavungu, Rodah Membe, Deborah Membe and Frank Membe (children of Rev. J.L.C. Membe) and later Louis Kafusu. Others are Regina Mwango, Mrs. Dorothy Chishimba, Mrs. Victoria Samuchapi and Charles Kaunda who was at Zambia Institute of Technology (ZIT) now Copperbelt University in Kitwe. He was in YPD and a great singer. He left to work in Botswana in the 1990s. Other names worth remembering are Br. Kelvin Mwitwa and Brother Westone Mutale Bowa.

Mr. Samuchapi (a member of Anglican church), Mrs. Victoria Samuchapi (former South Zambia Conference YPD Director) and Pastor, Rev. Wilson Mpundu at Bright Chapel, Kitwe 1991.

Covenant A.M.E. Church was started in 1998 at Ndeke Village in Kitwe by Rev. David D. Musole. He was a Pastor of Jordan Chapel and he initially began Calvary in 1994 where I was among the first organisers. Covenant was organized by Br. Alfred Mwambuyu Sitwala who had come from St. Peter's at Ndeke. A Bro. Jere, was a member of St. Peter but he was made to leave by a Pastor who was uncomfortable with him acknowledging to his messages with "Amens!" Bro. Julius Mutalu, Sis. Grace Mvula and Pastor Bright Mumba (Lay Pastor) and his son Martin Chibale were among the earliest organisers. Later, Rev. Anderson Tembo from Ndola, Rev. Shadreck Chinyanta, Rev. Ben Chiokola from Chief Nkana area and Rev. Everisto Siulapwa served at the church. Rev. Siulupwa came from Calvary in 2015 but left the church hardly two weeks later to begin another denomination. At Thomas in Luanshya Mr. and Mrs. Abraham Sachikola and Br. Langster D. Zulu were household names. Br. Zulu later became a Pastor then a Presiding Elder in Eastern Province after retirement from the Mines.

Ebenezer in Lusaka has had many prominent personalities. Honourable Wilson Chakulya, a former Cabinet Minister in the Kaunda's government was a member here. He attended Bright Chapel in Kitwe after his retirement from the government until his passing away. Bro. George Mwambazi was a well-known leader and businessman while Br. Alberto Mwansa who had joined from Bethel in Lusaka was another prominent member of the Lay Organisation. He had served in the YPD earlier as did Bro. Ojoni Gondwe. Sister Irene Nakazwe, Sister Mabel Chipelo Mwelwa and Sister Jane Masunga who were among memorable names at Ebenezer. Sisters Irene and Mabel were among the light bearers of the gospel and revival at the church who we worked with to bring about revival in Lusaka. Others were the Rev. and Mother Simfukwe's children Maybin Simfukwe, Faith Simfukwe, Chansa Simfukwe, Chisha Namfukwe, David Simfukwe, Jr., Philip Simfukwe and late Samuel Simfukwe.

At Mother Lesabe, Chelston in Lusaka were a few memorable names too. Sister Vera Nachilima was among the revivalists we had worked together with in the late 1980s and 1990s to bring salvation to souls. Other notable names here are Rev. Kingsley Bwali who had been recommended into ministry after working hard in ministry at the church, Deaconess Namonje, Sister Elizabeth Chifunda and Bro. Oswell Sinyangwe. Rev. Jones Sinyangwe was another great man of God who loved to sing and preach articulately in English.

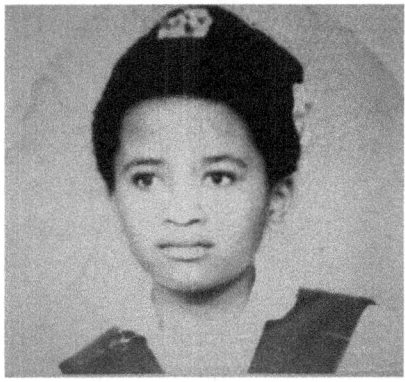

Charity Nakazwe daughter of Presiding Elder Rev. Field Sikazwe

At Bright Matero, were Victor Nyasulu and Sister Charity Nakazwe who helped in bringing about the revival in Lusaka. Others were Damira Chiwende and Rev. Ntinda Sikazwe during the same era. Mother Sikazwe, the wife, worked as a Manager for BP Zimbabwe before she returned to Zambia and retired. She has now gone to be with the Lord. I met her in Charleston, South Carolina in the U.S. in 2008. Another notable couple is Rev. Field Timu Sikazwe and Mother Enika Kasitu Sikazwe, Sister Charity's parents. They had led Bright Temple at Matero for years.

Br. Gilbert Masongo and Br. Richard Ngulube were household names at Kaunda Square Stage I (Chamba Valley) in Lusaka. The duo became ministers and was pastors of Ebenezer and Bethel in Lusaka, respectively. They were churchmates when I was a student in Lusaka in the 1980s. I was an affiliate member at Chamba Valley which changed later to Mother Lubemba. Rev. Masongo went to be with the Lord in 2019. Sister Joyce Masongo, wife of the late Rev. Gilbert Masongo, was also a member of this church as was Br. Paul Shimunza now a minister in Lusaka. At Bethel, Lusaka we had Gladys Wapamesa, Mainsa Mumpanshya, Mrs. Victoria Samuchapi who had left Bright Chapel in Kitwe and Mrs. Susanne Membe Matale now Rev. Matale. When Rev. Aaron Siwale became the Pastor here in the 1990s, he brought a great awakening to the church.

In the 1990s, Rev. Hoppes Jacob Chiluba was a Pastor at Maranatha A.M.E. Church in Lusaka. They used to meet at Evelyn Hone College. Bro. Happy Mulwe (later Rev. Mulwe) and Musenge Matibini (later Dr. Musenge, a medical doctor from University of Zambia School of Medicine) were prominent members here. They organized revival meetings and were instrumental in the reviving of the Midlands. When Rev. Aaron Siwale was transferred to Lusaka (Mandevu) in 1990 and later as Pastor of Bethel, he brought about a great awakening to Lusaka churches and in the A.M.E. Church. He experienced great opposition against his ministry especially at Bethel but he became a leading figure who brought the salvation message to the Church in the Midlands and surrounding regions.

Some prominent names come to memory when you think about Mindolo (Judah A.M.E. Church) in Kitwe. Sister Elizabeth Simwanza was among the people who received Jesus in our outreach there in the late 1980s. She later married Rev. Aaron Siwale. When Rev. Richard Kasanda was appointed Pastor there in 1996, he renamed the church Judah. Many people came to the Lord including Hope Muluka, and Humphrey Muyemba and Herbert Muyemba, brothers to Br. Richard's later to be wife, Mother Pamela Kasanda. Bro. John Mwamba was a prominent person at Membe, Twatasha in Kitwe. He was in my YPD Kitwe District Executive. Br. Floribert Chama was a Senior Steward and he became a Pastor in Redeemed Methodist when they left the church with Mrs. Chama, his wife. He went to be with the Lord in June 2020. Others are Br. Chibwe a Trustee and Bro. Kajimo.

This, therefore, is the history of the A.M.E. Church in Zambia, in Southern, East and Central Africa. Are you born again? If not, then you do not belong to His Church! Are you with zeal serving the House of Saul and not the House of David? He came that we may have life and have it more abundantly! He is coming back to get his Church – one with no wrinkle or spot – one washed in his blood! I pray that you can repent of your sins, invite Jesus in your heart today and belong to his Church – the body of Christ and not just your denomination! Jesus is coming for his Church and not your denomination! We accepted him and preached him crucified for our sins, died, buried and risen, a stumbling block to the "Natives," the lost and misguided staunch traditionalists in the Church! Will you accept him too? May the people you have read about in this work challenge you so that you too can labour for your Master in the same way they did and much more! God be with you!

Photos

Rev. Charles Kapungwe, Djeunou Tchamba (now MD., from Cameroon) and Lorenzo Jackson graduating with B.Sc. degree in Biology – Allen University in Columbia, South Carolina U.S.A., 1st May, 2004.

Dominique Langira (now MD, classmate in medical school and graduate school from Congo DR) and Rev. Charles Kapungwe graduate with a Master's in Health Services Administration from St. Joseph's College of Maine in Standish, Maine U.S.A. 10th May, 2008.

Biomedical Science Summer Research Internship at USC School of Medicine, Columbia, South Carolina U.S.A. Rev. Charles Kapungwe 31st July, 2003.

Charles Kapungwe worked at Kitwe Central Hospital, Kitwe Zambia. He worked for the Ministry of Health from 1st October, 1987 to 30th September, 1999. Above, screening a patient in Outpatients Department I, 1995. Photo by Robert Moyo.

Rev. Charles Kapungwe at Kitwe Central Hospital in Outpatients Department II, months before leaving Zambia for the U.S. 2000. Photo by Robert Moyo.

Rev. Charles Kapungwe at work – Kitwe Central Hospital, Kitwe Zambia 1997. Photo by Robert Moyo.

Rev. Charles Kapungwe at St. Matthew's University School of Medicine in Grand Cayman, Cayman Islands 22nd July, 2005.

Rev. Charles Kapungwe in Grand Cayman, Cayman Islands attending St. Matthew's University School of Medicine – 2005.

Rev. Charles Kapungwe in Kingston, Jamaica – 24th November, 2005.

Biomedical Science Summer Research Internship at USC School of Medicine, Columbia, South Carolina. Rev. Charles Kapungwe 31st July, 2003.

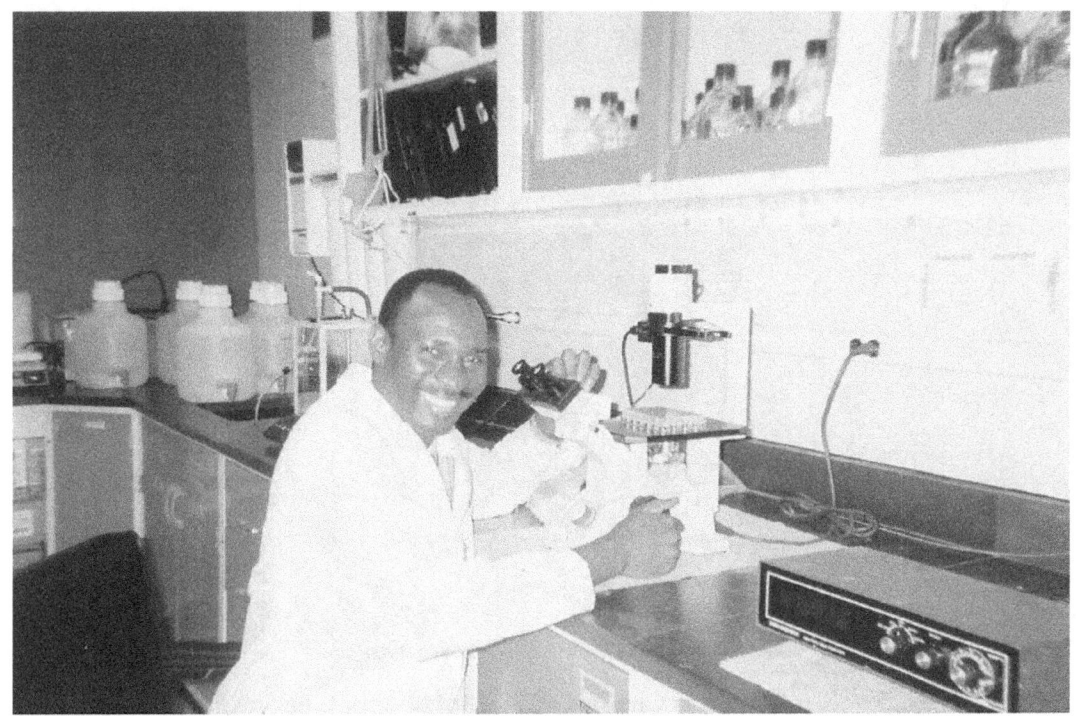

Biomedical Science Summer Research Internship at USC School of Medicine, Columbia, South Carolina. Rev. Charles Kapungwe 31st July, 2003.

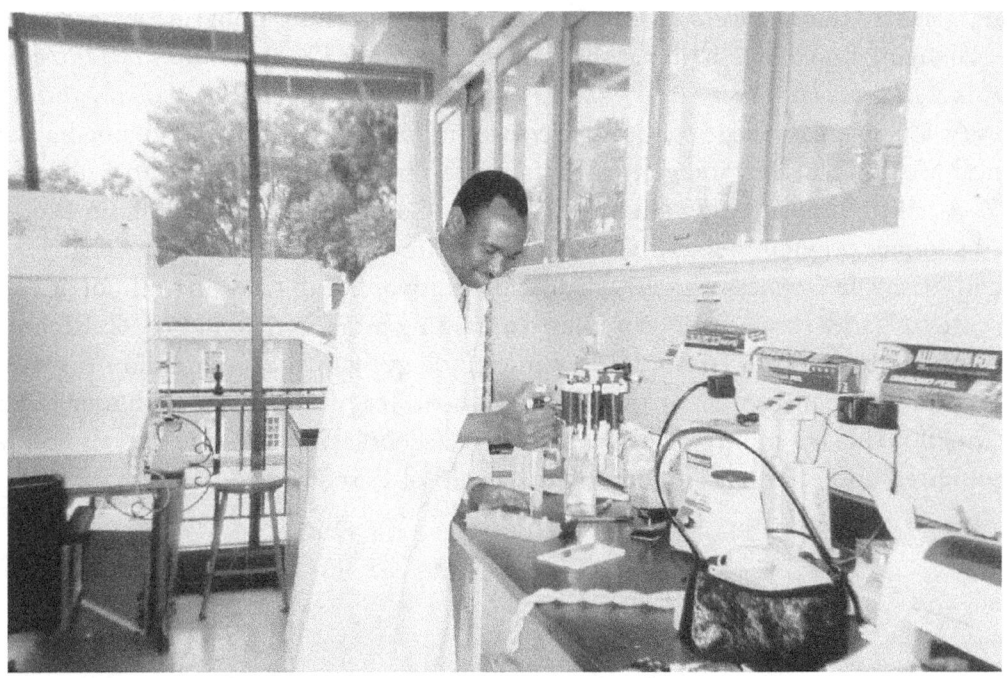

Biomedical Science Summer Research Internship at USC School of Medicine, Columbia, South Carolina. Rev. Charles Kapungwe 31st July, 2003.

Rev. Charles Kapungwe, guest preacher at Christian Methodist Episcopal Church (CMEC) – a Non-A.M.E. denomination in the Pastor's Office of Rev. Hosey in Batesburg, South Carolina U.S.A. before preaching on Sunday. 2004.

Rev. Charles Kapungwe is the author of many best-selling books. They are must-read and life-changing books. He is the author of *Soldiers of the Cross*, *Ministry of Deliverance*, *So God Created Man in His Own Image*, *The Cry of Mother Africa*, *Church Growth*, and *Ministry of Helps*. At Chainama College of Health Sciences in Lusaka, Zambia he obtained a Diploma in Clinical Medical Sciences and graduated as the best student in Medical Laboratory Sciences in 1987. At Allen University, he graduated Summa Cum Laude with a B.Sc. in Biology. He attended summer programmes at South Carolina State University in 2001, Meharry Medical College in Nashville, Tennessee in 2002 and University of South Carolina School of Medicine in 2003. Rev. Charles satisfactorily completed a training programme in MFSP2: Recombinant DNA Methodology & Special Topics in Biotechnology with the Foundation for Advanced Education in the Sciences, Inc. at the National Institutes of Health in Bethsaida, Maryland U.S.A., in 2001. He has multiple degrees from other schools. In 1993, the City of Fort Worth, Texas conferred upon him an Honorary Citizenship of Fort Worth.

Ministers' Ordination Certificates and Appointments

Under The Protection Of Almighty God

Certificate of
PASTOR APPOINTMENT

"Study to show thyself a workman approved unto God"

African Methodist Episcopal Church

This is to Certify that the

Reverend .... C. KAPIONGWE ....

is appointed to the pastoral charge of ..... TRINITY .....

the said charge being under the jurisdiction of the ..... SOUTH WEST ZAMBIA ..... Annual Conference of the African Methodist Episcopal Church.

Given under my hand and the Denominational seal at the Episcopal Room this ..... 1ST ..... day of ..... DEC ....., 19 96

Signed in behalf of the ..... SWZ ..... Annual Conference.

T. Larry Kirkland
Presiding Bishop

Under The Protection Of Almighty God

Certificate of
PASTOR APPOINTMENT

"Study to show thyself a workman approved unto God"

African Methodist Episcopal Church

This is to Certify that the

Reverend ......C. KAPUNGWE......

is appointed to the pastoral charge of ......TRINITY......
the said charge being under the jurisdiction of the ......SOUTH WEST ZAMBIA...... Annual Conference of the African Methodist Episcopal Church.

Given under my hand and the Denominational seal at the Episcopal Room this ...5TH... day of ...OCT..., 19..97..

Signed in behalf of the ...SWZ... Annual Conference.

T. LARRY KIRKLAND BISHOP
Presiding Bishop

CERTIFICATE OF ORDINATION
ITINERANT DEACON

"Study to show thyself a workman approved unto God"

T. LARRY KIRKLAND BISHOP   17TH

Presiding Bishop   Episcopal District

Having satisfied the Board of Examiners

CHARLES KAPUNGWE

Name of Itinerant Deacon

has duly fulfilled the educational requirements prescribed by the Discipline and passed the test for Ordination.

I, T. LARRY KIRKLAND BISHOP, One of the Bishops of the

African Methodist Episcopal Church

by the imposition of my hands and prayer, have this day set apart for the office of Itinerant Deacon in the African Methodist Episcopal Church CHARLES KAPUNGWE a person whom the SOUTH WEST ZAMBIA

Name of Itinerant Deacon   Name of Conference

Conference judges to be well qualified for the work, granting him/her the rights to administer the

Baptism, Perform Marriages, the Burial of the Dead and the Lord's Supper

after the Elements have been consecrated by an Elder. And to feed the flock of Christ so long as his/her spirit and practice are such as become the Gospel of Christ and the Discipline of the African Methodist Episcopal Church.

In Witness Whereof I have hereunto set my hand and the Denominational seal this 5TH day of OCT in the year of our Lord, One Thousand Nine Hundred and 97.

T. LARRY KIRKLAND BISHOP

Presiding Bishop

Certificates and Appointments • History of the A.M.E. Church in Zambia

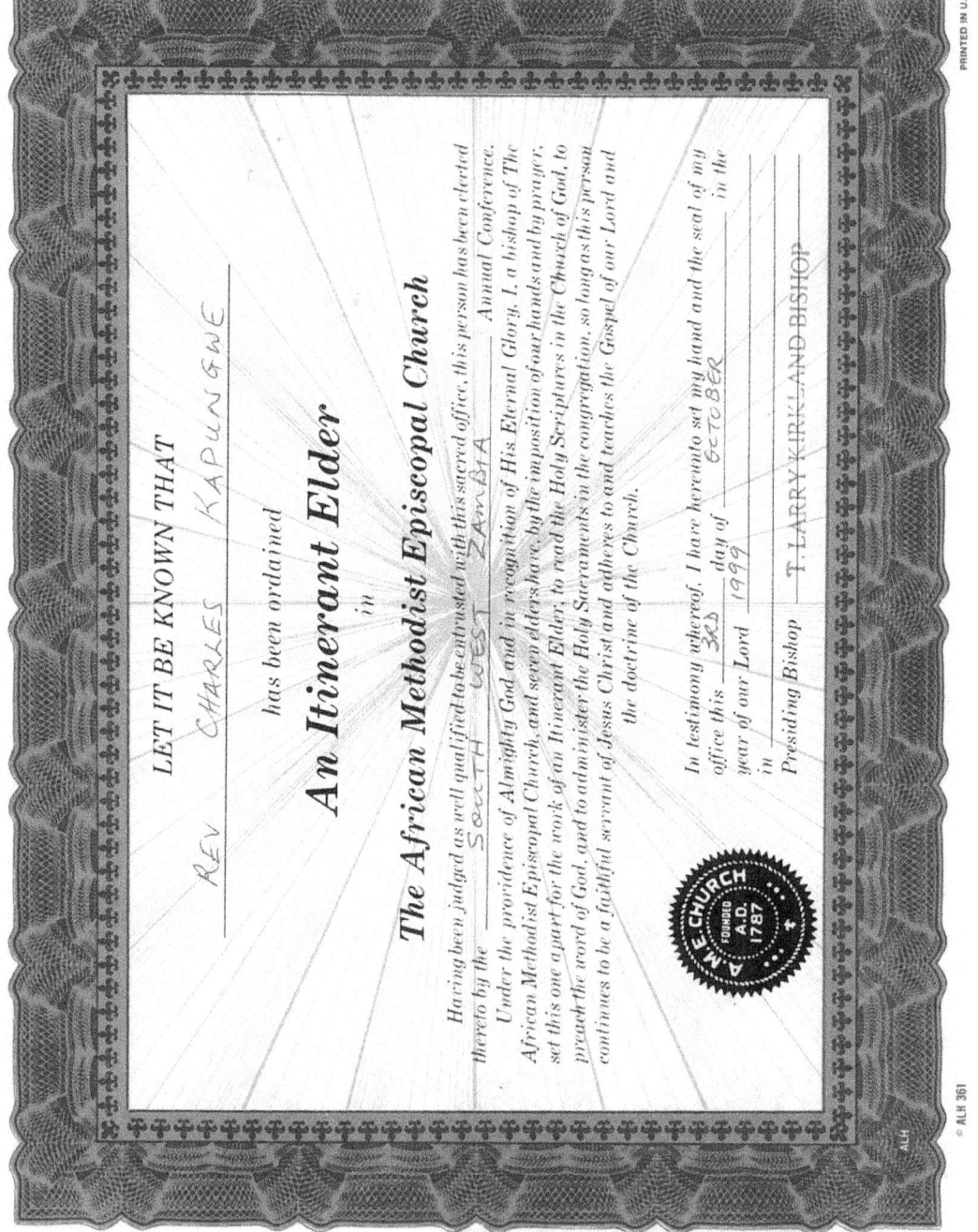

The BIBLE COLLEGE of CENTRAL AFRICA

This is to Certify that

PETER MWENYA

having successfully completed the prescribed
Three-Year Course of Study
and
having given evidence of Christian character
is hereby awarded this

Diploma in Biblical Instruction

Given at Ndola, Zambia, this 6th day of April 1982

Principal   *Registrar*

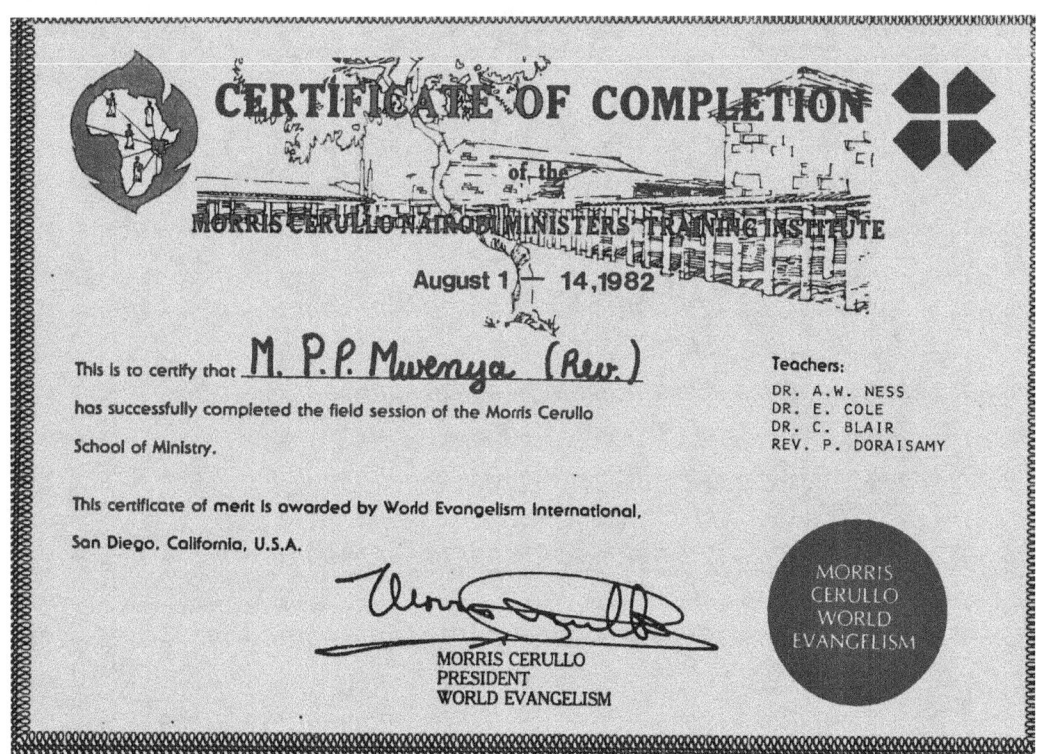

CERTIFICATE OF COMPLETION
of the
MORRIS CERULLO NAIROBI MINISTERS' TRAINING INSTITUTE
August 1 — 14, 1982

This is to certify that **M. P. P. Mwenya (Rev.)** has successfully completed the field session of the Morris Cerullo School of Ministry.

Teachers:
DR. A.W. NESS
DR. E. COLE
DR. C. BLAIR
REV. P. DORAISAMY

This certificate of merit is awarded by World Evangelism International, San Diego, California, U.S.A.

MORRIS CERULLO
PRESIDENT
WORLD EVANGELISM

MORRIS CERULLO WORLD EVANGELISM

Mindolo Ecumenical Foundation

CONFERENCE, CONSULTATIONS RESOURCE PROGRAMME

CERTIFICATE

This is to Certify that

PETER M. P. MWENYA

has successfully completed a Course in

ADVANCED IN-SERVICE THEOLOGICAL STUDIES

from 7th September 1982 to 1st December 1984

Date 27th November, 1984

COORDINATOR   *DIRECTOR*

Mindolo Ecumenical Foundation

Industry and Commerce Programme

CERTIFICATE

MANAGEMENT DEVELOPMENT

This Certifies that REV. PETER M. P. MWENYA

has attended and successfully completed Course Number 1

from 7th September 1982 to 1 December 1984

which included the following subjects- Basic Objectives of Industry, Management Principles and Functions, Leadership Styles and Delegation, The Art of Supervision, Morale and Discipline, Human Motivation and Communications, Job Analysis and Job Instructions, Uses and Abuses of Management Power, Management By Objectives, Time Management, Management Integrity, Measuring Efficiency, Value Analysis, Industrial Psychology, Group Dynamics, Creativity and Innovation, Human Relations, Decision Making.

DIRECTOR
HEAD OF PROGRAMME
COURSE LEADER

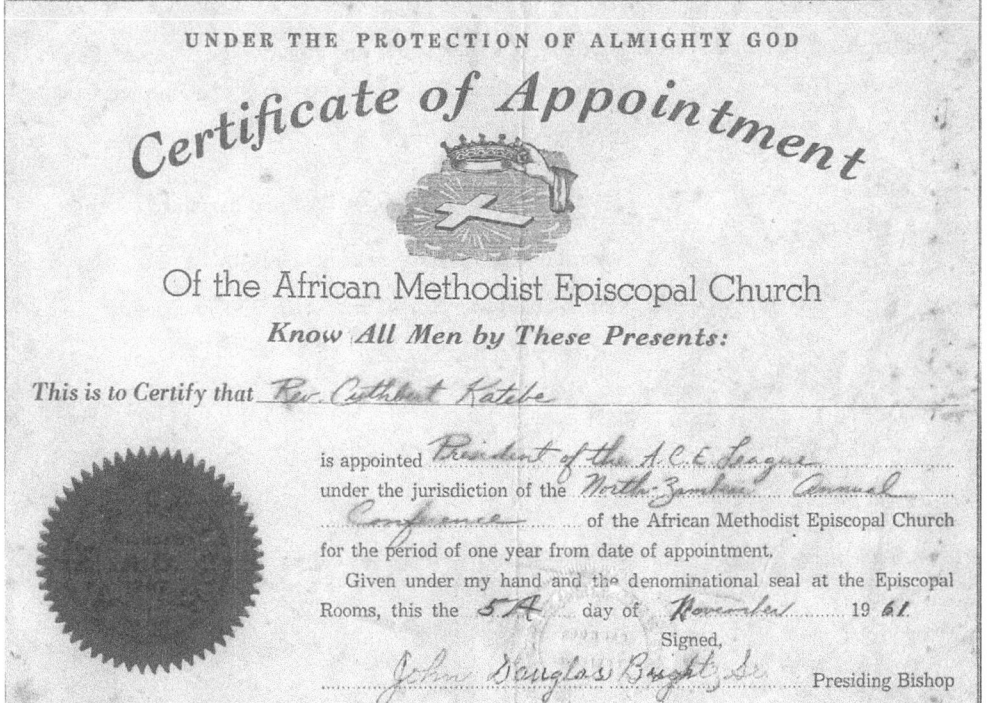

Certificates and Appointments • History of the A.M.E. Church in Zambia

Under the Protection of Almighty God.

Know all Men by these Presents, That I,

ONE OF THE BISHOPS OF THE

African Methodist Episcopal Church,

Under the protection of Almighty God, and with a single eye to His glory, by the imposition of my hands and prayer, have this day set apart

___CUTHBERT   KATEBE___
ITENERANT
for the office of ELDER in the said African Methodist Episcopal Church, a man whom the Annual Conference judges to be well qualified for that work; and do hereby recommend him to all whom it may concern, as a proper person to administer the ordinances of the

𝕷𝖔𝖗𝖉'𝖘 𝕾𝖚𝖕𝖕𝖊𝖗, 𝕭𝖆𝖕𝖙𝖎𝖘𝖒, 𝕸𝖆𝖗𝖗𝖎𝖆𝖌𝖊 𝖆𝖓𝖉 𝖙𝖍𝖊 𝕭𝖚𝖗𝖎𝖆𝖑 𝖔𝖋 𝖙𝖍𝖊 𝕯𝖊𝖆𝖉

and to feed the flock of Christ so long as his spirit and practice are such as become the Gospel of Christ, and he continueth to hold fast the form of sound words, according to the established doctrine of the Gospel.

In Witness Whereof I have hereunto set my hand and the Denominational Seal, this 12th day of Dec in the year of our Lord, One Thousand 9 Hundred and 77

C. E. Thomas, Bishop

Done in South Zambia Conf

Under the Protection of Almighty God

CERTIFICATE OF

Pastor's Appointment

"Study to show thyself a workman approved unto God"

This is to Certify, That the Rev. C Y Katebe is appointed to the pastoral charge of Presiding Elder Copperbelt the said charge being under the jurisdiction of the South Zambia Annual Conference of the African Methodist Episcopal Church

Given under my hand and the Denominational seal at the Episcopal Rooms this 30th August 1987

Signed in behalf of said Annual Conference

Robert L. Pruitt
BISHOP
Presiding Bishop

Under The Protection of Almighty God

CERTIFICATE OF

Presiding Elder's Appointment

"Study to show thyself a workman approved unto God"

This is to Certify, That the Rev. _C. Y. Katebe_ is appointed Presiding Elder of the _Lusaka District_ District, the said District being under the jurisdiction of the _South Zambia_ Annual Conference of the African Methodist Episcopal Church.

Given under my hand and the Denominational seal at the Episcopal Rooms this _May 3,_ 19_81_

Signed in behalf of said Annual Conference

C. Egbert Thomas
Presiding Bishop.

Under The Protection Of Almighty God

Certificate Of

Presiding Elder's Appointment

"Study to show thyself a workman approved unto God"

This is to Certify that the Rev. _C. Y. Katebe_ is appointed Presiding Elder of the _Copperbelt_ District, the said District being under the jurisdiction of the _South Zambia_ Annual Conference of the African Methodist Episcopal Church.

Given under my hand and the Denominational Seal at the Episcopal Rooms this _December 5_ 19_82_

Signed in behalf of said Annual Conference.

C. E. Thomas
Presiding Bishop.

Under the Protection of Almighty God

CERTIFICATE OF
Pastor's Appointment

This is to Certify, That the Rev. F.T. Sinazo is appointed to the pastoral charge of MATERO the said charge being under the jurisdiction of the SOUTH AFRICA Annual Conference of the African Methodist Episcopal Church.

Given under my hand and the Denominational seal at the Episcopal Rooms this 23rd NOVEMBER 19__

Signed in behalf of said Annual Conference

_____
Presiding Bishop

UNDER THE PROTECTION OF ALMIGHTY GOD

CERTIFICATE OF
PRESIDING ELDER'S APPOINTMENT

"Study to show thyself a workman approved unto God."

This is to Certify that

The Rev. H. M. LUKAMBA

is appointed Presiding Elder of the COPPERBELT

District, the said district being under the jurisdiction of the

SOUTH ZAMBIA Annual Conference

of the African Methodist Episcopal Church

Given under my hand and the denominational seal at the Episcopal Rooms this 2nd day of January 19 72

Signed in behalf of said Annual Conference

_____
Presiding Bishop

UNDER THE PROTECTION OF ALMIGHTY GOD

CERTIFICATE OF

Pastor's Appointment

"Study to Show thyself a workman approved unto God."

This is to certify that the Rev. Brother H. L. Lukamba is appointed to the pastoral charge of Nkana the said charge being under the jurisdiction of the Zambesi Annual Conference of the African Methodist Episcopal Church.

Given under my hand and the Denominational Seal at the Episcopal Rooms this 9th November 1947

Signed on behalf of said Annual Conference.

Theo R. Mareka, Assist.
General Presiding Bishop

UNDER THE PROTECTION OF ALMIGHTY GOD

CERTIFICATE OF

Pastor's Appointment

"Study to Show thyself a workman approved unto God."

This is to certify that the Rev. H. M. Lukumba is appointed to the pastoral charge of Nkana the said charge being under the jurisdiction of the Zambese Annual Conference of the African Methodist Episcopal Church.

Given under my hand and the Denominational Seal at the Episcopal Rooms this 12th November, 1950.

Signed on behalf of said Annual Conference.

J. H. Bonner
Presiding Bishop.

Certificates and Appointments • History of the A.M.E. Church in Zambia

UNDER THE PROTECTION OF ALMIGHTY GOD.

CERTIFICATE OF

Pastor's Appointment

"Study to show thyself a Workman approved unto God."

This is to Certify that

Rev. H. M. Lukamba is appointed to the

Pastoral Charge of Mukutuma the said

Charge being under the Jurisdiction of the

N. Rhodesia Annual Conference of the African

Methodist Episcopal Church.

Given Under my Hand the and Denominational Seal

at the Episcopal Rooms 24 January 1954

Signed on behalf of said Annual Conference.

Presiding Bishop

UNDER THE PROTECTION OF ALMIGHTY GOD

CERTIFICATE OF

Pastor's Appointment

"Study to show thyself a workman approved unto God"

This is to Certify that

Rev. _H. M. Lukamba_ is appointed to the pastoral charge of _Mukutuma_ the said charge being under the Jurisdiction of the _Northern Rhodesia_ Annual Conference of the African Methodist Episcopal Church.

Given under my hand and the Denominational Seal at the Episcopal Rooms _27th February_, 19_55_

Signed in behalf of said Annual Conference

Frederick Jordan
Presiding Bishop

UNDER THE PROTECTION OF ALMIGHTY GOD.

CERTIFICATE OF
Presiding Elder's Appointment

"Study to show thyself a Workman approved unto God."

This is to Certify that Rev. H. M. Lukamba is appointed to the Presiding Elder of the Kasempa District. The said District being under the Jurisdiction of the No. Rhodesia Annual Conference of

The African Methodist Episcopal Church.

Given Under my Hand and the Denominational Seal.

at the Episcopal Rooms this .... 19......

Signed on behalf of said Annual Conference.

....
Presiding Bishop

Under The Protection Of Almighty God

Certificate Of

Presiding Elder's Appointment

"Study to show thyself a workman approved unto God"

This is to Certify that the Rev. H. M. Lukamba is appointed Presiding Elder of the LAMBALAND District, the said District being under the jurisdiction of the _____ Annual Conference of the African Methodist Episcopal Church.

Given under my hand and the Denominational Seal at the Episcopal Rooms this 20th Day of October 1957

Signed in behalf of said Annual Conference.

William F. Ball
Presiding Bishop.

REFERENCE

Gray, Richard. (2009, May 09) Science Correspondent. African tribe populated rest of the world. Retrieved October 3, 2018, from https://www.telegraph.co.uk/news/science/science-news/5299351/African-tribe-populated-rest-of-the-world.html

Lambert, Tim. A brief history of Africa. Accessed from http://www.localhistories.org/africanhistory.html Sep.5 2018

Andrews, Evan. History Stories. 7 Influential African Empires (January 11, 2017). https://www.history.com/news/7-influential-african-empires. Accessed Sep/5/2018

Lambert, Tim. A short history of Zambia. Accessed from http://www.localhistories.org/zambia.html Sep.5 2018

Lyons, D.C. (1987, November). Bicentennial of The A.M.E. Tradition. Retrieved October 18, 2017, from http://connection.ebscohost.com/c/articles/50914248/bicentennial-a-m-e-tradition

Christianity Today. Richard Allen Founder of the African Methodist Episcopal Church. Retrieved August 18, 2018, from https://www.christianitytoday.com/history/people/denominationalfounders/richard-allen.html

Encyclopedia of World Biography. Sarah Allen Biography. Retrieved August 18, 2018, from http://www.notablebiographies.com/supp/Supplement-A-Bu-and-Obituaries/Allen-Sarah.html

Galli, M. (2017). Richard Allen Founder of the African Methodist Church. Retrieved October 27, 2017, from http://www.christianitytoday.com/history/people/denominationalfounders/richard-allen.html

Holsoe, S. E., Petterson, D. R., & Jones, A. B. (2018, June 27). Liberia. Retrieved September 5, 2018, from https://www.britannica.com/place/Liberia

The General Missionary Conference of Northern Rhodesia. (8-15th August, 1939). http://www.historicalpapers.wits.ac.za/inventories/inv_pdfo/AD1715/AD1715-15-8-8-001-jpeg.pdf Accessed July 30, 2018

Princeton University Press. Christian Missionaries and the Creation of Northern Rhodesia 1880-1924 (2015). https://muse.jhu.edu/chapter/1680921 Accessed July 30, 2018.

D.D. Khomela, (1949) African Methodist Episcopal Church Introduced in Northern Rhodesia 1929.

Heres. What you need to know about Zambia (2018). https://www.africa.com/heres-what-you-need-to-know-about-zambia/ Retrieved August 1, 2018.

Gomez-Jefferson, A. L. (1998). In darkness with God: The life of Joseph Gomez, a bishop in the African Methodist Episcopal Church. Kent, OH: Kent State University Press.

[1]Author's note (Kapungwe, Charles). The history of the establishment of 19th Episcopal District - Mangena Maake Mokone conference Women's Missionary Society (WMS). (2015). Retrieved from http://wmsmmmokone.org.za/wms-mmmokone.php. Uniforms used in the U.S.A. have no leopard skins and usually are ordinary attires which the leadership may call on women to dress in cream or white depending on occasion. It is not adorned routinely or regularly as is the case in Africa.

Yusuf Simmonds (May 23, 2012). Bishop H.H. Brookins. https://lasentinel.net/the-rt-rev-bishop-h-h-brookins-a-giant-among-men-passes-on.html Accessed 7-26-2018

Rev. Mangena Maake Mokone. (2011, February 17). Retrieved April 25, 2019, from https://www.sahistory.org.za/people/rev-mangena-maake-mokone

South African History Online. (1998) https://www.sahistory.org.za/ Retrieved April 25, 2019.

Petruzzello, M. (2019). Ethiopianism AFRICAN RELIGION. Retrieved April 25, 2019, from https://www.britannica.com/topic/Ethiopianism Encyclopaedia Britannica

Williams, P. W. (2016). Williams, Preston Warren II. Retrieved October 16, 2018, from https://www.encyclopedia.com/education/news-wires-white-papers-and-books/williams-preston-warren-ii Select

Langfitt, F. (2004, July 12). AME faithful ponder Reid's words. The Baltimore Sun. Retrieved December 28, 2018, from https://www.baltimoresun.com/news/bs-xpm-2004-07-12-0407120118-story.html

Sikalumbi, W.K. Eulogy on Rev. J.L.C. Membe Funeral/Rev. Dr. John Lester Coward Membe The Legend. 11 Nov. 2016.

Frazier, M. (2010, June 15). Rev. William Tecumseh Vernon. Retrieved April 17, 2019, from https://www.findagrave.com/memorial/53740213/william-tecumseh-vernon

African Methodist Episcopal Church Historic Timeline 1703-1987. (1997). Retrieved August 17, 2018, from http://s3.amazonaws.com/gcah.org/African_Methodist_Episcopal_Church-1.pdf

Transcription of The A.M.E. Church Review, The Book Shelf 1997 Columns

Pastors' widows threaten to sue bishop. (2015, August 17). Retrieved from http://www.lusakavoice.com/2015/08/17/pastors-widows-threaten-to-sue-bishop/

Chihane, Christine. (2020). Reverend, congregants sue bishop Zambia. Daily Mail 20th March, 2020.

Index

Abercorn 17, 19, 57, 61-62, 72, 83-89, 92-96, 126, 135, 145-146, 150, 161, 163-164, 170, 174, 177, 179, 190, 317, 427.
Aksum/Axum 7.
Alimasi, Henry Rev. v, 51, 53, 137, **160-161**, 184, 188, 197, 219, 356-357, 388, 431.
Allen, Richard vi, **24-25**.
Allen, Sarah **25**.
Allen Temple, Mufulira 51, 199, 215, 315, 434.
Allen University 25, 29, 31, 108-109, 181, 194, 246-247, 251, 258, 277, 337, 389, 391, 471, 431-432, 450.
A.M.E. Church Press viii.
America/Americans ix, 11, 24-26, 29-30, 39, 46, 51, 81, 83, 90, 107-110, 117-*120*, 124, 242, 248, 262, 269-271, 279, 287, *297*, 301, 308, 312, 383, 388, 392, 415.
American Colonization Society 26.
American Methodist Episcopal Church 44, 124, 146, 148, 157, 164.
Arabs 7, 9, 10, 11.
Asbury, Francis – Bishop 24-25.
Banda, Francis Chiku Paikua. Rev. **176-177**.
Barotse/Barotseland vii, *38*, 39-40, 76, 78, *83*, *144*, 155-156, 170, 177.
Basutoland 12, 32, 108.
BBC 6.
Bechuanaland 12, 33, 111, 143,
Belgian Congo 124, 146, 147.
Belgians 11.
Berlin Conference 11, 12.
Bicentennial 24.
Bishop Baber, George Wilbur 109.
Bishop Ball, William F. 48, 110.
Bishop Bearden, Harold Irwin 112
Bishop Becket, William Wesley 108
Bishop Bonner, Isaiah H. 112.
Bishop Bright, John Douglas **110-112**, 137, 175, 177.
Bishop Brookins, Hartford H. **112**, 137, 242, 291, 322, 326.

Bishop Chappelle, Richard Allen **113-114**, 118, 139-140, 142, 158, 165, 182-184, 187, 192-193, 197, 205, 210, 218-219, 254, 316, 327, 350-351, 424-425, 433.
Bishop Collins, George Napoleon **111-112**, 117.
Bishop Coppin, Levi J. 31, **107-108**.
Bishop Derrick, William Benjamin 108.
Bishop Gomez, Joseph 27, **112**, 118-119.
Bishop Gow, Francis Herman 110
Bishop Gregg, John Andrew 32, **108**, 178.
Bishop Johnson, James Albert **108**, 117.
Bishop Jordan, Frederick Douglas **110**.
Bishop Kawimbe, Paul **116**, 118, 180-181, 187, 208, 244, 248, 327-328, 350.
Bishop Kirkland, Larry Theodore 3, 113, **115-116**, 193, 327, 337, 369.
Bishop Messiah, Wilfred/Incompetence & Maladministration **116-117**, 187, **259**, 270, 276, **288, 296, 303, 312, 327-328, 431**.
Bishop Pruitt, Robert Lee **113**, 139, 141-142, 193, 239, 242, 325.
Bishop Reid, Frank Madison **109**.
Bishop Shaffer, Cornelius Thaddeus 28.
Bishop Sims, David Henry **109**, 126.
Bishop Spencer, Charles Smith **108**.
Bishop Springer, John **44-45**, 148.
Bishop Thomas, Cornelius Egbert **113**, 138, 183.
Bishop Turner, Henry M. 29, **107**.
Bishop Webster, Robert V. **114-115**.
Bishop Williams, Preston **116**, 310.
Bishop Wright, Richard Robert **109**.
Bishop Young, George B. **108-109**, 296.
Bishop Vernon, William T. 108.
Blantyre 99-100.
Bloemfontein 32-33, 41, 94, 126, 130, 146.
BOMA 37, 41, 61, 125, 155, 223, 420.
Botswana 10, 12, 16, 22, 213, 339, 438,
Britain/British 11-*12*, 16-*23*, *26*, 37, 39, 112,

123-24, 128-129, 136, 159, *218*,
British South African Company (BSAC) 16, 17, 123.
Broken Hill 37, 38, 40-43, 45.
Brooms, Winston. Dr. Rev. **359-361**, 363.
Bulawayo 31-34, 37-42, 46, 56, 75-76, 81, 94, 100, 102, 108, 125-126, 143, 145-146, 171, 177-179, 419.
Bupe, Paul. Dr. Rev. 22, 25, 113-114, 192-194, 205, 220, 227, 234, 251, 308, 325, 366-367, 370, 378, 431, 434.
Byzantine Empire 7.
Cape Mesurado 26.
Carthage 6, 7.
Cecil Rhodes 16-17.
Central Africa 23, 30, 106-107, 110-111, 120, 122, 129, 131, 136, 146, 187, 213, 246, 271, 358, 440.
Chainama College of Health Sciences 1, 134, 140, 336-338, 383, 450.
Chakulya, Wilson Honourable 119, 141, 439.
Chalomba, Benjamin W. Rev. vii, 54, 56, 65, 77, 83, **145**, 163.
Chief Chinakila, James 85, 88.
Chifunda, Stephen. Dr. Rev. **182**, 221, 349, 379.
Chiluba, Frederick T.J., President v, 240, 361-362.
Chimba, Justin Honourable **118-119**, 384.
Chisela, Benjamin Ben. Rev. vii, 42, 44-48, 56, 67, **143**, 145, 174.
Chisela, B.B. Mrs. vii.
Chisela, Samson 45.
Chisholm, James Alexander. Dr. Rev. 124-125, 145.
Chiyanga Mission 68, 70, 72, 84, 87-88, 92-96, 128, 156, 161, 163-164.
Congo DR 28, 112, 139, 142, 147, 171, 184, 196, 213-214, 218, 222, 226-227, 231, 262, 272, 315, 320, 327, 330, 370, 430, 442.
Constantinople 7.
Copperbelt vii, ix, 16, 18-20, 43-44, 46-47, 49-52 …

Daniels, J. A. Rev. 81.
Dupont, Joseph-Marie-Stanislas (Moto-Moto) 17, 96.
Dutch 11, 107, 147, 152, 161, 333.
Early Africa 6, 7.
Ebenezer A.M.E. Church 1, 50, 110, 126, 134, 141, 187, 239, 315, 341.
Elizabethville 44, 124, 213.
Ethiopia 6-7, 10-11, 26, 195.
Ethiopian Church 29, 107, 195.
Ethiopian Orthodox Church 7.
Europe 6-7, 9-12, 15-17, 26, 30, 119-120, 195.
Federation of African Societies of Northern Rhodesia 19.
Formalism 3, 249-250.
Fort Jameson 17, 19, 73, 77, 82, 144, 151, 153, 163, 168, 173, 178, 187.
France 11.
French 11, 17, 96.
Gabashane, Daniel K. Rev. 31.
Germans 11, 17.
Gray, Richard 6.
Gwamba, Paul M. 54, 436.
Healthcare Christian Fellowship of Zambia (HCFZ) 79, 362, 371, 382.
Heath, Annie E. 111.
Herodias 294, 301, 393, 410, 415.
Historical Committee vi, 1, 81, 134.
Honoko, Jonas Lesapi Rev. 42, 57, 76, 82, 126, **177**.
Hughes, L.M. Mother 48, **83**, 109, 116, 117, …
Hymnal **2, 131-132**, 173, 176, 183.
Iniquity 3, 232-233, 237, 241, 251, 256, 291.
Istanbul 7.
Islam 7, 30, 131.
Jezebel 301, 393, 410, 415.
Jones, Absalom 24.
Jordan Chapel A.M.E. Church, Wusakile Kitwe iii, 234, 276, 278, 279, 280, 333, 336, 343, 346, 424, 436.
Kalobwe, Alfred Mwika. Rev. **186**, 221, 370.
Kalumba, Theodore. Rev. **183-184**, 218, 220, 392.

Kamdgshariwa, S.M. Rev. vi, 33, 81, 155.
Kanyembo, G.W. Rev. 51, 137, 160, 184, **188**, 191, 220.
Kapufi, Samson Mulonga Rev. iii, v, 47-48, 64, 67, 123, **171-173**, 188, 211, 216, 367.
Kapungwe, Charles. Rev. 54, 75, 78, 106, 108, 110, 112-123, 126, 135, 140-141, 149-150, 153, 158, 165, 171, 173, 175, 177-178, 179, 181, 183-186, 189, 192-193, 195, 208-209, 211, 212, 215, 221, 234, 247, 248, 250, 256, 260-261, 268, 269, 270, 271-276, 281, 285, 292-293, 295, 301-302, 307, **331-418**, 432-433, 435-438, **442-454**.
Kariba Dam 20.
Karonga 99, 109, 144, 151, 153-154, 161.
Kasanda, Richard. Dr. Rev. 54, **211-213**, 220, 345, 347-350, 356-357, 363, 366, 367-369, 372, 379, 380, 388, 437, 440.
Katanga Annual Conference 231.
Katebe, Cuthbert Yoram Rev. v, 113, 115, 141, 150, **158-159**, 184, 188, 201-203, 215, 219, 349, 368, 421, 422.
Katebe, Daisy Mrs. 368, **421-422**.
Kaunda, Kenneth D., President iv, 2, 20-22, 118-121, 123, 131, 135, 141, 175, 206, 439.
Kawala, Augustus Rev. vii, 44, 82, 97-98.
Kawala, Augustus Mrs. vii.
Khaile, Joseph J. Rev. 32.
Khomela, David Dafite Rev. v, vi, 33, 41-43, 46, 57, 75-76, 78, 81-83, 125-126, **143**, 152, 154-155, 157, 169.
Kingdoms 6-7, 10-11, 15, 195.
Kitwe 16, 18, 47, 48, 51, 54, 55, 116, 119, 126, 127, 130, 149, 210, 212, 216, 217, **307**, 331, **332**, 335 …
Kush 6.
Kuyumba, Joel Perhaps Mumbili Rev. 75, **150-151**.
Legalism 249-250.
Lesotho 22, 113, 433.
Liberia 11, **26**, 28, 116, 246, 247.
Livingstone 16, 35, 36-43, 46, 56, 76-79, 82, 106, 110, 115, 124-126, 143-145, 155-156, 172, 177-178, 191, 219, 221, 227, 243, 245, 255, 348-349, 355, 361, 382-383, 421, 433.
Livingstone, David Dr. **15-16**, 36.
Livingstonia Mission 124, 146, 153-154, 161.
London Missionary Society 44, 61, 81, 85, 126, 135, 147, 150-152, 156-157, 162-164, 169, 170, 174, 317.
Lukamba, Henrique Matenda Rev. v, 81, 131-132, **148-150**, 179, 219, 344.
Lusaka 82, 83, 104, 110-114, 118-**119**, **121**, 126-128, **134**-145, 151, 153, 155 …
Mabombo, Johannes Rev. 83, 131, 156, 161, 164, 175, **177-178**.
Mabote, S.J. Rev. 31.
Makghato, E.M. Rev. vi, 81.
Mandah, George Green Rev. **168**.
Mapoma, Abraham Phillip Chibwe Rev. **164-165**, 429.
Marumo, Johannes Rev. vi, 33, 56, 57, 76-78, 81-83, 127, **144**, 156.
Mashonaland 33, 34, 111.
Matabeleland 33.
Maya, John Oliver Rev. 33.
Mazimba, Joel Manda Rev. 47, 189, **190**.
Mbereshi Mission 147, 150, 152, 156-157, 162-163, 170, 174-175, 177, 188.
Mbunjimayi West Annual Conference 226.
Mbunjimayi South West Annual Conference 231.
Membe, John Lester C. Rev. 35-42, 48, 84, 97-104, **122-133**, 233.
Membe, Fanny. Mother 48, 122.
Middle Ages 6, 7.
Middle East 6.
Mkhwanazi, Clement Rev. 160, **171**.
Mkhwanazi, Daniel Rev. v, 138, 159, **170**, 171, 219.
Mkwayi, John Richard Rev. 42, 82, 126, **145**, 152, 155.
Modern Africa 6.
Mokone, Mangena M. Rev. **29**, 107, 109, **195**.
Molebatsi, J. Daniel Rev. 31.

Monrovia 26.
Mother Bethel A.M.E. Church 24, 25.
Moto Moto/Museum 96.
Mpundu, Wilson Rev. v, 3, 49, 113-116, 130, 142, 160, 189, **194-208**, 220, 241, 244-246, 249, 308, 325, 327, 364, 370, 378, 434, 438.
Mtshwello, Z.C. Rev. 32-33, 37-41, 45-48, 82, 125, 145, 154, 173.
Mugala, Nathan. Rev. 182, 434-435.
Mukeya, John. Rev. **213-214**, 220-221, 308, 370.
Mulwe, Happy. Rev. 211, **215**, 221, 344, 349, 366-368, 440.
Mumba, Bright. Pastor **217**, 348, 349-350, 356-357, 364-366, 382, 383, 439.
Mumba, Philemon Chakalipa. Rev. **182-183**, 214, 220, 368, 435.
Mumpanshya, Isaac C. Rev. v, 50, 141-142, **158**, 219, 239.
Musole, David Damus. Rev. **192-193**, 217, 221, 255, 308, 337, 351, 365, 437, 439.
Musonda, Elsie. Rev. 51, 184, **185-186**, 221, 241, 379.
Mvula, Ernest Aaron. Rev. 60-63, 65-66, **152**.
Mwamba, Ernest Alexander 45-46, 49, 54, 82.
Mwenya, Peter M.P. Rev. v, ix, 52, 165, 192, 199, 219-220, 223, 253-254, **313-330**, 351, 356, 367, 370, 434.
Mwenyo, Rowland Katemba. Rev. 132, **175-176**, 184, 197, 201-203, 208, 220.
Mwenzo Mission 123-124, 128, 145, 163.
Nakapizye, Mirriam. Rev. **216-217, 345, 346**, 437.
Nakazwe, Charity **58**, 184, 349, **439-440**.
Native(s) 63, 76, 89, 328, 334, **441**.
Native Christian Church 44-46.
Ncube, Mikia C. Rev. 31.
Ndola 41-43, **45-53**, 56-57, 60, 61-63, …
Nelson Mandela 191.
Ngalala, Emmanuel Rev. iii, 47, 59, 64-67, **215-216**, 228.
Ngoma, Caleb Rev. v, 141, 160, **187-188**, 207, 219, **370**.

Nomazele, William Rev. 33.
North East Zambia Conference 64, 68, 180, 190, 305-306.
North-Eastern Rhodesia 17.
Northern Rhodesia **17-19**, …
North-Western Rhodesia 17.
North West Zambia Conference 64, 311.
Nubian 6.
Nyasaland 12, 19, 21, …
Partition of Africa 11.
Penxa, J.H. Rev. 33.
Phiri, Hanock Msokera Rev. 29, **32**, 45, 56, 61-63, 65, **146**.
Phiri, Isaiah Rev. **191**, 220.
Phiri, Minerva Mrs. 54, 153, 241, **423-425**, 430, 436-437.
Phoenicians 6.
Portuguese 10, 11, 15, 23.
Portuguese East Africa 11, 12, 15, 110, 176, 177.
Portuguese West Africa 11, 12, 15, 148, 153, 175, 419-420.
Rituals 250.
Rush, Benjamin Dr. 24.
Roll Call (South Zambia Conference) 219-221.
Roman Empire 6, 7.
Saka, Lazarus Samuel Sekandiyani Rev. 50, **154**.
Salisbury 31-34, 48, 77, 83, 109, 143, 146, 148, 150-151, 179.
Sangweni, Solomon N. Rev. vi, 33, 38-39, 41, 46, 56, 81-82, **145-146**, 148, 151.
Scramble for Africa 11.
Scripture Union 198-199, 338, 344, 358-361, 363.
Shaka 15.
Sichone, N.J. Rev. vii, 49, **161-162**.
Sikalumbi, W.K. 118, 119, 127, 326.
Sikazwe, Field T. Rev. **184-185**, 439-440.
Simfukwe, David K. Rev. v, viii, 1-2, 50, 123, **134-142**, 219, 239, 291, 315, 341, 367, 427-428, 433.
Simfukwe, Rose Mrs. iii, v, 1-2, 48, 51-52, 133, 135, 137, 139, 189, 236, 240, **427-428**.
Simukwai, Idah Rev. **189**, 220, 244, 351, 367,

428.
Simyembe, Warren K. Rev. v, 29, 81, 149, **179-180**, 344, 420-421.
Simyembe, Elizabeth Nelinya Mrs. v, 55, 81, 122, 132, 149-150, 176, 179, 344, 419, **420-421**.
Siska, Manasae Rev. 75, **151-152**.
Siwale, Aaron Rev. **209-211**, 220, 238, 345-347, 351-355, 363, 366-368, 378, 435-436, 440.
Siwila, Gift 359-360.
Siyame, Benjamin Brown Burton Rev. **163-164**.
Slave trade 11, 13, 15.
Southern, East and Central Africa 23, 30, 107, 117, 131, 187, 213, 440.
Southern Rhodesia vi, 17-21, 23, ...
South East Zambia Conference 219.
South West Africa 11, 23.
South West Zambia Conference 219, 309, 350, 356-357, 422-425, 430, 432.
Spanish 11.
Sub-Saharan Africa 6, 9, 13.
Suez Canal 6.
Sumbwanga 84-96.
Superintendent 33, 37-39, 43, 46, 83, 100, 109, 125, 127, 143, 146, 178, 433.
Swaziland 12, 22, 113, 433.
Tanganyika Territory 17-18, 29, 84-86, 88, 90-91, 95-104, 110, 126, 128, 154, ...
Taxation 18, 218.
Traditions 214, 215, 249, **250-252**.
Trinity A.M.E. Church, Garneton Kitwe 259, 260, **263-303**. 396-416.
Tshaka, J. Rev. vi, 32-33, 81, 151.
Ufipa Province 62, 84, 85.
Union of South Africa 26, 29, 31-33, 41, 82-83, 126, 146, 179.
Wakunguma, Mundia K. Rev. vii, 119, **155**, 219, 233.
Washiama, Foodson B.S. Rev. vii, 52, 59, 105, 131, **146-147**, 219, 429.
Webb, James Dr. Rev. 118, **190-191**.
Wesleyan Methodist Church 37, 125, 145, 155, 158, 177, 195.

White Hall A.M.E. Church, Jenkinsville, South Carolina 181, 277, 297, 337, 390, 391, 393, 417.
Wilberforce College 29.
World War I 17, 23.
Yanduli, Samuel. Rev. 51, **175**, 219.
YMCA 212, 351, 358, 363, 378.
Young's Chapel A.M.E. Church 34, 42, 56, 75-76, 126, 179.
Zambezi Annual Conference vi, **33**, 41-42, 75-76, 81, 130, 143, 153, 178, 225*, 237*, 420.
Zambezi Conference 75*, 80*, 219*.
Zimba, D.D. Rev. 78, **152**.
Zambia Fellowship of Evangelical Students (ZAFES) 337, 362.
Zimbabwe 10, 12-13, 23, 27-28, 30, ...
Ziyezwa, Hannington N. Rev. 83, 131, 143, **178**, 435, 438.
*Modern, created in 2008. Distinguish it from the historical Conference created in 1929.

www.ingramcontent.com/pod-product-compliance
Lightning Source LLC
Chambersburg PA
CBHW080721230426

43665CB00020B/2577